*Eighth Edition*

# AN EXPERIENTIAL APPROACH TO ORGANIZATION DEVELOPMENT

Donald R. Brown

*Antelope Valley College*

D1430671

**Prentice Hall**
Boston   Columbus   Indianapolis   New York   San Francisco   Upper Saddle River
Amsterdam   Cape Town   Dubai   London   Madrid   Milan   Munich   Paris   Montreal   Toronto
Delhi   Mexico City   Sao Paulo   Sydney   Hong Kong   Seoul   Singapore   Taipei   Tokyo

**Editorial Director:** Sally Yagan
**Editor in Chief:** Eric Svendsen
**Acquisitions Editor:** Jennifer M. Collins
**Editorial Assistant:** Meg O'Rourke
**Editorial Project Manager:** Susie Abraham
**Director of Marketing:** Patrice Jones
**Marketing Manager:** Nikki Jones
**Senior Marketing Assistant:** Ian Gold
**Operations Specialist:** Renata Butera
**Creative Art Director:** Jayne Conte
**Cover Designer:** Bruce Kenselaar
**Full-Service Project Management:** Mohinder Singh/Aptara®, Inc.
**Composition:** Aptara®, Inc.
**Printer/Binder:** Bind-Rite Graphics, Inc.
**Cover Printer:** Lehigh-Phoenix, Hagerstown
**Text Font:** Times

Credits and acknowledgments borrowed from other sources and reproduced, with permission, in this textbook appear on appropriate page within text.

**Library of Congress Cataloging-in-Publication Data**
Brown, Donald R.
  An experiential approach to organization development / Donald R. Brown.—8th ed.
    p. cm.
  Includes bibliographical references and index.
  ISBN-13: 978-0-13-610689-0 (alk. paper)
  ISBN-10: 0-13-610689-7 (alk. paper)
  1. Organizational change.   2. Organizational effectiveness.   I. Title.
  HD58.8.H37 2011
  658.4'063—dc22

                      2009037710

10 9 8 7 6 5 4 3 2 1

**Prentice Hall**
is an imprint of

www.pearsonhighered.com

ISBN 10:   0-13-610689-7
ISBN 13: 978-0-13-610689-0

# BRIEF TABLE OF CONTENTS

# CONTENTS

# CONTENTS

# PREFACE

The first edition of this text appeared over three decades ago, and what changes have taken place! We live in a world that has been turned upside down. Fortune 500 companies are pouring money, technology, and management expertise into regions that were once off limits, acquiring new enterprises, forming joint ventures, and creating new global businesses from the ground up. Many major companies are going through significant changes, including outsourcing, downsizing, breaking into smaller companies, radically transforming themselves, reengineering, using self-managed work teams, flattening their organizations, and doing routine jobs with automation and computers. And some other major companies have gone into bankruptcy or no longer exist. Some experts contend that if you can describe a job precisely or write rules for doing it, the job will probably not survive. The added stress on people makes it increasingly a challenge to create and maintain a culture that motivates and satisfies human potential.

In the past, managers aimed for success in a relatively stable and predictable world. In the hyperturbulent environment of the twenty-first century, however, managers are confronting an accelerating rate of change. They face constant innovation in computer and information technology and a chaotic world of changing markets and consumer lifestyles. Today's organizations must be able to transform and renew themselves to meet these changing forces.

This is a book about organization development (OD): the management discipline aimed at improving organizational effectiveness by increasing use of human resources. OD is an emerging behavioral science discipline that provides a set of methodologies for systematically bringing about high-performing organizations. The goals of OD are to make an organization more effective and to enhance the opportunity for the individuals to develop their potential. OD is also about effectively managing in a changing world.

Much like the changing world we live in, this eighth edition has undergone changes. This text offers a practical and realistic approach to the study of OD. Through the application of a new paradigm—the OD process model—each of the OD stages is described from the standpoint of its relationship to an overall program of change. The book is written primarily for those who are learning about OD for the first time. You will learn of the real world through the use of concepts, theories, and numerous illustrations and company examples that show how OD is being applied in today's organizations.

*An Experiential Approach to Organization Development* differs from most OD texts in providing both conceptual and experiential approaches to the study of OD. A revolution is under way in how individuals use education to improve their performance. The approach in this text focuses on the development of interpersonal skills. You are provided with the conceptual framework necessary for understanding the relevant issues in OD. In addition, you will actively participate in individual and team exercises that require the application of chapter content to specific organizational situations. This approach is aimed at developing the critical interpersonal skills needed to manage in a changing world. The word that best summarizes the text's approach to teaching and learning is experiencing. Experiencing captures the importance of engaging with new ideas and new personalities. It also implies a deeper involvement in the learning process that will produce a lasting impact or meaning.

This text is the first to relate directly student learning experiences in OD with skills judged to be essential for OD practitioners and managers. Recent studies have been critical of today's business graduates for their deficiencies in a number of areas, including communication skills, problem solving, decision-making ability, and leadership potential. This text covers OD topics and also develops student skills in a "learn by doing" context.

## NEW TO THIS EDITION

Some of the significant additions, changes, and revisions in this edition include:

- Approximately 35 percent of the material is new or revised.
- OD Applications and examples of organizations are fresh and reflect current business practices.
- Links are provided to Internet locations of organizations used in the applications.

- New material reflects current academic research in OD topics.
- Illustrations have been added to provide a better overview of the OD process.
- New material, including illustrations, better describes and introduces the five parts of the book.
- Enhanced documentation and suggested material for further reading and research is included in the references.
- New design for illustrations enhances their use.
- Simulations including instructions, forms, and tables are revised to improve readability.
- Some of the chapters are reordered to improve the flow for learning OD concepts.
- Material within chapters is reorganized to improve the continuity.

## THE EXPERIENTIAL APPROACH TO LEARNING

To learn OD techniques, a manager or student needs both the knowledge of content material and the experience of putting theory into practice. Consequently, to create a learning environment for the field of OD at either the undergraduate or graduate level, the emphasis should be on experience. In this book, you will be experiencing OD techniques by means of simulations and cases while at the same time you are learning OD theories.

You will perhaps discover a different approach to the study of organizational change. Many courses in OD approach change in a structured and traditional manner. By means of lectures and readings, useful concepts and theories are presented to the student, whose role is largely passive. This book utilizes an innovative and significantly different approach to teaching OD: the experiential approach. It is based on learning OD techniques by experiencing simulated organizational situations. You will experience situations in which you are developing relationships with other students and diagnosing problems rather than simply reading about them.

Experiential learning is based upon three basic concepts:

1. You learn best when you are involved in the learning experience.
2. As a learner, you have to experience or discover concepts, if they are to change your behavior.
3. Your commitment to learning will be greatest when you are responsible for setting your own learning objectives.

In the experiential approach, the major responsibility for learning is placed upon you, the learner. You will determine your own learning objectives and influence how the class goes about achieving these objectives. You set your own goals, decide which theories you want to learn, practice the skills or techniques you want to improve, and develop the behavioral style you want to develop. Concurrently, you will be receiving feedback from class members pertaining to what you do that is effective and ineffective.

Experiential learning also involves an active, rather than a passive role. Often you may sit in a class, listen, take notes, or perhaps daydream while the instructor lectures. In this class, you will be actively deciding what to do and how to do it. You will be doing, communicating, and participating in learning. You will find that you cannot learn in isolation. As in a job situation, you are dependent upon others and they upon you for ideas, reactions, experiences, and feedback about behavior. The same will be true in this class. Experiential learning is also the method most corporations use to teach OD concepts to their employees. So, you will be experiencing the same kinds of activities that occur in most "real world" OD programs.

What is different about the experiential learning process? First, you will generate from your own experiences in this class a set of concepts that will guide your behavior. These concepts will be continually modified over time and in various managerial situations to improve your effectiveness. The experiential learning process, depicted in Figure 1, can be presented as a four-stage cycle:

1. *Gaining conceptual knowledge and theories*—you will be reading about OD concepts and theories and doing preclass preparation.
2. *Activity in a behavioral simulation*—you will be problem solving, making decisions, communicating, and actively practicing the concepts and theories.
3. *Analysis of activity*—you will be analyzing, critiquing, and discussing the way you solved problems, and comparing the results of different approaches.
4. *Connecting the theory and activity with prior on-the-job or life situations*—you will be connecting your learning to past experiences, receiving feedback, reflecting upon the

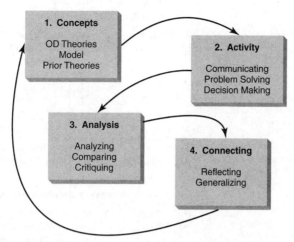

**FIGURE 1** Experiential Learning Process

results, and generalizing into the future. The end result should be improved skill and performance in applying these things learned to life and job situations.

"Student-centered" learning places the learning responsibility upon you. There will be an opportunity in the class for a high level of participation and for a challenging learning experience. Small-group learning environments will be formed wherein you may share learning with others, thus encountering feedback. Each of the learning units presents a conceptual background and a framework for a behavioral simulation. The focal point for each chapter is the action-oriented behavioral simulation.

As part of the experiential learning model in OD, feelings and emotions represent important data for learning. Open and authentic relationships in which you share your feelings with others and provide honest feedback are a necessary part of the learning situation. Each chapter is organized to help you learn concepts and skills, and chapters provide cases, simulations, and diagnostic instruments to help you learn more about OD. Although experiential learning can be stimulating and is often fun, it is important to remember that you learn from the combination of theory and experience.

## ORGANIZATION OF THIS TEXTBOOK

Both the theory and practice of OD is presented in this text. The material has been selected to provide you with most of what is known at this time about the field of OD. This includes issues, critiques, and controversy as well, for the field of OD is itself evolving and being questioned.

The book is intended to assist the student, manager, and future OD practitioner in understanding the strategies and techniques of OD and moves from the more basic elements to the more complex. The five parts of the text are:

*Part 1: Anticipating Change.* This introduces the concepts and techniques of organization development and organization renewal. This includes understanding planned change, what OD is, why it has emerged, and the nature of changing the corporate culture.

*Part 2: Understanding the OD Process.* In this part, the basic roles and styles of the OD practitioner are presented. Then the diagnostic process and overcoming resistance to change are discussed.

*Part 3: Improving Excellence in Individuals.* The text moves into a discussion of OD on an individual level. This covers an overview of intervention strategies, personal intervention skills, and employee empowerment.

*Part 4: Developing High Performance in Teams.* This part focuses on team development, interteam interventions, and goal-setting strategies.

*Part 5: Building Success in Organizations.* This last part focuses on system-wide OD approaches. Specific areas discussed are high-performing organizations, organization transformation, and strategic change. Part 5 concludes with a discussion of the challenge and the future for organizations.

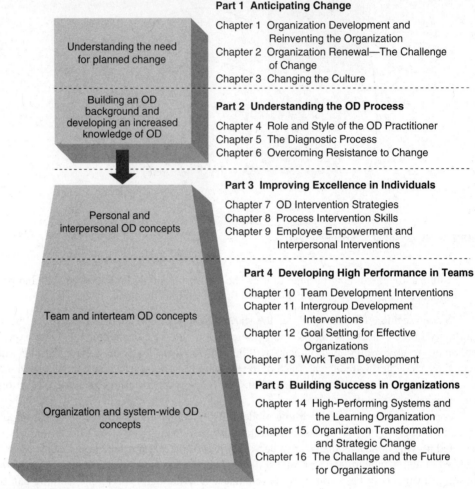

**Part 1 Anticipating Change**

Chapter 1 Organization Development and Reinventing the Organization
Chapter 2 Organization Renewal—The Challenge of Change
Chapter 3 Changing the Culture

**Part 2 Understanding the OD Process**

Chapter 4 Role and Style of the OD Practitioner
Chapter 5 The Diagnostic Process
Chapter 6 Overcoming Resistance to Change

**Part 3 Improving Excellence in Individuals**

Chapter 7 OD Intervention Strategies
Chapter 8 Process Intervention Skills
Chapter 9 Employee Empowerment and Interpersonal Interventions

**Part 4 Developing High Performance in Teams**

Chapter 10 Team Development Interventions
Chapter 11 Intergroup Development Interventions
Chapter 12 Goal Setting for Effective Organizations
Chapter 13 Work Team Development

**Part 5 Building Success in Organizations**

Chapter 14 High-Performing Systems and the Learning Organization
Chapter 15 Organization Transformation and Strategic Change
Chapter 16 The Challange and the Future for Organizations

**FIGURE 2** Organization of This Text

The five parts are, in turn, divided into a total of 16 chapters. Figure 2 illustrates how the text progresses from establishing a need for planned change in organizations to establishing fundamental knowledge of OD. The text then discusses OD in more depth by showing how effectiveness and high performance is built on an individual basis, into teams and between teams, and finally into organization-wide systems.

The 16 chapters of the text are designed to fit a one-semester course, and it has been thoroughly edited to improve readability. It is one of the most "user-friendly" texts on OD available. Illustrations and figures add to the book's visual appeal. Tables, facts, figures, references, and current examples are provided within the text materials.

## LEARNING AIDS

This book presents many learning aids to help you learn about OD. The main ones are:

*Chapter Objectives.* Each chapter presents a brief list of objectives that prepare you for the chapter material and point out learning goals.

*Premeeting preparation.* This section is on the first page of a chapter and specifically lists what you need to do to prepare for that chapter before class meeting time. This section is especially helpful when you refer to it near the conclusion of the preceding chapter. It specifies if teams need to be formed prior to the class meeting, the number of participants in a team, and role assignments that need to be made. Additional premeeting preparations are clearly specified.

*Illustrations including figures and tables.* Throughout a chapter, key concepts, theories, and applications are illustrated with strong, visual materials. Illustrations have been redrawn to improve their visual appeal and clarity.

*OD Applications.* Within each chapter are one to three OD Applications that provide information about how large organizations such as Google and P&G as well as smaller, less well known organizations such as Setpoint Systems and the Chugach School District are applying the OD concepts or interventions discussed in that chapter. Issues such as culture, economic impact, globalization, joint ventures, and approaches to change are featured. The material comes from business publications such as *Business Week*, *Fortune*, and the *Wall Street Journal*. Applications are well-documented, including Internet Web site addresses, so that you can conduct additional research.

*Current Examples of Business Practices.* A concerted effort has been given to bridge OD theory with actual examples from businesses and other organizations. Interwoven throughout the text are brief and current examples of good and poor business practices. A cartoon strip in each chapter helps to illustrate OD concepts. Many examples are quotes from company managers that illustrate a specific point. As in the OD Applications, examples are derived from business publications and are referenced so that you may do additional research. The objective is to show how OD theory is relevant and used in organizations.

*Summaries.* Each chapter concludes with a summary that wraps up the main points and concepts.

*Review Questions.* A set of review questions covering the main chapter points are provided to test your understanding of some of the primary topics.

*Key Words.* Key terms are highlighted within each chapter, and a list of the terms is provided near the end of the chapter.

*OD Skills Simulations (Exercises).* These self-learning, experiential exercises include both individual and team learning. The exercises take theories and principles covered in the text and bring them to life in team activities. The hands-on, team interaction serves to generate feedback, lively discussions, testing of personal ideas, and sharing of information. The simulations are often fun and engaging, and always present a very real learning opportunity.

*Case Studies.* Cases are provided at the end of each chapter for class discussion or written assignment. The cases challenge you to apply OD principles to organizations.

*References.* This text is thoroughly documented to allow you to do additional research. At the conclusion of each chapter are endnotes that include the referenced material. The references also point to books and articles that you can read to gain additional information. Internet Web site addresses are provided so that you may conduct your own research. In addition, by using Internet search engines and academic data base services that are typically available at a library, it is relatively easy to conduct research.

*Index.* A subject and name index helps you quickly find information and examples in the book.

## ACKNOWLEDGMENTS

I am grateful to the many people who have contributed to this eighth edition. Many students, users of the text, colleagues, and managers for over 30 years have been involved in the development of the simulations and cases. My thanks to all of them for their contributions. I want to especially acknowledge and thank Kent Nealis of Harvard-Westlake School, Los Angeles, for his assistance in preparing and reading the manuscript. My thanks also goes to Janice Schnorr for her assistance in the preparation of the instructor's material that accompanies this text.

For the team at Prentice Hall, I want to acknowledge the assistance of Jennifer Collins, acquisitions editor, who moved the text through to completion. She successfully solved some challenging problems in getting this book to print. Susie Abraham, assistant editor, and Debbie Ryan, the production editor, got everyone working together and took care of all the big and little things that got this book published.

I will greatly appreciate hearing from you and receiving your suggestions for how the text can be improved—what worked and what did not. Best wishes for your future.

# PART ONE

# Anticipating Change

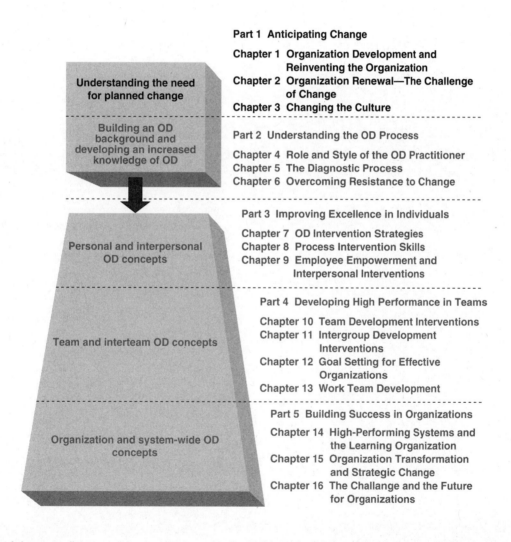

Understanding the need for planned change

Building an OD background and developing an increased knowledge of OD

Personal and interpersonal OD concepts

Team and interteam OD concepts

Organization and system-wide OD concepts

The successful twenty-first-century manager must deal with a chaotic world of new competitors and constant innovation. In the future, the only winning companies will be the ones that respond quickly to change. Preparing managers to cope with today's accelerating role of change is the central concern of this book. Modern managers must not only be flexible and adaptive in a changing environment, they must also be able to diagnose problems and implement change programs.

Many of the ways of managing and doing things in the past will not work in the organizations of the future. Managers and their organizations must anticipate the future and become proactive players. To wait and let the marketplace change and then stabilize is not a strategy for managing change. The first decade of this century painfully taught many companies—big and small—the lessons of not managing for the future. Once-powerful companies like Lehman Brothers and General Motors who saw themselves as too powerful to fail did fail. Other large companies and even industries, such as the U.S. financial and auto industry, found themselves looking to the government for assistance in order to survive.

In *Part 1: Anticipating Change*, we will study what organization development is and how it plays a part in helping organizations to reinvent themselves. We will examine different approaches to changing an organization and the effectiveness of these approaches in a range of situations. Part 1 will conclude with a study of what organization culture is and how it plays a role in shaping and changing an organization.

# Organization Development and Reinventing the Organization

**LEARNING OBJECTIVES**

**Upon completing this chapter, you will be able to:**

1. Define the concept of organization development and recognize the need for change and renewal.
2. Describe organization culture and understand its impact on the behavior of individuals in an organization.
3. Understand the expectations of the psychological contract formed on joining an organization.
4. Describe the five stages of organization development.

## PREMEETING PREPARATION

1. Read Chapter 1.
2. Read and prepare analysis for Case: TGIF.

## CHANGE IS THE CHALLENGE FOR ORGANIZATIONS

Change is coming down upon us like an avalanche, and most people are utterly unprepared to cope with it. Tomorrow's world will be different from today's, calling for new organizational approaches. Organizations will need to adapt to changing market conditions and at the same time cope with the need for a renewing rather than reactive workforce. Every day managers confront massive and accelerating change. As one writer comments, "Call it whatever you like—reengineering, restructuring, transformation, flattening, downsizing, rightsizing, a quest for global competitiveness—it's real, it's radical and it's arriving every day at a company near you."[1]

Global competition and economic downturns have exposed a glaring weakness in American organizations: the fact that many of them have become overstaffed, cumbersome, slow, and inefficient. To increase productivity, enhance competitiveness, and contain costs, organizations have changed and continue to change the way they are organized and managed.

Organizations are never completely static and they do not exist in isolation of other entities. They are in continuous interaction with external forces including competitors, customers, governments, stockholders, suppliers, society, and unions. Their interactions with their environment are illustrated in Figure 1.1. The conditions facing today's organizations are different from those of past decades. Many companies face global as well as domestic competitors. Changing consumer lifestyles and technological breakthroughs all act on the organization to cause it to change. Government regulation and deregulation are continually changing, while at the same time, international trade agreements present both new opportunities and obstacles. Stockholders are demanding more accountability. Suppliers, providing both products and services to organizations, come more and more from the world economy. The society within which an organization operates influences the modes, values, and norms that are developed within the organization. The employees and unions have a direct and substantial influence on how well an organization functions. The CEO of Intel Corporation, Paul Otellini, expressed his frustration with operating in an environment of unknowns in a *Wall Street Journal* interview. "The problem is that there used to be one set of rules out there—U.S. antitrust laws were the de facto rules of the world. Now with globalization, we have different sets of rules for different regions, such as the EU, written around entirely different philosophies. It would sure make things easier if we decided on a single set of rules once again—whatever they are. Then we'd know how to behave and we could plan better for the future."[2]

The type and degree of external forces vary from one organization to another, but all organizations face the need to adapt to these forces. Many of these changes are forced upon the organization, whereas others are generated internally. Because change is occurring so rapidly, there is a need for new ways to manage it. General Mills is one of a number of

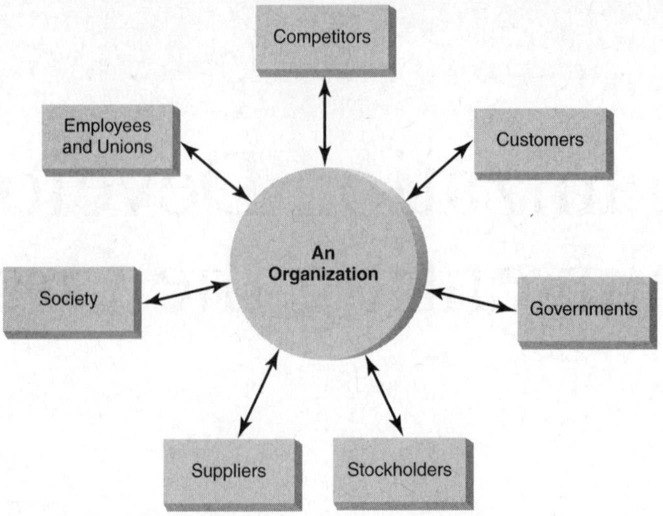

**FIGURE 1.1**  The Organization Environment

companies that has recognized the challenges confronting it. As the economy unraveled during the first few years of the 2000s, General Mills looked far afield to come up with ways to cut costs. "We can't get by doing what we did yesterday," says retired CEO Stephen Sanger.[3] Organizations are changing and will continue to do so in order to survive in this complex environment.

This book has been written to help managers and would-be managers learn about organization development (OD) and the part it can play in bringing about change in organizations. The purpose is twofold: (1) to create an awareness of the changing environmental forces confronting the modern manager and (2) to provide the techniques and skills needed for dealing with change in organizations.

Organizations are using OD techniques to increase their effectiveness and their adaptability to changing conditions. In this chapter, you will learn about this exciting field: What OD is, why it has emerged, and some basic concepts pertaining to the process of organization change. The chapter concludes with a model for organizational change describing the stages of the organization development process.

## WHAT IS ORGANIZATION DEVELOPMENT?

What makes one organization a winner, whereas another fails to make use of the same opportunities? The key to survival and success lies not in rational, quantitative approaches, but rather in a commitment to irrational, difficult-to-measure things like people, quality, customer service, and, most important, developing the flexibility to meet changing conditions. Employee involvement and commitment are the true keys to successful change.

**Organization development (OD)** comprises the long-range efforts and programs aimed at improving an organization's ability to survive by changing its problem-solving and renewal processes. OD involves moving toward an adaptive organization and achieving corporate excellence by integrating the desires of individuals for growth and development with organizational goals. According to a leading authority on OD, Richard Beckhard, "Organization development is an effort: (1) planned, (2) organization-wide, (3) managed from the top, (4) to increase organization effectiveness and health, through (5) planned interventions in the organization's processes using behavioral science knowledge."[4]

Organization development efforts are planned, systematic approaches to change. They involve changes to the total organization or to relatively large segments of it. The purpose of OD efforts is to increase the effectiveness of the system and to develop the potential of all the individual members. It includes a series of planned behavioral science intervention activities carried out in collaboration with organization members to help find improved ways of working together toward individual and organizational goals.

Another way of understanding OD is to explain what it is not:

- **OD is not a micro approach to change.** Management development, for example, is aimed at changing individual behavior, whereas OD is focused on the macro goal of developing an organization-wide improvement in managerial style.

- *OD is not any single technique.* OD uses many different techniques, such as total quality management or job enrichment, and none of them by itself represents the OD discipline.
- *OD does not include random or ad hoc changes.* OD is based on a systematic appraisal and diagnosis of problems, leading to planned and specific types of change efforts.
- *OD is not exclusively aimed at raising morale or attitudes.* OD is aimed at overall organizational health and effectiveness. Participant satisfaction may be one aspect of the change effort, but it includes other effectiveness parameters as well.

Organization development is an emerging discipline aimed at improving the effectiveness of the organization and its members by means of a systematic change program. Chester Barnard and Chris Argyris, among other management theorists, have noted that a truly effective organization is one in which both the organization and the individual can grow and develop. An organization with such an environment is a "healthy" organization. The goal of organization development is to make organizations healthier and more effective. These concepts apply to organizations of all types, including schools, churches, military forces, governments, and businesses.

Change is a way of life in today's organization, but organizations are also faced with maintaining a stable identity and operations in order to accomplish their primary goals. Consequently, organizations involved in managing change have found that the way they handle it is critical. There is a need for a systematic approach and for the ability to discriminate between features that are healthy and effective and those that are not. Erratic, short-term, unplanned, or haphazard changes may introduce problems that did not exist before or result in side effects that may be worse than the original problem. Managers should also be aware that stability or equilibrium can contribute to a healthy state. Change inevitably involves the disruption of that steady state. Change just for the sake of change is not necessarily effective; in fact, it may be dysfunctional.

## The Characteristics of Organization Development

To enlarge upon the definition of OD, let us examine some of the basic characteristics of OD programs (see Table 1.1).

- *Change.* OD is a planned strategy to bring about organizational change. The change effort aims at specific objectives and is based on a diagnosis of problem areas.
- *Collaborative approach.* OD typically involves a collaborative approach to change that includes the involvement and participation of the organization members most affected by the changes.
- *Performance orientation.* OD programs include an emphasis on ways to improve and enhance performance and quality.
- *Humanistic orientation.* OD relies on a set of humanistic values about people and organizations that aims at making organizations more effective by opening up new opportunities for increased use of human potential.
- *Systems approach.* OD represents a systems approach concerned with the interrelationship of divisions, departments, groups, and individuals as interdependent subsystems of the total organization.
- *Scientific method.* OD is based upon scientific approaches to increase organization effectiveness.

**TABLE 1.1** Major Characteristics of the Field of OD

| Characteristics | Focal Areas |
| --- | --- |
| 1. Change | Change is planned by managers to achieve goals. |
| 2. Collaborative Approach | Involves collaborative approach and involvement. |
| 3. Performance Orientation | Emphasis on ways to improve and enhance performance. |
| 4. Humanistic Orientation | Emphasis upon increased opportunity and use of human potential. |
| 5. Systems Approach | Relationship among elements and excellence. |
| 6. Scientific Method | Scientific approaches supplement practical experience. |

In more general terms, organization development is based on the notion that for an organization to be effective (i.e., accomplish its goal), it must be more than merely efficient; it must adapt to change.

An **OD practitioner** is a person in an organization responsible for changing existing patterns to obtain more effective organizational performance. People using organization development have come to realize that conventional training techniques are no longer sufficient for achieving the types of behavioral changes needed to create adaptive organizations. Going to a company's management class and listening to someone lecture about the need to change or the importance of effective organizations may be a good beginning, but speeches will not produce exceptional organizational performance. New techniques have been developed to provide organization members with the competence and motivation to alter ineffective patterns of behavior.

There are many OD techniques, and any individual using OD may rely on one or a combination of approaches. Regardless of the method selected, the objectives are to work from an overall organization perspective, thus increasing the ability of the "whole" to respond to a changing environment.

Organizations have objectives, such as making profits, surviving, and growing; but individual members also have desires to achieve, unsatisfied needs to fulfill, and career goals to accomplish within the organization. OD, then, is a process for change that can benefit both the organization and the individual. In today's business environment, managers must continuously monitor change and adapt their systems to survive by staying competitive in a turbulent arena.

## Why Organization Development?

Why has such a fast-growing field emerged? Organizations are designed to accomplish some purpose or function and to continue doing so for as long as possible. Because of this, they are not necessarily intended to change. But change can affect all types of organizations, from giants like IBM, GE, and Google to the smallest business. The year 2008 can lay claim to some of the greatest failures or near-failures of corporations blindsided by fast-developing economic and market conditions. The lists include some of the titans of American capitalism: American International Group (AIG), General Motors, Chrysler, and Lehman Brothers. No organization or person can escape change, and change is everyone's job. Managers at all levels must be skilled in organization change and renewal techniques.

Typical factors for an organization to initiate a large-scale change program include a very high level of competition, concern for survivability, and declining performance. Goals for change include changing the corporate culture, becoming more adaptive, and increasing competitiveness. In today's business environment, managers must continuously monitor change and adapt their systems to survive by staying competitive in a turbulent arena. Kodak, for example, is trying to change by focusing on consumers who use digital cameras instead of film cameras. "If they don't invest in digital, that's the end of Kodak," according to Frank Romano, professor of digital printing at the Rochester Institute of Technology.[5] In the coming decades, changes in the external environment will occur so rapidly that organizations will need OD techniques just to keep pace with the accelerating rate of innovation.

## The Emergence of OD

Organization development is one of the primary means of creating more adaptive organizations. Warren Bennis, a leading OD pioneer, has identified three factors as underlying the emergence of OD.

1. *The need for new organizational forms.* Organizations tend to adopt forms appropriate to a particular time; the current rate of change requires more adaptive forms.
2. *The focus on cultural change.* Every organization forms its own culture—a distinctive system of beliefs and values; the only real way to change is to alter the organizational culture.
3. *The increase in social awareness.* Because of the changing social climate, tomorrow's employee will no longer accept an autocratic style of management; therefore, greater social awareness is required in the organization.[6]

## THE ONLY CONSTANT IS CHANGE

Although many organizations have been able to keep pace with the changes in information technology, fewer firms have been able to adapt to changing social and cultural conditions. In a dynamic environment, change is unavoidable. The pace of change has become so rapid that it is difficult to adjust to or compensate for one change before another is necessary. Change is, in essence, a moving target. The technological, social, and economic environment is rapidly changing, and an organization will be able to survive only if it can effectively anticipate and respond to these changing demands. The first decade of the twenty-first century has seen change in political, not-for-profit, and business institutions that were hardly imaginable in the last decade of the previous century. As we move into the second decade, there will, undoubtedly, be additional changes that will provide both challenges and opportunities for corporations to compete effectively.

Given this increasingly complex environment, it becomes even more critical for management to identify and respond to forces of social and technical change. In attempting to manage today's organizations, many executives find that their past failures to give enough attention to the changing environment are now creating problems for them. In contrast, 3M Corporation has developed an outstanding reputation for innovation. 3M is big but acts small. 3M's 15 percent rule allows its people to spend up to 15 percent of the work week on anything as long as it is product related. The most famous example to come out of this is the Post-it note. General Electric (GE), another company that cultivates a climate for change, has a Leadership Center, a tool that GE uses to spread change throughout the company. For more information about GE's Leadership Center, see **OD Application: GE's Epicenter of Change.**

## OD Application: GE's Epicenter of Change[7]

General Electric Company is well known the world over for its light bulbs, jet engines, refrigerators, locomotive engines, NBC, wind turbines, and toasters. But one of its most successful and important accomplishments is their "university" that it operates the world over. It is headquartered at the John F. Welch Leadership Center at Crotonville, located in Ossining, N.Y. Here, GE turns out the internal leaders it needs, which was the center's initial mission when it was founded over 50 years ago.

Through the years and particularly during the tenure of CEO Jack Welch, now retired, the center evolved to become much more than a training center for future GE managers. The center is now the tool to spread change throughout GE. The company's Web site says the center "has been at the forefront of real-world application for cutting-edge thinking in organizational development, leadership, innovation and change." With the current CEO, Jeff Immelt, the center is branching out by inviting its customers to join with GE employees to discuss and solve big issues.

GE invests about $1 billion world-wide every year on training and education for its people. This has been the case even in the recessionary years of 2008 and 2009. "We have always believed that building strong leaders is a strategic imperative," says CEO Immelt. "When times are easy, leadership can be taken for granted. When the world is turbulent, you appreciate great people." An indication of Immelt's personal commitment to leadership and learning is that he spends approximately 30 percent of his time on leadership development.

The Leadership Center at Crotonville is the epicenter for GE learning, but the students are not just top executives. It hosts around 10,000 employees and customers ranging from entry-level to the highest-performing executives. For many, it is a defining career event. The courses, typically running one to three weeks, cover a broad range of topics including:

- Essential skills courses such as hiring, team building, and presentations.
- Leadership courses for new managers.
- Executive courses in leadership, innovation, strategy, and manager development.
- Customer programs including change management and integration.

The classes have a broad functional and global mix with courses typically having 50 percent non-U.S. participation. With GE having such a large worldwide presence, there are now leadership courses that are taught in places that include Shanghai, Munich, India, Africa, and, Dubai.

A recent program at the Leadership Center was Leadership, Innovation, and Growth (LIG). The program brought together all the senior managers of a business unit for four days with the expressed purpose of expanding GE's businesses and creating new opportunities. GE calls this "filling in the white spaces." Attending each session were several teams from around the world. This was a new approach at the Leadership Center as it brought in existing teams at one time to work on a specific issue. In addition to intensive work sessions, there were external speakers who frequently came from a university and internal speakers who were GE managers and had applied the concepts that the teams were learning. On the last day, all the teams at the session delivered a 20-minute presentation to CEO Immelt that covered what the team members had decided they should do to optimize growth. Once back at their home office, they had to refine their presentation into a letter to Immelt that was no longer than two pages. From 2006 to 2008, 2,500 people and their 260 teams went through the program with a follow-up in 2009.

GE discovered over 50 years ago when the CEO at that time, Ralph Cordiner, established the Leadership Center that their success depended upon having well-trained and developed leaders. Though GE has experienced some critical challenges during recent recessionary times, their success for the future will in part depend upon how well their employees learned their lessons at the Leadership Center.

### Questions

1. How does the Leadership Center serve as a center for change at GE?
2. Visit GE's Web site to learn about the Leadership Center's current programs at www.ge.com/ and www.ge.com/company/culture/leadership_learning.html.

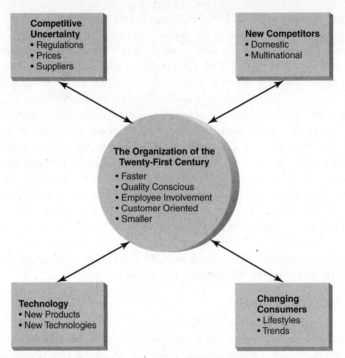

**FIGURE 1.2** The Changing Organization of the Twenty-First Century

The fundamental nature of managerial success is changing. The pace of this change is relentless, and increasing past sources of competitive advantage, such as economies of scale and huge advertising budgets, are no longer as effective in the new competitive landscape. Moreover, the traditional managerial approach can no longer lead a firm to economic leadership.

Today's managers need a new mind-set—one that values flexibility, speed, innovation, and the challenge that evolves from constantly changing conditions. Virtual organizations can spring up overnight as networks of free agents combine expertise for a new project or product. Management theorists believe that to be successful in the twenty-first century, organizations will require changes of the kind shown in Figure 1.2. They suggest that predictability is a thing of the past, and that the winning organization of today and tomorrow will be based upon quality, innovation, and flexibility.[8] Yogi Berra, foreshadowing this sentiment, reportedly once said, "The future ain't what it used to be."

These successful firms will share certain common traits. They will all be:

- *Faster*—more responsive to innovation and change.
- *Quality conscious*—totally committed to quality.
- *Employee involved*—adding value through human resources.
- *Customer oriented*—creating niche markets.
- *Smaller*—made up of more autonomous units.

## THE EVOLUTION OF ORGANIZATION DEVELOPMENT

It is not within the scope of this book to provide a detailed history of organization development, but a brief explanation of the evolution of the field may give you a better understanding of its application today. OD has evolved over the past 55 years from its beginnings as the application of behavioral science knowledge and techniques to solving organizational problems. What has become OD started in the late 1940s at MIT and is deeply rooted in the pioneering work of applied social scientists like Kurt Lewin. It is also strongly influenced by the work of psychologists like Carl Rogers and Abraham Maslow. The term "organization development" is widely attributed to Robert Blake and Jane Mouton (the originators of the Managerial Grid[9]) and Herbert Shepard (a leading OD pioneer); but Richard Beckhard[10] claims this distinction as well. Regardless of who first coined the term, it emerged in about 1957 and is generally conceded to have evolved from two basic sources: the application of laboratory methods by the National Training Laboratories (NTL) and the survey research methods originated by the Survey Research Center. Both methods were pioneered by Kurt Lewin around 1946.[11]

## NTL Laboratory-Training Methods

In the late 1940s and early 1950s, laboratory-training methods were developed and applied by a group of behavioral scientists in Bethel, Maine. Douglas McGregor (the originator of Theory X and Theory Y[12]), working with Richard Beckhard, began applying laboratory-training methods to industry at General Mills in 1956 and at Union Carbide in 1957. At Union Carbide, McGregor and his colleague John Paul Jones formed the first internal OD group.

About the same time, Herbert Shepard and Robert Blake were initiating a series of applied behavioral science interventions at Esso (the international trade name for ExxonMobile), mainly using laboratory-training techniques to improve work team processes (see Chapter 9). These early training sessions provided the basis for what Blake and Mouton later developed as an instrumented training system, which they called the Managerial Grid (see Chapter 14). The success of these programs led to the dissemination of such efforts to other corporations.

## Survey Research and Feedback

Meanwhile, a group at the Survey Research Center at the University of Michigan began to apply Kurt Lewin's action research model to organizations. Rensis Likert and Floyd Mann administered an organization-wide survey at Detroit Edison Co. involving the systematic feedback of data to participating departments. They used what is termed an "interlocking series of conferences," feeding data back to the top management group and then down to work teams throughout the organization. Since that time, many organizations have used the survey feedback approach.

In summary, the major sources of current OD practice were the pioneering work at NTL (laboratory-training techniques) and the Survey Research Center (survey feedback methods). This brief look at the past is important because OD is a new and still developing field, and in the future, you may build upon these earlier foundations in pioneering other new OD approaches.

## The Extent of OD Applications

From these early beginnings, OD has experienced rapid growth. A growing number of organizations worldwide are applying OD techniques. The OD Network,[13] an organization of people practicing or advocating OD, was started in 1964 and now has more than 3,000 members from all over the world. The NTL, the American Psychological Association, the American Society for Training and Development, Outward Bound, and the Academy of Management all have professional divisions related to organization development. The first doctoral program for training OD specialists, called the Organizational Behavior Group, was started by Shepard in 1960 at what is now the Organizational Behavior Department at Case Western Reserve University. In addition to OD programs at small to large organizations in the United States, OD programs abound globally in both developed and developing economies with democratic and authoritarian governments.[14]

Organization development is an exciting and rapidly growing field. OD efforts have grown into a multitude of different approaches and are now applied in organizations around the world by a growing number of people practicing OD.[15]

## WHO DOES ORGANIZATION DEVELOPMENT?

The people who do OD, OD practitioners, come primarily from two areas. The first area consists of **OD specialists,** who are professionals that have specialized and trained in organization development and related areas, such as organization behavior, applied social sciences, interpersonal communications, and decision making. These specialists are often referred to as OD practitioners and consultants. They may be members of the organization, **internal practitioners,** or come from outside the organization, **external practitioners.** Historically, OD programs were established in organizations by external practitioners. These practitioners were usually individuals, perhaps a university professor who had written in the area and had assisted other organizations in developing OD programs. In some cases, specialists joined together to form a small business offering their consulting expertise. OD external practitioners are still used extensively by organizations, particularly with upper management, to help design and implement OD programs. The OD program may not use the term "organization development" or "OD," but nevertheless it is likely to encompass many of its values and methods. Instead of using external practitioners, an organization may have its own team of internal practitioners. They are employed by the organization and are an ongoing part of it. Some organizations have a group or division solely responsible for implementing OD; in other organizations the OD program may be part of the human resource department. In some cases, the OD program reports directly to the CEO or president.

The second area of people doing OD consists of people in a managerial or leadership position who apply OD to their work. With growth in the use of OD, the way it is used in organizations has also evolved. It is increasingly common to find people in different parts of organizations—team leaders, supervisors, and managers at all levels—practicing and applying OD. They may have picked up OD concepts and ideas in a college course or a leadership program offered by their company. They probably do not call what they are doing OD. As they see it, organization development is not a noun but an action verb. That is to say, OD is not so much a program as an activity; it is managing and leading. These OD practitioners include team leaders who practice planned change, act as coaches to their team, develop effective and efficient teams, and build leaders. They are also CEOs who build effective management teams by doing many of the same things that a team or group leader does. As CEOs operate organization-wide, they are OD practitioners by building learning organizations, implementing total quality management programs, creating boundaryless organizations, and implementing organization development programs.

This text will generally use the term "OD practitioner." **OD practitioners** are the people who use, advocate, and assist others to implement OD.[16] Practitioners are the internal and external specialists who are professionally trained in OD and related fields. Also, they are the people who use and apply OD to their work.

"Change agent" is another term frequently used to describe an OD practitioner. A **change agent** is a person attempting to bring about planned change to an organization or system. The organization that is the subject of the change is the **client system.** Just as an OD practitioner is external or internal to the organization, so too is the change agent.

Some of the subjects discussed in this text are aimed more at OD specialists, but in most cases these subjects can be adapted by the manager and team leader practicing OD. For example, there is a discussion in Chapter 4 on the initial intervention into an organization that OD specialists typically will go through. It describes a more formal and lengthy process that a manager practicing OD will need to follow when introducing team development to a work team. The ideas and procedures, though, can be adapted by the manager.

## THE ORGANIZATION CULTURE

One element of an organization system that a manager needs to understand is the **organization culture.**[17] The term "culture" refers to a specific civilization, society, or group and its distinguishing characteristics. As B. F. Skinner commented: "A culture is not the behavior of the people 'living in it'; it is the 'it' in which they live—contingencies of social reinforcement, which generate and sustain their behavior."[18] One company, Unum Group (formerly Unum Provident), gave out "Hungry Vulture" awards for top performers. The award carried the motto "Patience my foot... I'm gonna kill something." Unum Group, the largest disability insurer worldwide, has been investigated by 45 states in regard to how it handles claims. A senior vice president says the award was never given to workers for denying claims but was given in recognition of good performance. However, plaintiffs' attorneys and former employees who have seen company files paint a picture of an aggressive corporate culture.[19]

The term "organization culture" refers to a system of shared meanings, including the language, dress, patterns of behavior, value system, feelings, attitudes, interactions, and group norms of the members. Examine the patterns of behavior on your campus or in your company. How do people dress? What jargon or unique terms do they use? These are the elements that make up a culture: the accepted patterns of behavior.[20] This provides a set of values and behavioral norms for the organization. For an example of learning the jargon of an organization, see Figure 1.3.

**Norms** are organized and shared ideas regarding what members should do and feel, how this behavior should be regulated, and what sanctions should be applied when behavior does not coincide with social expectations. The values and behaviors of every organization are unique. Some patterns of behavior may be functional and may facilitate the accomplishment of organizational goals. Other patterns of behavior or cultural norms may actually inhibit or restrict their accomplishment.

**FIGURE 1.3**  **It's Important to Learn the Jargon**
*Source:* B.C. by permission of Johnny Hart and Creators Syndicate, Inc.

A look at the types of norms that exist in an organization will help in gaining a better understanding of the organization's culture. Norms are generally enforced only for the behaviors viewed as most important by most group members.[21] Norms essential to accomplishing the organization's objectives are called **pivotal norms.** Norms that support and contribute to the pivotal norms but are not essential to the organization's objectives are called **peripheral norms.** For example, dress codes that are enforced Monday through Thursday are probably peripheral in light of Friday's being a casual dress day. Pivotal and peripheral norms constantly confront individuals in an organization, and they must decide whether or not to conform. The pressure to conform to norms varies, allowing individuals some degree of freedom in responding to these organizational pressures, depending on how they perceive the rewards or punishments. The organization also has latitude in the degree of conformity it requires of its members.

## THE SOCIALIZATION PROCESS

Even if an organization does an effective job of recruiting, new employees must still adjust to the organizational culture. Because they are not aware of the culture, new employees are likely to disagree with or question the customs and values that exist. **Socialization** may be defined as the process that adapts employees to the organization's culture. For a new employee, the socialization process evolves through four stages: entering an organization with initial expectations, encountering the organization's culture, adjusting to the culture and norms, and receiving feedback. This is illustrated in Figure 1.4.[22] The socialization of employees at Procter and Gamble Co. (P&G) starts at an early age because employees often begin their careers there and grow up together. The culture is one of being resistant to new ideas and even being insular. P&G is, by many measures, a

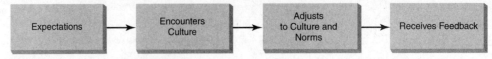

**FIGURE 1.4**   The Socialization Process

family company and only promotes from within. It is located in a relatively small city, Cincinnati, where employees live near one another, go to the same social functions, and eat at the same restaurants. Chairman of the Board and retired CEO A. G. Lafley admits, "I am worried that I will ask the organization to change ahead of its understanding, capability, and commitment."[23]

## Expectations of New Employees

To function effectively, managers and members must be aware of the organization's norms. They must recognize how sharply norms are defined and how strongly they are enforced. Entry into a new situation often results in some degree of anxiety or stress. The less an individual can relate the new situation to previous situations, the greater the feelings of anxiety and discomfort. The more the individual can meet expectations, the less the feelings of anxiety and discomfort.

Some organizations assign current employees to act as mentors to new employees. W. L. Gore & Associates assigns each person hired by the company a sponsor who acts as a mentor. Twenty percent of Gore's associates (employees) are sponsors, and the sponsor is typically the person who has the most at stake in making the new associate successful. The Gore philosophy is that if you sponsor someone, you want them to be successful, and therefore, will offer them opportunities, such as sitting in on meetings. If the new associate is successful, the team will be successful, and Gore will be successful.[24]

## Encountering the Organization's Culture

The organizational culture provides a way for organization members to meet and get along. Three important aspects of socialization when joining an organization are:

1. Deciding who is a member and who is not.
2. Developing an informal understanding of behavioral norms.
3. Separating friends from enemies.

To work together effectively, individuals need to understand things like power, status, rewards, and sanctions for specific types of behaviors. For instance, what behavior gets one a good grade, and so on.

While the individual employees are experiencing a new situation, the organization may be attempting to influence them. If new members come to an organization expecting to find a certain set of norms, they are looking for their expectations to be affirmed. If their expectations reflect the actual norms of the organization, the integration process for both the new members and the organization is relatively painless.

## Adjusting to the Culture and Norms

New members often find that the norms are unclear, confusing, and restrictive. As a result, they may react in different ways when entering an organization. This is illustrated in Figure 1.5. At one extreme, a new member may choose to conform to all the norms of the organization, resulting in uniformity of behavior and complete acceptance of organizational values. This conformity may result in stagnation, nonresponsiveness, and a loss of creativeness. At the other extreme, a new member may choose to rebel, to reject all the values, or to leave the organization altogether.[25]

**FIGURE 1.5**   Basic Responses to Socialization

A less obvious alternative is for new members to accept the pivotal norms and seriously question the peripheral norms, which can be termed **creative individualism.** This is the ideal behavior for a healthy and effective organization, but it is often difficult for a newcomer to correctly determine which norms are peripheral and which are pivotal. What may be a pivotal norm in one department may be a peripheral norm or not a norm at all in another department of the same organization. Since norms are changing and dynamic, the organization member must have the awareness to discern the differences between pivotal and peripheral norms.

## Receiving Feedback

Only the more healthy organizations allow their members to challenge their norms. The aim of OD is to develop an organizational climate that is appropriate to the organization's mission and members. In a sense, OD involves changing the culture of organizations and work groups so that a more effective means of interacting, relating, and problem solving will result. OD seeks to develop the organization to the point that it feels comfortable about allowing its members to openly examine the norms, both pivotal and peripheral, with the ultimate goal of building a more effective organization. The reaction of the individual to the norms results in the formation of an unwritten agreement with the organization.

For example, at one organization, employees believe that it is their responsibility to innovate and be creative. They develop new and improved products, processes, and ways to serve their customers. They believe that team discussion, challenging ideas, and taking risks are appropriate behaviors for achieving goals. However, another organization's employees believe that following procedures, reaching numerical outcome targets, doing no more or less than what is required, and not saying anything that the boss does not want to hear are the appropriate behaviors. These two organizations have very different types of cultures. In both of these organizations, each person tends to do the following:

1. Separate more important from less important goals.
2. Develop ways to measure his or her accomplishments.
3. Create explanations for why goals may not always be met.

For an example of how Starbucks Coffee Company uses socialization to integrate new employees into their organization, see **OD Application: Leave No One Behind at Starbucks.**

---

## OD Application: Leave No One Behind at Starbucks[26]

Howard Schultz's vocabulary, at least in formal interviews, makes him sound like a college professor of management. The interviews are peppered with words like "collaborative," "teams," "empowerment," "empathetic," "vision," and "partners."

Schultz just happens to be one of the founders, chairperson of the board, president, CEO, and chief strategist of Starbucks Coffee Company. The firm has more than 176,000 partners who handle approximately 50 million transactions every week in nearly 17,000 retail stores in 49 countries. Starbucks has one of the highest frequencies of customer visits than just about any other retailer in the U.S.

Besides a good cup of Joe, what is the Starbucks formula for success? Perhaps it is the firm's vision. Says former U.S. Senator and current Starbucks board member Bill Bradley, "Howard is consumed with his vision of Starbucks. That means showing the good that a corporation can do for its workers, shareholders, and customers." On Starbucks' six-point mission statement is "We're called partners, because it's not just a job, it's our passion. Together, we embrace diversity to create a place where each of us can be ourselves. We always treat each other with respect and dignity. And we hold each other to that standard."

Central to Starbucks is the philosophy "Leave no one behind." This philosophy shows up in new employees receiving 24 hours of in-store training, higher-than-average salaries, and benefit packages. All employees who work more than 20 hours a week receive stock options and full health care benefits. Schultz says, "The most important thing I ever did was give our employees stock options. That's what sets us apart and gives a higher-quality employee, an employee that cares more."

Starbucks consistently shows up on *Fortune's* annual lists of "100 Best Companies to Work For" and "America's Most Admired Companies." In employee surveys, Starbucks ranks ahead of other companies. Starbucks employees show an 82 percent job-satisfaction rate compared to a 50 percent rate for all employers. It has the lowest employee turnover rate of any restaurant or fast-food company. Another survey found that the two principal reasons people work for Starbucks are "the opportunity to work with an enthusiastic team" and "to work in a place where I feel I have value." A Starbuck spokesperson says, "We look for people who are adaptable, self-motivated, passionate, creative team players." Maintaining this spirit is not easy in a company with over 170,000 employees. "Getting big and staying small" is the Starbucks objective, says Schultz.

*(continued)*

Starbucks is also confronted with some challenges. Like most retailers operating in a recession, Starbucks sales and profits have been negatively affected. This has especially been the situation with Starbucks, which offers a premium product at a premium price. Competition for the coffee consumer has intensified with McDonalds' strategy of opening coffee and beverage stations with Starbucks-style baristas in their restaurants. McDonalds' premium coffees are priced an average of 60 cents less per drink than Starbucks'. In response to declining sales, Starbucks has closed underperforming stores and reduced the number of new store openings within the U.S. To help solve the problem, Schultz is focusing on "reigniting" the connection with consumers through better products and better store design. In a press release for Starbucks, Shultz says, "Our customers are telling us they want value and quality and we will deliver that in a way that is both meaningful to them and authentic to Starbucks."

**Questions**

1. What do you think Schultz meant when he said that Starbucks' objective is "Getting big and staying small?"
2. If possible, interview a present or former employee of Starbucks to get his or her impression of the company.
3. If you have visited a Starbucks, did you see any examples of teamwork among its employees?
4. Research the current lists of *Fortune*'s "100 Best Companies to Work For" and "America's Most Admired Companies." Information is available at www.money.cnn.com/magazines/fortune/fortune_archive/.
5. Research current information about Starbucks' sales and revenue. Information and their annual report can be found at www.starbucks.com/.

## PSYCHOLOGICAL CONTRACTS

A **psychological contract** may be defined as an unwritten agreement between individuals and the organization of which they are members. It describes certain expectations that the organization has of the individual and the individual's expectations of the organization.[27] Because the two parties are growing and changing, the contract must be open-ended, so that old issues and new issues can be renegotiated.

An organization has certain expectations of its members. If it is a business organization, its expectations of member behavior will probably be spelled out very clearly. It undoubtedly expects its members to be on the job during certain hours of the day. It is probably concerned with the quality and quantity of the work they do, their loyalty, their appearance, and various other things unique to the organization. For the organization to be satisfied, the individual will need to comply to some degree with its expectations. In other words, the organization has certain requirements, and the individual must do certain things to meet them if there is to be a lasting and healthy relationship. In many instances, unfulfilled expectations result in high turnover, absenteeism, sabotage, and worker alienation. Research into the effectiveness of psychological contracts has shown that the obligations of both the employee and the organization are important determinants of organizational commitment.[28]

Similarly, the individual has certain expectations of the organization. An individual may expect to gain work experience, security, and advancement. The individual probably expects to have an opportunity to meet people, make friends, and form social relationships and undoubtedly expects remuneration from the organization. For the individual to be satisfied and stay, the organization will have to meet the individual's expectations.

When either the organization's or the individual's expectations are not being satisfied adequately by the other party, friction and difficulties may develop. If these problems cannot be solved, they may culminate in the individual's leaving the organization, either voluntarily or by the organization's choice. All too often, the problem is solved by not solving it: it takes too much effort to reach a real solution, so both parties must continue with a tenuous and unharmonious relationship.

Sometimes, the psychological contract between the organization and the individual does not even address certain key expectations. One or both parties may assume that the other party agrees to some unstated expectations. The phrase "it is intuitively obvious to the most casual observer" may be the underlying assumption of one or both parties. Unstated or assumed expectations can lead to an organization of individuals who feel cheated or of managers who are disappointed in their subordinates. To avoid such misunderstandings, both parties—the members and the representatives of the organization—should formulate a psychological contract that can be continually renegotiated.

## A MODEL FOR ORGANIZATIONAL DEVELOPMENT

Organization development is a continuing process of long-term organizational improvement consisting of a series of stages, as shown in Figure 1.6. In an OD program, the emphasis is placed on a combination of individual, team, and organizational relationships.

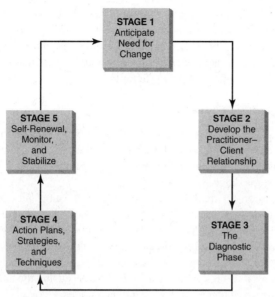

**FIGURE 1.6** Organization Development's Five Stages

The primary difference between OD and other behavioral science techniques is the emphasis upon viewing the organization as a total system of interacting and interrelated elements. Organization development is the application of an organization-wide approach to the functional, structural, technical, and personal relationships in organizations. OD programs are based upon a systematic analysis of problems and a top management actively committed to the change effort. The purpose of such a program is to increase organizational effectiveness by the application of OD values and techniques. Many organization development programs use the **action research model.** Action research involves collecting information about the organization, feeding it back to the client system, and developing and implementing action programs to improve system performance. The manager also needs to be aware of the processes that should be considered when one is attempting to create change. This section presents a five-stage model of the total organization development process. Each stage is dependent on the preceding one, and successful change is more probable when each of these stages is considered in a logical sequence.

## Stage 1: Anticipate a Need for Change

Before a program of change can be implemented, the organization must anticipate the need for change. The first step is the manager's perception that the organization is somehow in a state of disequilibrium or needs improvement. The state of disequilibrium may result from growth or decline or from competitive, technological, legal, or social changes in the external environment. There must be a felt need, because only felt needs convince individuals to adopt new ways. Managers must be sensitive to changes in the competitive environment, to "what's going on out there."

## Stage 2: Develop the Practitioner–Client Relationship

After an organization recognizes a need for change and an OD practitioner enters the system, a relationship begins to develop between the practitioner and the client system. The client is the person or organization that is being assisted. The development of this relationship is an important determinant of the probable success or failure of an OD program. As with many interpersonal relationships, the exchange of expectations and obligations (the formation of a psychological contract) depends to a great degree upon a good first impression or match between the practitioner and the client system. The practitioner attempts to establish a pattern of open communication, a relationship of trust, and an atmosphere of shared responsibility. Issues dealing with responsibility, rewards, and objectives must be clarified, defined, or worked through at this point.

The practitioner must decide when to enter the system and what his or her role should be. For instance, the practitioner may intervene with the sanction and approval of top management and either with or without the sanction and support of members in the lower levels of the organization. At one company, OD started at the vice presidential level, and by using internal OD practitioners, the OD program was gradually expanded to include line managers and workers. At another company, an external practitioner from a university was invited in by the organization's industrial relations group to initiate the OD program.

### Stage 3: The Diagnostic Process

After the OD practitioner has intervened and developed a working relationship with the client, the practitioner and the client begin to gather data about the system. The collection of data is an important activity providing the organization and the practitioner with a better understanding of client system problems: the diagnosis.

One rule of operation for the OD practitioner is to question the client's diagnosis of the problem, because the client's perspective may be biased. After acquiring information relevant to the situation perceived to be the problem, the OD practitioner and client together analyze the data to identify problem areas and causal relationships. A weak, inaccurate, or faulty diagnosis can lead to a costly and ineffective change program. The diagnostic phase, then, is used to determine the exact problem that needs solution, to identify the forces causing the situation, and to provide a basis for selecting effective change strategies and techniques.

Although organizations usually generate a large amount of "hard" or operational data, the data may present an incomplete picture of organizational performance. The practitioner and client may agree to increase the range or depth of the available data by interview or questionnaire as a basis for further action programs. One organization, for instance, was having a problem with high employee turnover. The practitioner investigated the high turnover rate by means of a questionnaire to determine why the problem existed, and from these data designed an OD program to correct it. The firm's employees felt it had become a bureaucratic organization clogged with red tape, causing high turnover. OD programs have since reduced employee turnover to 19 percent, compared with 34 percent for the industry.

At a major food company, a new executive vice president needed to move quickly to improve the division's performance. With the help of an external practitioner, data were gathered by conducting intensive interviews with top management, as well as with outsiders, to determine key problem areas. Then, without identifying the source of comments, the management team worked on the information in a 10-hour session until they were able to hammer out the problems and develop a plan of action.

### Stage 4: Action Plans, Strategies, and Techniques

The diagnostic phase leads to a series of interventions, activities, or programs aimed at resolving problems and increasing organization effectiveness. These programs apply such OD techniques as total quality management (TQM), job design, role analysis, goal setting, team building, and intergroup development to the causes specified in the diagnostic phase (all of these techniques are discussed in detail in subsequent chapters). In all likelihood, more time will be spent on this fourth stage than on any of the other stages of an OD program.

### Stage 5: Self-Renewal, Monitor, and Stabilize

Once an action program is implemented, the final step is to monitor the results and stabilize the desired changes. This stage assesses the effectiveness of change strategies in attaining stated objectives. The system members need to know the results of change efforts in order to determine whether they ought to modify, continue, or discontinue the activities. Once a problem has been corrected and a change program is implemented and monitored, means must be devised to make sure that the new behavior is stabilized and internalized. If this is not done, the system will regress to previous ineffective modes or states. The ideal OD program will create a client system that has a self-renewal capability that can maintain innovation without outside support.

### Continuous Improvement

In today's environment, companies seeking to be successful and survive are faced with the need to continually introduce changes. The unlikely has become commonplace, and the unthinkable has become almost inevitable. The most important lesson managers need to learn is that there are only two kinds of companies—those that are changing, and those that are going out of business. Continual change is a way of life. A critical challenge for managers who are leading change efforts is to inspire individuals to work as a team.

This five-stage model shows how different OD methods and approaches are used to continuously improve performance so that the vision can be achieved. It is important to remember that no model or paradigm is perfect, but it can still provide useful approaches to change.

As an OD program stabilizes, the need for the practitioner should decrease. If the client moves toward independence and evidences a self-renewal capacity, the gradual termination of the practitioner-client system relationship is easily accomplished. If the client system has become overly dependent upon the practitioner, termination of the relationship can be a difficult and awkward issue. An important issue in the implementation of an OD program is whether or not the practitioner is able to deal effectively with power and political infighting. Hierarchical organizations, whether they are business, governmental, for-profit, or not-for-profit, rely on power. The individuals in positions of influence generally constitute the power structure and frequently are power-motivated people. Managers compete for promotions, and departments and divisions have disagreements over budget allocations. In addition to power issues, political infighting is a reality (and often a dysfunctional factor) in most organizations. The issue is whether OD practitioners deal with these power and political issues in bringing about a change. Given the nature of OD, an OD program is not a political/power type of intervention. Still, the OD practitioner must be aware of politics and use a problem-solving approach that is compatible with power-oriented situations.

## Summary

This chapter focused on several major issues. One is that organizations operate in a dynamic and changing environment and consequently must be adaptive. You have been introduced to the emerging field of organization development (OD) and the ways it is used to improve organizational effectiveness.

- **Challenge.** One of the manager's most difficult tasks is initiating organization change and renewal. As a manager, you must be sensitive to changes in markets, products, and competition, and be aware of the need for an adaptive and flexible organization.
- **Organization Development.** Organization development is the discipline that applies behavioral science techniques to management problems. Because the essential task of management is to deal with change, it is the purpose of this book to better prepare managers for this task.
- **Change is Constant.** Change in our dynamic environment is unavoidable. And change is occurring so rapidly that it is a moving target. An organization will be able to survive only if it can effectively respond and anticipate the technological, social, and economic environment.
- **Evolution of OD.** OD has evolved over the past 55 years from its beginnings as the application of behavioral science knowledge and techniques. It has been strongly influenced by the works of Kurt Lewin, Abraham Maslow, Robert Blake, Richard Beckhard, and Douglas McGregor.
- **OD Specialists.** These are professionals who have specialized and trained in organization development and related areas, such as organization behavior, applied social sciences, interpersonal communications, and decision making. If they are members of the organization, they are internal practitioners. If they come from outside the organization, they are external practitioners.
- **Culture.** Culture is the set of characteristics of a specific civilization, society, or group. Organizational culture is the shared language, dress, patterns of behavior, value system, interactions, and group norms of the members of an organization.
- **Socialization.** Socialization is the process that adapts employees to the organization's culture. Entering a class for the first time is very similar to the first day on a new job. You may decide to rebel and reject the classroom norms, you may conform by accepting the classroom norms, or you may respond with creative individualism.
- **Psychological Contract.** A psychological contract brings many underlying expectations out into the open, explains them, and defines the interdependence and shared responsibility between the individual and the organization.
- **OD Model.** Organization development involves the long-term, system-wide application of behavioral science techniques to increase organization effectiveness. OD works on the idea that organizational change involves improving the way people work together on teams and the way team activities are integrated with organizational goals.

## Review Questions

1. How would you define "organization development"?
2. How does OD differ from a single-change technique such as management training?
3. Identify and demonstrate the uses of the psychological contract.
4. Explain the difference between pivotal and peripheral norms.

5. Explain three basic responses an individual may have to socialization.
6. Read a book or an article and identify the organizational culture and norms it embodies.
7. Identify and explain the five stages of organization development.

## Key Words and Concepts

Action Research Model
Change Agent
Client System
Creative Individualism

External Practitioner
Internal Practitioner
Norms
Organization Culture

Organization Development
  (OD)
OD Practitioner
OD Specialist

Peripheral Norms
Pivotal Norms
Psychological Contract
Socialization

## OD Skills Simulation 1.1

### Auditioning for the *Saturday Night Live* Guest Host Spot

*Total time suggested: 60 minutes.*

### A. Purpose

The goal of this exercise is to begin building trust within the class by sharing information about yourself with others and exploring values and norms. You will gain experience interviewing another person, which is a key skill for an OD practitioner.

### B. Procedures

*Step 1.* Members form into pairs.

*Step 2.* Each member of the pair interviews the other member to find out who she/he is. The purpose is to gain enough information to introduce the other person to the class, with an emphasis on behavior. A set of questions is provided as a departure point for your discussion on the Interview Format. See the Interview Format.

*Time suggested for Steps 1 and 2: 20 minutes.*

*Step 3.* The total class is reformed. Each member of the pair introduces the other member. Introduce your partner to the class with a focus on positive accomplishments, but add some humor and demonstrate your own "guest host" style. Try not to appear as though you are reading "que cards" but instead introduce your partner in a conversational manner. The class may ask questions to find more relevant information about the partner you are introducing. This continues around the class until everyone has been introduced.

*Step 4.* In a meeting with the entire class, discuss the following questions:

1. How many potential guest hosts did you discover?
2. In the introduction process, did you learn more about the person being introduced or the person doing the introduction?
3. Based on the introductions, can you foresee the formation of any norms?
4. What seems to be the type and level of participation of the members?

*Time suggested for Steps 3 and 4: 40 minutes.*

**INTERVIEW FORMAT**

*Possible questions and topic:*

Name of Person Interviewed _____

1. Tell me a little bit about yourself.

     a. _____

     b. _____

     c. _____

2. How would you describe the strengths you bring to the class?

     a. _____

     b. _____

     c. _____

3. What do you consider your past accomplishments or highlights?

     a. _____

     b. _____

     c. _____

4. What are your hobbies, interests, and astrological sign?

     _____

5. What is your favorite:

     Color _____

     Music _____

     Car _____

     Food _____

     TV Star _____

     Other _____

6. What are your goals for this class?

     a. _____

     b. _____

     c. _____

7. What resources can you contribute?

     _____

8. Anything else we've not covered?

     _____

     _____

     _____

## OD Skills Simulation 1.2

### The Psychological Contract[29]

*Total time suggested: 15 to 115 minutes depending on the parts used.*

### A. Purpose

The goal of this exercise is to make explicit and share some of the major expectations and obligations between students and instructor. It provides an opportunity for the instructor to find out what the class expects and for the students to learn what the instructor expects.

### B. Procedures

#### Part A. Instructor's Interview of Students

*Step 1.* The class forms into groups of four or five members.

*Step 2.* Each group elects one person as representative.

*Step 3.* Each group prepares its representative for the interview by the instructor. The representative should understand the group's position and be prepared to answer the instructor's questions. (See the Suggested Question Guide for Instructor's Interview of Students.)

*Time suggested for Steps 1 to 3: 15 minutes.*

*Step 4.* The representatives meet with the instructor. The instructor interviews them about their expectations while the rest of the class observes.

*Time suggested for Step 4: 20 minutes.*

**SUGGESTED QUESTION GUIDE FOR INSTRUCTOR'S INTERVIEW OF STUDENTS**

1. What are your objectives for this course?

   a. To learn theories?

   b. To reach some desired level of knowledge?

   c. To learn new skills?

   d. To gain new behaviors?

   e. To get a good grade?

   f. To get required credit hours?

2. How can the instructor best help you to achieve your goals?

   a. By giving lectures?

   b. By assigning and discussing readings?

   c. By conducting exams?

   d. By leading seminar discussions?

   e. By relating personal experiences?

   f. By letting you work on your own?

   g. By being a stern task master?

   h. By being warm and supportive?

3. How can other class members help you achieve your goals?

   a. By sharing prior experiences?

   b. By participating in group discussions?

   c. By coming to class prepared?

   d. By sharing educational background?

   e. By doing nothing?

   f. By being enthusiastic and supportive?

   g. By being critical?

   h. By being flattering?

   i. By giving honest appraisals?

4. How should class members be evaluated?

   a. By quizzes, exams, and tests?

   b. By instructor?

   c. By peers?

   d. By quantity or quality of work?

**Part B. Students' Interview of Instructor**

*Step 1.* The class forms into the same groups.

*Step 2.* Elect a different representative.

*Step 3.* Each group discusses the questions it would like its representative to ask the instructor. The representative should be sure to understand the group's questions and concerns. (See the Suggested Question Guide for Students' Interview of Instructor.)

*Time suggested for Steps 1 to 3: 15 minutes.*

*Step 4.* In a class meeting, the representatives interview the instructor to clarify the instructor's expectations of the class. The representatives and the instructor should write on the blackboard a consensus of course objectives. This will not only reaffirm and support the objectives listed in the syllabus (by allowing the class to come up with the objectives), but will let the students and instructor delete or add other objectives that they feel may be important to the OD learning process.

*Time suggested for Step 4: 20 minutes.*

---

**SUGGESTED QUESTION GUIDE FOR STUDENTS INTERVIEW OF INSTRUCTOR**

You may ask the instructor any questions you feel are relevant to effective learning. Some areas you may want to discuss are:

1. How do people learn?

2. What is the instructor's expectations about attendance?

3. What is his/her philosophy of evaluation? How are students evaluated?

4. What is the instructor's role in the class?

5. What stereotypes about students are held?

6. Is there anything else that you feel is important?

### Part C. Identifying and Establishing Norms

Note: Part C is optional and may be omitted or used instead of Parts A, B and D.

*Step 1.* Meeting as a class, do or discuss the following:

1. Identify the pivotal and peripheral norms that are being established.
2. Which of these norms are functional or dysfunctional to the class?
3. Which of these norms would you like to change?
4. Do you have any additional behaviors you would like to see become norms?
5. How much trust is being developed among students, and between students and instructor?

*Step 2.* For the norms you would like to change, make some specific plans for the changes.

*Time suggested for Steps 1 and 2: 15 minutes.*

### Part D. Finalizing the Psychological Contract

Note: Part D is optional and may be omitted or used instead of Parts A, B and C.

*Step 1.* Individually complete Column 1 of the Psychological Contract Worksheet.

*Step 2.* In small groups, exchange views, and achieve consensus in completing Column 2 of the Worksheet. Select a representative to report to the class.

*Time suggested for Steps 1 and 2: 15 minutes.*

*Step 3.* The representatives share with the class their group's responses. As a class, and including the instructor, reach an agreement on a psychological contract for the course. Appoint a class member to serve as a recorder and write the contract on the board. Also, the recorder is to make a permanent copy where it will be posted in the class meeting room for future classes. All class members are to record the results on their Final Psychological Contract.

*Time suggested for Step 3: 15 minutes.*

**THE PSYCHOLOGICAL CONTRACT WORKSHEET**

| Issues | Column 1<br>Individual Responses | Column 2<br>Group Response |
|---|---|---|
| 1. What were your expectations from this course when you enrolled in it? | | |
| 2. What do you expect to get out of this course? | | |
| 3. What will be the most enjoyable part of the course? | | |
| 4. What skills do you feel will be the most critical to becoming an effective manager? | | |
| 5. What skills and topics must you work on? | | |

**FINAL PSYCHOLOGICAL CONTRACT**

_____

_____

_____

_____

_____

_____

_____

_____

_____

_____

_____

_____

_____

_____

_____

_____

## Case Analysis Guidelines

### Why Use Cases?

Case studies allow a learning-by-doing approach. The material in the case provides the data for analysis and decision making. Cases require you to diagnose and make decisions about the situation and to defend those decisions to your peers.

### Objectives of the Case Method

1. Helping you to acquire the skills of putting textbook knowledge about management into practice.
2. Getting you out of the habit of being a receiver of facts, concepts, and techniques, and into the habit of diagnosing problems, analyzing and evaluating alternatives, and formulating workable plans of action.
3. Training you to work out answers and solutions for yourself, as opposed to relying upon the authoritative crutch of the professor or a textbook.
4. Providing you with exposure to a range of firms and managerial situations (which might take a lifetime to experience personally), thus offering you a basis for comparison when you begin your own management career.

### How to Prepare a Case

1. Begin your analysis by reading the case once for familiarity.
2. On the second reading, attempt to gain full command of the facts, organizational goals, objectives, strategies, policies, symptoms of problems, problems, basic causes of problems, unresolved issues, and roles of key individuals.
3. Who are the key players in this situation? What are their roles and their styles?
4. Arrive at a solid evaluation of the organization, based upon the information in the case. Developing the ability to evaluate organizations and size up their situations is the key to case analysis.
5. Decide what you think the organization needs to do to improve its performance and to set forth a workable plan of action.

# CASE: TGIF

It's 4:30 on a Friday afternoon, and the weekly beer bust is in full swing at Quantum Software's Denver headquarters. The sun shines on the volleyball court and beyond; the patio sparkles over a skyline of the Rocky Mountains. Every week, most of the employees drop in to unwind and relax at the beer bust for an hour as a reward for extra effort.

Quantum Software was founded three years ago by Stan Albright and Erin Barber, based upon an idea they came up with in college for forming a business aimed at developing and selling computer software specifically oriented to the needs of independent oil businesses. Few of these firms grow large enough to do their own data-processing systems. Quantum has grown to more than 200 employees and $95 million in sales over the past three years. One Friday afternoon, Bill Carter, the corporate attorney, dropped in to attend a business meeting. After the meeting, he was invited to mix in with employees at the weekly beer bust.

"What a great place to work!" several people told Bill. The spirit of Quantum continually amazed Bill. Stan and Erin knew how to keep things hopping and yet hold morale at an enthusiastic level. To counter the frantic work pace of 16-hour days and six-day weeks, Quantum had a beer bust every Friday afternoon. Everyone was invited, from Stan and Erin to the part-time janitor who worked nights.

No ties, no suit coats, first names only: this was a great way to encourage the team concept. Lately though, Bill Carter had been having second thoughts about serving alcohol at a company-sponsored party. He made up his mind to speak to CEO Stan Albright about it and started toward the pool where Stan and Erin were holding a lively discussion with three employees. Just then, John Hooker, a new programmer in software development, lost his balance and fell on the snack table, sending finger sandwiches flying in all directions and getting a round of applause. "All right, John!" several people called out. More determined than ever, Bill approached Stan and Erin and said, "Don't you think this party thing is getting a little out of hand? It used to be a lot of fun, but now maybe we're growing too fast. We're getting more people like John there, who just seem to overdo it."

"Take it easy, Bill," said Stan. "The atmosphere around here would get stale real fast if we couldn't blow off a little steam now and then."

"Come on, Bill," Erin added, "lighten up. We need this time to relax and for everyone to socialize over a beer without the pressure of work."

"You should know, Bill, how much these parties mean to our success. I really feel that one of the keys to our continued growth has been the family feeling among our employees. On Fridays at our TGIF get-togethers, we all get to know one another as equals. That gives me the right to kick butts when I have to because they know I like them and want them to succeed. That's the real value of these parties."

"Okay, Stan, so you tell me," asked Bill, "what's the value in having someone like John who has had too many beers driving home and possibly causing a serious accident? Do you realize that Quantum could be held liable in such an instance?"

"Bill," responded Erin, "you know I'm the one who first thought up the idea of having a Friday bash and I still think it's a great idea. I agree with Stan that this company is a success thanks to our employees and the esprit de corps that we've developed. If we drop the TGIFs as a time to unwind, what can we replace it with? I can see the point you're trying to raise. I agree that something bad could come out of this, but if we can't take a few risks we may as well close the doors. These parties are great for recruitment and they define our corporate culture. I feel it would be a big mistake to drop the parties."

"I think you two are missing the point," answered Bill. "Of course, I realize how important it is to keep our team spirit. What I'm trying to say is, isn't there a way to keep that spirit and put some limit to our liability exposure at the same time?" (Use Case Analysis Form.)[30]

**TGIF CASE ANALYSIS FORM**

Name: _____

I. Problems

  A. Macro

    1. _____

      _____

    2. _____

      _____

  B. Micro

    1. _____

      _____

    2. _____

      _____

II. Causes

    1. _____

      _____

    2. _____

      _____

    3. _____

      _____

III. Systems affected

    1. _____

      _____

    2. _____

      _____

    3. _____

      _____

IV. Alternatives

    1. _____

      _____

    2. _____

      _____

    3. _____

      _____

V. Recommendations

_____

_____

_____

_____

_____

## Chapter 1 Endnotes

1. Laura Rubach, "Downsizing: How Quality Is Affected as Companies Shrink," *Quality Progress*, vol. 28, no. 4 (April 1995), p. 23.

2. Michael Malone (interviewer), "Intel Reboots for the 21st Century," *Wall Street Journal*, September 27–28, 2008, p. A17.

3. Pallavi Gogoi, "Thinking Outside the Cereal Box," *Business Week*, July 28, 2003, pp. 74–75.

4. Richard Beckhard, *Organizational Development: Strategies and Models* (Reading, MA: Addison-Wesley, 1969), p. 9. Also see Jyotsna Sanzgiri and Jonathan Z. Gottlieb, "Philosophic and Pragmatic Influences on the Practice of Organization Development, 1950–2000," *Organizational Dynamics*, vol. 21, no. 2 (Autumn 1992), pp. 57–59.

5. William C. Symonds, "The Kodak Revolt Is Short-Sighted," *Business Week*, November 3, 2003, p. 38.

6. Warren G. Bennis, *Organization Development: Its Nature, Origins, and Prospects* (Reading, MA: Addison-Wesley, 1969).

7. www.ge.com; Steven Prokesch, "How GE Teaches Teams to Lead Change," *Harvard Business Review*, January 2009, pp. 99–106; and Fay Hansen, "Building Better Leaders . . . Faster," *Workforce Management*, vol. 87, no. 10 (June 9, 2008), pp. 25–28.

8. Robert B. Reich, "The Company of the Future," *Fast Company*, November 1998, p. 124.

9. Robert R. Blake, Jane S. Mouton, L. Barnes, and L. Greiner, "Breakthrough in Organization Development," *Harvard Business Review*, November–December 1964, pp. 133–55.

10. See Richard Beckhard, *Organization Development Strategies and Models* (Reading, MA: Addison-Wesley, 1969).

11. For more information, see www.ntl.org/.

12. Douglas McGregor, *The Human Side of Enterprise* (New York: McGraw-Hill, 1960); Douglas McGregor, *The Human Side of Enterprise*, updated and with new commentary by Joel Cutcher-Gershenfeld (New York: McGraw-Hill, 2006); and Douglas McGregor, *The Professional Manager*, edited by Caroline McGregor and Warren G. Bennis (New York: McGraw-Hill, 1967).

13. For more information, see www.odnetwork.org/.

14. Therese F. Yaeger, Thomas C. Head, and Peter F. Sorensen. *Global Organization Development: Managing Unprecedented Change* (Greenwich, CT: IAP, 2006).

15. For additional information, see David L. Bradford and W. Warner Burke (Editors), *Reinventing Organization Development: New Approaches to Change in Organizations* (San Francisco: Pfeiffer, 2005).

16. See Bennis, *Organization Development: Its Nature, Origins, and Prospects,* for one of the first discussions of OD practitioners.

17. For more information on organizational culture, see Edgar Schein, *Organizational Culture and Leadership* (San Francisco: Jossey-Bass, 2004); Hasan Danaee Fard, Ali Asghar Anvary Rostamy, and Hamid Taghiloo, "How Types of Organizational Cultures Contribute in Shaping Learning Organisations" *Singapore Management Review*, January 2009, pp. 49–61; Davide Ravasi and Majken Schultz, "Responding to Organizational Identity Threats: Exploring the Role of Organizational Culture," *Academy of Management Journal*, June 2006, pp. 433–58; Joanne Martin, *Organizational Culture: Mapping the Terrain* (Thousand Oaks, CA: Sage, 2002); Neal Ashkanasy, Celeste P. M. Wilderom, and Mark F. Peterson, eds., *Handbook of Organizational Culture and Climate* (Thousand Oaks, CA: Sage, 2000); Cary L. Cooper, Sue Cartwright, and P. Christopher Earley, eds., *The International Handbook of Organizational Culture and Climate* (New York: Wiley, 2001).

18. B. F. Skinner, *Contingencies of Reinforcement* (Upper Saddle River, NJ: Prentice Hall, 1969), p. 13.

19. Dean Foust, Anand Natarajan, and Brian Grow, "Disability Claim Denied!" *Business Week*, December 22, 2003, pp. 62–64.

20. See H. S. Becker, "Culture: A Sociological View," *Yale Review*, Summer 1982, pp. 513–27; and Edgar H. Schein, *Organizational Culture and Leadership* (San Francisco: Jossey-Bass, 1985), p. 168.

21. Edgar H. Schein, "Coming to a New Awareness of Organizational Culture," *Sloan Management Review*, Winter 1984, pp. 3–16; Daniel C. Feldman, "The Development of Group Norms," *Academy of Management Review*, vol. 9, no.1 (1984), pp. 47–53.

22. See, for example, Daniel M. Cable and Charles K. Parsons, "Socialization Tactics and Person-Organization Fit," *Personnel Psychology*, vol. 54, no.1 (Spring 2001), pp. 1–23; J. Hebden, "Adopting an Organization's Culture," *Organizational Dynamics*, Summer 1986, pp. 54–72; G. R. Jones, "Socialization Tactics," *Academy of Management Journal*, June 1986, pp. 262–79.

23. Robert Berner, "P&G, How A. G. Lafley Is Revolutionizing a Bastion of Corporate Conservatism," *Business Week*, July 7, 2003, pp. 52–63.

24. Glenn Hasek, "The Right Chemistry," *Industry Week*, vol. 249, no. 5 (March 6, 2000), p. 36–40.

25. Edgar H. Schein, "Organization Socialization and the Profession of Management," *Industrial Management Review*, vol. 9, no. 2 (Winter, 1968), p. 8.

26. www.starbucks.com; Judith Crown, "Coffee Gets Hotter at McDonald's," *Business Week*, January 9, 2008, www.businessweek.com/; Moira Herbst, "Starbucks' Karma Problem," *Business Week*, January 12, 2009, p. 26; Burt Helm and Jena McGregor, "Howard Schultz's Grande Challenge," *Business Week*, January 21, 2008, p. 28; Andy Serwer and Kate Bonamici, "Hot Starbucks to Go," *Fortune*, January 26, 2004, p. 60; Interview of Howard Schultz on National Public Radio, *The Monthly Fool* show, April 23, 2004; Maryann Hammers, "Pleasing Employees, Pouring Profit," *Workforce Management,* October 2003, p. 58; Stanley Holmes, Drake Bennett, Kate Carlisle, and

Chester Dawson, "Planet Starbucks," *Business Week,* September 9, 2002, p. 100.

27. For some of the original material on psychological contracts, see C. Argyris, *Understanding Organizational Behavior* (Homewood, IL: Dorsey Press, 1960); Schein, "Organization Socialization and the Profession of Management"; Schein, *Organizational Psychology*, 3rd ed. (Englewood Cliffs, NJ: Prentice-Hall, 1980); H. Levinson, C. Price, K. Munden, H. Mandl, and C. Solley, *Men, Management, and Mental Health* (Cambridge, MA: Harvard University Press, 1962). For more current information, see Charissa Freese and René Schalk, "How to Measure the Psychological Contract? A Critical Criteria-Based Review of Measures," *South African Journal of Psychology,* June 2008, pp. 269–86; Rene Schalk and Robert E. Roe, "Towards a Dynamic Model of the Psychological Contract," *Journal for the Theory of Social Behaviour*, June 2007, pp. 167–82; Simon Restubog, Prashant Bordial and Robert L. Tang, "Effects of Psychological Contract Breach on Performance of IT Employees: The Mediating Role of Affective Commitment," *Journal of Occupational and Organizational Psychology*, June 2006, pp. 299–306.

28. Schalk and Roe, "Towards a Dynamic Model of the Psychological Contract."

29. This exercise is adapted from David A. Kolb, Irwin M. Rubine, and James M. McIntyre, *Organizational Psychology: An Experiential Approach*, 2nd ed. (Upper Saddle River, NJ: Prentice Hall, 1974), pp. 9–17.

30. Don Harvey, John Hulpke, and Joe Hudson, California State University, Bakersfield, Bakersfield, CA, 1994. Modified and edited by Don Brown.

# Organization Renewal: The Challenge of Change

## LEARNING OBJECTIVES

**Upon completing this chapter, you will be able to:**

1. Recognize the factors contributing to the accelerating rate of change.
2. Identify the ways an organization uses renewing processes to adapt to change.
3. Determine the individual and group methods of coping with change.
4. Understand and apply the sociotechnical-systems approach to OD.

## PREMEETING PREPARATION

1. Read Chapter 2.
2. Read the instructions for OD Skills Simulation 2.1. Before coming to class, complete Part A, Steps 1 and 2, which includes completing the Profile Survey, Profile Form, Class Performance Form, and Objectives Form. Familiarize yourself with the "Instructions for Developing OD Practitioner Roles and Skills" at the end of the simulation.
3. Read and prepare analysis for Case: The NoGo Railroad.

## THE CHALLENGES OF CHANGE

Change is the name of the game in management today. Market, product, and competitive conditions are rapidly changing. Under these pressures, organizations are changing. They are downsizing, reengineering, flattening structures, going global, and initiating technologies that are more sophisticated. However, many organizational changes, such as downsizing, often have unintended effects or consequences on the productivity of individual work units.[1] As the environment changes, organizations must adapt if they are to be successful. For example, through changing times, 3M has managed to keep its creative spirit alive. The company is consistently in the list of top 20 innovative companies in the world in the *Business Week*—Boston Consulting Group ranking.[2] Almost everyone now uses Post-It notes, yet they were an accidental discovery of 3M scientist Art Fry, who became the product champion for Post-Its. The outcome is a big company that still manages to develop new products faster than its competition. The reason: Commitment to innovation and lack of corporate rules leave room for plenty of experimentation—and failure.[3]

### Renewal

Organization renewal requires that top managers make adaptive changes to the environment. Strategic models of top managers play a crucial role in directing organizational responses to keep pace with changing industry conditions. In today's business environment, more than at any time in history, the only constant is change. Business consultant and author Jim Collins wrote in *Fortune*, "Companies do not fall primarily because of what the world does to them or because of how the world changes around them; they fall first and foremost because of what they do to themselves."[4]

The fact is that managers will have to become masters of change and renewal to be effective in the future. The changes facing management in the twenty-first century are likely to be even more dynamic and challenging than in the past. Therefore, the focus of organization development is on changing organizational systems, stressing the situational nature of problems and their system-wide impact. In solving a given problem, managers must analyze the organization, its departmental subsystem interrelationships, and the possible effects on the internal environment. This approach, termed the **systems approach,** provides a way of observing, analyzing, and solving problems in organizations. The systems approach, then, is concerned with relationships among departments and the interdependencies between these elements and the external environment.

The changing conditions that face organizations can be seen in the sudden decline in the sewing machine market compared to the projected increase in the cell phone market. After Singer N. V. (the Singer Company) came out of bankruptcy, it had to reorganize, sell off unprofitable units, and change the marketing strategy because the number of people buying sewing machines had declined drastically. Meanwhile, the market for smart cell phones, virtually nonexistent a decade ago, today constitutes a several-billion-dollar market.

## Constant Change

Because of the rapid pace of technology, firms are confronted with the early technological obsolescence of products. In the past, companies could grow during the long lifespan of a proprietary invention, but today their innovations are often quickly overtaken by competitors with technological improvements. These problems are the result of the increasing rate of change and are made more difficult because of the impact of future shock on management. Managers today face risk situations unlike those of the past, and in an era of accelerating change, managerial excellence derives from the ability to cope with these changes. Organizations either become more adaptive, flexible, and anticipative, or they become rigid and stagnant, reacting to change after the fact, often when it is too late. Seldom can managerial decisions be based solely on extrapolations of historical experience. Many decisions are unique, innovative, and risky, involving new areas of opportunity. Putting a new product or a new process into production is a major business decision.

Organizations exist in a changing environment and, therefore, must have the capacity to adapt. As Apple Computer's evangelist for the Macintosh, Guy Kawasaki was one of the driving forces behind a revolutionary new product. Kawasaki's first rule: If you want to make a revolution, you have to start by unleashing revolutionary products and ideas. You have to "create like God," but thinking differently is just the first step.[5] Business revolutionaries (or change agents) also have to keep rethinking—and just as important, they have to keep doing, if they are to turn radical ideas into real accomplishments.

In the previous chapter, a model for five stages of the organization development process was described. Stage 1 of this model is to anticipate a need for change and is depicted in Figure 2.1. In this chapter, we will concentrate on the first stage and examine the way managers

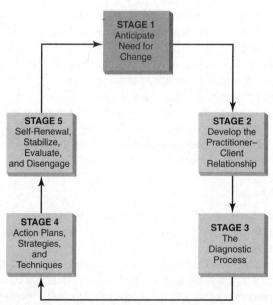

**FIGURE 2.1    Stage 1 of Organization Development's Five Stage**

react to the accelerating rate of change. The pressure of future shock results in new perspectives for management strategies and decisions. Managers must do more than just react: they must be able to anticipate the changing patterns of people, markets, products, and technology. Five areas will be covered:

1. Organization renewal.
2. The systems approach.
3. The sociotechnical system.
4. Future shock.
5. Organizational transformation and organization development.

## ORGANIZATION RENEWAL: ADAPTING TO CHANGE

Managing effectively is a major challenge facing organizations today.[6] When an organization fails to change, the cost of the failure may mean its very survival. Because the environment is composed of systems outside the immediate influence of the organization, the organization must adapt itself to these forces by introducing internal changes that will allow it to be more effective. Herb Kelleher, founder of Southwest Airlines and currently Chairman Emeritus, was asked in an interview with *Fortune* how one could renew a big organization. He replied, "The way that we accomplish that is that we constantly tell our employees . . . think small and act small, and we'll get bigger. Think big, be complacent, be cocky, and we'll get smaller."[7] To be successful, organizations must develop a managerial style and culture that can adequately handle the challenges and opportunities they face. A management style that was adequate under one set of conditions may become progressively less effective under changing circumstances. The OD practitioner, then, is ultimately interested in changing human behavior and organizational processes to create a more adaptive and flexible organization.

Organizational renewal is important. If a company is to survive in an increasingly competitive marketplace, the organization must continuously adapt to its environment; without renewal, management cannot maintain excellence. **Organizational renewal** may be defined as an ongoing process of building innovation and adaptation into the organization. Google, for example, encourages innovation by letting engineers spend about 20 percent of their time in projects other than their primary job. CEO Eric Schmidt explains why he thinks this model works: "I think it's cultural. You have to have the culture, and you have to get it right."[8] **See OD Application: Google's Culture.**

A dilemma with renewal is that stability is necessary but is also the major obstruction to change. For most organizations, it seems, the more effective they have been in the past, the more likely they are to resist change. **Entropy** is a principle of physics according to which everything that is organized will break down or run down unless it is maintained. Organization renewal, then, is an approach to preventing corporate entropy.

Why is change so difficult? Possibly because the culture of the organization becomes a part of the people who perform the work. In changing these old patterns, people must alter not only their behavior but also their values and their views of themselves. The organization's structure, procedures, and relationships continue to reinforce prior patterns of behavior and to resist the new ones. As a result, organizational change sometimes results in upheaval and dissatisfaction, and possibly even in resignations, dismissals, or transfers. Consequently, an organization must develop an adaptive orientation and management style that is geared to its environment. Managers in different organizations deal with situations that may be dramatically different. Some organizations exist in relatively stable environments, whereas others operate in highly dynamic settings. Each requires a different orientation to the environment.

### Approaches to Change

Every organization must have enough stability to continue to function satisfactorily and still prevent itself from becoming too static or stagnant to adapt to changing conditions. Both stability and adaptation are essential to continued survival and growth.

An organization that operates in a mature field with a stable product and relatively few competitors needs a different adaptive orientation than a firm operating in a high-growth market, among numerous competitors, and with a high degree of innovation. The former operates in an environment that is relatively stable, whereas the latter faces a more dynamic and turbulent set of

## OD Application: Google's Culture[9]

The company is Google, its product is a search engine, and it still operates under the same freewheeling managerial style that it started with. The company is managed by its designated grown-up, CEO Eric Schmidt. In practice, however, it is run by a triumvirate (from the Latin *triumviratus*, meaning "board of three"). Schmidt is joined in decision-making responsibilities by company cofounders Larry Page and Sergey Brin. Schmidt is a seasoned manager from Sun Microsystems and Novell.

CEO Schmidt was hired in 2001 to provide experienced leadership. He handles the day-to-day stuff. Decisions come from three-way discussions between Schmidt, Page, and Brin. Harvard Business School professor David Yoffie says of Google, "If multiple people are making decisions, decisions don't get made . . . Ultimately one person has to make a decision." Schmidt responds that the consensus-management structure at Google can be maddening at times but it is effective. Brin serves as president for technology and Page is president for products. "We try to run as a group, because partnerships make better decisions," says Schmidt. He adds, "I've tried very hard to have this be a founder-driven company."

Executives at Google keep a "Top 100" priority list, and managers rarely tell engineers what project to work on. Instead, engineers migrate to projects that interest them. This controlled-chaos type of strategy forms fluid working groups that can last weeks or months, but it is tough on planners. Engineers are also encouraged to spend 20 percent of their time working on their own research projects, no matter how esoteric and offbeat. CEO Schmidt says, "It has always been a small team of people who have a new idea, typically not understood by people around them and their executives. [This is] a systematic way of making sure a middle manager does not eliminate that innovation." A vice president says, "We're encouraging creativity and tolerating chaos." The three executives maintain that Google's freewheeling engineering culture is not a liability but an asset. "What we really talk about is how we can attract and develop this creative culture," says Schmidt.

Google has a unique culture, and with a lot of work it has been able to maintain its culture, even with a workforce of over 20,000 located around the world. Commitment to innovation at Google depends on everyone being comfortable sharing ideas and opinions. With each employee a hands-on contributor, everyone realizes they are an important part in Google's future success. This is evident at the weekly TGIF meetings where anyone is free to ask Page or Brin questions. "Nobody works the way we do. The Google culture makes sense if you're in it, and no sense if you're not in it," says Schmidt.

Part of the Google culture is its "ten things," which is the company's list of ten things it has found to be true:

1. Focus on the user and all else will follow.
2. It's best to do one thing really, really well.
3. Fast is better than slow.
4. Democracy on the Web works.
5. You don't need to be at your desk to need an answer.
6. You can make money without doing evil.
7. There's always more information out there.
8. The need for information crosses all borders.
9. You can be serious without a suit.
10. Great just isn't good enough.

With a worldwide marketplace full of competitors, Google must maintain breakthrough innovations. Brin says, "I've seen companies obsessed with competition, say, with Microsoft, that keep looking in their rearview mirror and crash into a tree head-on because they're so distracted. If I had one magic bullet, I wouldn't spend it on a competitor, I'd spend it to make sure we're executing as well as we possibly can. I think we're doing a pretty good job."

Google maintains its focus and strategy. The outward impression of kids playing in a sandbox belies the seriousness and intensity of the people at Google. At lunchtime, employees chow down on free food and pay little attention to Page as he passes by on skates. This is the same group of engineers that will still be around that evening working in groups or writing computer code. They emit an extreme sense of urgency.

Google is under siege from no less than Microsoft and Yahoo!. Both companies were sleeping while Brin and Page were developing new ways to build an efficient, effective search engine. Brin and Page came up with a breakthrough search algorithm and then put together about 10,000 servers to build their own supercomputer.

Google continues to innovate on a number of fronts. It continues to improve its search abilities and ways to attain revenue from the searches. But it is also building new lines such as online-productivity software and a cell phone.

All this intensity is for a piece of the Internet search business. As has recently become obvious, "Search is the key to the kingdom." This is a battle for the heart of the Internet, and Google controls about 70 percent of the Internet's search ad business. Google has revolutionized the way the world finds things out, and people now look for things previously considered unfindable. "The perfect search engine would understand exactly what you mean and give back exactly what you want," Page says. Though no search engine can do this to date, it is an endeavor that Google and its competitors are committed to developing.

### Questions

1. Do you think Google will be able to maintain its controlled-chaos type of culture? Support your position.
2. Research Google to determine if it has been able to maintain its culture-strategy mix and remain competitive. Google's Web site for corporate information is www.google.com/about.html.

conditions. A **stable environment** is characterized by unchanging basic products and services, a static level of competition, a low level of technological innovation, a formalized and centralized structure, and a slow, steady rate of growth. Such an environment remains relatively stable over long periods.

A **hyperturbulent environment,** on the other hand, is characterized by rapidly changing product lines, an increasing and changing set of competitors, rapid and continual technological

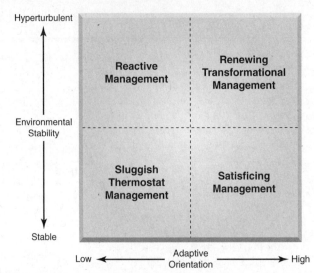

**FIGURE 2.2**   **Model of Adaptive Orientation in Organizations**

innovation, and rapid market growth. For today's organization, the idea of change is clear. A static organization can no longer survive. Yesterday's accomplishments amount to little in an environment of rapidly advancing markets, products, and lifestyles. To survive, organizations must devise methods of continuous self-renewal. Organizations must recognize when it is necessary to change, and they must develop the ability to implement change when needed. To meet these conditions, many companies have created specialized OD units whose primary purpose is the implementation of organizational changes. These units develop new programs to help the organization improve its adaptation to its environment and maintain a stable identity, so that change is not overwhelming.

## A Model of Adaptive Orientation

The topic of transformational change as opposed to gradual change has been receiving much attention. Some organizations resist change until a critical state of incongruence is reached, at which point change occurs. An illustration of an organization's orientation in adapting to change is illustrated in Figure 2.2.[10] One dimension in the figure represents the degree of change in an organization's environment, and the second represents the degree of flexibility present in its internal orientation. Organizations can vary greatly on these dimensions, and the many possible combinations of these orientations can lead to different adaptive styles. In addition, organizations operate on a continuum or blend of the orientations. Several of the orientations used by managers are described next.

## Sluggish-Thermostat Management (Stable Environment, Low Adaptation)

"Sluggish-thermostat management" is a term originated by David Miller to describe organizations that resist change until cost trade-offs favor it.[11] This term is a good metaphor because many organizations set their thermostats so low that they become insensitive to change.

**Sluggish management** refers to a managerial style based on low risk, with formalized procedures and a high degree of structure and control. Typically, organizations that utilize sluggish management have very stable goals and a highly centralized structure. They also tend to have more managerial levels, a higher ratio of superiors to subordinates, and an emphasis upon formal control systems. There may be a tendency to value tradition, to keep on doing things as they have always been done, to value seniority more than performance, and to be averse to accepting new ideas. Although this is a low-risk style of managing, it may lead to serious problems in the long run. Referring to Ford Motor Company's sluggish management and inability to meet new customer demands, a former Ford CEO said, "We learned that there's no market for lousy cars: we tested it."[12]

Without change, organizations may succumb to the forces of entropy. For some organizations, slowness to adapt stems not from failure but from success. These organizations become a victim of their own success. In the auto industry, for example, the rules for competing remained the same for around 60 years, and the assumptions about customers, markets, and suppliers remained valid.

## Satisficing Management (Stable Environment, High Adaptation)

**Satisficing management,** a term related to the word "satisfactory," is management that is adequate and average. It is a style of managing that emphasizes a more centralized decision-making structure with problems referred to the top. Because of the stable environment, there tend to be more levels of management, with coordination done by formal committees. Planning and decision making are usually concentrated at the top, with high clarity of procedures and roles. Change is accomplished at a rate that is "good enough" to keep up with the industry, but certainly well behind the state of the art. Company financial statistics, such as return on investment and employee turnover, are commensurate with industry averages. Such organizations often tend to accept strategies that are "good enough" because of the low level of pressure for change from the environment. Eighty-two percent of the respondents in a study reported that without change they would gradually suffer a decline in performance.[13]

## Reactive Management (Hyperturbulent Environment, Low Adaptation)

Organizations that have a low level of adaptation but exist in a rapidly changing environment tend to deal with problems on a short-run, crisis basis. **Reactive management** refers to the style of reacting to a stimulus after conditions in the environment have changed. It is a short-term, crisis type of adaptation, often involving replacement of key people, hasty reorganization, and drastic cutting of personnel and product lines. The reactive approach to change implies waiting until serious problems emerge that can no longer be ignored and then taking drastic and corrective measures. A major food corporation, for example, was feeling the pressures of changing business conditions, losing momentum, experiencing product failures, and reporting decreased earnings. The new chief executive instituted some massive changes, including a major managerial reorganization, a company-wide efficiency drive, cutting salaried personnel by 10 percent, and taking a very hard look at the firm's marketing programs. In another example, the Securities and Exchange Commission (SEC) has been criticized for sitting on the sidelines while corporate scandals were being uncovered by New York's attorney general. The SEC chairman said in 2003, "The commission has found itself in a position of reacting to market problems rather than anticipating them."[14] The *Wall Street Journal* reported, "Chief among the flaws of the SEC is a reactive culture that often fails to identify danger ahead of time, leaving the agency to respond after others expose problems."[15] In late 2008, the reactive culture at the SEC had changed little, as reported again in the *Wall Street Journal*.[16] This time the agency's inspector general said that the SEC failed to "vigorously" enforce securities law during the two years before the start of the 2008 financial and banking crisis.

## Renewing/Transformational Management (Hyperturbulent Environment, High Adaptation)

Organizations that exist in a hyperturbulent environment must not only respond to change, they must proactively take advantage of new opportunity and innovation. These organizations tend to fit the renewal/transformational orientation and to be champions of innovation; they are faster at developing new ideas, more responsive to competitive changes (a more sensitive thermostat), and more participative in getting the commitment and involvement of organization members in the renewal process. Organizations with a high level of adaptation existing in a rapidly changing environment tend to utilize the renewing managerial style.

**Renewing/transformational management** refers to introducing change to deal with future conditions before these conditions actually occur. Examples of renewing management include the innovations of corporations like General Electric (GE), 3M, and IBM, which have all actively initiated programs of innovation before conditions became critical. IBM has a program it calls on-demand computing that could transform the information technology industry. It will offer computing power to corporate customers as a service, whenever and wherever they need it. IBM's current annual budget allots $1.6 billion to research and development for on-demand products. The CEO, Samuel J. Palmisano, says, "IBM has a history of making bold moves in unsettled times. You don't make bold moves when there's stability because you're not going to capture any great advantage."[17] A renewing management orientation has both the ability and need to respond to a hyperturbulent environment. Most modern organizations are increasingly finding the need for this adaptive orientation.

Change can provide new opportunities for growth or an increase in the state of organizational entropy—inability to change. The renewing or transformational manager is constantly fighting entropy and proactively building for the future. Today, organizations need to develop a renewal/transformational orientation if they are to maintain a competitive edge and even to survive.

## THE SYSTEMS APPROACH: FINDING NEW WAYS TO WORK TOGETHER

The systems approach to managing change views the organization as a unified system composed of interrelated units. This gives managers a way to look at the organization as a whole and as a part of a larger external environment. In an organization engaged in downsizing, managers may use a systems approach to determine how to cut costs. One approach, the **horizontal corporation,** breaks the company into its key processes and creates teams from different departments to run them. It's about managing across, rather than up and down.

This suggests that managers can no longer function within the traditional pyramid organization chart, but must integrate their department with the goals and strategy of the whole organization. To accomplish this, managers must communicate with other departments as well as with employees and customers. By using a systems perspective, a manager can maintain a balance between the needs of various units of the enterprise as well as total system goals and objectives.

Downsizing, alone, does little to change the fundamental way that work gets done in a corporation. To do that takes a different organizational model: the horizontal corporation. Some of America's corporations, from DuPont, Cisco, GE, and W. L. Gore, are already moving toward this idea. In the quest for greater efficiency and productivity, they are beginning to flatten the hierarchical organization charts that have defined corporate life. The trend is toward flatter, more adaptive organizations. Some of these changes have been under way for several years, such as total quality management, reengineering, and process redesign.

### The Organization as a System

A **system** is a set of interrelated parts unified by design to achieve some purpose or goal. Organizations are systems. Every organization can be viewed as a number of interrelated, interdependent parts, each of which contributes to total organizational functioning and to the achievement of the overall organizational goal. The systems approach is one of the most important concepts in OD because it deals with change and interrelationships in complex organizations. The notion of system interdependency is critical because a change in one part of an organization system has consequences in other parts of the organization. When Mark Hurd initially became CEO of Hewlett-Packard, he recognized this concept in an interview he gave to the *New York Times,* saying, "We'll look at the entire enterprise" in reference to any changes that he might make.[18]

A system is "an organized unitary whole composed of two or more interdependent parts, components, or subsystems and delineated by identifiable boundaries from its environment."[19] The term is used in many different contexts: for example, defense system, weapons system, solar system, and eco system.

Systems have several basic qualities:

- A system must be designed to accomplish an objective.
- The elements of a system must have an established arrangement.
- Interrelationships must exist among the individual elements of a system.
- The basic ingredients of a process (the flows of information, energy, and materials) are more vital than the basic elements of a system.
- A system's overall objectives are more important than the objectives of its elements, and thus the narrow objectives of a system are deemphasized.

From an organizational perspective, the systems approach recognizes and focuses on the effect of managerial functions and the interrelationship between subelements of the organization.

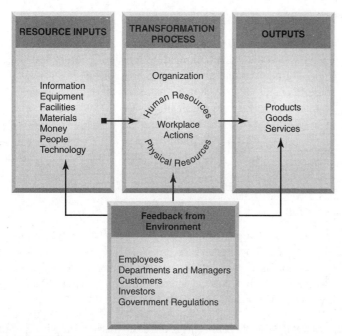

**FIGURE 2.3**  The Organization as an Open System

Rather than view the organization as a static set of relationships, it views the organization as a set of flows of information, personnel, and material. Time and change become critical aspects. The flow of inputs and outputs is a basic starting point in the description of a system (see Figure 2.3). Three basic elements make up such a system:

1. *Inputs* are the resources that are applied to the processing function.
2. *Processes* are the activities and functions that are performed to produce goods and services.
3. *Outputs* are the products and services produced by the organization.

A business firm takes such inputs as materials, people, and energy, and converts them into products or services desired by consumers. The organization receives inputs from its environment, acts on the inputs by transforming them, and returns the transformed elements to the environment as products. As an example, the resource inputs to a hospital include money, equipment, trained staff, information, patients, and physicians; the outputs include new research, well patients, improved medicine, and trained doctors and nurses.

## Open Systems

There are two basic types of systems: open and closed. A **closed system** is one that is self-contained and isolated from its environment. In the strictest sense, closed systems exist only in theory, for all real systems interact with their environment.

The open system is by far the most important type of system, and it will be emphasized in our treatment of organizations. An open system influences and is influenced by the environment through the process of interdependency, which results in a dynamic (changing) equilibrium. A business organization provides an excellent example of the process of reciprocity and, therefore, of an open system. The **open system** is in continual interaction with its environment and, therefore, achieves a steady state of **dynamic equilibrium.** The system could not survive without the continuous influence of transformational outflow. As the open system interacts with its environment, it continually receives information termed **feedback** from its environment, which helps the system adjust. The departments also interact with one another, because they have interacting tasks to perform. Therefore, the overall efficiency of the system depends upon the level and degree of interaction with other elements.

One of the current trends in OD is a shift toward using a more integrated systems approach to organizational improvement. The systems approach, then, allows managers to anticipate both immediate and far-reaching consequences of organizational changes.

## THE SOCIOTECHNICAL SYSTEM

Organization development and renewal may be referred to as a systems approach to change. An organization is viewed as an open **sociotechnical system**[20] of coordinated social and technical activities. Organizational functions and processes are not considered as isolated elements but as parts reacting to and influencing other system elements. As the social and technical functions are interdependent, they need to be jointly optimized to provide the best outcome for an organization.[21] The sociotechnical system uses the following approaches:

1. Organize around process—not tasks.
2. Flatten the hierarchy.
3. Use teams to manage everything.
4. Let customers drive performance.
5. Reward team performance.

Changes in any one of the organization's processes can have effects throughout the organization, because all processes are related. Therefore, by its very nature, OD seeks to consider the interrelationships among the basic elements of the system when changes are planned. The organization can be viewed as an open system in interaction with its environment and consisting of five primary components and represented in Figure 2.4.

**THE GOALS AND VALUES SUBSYSTEM**  This is the basic mission and vision of the organization. Such goals may include profits, growth, or survival and are often taken from the larger environment.

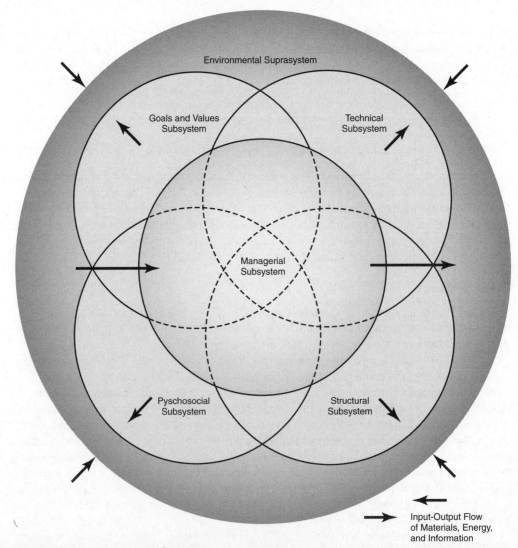

**FIGURE 2.4**   **The Sociotechnical System**

*Source:* Fremont, E. Kast and James E. Rosenzweig, *Organization and Management* (New York: McGraw-Hill, 1979, p. 19).

**THE TECHNICAL SUBSYSTEM**  This subsystem includes the primary functions, activities, and operations, including the techniques and equipment, used to produce the output of the system.

**THE STRUCTURAL SUBSYSTEM**  This is the formal design, policies, and procedures. It is usually set forth by the organization chart and includes division of work and patterns of authority.

**THE PSYCHOSOCIAL SUBSYSTEM (CULTURE)**  This subsystem is the network of social relationships and behavioral patterns of members, such as norms, roles, and communications.

**THE MANAGERIAL SUBSYSTEM**  This subsystem spans the entire organization by directing, organizing, and coordinating all activities toward the basic mission. The managerial function is important in integrating the activities of the other subsystems.

One of the earliest applications of the sociotechnical-systems concept was in British coal mining. The traditional "short wall" method utilized small, cohesive work groups working as autonomous teams. In light of technological advances, engineering efficiency experts determined that the short wall method was inefficient and introduced an improved technical system termed the "long wall" method. Unfortunately, the long wall method resulted in lower performance and higher absenteeism. Production decreased because the experts had failed to consider the impact of the changes on the psychosocial system. Researchers found that productivity and morale improved substantially when the team approach was restored and team pay incentives were provided. The sociotechnical-systems OD approach is considered one of the most sophisticated techniques, involving large-scale effort and considerable skill on the part of the OD practitioner.[22] As can be expected with a sophisticated approach, the sociotechnical-systems approach is more difficult to implement, as knowledge and expertise to implement it is widely dispersed among diverse groups.[23]

## High-Performance Systems

A more recent development is the application of the sociotechnical-systems approach in designing a high-performance organization. High-performance organizations do not occur by chance or by policy or decree: they are designed.

The high-performance model focuses on five key variables (similar to Figure 2.4) that need to be considered if managers wish to improve performance.[24] These key variables are:

1. The business situation (forces in the environment).
2. The business strategy (goals and values).
3. The design elements (technology, structure, etc.).
4. The culture.
5. The business results (the outputs produced).

The model can be used to identify the real drivers of organizational success used in organization development and renewal programs to improve system performance.

## The Contingency Approach: No One Best Way

Systems theory provides a conceptual overview of organizational functioning, but managers need to know how the subsystems of their own organization are uniquely related in the organization's specific environment in order to best deal with the organization's problems. Contingency theory recognizes that there are differences between organizations, and that what constitutes effective management in one system may not in another. Contingency views emphasize the characteristics of a specific organization and maintain that to organize and manage a change program, one must consider the set of conditions in that particular setting.[25]

The **contingency approach** holds that there is no one best way of managing in all situations. Given certain combinations of contingencies (such as a stable external environment and a low adaptive orientation to change), one can specify general approaches to change that are likely to be more effective than others. In other words, the contingency approach identifies various "if-then" relationships and suggests general directions for change, depending on the situation. The contingency approach relies on certain conceptual skills, such as diagnosing and understanding the various types of situations that are likely to confront the OD practitioner.

The contingency view suggests that managers in different departmental units face situations that may be very different on a number of dimensions, including degree of structure, levels of motivation, and potential for conflict. The OD practitioner, then, must recognize that there is no one best way for all organizations, although some practitioners would take issue with this statement.[26] The contingency approach to OD suggests that the effectiveness of practitioner styles, intervention techniques, or strategies is a factor of the circumstances. The contingency variables that need to be considered and the emphasis they are given will depend on the type of problem being considered.

## FUTURE SHOCK AND CHANGE

Alvin Toffler, in the book *Future Shock,* suggests that most people are utterly unprepared to cope with the accelerated rate of change. "Future shock is a time phenomenon, a product of a greatly accelerated rate of change in society. It arises from the superimposition of a new culture on an old one."[27] Future shock—too much change in too short a time—affects managers and organizations as well. When change occurs too rapidly, the capacity of management to react is strained, creating the danger of future shock. As a result, managers must become more adaptable and flexible than ever before.

The world is constantly changing in finance and economics, technology, and social values; and these changes seem to have accelerated in recent years. In so rapidly changing an environment, plans are sometimes out of date within three to six months. Changing trends will have a significant impact on organizations as managers develop new organizational models and find novel ways of motivating employees.

*Changes in finance and economics.* The lead sentence in a front-page article in the *Wall Street Journal* began: "The notoriously fragmented American banking system is going through a decade's worth of consolidation in a matter of weeks . . ."[28] The worldwide recession that began in late 2007 has introduced challenges and problems that previously were not imaginable to most managers. Managers are confronted with new challenges on diverse fronts: tighter credit, lack of consumer confidence, higher energy costs, increased environmental requirements, making cuts in departments, laying off of employees, and perhaps facing their own layoff notice. Managers will need to scan the environment to be aware of issues that will have a major impact on their industry or organization. History has shown that with economic crisis comes opportunity.

*Changes in technology.* Technological changes have shortened the life cycle of many products and services, and when product life cycles are shortened, organizations must become more adaptive by shortening their lead times to get into production. Technological advances are occurring so rapidly that the education of most scientists is technically obsolete within a few years after graduation from college. There is so much information that professionals operating in narrow fields often find it impossible to keep current on information pertinent to their specialties.

*Changes in social values.* Society has placed new demands on business firms for social responsibility, environment-friendly operations, and pollution controls. Other social changes also affect the organization. In the past, jobs were thought of as tasks to be done, not something to be questioned or evaluated. In the United States, more workers earn their pay in knowledge-based jobs than in skilled and nonskilled jobs. For many years to come, managers will be searching for newer, more relevant, and more effective ways of managing this increasingly intelligent and sophisticated workforce.

In *The Future of Management,* author Gary Hamel asks the question, "Could the practice of management change as radically over the first two or three decades of this century as it did during the early years of the 20th century? I believe so. More than that, I believe we must make it so. . . . Sure, we're bound by precedent, and most of us have a vested interest in the management status quo. But if human beings could invent the modern industrial organization, then they can reinvent it."[29] Meetup Inc., a recent Web-based start-up, serves as an excellent example of how fast-changing forces in economics, technology, and society have intersected to provide not obstacles but opportunities. As the world's largest network of local groups, Meetup provides a place where people with similar interests can easily organize a group or find one of the thousands of groups already formed and meet with them face-to-face. But Meetup's success and rapid growth brought about an organization with layers of bureaucracy. Consequently, it was not able to respond quickly to its customers. The CEO discarded the organization chart and replaced it with a strategy in which workers set priorities and picked their own projects. For some workers, the new system felt like chaos and they left, but other workers thrived. The system is still evolving, and a strategy group follows how changes and new services affect revenues. With a clearly articulated "Meetup Manifesto" providing the direction for the company, the CEO retains the authority to stop a project headed in the wrong direction.[30]

An organization must adapt to these changing conditions. Each day brings a new set of conditions, and internal realignment is often required. Product and market strategies need to be more flexible and must depend upon the ability of a company to recognize the need for change. Consequently, management will need to place an increased emphasis on human resource development. An unprecedented opportunity exists for the OD practitioner to apply specialized skills in seeking solutions for these problems of industry. In view of these factors, whether an organization can remain effective is largely dependent upon whether it is sufficiently adaptive to changing conditions. Apple Inc. is an example of a company that over the years has been able to develop new and innovative products. Some of its products, such as the iPod and iPhone, have become the benchmark by which competitors' products are measured. **OD Application: Apple and Renewal** looks more closely at how Apple is able to do this.

## ORGANIZATION TRANSFORMATION AND ORGANIZATION DEVELOPMENT

There are many ways to respond to the pressures for change. Some responses may be ineffective or even ultimately destructive. Many companies have been driven out of business because of competitive forces or of unwise financial maneuvers. In this section, we will examine two major approaches to change and present a model of the planned change process.

Organization transformation (OT) and organization development (OD) are both approaches to managing change in organizations. **Organization transformation** (discussed in more detail in Chapter 15) may be defined as the action of changing an organization's form, shape, or appearance, or changing the organization's energy from one form to another, which

---

### OD Application: Apple and Renewal[31]

When you review several business magazines, like *Fast Company*, *Business Week*, and *Fortune*, Apple Inc. consistently shows up on their "best" lists. On *Business Week*'s annual list of "The 25 Most Innovative Companies," Apple is at or near the top year after year. And on *Fast Company*'s list of "The World's Most Innovative Companies," Apple is again near the top. *Fortune* has a slightly different list, "America's Most Admired Companies," but Apple again leads this list. When all of these "best" lists are translated to dollars, a much more quantitative measure than "innovation" and "most admired," Apple is near the top once again. Based on the total return to shareholder of *Fortune* 500 companies, Apple ranks number 1 for the past five years.

Just when some technology analysts are forecasting that there are no more breakthrough innovations for Apple or they don't have many new products in the pipeline, Apple makes a surprise announcement about a new innovative product. Sometimes, as with the iPod and iPhone, the innovations are based on existing competitors' products like MP3 players and cell phones. But the delivery, package, quality, and feel, is so unique as to redefine a product with virtually no competition—and with a premium price.

The question begs as to what Apple does time after time, year after year to be so successful. In large measure, it is in the culture defined primarily by Steven Jobs. Jobs' vision of "providing computers as a tool to change the world," has helped to define Apple. Jobs has a perfectionist's approach to product development and an unwillingness to accept compromises. His dedication to excellence has created a culture of innovation at Apple. Though Jobs does not design the products, he meets extensively with his team during the development and has unquestioned authority. A fundamental belief of Jobs is that giving customers even more choices and better products will give Apple a reliably profitable and growing business.

Jobs' charismatic leadership and idiosyncrasies have caused some internal problems at Apple. Somewhat legendary in Silicon Valley is his management style that tends toward throwing tantrums and berating and humiliating employees who disagree with his ideas. His habit of making decisions and then suddenly changing his mind has also been cited as part of the reason he is difficult to work for. For this and Apple's unusual structure, a special kind of work force is required. COO Tim Cook says that collaboration is key within Apple as there are vague lines separating departments.

Perhaps no other CEO today is as closely associated with the company that they head than Steve Jobs. But in terms of strategy and execution, Tim Cook is critical to Apple's success. He has been running much of the day-to-day operations since Jobs brought him to Apple in 1998. Cook is frequently seen as a polar opposite to Jobs. While Jobs has a reputation of being unpredictable and hard to please, Cook is reputed to be cool and soft-spoken. But both Jobs and Cook are perfectionists, workaholics, and dedicated to Apple.

**Questions:**

1. Research Apple's product history to discover the progression of its major products.
2. What are its newest product innovations? Apple's Web site is www.apple.com/.
3. To what do you attribute Apple's ability for self-renewal?

normally occurs in a brief time interval. Organization transformation tends to focus on unplanned changes from within the system in response to crises and life-cycle considerations. The organization is in such peril that it must change quickly. "Transformational change" is a term often used by President Barack Obama to describe the kind of change that is necessary to solve the problems and challenges facing the United States. Transformational changes transform the very framework and assumptions of an organization. Organization development, on the other hand, focuses more on planned changes introduced by practitioners.

The difference between OT and OD centers on the magnitude and speed of the change—it is the difference between revolution and evolution. OT refers to significant changes introduced in a short, almost immediate time frame to deal with survival or crisis-type problems. As a contrast between OD and OT, see Figure 2.5. OD involves large-scale change over a longer time frame on a more gradual basis. Organizations must interact with their external environment to survive. The factors that interfere with the organization's ability to produce or market its products, or to attract the human, technical, and financial resources it needs, become a force for change.

OD, or planned organizational change, is a deliberate attempt to modify the functioning of the total organization or one of its major parts in order to bring about improved effectiveness.[32] The persons attempting to bring about this change will be referred to as practitioners, and the organization being changed will be referred to as the **client system.** Planned change efforts can focus on individual, team, and organizational behavior.

**FIGURE 2.5**   OT Is Similar to a Crash Diet
*Source:* B.C. by permission of Johnny Hart and Creators Syndicate, Inc.

## Individual Effectiveness

An organization is made up of individual members, and each member has unique values, beliefs, and motivations. The leadership style of top management and the norms, values, and beliefs of the organization's members combine to form the organization's culture. An organization's effectiveness can be increased by creating a culture that achieves organizational goals and at the same time satisfies members' needs. Empowering the individual employee by letting workers make decisions can often improve quality, productivity, and employee commitment. Recent use of empowerment in companies like Southwest Airlines, Costco Wholesale, and Google suggests that empowering employees pays off. Managers who can find the key to unlocking the human potential of their employees will be able to tap an immense source of productive energy.

Change efforts that focus on individual effectiveness range from empowerment training programs to high-powered executive development programs. These include empowerment activities designed to improve the skills, abilities, or motivational levels of organization members. The goals are improved managerial and technical skills or improved interpersonal competence. Such change efforts may also be directed toward improved leadership, decision making, or problem solving among organization members. The assumption underlying such efforts is that developing better managers and employees will make for a more effective organization.

## Team Effectiveness

Change efforts may also focus on the fundamental unit of an organization, the team or work group, as a means for improving the organization's effectiveness. Today, we are in the midst of revolutionary changes in how people are managed in organizations. Hewlett-Packard, Harley-Davidson Motor Company, and other organizations are moving toward what are called "self-managed" work teams (see Chapter 13). The premise of this emerging approach is that organizations must elicit the commitment of its employees if it is to achieve a sustainable competitive advantage in a turbulent marketplace. There is an emphasis on improving problem-solving processes while working through conflicts and issues surrounding ways the group can improve its effectiveness and productivity.

These activities are designed to improve the operations of work teams and may focus on **task activities,** what the team does, or **team process,** how the team works, and the quality of relationships among team members. Work teams are the primary unit of the organization, and more effective teams can lead to improved organizations. More effective teams may increase work motivation, improve performance, and decrease turnover and absenteeism.

One technique that is often used in examining groups is called **process observation.** As we observe and analyze work groups as systems, two separate dimensions may be identified:

1. *content*—the task of the group.
2. *process*—the way the group functions.

Group process includes such factors as leadership, decision making, communication, and conflict. The content is what is being discussed; the process is how the group operates. These concepts will be covered in Chapter 8.

By observing the behavior of group members, one can determine the way a group is functioning. The observer systematically describes group functioning: who talks to whom, who practices leadership behavior, who dominates in team work, and so on. The observations are then summarized and presented to the group. The purpose is to clarify and improve team functioning. It is helpful for the OD practitioner to develop skills in process observation and to learn to be a **participant-observer,** that is, to actively participate and at the same time be aware of group process. Such skills are particularly useful in developing an effective team.

## Organization Effectiveness

Another focus for OD planned change efforts is the organization system. The total organization may be examined by use of climate surveys. Planned change programs are then designed to deal with the specific problem areas identified in the survey. The activities aim at improving effectiveness by structural, technical, or managerial subsystem changes. The objective of such systemwide operations is to increase the effectiveness, efficiency, and morale of total organization functioning.

All of these planned change efforts aim at improving the overall goal attainment of the system, but each has a specific target or focus for the change program. Organization development occurs when the change effort is focused on the total system. OD may involve individual, group, and intergroup approaches, but it becomes OD only when the total system is the target for change. In an OD program, a set of goals or purposes is identified, and a course of action is undertaken involving the commitment of the members of the organization to its improvement.

## Summary

- **Change.** All around us we are confronted with change, and for managers the idea of future shock—too much change in too short a time—can be a very real problem. Managers and organizations face rapid changes in three areas: technological advances, environmental changes, and social changes. The organization must renew and adapt to these changing situations, because every day presents a new set of conditions.
- **Organization Renewal.** Most modern organizations feel an increasing need for organization renewal. Renewing management predicts future conditions and makes planned changes before the conditions actually occur. For an organization to have the capacity to adapt to change and become more effective, management must initiate and create a climate that encourages creativity and innovation.
- **Adaptive.** Organizations may adapt to changes with four different orientations. A sluggish management orientation has little ability to adapt to changes, but there is no great need for it to adapt because the environment is stable. A reactive management orientation has the need to respond to a rapidly changing environment but does not have the ability. A satisficing management orientation has the ability to respond to a changing environment but finds itself in a relatively stable environment. A renewing management orientation has both the ability and the need to respond to a rapidly changing environment.

- **Systems.** Every organization must maintain a dynamic equilibrium between stability and innovation. A systems model may be used to identify the sources of impetus for change. The environmental system has an impact on organizations through technological, economic, and cultural forces. Organizational change also comes from forces within the organizational subsystems.
- **Sociotechnical System.** An organization can be viewed as an open system of coordinated human and technical activities. The activities consist of five primary components: goals and values, technical, structural, psychosocial, and managerial.
- **Future Shock.** Future shock is too much change in too short a time and can affect managers and organizations. It occurs when there is a greatly accelerated rate of change. In order to meet the challenges of rapid change, managers need to become more adaptable and flexible.
- **Organization Transformation.** This is significant change to the form and assumptions of an organization. It is typically an unplanned response to crises.
- **Planned Change and Organization Development.** Organization development uses planned change to improve the effectiveness of the organization. Planned change can focus on individuals, teams, and the organization.

## Review Questions

1. What is the implication of organization renewal for today's organizations?
2. Contrast the differences between a stable and a hyperturbulent environment.
3. Compare and contrast the four types of management orientations used in relating to the environment.
4. Using companies who compete with one another (for example, Apple and Microsoft), position them on the adaptive orientation model in Figure 2.2. Support your position.
5. Explain a sociotechnical system and its five components.
6. What lessons can future shock provide for organizations?

## Key Words and Concepts

| | | | |
|---|---|---|---|
| Client System | Horizontal Corporation | Process Observation | System |
| Closed System | Hyperturbulent | Reactive Management | Systems Approach |
| Content | Environment | Renewing/Transformational | Task Activities |
| Contingency Approach | Open System | Management | Team Process |
| Dynamic Equilibrium | Organization Renewal | Satisficing Management | |
| Entropy | Organization | Sluggish Management | |
| Feedback | Transformation (OT) | Sociotechnical System | |
| Future Shock | Participant-Observer | Stable Environment | |

# OD Skills Simulation 2.1

## OD Practitioner Behavior Profile I

*Total time suggested: 60 to 75 minutes.*

## A. Purpose

In most organizations there is a lot of untapped human potential. In an excellent, renewing organization, this potential can be released, resulting in personal growth for the individual. Personal development and organization renewal involve changes in attitudes and behavior that are related to your self-concept, role, goals, and values.

The behavior profile that you will generate in this simulation is intended to illustrate some growth dimensions for interpersonal competence and career planning. By recognizing your strengths and accomplishments, you may be encouraged to improve your self-image and interpersonal skills. Hopefully, an honest self-appraisal may aid you in becoming a more effective individual and team member. During this course, you will be afforded additional opportunities to obtain information about yourself and how you behave in organizational situations. This feedback may provide the impetus for you to change, but the ultimate responsibility for change is with you. Retain this survey; it will be used again near the end of this course in Chapter 16.

## B. Procedures

### Part A. Before Class Surveys

*Step 1*. Before class, complete the Profile Survey, Profile Form, Class Performance Form, and Objectives Form.

How you respond reflects how you view yourself, which, in turn, reveals something of your behavioral style. Based on the profile scale of 1 through 10, select the number to indicate the degree to which you feel each description is characteristic of you. Record your choice in the blank to the right. ***Save the survey results; you will need the completed survey again in OD Skills Simulation 16.1.***

Record your responses on the Profile Form and in the column labeled "Score." Shade in the bar graph for Chapter 2 in the appropriate line, based on your score. Note that the 30 descriptions have been reordered to fit into 5 categories. Calculate and record on the Profile Form the averages for the five categories and an overall profile average. The profile provides information about your behavioral style and allows you to see where you stand in each category. It also lets you directly compare your score on different scales by looking at the difference in the bar graph. The profile may indicate items on which your score is less desirable than you would like. You may also find categories in which you have generally low ratings. These may suggest areas for improvement during this course and for assessing the kinds of changes you may wish to make in order to become a more effective OD practitioner or manager.

*Step 2*. After completing the Profile Form, list some of the specific objectives and expectations you have for this class on the Class Performance Form and Objectives Form. These objectives should describe what you will be able to do and the time required. Refer to the Profile Form you have just completed and select some behaviors you would like to emphasize for change. Sample: to develop more self-confidence in doing class presentation by making three short presentations in class.

Try referring to the Class Performance Form and the Objectives Form often and at least before coming to class for the remainder of the course. Do not hesitate to experiment with the new behaviors you would like to cultivate. You will be referring to these objectives again later in the book. ***Be sure to keep all of these surveys and forms; you will need to refer to them in OD Skills Simulation 16.1.***

### Part B. Refining Objectives with Practitioner

*Step 1*. The Profile Form, Class Performance Form, and the Objectives Form can be used as feedback tools. You will be able to learn more about yourself by assessing the kinds of changes you may need to make in order to become more effective. Form into trios, with one person acting as the client, the second as practitioner, and the third as observer. Use your Profile Form, Class Performance Form, and the Objectives Form as the basis of your discussion. Refer to the end of this simulation for "Instructions for Developing Practitioner Roles and Skills." The practitioner will help you develop a fuller understanding of how your styles play a part in your overall effectiveness and how you may build on your strengths during this course. The practitioner will review the client's Profile Form, Class Performance Form, and the Objectives Form for the following:

1. How accurate are the profile assessments?
2. Are they a complete and challenging set of goals?
3. Are they realistic and feasible?
4. Are they specific and measurable?
5. Are they things the client can do and demonstrate by the end of the course?

The observer can use the Observer Form to record his or her observations. At the end of each interview, the observer gives feedback to the practitioner using the Observer Form.

Then rotate roles so that each person has a chance to play each of the three roles. Continue the simulation by switching roles until everyone has performed each role.

*Time suggested for Step 1: 15–20 minutes per session. Total time is 45 to 60 minutes.*

*Step 2.* Meet with the entire class and discuss the following questions:

1. How can we improve performance?
2. What practitioner role seemed to work best?
3. Did we view change as positive or negative?
4. Was the role of the practitioner helpful? How? What could be improved upon?
5. How effective was our team?

*Time suggested for Step 2: 15 minutes.*

**PROFILE SURVEY**

| 1 | 2 | 3 | 4 | 5 | 6 | 7 | 8 | 9 | 10 |

| Not at All Characteristic | Somewhat Characteristic | Very Characteristic |

1. Having the ability to communicate in a clear, concise, and persuasive manner  *10*

2. Being spontaneous—saying and doing things that seem natural on the spur of the moment ___ *10*

3. Doing things "by the book"—noticing appropriate rules and procedures and following them  *9*

4. Being creative—having a lot of unusual, original ideas; thinking of new approaches to problems *10* others do not often come up with ___

5. Being competitive—wanting to win and be the best *10*

6. Being able to listen to and understand others  *10*

7. Being aware of other people's moods and feelings  *10*

8. Being careful in your work—taking pains to make sure everything is "just right"  *9* ___

9. Being resourceful in coming up with possible ways of dealing with problems  *10*

10. Being a leader—having other people look to you for direction; taking over when things are confused *10* ___

11. Having the ability to accept feedback without reacting defensively, becoming hostile, or withdrawing *9*

12. Having the ability to deal with conflict and anger  *9* ___

13. Having written work neat and organized; making plans before starting on a difficult task; organizing details of work  *9*

14. Thinking clearly and logically; attempting to deal with ambiguity, complexity, and confusion in a situation by thoughtful, logical analysis  *9* ___

15. Having self-confidence when faced with a challenging situation  *10*

16. Having the ability to level with others, to give feedback to others  *10* ___

17. Doing new and different things; meeting new people; experimenting and trying out new ideas or activities *9*

18. Having a high level of aspiration, setting difficult goals  *10* ___

19. Analyzing a situation carefully before acting; working out a course of action in detail before embarking on it *9*

20. Being effective at initiating projects and innovative ideas  *10* ___

21. Seeking ideas from others; drawing others into discussion  *10*

22. Having a tendency to seek close personal relationships, participating in social activities with friends; giving affection and receiving it from others  *9* ___

23. Being dependable—staying on the job; doing what is expected  *10*

24. Having the ability to work as a catalyst, to stimulate and encourage others to develop their own resources for solving their own problems  *10* ___

25. Taking responsibility; relying on your own abilities and judgment rather than those of others *10*

26. Selling your own ideas effectively  *10* ___

27. Being the dominant person; having a strong need for control or recognition *9*

28. Getting deeply involved in your work; being extremely committed to ideas or work you are doing  *10* ___

29. Having the ability to evaluate possible solutions critically  *10*

30. Having the ability to work in unstructured situations, with little or no support, and to continue to work effectively even if faced with lack of cooperation, resistance, or hostility  *10* ___

## Profile Form (part 1)

| | | Score | Not at All Characteristic | | | Somewhat Characteristic | | | | Very Characteristic | | |
|---|---|---|---|---|---|---|---|---|---|---|---|---|
| | | | 1 | 2 | 3 | 4 | 5 | 6 | 7 | 8 | 9 | 10 |
| *A. Communicating Skills* | | | | | | | | | | | | |
| 1. Communicates | Ch. 2 | 10 | | | | | | | | | | |
| | Ch. 16 | | | | | | | | | | | |
| 6. Listens | Ch. 2 | 10 | | | | | | | | | | |
| | Ch. 16 | | | | | | | | | | | |
| 11. Receives Feedback | Ch. 2 | 9 | | | | | | | | | | |
| | Ch. 16 | | | | | | | | | | | |
| 16. Gives Feedback | Ch. 2 | 10 | | | | | | | | | | |
| | Ch. 16 | | | | | | | | | | | |
| 21. Seeks Ideas | Ch. 2 | 10 | | | | | | | | | | |
| | Ch. 16 | | | | | | | | | | | |
| 26. Sells Ideas | Ch. 2 | 16 | | | | | | | | | | |
| | Ch. 16 | | | | | | | | | | | |
| **Average Score A** | Ch. 2 | 9.83 | | | | | | | | | | |
| | Ch. 16 | | | | | | | | | | | |
| *B. Interpersonal Skills* | | | | | | | | | | | | |
| 2. Is Spontaneous | Ch. 2 | 10 | | | | | | | | | | |
| | Ch. 16 | | | | | | | | | | | |
| 7. Is Aware | Ch. 2 | 10 | | | | | | | | | | |
| | Ch. 16 | | | | | | | | | | | |
| 12. Deals with Conflict | Ch. 2 | 9 | | | | | | | | | | |
| | Ch. 16 | | | | | | | | | | | |
| 17. Experiments | Ch. 2 | 9 | | | | | | | | | | |
| | Ch. 16 | | | | | | | | | | | |
| 22. Seeks Close Relationships | Ch. 2 | 9 | | | | | | | | | | |
| | Ch. 16 | | | | | | | | | | | |
| 27. Is Dominant | Ch. 2 | 9 | | | | | | | | | | |
| | Ch. 16 | | | | | | | | | | | |
| **Average Score B** | Ch. 2 | 9.33 | | | | | | | | | | |
| | Ch. 16 | | | | | | | | | | | |
| *C. Aspiration-Achievement Levels* | | | | | | | | | | | | |
| 3. Conforms | Ch. 2 | 9 | | | | | | | | | | |
| | Ch. 16 | | | | | | | | | | | |
| 8. Is Careful | Ch. 2 | 9 | | | | | | | | | | |
| | Ch. 16 | | | | | | | | | | | |
| 13. Is Organized | Ch. 2 | 9 | | | | | | | | | | |
| | Ch. 16 | | | | | | | | | | | |
| 18. Aspires | Ch. 2 | 10 | | | | | | | | | | |
| | Ch. 16 | | | | | | | | | | | |
| 23. Is Dependable | Ch. 2 | 10 | | | | | | | | | | |
| | Ch. 16 | | | | | | | | | | | |
| 28. Is Committed to Ideas or Work | Ch. 2 | 10 | | | | | | | | | | |
| | Ch. 16 | | | | | | | | | | | |
| **Average Score C** | Ch. 2 | 9.5 | | | | | | | | | | |
| | Ch. 16 | | | | | | | | | | | |

**continued on next page**

## Profile Form (part 2)

| | | Score | Not at All Characteristic | | | | Somewhat Characteristic | | | | Very Characteristic | | |
|---|---|---|---|---|---|---|---|---|---|---|---|---|---|
| *D. Problem-Solving Skills* | | | | | | | | | | | | | |
| 4. Is Creative | Ch. 2 | 10 | | | | | | | | | | | |
| | Ch. 16 | | | | | | | | | | | | |
| 9. Is Resourceful | Ch. 2 | 10 | | | | | | | | | | | |
| | Ch. 16 | | | | | | | | | | | | |
| 14. Is Logical | Ch. 2 | 9 | | | | | | | | | | | |
| | Ch. 16 | | | | | | | | | | | | |
| 19. Analyzes | Ch. 2 | 9 | | | | | | | | | | | |
| | Ch. 16 | | | | | | | | | | | | |
| 24. Is a Catalyst | Ch. 2 | 10 | | | | | | | | | | | |
| | Ch. 16 | | | | | | | | | | | | |
| 29. Evaluates | Ch. 2 | 10 | | | | | | | | | | | |
| | Ch. 16 | | | | | | | | | | | | |
| **Average Score D** | Ch. 2 | 9.83 | | | | | | | | | | | |
| | Ch. 16 | | | | | | | | | | | | |
| *E. Leadership Skills* | | | | | | | | | | | | | |
| 5. Is Competitive | Ch. 2 | 10 | | | | | | | | | | | |
| | Ch. 16 | | | | | | | | | | | | |
| 10. Is a Leader | Ch. 2 | 10 | | | | | | | | | | | |
| | Ch. 16 | | | | | | | | | | | | |
| 15. Is Confident | Ch. 2 | 10 | | | | | | | | | | | |
| | Ch. 16 | | | | | | | | | | | | |
| 20. Initiates | Ch. 2 | 10 | | | | | | | | | | | |
| | Ch. 16 | | | | | | | | | | | | |
| 25. Takes Responsibility | Ch. 2 | 10 | | | | | | | | | | | |
| | Ch. 16 | | | | | | | | | | | | |
| 30. Can Work in Unstructured Situations | Ch. 2 | 10 | | | | | | | | | | | |
| | Ch. 16 | | | | | | | | | | | | |
| **Average Score E** | Ch. 2 | 10 | | | | | | | | | | | |
| | Ch. 16 | | | | | | | | | | | | |
| **Overall Profile Average (A + B + C + D + E) ÷ 5** | Ch. 2 | 9.69 | | | | | | | | | | | |
| | Ch. 16 | | | | | | | | | | | | |

**CLASS PERFORMANCE FORM**

### 1. ATTENDANCE

What percentage of the class meetings will you attend?

| 100%–95% | 94%–90% | 89%–80% | 79%–70% | 69%–60% | 59%–50% | 49%–0% |
|---|---|---|---|---|---|---|
|  |  |  |  |  |  |  |

### 2. PREPARATION

What percentage of the time will you come prepared?

| | 100%–95% | 94%–90% | 89%–80% | 79%–70% | 69%–60% | 59%–50% | 49%–0% |
|---|---|---|---|---|---|---|---|
| Chapters read |  |  |  |  |  |  |  |
| OD Skills Prepared |  |  |  |  |  |  |  |
| OD Cases Prepared |  |  |  |  |  |  |  |

### 3. PROBLEM SOLVING

What percentage of the time will you:

| | 100%–95% | 94%–90% | 89%–80% | 79%–70% | 69%–60% | 59%–50% | 49%–0% |
|---|---|---|---|---|---|---|---|
| Understand key terms |  |  |  |  |  |  |  |
| Prepare text assignments |  |  |  |  |  |  |  |
| Develop correct answers |  |  |  |  |  |  |  |

### 4. INVOLVEMENT

What percentage of the time will you contribute to team performance by:

| | 100%–95% | 94%–90% | 89%–80% | 79%–70% | 69%–60% | 59%–50% | 49%–0% |
|---|---|---|---|---|---|---|---|
| Showing interest in meeting |  |  |  |  |  |  |  |
| Initiating discussion |  |  |  |  |  |  |  |
| Getting along with other team members |  |  |  |  |  |  |  |

**OBJECTIVES FORM**

Communicating Skills:

1. _____
   _____
2. _____
   _____
3. _____
   _____

Interpersonal Skills:

1. _____
   _____
2. _____
   _____
3. _____
   _____

Aspiration-Achievement Levels:

1. _____
   _____
2. _____
   _____
3. _____
   _____

Problem-Solving Skills:

1. _____
   _____
2. _____
   _____
3. _____
   _____

Leadership Skills:

1. _____
   _____
2. _____
   _____
3. _____
   _____

Other:

1. _____
   _____
2. _____
   _____
3. _____
   _____

## OBSERVER FORM

Your role during this part of the simulation is important because your goal is to give individuals feedback on their strategies of change. Following are listed 10 criteria of helping relationships. Rate the practitioner by circling the appropriate number.

| | | | NOTES: Words, behaviors |
|---|---|---|---|

1. Level of involvement:
   Cautious _____ Interested _____ Low 1: 2: 3: 4: 5: 6: 7: 8: 9: 10 High _____

2. Level of communication:
   Doesn't listen _____ Listens _____ Low 1: 2: 3: 4: 5: 6: 7: 8: 9: 10 High _____

3. Level of openness, trust:
   Shy, uncertain _____ Warm, friendly _____ Low 1: 2: 3: 4: 5: 6: 7: 8: 9: 10 High _____

4. Level of collaboration:
   Authoritative _____ Seeks agreement _____ Low 1: 2: 3: 4: 5: 6: 7: 8: 9: 10 High

5. Level of influence:
   Gives in _____ Convincing _____ Low 1: 2: 3: 4: 5: 6: 7: 8: 9: 10 High _____

6. Level of supportiveness:
   Disagrees _____ Supports _____ Low 1: 2: 3: 4: 5: 6: 7: 8: 9: 10 High _____

7. Level of direction:
   Easygoing, agreeable _____ Gives directions _____ Low 1: 2: 3: 4: 5: 6: 7: 8: 9: 10 High _____

8. Level of competence:
   Unsure _____ Competent _____ Low 1: 2: 3: 4: 5: 6: 7: 8: 9: 10 High _____

9. Reflects feelings and summarizes:
   Never _____ Often _____ Low 1: 2: 3: 4: 5: 6: 7: 8: 9: 10 High _____

10. Overall style:
    Ineffective _____ Effective _____ Low 1: 2: 3: 4: 5: 6: 7: 8: 9: 10 High _____

## Instructions for Developing Practitioner Roles and Skills

In this course, there has been an opportunity to develop the interaction and communication atmosphere conducive to experiential learning. The interrelationship among students in experiential learning is as important as the relationship between instructor and students. Some characteristics of the OD practitioner role are:

1. Two-way communication and influence. Use open-ended questions.
2. Openness of expression of views, feelings, and emotions. Being able to tell it like it is!
3. Supportiveness. When you are in agreement with others, give them your support. Learn to express differences without offending. Often two people in confrontation are 90 percent in agreement on the issues, but they focus only on their differences.
4. Awareness that conflict can be creative when differences are expressed appropriately.
5. Recognition of individual differences.
6. Confrontation of another person.
   a. The courage to express your own convictions.
   b. Can you give and take feedback?
   c. Are you worried about being shot down?
   d. Are you willing to attempt risk-taking behavior?
   e. Are you overusing your share of air time?
7. Reflections of the feelings of the other person. You might say, "You seem to feel very strongly about this."
8. Disclosure of something about yourself. You might say, "This is a problem for me also."
9. Use of silence or no response; just let the other person talk.
10. Use of nonverbal signals, such as eye contact or a nod of the head, to indicate that you hear what is said.

# CASE: THE NOGO RAILROAD

## Introduction

Allen Yates, the operations manager of the NoGo Railroad, promoted the chief dispatcher, Dave Keller, to communication manager of the division. Dave Keller was a recent graduate of State University, but his managerial experience was limited to only five years as chief dispatcher. Allen announced that Dave had demonstrated that he had the guts to do what was needed and the ability to act intelligently, rationally, and quickly in a crisis. He told Dave that his selection was based on his being single, willing to accept a temporary position, and amenable to extensive traveling, as well as on his effective, independent, decision-making capabilities.

## Background

NoGo is a small, privately owned, and regional railroad operating in the northwest states of Washington, Idaho, Montana, and Wyoming. It serves remote and mountainous areas and hauls primarily timber, coal, potash, and phosphorous. As a consequence of NoGo's unique operations, it has had little competition and no compelling reason to modernize operations.

Dave was originally hired as a dispatcher because of his military experience. After six years of outstanding service, he was promoted to chief dispatcher, due in part to his youth and his excellent physical condition, attributes needed to stand the stress of the position. The previous chief dispatcher had had a heart attack on the job and was unable to return to work. Dave's yearly performance evaluations as chief dispatcher were consistently rated satisfactory by Rex Kelly, the Rail Manager. See Figure 2.6 for NoGo's organization chart.

Rex was scheduled for retirement, and Nick Chacco, the communication manager, was going to assume Rex's responsibilities. Dave accepted the vacated communication manager position, but was uneasy about his ability to perform the tasks ahead. He felt extremely uncomfortable about his people skills, educational background, and experience. He told Allen about his concerns, but the division manager told him not to worry about it.

## Communications Department

Officially, Dave's responsibilities included managing the personnel who performed radio, teletype, telephone, and computer operations. These communication operations were performed by two groups of unionized employees: telegraph operators and clerks.

Unofficially, Allen had made arrangements for Dave to meet and travel with several experienced individuals. His purpose was to tour remote areas, observe different job functions, eliminate obsolete practices, and modernize wherever possible.

Dave discovered that the clerks were predominantly women. Their contract stipulated that they could not work directly with radio communications and train crews. The daily functions of the clerks varied from teletype and computer operations to general clerical duties. Their contract stated that they could not be sent more than 30 miles from home on assignments. In rural districts, this led to having a large force of clerks who could not cover for vacations and emergencies. Therefore, Dave found an overabundance of clerks without enough work to keep them all busy.

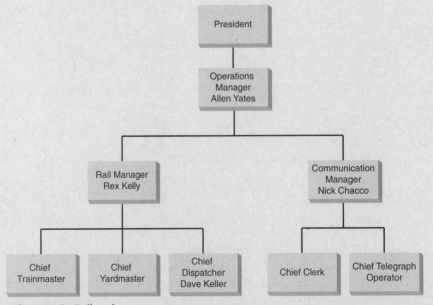

**FIGURE 2.6**  Organization Chart: NoGo Railroad

The telegraph operators, predominantly men, no longer had to know Morse code, but were highly trained in radio, teletype, and computer operations. However, such skills as knot tying were still essential. Proper knot tying was important in handing paperwork extended on a pole to the conductor and engineer passing by in a speeding train. The taller the employee, the easier and safer this practice.

Placing small "torpedoes" on the rails of the tracks to signal the crew of an oncoming train was another function of the telegraph operators. This loud explosion would alert the crew in the engine to a dangerous situation or inform them that there was new information to be picked up ahead. These and many other archaic traditions and procedures were still practiced in mountainous areas where communication by radio and cell phone was impossible or difficult between train dispatcher, train crews, and telegraph operators.

## Union Contracts

The telegraph operators had a contract guaranteeing them 40 hours of weekly pay even if no work was available. This concession had been granted years before because of the long periods of time they spent on call or away from home and family. Each telegraph operator managed to receive this benefit four to six weeks per year during the slow winter season. Their pay was also higher than that of the clerks.

The telegraph operators could be sent anywhere, but could only replace telegraph operators. Clerks could only replace other clerks. It was not uncommon during major derailments for telegraph operators to be hundreds of miles from their home, on overtime, living on expenses paid by the railroad, yet working next to clerks who had nothing to do.

## Rumors of Changes

Dave was aware of the rumors about lay-offs running rampant in the company and knew that these fears were justified. In addition, attempts to combine job descriptions and job functions in different departments were also under debate.

Dave knew that the removal of the fireman position from the engine of the train was meeting with an organized covert slowdown of work. The fireman position was a leftover from the days when the shoveling of coal was required to heat the boiler on the steam locomotive. The train crew in the engine consisted of the engineer, fireman, and brakeman. The fireman's only function, since the advent of the internal combustion engine, was to take over the controls of the engine should the engineer need assistance.

Since the decline of the steam engine, several unsuccessful attempts had been made to eliminate the fireman position by incorporating its duties with those of the brakeman.

Employees who believed they had enough seniority to remain after a layoff saw this as increasing their work without increasing their pay. When seasoned employees were asked to do a different task or function previously done by another job title, they would openly refuse. Backed by the union, they stated that it was not in their job description or their contract.

## Challenges

After extensive research, Dave realized he had two immediate problems facing him: reducing the crushing employee expenses necessary in day-to-day operations and improving the attitude of employees to accept necessary changes to ensure the railroad's survival.

He believed that the morale problem had been created by a recruitment process that traditionally favored the hiring of relatives. This was a common practice throughout the region. Dave had observed employees working beside spouses, brothers, cousins, and children. Nepotism saturated many different levels of the organization. Featherbedding proliferated because of the high degree of nepotism historically in the railroad industry. (Featherbedding is the practice of limiting work output in order to provide more jobs and prevent unemployment.) Resistance to change was high, especially when cooperation could result in loss of employment for one or more family members.

Dave believed that if he could eliminate the featherbedding, reduction in expenses would follow. This would help to prevent a major layoff of clerks and telegraph operators. Both groups would have to accept some changes and take on additional or different duties. But this action would reduce the yearly income of many individuals who had grown to count on their guarantees, expense accounts, and overtime pay.

A new union contract was still two years away, and experience had shown that the union was very rigid about concessions in these areas. Gathering enough information and evidence to substantiate changes in job descriptions with union representatives would be impossible without help from upper management.

The thing Dave was uncertain about was whether or not there would be any organized resistance by the employees under his jurisdiction. Twice during his 11 years with the railroad, he had witnessed such subversive group resistance. Its effects were extremely devastating to the company and the responsible managers. The present slowdown by the train crews over the fireman issue attested to the power, strength, and attitude of the employees.

## Conclusion

Dave was aware of his own career vulnerability if an organized effort took place against him. He wondered why someone with more experience hadn't been given these difficult tasks. Why was his being single an important criterion?

Originally, Dave was excited but also apprehensive about his promotion to communication manager. But once Dave was in the new position, Allan's unofficial duties for Dave cast a cloud over Dave's enthusiasm. Dave tried unsuccessfully to get written backing from Allen to support his unofficial directives. Allen's only advice was to do what was best for the railroad.

After much soul-searching, Dave begun to wonder whether he was being set up as the helmsman on a sinking ship or was just being paranoid. If he implemented the needed changes, he would lose employee support and fail to meet official expectations, possibly causing his dismissal if Allen didn't back him. If he didn't make the required changes, Allen would dismiss him, and thus the outcome would be the same. Dave felt forced to give Allen the changes he wanted, but didn't trust him for support afterwards.

Things were changing fast, and Dave wanted a fresh perspective. He felt the need for outside consultation before taking any action, but using company funds was out of the question. So for a small fee, out of his own pocket, he consulted and confided in a small group of outstanding business students at the local college. You are one of these students. What problems, recommendations, advice, and actions would your group identify? (Use Case Analysis Form.)[33]

**NOGO RAILROAD CASE ANALYSIS FORM**

Name: _____

I. Problems

  A. Macro

    1. _____

    _____

    2. _____

    _____

  B. Micro

    1. _____

    _____

    2. _____

    _____

II. Causes

    1. _____

    _____

    2. _____

    _____

    3. _____

III. Systems affected

    1. _____

    _____

    2. _____

    _____

    3. _____

    _____

IV. Alternatives

    1. _____

    _____

    2. _____

    _____

    3. _____

    _____

V. Recommendations

_____

_____

_____

_____

_____

## Chapter 2 Endnotes

1. Laura Rubuch, "Downsizing: How Quality Is Affected as Companies Shrink," *Quality Progress*, vol. 28, no. 4 (April 1995), p. 24.
2. "25 Most Innovative Companies: Smart Ideas for Tough Times," *Business Week*, April 28, 2008, pp. 61–63.
3. For additional information, see Paul Lukas, "3M: The Magic of Mistakes," *Fortune Small Business*, April 18, 2003 (www.Fortune.com).
4. Jim Collins, "The Secret of Enduring Greatness," *Fortune*, May 5, 2008, p. 76.
5. "Capitalists of the World: Innovate!" *Fast Company*, February/March 1999, p. 76.
6. For additional information on renewal and the role of leadership, see Teresa M. Amabile and Mukti Khaire, "Creativity and the Role of the Leader," *Harvard Business Review*, October 2008, pp. 98–109.
7. John Huey and Geoffrey Colvin, "Staying Smart, The Jack and Herb Show," *Fortune*, January 8, 2002 (www.Fortune.com).
8. Robert D. Hof, "How Google Fuels Its Idea Factory," *Business Week,* May 12, 2008, p. 54.
9. www.google.com/about.html; Michael Orey, "Why Google Wants to Make Nice," *Business Week*, May 11, 2009, pp. 54–56; Hof, "How Google Fuels Its Idea Factory," *Business Week*, May 12, 2008, pp. 54–56; Ben Elgin, "Web Search for Tomorrow," *Business Week,* May 17, 2004, p. 46; Robert Frank, "Two Founders Get a New Job: Handling All That Money," *Wall Street Journal,* April 30, 2004, pp. A1, A10; Ben Elgin, "Google: Why the World's Hottest Tech Company Will Struggle to Keep Its Edge," *Business Week,* May 3, 2004, pp. 82–90.
10. The following were used as sources for Figure 2.1: Joan Ash and Ellen West, "High Performance Systems and Transformational Change," paper presented at Academy of Management meeting, Washington, D.C., August 1989; Teresa J. Colvin and Ralph H. Kilmann, "A Profile of Large-Scale Change Programs," *Proceedings of the Southern Management Associations*, 1989, p. 202.
11. David Miller, "Evolution and Revolution: A Quantum View of Structural Change in Organizations," *Journal of Management Studies*, April 1982, pp. 131–51.
12. Ruth Simon, "What I Learned in the Eighties," *Forbes*, January 8, 1990, p. 100.
13. Colvin and Kilmann, "Profile of Large-Scale Change Programs," p. 202.
14. Mark Maremont and Deborah Solomon, "Behind SEC's Failings: Caution, Tight Budget, '90s Exuberance," *Wall Street Journal*, December 24, 2003, p. A1.
15. Ibid., p. A5.
16. Kara Scannell, "SEC Watchdog Faults Agency in a Bear Case," *Wall Street Journal*, October 11, 2008, p. A1.
17. Steve Hamm, Steve Rosenbush, and Cliff Edwards, "Tech Comes Out Swinging," *Business Week*, June 23, 2003, p. 64.
18. Laurie J. Flynn, "Technology; Hewlett Chief Has No Plans But Says All Is on the Table," *New York Times,* March 31, 2005, p. C11.
19. Fremont E. Kast and James E. Rosenzweig, *Organization and Management* (New York: McGraw-Hill, 1979), p. 11.
20. For additional information, see Eric Trist and H. Murray, ed. *The Social Engagement of Social Science, Volume II: The Socio-Technical Perspective* (Philadelphia: University of Pennsylvania Press, 1993); Eric Trist, B. Higgin, H. Murray, and A. Pollock, *Organizational Choice* (London: Tavistock, 1963); and Eric Trist and K. Bamforth, "Some Social and Psychological Consequences of the Longwall Method of Coal Getting," *Human Relations*, vol. 4, no.1 (February, 1951), pp. 3–38.
21. For an edited book of readings on technology and society, see Deborah G. Johnson and Jameson M. Wetmore, ed., *Technology and Society: Building Our Sociotechnical Future* (Cambridge MA: The MIT Press, 2009).
22. Marshal Sashkin, Ronald J. Burke, Paul R. Lawrence, and William Pasmore, "OD Approaches," *Training and Development Journal*, vol. 39, no. 2 (February 1985), p. 46.
23. Joe McConagh and David Coghlan, "Information Technology and the Lure of Integrated Change: A Neglected Role for Organization Development?" *Public Administration Quarterly*, Spring 2006, pp. 22–55.
24. David P. Hanna, *Designing Organizations for High Performance* (Reading, MA: Addison-Wesley, 1988), p. 42.
25. See Henry L. Tosi Jr. and John W. Slocum, Jr., "Contingency Theory: Some Suggested Directions," *Journal of Management*, vol. 10, no.1 (Spring, 1984), pp. 9–26.
26. See Robert R. Blake and Jane S. Mouton, "OD Technology for the Future," *Training and Development Journal*, November 1979, p. 55; Blake contends that there is "one best way."
27. From Alvin Toffler, *Future Shock* (New York: Random House, 1970). Reprinted by permission of Random House, Inc. Originally appeared in *Playboy* in a slightly different form. Also by permission of the Bodley Head, London. See also Alvin Toffler, *The Third Wave* (New York: Morrow, 1980).
28. For additional information see, Robin Sidel and Damian Paletta, "Industry Is Remade in a Wave of Mergers," *Wall Street Journal*, September 30, 2008, p. A1.
29. Gary Hamel, *The Future of Management* (Boston, MA: Harvard Business School Press, 2007); Gary Hamel, "Break Free!" *Fortune*, October 1, 2007, p. 120.
30. Heather Green, "How Meetup Tore up the Rule Book," *Business Week*, June 16, 2008, pp. 88–89; and www. meetup.com.
31. Arik Hesseldahl, "Tim Cook: A Steady Go-To Guide for Apple," *Business Week*, January, 14, 2009, available at www.businessweek.com; Adam Lashinsky, "Apple: the Genius Behind Steve," *Fortune*, November 24, 2008, pp. 71–80; Peter Elkind, "The Trouble with Steve,"

*Fortune*, March 17, 2008, pp. 88–98; Anne Fisher, "America's Most Admired Companies," *Fortune*, March 17, 2008, pp. 65–74.

32. Robert Chin and Kenneth D. Benne, "General Strategies for Effecting Changes in Human Systems," in *The Planning of Change*, ed. Warren G. Bennis, Kenneth D. Benne, and Robert Chin (New York: Holt, Rinehart & Winston, 1979), pp. 32–59.

33. Mark Mangiaracina and Don Harvey, Eastern Washington University, 1991. Revised and rewritten by Don Brown, 2009.

# Changing the Culture

## LEARNING OBJECTIVES

**Upon completing this chapter, you will be able to:**

1. Recognize the importance of corporate culture to organizational success.
2. Identify the key factors used in assessing corporate culture.
3. Describe the culture and organizational factors that lead to effective organizations.
4. Describe the major ethical, value, and goal considerations of an OD program.

## PREMEETING PREPARATION

1. Read Chapter 3.
2. Prepare and read the instructions for OD Skills Simulation 3.1. Prior to class, form into teams of six and select roles. Complete Step 1.
3. Read and analyze Case: The Dim Lighting Co.

## CREATING A CLIMATE FOR CHANGE

Change, massive change, is having an impact on all facets of society, creating new dimensions and great uncertainty. The issue facing us today is how to manage change. Organization development provides a renewal process that enables managers to adapt their style and goals to meet the changing demands of the environment. These changes—improving quality, increasing innovation, adopting a customer orientation—are so fundamental that they usually mean changing the organization's culture.[1]

Change for an organization is inevitable, and successful organizations are a dynamic engine of change. Executives are adapting to changing market conditions and, at the same time, facing the need to create a "renewing" rather than a "reactive" managerial system. They are searching for ways to manage an increasingly complex technology and a more sophisticated workforce. To accomplish these diverse goals, managers need more than piecemeal, ad hoc change programs dealing only with current crises. They need long-term efforts to prepare for future organizational requirements. In this chaotic world, the only excellent managers will be those who are constantly adapting to change—those able not only to deal proactively with shifting forces, but also to take advantage of the opportunities that arise.

The lessons of management seem to point out that companies with outstanding financial performance often have powerful corporate cultures, suggesting that "culture" is the key to an organization's success. Changing the culture of an organization does not just happen; it is usually the result of a complex change strategy implemented by the company's management.

In this chapter, we will examine (1) the concept of corporate culture, (2) cultural resistance to change and ways to bring about change, and (3) ethical, value, and goal considerations of an OD program.

## UNDERSTANDING CORPORATE CULTURE

In today's organization, change leaders are seeking to make a more fundamental shift in the capabilities of their organizations. They are not looking for marginal improvements; their goal is to reinvent themselves. Reinventing lies not in marginally

## OD Application: The Culture at Setpoint Systems[2]

The founders of Setpoint Systems had a pretty good idea of the sort of company culture they wanted to build. It didn't occur to them that what they came up with would become one of the company's most valuable assets.

Setpoint is an industrial automation integration firm employing only about 50 employees. Most of its revenues come from designing and building factory-automation equipment for companies like Honeywell and Kimberly-Clark. For many of its customers, the automation equipment that Setpoint builds is unique to fill specific customer requirements. This requires exceptionally self-motivated employees who can solve problem and continually look for ways to improve processes and functions. For over 15 years, Setpoint has been actively practicing project management and open-book accounting. On one occasion, a visitor touring Setpoint being led by CFO Joe Knight encountered ten employees or so on the shop floor working on building half a dozen machines. Off to the side was a whiteboard. Scribbled across the board were about 20 rows and 10 columns of numbers forming a table of some sort.

"What's that?" the visitor asked.

"That's our board," Knight said. "It's how we track our projects and figure out whether or not we're making money." Knight began explaining what the numbers were and where they came from. Then Knight stopped. "You know," he said, "you really shouldn't take my word for it. You should get these guys to tell you about it." He called out to one of the technicians, introduced him, and asked him to explain what was on the board.

"Sure," the young man said and proceeded to walk them through it. He talked about calculating the gross profit that he and his colleagues had earned the previous week on each project. He pointed out the column showing each project's gross profit per hour and explained the importance of keeping that

number in mind. He said that he also watched the ratio of overall gross profit to operating expenses, because that's how he knew if the company was making money. He added that he liked to see it running at about 2.0.

"I was just amazed," the visitor recalled later. "He knew that board inside and out. He knew every number on it. He knew exactly where the company was and where they had to focus their attention. There was no hesitation. He had great confidence in what was up there. I could see that the board was a cherished possession, and I was so impressed, not that Joe Knight understood it, but that the people on the shop floor had it down like that. It was their scoreboard. It was the way they could tell if they were winning or losing. I talked to several of them, and I just couldn't get over the positive attitude they had and their understanding of business." Joe Knight has been so successful in explaining accounting concepts to nonaccountants that he has co-authored a book on the subject, *Financial Intelligence: A Manager's Guide to Knowing What the Numbers Really Mean*, published by Harvard Business School Press.

Companies are bought for a limited number of reasons. Yet Setpoint has an asset that is worth something for the bottom line. Though it is hard to value, some companies would be willing to pay a substantial price for a particular type of corporate culture with a thorough attention to the financials.

### Questions

1. Is it reasonable to expect other manufacturing companies to be able to duplicate the culture that Setpoint has developed? Support your position.
2. Can culture be bought?
3. What dangers would a merger pose for the culture at Setpoint?

changing the current way of doing business, but in creating totally new approaches, new technologies, and new markets.

Given an environment of rapid change, a static organizational culture can no longer be effective. Managers must be able to recognize when changes are necessary and must possess the skills and competence to implement these changes. The organization must adapt itself to a dynamic environment by introducing internal changes that will allow it to become more effective. Organization development is one method for bringing about a proactive managerial culture. OD, as was explained in Chapter 1, is a long-range effort to introduce planned change throughout an organization. Setpoint Systems is an example of a small company that has been able to remain successful in a highly competitive marketplace. To learn more about how they have done this, see **OD Application: The Culture at Setpoint Systems**.

## What Is Corporate Culture?

A corporate culture is a system of shared values and beliefs that interact with an organization's people, structure, and systems to produce behavioral norms ("the way things are done around here"). It is the tangible and intangible characteristics of an organization including aspirations, reward systems, behaviors, assumptions, performance, rituals, communications, and heritage.[3] (See Figure 3.1). **Corporate culture** is defined as "an interdependent set of beliefs, values, ways of behaving, and tools for living that are so common in a community that they tend to perpetuate themselves, sometimes over long periods of time. This continuity is the product of a variety of social forces that are frequently subtle, bordering on invisible, through which people learn a group's norms and values, are rewarded when they accept them, and are ostracized when they

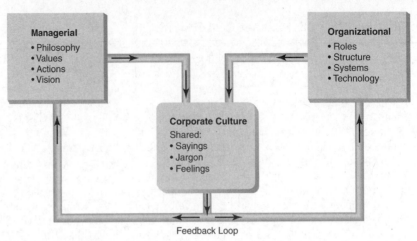

**FIGURE 3.1** Culture Formation

do not."[4] Southwest Airlines is so serious about developing an appropriate culture that in 1990 the president and COO, Colleen Barrett, started their Culture Committee.[5] Herb Kelleher, founder of Southwest Airlines, has said, "Culture is one of the most precious things a company has, so you must work harder on it than anything else."[6] Culture is the glue that holds an organization together.

An organization may also have subcultures with differing or even conflicting corporate cultures. We shall use the term "corporate culture" to refer to the culture of all types of organizations; thus, a university and a city government each have a corporate culture, even though they are not corporations.

Every organization has a culture, though some cultures are stronger and more pronounced than others. Starbucks is an example of a company that exhibits a strong internal culture. Its CEO, Howard Schultz, put it this way: "If people relate to the company they work for, if they form an emotional tie to it and buy into its dreams, they will pour their hearts into making it better."[7] But companies with strong cultures need to be cautious. Yale University's associate dean of the School of Management, Jeffrey A. Sonnenfeld, warned, "[A company] is not a museum. It's not a religion."[8] Cofounder Sergey Brin of Google echoed this belief in an interview saying, "I actually don't think keeping the culture is a goal. I think improving the culture is. We shouldn't be, like, looking back to our golden years and saying, 'Oh, I wish it was the same.'"[9]

Culture is derived from both the management and the organization itself. Managers, through their actions and words, define a philosophy of how employees are treated. Sam Walton, the founder of Wal-Mart, used to say that it takes a week to two weeks for employees to start treating customers the same way the employer is treating the employee.[10] Values and ways of behaving are defined—and a vision is usually articulated by the top management. All of these factors coming from management help define the culture. Simultaneously, factors brought in by the organization also help define the culture. The technology a company utilizes will influence the culture. A company in a fast-changing industry will probably develop a different culture than a company in a slower-changing industry. For example, the organization that publishes the *Wall Street Journal*, a traditional print media company that dates its first publication to 1889, will have a far different culture and business model than *The Huffington Post,* an Internet newspaper with accompanying blogs and video. The job descriptions and the way an organization is structured, such as a tall hierarchy versus a flat hierarchy, will influence the development of the culture.

Management style and corporate culture are central factors in the success of a company. Managerial style and culture constitute one of the most critical factors in organizational strategy. They set the tone for the whole organization and influence the communication, decision-making, and leadership patterns of the entire system. There is no basic culture that works best for all organizations. The managerial style and the set of norms, values, and beliefs of the organization's members combine to form the corporate culture. According to Terrence Deal and Allan Kennedy, "A shared history between members builds a distinct corporate identity or character."[11]

A corporate culture must achieve goals as well as satisfy the needs of members if the organization is to be effective. Culture influences how managers and employees approach problems, serve customers, react to competitors, and carry out activities. Sam Walton created a culture for his firm that reflected his own personal values. Although he was worth some $8 billion, Walton lived in a modest home in Bentonville, Arkansas. He drove a Ford pickup truck and ate breakfast almost daily at the local Ramada Inn. He went out on Friday nights to Fred's Hickory Inn for ribs and cheesecake. He worked out of a small office with plywood paneling. He visited every store and led the company cheer.[12]

A strong, widely internalized corporate culture is frequently cited as a reason for the success of such companies as 3M, Google, and Disney.[13] In these organizations, the rewards, ceremonies, and other symbolic forms of communications maintain a culture that guides the actions of its members. In a study of 24 organizations, Henry Migliore identified a set of 20 cultural factors, termed the Corporate Culture Index that can be used to measure an organizational culture.[14] These factors include the following characteristics:

- *Member Identity:* employees identify with their profession or the organization.
- *Team Emphasis:* the degree to which work activities are organized around teams rather than individuals.
- *People Focus:* the degree to which management empowers the employees within the organization.
- *Autonomy:* the degree to which departments within the organization are encouraged to operate in a coordinated or interdependent manner.
- *Control:* the degree to which rules, regulations, and direct supervision are used to control employee behavior.
- *Risk Tolerance:* the degree to which employees are encouraged to be aggressive, innovative, and risk-seeking.

## The Corporate Culture and Success

A corporate culture gives the whole organization a sense of how to behave, what to do, and where to set the priorities in getting the job done. Culture helps members fill in the blanks between formal directives and how work is actually done. Because of this, culture is of critical importance in the implementation of strategy.

A great majority of outstanding companies trace their culture back to an influential founder who personified a value system and relentlessly hammered in a few basic values that become the cultural core of the company. However, in today's rapidly changing environment, many corporate cultures fail to adapt to change and, therefore, fail as economic entities.

For some organizations, especially those in the service sector, the company's culture is what helps set it apart from its competition. The Walt Disney Company is one organization where this is the case. Disney's corporate culture, formed over a period of 80 years, is one of the world's most deeply rooted corporate cultures—"a planet unto itself ruled by the iconography of the company's twin deities, Walt Disney and Mickey Mouse."[15] It is this culture, unique to Disney, that sets the firm apart from virtually every other business organization and is responsible for much of the company's success. Indeed, many of the once-great corporations, such as Sears and General Motors, previously thought of as model organizations incapable of losing their dominating position in the marketplace, almost met ruin because their culture embodied a reluctance to change.

Cultures often clash following corporate mergers, downsizings, or other restructurings. Both mergers and internal restructurings involve bringing groups together that may have very different goals, operating methods, and cultures. Using Disney again as an example, the company has been careful to protect the culture of Pixar Animation Studios since it purchased Pixar in 2006. Disney and Pixar have very different cultures. Disney has a legacy going back to its founding in 1923 as an animation studio by brothers Walt and Roy Disney. Pixar grew out of the computer division at Lucasfilm Limited when in 1986, it was purchased by Apple's Steve Jobs and given its current name. Disney's CEO, Bob Iger, said of the Pixar purchase in an interview, "A major priority when we did the deal was to protect their culture."[16] International mergers can be even more complex because they entail bringing national cultures together and, perhaps, language differences. The complexities involved in mergers, both domestic and international, require that issues regarding the organizations' culture be carefully managed.[17]

Following a merger, differences in corporate beliefs, goals, policies, management style, values, norms, gender, race, religion, and nationalism can manifest a nonproductive "we" versus "they" situation if the parties involved are not made aware of, and sensitive to, the cultural differences. Here are some important guidelines:

1. Do everything possible to accelerate and to create a culture of quicker reflexes.
2. Cool-headed thinking, a clear focus, and well-aimed action are required.
3. Self-directed behavior is essential in today's world of accelerating change.
4. Redirect conflict, anger, or worry into the passionate pursuit of results.
5. A culture unwilling to experiment has little chance to innovate.

What makes for excellence in the management of an organization? Today's key words are flexibility and innovation. Organizations are being forced to make dramatic changes just to remain competitive. These changes, such as improving product quality, increasing speed of responsiveness, and expanding customer orientation, are so basic and fundamental that managers must alter the corporate culture. However, cultural change implies a change in the basic values of the organization and in the hearts and minds of the individual employees.

## The Impact of Key Factors

In order to create a winning culture, managers need to adapt their managerial style, values, and goals to fit the changing demands of the environment.

As we move into the twenty-first century, the question is not whether corporate cultures will continue to exist, but what type of corporate culture will be most effective in enabling a company to survive and excel. To understand the performance of an organization, one must first investigate the corporate culture. The focus of OD is on improving an organization's self-renewal process so that managers can quickly initiate changes to the corporate culture to meet emerging new problems. Tomorrow's leaders will be those who are the most flexible and innovative.

There are several key factors that organizations need to be aware of to improve their effectiveness:

- *Create a Vision for the Future.* A shared vision provides direction, focus, and commitment. Harold Leavett terms this action "pathfinding" and observes that it involves the dreamer, the innovator, the creator, and the entrepreneur.[18] Some very successful organizations began with a vision. Since Steve Jobs' early days at Apple Computer, for example, he dreamed of computers for everyone, "one person, one computer," as a way toward a better world. Fred Smith, founder and CEO at Federal Express, bet his personal fortune on overnight delivery, on the need for faster information processing in a high-speed world. These visions are compelling and involve all members in striving toward goals: vision provides meaning.
- *Develop a Model for Change.* Total organization change often starts in one unit or subculture of an organization. When Steve Jobs started to develop the Macintosh at Apple, he started with a group he called his "pirates," a handpicked team of dedicated young designers working under a black skull-and-crossbones flag. Similarly, at a large utility, one department manager instituted a management by objectives (MBO) program even though most of the other corporate managers said it would never work. This change led to increased performance of this department, and ultimately the whole organization was motivated to use this system. Although it may be coincidental, this manager is now the president of his company.
- *Reward Changes.* One of the basic underlying concepts of motivation is that people tend to behave in ways that provide rewards or reinforcement. If the system still rewards the old culture, then it won't make sense for people to change. This, of course, includes not only pay and promotion, but other incentives as well.

Corporate cultures are the very essence of organizations. Whether effective or ineffective, organizational cultures exist—usually reflecting the personality of the top executive. Corporate cultures often affect the success or failure of the organization and are shaped in various ways by the employees. There is considerable debate over whether it is possible to change these deeply held values. In the next sections, we examine cultural resistance to change and some tools to use in change programs.

## CULTURAL RESISTANCE TO CHANGE

Changing a corporate culture is not easy. Culture emerges out of the shared behaviors and the working relationships of organization members that have developed over time. Consequently, it takes time for a cultural transformation to take effect. Many firms, confronted with international competition and technological change, have no choice but to slim down. Though accelerated by recession, this trend is likely to continue even after economic growth returns. Whether it is called "reengineering," "downsizing," or "delayering," the goals are the same: to eliminate layers of middle management in order to delegate responsibility to those actually making products or dealing with customers. Ideally, companies should emerge from these reorganizations more flexible, entrepreneurial, and effective. However, unless they find new ways to motivate the remaining employees, most managers are unlikely to achieve the gains that are supposed to justify such drastic changes.

A culture can also prevent a company from remaining competitive or adapting to a changing environment. In the case of General Motors (GM), culture got in the way of the firm's remaining a competitive force in the automobile industry. Since the early 1970s, there have been GM executives and board members who have publicly pointed out that GM's culture was one where conformity was encouraged and rebellion was frowned on. Former manager of GM's Chevrolet Division, John DeLorean, said approximately 40 years ago in 1973, "There's no forward response at General Motors to what the public wants today. It's gotten to be a total insulation from the realities of the world."[19] Even GM's own History Project pointed out that in the early 1980s, the company was still making decisions under a structure that was similar to what existed 50 years earlier. And in the mid-1980s, GM board member, H. Ross Perot said, "I come from an environment where, if you see a snake, you kill it. At GM, if you see a snake, the first thing you do is organize a committee on snakes. Then you go hire a consultant who knows a lot about snakes. Then you talk about it for a year."[20] GM has shown through at least 40 years to be an example of the importance of changing the culture in order to successfully implement a change strategy.

The need for devising and executing better strategies is becoming readily apparent. Recession, deregulation, technological upheavals, social factors, global competition, outsourcing, and markets that seem to suddenly emerge and then vanish just as quickly have increased the pressure on companies to be flexible and adaptable. An inappropriate culture is often one of the biggest stumbling blocks on the path to adaptation.

## TOOLS FOR CHANGE

Management changes to improve strategy are more likely to succeed if the factors that shape the culture can be identified and managed. In a comparison of high-innovation companies with low-innovation ones, Rosabeth Moss Kanter describes how change masters and corporate entrepreneurs are allowed to flourish in high-innovation companies.[21] Three organizational tools are required in the adaptive organization: information, support, and resources.

### Information

The first tool provides people with information or the ability to gather information. People feel free to go outside their own department to gather information and engage in open communication patterns across departments. Some companies have rules prohibiting closed meetings. Other organizations have information-exchange meetings that cut across employee levels. Making information available at every level increases employee motivation and permits faster decision making. This helps employees to identify with organizational goals.

One new trend is termed **open-book management.** Open-book organizations teach employees to understand accounting and financial statements and to use that knowledge in their work and planning, similar to Setpoint Systems, which was discussed in the OD Application earlier in this chapter. The basic element involves giving key information to employees so that work teams can make job decisions. A major benefit is that employees are able to analyze and understand the problems for themselves.[22]

### Support

The second tool provides the corporate entrepreneur with the support and necessary "go ahead" from higher management as well as the cooperation of peers and subordinates. If the project cuts across organizational lines, support and collaboration from other departments is needed. For example, interdepartmental meetings and training sessions that bring people together can provide the opportunity to build support for projects. Organizations can remove the fear of failure and provide a climate that supports people in taking risks.

## Resources

The third tool provides the resources, including funds, staff, equipment, and materials, to carry out the project. Budgetary channels are the normal vehicle of funding innovation, but in most instances this process is too time-consuming to respond to a project in a timely manner. Some organizations support projects from bootlegged funds budgeted for other projects. "Venture capital" and "innovation banks" also provide support for innovative projects. W. L. Gore and Associates, an example of a highly adaptive company, does not have employees; instead it has associates, and the company encourages people to develop their ideas into projects. This provides a team focus and ownership of operations.

Changing the organization's culture does not take place quickly in a strongly established culture. Any changes to the organization's culture must focus on what people value and what they do. Cultural changes are likely to be more successful when the following are considered:

- *Understand the old culture.* Managers should understand the existing culture.
- *Follow outstanding units.* Recognize exemplary units and use them as a model for change.
- *Encourage change in employees.* Encourage employees to change and improve the current culture.
- *Involve employees.* Avoid imposing cultural change and instead involve employees in discovering new ways of operating.
- *Lead with a vision.* The vision provides a guiding principle for change, but must be brought into by employees.
- *Recognize that large-scale change takes time.* It may take three to five years for significant, organization-wide cultural change to take effect.
- *Live the new culture.* The actions of managers carry more impact than their words.

Trilogy Software has been successful in building a strong culture by using many of the foregoing factors. **OD Application: How Trilogy's University Helps to Build Its Culture** discusses this in more detail.

---

## OD Application: How Trilogy's University Helps to Build Its Culture[23]

Trilogy Software Inc. is a small, rapidly growing software firm based in Austin, Texas, with offices in India and China. Trilogy, on the cutting edge of sales-and-marketing software, also has a very unique orientation program for new hires.

### Stanford Dropout

Joe Liemandt founded Trilogy in 1989, after dropping out of Stanford only a few months before graduation. To finance the startup, Liemandt charged up 22 credit cards. In four years, Trilogy grew from 100 to 1,000 employees. Today, Trilogy is among the world's largest privately held software companies and is a leading provider of industry-specific software for the automotive, consumer electronics, and insurance industries. To call Trilogy workers "employees" misses the point. They're all shareholders. They're all managers. They're all partners.

Joe Liemandt knows that Trilogy depends on talented people. He also knows that people can go anywhere, which means that his biggest competitive headache isn't companies like SAP AG and Oracle—businesses he has to compete with in the marketplace. His biggest worry is holding onto talented people. "There's nothing more important than recruiting and growing

people," he says. "That's my number one job." Management consultant and author Noel Tichy says, "Trilogy is going head-to-head with Microsoft and other biggies in the talent war. On their side, they have a very clear teachable point of view of what Trilogy is and what they practice. They are confident of their ideas and values. They know how to energize people, how to make courageous decisions."

### Trilogy University

Trilogy University (TU) is a corporate boot camp experience, modeled after Marine Corps basic training, where the new employee goes through a three-month high-pressure program. Liemandt, along with others in top management, teach a large portion of the classes. The first month places the candidates in teams of about 20 where they participate in fast-paced creative projects. In the second month, the teams are broken into smaller teams, where they develop a business model, marketing plans, and a prototype for a new product or service. During the third month, the candidates demonstrate personal initiative by working on their project either with their team or finding a sponsor somewhere in the company. At the conclusion of the program,

*(continued)*

the candidates go through a comprehensive evaluation and feedback session given by their peers, section leaders, and senior managers.

TU makes diverse contributions to the Trilogy organization. Joe Liemandt realized early on that as the company rapidly grew, the new employees needed to learn not only the skills for their new job, but, perhaps more importantly, also the values and culture of Trilogy. During the time of close to 20 years that TU has been around, TU has become the primary source for research and development as well as a major source for self-renewal and transformation. Ideas that start as projects in month two sometimes go on to become new products and services. In addition, the program has helped employees form relationships that last throughout their careers. And for the long-term viability of Trilogy, TU serves as a place where a new generation of leaders is created. Noel Tichy says, "Most companies' orientation programs were designed to help new hires hit the ground running. Trilogy's boot camp has a bigger goal: keep the company running."

### The Business Model

Trilogy has a unique business model in the software industry and most other service-oriented businesses. Its model ties Trilogy's revenue and 100 percent of employee incentives directly to the economic value that it delivers to its clients. Trilogy is so commit-

ted to the practice that it delivers guaranteed business value for its clients. Trilogy is paid only once the customer receives the promised business value.

Trilogy's unusual business model extends to its relationships with its employees. It provides perks like fully stocked kitchens and keg parties every Friday. And there are spontaneous rewards, such as a trip to Las Vegas, for good work. Bonuses are given to top performers that are equal to 50 to 100 percent of their regular salaries. The company offers to its employees many of the advantages of a free agency: flexibility in how, when, and where you work; compensation linked to what you contribute; and freedom to move from project to project. It also offers advantages of belonging to an organization in which mutual commitment builds continuity.

Trilogy fosters new methods in the way it relates with its clients and employees. The company has been highlighted as an innovative and ambitious company by leading business titles like *Harvard Business Review*, *Fortune*, and *Forbes*.

### Questions

1. Do you think the practices of Trilogy will help it remain competitive? Why?
2. How does Trilogy transfer its culture to new employees?
3. What other companies would you consider to be "enterprises of the future?"

## ETHICAL, VALUE, AND GOAL CONSIDERATIONS

Now that we have described a macro approach to organizational change, let us examine some of the micro issues: how ethics, values, and goals can be compatible and incompatible within an OD program. The ultimate purpose of increasing an organization's ability to adapt to a changing environment is to make it more effective. What makes an organization effective or ineffective? From an organization's perspective, effectiveness is the degree of goal achievement—or, to put it another way, the amount of resources the organization uses in order to produce units of output.[24] Some organizations are very good at getting a new product out with very few resources, whereas other organizations can spend a lot of money and still have few results.

In general, OD programs are aimed at three basic organizational dimensions that affect performance: managerial effectiveness, managerial efficiency, and motivational climate. **Managerial effectiveness** refers to the accomplishment of specific organizational goals and objectives, or "doing the right thing." If organizations are using their resources to attain long-term goals, the managers are being effective. The closer an organization comes to achieving its strategic goals, the more effective it is. **Managerial efficiency** refers to the ratio of output (results) to input (resources), or "doing the things right." The higher this proportion, the more efficient is the manager. When managers are able to minimize the cost of the resources used to attain performance, they are managing efficiently. An organization may be efficient but not effective, or vice versa. **Motivational climate** consists of the set of employee attitudes and morale that influences the level of performance. The goal of OD is to improve and maximize all three dimensions: effectiveness, efficiency, and motivational climate. The organization is not only doing the "right thing," but doing it well.

Three other criteria that serve as indicators of organizational effectiveness and health are adaptability, vision, and reality testing.

- Adaptability is the ability to solve problems and to react with flexibility to changing environmental demands.
- A sense of identity and vision is the organization's knowledge and insight about what its goals are and what it has to do.
- Capacity to test reality is the ability to search out and accurately and correctly interpret the real properties of the environment, especially those that have relevance for the functioning of the organization.

Some OD practitioners maintain that organizational effectiveness comes from conditions that permit the integration of organizational goals with individual goals. In a similar vein, others indicate that organizational effectiveness is derived from the integration of concern for production with concern for people. Organizational effectiveness is a multiple rather than a singular goal, involving all of these factors.

OD seeks to improve the anticipative nature of the culture and the way the organization's mission is accomplished. Organizations that only react to change become less able to adapt as the rate of change increases. Organizations that anticipate change are able to adapt to changing conditions and are consequentially more effective. Because of the impact of corporate culture, the OD practitioner must also examine the relationship between the values of OD and those of the client system.

## Ethical and Value Issues

Almost every organizational decision involves ethical questions, such as how people should treat others, conflicts of interest, and so on. In attempting to change organizations, OD practitioners must consider the ethical consequences of various actions and develop a set of ethical standards to guide them when competing interests collide.

There is also the question of professional values. OD is an emerging profession, and its practitioners tend to describe themselves as professionals. However, individuals working in the field may vary greatly in respect to their degree of professionalism. By **professionalism,** we refer to the internalization of a value system that is a part of the concept of the profession.

Whether a person can be deemed a professional is determined by the degree to which he or she has internalized certain values pertinent to the profession. Although there is some disagreement, four areas appear to be important.

1. *Expertise.* The professional requires some expertise. This includes specialized knowledge and skills that can be obtained only through training (usually through academic study and experience).
2. *Autonomy.* The professional claims autonomy. Professionals reserve the right to decide how their function is to be performed and to be free from restrictions.
3. *Commitment.* Professionals feel a commitment to the discipline. They are more likely to identify with members of their profession in other organizations than with their own organization.
4. *Code of ethics.* Finally, there is a responsibility to society for the maintenance of professional standards of work. They adhere to professional self-discipline and a code of ethics.

In any program of organizational change, the OD practitioner must take into account the individual members whose lives and livelihood could be affected by the change being introduced. Lou Holtz (retired football coach, University of Notre Dame) laid out three principles to live by that can also be useful to OD practitioners: do what is right, do your best, and treat others the way you want to be treated.

## OD Implementation Issues

It is important to recognize that the success of an OD program is, to a great extent, dependent upon the fit between OD values and the organization's values. One of the key issues to be resolved between the OD practitioner and the client concerns the value orientations of each party. These include beliefs about people, the methods used to reach change goals, and the purpose of the change program.

The value system underlying OD approaches emphasizes increasing individual growth and effectiveness by creating an organizational climate that develops human potential while achieving organizational goals. The value systems underlying OD are derived from a number of basic ideas and approaches, including those of Chris Argyris, Warren Bennis, Abraham Maslow, Douglas McGregor, Frederick Perls, and Carl Rogers. As Wendell L. French and Cecil H. Bell Jr. have written:

Organization development activities rest on a number of assumptions about people as individuals, in groups, and in total systems, about the transactional nature of organization improvement, and about values. These assumptions tend to be humanistic, developmental, and optimistic. Assumptions and values held by change agents need to be made explicit, both for enhancing working relationships with clients, and for continuous testing through practice and research.[25]

To achieve the OD goals, practitioners must consider certain ethical or value implications of their role in initiating a change program. A range of ethical issues may be involved in a change program. Important issues include (1) the compatibility of the values of the OD practitioner and the organization, (2) the changes imposed on the members, and (3) determining the priority of the goals.

## Compatibility of Values

The OD practitioner's values may not be compatible with the organizational culture of the client system. The practitioner brings a certain set of values to the client organization, which has its own basic values and mission. The question, then, is the degree to which the practitioner's personal values are congruent with those of the client. For example, should an OD practitioner help an organization doing research on biochemical warfare to become more effective if his or her personal value system is opposed to the organization's methods or mission?

Many OD practitioners feel that this is a preliminary issue to be considered before one enters any relationship. If the client's goals are unacceptable, the practitioner should not try to make the client's system more effective. To do so, these practitioners feel, would be unethical.

Others argue that such companies are legal and are following directions chosen by elected governmental representatives, and therefore, organization development is valid in these situations. These practitioners believe that OD should have a value-free orientation. Just as a doctor treats both friend and foe, the OD practitioner works to help organizations of all types and the individuals within them to develop a more healthy orientation.

A related issue concerns which client systems the practitioner chooses to help or not to help. Some OD practitioners offer their professional assistance to all potential clients regardless of financial remuneration; others limit themselves to client systems that can afford their professional fees. The latter of the two is illustrated in Figure 3.2.

## Imposed Change

Since organizations are political systems, another ethical consideration for the OD practitioner is the question of choice in deciding to implement a change program. The decision to initiate an OD program is usually made by the top management group, yet it is likely to affect all the members and parts of the organization. At one major company, for example, the top executives and the OD practitioner decided on the OD program, which involved all members. Lower-level members may or may not have a real choice regarding their participation in the program. If organization members do not have a choice, the practitioner may become an instrument for imposing change upon the rest of the organization.

Organizational politics are also a factor in any change program, because change has the potential to disrupt the current balance of power among members and units. The OD practitioner cannot afford to ignore the reality of power and politics in implementing change.

## Determining the Priority of the Goals

A third issue involves which of the goals of an OD program is likely to be given precedence. As noted earlier, change programs generally are aimed at improved effectiveness, efficiency, and participant satisfaction. It then becomes necessary to decide how much emphasis, if any, to put on each goal. Are organizational or individual goals to take precedence? This sounds relatively simple in theory, but in practice, the executives who are paying for the OD program are frequently under pressure to improve efficiency and profitability, even though they also seek increased participant satisfaction and morale. The question is: How can the OD practitioner help improve the productive efficiency of the organization and at the same time improve the quality of work for its members?

So one challenge for the OD practitioner is to try to develop a balanced intervention—one that considers member rights and well-being along with improvements in productivity. Underlying the challenges and dilemmas of OD is a set of values about the nature of human beings and

**FIGURE 3.2** Help for a Price
*Source:* B.C. By permission of Johnny Hart and Creators Syndicate, Inc.

their positions in an organizational context, as shown in Table 3.1. In this environment of change, OD practitioners face both exciting challenges and serious dilemmas over how to fully meet the changing values and processes of change.

There has been growing concern about the philosophical issues surrounding the field of OD. These issues arise from the basic inconsistencies between the values of OD practitioners and those held by client organizations. The technology and value system of OD is itself undergoing change and revitalization.

**TABLE 3.1** OD Values

| | |
|---|---|
| *Respect for people* | Individuals are allowed to function as human beings, perceived as responsible, authentic, and caring. People should be treated with dignity and respect, not just as resources. |
| *Trust and support* | Develop an effective, healthy organization characterized by trust, authenticity, openness, and a supportive climate. |
| *Power equalization* | Provide opportunities for people to influence their work environment. Effective organizations have less reliance on hierarchical authority and control. |
| **Confrontation** | Provide an environment of open communication where problems aren't swept under the rug. Issues and strategies should be openly confronted and decided. |
| *Participation* | Provide opportunities for individuals to develop their full potential. The more that people affected by a change are involved in the decisions leading to that change, the more they will be committed to implementing the change. |

To sum up, the objectives of OD are to create organizational cultures that are more effective, more potent, more innovative, and better equipped to accomplish both organizational and member goals. The following 10 chapters examine each stage of an OD program and explain them in greater depth.

## Summary

- **Change.** Change is an inevitable consequence of operating in a dynamic environment. For OD practitioners and managers, it is important to recognize that organizational changes can be initiated by its members or as a reaction to external forces. This chapter focuses on the idea that a key aspect of implementing change is the need to institutionalize the change into organizational value systems. Consequently, the corporate culture is an important element in implementing a change program.
- **Corporate Culture.** Corporate culture has been defined as the shared values and behaviors of organizational members and represents a key factor in implementing planned change in organizations. Whether anticipative or reactive, change is likely to be most successful when the organization proceeds with a planned approach that takes the nature of the culture into account. In recent years, corporate culture has been reorganized as a pervasive force influencing organizational effectiveness.
- **Cultural Resistance to Change.** Culture emerges out of the shared behaviors of organization members and the working relationships that have developed over time. An

inappropriate culture is often one of the biggest stumbling blocks on the path to adaptation. A culture can prevent a company from remaining competitive or adapting to a changing environment.
- **Tools for Change.** Three organization tools are required in the adaptive organization: information, support, and resources. Employees need to have information or the ability to gather information. Support is necessary from higher management, and so is the cooperation of peers and subordinates. Resources, including funds, staff, equipment, and materials to carry out the project, are also required.
- **Goals and Values of OD.** It is important to understand the underlying goals, assumptions, and values basic to most OD programs. OD programs are aimed at improving and maximizing basic organizational dimensions that affect performance: managerial effectiveness, managerial efficiency, and motivational climate. OD practitioners must consider the ethical consequences of various actions and develop a set of ethical standards to guide them when competing interests collide.

## Review Questions

1. Describe or compare the corporate cultures of organizations you have worked in. What makes one more effective than another?
2. Compare and contrast managerial efficiency and effectiveness.

3. Identify the key factors in cultural change.
4. Explain the role of tools for change in an OD program.

## Key Words and Concepts

Corporate Culture
Managerial
  Effectiveness

Managerial Efficiency
Motivational Climate

Open-Book
  Management

Professionalism

# OD Skills Simulation 3.1

## Downsizing: A Consensus-Seeking Activity

*Total time suggested: 75 minutes.*

### A. Purpose

The purpose of this simulation is to examine the interdependence among team members and to provide insights into the concept of culture. To study culture, we may examine the culture of a group that shares certain cultural traits. The goals include:

1. To compare decisions made by individuals with those made by the group.
2. To practice effective consensus-seeking techniques.
3. To gain insights into the concept of cultural values.

### B. Procedures

*Step 1.* Prior to class, form into teams of six members. Any extra class members may serve as additional observers. Each individual is to select and prepare one role from the following:

Executive Vice President, Marketing

Executive Vice President, Finance

Executive Vice President, Manufacturing

Executive Vice President, Human Resource Management

Executive Vice President, Research and Development

Observer(s)

Before class and after you know which vice president role you will have, individually read the Downsizing: Delta Corporation background information and the Employee Profiles that follow. Rank order the 10 employees from 1, for least likely to be expendable, to 10, for most likely to be expendable. Record your ranking on the Individual Decision Work Sheet. Then transfer your ranking to column 2 on the Executive Committee Decision Work Sheet. The observer(s) will read the Downsizing: Delta Corporation background information and Employee Profiles but will not complete the Individual Decision Work Sheet.

*Step 2. Executive Committee Meeting*

Through group discussion, exploration, and examination, try to reach a *consensus decision* reflecting the integrated thinking and consensus of all members. A consensus decision involves reaching a mutual agreement by discussion until everyone agrees on the final decision.

Follow these instructions for reaching a consensus:

1. Try to reach the best-possible decision while at the same time defending the importance of your department.
2. Avoid changing your mind simply to reach an agreement and to avoid conflict, but support solutions with which you are able to agree.
3. Avoid conflict-reducing techniques, such as majority vote, averaging, or trading, in reaching your decision.
4. View differences of opinion as a help rather than a hindrance in decision making.

At this point, meet together as the Executive Committee and enter your results in Committee Ranking (column 3) on the Executive Committee Decision Work Sheet. The observer(s) will not take part in the discussion, but will record their observations on the Observer Form so that they can provide feedback in Step 5b.

*Time suggested for Step 2: 35 minutes.*

*Step 3.* Each team lists its results on the blackboard, and the instructor posts the actual performance ranking. Enter the performance ranking in column 4.

*Time suggested for Step 3: 5 minutes.*

*Step 4.* Using the answers given by the instructor, score your individual and team answers by subtracting the Personal Ranking (column 2) and Committee Ranking (column 3) from the Actual Performance Ranking (column 4). Then, record the absolute difference as the Individual Score (column 5) and Team Score (column 6), respectively. By totaling the points, an individual and a team score can be calculated. Column 5 provides an indication of the individual participant's "correctness," and column 6 provides an equivalent measure of each group's performance.

Individuals and teams can be compared based on these scores. However, the final score may not reflect how decisions were made during the team discussion.

*Time suggested for Step 4: 5 minutes.*

*Step 5a.* Team members individually complete the Values Survey and Conflict Survey Forms. Record your individual responses in column 1 of both surveys.

*Step 5b.* As a team, discuss and come to a team rating on the Values Survey and Conflict Survey Forms. The observer feeds back information on the team process using the Observer Form as a guide.

*Time suggested for Step 5: 15 minutes.*

*Step 6.* The instructor leads a discussion of the activity, letting each team explain its scores on the Value Survey and Conflict Survey Forms. Consider the following points, and compare the results for each team:

1. The consensus process within each group: things that went well and difficulties, whether the rules were followed, and the dynamics behind the posted scores.
2. The extent to which efficiency, effectiveness, and member satisfaction were emphasized in the meeting.
3. The culture that will likely develop at Delta as a result of the decisions made in the meeting.
4. How could an OD program help Delta and your management team?

*Time suggested for Step 6: 15 minutes.*

## Downsizing: Delta Corporation

Delta, started in 1988, is a small, family-owned firm in the microcomputer business. The company grew rapidly because of its development of optical and backup drives, and innovative approaches to solving computer hardware problems. Managers and workers have all put in long hours, often sacrificing their personal time to get the company off the ground.

Unfortunately, a significant downturn in the economy has caused a reduction in sales, and it is increasingly apparent that some adjustments will have to be made if the company is to survive.

Your committee will have to make a series of recommendations for a downsizing (layoff) of employees, all of whom are married, the same age (28), and had no work experience before joining Delta.

The president has asked you to examine the personal information of the 10 employees who are the most expendable. They are all good employees, but because of reduced sales and earnings and a declining economy, Delta needs to be prepared for a 5 percent reduction in workforce (RIF). Therefore, you are meeting to rank-order from 1, for least likely to 10 for most likely to be "riffed." There are at least 15 employees in each of the five departments. The employees other than those on the list given to you have been with the company at least eight years, and it is not feasible to RIF them at this time.

Among the criteria you may want to consider are:

1. Education
2. Performance
3. Seniority
4. Technical ability
5. Attitude
6. Leadership
7. Effectiveness
8. Efficiency
9. Job function
10. Social ability

You do not have to consider any of these criteria, and you are free to develop your own criteria and methods for the layoffs.

### Employee Profiles

#### Finance

*Gwen*—seniority three and one-half years; four-year college education; has performed about average on annual appraisal (75 percent); average technical ability and leadership potential; a steady, grinding worker; works long hours, has been working on employee benefit plan for two years; is a nonsmoker and nondrinker; has frequently complained about working with cigarette smokers.

*Sanjay*—seniority five and one-half years; four-year college education; has been rated average and above in annual appraisals (80 percent); high technical ability; average leadership; always in on Saturday mornings; frequently works through lunch hour; has been working on committee to computerize payroll for past 18 months; is well liked and gets along with fellow workers; is a very neat and stylish dresser.

## Research and Development

*Carole*—Ph.D. in engineering; seniority two and one-half years; has been an above-average research engineer in performance appraisal (90 percent); high technical and leadership ability; works unusual hours (sometimes works late at night, then doesn't come in until noon the next day); developed a patent on a new solid-state circuit device last year; seldom attends social events; is said to be friendly but often disagrees with fellow workers.

*Dave*—M.S. in engineering; seniority three and one-half years; has been average to above average on performance appraisal (75 percent); average technical ability; average leadership; works steadily from 8 a.m. to 5 p.m. is working on several R&D projects but none yet completed; always ready for a coffee break or joke-telling session; is well liked by coworkers; never complains about bad assignments.

## Marketing

*Tony*—MBA degree; seniority two years; has been rated as performing better than 90 percent on performance appraisal; high technical ability; above-average leadership; works erratic hours (often comes into office at 9:30 a.m. and frequently plays golf on Wednesday afternoons); sold the highest number of product units in his product line; seldom socializes with fellow workers; is often criticized because his desk is messy and disorganized, piled with correspondence and unanswered memos.

*Ken*—four-year college degree; seniority 18 months; has been rated an above-average to outstanding performer (80 percent); high technical ability; average leadership; has been criticized for not making all his sales calls, but has a good sales record and developed an advertising campaign for a new product line; although a good bowler, refuses to bowl on company team; rumored to drink quite heavily on occasion.

## Human Resources Management

*Eduardo*—four-year college degree; seniority 18 months; has been rated above average as performer (80 percent); average technical ability; high leadership; is frequently away from desk and often misses meetings; has designed and implemented a new management development program; is well liked although frequently has differences of opinion with line managers; often takes long coffee breaks and lunch hours.

*Frank*—two-year college degree; seniority four years; has been rated average to above average as performer (70 percent); low technical ability; above-average leadership; works long hours; regularly attends all meetings; has been redesigning performance-appraisal systems for the past two years; is involved in many company activities; belongs to Toast Masters, Inc.; is known as a friendly, easy-going guy.

## Manufacturing

*Irv*—four-year college degree; seniority 15 months; rated an outstanding performer (90 percent); high technical ability; moderate leadership; has been criticized for not attending committee meetings; designed and implemented the computerized production-control process; does not socialize with fellow employees; is a sloppy dresser (often wearing white or red socks with a suit).

*Jackie*—high school; seniority six years; rated an average performer (75 percent); average technical ability; low leadership; always attends meetings; works steadily from 8 a.m. to 5 p.m. and Saturday mornings; has chaired a committee to improve plant safety for past two years; participates in all social events; plays on company bowling and softball teams; is known for a very neat, organized office.

## INDIVIDUAL DECISION WORK SHEET

Instructions: Rank in order the 10 employees from 1 for least likely to 10 for most likely that are expendable.

| Employee | Department | Education | Performance | Seniority | Technical Ability | Attitude | Leadership | Effectiveness | Efficiency | Job Function | Social Ability | My Ranking |
|----------|------------|-----------|-------------|-----------|-------------------|----------|------------|---------------|------------|--------------|----------------|------------|
| Gwen | Finance | | | | | | | | | | | |
| Sanjay | Finance | | | | | | | | | | | |
| Carole | R&D | | | | | | | | | | | |
| Dave | R&D | | | | | | | | | | | |
| Tony | Marketing | | | | | | | | | | | |
| Ken | Marketing | | | | | | | | | | | |
| Eduardo | HR | | | | | | | | | | | |
| Frank | HR | | | | | | | | | | | |
| Irv | Manufacturing | | | | | | | | | | | |
| Jackie | Manufacturing | | | | | | | | | | | |

**EXECUTIVE COMMITTEE DECISION WORK SHEET**

*Instructions: As a team, rank in order the 10 employees from 1 for least likely to 10 for most likely that are expendable.*

| 1 Employee | 2 Personal Ranking | 3 Committee Ranking | 4 Actual Performance Ranking | 5 Individual Score | 6 Team Score |
|---|---|---|---|---|---|
| Gwen | | | | | |
| Sanjay | | | | | |
| Carole | | | | | |
| Dave | | | | | |
| Tony | | | | | |
| Ken | | | | | |
| Eduardo | | | | | |
| Frank | | | | | |
| Irv | | | | | |
| Jackie | | | | | |
| | | | Total Scores | | |

**VALUES SURVEY FORM**

Below are several value orientations. Based on the following scale, individually rate the values at Delta based on your team's decision. Record your choice in the left column (Step 5a) and record the team rating in the right column (Step 5b).

| 1 | 2 | 3 | 4 | 5 | 6 | 7 |
|---|---|---|---|---|---|---|
| Not at All Characteristic | | | Somewhat Characteristic | | | Very Characteristic |

| Values | Individual Rating | Team Rating |
|---|---|---|
| 1. High Productivity | _____ | _____ |
| 2. Effective Relationships | _____ | _____ |
| 3. High Quality | _____ | _____ |
| 4. High Achievement | _____ | _____ |
| 5. Seniority | _____ | _____ |
| 6. Time Consciousness | _____ | _____ |
| 7. Dress/Neatness | _____ | _____ |
| 8. Amount of Education | _____ | _____ |
| 9. Positive Attitudes | _____ | _____ |
| 10. High Professionalism | _____ | _____ |

**CONFLICT SURVEY FORM**

Rate your team, individually, on how differences were resolved during your team's meeting. Record your choice in the left column (Step 5a) and your team rating in the right column (Step 5b).

```
::                :              :                    :                    :                :            ::
 1                2              3                    4              5      6                7
```

Not at All                                      Somewhat                                      Very
Characteristic                                 Characteristic                              Characteristic

| Factor | Individual Rating | Team Rating |
|---|---|---|
| 1.  Not Afraid of Conflict | _____ | _____ |
| 2.  Express Differences | _____ | _____ |
| 3.  Ignore Disagreements | _____ | _____ |
| 4.  Open Discussion | _____ | _____ |
| 5.  Analysis of Differences | _____ | _____ |
| 6.  Debate of Issues | _____ | _____ |
| 7.  Trust | _____ | _____ |
| 8.  Confrontation | _____ | _____ |
| 9.  Encourage Openness | _____ | _____ |
| 10. Flexibility | _____ | _____ |

**OBSERVER FORM**

Instructions: Complete this form on the team you are observing. Draw direction arrows for communication flow. Identify behaviors shown.

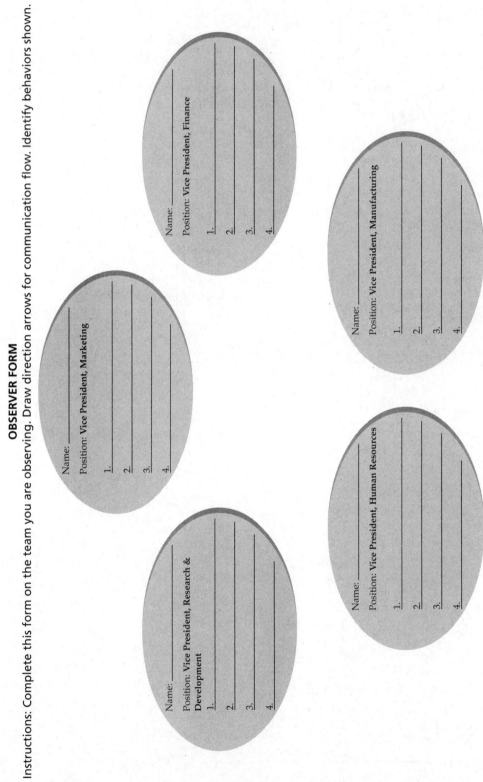

Name: _____
Position: **Vice President, Finance**

1. _____
2. _____
3. _____
4. _____

Name: _____
Position: **Vice President, Manufacturing**

1. _____
2. _____
3. _____
4. _____

Name: _____
Position: **Vice President, Marketing**

1. _____
2. _____
3. _____
4. _____

Name: _____
Position: **Vice President, Research & Development**

1. _____
2. _____
3. _____
4. _____

Name: _____
Position: **Vice President, Human Resources**

1. _____
2. _____
3. _____
4. _____

# CASE: THE DIM LIGHTING CO.

The Dim Lighting Company is a subsidiary of a major producer of electrical products. Each subsidiary operates as a profit center and reports to regional, group, and product vice presidents at corporate headquarters. The Dim Lighting subsidiary produces electric lamps and employs about 2,000 workers. The general manager is Jim West, an MBA from Tri-State University, who has been running this subsidiary successfully for the past five years. See the organization chart in Figure 3.3. However, last year the division failed to realize its operating targets, and profit margins dropped by 15 percent. In developing next year's budget and profit plan, Jim West feels that he is under pressure to have a good year because two bad years in a row might hurt his long-term potential for advancement.

## Mr. Spinks, Director of R&D

Robert Spinks, director of R&D, was hired by West three years ago, after resigning from a major competitor. Mr. Spinks has received a number of awards from scientific societies. The scientists and engineers in his group respect his technical competence and have a high level of morale.

Although Spinks is recognized as a talented scientist, other managers feel that he is often autocratic, strong-willed, and impatient. Spinks has said that he left his former company because the management lacked creativity and innovation in R&D.

## The Proposal

Spinks has submitted a budget request for a major research project, the micro-miniaturization of lighting sources so as to greatly reduce energy requirements. He sees this as the Lamp of the Future, and if successful, it would be the successor to LED lights. The proposed budget would require $1.2 million per year for two years, plus another $500,000 to begin production. Jim West immediately contacted corporate headquarters, and although top management praised the idea, they were reluctant to spend on the proposed project. Spinks feels the project has a 70 percent chance of success. The first two years of production are projected to break even, and the third-year profits are anticipated to be $1 million. Profits should increase by 20 percent each year for the fourth through eighth years. Beginning in the ninth year, profits will likely hold steady at around $3 million and then decline as new competitive products enter the market.

## The Budget Meeting

West called a meeting of his management group on Wednesday morning to discuss the proposed budget. Spinks presented a well-reasoned and high-powered sales pitch for his project. He suggested that the energy crunch had long-term implications, and if they failed to move into new technologies, the firm would be competitively obsolete.

Carol Preston, accountant, presented a financial analysis of the proposed project, noting the high risk, the uncertain results, and the length of time before it would contribute to operating profits. "We can't afford to wait for long-term results. Unfortunately, if we don't do something about the bottom line right now, we may not be here to enjoy it," she noted.

Bill Boswell, production manager, agreed with Preston: "We need new machinery for our current production line also, and that has a very direct and immediate payback."

Pete Newell, marketing, agreed with Spinks: "I don't feel we can put our heads in the sand. If we don't keep up competitively, how will our salespeople be able to keep selling obsolete lighting products? Besides, I'm not sure that Carol's figures are completely accurate in measuring the actual return on this low-energy project." A stormy debate followed, with heated arguments both for and against the project, until West called the meeting to a halt.

**FIGURE 3.3   The Organization Chart**

Later, thinking it over in his office, West considered the situation. Going ahead with the micro-miniaturization project was a big gamble. He realized that the long-term success for Dim Lighting required new product lines such as the micro-miniaturization project. But such projects would require capital from corporate headquarters, plus strain the needs of current products at Dim Lighting. West is in a quandary as to how much he should make a case for funding from headquarters. If he obtains funding and the project is not as successful as projected, what will this do to his career at Dim Lighting or even some other company? On the other hand, if he rejects the project, what chance does Dim Lighting have for turning around the decline experienced last year? Further, if he decides against it, it is quite possible that Spinks will resign, which will shatter the R&D department West had worked so hard to assemble. (Use the Case Analysis Form.)

**THE DIM LIGHTING CO. CASE ANALYSIS FORM**

Name: _____

I. Problems

  A. Macro

    1. _____

      _____

    2. _____

      _____

  B. Micro

    1. _____

      _____

    2. _____

      _____

II. Causes

    1. _____

      _____

    2. _____

      _____

    3. _____

      _____

III. Systems affected

    1. _____

      _____

    2. _____

      _____

    3. _____

      _____

IV. Alternatives

    1. _____

      _____

    2. _____

      _____

    3. _____

      _____

V. Recommendations

_____

_____

_____

_____

_____

_____

## Chapter 3 Endnotes

1. For additional information, see Ruth Alas, "The Triangular Model for Dealing with Organizational Change," *Journal of Change Management*, September 2007, pp. 255–71; Geert Devos, Marc Buelens, and Dave Bouckenooghe, "Contribution of Content, Context, and Process to Understanding Openness to Organizational Change: Two Experimental Simulation Studies," *Journal of Social Psychology*, vol. 147, no. 6 (December 2007), pp. 607–29; Joanne Martin, *Mapping the Terrain* (Thousand Oaks, CA: Sage Publications, 2002); Larry Hirschborn, "Campaigning for Change," *Harvard Business Review,* July 2002, pp. 98–104; John S. Carrol and Sachi Hatakenaka, "Driving Organizational Change in the Midst of Crisis," *Sloan Management Review,* Spring 2001, pp. 70–79.

2. www.setpointusa.com; Bo Burlingham, "What's Your Culture Worth," *Inc. Magazine,* September 2001, www.inc.com; Karen Berman and Joe Knight, *Financial Intelligence: A Manager's Guide to Knowing What the Numbers Really Mean* (Boston: Harvard Business School Press, 2006).

3. For additional information on culture, see Jerome Want, *Corporate Culture: Illuminating the Black Hole* (New York: St. Martin's Press, 2007); Susan C. Schneider and Jean-Louis Barsoux, *Managing across Cultures* (New York: Financial Times Prentice Hall, 2003); Terrence E. Deal and Allan A. Kennedy, *The New Corporate Cultures: Revitalizing the Workplace after Downsizing, Mergers, and Reengineering* (Reading, MA: Perseus Books, 1999).

4. See Karen Bemowski, "Codes, Cultural, Archetypes and the Collective Cultural Unconscious," *Quarterly Progress*, vol. 28, no. 1 (January 1995), p. 34; Warren Wilhelm, "Changing Corporate Culture—or Corporate Behavior? How to Change Your Company," *Academy of Management Executive,* vol. 6, no. 4 (November 1992), p. 72.

5. To learn more about the Southwest Airlines Culture Committee, see Jody Hoffer Gittell, *The Southwest Airlines Way* (New York: McGraw Hill, 2003), p. 119–20; www.blogsouthwest.com/ and search for "culture committee."

6. Deal and Kennedy, *The New Corporate Cultures*, p. 22.

7. Ibid.

8. Burt Helm and Jena McGregor, "Howard Schultz's Grande Challenge," *Business Week,* January 21, 2008, p. 28.

9. Adam Lashinsky, "Back2Back Champs," *Fortune,* February 4, 2008, p. 70.

10. John Huey and Geoffrey Colvin, "Staying Smart, the Jack and Herb Show," *Fortune,* January 11, 1999, p. 163.

11. Terrence E. Deal and Allan A. Kennedy, "Culture: A New Look Through Old Lenses," *Journal of Applied Behavioral Science,* vol. 19, no. 4 (December 1983), p. 108l; http://corporatecultureindex.com/.

12. Sam Walton and John Huey, *Made in America: My Story* (New York: Doubleday, 1992), pp. 156–58.

13. See Rajendra S. Sisodia, David B. Wolfe, and Jagdish N. Sheth, *Firms of Endearment: How World-Class Companies Profit from Passion and Purpose* (Upper Saddle River, NJ: Wharton School Publishing, 2007).

14. Henry Migliore, R.T. Martin, Tim Baer, and Jeffrey L. Horvath, "Corporate Culture Index," *Proceedings of the Southern Management Association,* 1989, p. 217.

15. Bruce Orwall and Emily Nelson, "Hidden Wall Shields Disney's Kingdom: 80 Years of Culture," *Wall Street Journal,* February 13, 2004, p. A1.

16. Richard Siklos, "The Iger Difference," *Fortune*, April 28, 2008, p. 92.

17. Marie H. Kavanagh and Neal M. Ashkanasy, "The Impact of Leadership and Change Management Strategy on Organizational Culture and Individual Acceptance of Change During a Merger," *British Journal of Management*, vol. 17, (March 2, 2006), pp. S81–S103; Mitchell L. Marks, "Managing the Diversity That Follows Mergers and Restructurings," *Employee Relations Today,* Winter 1991/1992, pp. 453–58.

18. Harold Leavitt, *Corporate Pathfinders* (Homewood, IL: Dow Jones-Irwin, 1986), pp. 10–11.

19. "The Automobile Industry Has Lost Its Masculinity," *Fortune*, September 1973, p. 187.

20. Maryann Keller, *Rude Awakening: The Rise, Fall, and Struggle for Recovery of General Motors* (New York: William Morrow and Company, Inc., 1989), p. 181.

21. Rosabeth Moss Kanter, "SMR Forum: Innovation—The Only Hope for Times Ahead," *Sloan Management Review,* vol. 25, no. 4 (Summer 1984), pp. 51–55.

22. Rick Mauer, "Making a Strong Case for Change," *Journal for Quality and Participation*, vol. 26, no. 3 (Fall 2003), pp. 41–42; John Case, *The Open-Book Experience: Lessons from over 100 Companies Who Successfully Transformed Themselves* (Reading, MA: Addison-Wesley Longman, 1998).

23. www.trilogy.com; Tamara J. Erickson and Lynda Gratton, "What It Means to Work Here," *Harvard Business Review*, March 2007, pp. 104–12; Noel M. Tichy, "No Ordinary Bootcamp," *Harvard Business Review*, April 2001, pp. 63–70.

24. A. Etzioni, *Modern Organizations* (Upper Saddle River, NJ: Prentice Hall, 1964), p. 8.

25. Wendell L. French and Cecil H. Bell Jr., *Organization Development: Behavioral Science Interventions for Organization Improvement,* 4th ed. (Upper Saddle River, NJ: Prentice Hall, 1990), p. 18.

# PART TWO

# Understanding the OD Process

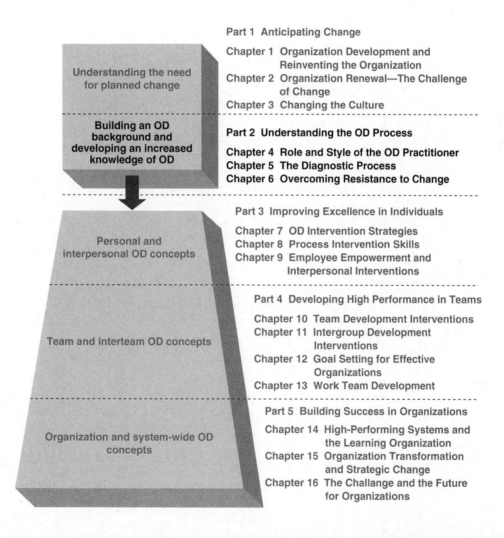

Successful change in organizations happens with a specific purpose and requires leadership. The OD practitioner proactively brings change to an organization by bringing together competitive elements within the organization to build a consensus. Change in an OD program is planned and deliberate, not random or haphazard.

The OD process involves a collaborative relationship between a practitioner and a client system. Though the practitioner has a variety of styles or approaches to work with the client system, it is important to build a relationship of trust and create a climate for change.

As a successful relationship is built, the change program moves to a stage where problems are identified and diagnosed. The diagnosis is a systematic approach to understanding the present state of the organization. The purpose of the diagnostic phase is to gather information to specify the exact nature of the problem requiring solution, to identify the underlying causal forces, and to provide a basis for selecting effective change strategies and techniques.

As the change program progresses, resistance is likely to occur. This will particularly be the situation when the change represents alterations of set patterns of behavior and relationships with others. On an organizational level, change means that policies, procedures, structures, manufacturing processes, and workflows will no longer be the same. Both people and organizations have stakes in the status quo. Those advocating change must deal with the possible resistance to change before implementing any OD strategy or technique.

In *Part 2: Understanding the OD Process,* we will initially look at the styles the OD practitioner can use to intervene with the client system. We will examine the diagnostic process including the identification of problems and cause-effect relationships. As resistance to change on individual and organization levels can be expected, Part 2 will conclude with a study of restraining and driving forces of change and strategies to lessen resistance.

# Role and Style of the OD Practitioner

## LEARNING OBJECTIVES

**Upon completing this chapter, you will be able to:**

1. Define the role of an OD practitioner.

2. Identify your strengths and areas of improvement as a potential practitioner.

3. Experience and practice your own style of intervention and influence in a team.

## PREMEETING PREPARATION

1. Read Chapter 4.

2. Read and complete Steps 1 through 4 of OD Skills Simulation 4.1.

3. Read and prepare Case: The Grayson Chemical Company.

## HAPHAZARD VERSUS PLANNED CHANGE

The globalization of markets, the downsizing of workforces, the flattening of hierarchies, the reengineering of work processes, and the spread of information technology are all part of a revolution in the way we do business. These changes are happening at the same time and fast. Because these changes interact, business and society are in the midst of a revolution comparable to the Industrial Revolution. In a turbulent and changing environment, managers are concerned not only with managing organizations as they exist now, but also with changes to meet future conditions. Alan Feldman, CEO of Midas Inc., says, "Any company today has to be very vigilant about their business model and willing to break it, even if it's successful, to make sure they stay on top of the changing trends." Reflecting on his experience as COO at McDonald's, Feldman continues, "You can't just go on cloning your business into the future."[1]

Change programs do not happen accidentally. They are initiated with a specific purpose and require leadership to function properly. The OD practitioner must deal proactively with these changing competitive forces. The practitioner tries to build a consensus among management to initiate changes quickly in order to take advantage of shifting circumstances. For example, in the new horizontal corporation, self-managed teams are the building blocks of the changing organization. In effective change programs, everyone in the organization plays a crucial part.

One study reports that large-scale change efforts are typically initiated in response to, or in anticipation of, external environmental changes.[2] Change programs often represent a major alteration of organizational processes. For example, organizations are reengineering, restructuring, and downsizing to meet changing times. Organizations consist of groups of people working together. Changes alter the way the people work together, how they relate to others, and even how they see themselves. The OD practitioner facilitates such changes by training, educating, and collaboratively designing new ways of functioning.

There are two types of change that may take place in an organization. The first type, termed "random" or "haphazard" change, is forced on the organization by the external environment. This type of change is not prepared for; it simply occurs and is dealt with as it happens, a practice sometimes called firefighting. This type of change includes downsizing, where sizable numbers of employees are laid off. Commenting on flare-ups and the reactive style of handling problems at Ford Motor Company, the CFO quipped, "We're running a fire department these days," referring to the fast and unpredictable

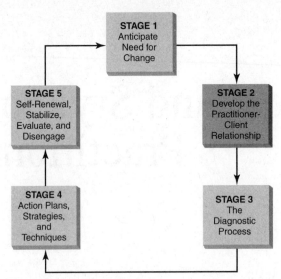

**FIGURE 4.1** Stage 2 of Organization Development's Five Stages

changes occurring at Ford.[3] When large organizations like Ford implement a downsizing program, the change can be extremely difficult, because it involves a major cultural transformation.

The second type of change results from deliberate attempts to modify organizational operations in order to promote improvement. One example of this type of program is total quality management (TQM), which focuses on continuous improvement.

Sustaining the long-term success of OD programs requires commitment and leadership as organizational relationships change. Such changes do not automatically occur simply because someone in the organization decided that an OD program would be helpful. The implementation of these steps depends largely on the practitioner's abilities. Before an OD program begins, there must be an awareness of the need for change—usually some problem or disequilibrium causing the client system to seek help. To implement a program of planned change, the management must first identify a gap between the current situation and some desired condition. OD change programs are then designed to improve effectiveness, efficiency, and participants' well-being. All too often, the management will have introduced short-run, expedient change programs aimed solely at cost savings. Such programs often have unintended dysfunctional effects on participants' satisfaction and the long-term goals of the organization. The OD practitioner helps the organization identify the differences between where it is and where it would like to be, and then proceeds to design and implement appropriate OD interventions. The development of a shared vision, for example, is an important element in developing a TQM culture. The practitioner involves everyone in the organization in developing a vision and improving the corporate culture.

An OD program must begin with a good working relationship between the OD practitioner and the individual or department being helped. If this relationship is weak or superficial, the program is unlikely to succeed. The success of almost any OD project depends, to a large degree, on the nature of this relationship, which must be developed in the initial stages of the change program.

This chapter discusses the second stage, development of the practitioner-client relationship, of an OD program, and is illustrated in Figure 4.1. Here, we will focus on the initial contact of OD practitioners with the client system and on forming an appropriate relationship. We will examine the initial intervention into the ongoing organization system, major OD practitioner styles, the intervention process, the practitioner-client relationship, and basic ground rules and warning signs in the relationship.

## EXTERNAL AND INTERNAL PRACTITIONERS

In every large-scale planned change program, some person or group is usually designated to lead the change; sometimes it is the OD practitioner. The practitioner, then, is a change leader, a person leading or guiding the process of change in an organization. Internal practitioners are already members of the organization. They may be either managers practicing OD with their work groups or OD specialists who may be from the organization development or human resources department. External practitioners are brought in from outside the organization as OD specialists and are often referred to as consultants. The use of both external and internal practitioners has advantages and disadvantages.

The OD practitioners who are specialists, whether from within or outside of the organization, are professionals who have specialized and trained in OD and related areas, such as the social sciences, interpersonal communications, decision making, and organization behavior. These specialists, often referred to as OD consultants, have a more formal and involved process when they enter the client system than managers who are doing OD with their work group. Although much of the chapter is directed at OD practitioners who are specialists, the concepts also apply to OD practitioners who are managers and team leaders implementing OD.

## The External Practitioner

The **external practitioner** is someone not previously associated with the client system. Coming from the outside, the external practitioner sees things from a different viewpoint and from a position of objectivity. Because external practitioners are invited into the organization, they have increased leverage (the degree of influence and status within the client system) and greater freedom of operation than internal practitioners. Research evidence suggests that top managers view external practitioners as having a more positive role in large-scale change programs than internal practitioners.[4]

Since external practitioners are not a part of the organization, they are less in awe of the power wielded by various organization members. Unlike internal practitioners, they do not depend upon the organization for raises, approval, or promotions. Because they usually have a very broad career base and other clients to fall back on, they tend to have a more independent attitude about risk taking and confrontations with the client system.

The disadvantages of external practitioners result from the same factors as the advantages. Outsiders are generally unfamiliar with the organization system and may not have sufficient knowledge of its technology, such as aerospace or chemistry. They are unfamiliar with the culture, communication networks, and formal or informal power systems. In some situations, practitioners may have difficulty gathering pertinent information simply because they are outsiders.

## The Internal Practitioner

The **internal practitioner** is already a member of the organization: either a top executive, an organization member who initiates change in his or her work group, or a member of the organization development or human resources department. Many large organizations have established offices with the specific responsibility of helping the organization implement change programs. In the past few years, a growing number of major organizations have created internal OD practitioner groups. These internal practitioners may report directly to the president of the organization.

Internal practitioners have certain advantages inherent in their relationship with the organization. They are familiar with the organization's culture and norms and, probably, accept and behave in accordance with the norms. This means that they need not waste time becoming familiar with the system and winning acceptance. Internal practitioners know the power structure, who are the strategic people, and how to apply leverage. They are already known to the employees and have a personal interest in seeing the organization succeed. Unfortunately, it is by no means easy for internal practitioners to acquire all the skills they will need. The proof is in the problems encountered by new, not quite ready internal practitioners or managers who take on projects before they are fully comfortable with their practitioner roles in the organization, and before they understand and have developed critical skills.

The position of an internal practitioner also has disadvantages. One of these may be a lack of the specialized skills needed for organization development. The lack of OD skills has become a less significant factor now that more universities have OD classes and programs and their graduates have entered the workforce. Another disadvantage relates to lack of objectivity. Internal practitioners may be more likely to accept the organizational system as a given and accommodate their change tactics to the needs of the management. Being known to the workforce has advantages, but it can also work against the internal practitioner. Other employees may not understand the practitioner's role. They are influenced by his or her previous work and relationships in the organization, particularly if the work and relationships have in any way been questionable. Finally, the internal practitioner may not have the necessary power and authority; internal practitioners are sometimes in a remote staff position and report to a mid-level manager.

### The External-Internal Practitioner Team

The implementation of a large-scale change program is almost impossible without the involvement of all levels and elements of the organization. One approach to creating a climate of change uses a team formed of an external practitioner working directly with an internal practitioner to initiate and facilitate change programs (known as the **external-internal practitioner team**). The partners bring complementary resources to the team; each has advantages and strengths that offset the disadvantages and weaknesses of the other. The external practitioner brings expertise, objectivity, and new insights to organization problems. The internal practitioner, on the other hand, brings detailed knowledge of organization issues and norms, a long-time acquaintance with members, and an awareness of the strengths and weaknesses of the system. For change programs in large organizations, the team will likely consist of more than two practitioners.

The collaborative relationship between internal and external practitioners provides an integration of abilities, skills, and resources. The relationship serves as a model for the rest of the organization—a model that members can observe and see in operation, one that embodies such qualities as trust, respect, honesty, confrontation, and collaboration. The team approach makes it possible to divide the change program's workload and share in the diagnosis, planning, and strategy. The external-internal practitioner team is less likely to accept watered-down or compromised change programs, because each team member provides support to the other. As an example, during the U.S. Navy's Command Development (equivalent to OD) Program, the internal change agents recommended that training seminars be conducted away from the navy environment (i.e., at a resort) and the participants dress in civilian clothing to lessen authority issues. Higher authority, however, ordered the seminars to be held on naval bases and in uniform—ground rules that the internal practitioners reluctantly accepted. In this situation, an external practitioner with greater leverage might have provided enough support and influence to gain approval of the desired program.

Another reason for using an external-internal practitioner team is to achieve greater continuity over the entire OD program. Because external practitioners are involved in other outside activities, they are generally available to the organization only a few days a month, with two- or three-week intervals between visits. The internal practitioner, on the other hand, provides a continuing point of contact for the organization's members whenever problems or questions arise. Because many OD programs are long-term efforts, often lasting three to five years, the external-internal combination may provide the stimulation and motivation needed to keep the change program moving during periods of resistance. The team effort is probably the most effective approach because it combines the advantages of both external and internal practitioners while minimizing the disadvantages.

## OD PRACTITIONER STYLES

The OD practitioner, as we have discussed, is the person who initiates, stimulates, or facilitates a change program, and may come from inside or outside the organization. Change begins with the intervention of the practitioner in the system to be changed. Intervention refers to the practitioner's entry into the client system and includes several different roles and activities.

Practitioners, be they internal or external, have a variety of practitioner styles or approaches. One way to view the styles is based on the degree of emphasis the practitioner places upon two interrelated goals or dimensions of the change process. One of the goals is effectiveness, the degree of emphasis upon goal accomplishment. The other goal is morale, the degree of emphasis upon relationships and participant satisfaction. Based upon the two dimensions of accomplishing goals and member morale, five different types of practitioner styles or roles can be identified, as illustrated in Figure 4.2

### The Stabilizer Style

The goal of the **stabilizer style** is neither effectiveness nor participant satisfaction. Rather, the practitioner is trying to keep from rocking the boat and to maintain a low profile. The underlying

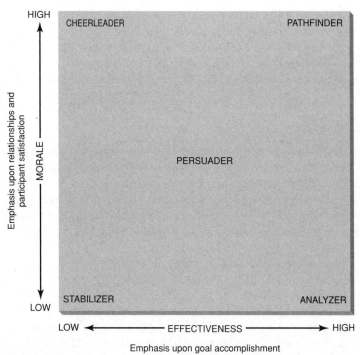

**FIGURE 4.2**    **Practitioner Styles**

motivation is often survival, or merely following the directives of top management. Such a role is typically found in large organizations where development programs may be part of the staff function and are not highly regarded by top management. This style is usually forced upon the practitioner by organizational pressures, so that the practitioner learns to conform and to suppress any other motivations.

## The Cheerleader Style

The **cheerleader style** places emphasis on the satisfaction of organization members and is chiefly concerned with employee motivation and morale. The cheerleader practitioner seeks warm working relationships and, in general, is more comfortable in nonconfrontational situations. Effectiveness per se is not emphasized, the assumption being that if member satisfaction is high, effectiveness will also be high. Unfortunately, there is a great deal of evidence that contradicts these assumptions. The cheerleader style strongly minimizes differences and maintains harmony.

## The Analyzer Style

The **analyzer style** places great emphasis on efficiency, and gives little emphasis to member satisfaction. The analyzer feels most comfortable with a rational assessment of problems and assumes that the facts will lead to a solution. Practitioners of this type may be quite confrontational, usually relying on authority to resolve conflicts and on rational problem-solving processes.

The analyzer style has a background of specialized expertise, knowledge, and experience applicable to the solution of specific problems. The client needs to have a problem solved, a service performed, or a study made; the analyzer practitioner takes responsibility for providing these functions. This style is based on the belief that the client does not need to know or cannot learn the skills to solve its problems. The success of the practitioner is largely dependent on the client's having properly diagnosed its problem and called in the right kind of practitioner.

## The Persuader Style

The **persuader style** focuses on both dimensions, effectiveness and morale, yet optimizes neither. Such a style provides a relatively low-risk strategy, yet avoids direct confrontation with other forces. This approach may be used when the practitioner has little power or leverage relative to other participants. It is motivated primarily by a desire to satisfy, that is, to achieve something that is "good enough." A great deal of effort is applied in attempting to satisfy the different forces, thus gaining a majority bloc of support for prepared changes. The resulting change program is often watered down or weakened to the point where organization improvement is unlikely.

### The Pathfinder Style

The **pathfinder style**[5] seeks both a high degree of effectiveness and a high degree of member satisfaction, believing that greater effectiveness is possible when all members are involved and problem solving is done through teamwork. There is an awareness that confrontation and conflict are often a means to a more effective organization and to more satisfied individual members. The pathfinder approach uses collaborative problem solving and challenges the underlying patterns of member behavior. The pathfinder practitioner helps the organization to focus on its most critical issues and questions.

OD practitioners have found that listening, integrity, and organizational diagnosis are some of the most important OD skills. The pathfinder practitioner uses these skills to give the client new insights into its activities and to help the client system determine how it wishes to change and how it might go about implementing changes. The practitioner rarely informs or instructs the client system, but instead tries to discover client system problems and to challenge the underlying patterns of behavior of organization members. The pathfinder practitioner focuses on six processes essential for effective organization performance: (1) communication, (2) member roles and functions in groups, (3) group problem solving and decision making, (4) group norms and growth, (5) leadership and authority, and (6) intergroup cooperation and competition.[6]

We have identified five different practitioner styles in this section. In OD Skills Simulation 4.1 at the end of the chapter, you will have an opportunity to find out where your own style fits in this classification system. Most organizational problems are complex situations, however, and may not neatly fit with any one change approach but will depend upon the practitioner, the nature of the problem, and the organizational climate.

In summary, these five practitioner styles are not mutually exclusive. All the styles can be effective, and they are interrelated. A practitioner may transition from one style to another to meet the changing needs of the client system and deal with diverse situations. Frequently, some combination of the styles may be applied.

## THE INTERVENTION PROCESS

The OD process involves a collaborative relationship between a practitioner and a client system. OD practitioners may have a variety of styles, philosophies, and approaches, but they generally perform a certain set of functions with regard to the client system. These functions include (1) helping the client determine its current level or state (data gathering), (2) assisting in a collaborative analysis of problem areas and planning strategies of change (diagnosis), and (3) intervening and facilitating change from the current level to some ideal or desired level. Consulting firms like McKinsey & Company, The Boston Consulting Group, and Bain & Co. offer a variety of services and approaches to serve the needs of their clients. **OD Application: Bain & Co.** has additional information on one of the largest consulting firms that sometimes does OD work.

### The Readiness of the Organization for OD

Upon first contacting the client system, the OD practitioner begins evaluating its receptiveness for an OD program. It is a mistake to assume that all organizations must, and should, have an OD program simply because most organizations can benefit greatly from one. Ironically, the very organizations, most in need of such programs, are precisely the least receptive. Their inflexibility and insensitivity to the need for change seem almost proverbial: "There are none so blind as those who will not see." Rather than imposing organization development upon them, the practitioner needs to wait until key personnel, typically top management in an organization-wide program, decide whether change is really needed. The motivation for a change program

## OD Application: Bain & Co.[7]

Bain & Co., a management consulting firm founded by Bill Bain in 1973, is one of the major consulting firms worldwide. Bain consultants have worked with more than 4,150 major corporations in all parts of the world and in virtually every industry. It has more than 3,500 people in 39 offices in 26 countries. Bain consultants work with governments and businesses alike. Industry sectors that Bain works with include retail, financial services, medical, entertainment, technology, and environmental services.

The firm's clients have included the governments of Japan and Korea. It also provides pro bono consulting services to nonprofit organizations, such as The Boys and Girls Clubs of America, to help them with their growing needs, and the Business Action on Homelessness in London to increase the help from businesses to tackle the homeless problem. An independent venture that Bain has helped to create is the Bridgespan Group, a nonprofit group dedicated to serving the nonprofit sector. Bain's former CEO, Tom Tierney, quit his job at Bain and helped establish the Bridgespan Group, and now heads it up for no pay. Its clients include the Bill and Melinda Gates Foundation and the Packard Foundation.

In 1973, William W. "Bill" Bain created a new type of management consultant role—a quasi insider who is privy to the client's secrets and works directly with the CEO and others in top management to implement the strategy. Bain & Co. was founded on the principle that "consultants must measure their success in terms of their client's financial results." Bill Bain is known as the creator of "relationship consulting." The consultants build their business on the close relationship they develop with clients. Bain focuses on the total system and on the profitability of the entire organization. Such knowledge demands lots of data gathering and a great deal of time for analysis. Bain consultants insist on working directly with the chief executive, because they feel that the CEO is the key to a firm's success.

Bain is known for the shrewd, suave people it employs. The Bain consultant tends to be articulate, meticulously groomed, well mannered, and exceedingly charming. Bain employees are notoriously secretive about their organization and their clients, and dedicate themselves to improving their customers' competitive position. Business is a war their clients must win.

Other consultants may come in and study a situation, write up a report with recommendations, and then leave. This is not Bain's approach. Bain consultants work collaboratively with the client to study, define, and assist in the implementation of the solution. And because Bain consultants have experience working with such a wide group of clients, they tend not to have the tunnel vision that too often afflicts employees within an organization.

The company CEOs may know their organization and their industry, but may not be able to bring in new ideas from across a multitude of industries and countries. Bain helps its clients to make the big decisions in areas of strategy, organization, operations, technology, and mergers and acquisitions. Though Bain does not make the decisions, its consultants serve as a catalyst to help in the process.

According to Bain, some of the things that make this consulting company unique are:

- It rejects the old advice model to focus on strategy and implementation.
- It is forthright with the client even if it is not what management wants to hear.
- It uses clear communications and no jargon.
- Its consultants work well with people at all levels.
- It accepts equity in lieu of fees to align incentives with client results. Bain prospers only if the clients prosper.

### Questions

1. Do you agree with the relationship-consulting approach?
2. Visit Bain's Web site (www.bain.com) and explore the firm's current approaches to consulting.
3. Contrast the approach of a company trying to solve its own problems versus bringing in outside consultants.
4. What are the pros and cons of the external versus internal consultants?

is then built in, not artificially contrived. To gauge the preparedness of an organization for an OD program, there are four questions the practitioner needs to answer before venturing further:

1. Are the learning goals of OD *appropriate*?
2. Is the cultural state of the client system *ready* for organization development?
3. Are the key people *involved*?
4. Are members of the client system *prepared* and *oriented* to organization development?[8]

Once these questions have been satisfactorily answered, then, and only then, should the practitioner proceed.

## The Intervention

Practitioners, whether external or internal, actually begin to intervene when they contact the client system. The intervention process refers to a coming between or among members or groups of an organization for effecting change. More specifically, **intervention** refers to an array of planned activities participated in by both the practitioner and the client, including shared observations of the processes occurring between members of a group or of an organization for the purpose of improving the effectiveness of the processes. The intent of the intervention is to alter the status quo. OD practitioner and writer, Richard Beckhard, suggests that a planned intervention consists of "moving into an existing organization and helping it, in effect, 'stop the music'; examine its present ways of work, norms, and values; and look at alternative ways of working, relating, or rewarding."[9]

In a very broad sense, stages 2 through 5 of the OD process (explained in Chapter 1 and in the succeeding chapters of this book) describe the intervention process. During the course of an OD program, there will be many interventions: interventions for gathering data, team-building activities, and so forth, but here we are concerned with the practitioner's initial contact with the client system. The initial contact with the client system is an intervention, if for no other reason than it is a message to the organization's members that the climate of the organization is under scrutiny and that new and more effective ways of doing things are being sought. The promise of a better future, in itself, can effect change and, therefore, constitutes an intervention.

The external practitioner generally intervenes through a top manager or a human resources director. It is easier to bring about change when the intervention is made at higher levels of the client system, because greater power to influence others is concentrated there. Bain & Co., for example, insists on working directly with the top management team. Change programs have been initiated at lower levels, and some OD practitioners feel that change will only be real and lasting if it begins at this level. Of course, the lack of support from the top increases the risk involved.

The practitioner faces many different types of situations when intervening in an organization. These may be categorized in terms of client system support. In the most favorable type of situation, every level of the organization recognizes the need for change programs and supports them. In another type of situation, top management recognizes the need for change and provides support, but lower levels are nonsupportive or resistant. Still another type of situation occurs when lower levels of the organization are supportive, whereas top management is resistant to change.

## Who Is the Client?

"Who is the client?" at first may seem to be an unimportant question, or one with an obvious answer. In reality, it is one of the most critical questions facing the practitioner. This is because dealing with the wrong client or a misidentified client may lead to ineffective or even disastrous consequences. Deciding who the client is becomes more complex as the practitioner intervenes into more segments of the organization. At some point, the practitioner needs to determine who the client actually is. Is it the organization? Is it certain divisions, departments, or groups? Or is it the individual who contracted for the services? The answer sometimes looks easy at the beginning of an OD program but becomes increasingly unclear as the program develops. The client will initially be the person with whom the practitioner first makes contact. But it may soon become apparent that the organization is more realistically the client. The practitioner's concern may thus extend to include work groups or subsystems of the organization and even the individual members of the system.

## The OD Practitioner's Role in the Intervention

As noted earlier in this chapter, the OD practitioner can be categorized into five general styles: stabilizer, persuader, analyzer, cheerleader, and pathfinder. Practitioners tend to work in the pathfinder style. This style is similar to that of the process practitioner, documented by Edgar Schein in his *Process Consultation: Its Role in Organization Development, Volume 1*[10] and discussed in Chapter 8 of this book. The OD process practitioner operates on the belief that the team is the basic building block of an organization. One OD intervention is the self-managed work team, which gives workers more autonomy and control over their immediate behavior. The workers are organized into teams on the basis of task functions. Self-managed work teams are discussed in more detail in Chapter 13. They make decisions on many key issues, including work schedules and assignments and how to deal with quality problems. Therefore, team behavior is analyzed in terms of (1) communications, (2) members' roles and functions in groups, (3) group problem solving and decision making, (4) group norms and growth, and (5) leadership and authority.[11]

OD practitioners are concerned with how these five processes occur in an organization. Their role involves sharing observations of these five processes and thus helping the client to improve the organization's effectiveness. Simultaneously, and equally important, the client is learning to observe and improve its own process skills and problem-solving abilities for use in the future as well as in the present. In learning to make process interventions, similar to those made by the practitioner, the client is also learning how to solve its own problems without having to rely on the practitioner.

A basic assumption underlying the OD practitioner's role holds that the client needs to learn to identify problems, participate in the diagnosis, and be actively involved in finding a solution to the problem. The practitioner recognizes that the client either has useful skills and resources but does not know how to use them effectively or does not have the requisite skills but has the capacity to develop them. As a result, the client solves its own problems with the practitioner "helping to share the diagnosis and in providing alternative remedies which may not have occurred to the client."[12] The OD practitioner operates on the notion that assisting the client instead of taking control will lead to a more lasting solution of the client's problems. Meanwhile, the client will have increased its skills so that it will be able to solve future problems. The process practitioner teaches the client how to diagnose and solve its own problems but does not advise or suggest solutions. Initially, the client may fumble a bit and take longer than it would with expert assistance, but in the long run, the client will grow and mature.

Although most writers on OD support the idea of OD process interventions, they also recognize that clients have various needs and maturity levels, and, therefore, it may be necessary at times to provide expert and technical advice. The need for working in a style other than the pathfinder style may be more apparent at the beginning of the relationship. As a rule of thumb, however, the OD practitioner should not encourage and perpetuate a dependency relationship. As the maturity of the client increases, the practitioner tends to operate more in the pathfinder style.

## OD Practitioner Skills and Activities

The role of the OD practitioner is changing and becoming more complex. Ellen Fagenson and W. Warner Burke found that the most practiced OD skill or activity was team development, whereas the least employed was the integration of technology. Table 4.1 shows more information about the results of the research.[13]

The results of this study reinforce what other theorists have also suggested. The OD practitioners of today are no longer just process facilitators, but are expected to know something about strategy, structure, reward systems, corporate culture, leadership, human resource development, and the client organization's business. As a result, the role of the OD practitioner today is more challenging and more in the mainstream of the client organization than in the past.

Susan Gebelein lists six key skill areas that are critical to the success of the internal practitioner. These are shown in Figure 4.3.[14] The relative emphasis on each type of skill will depend upon the situation, but all are vital in achieving OD program goals. The skills that focus on the people-oriented nature of the OD practitioner include:

- *Leadership Skills.* Leaders keep members focused on key company values and on opportunities and need for improvement. A leader's job is to recognize when a company is headed in the wrong direction and to get it back on the right track.
- *Project Management Skills.* This means involving all the right people and departments to keep the change program on track.
- *Communication Skills.* It is vital to communicate the key values to everyone in the organization.

**TABLE 4.1** OD Practitioner Skills and Activities

| Activity | Average Use |
|---|---|
| 1. Team development | 2.97 |
| 2. Corporate change | 2.91 |
| 3. Strategy development | 2.60 |
| 4. Management development | 2.45 |
| 5. Employee (career) development | 2.04 |
| 6. Technology integration | 1.97 |

Note: Ratings on 5-point scale with 5.0 being high.

**FIGURE 4.3** Practitioner Skills Profile

- *Problem-Solving Skills.* The real challenge is to implement a solution to an organizational problem. Forget about today's problems: focus constantly on the next set of problems.
- *Interpersonal Skills.* The number-one priority is to give everybody in the organization the tools and the confidence to be involved in the change process. This includes facilitating, building relationships, and process skills.
- *Personal Skills.* The confidence to help the organization make tough decisions, introduce new techniques, try something new, and see if it works.

The OD practitioner's role is to help employees create their own solutions, systems, and concepts. When the practitioner uses the above-listed skills to accomplish these goals, the employees will work hard to make them succeed, because they are the owners of the change programs.

## FORMING THE PRACTITIONER-CLIENT RELATIONSHIP

The practitioner-client relationship can be examined by viewing it as a system of interacting elements, as shown in Figure 4.4. One element is the practitioner: the internal or external OD practitioner or manager who initiates the change program aimed at improving the effectiveness of the client system. A second element within the client system is the **client sponsor** or contact. This is the person or group within the client organization who has requested the practitioner's help and interfaces with

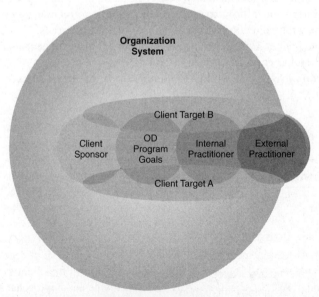

Organization Environment

**FIGURE 4.4 A System's View of the Change Relationship**

the practitioner. The third element consists of the organizational unit or units that are to be changed (Client Targets A and B in Figure 4.4) and the set of behaviors and values that have been traditionally practiced. This element is the **client target system**: the actual target of the OD intervention.

For example, in an OD program for a division of a medium-sized manufacturing company, the client contacts were the vice president of industrial relations and the division manager (also a vice president). The target system was the division, with the goal of developing a more participative managerial style and increasing productivity. The members of the division, however, had little voice in determining the proposed change program. It was found in preliminary discussions that some were strongly in favor of such changes, whereas others were strongly opposed or even hostile to them. This combination of elements would need to be considered before beginning any change program.

## Initial Perceptions

The first stage in developing a practitioner-client relationship involves an interaction between the parties that includes initial perceptions and assessments by each of the other. Such assessments involve the practitioner's determination of whether or not to enter into a relationship. This decision is based upon the practitioner's assessment of the degree of congruence between his or her values and those of the client system. These include the attitudes of the client system toward OD and change, the ability of OD techniques to deal with the problems, and the potential of the practitioner's efforts to help solve the client's problems.

The practitioner's first intervention will probably be tentative. OD practitioner Warren Bennis comments: "I enter a relationship on the basis that neither the client nor I know what the underlying problems are and that I need to explore and get a 'feel' for the situation before committing myself fully to the client system and before it fully entrusts itself to me."[15] This initial intervention might therefore be termed a reconnaissance on both sides. The OD practitioner is trying to evaluate the organization's readiness and commitment for change, while the client system is assessing the practitioner's capabilities.

Power networks are important because they will influence the choice of an OD strategy. The practitioner has to be aware of where the power is in the organization, because that represents the major lever for change. First impressions obtained in these exploratory interactions are rather important in setting the climate for any future relationships. An example of this is in Figure 4.5.

**Perception** is the process individuals use to give meaning to their environment by interpreting and organizing sensory impressions; however, what one perceives can be substantially different from reality. Perception is a basic factor in understanding behavior in the practitioner-client relationship because an impression is difficult to change once it is made, regardless of its correlation with reality. Clients form early impressions that become very quickly entrenched. Several studies indicate that impressions are formed very early, possibly in the first four or five minutes of the meeting. This is because people behave on the basis of what they perceive rather than on the basis of what really is. Figure 4.6 shows a basic model of the way such perceptions are formed. Many factors are involved, including one's past experiences, the system of rewards, the degree of stress in the situation, the amount of group pressure, and the type of role system involved. Selective perception, interpretation, and closure are all basic factors affecting the formation of perceptions.

**Selective perception** refers to the selectivity of the information perceived. People tend to ignore information that they do not want to hear because it might be distracting or conflict with other ideas or values. However, people tend to accept information that is satisfying, pleasurable, and in agreement with their ideas and values. Individuals may interpret the same stimulus differently. Every **interpretation** depends upon the individual's unique background and experience. Consequently, individuals tend to interpret situations in ways that reflect more favorably upon themselves.

Another process involved in perception is termed **closure.** This refers to the tendency of the individual to fill in any missing information, to complete the perception, and give it meaning and wholeness. Closure may lead a person to perceive more in a situation than is already there, adding information to make the picture seem complete.

During this initial intervention, each party may be selling itself to the other and trying to second-guess the other party's expectations. Often the client system seems to be seeking assurance that the potential practitioner is different enough from the client system to be a real expert and yet enough like it to be thoroughly understandable and approachable. For the practitioner, however, the process of selling oneself has certain dangers and could possibly lead to future problems. The practitioner should ideally be free of the pressure of needing the work, so as

**FIGURE 4.5** First Impressions Are Critical for Future Relationships
*Source:* B.C. By permission of Johnny Hart and Creators Syndicates, Inc.

to remain neutral in judging whether the client system needs the service and whether the practitioner could be helpful. The internal practitioner is in an especially precarious situation regarding personal independence and neutrality.

These elements are often termed **dilemma interactions.** They result from questions by the practitioner about the client's definition of the problem and awareness of the need for change, efforts to reduce the client's unrealistic expectations, the client's misuse of power, and value

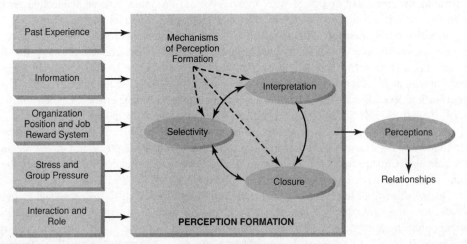

**FIGURE 4.6** Perception Formation and Its Effect on Relationships
*Source:* Adapted from Joseph A. Litterer, *The Analysis of Organizations* (New York: John Wiley, 1965), p. 64

differences between client and practitioner. The issue of dependency is a real problem in many practitioner-client relationships. At the beginning of any OD relationship, there is bound to be some amount of dependence on the practitioner by the client.

As the relationship continues, the client is likely to become more independent of the practitioner and to want to reject either the help or the helper or both. This is a critical point in the relationship, and the effective OD practitioner must be able to let this independence flourish while maintaining the relationship. Operationally, this may mean altering roles and letting the client assume a greater role in the change process. A mature relationship is characterized by a condition of interdependence. In this situation, the client is able to make optimum use of the practitioner's resources, knowing when to use expertise, when to take the initiative, and how to accept suggestions or ideas for consideration. The practitioner feels free to give ideas and suggestions, knowing that the client will use these as appropriate. Mutual confidence between practitioner and client is an essential condition of a sound relationship.

## Practitioner Style Model

There is often a gap between the practitioner's and the client's understandings about OD and change. The practitioner needs to assess the degree of this gap, because a relationship is possible only if the practitioner can be flexible enough to understand where the client is and help the client to learn about the OD change process. In this sense, the practitioner must have clarity about the purpose of OD in the organization. The practitioner brings certain knowledge, skills, values, and experience to the situation. In turn, the client system has its own values and a set of expectations for the practitioner. The target organization within the client system has its own subculture and level of readiness for change.

The practitioner's task and the scope, difficulty, and complexity of the changes to be implemented affect the relationship as well. Finally, the target organization's readiness for change, level of resistance, and culture also influence the practitioner's style and the change approaches that may be successful in a given situation. The OD practitioner needs to involve the organization's members at all levels and convince them to "buy in" on the change program—in effect, to get involved in solving the problems. Taken together, all of these elements help to fashion the style and approaches used by the practitioner, as illustrated in Figure 4.7.

## Developing a Trust Relationship

The development of openness and trust between practitioner and client is an essential aspect of the OD program. It is important because trust is necessary for cooperation and communication. When there is no trust, people will tend to be dishonest, evasive, and not authentic with one another, and communication will often be inaccurate, distorted, or incomplete. There are several basic responses that the practitioner may use in the communication process aimed at developing a trust relationship:

- *Questions*—"How do you see the organization?"
- *Applied expertise (advising)*—"One possible intervention is team building."

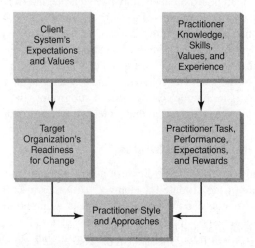

**FIGURE 4.7**   Practitioner Style Model

- *Reflection*—"It sounds like you would like to see a participative form of leadership."
- *Interpretation*—"From your description, interteam conflict could be the problem."
- *Self-disclosure*—"I've felt discouraged myself when my ideas were rejected."
- *Silence*—Say nothing, let the client sort out his or her thoughts.

How these basic responses are used is important in developing the practitioner-client relationship. In general, the more balanced the practitioner's use of these responses and the more open the range of responses, the higher the level of trust. For example, some practitioners rely almost exclusively on questions without sharing their own ideas and feelings. This tends to create a one-way flow of information. Other practitioners rely heavily on advisement responses, which may tend to develop a dependency relationship. It is important for the practitioner to be aware of the range of responses and to use those that will build an open and trusting relationship.

During the first several contacts with the client system, the following types of questions may be reflected upon:

- What is the attitude of the client system toward OD? Is there a real underlying desire for change? Or is the attitude superficial?
- What is the gut-level meaning of the client's problem? How realistic is the client's appraisal of its own problems?
- What are the possibilities that an OD program will alleviate the problem? Can OD solve the problem, or are other change programs more appropriate?
- What is the practitioner's potential impact on the system? Based on feedback from the client, how probable is it that the practitioner can bring about significant change?

Once these questions are answered, the practitioner can decide whether to continue the change efforts or to discontinue and terminate the relationship. Most OD practitioners recommend an open discussion with the client on these issues at an early stage.

## Creating a Climate for Change

Most OD practitioners would agree that an open give-and-take relationship with the client is desirable. To some extent this depends on the ability of the practitioner to form relationships of openness and trust. Good relationships do not fit into a formula or equation, but OD practitioners have noted a number of recognizable characteristics of which the practitioner may be aware. "The change agent should act congruently (authentically), in accordance with the values he or she is attempting to superimpose upon the client system's value system."[16] To use an old expression, the practitioner should practice what he or she preaches. The practitioner must think and act in ways that will create and enhance a positive climate for participation and learning.[17]

The basic value system of the OD practitioner may not be compatible with the organization's culture. As a result, there may be conflicts between the value systems of the practitioner and the client system. An assessment of the degree of difference and the likelihood of working these differences through should be part of the OD practitioner's initial intervention. The practitioner may desire to create a relationship of openness, authenticity, and trust. The client system managers, however, may tend not to be open, may have learned not to behave authentically, and may even feel threatened by an exploration of feelings or confrontation by the practitioner. If the discrepancy between values is too great, the practitioner may have reservations about the probability of a successful program. The practitioner also examines the degree of conflict and collaboration between the organization's units and needs to be aware of this to avoid being party to any existing conflicts. "One of the most frequent forms of resistance to change," comments OD authority Ronald Lippitt, "is the perception by certain subgroups, that the consultant is more closely related to other subgroups and is 'on their side' in any conflict of interests."[18]

## Practitioner-Client Relationship Modes

Eric H. Neilsen has identified several basic dimensions in the practitioner-client relationship that can be used as indicators of the climate for change.[19] In order to collaboratively change the organization's culture, members need to (1) share their ideas, assumptions, perceptions, and feelings, and (2) accept personal responsibility for their own behavior. Based upon these two dimensions, Neilsen has identified four possible modes in the practitioner-client relationship, which are illustrated in Figure 4.8.

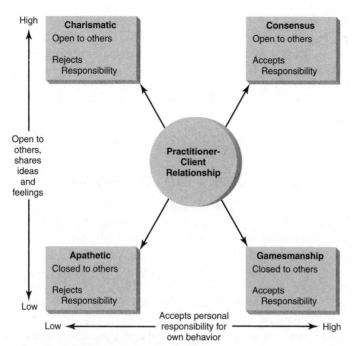

**FIGURE 4.8** **Four Practitioner-Client Relationship Modes**

*The apathetic mode.* Members keep their true ideas about self-fulfillment and organization effectiveness to themselves. They assume that sharing this information will not make any difference, so why bother? They follow established routines, take no responsibility for their actions, and simply do as they are told. They relate to the practitioner in the same way, assuming that higher authority has sanctioned the change but viewing it with skepticism.

*The gamesmanship mode.* Members keep their true feelings about self-fulfillment and organizational effectiveness to themselves, under the assumption that sharing information may threaten personally desired outcomes. They make their own decisions about how to behave, thus taking responsibility for their behavior. This may include conforming outwardly to any decision-making procedure but manipulating strategic factors to gain personal goals. Members may favor change if they can see ways in which it can serve their personal interest.

*The charismatic mode.* A limited number of members openly share ideas and feelings with the rest, based on perceptions of leadership. The followers are looking for cues from their leaders, so responsibility is low for most members. Members view the change process as desirable if the leaders approve, but they rely on the leaders to interpret the results.

*The consensus mode.* Members continuously share perceptions and feelings openly, both on self-fulfillment and organizational effectiveness. Personal viewpoints are seen as relevant to organization functioning and are expressed. Decisions are made and differences are resolved through the sharing of viewpoints. This process involves both sharing of data and maintaining one's responsibility for actions. Members see the OD process as consistent with their way of operating and find the results interesting and useful.

The practitioner's attitudes and behavior make it possible for the client to create a climate where feelings about the client system can be freely and honestly expressed. The practitioner also has the ability to listen effectively and express ideas clearly and concisely. The practitioner is honest with the client, because facades have no place in the relationship. By operating based on power equalization, the practitioner ensures that the power differential between practitioner and client is not too great, for otherwise it will be difficult to develop a collaborative relationship. This is particularly true with internal practitioners, who may be in a subordinate position in the organization's power structure. The practitioner also makes certain that all the key parties in the client system are involved in the OD program to some extent. The practitioner must determine how much involvement by different individuals or groups is appropriate. The outcome of ignoring key people is increased resistance and probable ineffectiveness in the change program.

These are not the only dimensions that are involved in a complex practitioner-client relationship, but they have been discussed here to provide the beginning practitioner with an awareness of some of the important dimensions that should be examined and considered. The practitioner must keep in mind that this relationship is analogous to one's impact on the total system. The practitioner's behavior will actually be a model for the organization between organization members. In attempting to create a climate of openness and collaboration between organization members and departments, one strives to develop personal relationships based on similar qualities. A good relationship increases the probability of a successful OD program. A tenuous or superficial relationship increases the probability that the OD program will be ineffective or unsuccessful.

## THE FORMALIZATION OF OPERATING GROUND RULES

The first contact between practitioner and client is generally informal, exploratory, and tentative. As Beckhard, Bennis, and Schein all point out in their writings, successful practitioner-client relationships require some definition of roles and procedures.[20] The formalization of obligations in the form of a contract is usually advisable for an external practitioner. The internal practitioner does not need a contract, but operating ground rules should be formalized in some manner. These are in many ways similar to the psychological contract discussed in Chapter 1. Instead of each party having a separate set of assumptions about the OD program, the key ideas are written down for everyone to see, discuss, and reach agreement.

The contract with the external practitioner may be incorporated in letters between the practitioner and the client, though a formal contract is strongly recommended to attenuate future misunderstandings. The formalization or contract normally specifies such items as:

1. *The point of contact.* Who in the client system will the practitioner be contacting, and who will be contacting the practitioner?
2. *The role of the practitioner.* Is the practitioner to be an expert or a process helper, or have some other role?
3. *The fees.* The amount the practitioner charges for services varies, depending on the financial status of the client system and the amount of time involved. Fees are usually charged on an hourly or daily basis, on a project basis, or on a retainer basis.
4. *The schedule.* For example, "The objective can be accomplished over an anticipated two-year program devoting five days of time per month." The schedule might also include a tentative list of activities and meetings.
5. *The anticipated results.* The outcome should be stated as specifically as possible, but some practitioners warn against providing any guarantee of value to the organization, because this tends to put the responsibility for change with the practitioner instead of with the client. The practitioner may promise to develop a valid diagnosis of organization problems and may suggest, in a very general way, areas of change that will develop.
6. *The operating ground rules.* Such ground rules could include but are not limited to:
   • The point of contact, which will usually include the top manager.
   • The requirements of the organization members, such as being prepared for meetings.
   • The confidentiality of information.
   • The process role, rather than having an expert coming in to define problems and implement solutions.

These are not the only factors involved in an agreement; they are offered here as guidelines for the beginning practitioner.

## WARNING SIGNS IN THE PRACTITIONER-CLIENT RELATIONSHIP

As noted above, the initial meeting is a critical stage in the OD process. Practitioners must decide whether or not to obligate themselves to a change project at this time. An unpromising beginning may lead to a frustrating change effort and to an OD program predestined to end as an unrewarding experience. Some of the critical warning signals for the practitioner to consider are discussed below.

### The Level of Commitment to Change

At times the client system is not really committed to a change program. Members may verbally express commitment to the proposed OD program, but their behaviors are not congruent with their words. They may be going through the motions only to please top management. In other situations, the client system is dominated by members who are genuinely enthused about the prospect of change.

### The Degree of Leverage or Power to Influence Change

Sometimes, a lower-level manager invites the practitioner into the organization. This member is committed to change but lacks any real capability to influence the system. Here the practitioner must realistically assess the probability of gaining enough leverage to effectively bring about change in such a situation. If a member of the human resources department invites the practitioner into the organization, the practitioner may first wish to ascertain the degree of top management's receptiveness and support for any proposed change before entering into an OD program.

### The Client's Manipulative Use of the Practitioner

In certain situations, there may be a conflict or an internal power struggle, and the client may wish to involve the practitioner as a weapon against other factions or individuals within the organization system. The person in the client system requesting external assistance may want others in the organization to change their ideas or may want to use the practitioner to enforce a position that is already determined. The resulting conflict would probably result in a destructive rather than constructive type of change effort, with the practitioner caught in the middle. In other situations, the client may intend to use the practitioner only to gather information about others in the organization that would otherwise be unobtainable.

## Summary

- **Planned Change.** Change within an organization may be random or haphazard where the change is forced upon the organization by the external environment. But another type of change, planned change, is the result of deliberate attempts to modify the organization in order to promote improvement.
- **Internal and External OD Practitioners.** The internal OD practitioner is already a member of the organization—typically someone from the human resource or organization development department who has received specialized training. An external practitioner is not previously associated with the client system. Internal and external practitioners have their own advantages and disadvantages. An approach that attempts to maximize the advantages while minimizing the disadvantages is to use both internal and external practitioners.
- **Practitioner Styles.** OD practitioner styles can be categorized in terms of the emphasis a practitioner places on (1) accomplishing goals and (2) member satisfaction. Based upon these two dimensions, there are five differ-

ent styles: stabilizer, cheerleader, analyzer, persuader, and pathfinder.
- **Intervention Process.** The practitioner must decide exactly when, how, and with whom to intervene. The receptivity of the system to change must not be overlooked or taken for granted but ought to be carefully probed and realistically determined prior to further intervention.
- **Practitioner-Client Relationship.** The practitioner-client relationship is a system of interacting elements: the internal or external practitioner, client sponsor, and client target system. The client will probably be dependent on the practitioner in the beginning stages of the relationship but become more independent as the relationship continues. The development of openness and trust between practitioner and client is essential.
- **Operating Ground Rules.** These are the formalized definition of roles and procedures for both the practitioner and client. The rules may take the form of a contract or be incorporated in letters between the practitioner and the client.

## Review Questions

1. What are the pros and cons of external and internal practitioners? Why is the team approach a viable alternative?
2. Compare and contrast the five basic practitioner styles.
3. Why is it important for an organization to be ready for an OD program?
4. Identify basic problems in the practitioner-client relationship.
5. Explain the process of perceptions and how perceptions play a part in forming the relationship between the client and the OD practitioner.

## Key Words and Concepts

| | | | |
|---|---|---|---|
| Analyzer Style | Client Target System | External Practitioner | Pathfinder Style |
| Apathetic Mode | Closure | Gamesmanship Mode | Perception |
| Charismatic Mode | Consensus Mode | Internal Practitioner | Persuader Style |
| Cheerleader Style | Dilemma Interactions | Interpretation | Selective Perception |
| Client Sponsor | External-Internal Team | Intervention | Stabilizer Style |

# OD Skills Simulation 4.1

## Practitioner Style Matrix

*Total time suggested: 30 to 45 minutes.*

## A. Purpose

The role of the OD practitioner is both difficult and challenging. The practitioner style matrix has been designed to give you information about your characteristic approaches to a practitioner-client relationship. This information may serve to reinforce existing strengths, or it may indicate areas that need improvement. In either case, the data from the survey should prove helpful in learning more about your style.

Many people may be involved in trying to bring about change. They probably do not operate under the guise of "practitioner" but are more commonly referred to as managers, teachers, social workers, ministers, parents, and so on. Even now you may be a practitioner in some aspects of your life, and at some time in the future you will most certainly be a practitioner. That is, you are now trying to initiate and implement change in an individual or organization, or are trying to do so. This survey will help you gain some insights into the ways you implement change.

## B. Procedures

In order to conserve class time and ensure that you have as much time as you need, Steps 1 through 4 should be completed before class.

*Step 1.* This survey includes 10 situations that call for responses. Each of the situations presents five alternative ways of responding. Because you will be asked to rank these five responses to the situation, it is important for you to read through all the responses before answering. Once you have read through all five responses, select the one that is most similar to the way you think you would actually behave or think in such a situation. Place the letter corresponding to that response (a, b, c, d, or e) somewhere on the "Most Similar" end of the 10-point scale appropriate to the intensity of your feeling. Next, select the response that is least similar to the way you would actually act or think. Place the letter corresponding to that response somewhere on the "Least Similar" end of the scale. Complete the answers by placing the remaining three responses that reflect your actions or thoughts for those responses within the range of previously selected most-least points.

As an example, the answer to a situation could be:

| Most Similar | 10 | 9 | 8 | 7 | 6 | 5 | 4 | 3 | 2 | 1 | Least Similar |
|---|---|---|---|---|---|---|---|---|---|---|---|
| | | | c | b | | | e | d | | a | |

## The Practitioner Style Matrix Survey

In answering these questions, think about how you would actually handle or act in the situation or how you think about change and the nature of change.

1. As a practitioner relating to a client, I will
   a. support the client in working out its goals aimed at high morale.
   b. generally set ground rules and then leave it up to the client.
   c. join with the client in identifying the goals of the change program and then jointly work through the alternatives.
   d. try to develop a friendly relationship, while suggesting change goals.
   e. provide expertise and use logic to convince the client.

| Most Similar | 10 | 9 | 8 | 7 | 6 | 5 | 4 | 3 | 2 | 1 | Least Similar |
|---|---|---|---|---|---|---|---|---|---|---|---|
| | C | | | | | | E | D | A | B | |

2. As a practitioner, change in a client can best be initiated when
   a. I avoid involving too many people.
   b. the logic for the change is pointed out and results emphasized.
   c. the client first has a good opinion of me and then I urge changes.
   d. I help the client to gain self-confidence and satisfaction.
   e. the client makes a choice for change on the basis of mutual needs and goals.

| Most Similar | 10 | 9 | 8 | 7 | 6 | 5 | 4 | 3 | 2 | 1 | Least Similar |
|---|---|---|---|---|---|---|---|---|---|---|---|
| E | | | | | | | B | C | D | A | |

3. If I am talking with a client, I usually
  a. try to be supportive by letting the client do most of the talking.
  b. try to let the client talk and then slowly sell the client on my methods of change.
  c. try to be sure the client understands the logic of the decision.
  d. participate equally in the conversation and attempt to reach a shared conclusion.
  e. say very little and only present my opinion when asked.

| Most Similar | 10 | 9 | 8 | 7 | 6 | 5 | 4 | 3 | 2 | 1 | Least Similar |
|---|---|---|---|---|---|---|---|---|---|---|---|
| D | | | | | | | B | C | A | E | |

4. To achieve change in the client, I feel that
  a. the client has to be convinced that the plan for change has benefits as well as employee satisfaction.
  b. the client and the practitioner can mutually agree on alternatives.
  c. the change and its implementation are left up to the client.
  d. the client decides what change is needed with support given by the practitioner.
  e. the change is to be logically presented by the practitioner.

| Most Similar | 10 | 9 | 8 | 7 | 6 | 5 | 4 | 3 | 2 | 1 | Least Similar |
|---|---|---|---|---|---|---|---|---|---|---|---|
| B | | | | | | | E | A | D | C | |

5. If I have made a suggestion or proposal and someone reacts negatively to it, I am likely to
  a. accept the client's position and search for mutual agreement.
  b. suggest the best course of action and make a logical case for what will happen if that course of action is not followed.
  c. allow the client to fully express his or her ideas and go along with what the client thinks.
  d. point out the requirements of the situation but avoid becoming involved in fruitless argument.
  e. search for a compromise position that satisfies both points of view.

| Most Similar | 10 | 9 | 8 | 7 | 6 | 5 | 4 | 3 | 2 | 1 | Least Similar |
|---|---|---|---|---|---|---|---|---|---|---|---|
| A | | | | | | | B | E | C | D | |

6. A client will probably be more accepting of changes if I
  a. emphasize the rewards and downplay any disadvantages.
  b. discuss how the change will result in increased personal satisfaction and simultaneously provide help and support.
  c. leave the responsibility to the client for taking a course of action he or she deems appropriate.
  d. explain how not carrying out the change will effect the bottom line.
  e. as an active participant along with the client, plan for the change.

| Most Similar | 10 | 9 | 8 | 7 | 6 | 5 | 4 | 3 | 2 | 1 | Least Similar |
|---|---|---|---|---|---|---|---|---|---|---|---|
| E | | | | | | | D | A | B | C | |

7. As a practitioner, a decision to change is most effective when I
  a. tell the client logically what is expected and how to best accomplish the change.
  b. gain the approval and friendship of the client to get acceptable changes.
  c. actively participate with the client in setting the change goals.
  d. point out the need for change but leave the situation open to the client to make his or her own decision whether or not to change.
  e. allow the client to take responsibility for the changes while giving personal support.

| Most Similar | C | | | | | | B | A | E | D | Least Similar |
|---|---|---|---|---|---|---|---|---|---|---|---|
| | 10 | 9 | 8 | 7 | 6 | 5 | 4 | 3 | 2 | 1 | |

**8.** In evaluating my effectiveness as a practitioner, the criterion I normally use is

    **a.** the degree to which the client complies with the change as well as the amount of pushing from me needed to gain compliance.

    **b.** the client's performance as measured by goals jointly set by the client and myself.

    **c.** the client's evaluation of his or her performance.

    **d.** a moderate degree of satisfaction of the client so that there is compliance in meeting change requirements.

    **e.** a high level of morale in the client as well as a friendly relationship between the client and myself.

| Most Similar | B | | | | | | A | D | E | C | Least Similar |
|---|---|---|---|---|---|---|---|---|---|---|---|
| | 10 | 9 | 8 | 7 | 6 | 5 | 4 | 3 | 2 | 1 | |

**9.** In evaluating the client's performance, I should

    **a.** look at evaluation as a mutual responsibility.

    **b.** use a standard evaluation form to ensure objectivity and equal treatment among persons.

    **c.** present my ideas, then allow questions, but casually push for specific improvement.

    **d.** compare performance with quantitative productivity standards and specify the corrections that need to be made.

    **e.** encourage the client to make his or her own evaluation with my moral support.

| Most Similar | A | | | | | | D | C | E | B | Least Similar |
|---|---|---|---|---|---|---|---|---|---|---|---|
| | 10 | 9 | 8 | 7 | 6 | 5 | 4 | 3 | 2 | 1 | |

**10.** As a practitioner, if there seems to be a personality conflict, I usually

    **a.** try to ignore the conflict.

    **b.** confront the client and use logic to gain acceptance of my position.

    **c.** try to relieve tension and smooth over differences.

    **d.** try to explore differences, resolve conflicts, and reach mutual goals.

    **e.** try to find areas of commonality, maintain morale, and seek compromise.

| Most Similar | D | | | | | | E | B | C | A | Least Similar |
|---|---|---|---|---|---|---|---|---|---|---|---|
| | 10 | 9 | 8 | 7 | 6 | 5 | 4 | 3 | 2 | 1 | |

*Step 2.* Scoring instructions for Table 4.2

In Step 1, you wrote your answers (a, b, c, d, and e) above a number. For each of the 10 situations, look at the questionnaire to determine what number value you assigned to that letter and then place the number in the appropriate columns of Table 4.2. The sum of each of the five columns is your score for each of the practitioner styles. There is further explanation of the five styles in Step 4.

*Step 3.* Scoring instructions for Table 4.3:

**1.** Transfer the numerical sums from the score sheet in Table 4.2 to column 3 of Table 4.3 by rearranging them from highest to lowest score.

**2.** In column 2, write the appropriate word description of Approach to Change beside the score.

**3.** Take the difference between the scores in column 3 for your first and second choices and record it on the first line of column 4. Then take the difference for your second and third choices and record it on the second line of column 4. Continue taking the differences between the third and fourth choices, and the fourth and fifth choices. The difference between the scores indicates the likelihood that you will shift styles: a low score (1–10) suggests switching, a high score (over 20) suggests resistance to shifting.

**TABLE 4.2 Scoring of Practitioner Style Matrix Survey**

| Situation | Aalyzer Style | Cheerleader Style | Stabilizer Style | Persuader Style | Pathfinder Style |
|---|---|---|---|---|---|
| 1. | e = 4 | a = 2 | b = 1 | d = 3 | c = 10 |
| 2. | b = 4 | d = 2 | a = 1 | c = 3 | e = 10 |
| 3. | c = 3 | a = 2 | e = 1 | b = 4 | d = 10 |
| 4. | e = 4 | d = 2 | c = 1 | a = 3 | b = 10 |
| 5. | b = 4 | c = 2 | d = 1 | e = 3 | a = 10 |
| 6. | d = 4 | b = 2 | c = 1 | a = 3 | e = 10 |
| 7. | a = 3 | e = 2 | d = 1 | b = 4 | c = 10 |
| 8. | a = 4 | e = 2 | c = 1 | d = 3 | b = 10 |
| 9. | d = 4 | e = 2 | b = 1 | c = 3 | a = 10 |
| 10. | b = 3 | c = 2 | a = 1 | e = 4 | d = 10 |
| Total Points | 37 | 20 | 10 | 33 | 100 |

*Time suggested for Steps 2 and 3 if class members need assistance in completing Tables 4.2 and 4.3: 15 minutes.*

*Step 4.* You have just completed and scored your practitioner survey. Following is a brief explanation of the five styles.

***The analyzer style.*** This practitioner style has maximum concern for the efficient accomplishment of the change goals and little concern about whether the people involved in implementing the goals are personally committed to them. The analyzer style sees people as a means to accomplish the change and believes they must be closely guided and directed because they lack the desire or capacity to change. A practitioner using this style tends to use an expert-based style and sets demanding performance standards as a method of implementing change.

***The cheerleader style.*** The practitioner using this style has minimum concern about whether the stated change goals are accomplished but maximum concern that the people involved in the change program are personally committed to and happy with the change. There may be as many change programs as there are people, because the cheerleader-style practitioner encourages members of a system to design and implement their own programs of change. The emphasis is on morale and friendly relationships.

***The stabilizer style.*** This practitioner style has very minimum concern for goal accomplishment and also has minimum concern for the people involved. The practitioner does not care to get involved and is only biding time until new orders come down. Change is viewed as a disruption of a well-ordered and secure environment.

***The persuader style.*** This practitioner style has moderate concern for achievement of the change goals and that the people implementing the change are committed to the change goals. As a result, the practitioner using this style is not consistent and often shifts the emphasis from concern for change goals to concern for the people involved in the change program. The practitioner believes that too rapid a change will be disruptive and, therefore, attempts to implement change in small steps that allow people to become gradually accustomed to the changes and avoid conflict.

**TABLE 4.3 Practitioner Style Matrix Summary**

| (1) Your Choice | (2) Word Description of Approach to Change | (3) Score (High to Low) | (4) Difference Between Scores |
|---|---|---|---|
| 1st Primary | Pathfinder | 100 | 63 |
| 2nd Backup | Analyzer | 37 | 4 |
| 3rd Backup | Persuader | 33 | 13 |
| 4th Backup | Cheerleader | 20 | 10 |
| 5th Backup | Stabilizer | 10 | |

***The pathfinder style.*** The practitioner using this style constantly strives for achievement of the change goals by other people in the change program and, at the same time, has maximum concern that the people involved in implementing the change are personally committed to the change and to the vision of the future.

You may now plot your average style scores on the graph in Table 4.4. Complete the bar chart by shading in the score for each style. This provides a profile of your scores.

A person does not operate using one style to the exclusion of others. The purpose of the scoring in Steps 2 and 3 was to give you an indication of the importance you place on each of the five styles. The difference between your primary and backup styles indicates the strength of your preference and how quickly you will fall back on another style. Little difference between scores could indicate a tendency to vacillate between styles or vague thoughts about how to handle change. A large difference could indicate a strong reliance on the predominant change style.

This survey should be used as a point of departure for further reflection and observation concerning the way you attempt to change and influence other people. To obtain a better understanding of your change style, try to become aware of how you handle change in your associations with class members, friends, peers, and work associates. It may also be helpful to observe other people when they try to change or influence your behavior and to become aware of how you react to their change methods.

*Step 5.* Discuss the five practitioner styles in class. Do the scores for your primary and backup change styles seem congruent with the way you think you operate in change situations? Share your scores with class members with whom you have been working and get their feedback. Does this feedback correlate with your scores on the survey?

*Time suggested for Step 5: 30 minutes.*

**TABLE 4.4  Practitioner Styles**

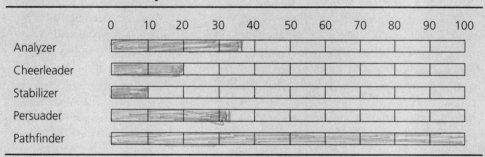

|  | 0 | 10 | 20 | 30 | 40 | 50 | 60 | 70 | 80 | 90 | 100 |
|---|---|---|---|---|---|---|---|---|---|---|---|
| Analyzer | | | | | | | | | | | |
| Cheerleader | | | | | | | | | | | |
| Stabilizer | | | | | | | | | | | |
| Persuader | | | | | | | | | | | |
| Pathfinder | | | | | | | | | | | |

# OD Skills Simulation 4.2

## Conflict Styles

*Total time suggested: 50 to 70 minutes.*

## A. Purpose

This simulation is designed to give you an opportunity to influence and change other individuals as well as to be influenced and changed by others. Although the story may seem contrived, it describes a situation about which most of us have some rather strong feelings and ideas. The story can be a means to quickly get involvement and commitment to certain issues that you will select. This personal involvement is necessary so that there will be a real and prior commitment to these ideas in a later part of the simulation that requires you to change others' ideas and others to change your ideas. The goals include: (1) identify ways of dealing with organizational or team conflict, (2) discuss when and why different methods of resolving conflict are appropriate to different situations, and (3) provide an experience in team decision making.

## B. Procedures

*Step 1.* Form teams of five members. Any extra persons may join as additional members of a team, but ideally no team should have more than six or fewer than four members.

*Step 2.* Read the following short story. Answer the question that directly follows the story individually. Space is provided on Line A for your answer.

*Time suggested for Steps 1–2: 5 minutes.*

## The Young Woman

In a house is a young woman married to a man who works very hard. She feels neglected. When her husband goes off on another trip, the young wife meets an attractive man who invites her to his house. She spends the night and at dawn she leaves, knowing her husband is coming home. Alas! The bridge is blocked by a madman who kills everyone who comes near him. The young wife follows the river and meets the ferryman, but he demands 100 francs to take her to the other side. The young wife has no money. She runs back to her lover and asks for 100 francs; he refuses to help. The woman remembers that a platonic friend lives nearby. She runs to him and explains her plight. The friend refuses to help; she has disillusioned him by her conduct. Her only choice is to go by the bridge in spite of the danger, and the madman kills her. That is the story.[21]

In what order do you hold the principals (woman, husband, lover, madman, ferryman, and friend) responsible for the tragedy? Record your answer on Line A.

| Individual Decision | Line A | 1. | 2. | 3. | 4. | 5. | 6. |
|---|---|---|---|---|---|---|---|
| Team Decision | Line B | 1. | 2. | 3. | 4. | 5. | 6. |
| Individual Decision | Line C | 1. | 2. | 3. | 4. | 5. | 6. |

*Step 3.* In your teams, reach a team consensus for the answer to the question. Remember, a consensus decision involves reaching a mutual agreement by discussion until everyone agrees on the final decision. It is important that your team make its decision in 15 minutes. Place the team's answer on Line B.

*Time suggested for Step 3: 10 to 15 minutes.*

*Step 4.* Meeting with the entire class and focus your discussion on the following questions:

1. Was there much disagreement within your team?
2. If there was, to what could it be attributed?
3. How did your team reach its decision (consensus, voting, etc.)?
4. To what extent do you feel that the other members of your team support the team's decision?

*Time suggested for Step 4: 5 to 10 minutes.*

*Step 5.* Go back to the story and on Line C, answer the question again, but on an individual basis. Your answer may be the same as when you first responded to the story, or you may alter your original position because of new information.

**TABLE 4.5** Team Member Styles

| Team Member's Name | Primary Style | Backup Style | Comments/ Observations |
|---|---|---|---|
| | | | |
| | | | |
| | | | |
| | | | |
| | | | |
| | | | |

*Step 6*. Meet back in your team to find out how everyone responded on Line C. Are the Line C answers the same as those on Line B? On Line A? Or are they different from the previous answers?

*Time suggested for Steps 5 and 6: 5 minutes.*

*Step 7*. Complete Table 4.5 by recording what you observed to be the primary and backup practitioner styles (analyzer, cheerleader, stabilizer, persuader, or pathfinder) of the members of your team. Add any observations or comments about why that style seems to fit.

*Time suggested for Step 7: 5 minutes.*

*Step 8*. In Table 4.6, transfer the information from what the other team members recorded about you in their Table 4.5. From Table 4.6, try to draw some conclusion about your practitioner style. Discuss your conclusions with the other team members.

1. How did your survey results from Simulation 4.1 compare with the information received from your team?
2. Did the members of the team agree about your practitioner style?
3. If there were differences, to what can they be attributed?

*Time suggested for Step 8: 10 to 15 minutes.*

*Step 9*. Meeting with the entire class, discuss the following questions:

1. How congruent were your scores from Table 4.3, of Simulation 4.1 with the feedback from your team members in this simulation?
2. If there was any difference, to what could it be attributed?
3. What practitioner styles do you feel are most effective in an OD program? Why?

*Time suggested for Step 9: 5 to 10 minutes.*

**TABLE 4.6** Individual Style Feedback

| | Information Received From | Primary Style | Backup Style | Comments/ Observations |
|---|---|---|---|---|
| 1 | | | | |
| 2 | | | | |
| 3 | | | | |
| 4 | | | | |
| 5 | | | | |
| 6 | | | | |
| Consensus | | | | |

## OD Skills Simulation 4.3

### Perception

**(Do not read Simulation 4.3 until instructed to do so by your instructor in class.)**

*Total time suggested: 20 minutes*

### A. Purpose

As mentioned in the chapter, practitioners must be especially perceptive in their relationships with clients, and it is important that the perceptions be accurate. Developing an effective relationship with a client and accurately answering some initial questions about the client requires perceptions that reflect reality. But what is reality? Is it what we see or what we think we see? Our perceptions, whether they reflect reality or not, most definitely influence our actions. The following brief simulation will provide some insight into the accuracy of your perceptions, how they influence your behavior, and how individuals perceive different signals from the same visual data.

### B. Procedures

*Step 1*. Read quickly and only once the sentence enclosed in the following box:[22]

> **FORMS ARE FREQUENTLY COMPLETED ON TIME, BUT OF COURSE THE RESULTS OF THE INFORMATION WOULD NOT BE OF USE TO ANYONE.**

*Step 2*. Now count the F's in the above sentence. Count them only once; do not go back and count them again. Enter the number of F's _____.

*Step 3*. Compare your perceptions with those of other members of the class, remembering that we all believe that our own perception is the only accurate one.

*Step 4*. Reconsider your initial perceptions, reread the sentence, and count the F's in the box. Did you alter your initial perceptions?

*Time suggested for Steps 1–4: 10 minutes*

*Step 5*. As a class, discuss the following:

1. How can people come to different conclusions when they are looking at the same thing?
2. Discuss how individuals perceive things differently and how this influences behavior.

*Time suggested for Step 5: 10 minutes*

# CASE: THE GRAYSON CHEMICAL COMPANY

## The Company

The Grayson Chemical Co. manufactures industrial chemicals for sale to other industrial companies. The company is about 40 years old and has been run by a stable management in which there have only been two presidents. Within the past few years, however, declining earnings and sales have brought pressure from the board of directors, investment bankers, and stockholder groups to name a new president. The company has become increasingly stagnant—although at Grayson they refer to it as conservative—and has steadily lost market standing and profitability. Finally, the board decided to go outside the company to find a new CEO and was able to recruit a dynamic manager from another major corporation, Tom Baker. Baker was 47 and had helped build his former company into a leadership position. However, when another executive was chosen for the top job, Baker decided to accept the position with Grayson.

Baker was clear about what he needed to do. He knew that he needed to develop a top management team that could provide the leadership to turn the company around. Unfortunately, the situation at Grayson was not very favorable.

Decisions were made by the book or taken to the next-higher level. Things were done because "they have always been done this way," and incompetent managers were often promoted to high-level jobs.

## The Meeting

Baker met with three members of the board, Robert Temple (chairman), James Allen, and Hartley Ashford. Each had a different bit of advice to offer.

Robert Temple said: "Look, Tom, you can't just get rid of the old organization if you want to maintain any semblance of morale. Your existing people are all fairly competent technically, but it's up to you to develop performance goals and motivate them to achieve these standards. Make it clear that achievement will be rewarded and that those who can't hack it will have to go."

James Allen noted: "Let's face it, Tom, you need to bring in a new top management team. Probably only six or so, but people who know what top performance means, people who are using innovative methods of managing and, above all, people you trust. That means people you've worked with closely, from your previous employer or other companies, but people you know. You can't retread the old people, and you don't have time to develop young talent, so you need to bring in your own team even though it might upset some of the old-timers."

Hartley Ashford smiled and said: "Well, my take on this is a little different. Sure, you're going to have to bring in a new team from the outside, but rather than bring in people you've worked with before, bring in only managers with proven track records. People who have proven their ability to lead, motivate, and perform from different industries. This way, you'll get a synergistic effect from a number of successful organizations. And the old people will see that favoritism is not the way to get ahead. So get a top performance team, and if you lose a few old-timers, so much the better." (Use the Case Analysis Form on the following page.)

**THE GRAYSON CHEMICAL COMPANY CASE ANALYSIS FORM**

Name: _____

I. Problems

  A. Macro

    1. _____

      _____

    2. _____

      _____

  B. Micro

    1. _____

      _____

    2. _____

      _____

II. Causes

    1. _____

      _____

    2. _____

      _____

    3. _____

      _____

III. Systems affected

    1. _____

      _____

    2. _____

      _____

    3. _____

      _____

IV. Alternatives

    1. _____

      _____

    2. _____

      _____

    3. _____

      _____

V. Recommendations

_____

_____

_____

_____

_____

_____

## Chapter 4 Endnotes

1. Pallavi Gogoi and Michaiel Arndt, "Hamburger Hell," *Business Week*, March 3, 2003, p. 108.
2. Teresa Colvin and Ralph Kilmann, "A Profile of Large-Scale Change Programs," *Proceedings of the Southern Management Association,* 1989, p. 202.
3. Alex Taylor, "CEO Bill Ford Must Cut Costs and Stop Feuds to Turn His Company Around," *Fortune,* vol. 147, no. 9 (May 12, 2003), p. 106.
4. Shari Caudren, "Change Keeps TQM Programs Thriving," *Personnel Journal*, vol. 72, no. 10 (October 1993), p. 104.
5. See Harold J. Leavitt, *Corporate Pathfinders* (Homewood, IL: Dow Jones–Irwin, 1986), p. 10.
6. Edgar Schein, *Process Consultation: Its Role in Organization Development,* vol. 1 (Reading, MA: Addison-Wesley, 1988), p. 13.
7. www.bain.com; "Running the Show," *Wall Street Journal,* October 31, 2005, p. R4.
8. Warren Bennis, *Organization Development: Its Nature, Origins, and Prospects* (Reading, MA: Addison-Wesley, 1969), p. 48.
9. See Richard Beckhard, *Organization Development Strategies and Models* (Reading, MA: Addison-Wesley, 1969), p. 13.
10. Schein, *Process Consultation: Its Role in Organization Development*, vol. 1, pp. 5–38.
11. Ibid., p. 11.
12. Ibid.
13. Ellen Fagenson, and W. Warner Burke, "The Current Activities and Skills of OD Practitioners," *Academy of Management Proceedings,* 1989, p. 251; W. Warner Burke, *Organization Change: Theory and Practice* (Thousand Oaks, CA: Sage Publications, 2002).
14. Susan Gebelein, "Profile of an Internal Consultant: Roles and Skills," *Training & Development Journal,* March 1989, p. 52.
15. Bennis, *Organization Development*, p. 43.
16. Ibid., p. 50.
17. For a review of some of the research regarding the importance of the change agent in creating a climate for change, see Liane Ginsburg and Deborah Tregunnno, "New Approaches to Interprofessional Education and Collaborative Practice: Lessons from the Organizational Change Literature," *Journal of Interprofessional Care*, vol. 19, supplement 1, (May 2005), pp. 177–87.
18. Ronald Lippitt, "Dimensions of the Consultant's Job," *The Planning of Change,* ed. W. Bennis, K. Benne, and R. Chin (New York: Holt, Rinehart & Winston, 1961), p. 160.
19. Eric H. Neilsen, "Reading Clients' Values from Their Reactions to an Intervention Feedback Process," *Academy of Management Proceedings,* 1978, p. 318.
20. Beckhard, *Organization Development Strategies and Models;* Bennis, *Organization Development;* Schein, *Process Consultation: Its Role in Organization Development*, vol. 1.
21. The author of this classic story could not be traced.
22. The author of this sentence could not be traced.

# The Diagnostic Process

**LEARNING OBJECTIVES**

**Upon completing this chapter, you will be able to:**

1. Identify system parameters and recognize the symptoms, problems, and causes of organizational ineffectiveness.
2. Recognize the various techniques for gathering information from client systems.
3. Describe the major diagnostic models and techniques used in OD programs.
4. Apply a systematic diagnosis to organizational situations.

## PREMEETING PREPARATION

1. Read Chapter 5.
2. Prepare for OD Skills Simulation 5.1. Prior to class, form teams of six and select roles. Complete Step 1.
3. Read and analyze Case: The Old Family Bank.

## DIAGNOSING PROBLEM AREAS

To be successful in the twenty-first century, organizations must have flexibility and the ability for rapid transformation. However, many organizations move along a well-worn path, and problems are often concealed or hidden.

The identification of problems and areas for improvement is an important element in developing a high-performance organization. In a time of downsizing and restructuring, many companies are finding that they must learn to manage more effectively. Organizational problem solving means that every member of an organization participates in developing a vision and improving the corporate culture. In any change program, you must know where you are before you can chart a course for where you want to be. Therefore, before implementing TQM or some other program, it is important to assess the organization's current quality or performance and to define the level of performance or quality you wish to achieve.

Organization diagnosis provides information that allows a faster-reacting organization to emerge, one that can deal proactively with changing forces. Diagnosis rigorously analyzes the data on the structure, administration, interaction, procedures, interfaces, and other essential elements of the client system. Using a systematic approach throughout the process, the diagnosis serves as a basis for structural, behavioral, or technical interventions to improve organizational performance. If organization change is to be effective, it must be based on a specific diagnosis of the problem.

Questioning the client's diagnosis of the problem is a good rule for organization development practitioners to follow. The client is part of the system that has a problem and, therefore, may be unable to take an objective view of the situation. Also, the client will probably be operating from one part of a larger system and may find it difficult, if not impossible, to see the total system. It is appropriate to listen to the client's definition of and ideas about the problem, but the practitioner should then openly ask permission to verify these ideas with properly conducted research. Diagnosis is a process that helps organizations improve their capacity to assess and change inefficient patterns of behavior as a basis for developing greater effectiveness and ensuring continuous improvement.

An OD program must be based on a sound analysis of relevant data about the problem situation. To make a sound diagnosis, it is important to have valid information about the situation and to arrange available data into a meaningful pattern. The simple fact of sharing performance information can become a powerful force for change.

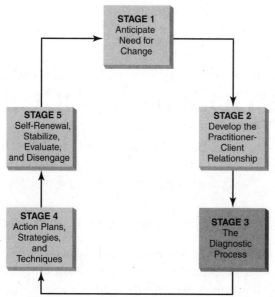

**FIGURE 5.1**   **Stage 3 of Organization Development's Five Stages**

This chapter examines stage 3, the diagnostic process, of an OD program, and is shown in Figure 5.1. The subjects discussed include a general definition of diagnosis, the process of collecting data, implementation of data collection, the major diagnostic models, and situations where caution is warranted.

## WHAT IS DIAGNOSIS?

Today's intense global competition and deregulation have created great uncertainty for firms in virtually every industry. Increased competition requires constant response to initiatives by other firms. It calls for continuous improvement of quality and products while decreasing costs. Diagnosis is a method of analyzing organizational problems and learning new patterns of behavior. It can help organizations by doing the following:

1. Enhancing the organization's capacity to assess and change its culture.
2. Providing an opportunity for organizational members to acquire new insights into the dysfunctional aspects of their culture and patterns of behavior as a basis for developing a more effective organization.
3. Ensuring that the organization remains engaged in a process of continuous improvement.[1]

Because diagnosis provides these opportunities, it is an indispensable step in the process of organizational revitalization. Organization development is a data-based activity. OD relies on valid information about current problems and possible opportunities for improvement. Diagnosis provides a starting point (a set of current conditions) and the change objective (an ideal or desired set of conditions).

Diagnosis usually examines two broad areas. The first area for diagnosis comprises the various interacting subelements that make up the organization. These include the divisions, departments, products, and the relationships between them. The diagnosis may also include a comparison of the top, middle, and lower levels of management in the organization. The second area of diagnosis concerns the organizational processes. These include communication networks, team problem solving, decision making, leadership and authority styles, goal-setting and planning methods, and the management of conflict and competition.

In organizational diagnosis, the practitioner is looking for causality—that is, an implication that change in one factor (such as compensation) will cause change in another factor (productivity): a cause-effect relationship. The client is often aware of the evidence of the problem, such as declining sales, high turnover, or loss of market share—the symptoms of a problem. In the diagnostic phase, the practitioner tries to identify what factors are causing the problem, and, therefore, what needs to be changed to fix it.

The critical issues in diagnosis include:

*Simplicity.* Keep the data as simple as possible and use simplicity in presentation.

*Visibility.* Use visible measures of what's happening.

*Involvement.* Emphasize the participation and involvement of organization members in the diagnosis.

*Primary factors.* Use an undistorted collection of primary operating variables in the diagnosis.

*Measure what is important.* Pursue the straightforward assessment of the variables critical to success.

*Sense of urgency.* During diagnosis, gain an overall sense of urgency for change.[2]

At management consulting firm McKinsey & Co., the diagnostic process is "hypothesis driven." The practitioner team develops hypotheses, such as "People who sell big orders make more money for the company." The practitioner team may interview the managers at many companies and collect factual data to prove or disprove the hypothesis. They may discover, in fact, that large sales orders are the least profitable. The secret of diagnosis, then, is in the rigor of fact finding; things are proved with facts, not opinions.

**Diagnosis** is a systematic approach to understanding and describing the present state of the organization. The purpose of the diagnostic phase is to gather information to specify the exact nature of the problem requiring solution, to identify the underlying causal forces, and to provide a basis for selecting effective change strategies and techniques. The outcome of a weak, inaccurate, or faulty diagnosis will be a costly and ineffective OD program. Organization diagnosis, then, involves the systematic analysis of data regarding the organization processes and culture with the intention of discovering problems and drawing conclusions about action programs for improvement. Andrew Grove, Intel Corporation's legendary CEO for over 10 years, said regarding the investigation of problems, "Ask why, and ask it again five more times, until all of the artifice is stripped away and you end up with the intellectually honest answer."[3]

### The Process

Diagnosis is a cyclical process that involves data gathering, interpretations, and identification of problem areas and possible action programs, as illustrated in Figure 5.2. The first step is the preliminary identification of possible problem areas. These preliminary attempts often bring out symptoms as well as possible problem areas.

The second step involves gathering data based on the preliminary problem identified in the preceding step. These data are categorized, analyzed, and presented to the client in a feedback session (steps 3 and 4). If it is determined that more data is required to make a diagnosis (step 5), the process reverts to the second step where additional data is collected. Otherwise, the client and practitioner jointly diagnose and identify likely problem areas (step 6). At this point, the client's level of motivation to work on the problems is determined (step 7). Based upon the diagnosis, the target systems are identified and the change strategy is designed (step 8). Finally (step 9), the results are monitored to determine the degree of change that has been attained versus the desired change goals.

### The Performance Gap

One method in the diagnostic process is to determine the **performance gap**—the difference between what the organization could do by virtue of its opportunity in its environment and what it actually does. This leads to an approach that may be termed "gap analysis." In this method, data are collected on the actual state of the organization on a varying set of dimensions and also on the ideal or desired state, that is, "where the organization should be." As seen in Figure 5.3, the discrepancy between the actual state and the ideal forms a basis for diagnosis and the design of interventions. The gap may be the result of ineffective performance by internal units or may emerge because of competitive changes or new innovations. A performance gap may also occur when the organization fails to adapt to changes in its external environment.

Competent organizational diagnosis does not simply provide information about the system; it is also helpful in designing and introducing action alternatives for correcting possible problems. The diagnosis affirms the need for change and the benefits of possible changes in the client system. Important problems are very often hidden or obscure, whereas the more conspicuous and obvious

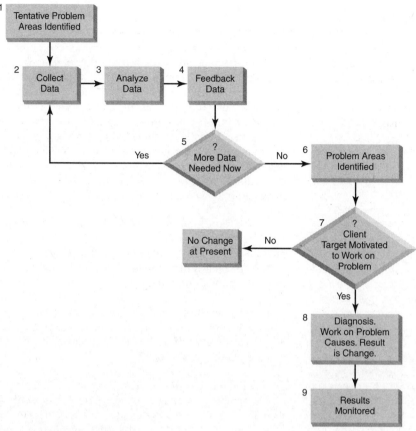

**FIGURE 5.2** The Diagnostic Process

problems may be relatively unimportant. In such situations, dealing with the obvious may not be a very effective way to manage change; this underscores the importance of the diagnostic stage.

A performance gap may continue for some time before it is recognized. In fact, it may never be recognized. On the other hand, the awareness of a performance gap may unfreeze the functions within the organization that are most in need of change. When this happens, conditions are present for altering the structure and function of the organization by introducing OD interventions.

A self-assessment version of gap analysis uses questionnaires to gather information in four key areas. Initially the strengths of the organization are determined. Then an assessment is made as to what can be done to take advantage of the strengths. Just as strengths are determined, the organization's weaknesses are likewise determined. The self-assessment concludes with an analysis of what is to be done to alleviate the weaknesses. The process of identifying the organization's strengths and weaknesses often leads to recognition of performance gaps and to

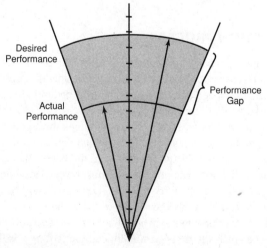

**FIGURE 5.3** The Performance Gap

## OD Application: The Performance Gap at eBay[4]

eBay has become the marketplace of the world and, in the process, it has become the world's largest recycling center. Its business of auctions and sales of merchandise exists solely on the Internet. Its business formula is to provide a worldwide market and collect a tax on transactions as they occur. Although eBay's sales are only a fraction of Wal-Mart's, eBay has no stores and warehouses. It does not take physical or legal possession of merchandise, so there is no inventory. eBay's revenue comes from listing fees and advertising. It also earns revenue from PayPal, the banking system it runs for its customers and other Internet-based merchants.

From the beginning, when eBay was founded in 1995, its business model was to bring together under one "roof" an array of goods that would attract buyers. To that end, eBay has become the world's largest online marketplace that averages around 81 million visitors a month with approximately $60 million annual sales of merchandise. This success has almost worked too well. "eBay's abundance [of merchandise] was one of its attractions," said CEO John Donahoe, a former Bain & Co. consultant. "But if you type in 'BlackBerry' and you get 23,000 search results, it's not that helpful."

The company already collected data about transactions so that by understanding the data, it could decide where to spend money, where employees are needed, and which projects are working and failing. But it did not know what customers were doing before they clicked the "Place Bid" or "Buy It Now" icons. So that eBay could provide a better shopping experience for its buyers, it needed to unravel all the mouse clicks to discover exactly what customers were doing. "If you start with the lowest level of detail, you can answer any question about the business," says chief information officer Matt Carey. He calls it a "culture of analytics" and says, "I want to eliminate feelings and get down to true math." To get this data, his team developed a new search engine so that browsing and sales are enhanced. Every mouse click is tracked to discover what leads shoppers to bid or buy.

Beginning around 2006, eBay and other Internet auction sites noticed a disturbing trend. As Internet commerce matured, people were less willing to spend days monitoring their bids to try and get a good deal. Furthermore, they frequently found that at the last moment someone else had come in and topped the highest bid with no chance of a counter bid. The practice of placing a bid at the last moment, called "sniping," had become more common because of automated software programs like "Bidnapper" and "Powersnipe." With Google and other search engines, buyers could find quickly almost anything and at the lowest price. The prospect of saving a few bucks by waiting days on auction results with no assurance of getting the item was mitigated by the convenience of buying things quickly at a set price.

The data that eBay tracked showed that its traditional strategy of online auctions had become obsolete. Fixed-priced sales were accounting for about half of all transactions. Auction sales made up less than a third of sales compared to 75 percent two years prior. Confronted with a significant decline in revenue and based on an analysis of the data, eBay decided to change its strategy by moving to fixed-price items. But instead of going up against Amazon, eBay decided to concentrate on making it easier for customers to find things like collectables, overstocked items, and last year's models.

"The business has continued to fall short of our expectations and customers' expectations," said CEO Donahoe. "That's not acceptable. The eBay you knew is not the eBay of today or the eBay of the future." In a critique of eBay's mistakes, he said, "We were the biggest and the best. And when you're the biggest and the best, there's a strong tendency to try to preserve that. eBay has a storied past. But frankly, it's a past we've held onto too much."

### Questions

1. What was the performance gap at eBay?
2. What are some advantages and disadvantages of gathering large quantities of data?
3. Visit the eBay Web site at www.ebay.com/ to further your understanding of its business model.

---

change programs. **OD Application: The Performance Gap at eBay** includes information about a performance gap at eBay and how it used data collection and diagnosis to identify the problem and solve it.

## THE DATA-COLLECTION PROCESS

The process of collecting data is an important and significant step in an OD program. During this stage, the practitioner and the client attempt to determine the specific problem requiring solution. After the practitioner has intervened and has begun developing a relationship, the next step is acquiring data and information about the client system.[5]

This task begins with the initial meeting and continues throughout the OD program. The practitioner is, in effect, gathering data and deciding which data are relevant whenever he or she meets with the client, observes, or asks questions. Of all the basic OD techniques, perhaps none is as fundamental as data collection. The practitioner must be certain of the facts before proceeding with an action program. The probability that an OD program will be successful is increased if it is based upon accurate and in-depth knowledge of the client system.

Information quality is a critical factor in any successful organization. Developing an innovative culture and finding new ways to meet customer needs are strongly influenced by the way information is gathered and processed. Organization development is a data-based change activity.

The data collected are used by the members who provide the data and often lead to insights into ways of improving effectiveness. The data-collection process itself involves an investigation, a body of data, and some form of processing information. For our purposes, the word **data,** which is derived from the Latin verb *dare,* meaning "to give," is most appropriately applied to unstructured, unformed facts. It is an aggregation of all signs, signals, clues, facts, statistics, opinions, assumptions, and speculations, including items that are accurate and inaccurate, relevant and irrelevant. The word **information** is derived from the Latin verb *informare,* meaning "to give form to," and is used here to mean data that have form and structure. A common problem in organizations is that they are data-rich but information-poor: lots of data, but little or no information.

An OD program based upon a systematic and explicit investigation of the client system has a much higher probability of success because a careful data-collection phase initiates the organization's problem-solving process and provides a foundation for the following stages. This section discusses the steps involved in the data-collection process.

## The Definition of Objectives

The first and most obvious step in data collection is defining the objectives of the change program. A clear understanding of these broad goals is necessary to determine what information is relevant. Unless the purpose of data collection is clearly defined, it becomes difficult to select methods and standards. The OD practitioner must first obtain enough information to allow a preliminary diagnosis and then decide what further information is required to verify the problem conditions. Usually, some preliminary data gathering is needed simply to clarify the problem conditions before further large-scale data collection is undertaken.

This is usually accomplished by investigating possible problem areas and ideas about what an ideal organization might be like in a session of interviews with key members of the organization. These conversations enable the organization and the practitioner to understand the way things are, as opposed to the way members would like them to be.

Most practitioners emphasize the importance of collecting data as a significant step in the OD process. First, data gathering provides the basis for the organization to begin looking at its own processes, focusing upon how it does things and how this affects performance. Second, data collection often begins a process of self-examination or assessment by members and work teams in the organization, leading to improved problem-solving capabilities.

## The Selection of Key Factors

The second step in data collection is to identify the central variables involved in the situation (such as turnover, breakdown in communications, and isolated management). The practitioner and the client decide which factors are important and what additional information is necessary for a systematic diagnosis of the client system's problems. The traditional approach was to select factors along narrow issues, such as pay and immediate supervisors. More recently, the trend has been to gauge the organization's progress and status more broadly. Broader issues include selecting factors that determine the culture and values of the organization.

Organizations normally generate a considerable amount of "hard" data internally, including production reports, budgets, turnover ratios, sales per square foot, sales or profit per employee, and so forth, which may be useful as indicators of problems. This internal data can be compared with competitors' data and industry averages. The practitioner may find, however, that it is necessary to increase the range of depth of data beyond what is readily available. Increasing the depth and scope of the data is illustrated in Figure 5.4. The practitioner may wish to gain additional insights into other dimensions of the organizational system, particularly those dealing with the quality of the transactions or relationships between individuals or groups. This additional data gathering may examine the following dimensions:

- What is the degree of dependence between operating teams, departments, or units?
- What is the quantity and quality of the exchange of information and communication between units?
- What is the degree to which the vision, mission, and the goals of the organization are shared and understood by members?
- What are the norms, attitudes, and motivations of organization members?
- What are the effects of the distribution of power and status within the system?

**FIGURE 5.4    The Importance of In-Depth Data Gathering**
*Source:* B.C. by permission of Johnny Hart and Creators Syndicate, Inc.

In this step, the practitioner and client determine which factors are important and which factors can and should be investigated.

## The Selection of a Data-Gathering Method

The third step in data collection is selecting a method of gathering data. There are many different types of data and many different methods of tapping data sources. There is no one best way to gather data—the selection of a method depends on the nature of the problem. Whatever method is adopted, data should be acquired in a systematic manner, thus allowing quantitative or qualitative comparison between elements of the system. The task in this step is to identify certain characteristics that may be measured to help in the achievement of the OD program objectives and then to select an appropriate method to gather the required data. Some major data-collecting methods follow.

**SECONDARY SOURCES OF DATA**    The data most needed by the practitioner are probably not available when the data-gathering process begins. Very often, however, there are large amounts of organizational data already generated for other purposes that can be used in identifying problem areas. These data may be termed secondary data or measures. Examples of secondary sources include accounting data, productivity data, quality data, and performance indicators, such as employee thefts, turnover, and absentee rates. Sears Holdings Corporation upgraded its software and data-mining capability to sift through customer-purchase information. Sears now understands that it needs to focus on customers with incomes of $50,000 to $100,000 and higher. This is a more upscale group than Sears customarily targets. The data helped a team develop a new marketing campaign that focuses on this new group of customers.[6]

There are certainly some limitations associated with the use of secondary data. Although available, the secondary data may not be in a usable format. For example, lateness and absentee figures may not provide information by department. An additional problem involves the interpretation of the data: What are the causes underlying a given absentee rate or number of grievance reports?

**EMPLOYEE SURVEYS AND QUESTIONNAIRES** Employee **surveys** or **questionnaires** (for our purposes here, the two words will be used interchangeably) are used to provide important information on past, present, and future improvement efforts. Questionnaires, the most frequently used method to gather information,[7] have two important functions:

1. Questionnaires serve as information/improvement tools. They can help identify opportunities for improvement and help evaluate the impact of changes being implemented.
2. Questionnaires are an effective communication tool. They facilitate dialogue on potential improvements between managers and employees.

Questionnaires are used to gather a large number of quantitative responses and lend themselves to quantitative analysis. At one extreme, the questionnaire may be administered by a person asking questions of a respondent in person and who is identified by name. At the other extreme, the questionnaire may be administered via a computer and submitted anonymously. The questionnaire is particularly useful for studies of the attitudes, values, and beliefs of respondents. On the other hand, questionnaire data tend to be impersonal, anonymous, and often lack feeling and richness.

There are many problems involved in designing and administering an effective questionnaire. Validity is often a problem: Does the questionnaire measure what it is intended to measure? The accuracy of the information obtained is another problem: Did the person answer it realistically or just to make a good impression? Or did the respondent feel comfortable to tell the interviewer his or her true feelings? These problems can be dealt with by means of statistical techniques that measure the reliability of the questionnaire responses. There are also problems of no response. If the response to a questionnaire is voluntary and anonymous, those who choose to respond may have strong feelings, either positive or negative, about the content of the questionnaire, but they may represent only a small percentage of the total sample.

The use of the questionnaire method depends upon the depth of information desired and the purpose of the information. In some organizations, questionnaire follows questionnaire, but without any effective change. This often leads to apathy and indifference in answering any subsequent questionnaires. Therefore, it is usually beneficial to inform the respondents beforehand about the purpose of the questionnaire, how the information will be used, and how feedback of the results will be made available to them. The OD practitioner has an obligation to the client to ensure confidentiality of data and feedback of data to everyone who participates.

Questionnaires seem to achieve better information in terms of quantity and validity if the questionnaire shows that the researchers are familiar with key issues in the organization. Such event-based questionnaires, making it clear that the researchers are acquainted with important aspects of the organization, are more likely to reveal information about the organization than vague, theory-based questionnaires.

**OTHER TYPES OF INSTRUMENTS** Another technique for collecting data on work groups is called the **sociometric approach.** This method, developed by Jacob Moreno, is a means of obtaining quantitative data about the network of interrelationships within groups, usually on certain given dimensions.[8] Sociometric analysis provides a means of analyzing data about the choices or preferences within a group. The sociometric instrument asks specific questions, such as "With whom do you prefer to work?" "With whom do you communicate?" "Who helps you the most with technical problems?" Such data enable the investigator to diagram the structure and patterns of group interaction. The results are usually presented in what is called a **sociogram,** illustrated in Figure 5.5. The sociogram is a type of picture graph that documents communication patterns within a team or group. The highly chosen individuals are called **stars;** those with few or no

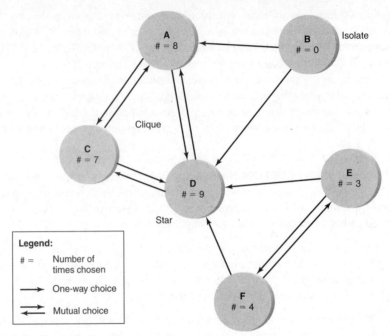

**FIGURE 5.5** Example of a Sociogram

choices are called **isolates.** Certain individuals will choose one another; this is known as **mutual choice.** When an individual chooses another but is not chosen in return, this designates a **one-way choice.** When three or more persons within a larger group select one another (mutual choices), this is termed a **clique.** The existence of subgroups may indicate lack of group cohesion and coordination.

The sociogram represents each member of the group by a circle, with choices designated by arrows indicating the direction of choice. The number of choices may be written in the circle under the person's name or code letter. Sociometric techniques are useful because they provide insights into the informal structure, give some indications of group cohesiveness, and aid in pointing out possible operating problems.

Other data-collecting methods include the use of indirect questions or ambiguous stimuli to gain information. An example of this would be the thematic apperception test (TAT), used to measure the intensity of achievement, power, and affiliation motivation profiles of organization members.[9] Some researchers have reported on the use of collages and drawings made by organization members as a means of inferring the organization's climate.[10]

**DIRECT OBSERVATION** Another important source of data for the OD practitioner is direct observation of member behaviors and interactions. The practitioner observes how people go about task performance and how they act or react in response to specific situations. The norms and attitudes expressed by members are also an important source of data. The observer looks for inconsistent or discordant behaviors: situations in which the observed actions differ from what was previously described or what is expected.

The practitioner may use a diagram (such as a sociogram) to chart the communication process in team meetings, identifying, for example, communications flows and patterns. Many practitioners recommend that the observer be as inconspicuous as possible, should not use a stopwatch (or other equipment), and should not take notes while observing. If making notes is unavoidable, the observer should leave the area before doing so. Some observers use indirect observation; that is, while seemingly observing one section, they may actually be observing another section across the room.

It is often valuable to visit work sites, field locations, or assembly-line operations to compare observed with reported behavior. This is obviously of greater value if the observer has a reasonably clear idea of what to look for. Observation varies from highly systematic, structured observations to nonsystematic, random observations. The more systematic the planning, recording, and observing, the greater the likelihood that observation will yield reliable and useful data. Too often, the observers' own biases influence what they see.

**INTERVIEWS** Interviewing is one of the most widely used data-gathering techniques in OD programs. Interviews are more direct, personal, and flexible than questionnaires and are very well suited for studies of interaction and behavior. Two advantages, in particular, set interviewing apart from other techniques. First, interviews are flexible and can be used in many different situations. For example, they can be used to determine motives, values, and attitudes. Second, interviewing is the only technique that provides two-way communication. This permits the interviewer to learn more about the problems, challenges, and limitations of the organization. Interviewing usually begins with the initial intervention and is best administered in a systematic manner by a trained interviewer. Data-gathering interviews usually last at least one hour; the purpose is to get the interviewees to talk freely about things that are important to them and to share these perceptions in an honest and straightforward manner. It is frequently the case that people really want to talk about things that they feel are important. If the OD practitioner asks appropriate questions, interviewing can yield important results.

The advantage of the interview method is that it provides data that are virtually unobtainable through other methods. Subjective data, such as norms, attitudes, and values, which are largely inaccessible through observation, may be readily inferred from effective interviews. The disadvantages of the interview are the amount of time involved, the training and skill required of the interviewer, the biases and resistances of the respondent, and the difficulty of ensuring comparability of data across respondents.

The interview itself may take on several different formats. It can be directed or nondirected. In a **directed interview,** certain kinds of data are desired, and therefore, specific questions are asked. The questions are usually formulated in advance to ensure uniformity of responses. The questions themselves may be open ended or closed. **Open-ended questions** allow the respondent to be free and unconstrained in answering, such as "How would you describe the work atmosphere of this organization?" The responses may be very enlightening, but may also be difficult to record and quantify. **Closed questions,** which can be answered by a yes, no, or some other brief response, are easily recorded and are readily quantifiable but may not reveal critical data.

In a **nondirected interview,** the interview's direction is chosen by the respondent, with little guidance or direction by the interviewer. If questions are used in a nondirected interview, open-ended questions will be more appropriate than closed questions. A nondirected interview could begin with the interviewer saying, "Tell me about your job here." This could be followed by "You seem to be excited about your work." The data from such an interview can be very detailed and significant but difficult to analyze because the interview is unstructured. An example of data-collection methods, including interviewing, is **OD Application: Data Collection and Diagnosis at McDonald's.** It also includes information on diagnosis and how the diagnosis was used to change McDonald's restaurant business.

---

## OD Application: Data Collection and Diagnosis at McDonald's[11]

Back in the later part of 2002, top managers of McDonald's Corporation became aware that they had a problem based on their earnings and profitability figures. Through a series of meetings where they made an assessment of where they were, they decided that McDonald's had to deliver a better experience for its customers. But just specifically, what was the problem and how to solve it remained a challenge. CEO James Skinner said, "We had lost our focus. We had taken our eyes off our fries, if you will." Continuing, he said, "To focus on our customers, we have to have a robust consumer-insight process."

Consequently, around 2003, McDonald's adopted a system of mining data that turned out to be something like mining gold. McDonald's had always checked in with customers, but the data were largely anecdotal. And there was a lack of consistency between reviewers doing customer interviews: a passing grade from two different reviewers did not mean the same thing in terms of quality of food and service.

McDonald's already had in place an information network that funneled real-time sales data to corporate headquarters. But sales data didn't say anything about the customer's opinion of the food or service. Declining sales figures indicated that there was a problem, but it left a lot to be desired in terms of discovering the underlying problems: Stale buns? Rubbery-tasting meat? Dirty tables? Long service lines? A promotion for a toy at the competition across the street? A 99¢ special at Burger King?

McDonald's started sending mystery-diners to restaurants—but not just to ding franchisees with a failing grade. They collected data in a manner that would be more useful to the individual store. The mystery-diners graded such things as speed of service, food temperature, cleanliness, and whether the counter crew smiled. Six-month and year-to-date averages for each store were made available on a McDonald's internal Web site, along with regional averages for other stores. Operators could find out where

*(continued)*

they had a consistent problem, maybe cold buns, and ignore a one-time problem, such as a dirty counter.

Simultaneously, McDonald's conducted in-depth interviews with repeat customers. What it discovered was that many customers ate at McDonald's because they had no better alternative. The interviews found that people didn't like things like the Big Mac sauce, the seasoning in the beef patties, limp and microwaved buns, and long lines at drive-up windows. In short, they found more people disliking the brand than liking it. The data indicated that the solution was in delivering a better experience for the customers rather than more restaurants. CEO Skinner said that they "were more willy-nilly before. The attitude was we'll make it and they'll buy it. We didn't spend enough time listening to our customers."

McDonald now has food studios in all its major geographic segments: Oak Brook, Illinois, Hong Kong, and Paris. The strategy to take on Starbucks by selling quality coffee and at a cheaper price is paying off. Coffee stations with Starbucks-style baristas separate from the main counter are being installed. The expanded menu into coffees and smoothies at beverage stations serves dual purposes of selling more beverages and attracting customers at nonpeak times. This builds on the strategy launched in 2003 to increase traffic at existing stores rather than opening more stores.

Data mining gives management at McDonald's, from the CEO to the local store, the information it needs to better serve customers in very specific ways. The data serve as the base for implementing a long-range strategy of changing McDonald's.

**Questions**

1. Research McDonald's and evaluate its strategy of separate beverage stations.
2. In lieu of in-depth interviews, what are some other methods McDonald's could have used to gather data? What are some advantages and disadvantages of McDonald's method and your suggestions?

## THE IMPLEMENTATION OF DATA COLLECTION

Data collection begins with a decision about from whom to obtain data and how many respondents there should be. The use of interviews may limit the number of respondents, whereas the use of a questionnaire may increase the number. Data should be collected from several levels and departments in the organization, but different questions may be needed for each of them.

Once an appropriate technique has been selected, the actual data-collection program must be accomplished. This includes the operational aspects of designing, printing, distributing, and collecting the data-collection instrument. Outside data-collection agents are typically more effective than internal personnel. The use of outside data-collection agents is recommended because it apparently makes respondents feel more secure and trusting that candid answers will not be used against them. There are companies that develop data-collection instruments, test them, and make them available commercially. The disadvantage is that such instruments may be too generalized and not focused enough for a specific organization to get reliable and useful data.

Once again, confidentiality of data is a critical issue. A small pilot study or beta test of the data-collection instrument is also a good idea. This should include a practice analysis before the large-scale data collection begins to ensure that every possible problem is corrected.

### The Analysis of Data

The techniques for analyzing data vary from relatively straightforward, simple methods to highly sophisticated statistical techniques. Several important questions must be considered before a data-collecting method is selected: How are the data to be analyzed? Are they to be analyzed statistically, and if so, what type of analysis is to be used? Will the data be processed by hand or by computer? Will they be coded, and if so, how? These questions must be taken into account prior to data collection so that the data can be used to draw inferences and conclusions. This is especially true with large-scale questionnaires or interviews, because the large amount of data makes processing a difficult task. The analysis may include comparisons of different divisions within the organization. Management levels can also be compared. To make comparisons, however, it is necessary to properly code the questionnaires or interviews.

### Evaluating the Effectiveness of Data Collection

A systematic data-collection program has to establish some criteria for how well the data meet the objectives in terms of quantity and quality. Obviously, the sample has to be large enough to enable generalization of results. The accuracy of the data, that is, the degree to which the data deviate from the truth, is also an important factor.

A number of criteria may be used to compare data-collection techniques. There is necessarily a trade-off between data quantity and accuracy, on the one hand, and collection cost and time spent collecting, on the other. Naturally, the practitioner wants to obtain the best available data that can be generated within the given cost and time constraints. The following criteria lay out some guidelines:

**THE VALIDITY OF THE DATA**  Probably the most important question is: Are we measuring and collecting data on the dimensions that we intend to measure? OD programs frequently have to deal with difficult subjective parameters such as attitudes and values.

**THE TIME TO COLLECT DATA**  How long will it take to gather the data using any given technique? How much time is available? Experience suggests that data collection usually takes longer than planned.

**THE COST OF DATA COLLECTION**  How much do the data cost? A large-scale interviewing program costs a great deal of time and money. The practitioner and the client must determine how much money can be spent in the data-gathering stage. They should also consider the problem of diminishing returns: What is the minimum number of interviews needed for a reliable measure?

**THE ORGANIZATIONAL CULTURE AND NORMS**  The practitioner has to decide what techniques are best suited to a given organization's culture and will yield the most valid data given these constraints. For example: Are people likely to be open and candid, or hidden and resistant? Does the climate call for open confrontation and questions or a more indirect form of data gathering?

**THE HAWTHORNE EFFECT IN DATA COLLECTING**  One of the most difficult factors to eliminate is the so-called **Hawthorne effect**—the effect the observer has on the subject. The very act of investigating and observing may influence the behavior of those being investigated.

One characteristic of successful change programs is that practitioners gather data about organizational problems before initiating a change effort. An effective data-collection process enables the change effort to focus on specific problems rather than rely upon a generalized program. The data-collection stage provides managers and organization members with hard data that can be compared with intuitive, subjective problem awareness.

## DIAGNOSTIC MODELS

Diagnosis is based on an understanding of how an organization functions. OD practitioners use diagnostic models to assess organizations. One method of diagnosis is the system approach discussed earlier in Chapter 2. **Diagnostic models** play a critical role in an organization development program. The models are useful as they assist in providing a conceptual framework to understand better the organization, its many components, and how well they function as a system. This enables the practitioner to focus attention on identified problem areas instead of using a shotgun approach. The trend now is to ask employees to rate the organization's progress on corporate change, empowerment, and similar issues. Each of the various diagnostic models may be used to analyze the structure, culture, and behavior of the organization. Several diagnostic models will be examined briefly in this section.

### Differentiation-and-Integration Model

The **differentiation-and-integration model,** sometimes referred to as the analytical model, stresses the importance of a sound analytical diagnosis as the basis for planned change in organizations.[12] The model was developed to study and understand interdepartmental issues by conducting a careful diagnosis of the organization's problem areas. Most organizations are composed of departments or divisions; that is, the organization is made up of differentiated functions or units that must be integrated into a unified effort if the organization is to be effective.

The model begins with a study of how much differentiation exists between the work units. Highly differentiated units may have developed within an organization because of geographic dispersion, competitive conditions in the marketplace, backgrounds of members, and so forth. In a study by the originators of the model, they found that members of work units differed not only in the type of work they did but in their ways of thinking and behaving.[13] There are obviously differences in the types of tasks that are performed between work units; for example, the tasks of the finance department and the advertising department are very different. But more subtle are the differences that may, or may not, exist in the ways these two departments have of solving problems, thinking, and behaving. These are differences that exist not as a result of any policy manual or organization chart. Furthermore, due to the culture and history of organizations, similar units but in different organizations will have degrees of differentiation. For example, the degree of differentiation of similar units at Microsoft will be different than at Google.

In conjunction with the analysis of the differentiation of the work units, the model also calls for an analysis of the integration required between work units. Various degrees of cooperation and collaboration are required between departments and divisions. Some units have little or no need to work together, while other units need to be highly integrated. For example, an analysis of one organization may show that marketing and engineering departments must be closely integrated for successful operations. But finance and human resources departments can function somewhat independently of one another and still be successful. Market and competitive conditions will also influence the degree of integration required of work units within the organization.

When work units are highly differentiated because of the nature of their work, it will be easier to obtain integration between them if the members have similar ways of solving problems and behaving. Conversely, it will be more difficult to achieve integration if the members have different and contradictory ways of solving problems and behaving. An even more difficult challenge to achieve integration exists if units need to be highly differentiated in their tasks, their ways of solving problems, and behaving, but yet they must be closely integrated. For example, in a software development company, a section is responsible for human interface elements, and another section is responsible for writing the computer program. The section working on the human interface elements (the look and feel) of the software is responsible for the wording and appearance of menus, the design of icons, and the flow of the program to accommodate the way a user of the software thinks. The people in this area may be specialists in cognitive reasoning and linguistics but they know little about the programming required. Likewise, the programming analysts are experts in developing computer code in languages such as Java, Delphi, and C++, but they have little expertise in human interface requirements. These two units are differentiated substantially in the nature of their work and their ways of solving problems and thinking. Even their language will be different. Yet the two units need to be well-integrated for them to develop an effective software program.

The tasks of the work units within an organization can be examined in respect to four characteristics of the organization's environment: (1) the degree of departmental structure, (2) the time orientation of members, (3) the interpersonal orientation of members toward others, and (4) organization members' orientation toward goals. One example of how this model can be used is shown in Table 5.1, which presents the survey results of four departments in a hypothetical company. The data show that the finance and research departments are fairly wide apart in how their members view time, orientation toward others, and goals. Despite these differences, the two departments must work together. The differentiation-and-integration model may make it possible for the two departments to understand why they have differences and to develop ways to work better together. The data on these four characteristics provide a basis for structural or cultural changes in the department.

**TABLE 5.1 Example of Survey Results Using the Differentiation-and-Integration Model**

| Organization Units | Degree of Departmental Structure | Members' Orientation Toward Time | Members' Orientation Toward Others | Members' Orientation Toward Goals |
|---|---|---|---|---|
| Finance Department | High | Short | Controlling | Investment |
| Research Department | Low | Long | Permissive | Science |
| Marketing Department | Medium | Short | Permissive | Market |
| Production Department | High | Short | Directive | Product |

## The Sociotechnical-Systems Model

The **sociotechnical-systems model,** developed from the work of Eric Trist and others at the Tavistock Institute of Human Relations in Great Britain, analyzes the organization as a sociotechnical system interacting with its external environment.[14] According to Trist and his colleagues, every organization comprises a social system consisting of the network of interpersonal relationships and a technological system consisting of the task, activities, and tools used to accomplish the organization's purpose. These two systems—the social system and the technological system—are interrelated and interdependent because they function together to accomplish work. Furthermore, the internal system is an open system and is part of a larger environmental suprasystem. (See Chapter 2 and Figure 2.4 for a more detailed discussion of the sociotechnical system.)

Diagnosis determines how the social, technical, and suprasystem interrelate, with emphasis on the feedback or lack of feedback between the various subsystems. The model is one of an open system that optimizes the relationship between the social and technical parts of the organization. As an example, the model describes new technology but also describes how people will use the technology.

## The Force-Field Analysis Model

The **force-field analysis model,** originated by Kurt Lewin, is a general-purpose diagnostic technique.[15] This model views organizational behavior not as a static pattern but as a dynamic balance of forces working in opposite directions. In any organizational situation, there are forces that push for change and forces that hinder change. The forces acting to keep the organization table are called **restraining forces;** they put pressure on the organization not to change. Opposite forces, called **driving forces,** put pressure on the organization to change. If the forces for change and the forces against change are equal, the result is equilibrium and the organization remains stable, as shown in Figure 5.6. Lewin termed this state "quasi-stationary equilibrium." This technique assumes that at any given moment, an organization is in a state of **equilibrium;** put differently, it is balanced.

Change takes place when there is an imbalance between the two types of forces and continues until the opposing forces are brought back into equilibrium. The imbalance can be planned, and specifically brought about, by increasing the strength of some of the forces, by adding a new force, by decreasing the strength of some of the forces, or by a combination of these methods. An example of how force-field analysis can be used may be helpful. The general manager of a hospital, employing 300 workers and her immediate subordinates, identified the

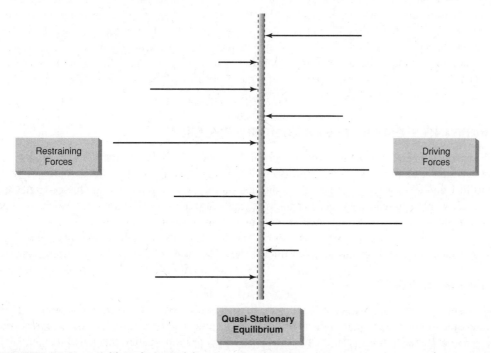

**FIGURE 5.6** Force-Field Analysis Model

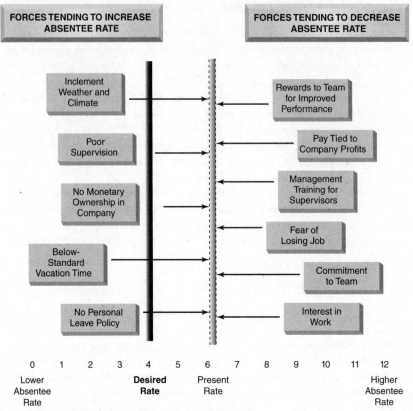

| FORCES TENDING TO INCREASE ABSENTEE RATE | FORCES TENDING TO DECREASE ABSENTEE RATE |
|---|---|
| Inclement Weather and Climate | Rewards to Team for Improved Performance |
| Poor Supervision | Pay Tied to Company Profits |
| No Monetary Ownership in Company | Management Training for Supervisors |
| | Fear of Losing Job |
| Below-Standard Vacation Time | Commitment to Team |
| No Personal Leave Policy | Interest in Work |

0   1   2   3   4   5   6   7   8   9   10   11   12

| | | | | |
|---|---|---|---|---|
| Lower Absentee Rate | | **Desired Rate** | Present Rate | Higher Absentee Rate |

**FIGURE 5.7   Example of the Use of Force-Field Analysis**

6 percent daily absentee rate as an area of concern. They determined that a 3 percent absentee rate would be much more acceptable. In other words, they found a "performance gap." After going over the survey results with the OD practitioner, it was decided to use force-field analysis to gain an improved diagnosis of this problem. In a brainstorming session, the work team listed all of the forces tending to restrain and increase absenteeism and assigned strengths to the forces. Figure 5.7 is a chart of what they produced.

The managers made the length of the arrows proportionate to the strength of the forces. They had a choice of several strategies to reduce the performance gap. They could decrease the strength of the restraining forces, increase the strength of the driving forces, or a combination of both. Generally, if the forces that put pressure on people (such as fear of losing their job) are increased, the tension within the system will also increase, possibly bringing about stronger resistance and unpredictable behavior. It is often better to increase forces that do not put pressure on people (for instance, a promotion policy that is more closely tied to an employee's absentee rate), to reduce restraining forces, or to add new driving forces.

## WARNING SIGNS IN THE DIAGNOSIS PROCESS

The change strategy and OD intervention techniques follow from the diagnosis. An inappropriate intervention can be very costly. Such programs can disrupt operations, generate resistance or even hostility among employees, and create additional problems. Using the wrong change strategies will either fail to produce the needed changes or lead to unnecessary changes at the expense of the client system. Ineffective change programs are usually the result of an inaccurate diagnosis.

The diagnostic phase presents some special problems. Because diagnosis is one of the most important stages in the OD process, the practitioner should be aware of the following warning signals.

### Confidentiality

The issue of confidentiality is a critical problem area in diagnosis. As noted in Chapter 3, in the discussion of practitioner ethics, the relationship of the client and practitioner is based upon privileged communication between the two. This often includes information that may be potentially damaging. The practitioner is entrusted with private information about the client. In one case, two practitioners carried on a casual conversation in the elevator about sensitive material revealed to them by the CEO, only to learn later that they had been overheard by an attorney who was a close personal friend of the CEO.

There are many similar examples indicating that practitioners cannot be too careful about how they handle confidential information. This goes back to the trust that the practitioner must be able to develop with organization members.

## Overdiagnosis

Sometimes a diagnosis goes on for so long that it is impossible to adopt a corrective program. The term "analysis paralysis" best describes this situation.[16] The diagnosis itself may become a ritual of continual analysis. An executive at one company, for example, commenting on his company's tendency to overdiagnose problems, said, "Everything has to be studied to death." The diagnosis may continue to a point where so many problems are identified that the client is overwhelmed by the complexity of the situation. While diagnosis is an important step, it can also be a delaying factor and prevent change programs from even getting started. In most situations, there are several problems that need correction. But if managers are faced with too many alternatives, the most important ones may be obscured or overlooked.

## The Crisis Diagnosis

The OD practitioner is often in danger of falling into the trap of attending only to the immediate, short-term crises that the client sees as immediate and important. Energy is often wasted on fighting symptoms or dealing with small crises as a way of avoiding the long-run change programs necessary to develop a more effective organization. Because of time pressures, a practitioner may go through an organization in a few days and quickly diagnose the problems. This often results in dealing only with the conspicuous problems, whereas more important but less visible ones may be missed.

## The Threatening and Overwhelming Diagnosis

An OD practitioner interacting with a client system and beginning to perceive possible problem areas may confront the client about them. There is a danger, however, that the practitioner may come across so blunt or so strong that the relationship with the client is weakened. Clients sometimes find it difficult to face and accept information about problem areas. The client may also be inundated with more information than can be dealt with in a meaningful way. If the diagnosis is too threatening or overwhelming, the client may resist or reject the entire change program.

## The Practitioner's Favorite Diagnosis

Practitioners have a tendency to fall victim to their own biases and selective perceptions. This may result in imposing a special or favorite diagnosis regardless of the nature of the problem. As an example, some practitioners see all problems as caused by organizational structure regardless of the actual circumstances. Other practitioners see every problem as arising from interpersonal behavior. The tendency to impose a favorite diagnosis on problems must always be kept in mind. Overreliance on a favorite technique may so distort the problem that it is impossible to find a solution. Variables that do not fit in are disregarded, and a well-designed solution is formulated for something that is not a problem.

As Lippitt, Watson, and Westley point out:

> The diagnostic orientation of the change agent is in many ways a self-fulfilling prediction. If he looks for difficulties in communication, for instance, he will find them; and if his help is directed toward improving communication patterns, success will demonstrate to the client system that a solution of communication problems necessarily results in a more satisfactory state of affairs. . . . The orientation of the change agent is a primary factor in determining the "facts" which the client system will discover to be true about its own situations.[17]

## The Diagnosis of Symptoms

As noted earlier, there is often a tendency to focus on the symptoms rather than on the underlying problems. The OD practitioner may be unduly influenced, say, by the data on high turnover rates and, in consequence, identify turnover as the problem. However, the turnover rate may only be a symptom of other problems, such as poor supervision, inadequate performance appraisal, or lack of compensation. An article in a business publication reported that revenues at one company fell by more than 40 percent over five years and that there were operating losses for 19 consecutive quarters. Falling revenues are the problem in some sense, but they are really a symptom of underlying problems. The problem was tracked further back to slowness in developing and delivering new products and consumer promotions to stores, inconsistent marketing, and the wasting of millions of dollars through inefficiency. Tracking back the problem even further disclosed a culture of past CEOs lording it over employees, and fiefdoms so fractious that they seldom communicated at all.[18]

In short, the diagnostic phase is an important and critical step in the OD process. The next chapter will expand the discussion of the diagnosis process by dealing with the process of OD practitioners identifying forces within individuals and organizations that cause resistance to change programs. The chapter will then cover the development of strategies that will increase the motivation to change.

## Summary

- **Diagnosis.** Organizational diagnosis is one of the most critsical and difficult elements in the OD process. Diagnosis has this importance because it leads to problem-solving action. A weak or inaccurate diagnosis prevents the practitioner and the client from identifying underlying forces and multiple causalities that would enable them to specify the nature of the problem.
- **Data Collection.** Intervention and data gathering take place throughout an OD program. Decisions about what information to collect and how it should be collected are difficult and important. No data-gathering method is right or wrong in itself; each method has its limitations as well as its strong points. The process of collecting information is an important step in an OD program because it provides a foundation for diagnosing problems and selecting change strategies and techniques. What must be determined is whether a given method is most appropriate for the specific objectives and climate of each unique situation.
- **Problem Solving.** In diagnosing an organization's problems, the practitioner and the client try to specify the problems, determine the underlying causes, and identify the opportunities for change. The practitioner sorts out factual from nonfactual information and searches for multiple sources of the problem condition. The outcome is an explicit and specific diagnosis upon which to base change efforts.

- **Diagnostic Process.** Diagnosis is not a simple process, because it encompasses both the client's needs and the system problems. The diagnostic process involves identifying the problems and assessing the readiness for change in the client system. It requires an understanding of the client's viewpoint. The practitioner must apply a system's approach by specifying the interrelationships of various elements of the client system. This requires organizing the available data or evidence into meaningful patterns.
- **Diagnostic Models.** Several diagnostic models have been described, including the analytical model, the emergent-group behavior model, the sociotechnical-systems model, and the force-field analysis model. The practitioner uses these models to facilitate the analysis of client system problems. The important factors and models in the diagnostic process have been described. This stage provides the foundation for subsequent OD interventions.
- **Implementation.** The practitioner needs maximum participation in the diagnostic process from members of the client system and needs to consider the impact of the diagnosis upon the relationship with the client. Since the practitioner may confront the client with unpleasant facts, the more objective the data and the more the analysis includes both strengths and weaknesses, the better the resulting OD program will be. During the diagnostic phase, the practitioner should be alert for danger signals or red-flag conditions.

## Review Questions

1. Describe the use of performance-gap analysis.
2. Compare and contrast the interview and survey methods of data collection.
3. List some possible types of organization data that you might find in your own organization or college that could be used in planning an OD program.

4. Explain the difference between symptoms and causes.
5. Identify and give examples of the force-field analysis model.

## Key Words and Concepts

| | | | |
|---|---|---|---|
| Clique | Directed Interview | Mutual Choice | Sociogram |
| Closed Questions | Driving Forces | Nondirected Interview | Sociometric approach |
| Data | Equilibrium | One-Way Choice | Sociotechnical-Systems |
| Diagnosis | Force-Field Analysis Model | Open-Ended Questions | Model |
| Diagnostic Models | Hawthorne Effect | Performance Gap | Stars |
| Differentiation-and- | Information | Questionnaires | Surveys |
| Integration Model | Isolates | Restraining Forces | |

# OD Skills Simulation 5.1

## The Acquisition Decision

*Total time suggested: 65 minutes.*

## A. Purpose

The purpose of this simulation is to experience and observe how information affects team decision making. Specifically, it will allow you to experience interdependence and to observe:

1. How team members share task information.
2. How various problem-solving strategies influence results.
3. How collaboration and competition affect team problem solving.

## B. Procedures

The two parameters of team effectiveness are (1) determination of an optimum solution to the problem and (2) completion in the shortest time.

*Step 1.* Prior to class, form teams of six members. Any extra persons may serve as additional observers. If there are fewer than six members, a member may play more than one vice president role, but each team should have at least one observer.

Each individual is to select and prepare one role from the following:

Vice President, Finance

Vice President, Human Resources

Vice President, Research and Development

Vice President, Marketing

Vice President, Production

Observer(s)

Read the Acquisitions Briefing Sheet and your role description before the class meeting. Review Table 5.2. Fill in the Individual Decision Work Sheet. Record your decision on the Executive Committee Decision Work Sheet, column 1. The observer should see Observer Forms A and B.

*Step 2.* Executive Committee Meeting. Your team is to select the correct acquisition candidate. Record your team's decision in column 2 of the Executive Committee Decision Work Sheet. Decisions are to be reached independently of the other teams in the class. The observer will not take an active part during this phase of the simulation.

*Time suggested for Step 2: 30 minutes.*

*Step 3.* In your teams, the observer will provide feedback and guide the discussion using Observer Forms A and B and the questions listed below. All team members are encouraged to ask questions and provide feedback. Conclude your discussion with the following questions:

1. What behaviors seemed to help your team to successfully complete its task?
2. What factors inhibited problem solving?
3. How much time was spent on deciding how to solve the problem?
4. How was information shared among the team? What does the sociogram for the team look like?
5. How did issues of authority or power affect the team?

*Time suggested for Step 3: 15 minutes.*

*Step 4.* Each team lists its committee decision on the board. Discuss the questions in Step 3 with the entire class.

*Time suggested for Step 4: 20 minutes.*

## Acquisition Briefing Sheet

Instructions to the team:

1. You are a committee made up of the key managers of SOS Corporation.
2. You must workout the problem as a team.

**3.** This is the meeting to make a decision about the acquisition from the possible candidates.

**4.** Basically, the data you bring with you are in your head.

**5.** Assume that there is an optimum solution.

**6.** Assume that all data are correct.

**7.** You may use a calculator or a personal computer.

**8.** There must be substantial consensus that the problem has been solved.

**9.** You have 45 minutes to workout the exercise.

## General Company Information

Your committee is made up of the managers of SOS Corporation, a young and growing medium-sized software company. Your mission is to locate and identify the best acquisition candidate for your firm. Your company is quick to sell units that don't offer high-growth, high-performance opportunities.

You have already examined the data on eight companies. Your first order of business is to arrive at a consensus on the best selection from among the candidates listed in Table 5.2.

## ROLE DESCRIPTIONS
## (READ ONLY YOUR ROLE)

**Vice President, Finance.** Your mission is to locate and identify the best financial acquisition candidate for your firm. Your company is quick to exit businesses that don't offer high-growth, high-performance opportunities.

You have already examined the data on eight companies. You think that the sales growth rate must be greater than 10 percent over the previous year in order to fit this criterion, and the price/earnings ratio should be 11 or less. Should you decide to consider payback (price paid divided by expected annual savings) in the acquisition decision, anything seven years or more is a low payback. You feel that the Wall Street reaction will be important, as will future earnings.

**Vice President, Human Resources.** Your mission is to locate and identify the best acquisition candidate for your firm. Your company is quick to exit businesses that don't offer high-growth, high-performance opportunities.

You have already examined the data on eight companies. You think that the reaction of the investment community on Wall Street must be better than fair if you are to maintain performance. Also, the company should have at least a moderate chance of being available. If you decide to consider the earnings growth rate, use the previous year's earnings as the base year. You want to avoid any large-scale downsizing, in order to achieve savings of over $30 million.

**Vice President, Research and Development.** Your mission is to locate and identify the best acquisition candidate for your firm. Your company is quick to exit businesses that don't offer high-growth, high-performance opportunities.

You have already examined the data on eight companies. You think that research and development should be at least 6 percent of sales in order to maintain technological capabilities, and annual sales must be at least $225 million. If you decide to consider the rate of sales growth, use the previous year's sales as the base year. The company has decided to use a modified price/earnings ratio of using the ratio of price paid for the company to its current earnings. You feel that availability is important so that prolonged negotiations can be avoided and the new company can be quickly integrated into current operations.

**Vice President, Marketing.** Your mission is to locate and identify the best acquisition candidate for your firm. Your company is quick to exit businesses that don't offer high-growth, high-performance opportunities.

You have already examined the data on eight companies. You think that the price should be less than $300 million to fit the performance goal, and the earnings growth rate should be greater than 5 percent over the previous year. Should you decide to consider an appropriate payback, anything less than five years is a high payback. The annual savings of the acquisition is an average projected for the next eight years. You are not concerned about antitrust reactions, because SOS and the companies being considered do not dominate the software industry.

**Vice President, Production.** Your mission is to locate and identify the best acquisition candidate for your firm. Your company is quick to exit businesses that don't offer high-growth, high-performance opportunities.

You have already examined the data on eight companies. You think that the payback should be moderate or high to gain economies of scale. You would like a favorable price/earnings ratio, but the lower the ratio the better. Antitrust reaction should be moderate or less. You want a high level of expected annual savings.

**Observer(s).** Your job is to collect information during the Executive Committee Meeting. Use Observer Forms A and B. Also, refer to the questions in Step 3. You should not take part in the decision that is made during the Executive Committee Meeting (Step 2). In Step 3, you will provide feedback from the Observer Forms.

**TABLE 5.2** Acquisition Alternative Summary Sheet

| Company | Previous Annual Sales (Millions) | Current Annual Estimated Sales (Millions) | Previous Annual Earnings (Millions) | Current Annual Estimated Earnings (Millions) | Price (Millions) | Research and Development (Millions) | Expected Annual Savings (Millions) | Antitrust Reaction | Availability for Purchase | Wall Street Reaction |
|---------|------|------|----|----|-----|----|----|----------|-------------|-----------|
| Altitude | 330 | 400 | 20 | 24 | 240 | 24 | 38 | Moderate | Most likely | Good |
| Bravado | 185 | 200 | 9 | 10 | 120 | 10 | 35 | Minimum | Moderate | Fair |
| Century | 325 | 350 | 27 | 30 | 315 | 21 | 65 | High | Most likely | Poor |
| DiGiTron | 210 | 250 | 10 | 13 | 172 | 20 | 35 | Low | Definite | Good |
| EcoTech | 135 | 150 | 7 | 8 | 75 | 6 | 10 | Extreme | Moderate | Fair |
| Firestorm | 350 | 380 | 20 | 22 | 228 | 23 | 50 | Absent | Low | Poor |
| GeoMark | 460 | 500 | 16 | 18 | 157 | 40 | 23 | Moderate | Moderate | Fair |
| Hypothesis | 185 | 220 | 10 | 14 | 185 | 14 | 30 | Minimum | Moderate | Excellent |

# INDIVIDUAL DECISION WORK SHEET

Role: Vice President of _____

Name: _____

| Previous Annual Sales | Current Annual Est. Sales | % Sales Growth | Previous Annual Earnings | Current Annual Est. Earnings | Price | P&E Ratio | R&D | Expected Annual Savings | Payback | Antitrust Reaction | Availability for Purchase | Wall Street Reaction | Total Reaction |
|---|---|---|---|---|---|---|---|---|---|---|---|---|---|
| Altitude | | | | | | | | | | | | | |
| Bravado | | | | | | | | | | | | | |
| Century | | | | | | | | | | | | | |
| DiGiTron | | | | | | | | | | | | | |
| EcoTech | | | | | | | | | | | | | |
| Firestorm | | | | | | | | | | | | | |
| GeoMark | | | | | | | | | | | | | |
| Hypothesis | | | | | | | | | | | | | |

## EXECUTIVE COMMITTEE WORK SHEET

| Company | (1)<br>Personal<br>Ranking | (2)<br>Team<br>Ranking |
|---|---|---|
| Altitude | | |
| Bravado | | |
| Century | | |
| DiGiTron | | |
| EcoTech | | |
| Firestorm | | |
| GeoMark | | |
| Hypothesis | | |

# OBSERVER FORM A

Instructions: Complete this sociogram on the team you are observing. Draw direction arrows for communication flow. Identify behaviors shown by participants.

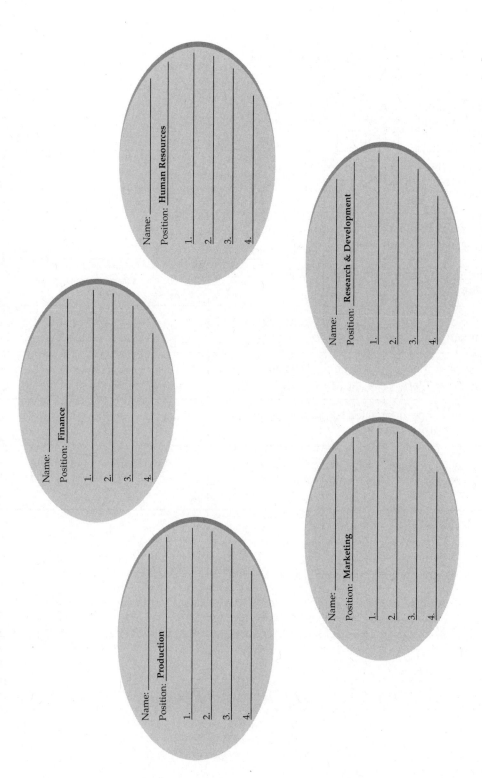

## OBSERVER FORM B

| Description of Behavior | Names of Individuals Observed |
|---|---|
| Encourager—friendly and responsive to others; offers praise; accepts others' points of view. | |
| Harmonizer—mediates differences; relieves tension in conflict situations; gets people to explore their differences. | |
| Compromiser—when own idea is involved in a conflict, offers compromise and admits error. Tries to maintain group cohesion. | |
| Expresses group feelings—senses the feeling or mood of the group, others, and self and shares this with group. | |
| Gatekeeper—keeps communications open; suggests procedures for sharing information with others. | |
| Initiator—proposes tasks or goals, suggests ways to solve problems. | |
| Information or opinion giver—offers facts; states own belief or opinion. | |
| Clarifier—interprets ideas or suggestions; clears up confusion; gives examples. | |
| Summarizer—pulls together related suggestions; offers conclusion for the group to accept or reject. | |
| Others: | |
| | |
| | |

# CASE: THE OLD FAMILY BANK

The Old Family Bank is a large bank in a southeastern city. As a part of a comprehensive internal management study, H. Day, vice president of management information systems, examined the turnover, absenteeism, and productivity figures of all of the bank's work groups. The results Day obtained offered no real surprises except in the case of the check-sorting and computer services departments.

## THE STUDY

The study revealed that, in general, the departments displaying high turnover and absenteeism rates had low production figures, and those with low turnover and absenteeism were highly productive. When the check-sorting and computer services figures were analyzed, Day discovered that the two departments were tied for the lead for the lowest turnover and absenteeism figures. What was surprising was that the check-sorting department ranked first as the most productive unit, whereas the computer services department ranked last.

This inconsistency was further complicated by the fact that the working conditions for check-sorting employees were very undesirable. They worked in a large open room that was hot in the summer and cold in the winter. They worked alone and operated high-speed, check-sorting machines requiring a high degree of accuracy and concentration. There was little chance for interaction because they took rotating coffee breaks.

The computer services room was air-conditioned, with a stable temperature year round; it had perfect lighting and was quiet and comfortable. Both groups were known to be highly cohesive, and the workers in each department functioned well with one another. This observation was reinforced by the study's finding of the low levels of turnover and absenteeism.

## THE INTERVIEW DATA

In an effort to understand this phenomenon, Day decided to interview the members of both departments in order to gain some insight into the dynamics of each group's behavior. Day discovered that the check-sorting department displayed a great deal of loyalty to the company. Most of the group members were unskilled or semiskilled workers; although they had no organized union, they all felt that the bank had made special efforts to keep their wages and benefits in line with unionized operations. They knew that their work required team effort and were committed to high performance.

A quite different situation existed in the computer services department. Although the workers liked their fellow employees, there was a uniform feeling among this highly skilled group that management put more emphasis on production than on support units. They felt that the operating departments had received better pay raises and that the wage gap did not reflect the skill differences between employees. As a result, a large percentage of the group's members displayed little loyalty to the bank, even though they were very close to one another. (Use the Case Analysis Form on the following page.)

# THE OLD FAMILY BANK CASE ANALYSIS FORM

Name: _____

I. Problems

  A. Macro

    1. _____

    _____

    2. _____

    _____

  B. Micro

    1. _____

    _____

    2. _____

    _____

II. Causes

    1. _____

    _____

    2. _____

    _____

    3. _____

    _____

III. Systems affected

    1. _____

    _____

    2. _____

    _____

    3. _____

    _____

IV. Alternatives

    1. _____

    _____

    2. _____

    _____

    3. _____

    _____

V. Recommendations

_____

_____

_____

_____

_____

_____

## Chapter 5 Endnotes

1. Michael Beer and Bert Spector, "Organizational Diagnosis," *Journal of Counseling & Development,* vol. 7, no 6 (July/August 1993), pp. 643–50.

2. John H. Johnson, "Another Look at Employee Surveys," *Training & Development,* July 1993, pp. 15–18.

3. Michael Malone, "Intel Reboots for the 21st Century," *Wall Street Journal,* September 27–28, 2008, p. A17.

4. Geoffrey A. Fowler, "Auctions Fade in eBay's Bid for Growth," *Wall Street Journal,* May 26, 2009, p. A1; Douglas MacMillan, "Good News from eBay," *Business Week,* April 23, 2009, www.businessweek.com; Peter Burrows, "eBay Outlines Three-Year Revival Plan," *Business Week,* March 12, 2009, www.businessweek.com; Douglas MacMillan, "eBay Sales: Going, Going . . .," *Business Week,* January 22, 2009, www.businessweek.com; Catherine Holahan, "eBay Auctions: Going, Going," *Business Week,* June 19, 2008, www.businessweek.com; Chuck Salter, "eBay's Chaos Theory," *Fast Company,* November 2007, pp. 101–7.

5. For a classic book on the role of data-based methods used in organization development, see David A. Nadler, *Feedback and Organization Development: Using Data-Based Methods* (Reading, MA: Addison-Wesley, 1977).

6. Amy Merrick, "Sears Orders Fashion Makeover from the Lands' End Catalog," *Wall Street Journal,* January 28, 2004, pp. A1, A8.

7. K. Lindström, M. Dallner, A. Elo, F. Gamberale, S. Knardahl, A. Skogstad et al., R*eview of Psychological and Social Factors at Work and Suggestions for the General Nordic Questionnaire (QPS Nordic)* (Copenhagen, Denmark: Nordic Council of Ministers. no. 1997:15 [1997]).

8. Jacob Moreno, *Who Shall Survive?* 2nd ed. (New York: Beacon House, 1953).

9. David C. McClelland, *The Achieving Society* (Princeton, NJ: Van Nostrand, 1961).

10. Jack Fordyce and Raymond Weil, *Managing with People* (Reading, MA: Addison-Wesley, 1971), pp. 146–52.

11. Judith Crown, "Coffee Gets Hotter at McDonald's," *Business Week*, January 9, 2008, www.businessweek.com/; "Online Extra: Skinner's Winning McDonald's Recipe," *Business Week,* February 5, 2007; Daniel Kruger, "You Want Data with That?" *Forbes,* March 29, 2004, pp. 58–60; Pallavi Gogoi and Michael Arndt, "Hamburger Hell," *Business Week,* March 3, 2003, pp. 104–8.

12. Paul Lawrence and Jay Lorsch, *Developing Organizations: Diagnosis and Action* (Reading, MA: Addison-Wesley, 1969), pp. 11–14.

13. Paul Lawrence and Jay Lorsch, *Organization and Environment: Managing Differentiation and Integration* (Boston: Harvard Graduate School of Business Administration Division of Research, 1967).

14. F. Emery, *Characteristics of Sociotechnical Systems* (London: Tavistock Institute, 1959).

15. Kurt Lewin, "Frontiers in Group Dynamics, Concepts, Methods and Reality in Social Science," *Human Relations,* June 1974, pp. 5–42.

16. For additional information on analysis paralysis, see Babette E. Bensoussan and Craig S. Fleisher, *Analysis without Paralysis, 10 Tools to Make Better Strategic Decisions* (Upper Saddle River, NJ: Pearson Education, Inc., 2008).

17. Ronald Lippitt, Jeanne Watson, and Bruce Westley, *The Dynamics of Planned Change* (New York: Harcourt Brace Jovanovich, 1958), p. 65.

18. Gerry Khermouch, "Putting a Pretty Face on Revlon," *Business Week,* November 3, 2003, pp. 92–94.

# Overcoming Resistance to Change

## LEARNING OBJECTIVES

**Upon completing this chapter, you will be able to:**

1. Identify the forces within individuals and organizations that cause resistance to change programs.
2. Recognize strategies that can increase the motivation to change.
3. Diagnose the forces driving and resisting organization change.
4. Experience reactions to a change situation.

## PREMEETING PREPARATION

1. Read Chapter 6.
2. Prepare for OD Skills Simulation 6.1. Complete Step 1 and read the Company Situation.
3. Read and analyze Case: The Hexadecimal Company.

## CHANGE AND REINVENT

Faced with continuing economic pressures and increasing competition, many organizations are being forced to radically change and reinvent their processes. Reengineering, right-sizing, transforming, and downsizing are frequent responses to these pressures. Especially in light of significant economic challenges, organizations today face a major challenge in managing change effectively. The costs are often high when an organization fails to change in the ways necessary for success. "A recession creates winners and losers just like a boom," says Mauro F. Guillen, a professor of management at the University of Pennsylvania's Wharton School.[1] Organizations in a dynamic environment must have the capacity to adapt quickly in order to survive. Fast-moving capability on the part of an organization is more than ever essential in an economic recession where growth will not bail out bad decisions. In a self-critique, Cisco's CEO John Chambers observes, "Without exception, all of my biggest mistakes occurred because I moved too slowly."[2]

The most serious challenges to improving programs all have the same focus: people. Managers developing and implementing programs to keep today's organizations competitive in a tough, constantly changing environment must deal with resistance to change. The team approach has proven to be successful, but only when cultural and communication barriers are overcome. In most cases, the speed and complexity of change may severely test the capabilities of managers and members. Unless members prepare themselves emotionally for change, the sheer speed with which change occurs can be overwhelming.

Solving organizational problems usually involves the introduction of change. If the required changes are small or isolated, they can usually be accomplished without major problems. However, there are often significant problems when the changes are on a larger scale and involve many individuals and subunits. As organizational problems emerge, managers attempt to take corrective actions. These corrective actions often affect patterns of work or values, and in consequence meet with resistance. Problems of many kinds may emerge when an organizational change program is initiated. The problems most likely to be encountered are associated with human resistance to changing patterns of work behavior.[3]

On a personal level, change represents the alteration of set patterns of behavior, defined relationships with others, work procedures, and job skills. On an organizational level, change means that policies, procedures, sunk costs, organization structures, manufacturing processes, and workflows will no longer be the same. Both people and organizations have vested interests in the status quo. Managers, change agents, and other change advocates must deal with the possible resistance to change before implementing any OD strategy or technique. "The single biggest reason organizational changes fail is that no one thought about endings or planned to manage their impact on people. Naturally concerned about the future, planners and implementers usually forget that people have to let go of the present first. They forget that while the first task of change management is to understand the destination and how to get there, the first task of transition management is to convince people to leave home."[4]

This chapter examines an issue important to any OD program: the motivation of the organization system. What makes an individual, a team, or an organization believe that a change would be beneficial? What forces interfere with and restrict the implementation of a change program? What phases of resistance does a typical change program encounter? Finally, what can a manager, change agent, and OD practitioner do to increase the probability that a change program will be accepted?

Once an organization or its key members decide to implement a change program, they have to energize the forces favoring it. This chapter will give you a better understanding of this process by explaining the phases of resistance to change programs, the driving and restraining forces, and the actions that increase the probability of change.

## THE LIFE CYCLE OF RESISTANCE TO CHANGE

Organization programs such as downsizing, reengineering, and TQM (discussed in future chapters) involve innovations and changes that will probably encounter some degree of resistance. This resistance will be evident in individuals and groups in such forms as controversy, hostility, and conflict, either overt or covert. The response to change tends to move through a lifecycle that typically consists of five phases.[5]

### Phase 1: Change Introduced

In the first phase, there are only a few people who see the need for change and take reform seriously. As a fringe element of the organization, they may be openly criticized, ridiculed, and persecuted by whatever methods the organization has at its disposal and thinks appropriate to handle dissidents and force them to conform to established organizational norms. The resistance looks massive. At this point, the change program may die, or it may continue to grow. Large organizations seem to have more difficulty bringing about change than smaller organizations.

### Phase 2: Forces Identified

As the movement for change begins to grow, the forces for and against it become identifiable. The change is discussed and is more thoroughly understood by more of the organization's members. Greater understanding may lessen the perceived threat of the change. In time, the novelty and strangeness of the change tends to disappear.

### Phase 3: Direct Conflict

In this phase, there is a direct conflict and showdown between the forces for and against the change. This phase will probably mean life or death to the change effort, because the exponents of the change often underestimate the strength of their opponents. Those in an organization who see a change as good and needed often find it difficult to believe how far the opposition will go to put a stop to the change.

### Phase 4: Residual Resistance

If the supporters of the change are in power after the decisive battles, they will see the remaining resistance as stubborn and a nuisance. There is still a possibility that the resisters will mobilize enough support to shift the balance of power. Wisdom is necessary in dealing with the overt opposition and also with the sizable element that is not openly opposed to the change but also is not convinced of its benefits.

### Phase 5: Change Established

In the last phase, the resisters to the change are as few and as alienated as the advocates were in the first phase. Although the description of the five phases may give the impression that a battle

## OD Application: The Five Phases of Resistance to Change

### Phase 1: Change Introduced

In the 1970s, the environmental movement began to grow. The first Earth Day was held in 1970. Widespread interest in environmental concerns subsided during the 1980s. Some political officials neglected environmental concerns, and environmentalists were often portrayed as extremists and radicals. The forces for change were small, but pressure for change persisted through court actions, elected officials, and group actions.

### Phase 2: Forces Identified

Environmental supporters and opponents became more identifiable in the 1980s. A Secretary of the Interior at the time, James Watt, was perhaps the most vocal and visible opponent of environmental concerns and served as a "lightning rod" for proenvironmental forces like the Sierra Club and the Wilderness Society. As time passed, educational efforts by environmental groups increasingly delivered their message. The public now had information and scientific data that enabled it to understand the problem.

### Phase 3: Direct Conflict

The Clean Air Act passed by Congress in 1990 represented the culmination of years of confrontation between pro- and antienvironmental forces. The bill was passed several months after national and worldwide Earth Day events. Corporations criticized for contributing to environmental problems took out large newspaper and television ads to explain how they were reducing pollution and cleaning up the environment. The "greening" of corporations became very popular.

### Phase 4: Residual Resistance

One example is the confrontation between Greenpeace (an environmental group) and Shell Oil. The Greenpeace group had been campaigning for weeks to block the Royal Dutch/Shell group from disposing of the towering Brent Spar oil-storage rig by sinking it deep in the Atlantic Ocean. As a small helicopter sought to land Greenpeace protesters on the rig's deck, Shell blasted high-powered water cannons to fend off the aircraft. This was all captured on film and shown on TV around the world. Four days after the incident, Shell executives made a humiliating about-face; they agreed to comply with Greenpeace's requests and dispose of the Brent Spar on land. This incident, like the *Exxon Valdez* oil spill, shows how high-profile cases can ignite worldwide public interest.

### Phase 5: Change Established

Much of the world now sees environmental-responsible behavior and energy conservation as a necessity. Near-zero automobile emissions are moving closer to reality. Reducing carbon emissions and recycling have become a natural part of everyday life for many people. But new ways to be environmentally responsible are still being sought.

### Questions

1. Do you agree that the environmental movement has moved into the fifth phase?
2. Where do you see the environmental movement going? Stronger or weaker?
3. Will the environmental movement be worldwide or regional? Will developed nations have different responsibilities than developing nations?
4. Will there be lasting public and corporate support?

is being waged between those trying to bring about change and those resisting the change (and sometimes this is the situation), the actual conflict is usually more subtle and may only surface in small verbal disagreements, questions, reluctance, and so forth.

Regardless of how much resistance there is to the organization's change program, the change will to some extent evolve through the five phases described above. Depending on the change program, however, some of the phases may be brief, omitted, or repeated, and at any point the process of bringing about change may fail. If the last phase is not solidified, the change process may move into the first phase again. Jack Welch, General Electric's retired CEO, wrote in an article for *Fortune*, "People always ask, 'Is the change over? Can we stop now?' You've got to tell them, 'No, it's just begun.' They must come to understand that it is never ending. Leaders must create an atmosphere where people understand that change is a continuing process, not an event."[6] **OD Application: The Five Phases of Resistance to Change** is an example of applying the phases to better understand a long-range change program.

## LEADING CHANGE

Changing an organization involves modifying its existing systems, structure, and culture to some different standard or level of performance. The purpose of change is to increase the organization's effectiveness or even to ensure its survival. Most managers agree that if an organization is to continue to be excellent, it must continually respond to significant environmental developments.

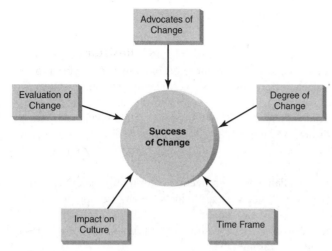

**FIGURE 6.1**   Change Factors

Change typically creates a conflict between the business side of an organization and its human side. A manager is likely to be well equipped and experienced to handle restructuring, altering production processes, making marketing decisions, and other operational issues. But these changes unavoidably create issues and conflicts on the human side of the organization. Many managers are more likely not to be as successful in the overall changes because of a failure to consider, or an inability to deal with, the human elements. Leading change is about bringing together both the business and human components of the change.[7]

Effectively managing change is not only a challenge for managers, it is necessary for survival. Toshiba Corporation's chief executive Atsutoshi Nishida said in a *Wall Street Journal* interview, "If you don't take risks, you make no progress. Situations change constantly, so if we can't change with them, then there's no future for us."[8] Some managers consider change so critical to the success of the organization that they continuously search for ways to make positive organizational changes. Major forces in the change process include advocates of change, degree of change, time frame, impact on culture, and evaluation of change (see Figure 6.1).

## Advocates of Change

The person who spearheads a change program is very often the most important force in the change process. Typically, this is a key person in the organization. In the case of a company-wide change, the CEO is likely the change advocate. For a change within a division, the change advocate is likely the divisional manager. In situations where an internal or external OD practitioner has been brought in to assist in the change project, he or she would also be an advocate, but the primary responsibility will be on a key person within the organization.

## Degree of Change

The degree of change will fall on a continuum of change ranging from minor to extreme. The greater the degree of change, the more difficult it is to implement it successfully. But what initially appears to be a minor change may well have a significant impact on others.

## Time Frame

The change may be implemented over several months or years, or it may be implemented immediately. In general, the more gradual the change and the longer the time frame, the greater the chance of success. Some organizations, however, have become so ineffective that any chance they have for survival depends on radical change introduced and implemented swiftly. And external economic conditions, such as a major recession, may dictate that the change be significant and immediate. As a rule, the length of time for a change program to take hold and become part of the bloodstream and fabric of an organization is measured in years. CEOs from

GE, Seagate Technology, and Intel provide some insights into the time required to make a change:

- GE's Jeffrey Immelt, referring to GE's plan to come out of the recession that began in late 2007: "A major change-management effort like this is a 10-year process. It takes a decade to build the talent, culture, and tools, and to learn from our mistakes."[9]
- Seagate Technology's Bill Watkins comment on Seagate evolving into a more consumer-focused company: "Organizations will fight organization changes up and down. You need to realize, it's not a six-month deal, its not a one year deal, it's a three-year endeavor. It's a minimum three years. And be braced for that, and realize you keep constantly going back and kind of tweaking it."[10]
- Intel Corporation's Paul Otellini reflecting on bringing back Intel to be a major force in the twenty-first century: "I knew what products we had coming out, and I knew the results of our efficiency efforts, so I was optimistic. But as Andy [Grove, CEO from 1987 to 1998] once told me, 'You won't believe how long it takes for the change you've started to work its way all of the way through the rank and file.'"[11]

### Impact on Culture

The greater the impact on the existing culture and norms, the greater the amount of resistance that is likely to emerge, and thus the more difficult it will be to implement the change program. On the other hand, an organizational culture that values change and innovation will positively influence the acceptance and support of a change program. GM has for decades been a leading example of having an organizational culture that valued the status quo. Former GM CEO Roger Smith, as long ago as the 1980s, referred to the tens of thousands of managers made complacent by the golden days of GM as the "frozen middle." For a number of reasons, including a GM culture that did not value change, Smith was not successful in many of the changes he attempted to make.

**EVALUATION OF CHANGE** Plans and levels of performance are developed to measure the degree of change and its impact on the organization's effectiveness. The evaluation is not a one-time activity that occurs near the end of the change process. It is, however, an ongoing part of the change. Continuous reviews of the progress are made for all the stakeholders so that corrections are made and accountability is maintained.

## A CHANGE MODEL

Two major considerations in organizational change are the degree of change and the impact on the organization's culture. Implementation is difficult, and resistance can be expected whenever a change involves a significant impact on the organization's traditional behavior, power, culture, and structure. The degree of change and the impact on the existing culture are shown in the change model in Figure 6.2. The areas in the divisions of the figure approximate the amount of resistance encountered in four possible change situations.

1. *Minor change, low impact on culture.* When the change to be introduced is relatively minor and the impact on the existing culture is low, resistance will be at the lowest level, and success will be most probable.
2. *Minor change, high impact on culture.* When the change is minor but the impact on the culture is high, some resistance can be expected, depending on the size of the threat and the speed of the change.
3. *Major change, low impact on culture.* When the change is major, but the impact on existing culture is minor, some resistance is likely, but good management can probably overcome it.
4. *Major change, high impact on culture.* When the change is large and the impact on the existing culture is high, the greatest resistance can be predicted. Concomitantly, the probability of success is low.

Experience suggests that both the level of resistance and the time needed to implement change tend to be underestimated. An alternative plan, assuming the organization has the time, is to break the change into smaller components that can be introduced over a longer time. Each component will encounter low resistance because it represents only a small degree of change and has a small impact on the culture.

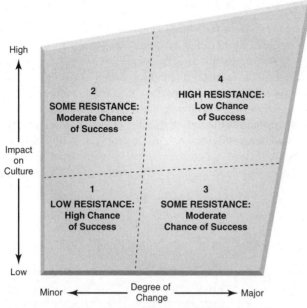

**FIGURE 6.2    Change Model**

# DRIVING FORCES TOWARD ACCEPTANCE OF A CHANGE PROGRAM

**Driving forces** are anything that increases the inclination of an organization to implement a proposed change program. They vary in intensity, depending on the specifics and the immediate situation. Some driving forces help to create the need for a change program or energize its initiation; others develop later, as the change program progresses.[12]

## Dissatisfaction with the Present Situation

Sometimes an organization is dissatisfied or even troubled by its situation. It may not know why it is dissatisfied, but it has a desire for relief. This could be likened to a person who is sick. When you are sick and you do not know what has caused your illness or how to cure yourself, you just want to be relieved of the pain. You can try some home remedies or seek the help of a doctor. Organizations sometimes find themselves in a similar situation; that is, they realize that they are unhealthy or ineffective. The more intense the dissatisfaction with the present situation, the greater the motivation to change. Members of an organization who are dissatisfied with their personal positions may push for change in the belief that things cannot get much worse.

Sometimes an organization and its members are aware of the need to change. Members may perceive a difference between the present situation and the situation as they would like it to be. They may not be greatly dissatisfied with the situation as it is, but they recognize a need for improvement, perhaps after observing other organizations. Although the organization's operating records are compatible with the standards for their type of organization, they are not satisfied with being average. They believe they have an untapped potential but are not sure how to release their talents in a way that will further the development of the organization.

In other organizations, the need to change may be more obvious. The organization may not be meeting its industry's standards on such matters as rate of return on invested capital. Internal goals, such as group production quotas, may not have been achieved. Or there may be an attempted stockholder revolt or an unfriendly takeover. As a consequence, internal pressures are brought to bear to change the situation. There is an obvious felt need that "we had better do something, anything, and fast." Lawrence Bossidy, the former CEO of AlliedSignal (also CEO of Honeywell after the merger with AlliedSignal), calls this the "burning platform" condition.[13] When Bossidy took over AlliedSignal, the company had poor profit margins, too much debt, and negative cash flow. Regarding AlliedSignal's need to change, he said, "The people of AlliedSignal obviously were on a burning platform. . . . To inaugurate large-scale change, you may have to create the burning platform. You have to give people a reason to do something differently. . . . Scaring people isn't the answer. You try to appeal to them. The more they understand why you want change, the easier it is to commit to it."[14]

### External Pressures Toward Change

An organization does not exist in a vacuum. It is part of a larger external environment that imposes certain forces upon it. Sometimes external pressures will cause the organization to change some of its methods of operation. These pressures range from voluntary actions to involuntary legal requirements. In industry, the corporation may need to adopt new technologies to remain competitive, or may be required by law to make a change necessitated by environmental or civil rights legislation. A worldwide recession, international competition, and lowering of trade barriers are probably doing more to force changes on organizations than any other external force. The newest technologies, such as electronic communications, the Internet, and computer software, are by their very nature products without boundaries.[15] For additional information on the impact of international competition, refer to **OD Application: The World of Business.**

---

## OD Application: The World of Business[16]

Of the 100 largest economies in the world, 53 percent are multinational corporations; the other 47 percent are nations. Based upon *Fortune*'s Global 500 list, Wal-Mart is the world's largest retailer and also the world's largest company in terms of revenue. It is also the world's largest private employer, with 2,055,000 employees in more than 7,300 stores around the world. There are 3,659 stores and 680,000 employees in 15 markets out of the United States. Wal-Mart is the largest private employer in Mexico and the United States, and more than 175 million customers worldwide shop every week in its stores.

Much has been reported in the general media, and especially in business and economic publications, about globalization and the effect it is having on businesses, competition, governments, workers, societies, and cultures. Several books devoted to the subject are *Hot, Flat, and Crowded*, *The World Is Flat*, *Managing across Cultures*, and *Global, Inc. Global, Inc.*, is subtitled "An Atlas of the Multinational Corporation," and its authors describe it as an effort "to conceptualize and to see globalization in a historical perspective."

For businesses, governments, and employees, this book and material like it are helpful in obtaining data that show the challenges and potentials of globalization. Learning as much as possible about globalization can help a business deal with the changes that will undoubtedly result from increased globalization.

Globalization is not a new concept on the landscape. World trade was going on even before the first caravans brought silk from China to Europe, and in the sixteenth century, European explorers set out to find a better route to Asia for the profits to be made in the spice trade. Globalization lumbered along for 500 years or so until the last 30 years, when it really picked up speed. Globalization has experienced exponential growth due in part to phenomenal improvements in communications and transportation; more efficient global banking systems; surpluses in capital in China, Japan, the United States, and Europe; and worldwide lowering of trade barriers.

As evidence of the rapid changes in globalization, there were about 2,400 multinational companies (MNCs) in 1869. By 1969, 100 years later, the number had tripled to 7,258. Approximately 30 years later, the number of multinationals had grown by a factor of nearly nine to above 63,000. Today the 1,000 largest MNCs account for 80 percent of the world's industrial production.

**TABLE 6.1** Fortune Top Global 500 Companies

|    |             | 2008 |     | 2005 |     |
|----|-------------|------|-----|------|-----|
| 1  | U.S.        | 153  | 31% | 176  | 35% |
| 3  | Europe      | 184  | 37% | 174  | 35% |
| 2  | Japan       | 64   | 13% | 81   | 16% |
| 4  | China       | 29   | 6%  | 16   | 3%  |
| 5  | South Korea | 15   | 3%  | 11   | 2%  |
| 6  | Canada      | 14   | 3%  | 13   | 3%  |
| 7  | Australia   | 8    | 2%  | 9    | 2%  |
| 8  | India       | 7    | 1%  | 5    | 1%  |
| 9  | Taiwan      | 6    | 1%  | 2    | 0%  |
| 10 | Mexico      | 5    | 1%  | 2    | 0%  |
| 11 | Russia      | 5    | 1%  | 3    | 1%  |
| 12 | Brazil      | 5    | 1%  | 3    | 1%  |
| 13 | Other       | 5    | 1%  | 5    | 1%  |

The nature of the MNC has also changed. In 1962, almost 60 percent of the 500 largest corporations were based in the United States. Today, only 31 percent of MNCs are U.S.-based. Japan accounts for about 13 percent, and Europe has 37 percent. Perhaps more important, MNCs are emerging in developing countries, all reaching out for a piece of the pie. For the most recent year and three years prior, Table 6.1 shows the breakdowns based upon *Fortune*'s list for the top 500 global companies.

In effect, U.S.-based MNCs have been decoupling from the U.S. economy over the last decade, as some companies are not exporting a product to another country but are taking their operations to that country. U.S.-based MNCs' growth has been largely overseas, increasingly in developing countries. Yet their headquarters are in the United States, they are listed on U.S. stock exchanges, and Americans own a majority of the stock. And to add a bit more complexity, there is political and economic debate as to how foreign earnings should be treated in the United States tax code. When MNCs like United Technologies and GE manufacture a product, for example a jet engine or a large turbine, it may be designed, manufactured, and used offshore. Of course, the

*(continued)*

same is also true for foreign companies, such as Toyota Motor Corporation, as they may design, manufacture, and sell an automobile in the United States.

MNCs help create markets by employing workers worldwide; 90 million people in all countries and 20 million in developing countries are employed by MNCs. They pay more than $1.5 trillion in wages and more than $1.2 trillion in taxes to governments. Though the world is becoming a global marketplace, the people in a country still retain a strong sense of identification with their country and culture. As a consequence, the trend has been for MNCs to blend into the local landscape. The Walt Disney Company discovered the folly of not adapting to the local culture when it opened up a theme park in France. CEO Bob Iger of Disney said, "We've discovered that pride in local culture and

demand to own it is much greater than we had previously thought." Wal-Mart has tried to avoid this mistake. In the United Kingdom, Wal-Mart is known as ASDA, in Mexico it is Walmex, in Japan it is Seiyu, and in Chile it is Hiper de Lider.

**Questions**

1. Why is it important for a business to understand globalization?
2. Do you think globalization is something that a business of any size can ignore? Support your position.
3. Research *Fortune's* "Global 500" list of companies to see how trend lines are developing. The Web site is http://money.cnn.com/. Search for "global 500 list" or something similar.

## Momentum Toward Change

When a change program is under way, certain forces tend to push it along. An OD program is built around involvement. The members of an organization play a major part in directing the change, and those involved in orchestrating the change will probably become committed to the program. Since change programs usually do not come cheap, an organization that spends money to begin a change will probably want to continue in order to get full value for its investment.

Once a change program is under way in one part of an organization, it may set off a chain reaction requiring or permitting changes in other parts of the organization. This is often the case with self-managed work teams, which are usually set up on a trial basis within a department. Other workers, hearing of the teams, may ask for self-managed teams in their units so that they can participate. This notion of change is compatible with the OD fundamental that effective change is organization-wide, or, if the change is in a subpart of an organization, the subpart is reasonably well-isolated or compartmentalized.

## Motivation by Management

The manager or advocate of change should not be overlooked as a motivating force. A CEO's words of assurance and encouragement to the department managers can have a strong motivating effect. More experienced and senior managers may have been involved in other planned change programs, but for some employees this may be the first major planned change program. Participants in the change program may be discouraged by the seemingly slow pace at which the change is moving, or, after having been involved in the diagnosis of problems, they may be overwhelmed by the variety and magnitude of the problems.

The behavior of key managers can often be a motivating force, especially if others hold them in high esteem. Members of the organization may be closed, untrusting, and dishonest in their relations with one other, whereas the change advocates believe that effective organizations are built on openness, trust, honesty, and collaboration. If the advocates of change personally behave in this manner and are held in high regard, others may change their own behavior.

## RESTRAINING FORCES BLOCKING IMPLEMENTATION OF CHANGE PROGRAMS

In addition to the driving forces of change, implementation of any OD change program needs to take account of the **restraining forces** of change. The advocates of the change may assume that everyone will actively support the change because its goals are worthwhile, but this is sometimes not what happens. Since change always alters the status quo, managers should anticipate some employee resistance and plan for this eventuality in the change strategy. The failure of management to win acceptance of the proposed changes can be one of the most significant hindrances to an OD change program.

The success of organization development programs may depend to a great extent on the ability of those doing the planning. Managers can benefit from the knowledge of sociologists, social psychologists, and cultural anthropologists who have studied the process of change. Resistance to organization development programs is a complex rather than a simple problem; it is the cumulative effect of many factors that make up the acceptance or rejection of change.

### Uncertainty Regarding Change: "The Comfort Zone"

Organization members may have a psychological resistance to change because they want to avoid uncertainty. Past ways of doing things are well known and predictable, and unwillingness to give up familiar tasks or relationships may cause resistance. Many people feel comfortable doing things the same way as always—they prefer to remain in "the comfort zone." Douglas Solomon, the chief technology strategist at IDEO, which is a consulting firm specializing in innovation, believes that companies who are in their comfort zone are not aware of a need to change and are likely to resist change. He says, "There are still people who say, 'If it ain't broke, don't fix it.' And I don't think these companies are in a good position to really change, because they're happy with where they are [their comfort zone]. So you have to have a certain degree of discomfort in your business to be willing to make the changes that are necessary."[17]

### Fear of the Unknown

A large part of the resistance to change stems from a fear of the unknown. People become anxious when they have to exchange the old and familiar for something new and uncertain. Lack of information or understanding often leaves a vacuum that is filled by rumor, speculation, and insecurity.

### Disruption of Routine

Proposed changes that disturb habitual routines or patterns are likely to encounter resistance because human behavior is governed largely by habit and routine. If a person tries to cope with a situation and succeeds, that person will usually continue to operate in the same way. The familiar is preferred, and this is especially true when the established behavior has been successful until now.

There is little incentive to change when the old way seems to work. Once habits and attitudes are firmly established, they become the framework through which people respond to their environment and to new ideas. Situations in conflict with the old attitudes are altered and perceived in a way that is congruent with them. The old adage "we hear what we want to hear" has some degree of truth. People may conveniently forget some learning if it is in conflict with their present behavior. The notion of selective perception means that people will successfully resist and negate the possible influence of new information upon their earlier attitudes and behavior.

### Loss of Benefits: "What's in It for Me?"

When a change causes employees to feel pressured, they may interpret the change as a loss of individual security. There may be an emotional loss associated with the change, a loss of the former "comfort zone."

Any proposed change is more readily accepted if it promises to benefit those affected by it, but the motivation of top management to change may not be shared at the operating level. In some cases, resistance may be due to a lack of interest or practical appreciation of the reason for the change. In a similar vein, the expectations of a group will influence its reception of a proposed change. A group that favors a change and expects to benefit from it will more readily change than one that starts with a negative attitude. People affected by a change will naturally be concerned about how the change affects them: Is my job safe? Will I have to move to another city? Can I get a promotion out of this? What's in it for me? So that more support for the change can be garnered, the change process should at least be initially presented and discussed in terms of how those affected will benefit from the change.

### Threat to Security

Change sometimes results in a disadvantage to an individual employee or group, and people tend to resist change that threatens the security of their environment. There may be concern about vested interests, such as loss of the job, reduced promotional potential, change in career opportunities, reduced wages or benefits, or greater job demands. There are many instances of work groups withholding a secretly invented tool or improved work method from management for fear the job will be restructured and people laid off or transferred. These fears induce a loss of security and result in resistance to change.

## Threat to Position Power

Any change that causes a manager or group to "lose face" will be resisted. Changes that threaten to lower the status or prestige of the individual or group will probably meet with resistance. For example, a department manager is not likely to favor a change perceived as reducing his or her sphere of authority. Where a proposed change appears to be detrimental to the vested interest of any group, the group will resist the change. Thus, even though a change to an organization's structure may benefit the organization as a whole, departments may view the change as a threat to their best interests and therefore resist.

## Redistribution of Power

A major factor in resistance to innovation is that reorganization invariably implies a redistribution of power and influence. Individuals or groups who perceive a change as lessening their influence will strongly resist it. Those who have the most to lose will be most likely to disapprove of or resist proposed changes.

## Disturb Existing Social Networks

Technical changes are more readily accepted when they do not disturb existing social networks. Friendships, social cliques, or informal teams may be threatened by changes. Research evidence indicates that the stronger the group ties, the greater the resistance to change.

## Conformity to Norms and Culture

Norms are organized and shared ideas about what members of an organization should do and feel. The members define the norms and enforce individual behavior to conform to them. The enforcement is imposed by the individuals and by the group through peer pressure upon those who do not conform. Norms cannot easily be changed because of their strong group support. This is especially true if an individual attempts to change a norm because of the possibility of exclusion from the group. When a person is external to the group (say, an upper-level manager), the change process may be even more difficult because of lack of familiarity with the group.

The organizational culture includes the language, dress, patterns of behavior, value systems, feelings, attitudes, interactions, and group norms of the members. Larger organizations will have subcultures formed around smaller units of work or social groups. According to the system view of organization behavior, it is difficult to change the ways of behaving in one part of the organization without influencing and being influenced by the other parts (perhaps through resistance). Unless the managers advocating a change begin by considering the possibility of resistance from the organization as a whole, the ultimate acceptance of the change program will be in serious doubt.

## Driving Forces and Restraining Forces Act in Tandem

Effective change programs try to increase the driving forces toward acceptance of change and simultaneously to decrease the restraining forces blocking the change. The force-field analysis model, discussed as a diagnostic model of change in Chapter 5, is helpful to understand and develop a strategy for implementing the change program. If the equilibrium point in change is to be shifted to the desired goal, strategies must be implemented that decrease the strength of the restraining forces and in tandem increase the strength of the driving forces. This is analogous to the changes in the weather due to high- and low-pressure systems. The weather is a dynamic system in which a high-pressure system increases or decreases while a nearby low-pressure system behaves in an opposite manner. Depending on the intensity of the two systems, there can be volatile changes in the weather or more gradual and subdued changes. Though organization development differs from weather systems in a variety of ways, one being that the OD practitioner attempts to control the change, there are some parallels. Unlike the saying commonly attributed to Mark Twain, "Everyone talks about the weather but nobody does anything about it," in OD someone is trying to do something about it.

# STRATEGIES TO INCREASE MOTIVATION

The chances of success for an OD program are improved if resistance to change can be minimized. It is important to recognize two things about resistance. First, resistance to change can be predicted. Second, resistance cannot be repressed effectively in the long run. In a change situation, resistance of some type is inevitable, and the resistance can be used to improve upon the changes. The task of the manager and change agent is to utilize creatively the conflict resulting from the resistance for the organizational good. In other words, since it is unwise, and even futile, to try to repress conflict, the objective is to turn the energies generated by the antichange resistance to good advantage.

Resistance to change can be used as feedback about the change. Researchers and consultants of organizational change, Jeffrey Ford and Laurie Ford, said in a *Harvard Business Review* article, "Resistance, properly understood as feedback, can be an important resource in improving the quality and clarity of the objectives and strategies at the heart of a change proposal. And, properly used, it can enhance the prospects for successful implementation."[18] Listening to comments and criticisms provides information that can be used to adjust the tempo and extent of the change program. In addition, resistance can provide functional conflict that contributes to the quality of the change program. Questions and objections to the change, which is interpreted by the change agent as resistance, may actually be reasonable concern for what the change may do to the organization or team. Furthermore, the absence of resistance may indicate a degree of disengagement and an indication of future problems.[19]

Though it is normal to expect some resistance to change, at some point continual resistance to change may be a signal that something is not working in the implementation of the program. The signals include delays and inefficiencies, failure to produce anticipated results, or even efforts to sabotage the change program. There are several methods for dealing with resistance to change.

## Climate Conducive to Change

The climate and culture of organizations are decisive in sustaining organizational change.[20] Creating a climate where everyone involved in a change program feels free and not threatened to communicate with others can minimize resistance in the long run. Attitudes of respect, understanding, and communication will help to break a cycle of reciprocal threat and aggressiveness on the part of the resisters and the advocates of the change program. Also, a climate that focuses attention on the basic issues and the relevant facts and ensures that parties do not sit in judgment of each other will more likely be productive.

## Clearly Articulated Vision

Closely tied to creating a climate conducive to change is to create a vision for a team, division, and organization. A **vision** describes a desired future state for an organization. A vision can provide the members with a mental image of the future and give them the enthusiasm and motivation to accomplish a common goal and purpose. This will help to give direction to a change program and to provide a benchmark to evaluate the success of the change. Without a well-understood vision, the change is likely to go haphazardly in many unintended directions. For a vision to become part of the fabric of an organization, it requires more than cleverly strung together words or a catchy slogan. The deeds and behaviors of key people in the organization will do more than words to communicate the vision. As an example, if a pharmaceutical company's vision statement includes the ethical testing of new drugs, and it is disclosed by the Food and Drug Administration that company executives tampered with the results, other employees are less likely to accept the professed vision.

Vision statements for organizations go by various titles. For example, at Johnson & Johnson they call it "Our Credo," Google has "ten things," the American Red Cross has a brief "Mission Statement" and a longer fundamental principles statement, and W. L. Gore & Associates has four basic guiding principles. The vision statement for the organization is usually drawn up by the CEO and a committee composed of senior executives. At lower levels, a team may create its own vision statement within the context of the vision of the larger organization. Along with a vision statement, some organizations have a brief motto, slogan, or rallying cry. To combat a reputation of delayed flights, US Airways has a rallying cry. "Airlines, or really any organization, need a rallying cry," says Robert Isom, the airline's COO, "especially one that has been the worst of the worst for so long."[21]

## Effective Communications

An effective communication program can minimize the uncertainty and fear of the unknown associated with change. For an illustration, see Figure 6.3. As the lack of reliable information leads to rumors and uncertainty, information concerning "the what and why" of the change program

**FIGURE 6.3    Reducing Uncertainty of Change with Communications**
*Source:* B.C. by permission of Johnny Hart and Creators Syndicate, Inc.

should be provided to all organization members.[22] A study reported in the *Wall Street Journal* found that employees are more likely to support decisions when they are told about the rationale. In the study, roughly 300 managers at more than 100 U.S. employers were asked what they knew of decisions and how supportive they were of the decisions. In companies that explained decisions more fully, the employees were more than twice as likely to support those decisions as workers who got less information. Ideally, those affected by the change will have participated in designing the change program. If the reality is that this is not feasible, then these people are more likely to buy in to the change if they are told the "why" of the change.[23]

Employees are much more likely to support changes when they are told about falling sales, sharply rising costs, declining profits, decreasing quality, customer complaints, high absenteeism, and other statistics that compare unfavorably with the competition or where the company would like to be. John Kotter, author of books on change and the role of leadership, has written, "Employees will not make sacrifices, even if they are unhappy with the status quo, unless they believe that useful change is possible. Without credible communication, and a lot of it, the hearts and minds of the troops are never captured."[24]

Change leaders find a way to communicate this information and establish a sense of urgency. General Mills, Aetna Life & Casualty, and other organizations are spending a significant amount of time training production-line employees to read accounting and production documents, and then making sure they have all the relevant cost and production information. This technique, sometimes referred to as **open-book management,** literally opens the books to employees, so that they can see the company's financial records, expenses, and sources of profit. A major benefit is that employees are able to analyze and understand the problems for themselves.[25] The importance of change is then appreciated directly by employees at all levels, from line workers to top executives. The longer that members are left to speculate without access to reliable facts, the more likely that resistance will emerge. Most managers underestimate the amount of communication needed, so it is better to use "overkill" than to understate the situation. At Delphi Automotive Systems, a GM spin-off, the chairperson and CEO allowed the union to bring in an independent auditor to examine the factory's books. "I'll do anything to improve communication," the CEO says. "It's important that people have trust."[26]

The advantages and rewards of the communication of proposed changes should be emphasized, because opposition to change disappears as the fears it generates are explained away. Once the benefits from a change program for individuals and the organization are made clear, employees involved can more readily understand and accept the impact of the change. In reference to bringing change to Intel, CEO Paul Otellini said in a *Wall Street Journal* interview, "I made it my job to communicate, communicate, communicate the positive message. I did open forums, I did Webcasts, I told the employees to send me any question via email and I'd answer them. I wasn't trying to sell them on the idea. . . . You have to convince them through reasoning and logic, the accuracy of your claims."[27]

## Leadership of Managers

The leadership of key managers in the organization is critical to the success of a change program. Today's managers cannot have an emotional commitment to the past. They cannot be afraid to shake things up. Employees affected by a change need to be involved and supportive. Leaders with loyal followers set high standards and strive to attain exceptional results. An ongoing project surveying tens of thousands of working people around the world on leadership was reported in *Harvard Business Review*. The question asked was, "What do you look for and admire in a leader (defined as someone whose direction you would willingly follow)?" The number one requirement of a leader was honesty and the second-highest requirement was that he or she be forward looking.[28] Additional research shows that workers who have open and strong leaders are more receptive to change than those working for leaders who are driven by politics, territoriality, and inconsistency.[29]

Through such methods as empowering employees and developing high-performance teams, the leader is able to accomplish things that he or she could not accomplish if acting alone. One of the most important roles of a leader is to communicate an image of the future and inspire a shared vision of the organization. The CEO of United Parcel Service, Inc. (UPS), Mike Eskew, expressed this idea well in a *Harvard Business Review* article he wrote: "[Leadership] requires relentless communication, which is a big part of my job. Perhaps more important, it requires a culture based on an authentic respect for employees and customers."[30]

## Participation of Members

Making sure that the individuals involved in a change are allowed to participate in the decision process rather than forced to go along with it is a basic technique for increasing the acceptance of change. The participation of employees in matters that concern them increases the probability that they will find the program acceptable. People who help to create a program have an interest and ownership in it that is likely to lead to better motivation and understanding. In a research study of employees' adaptation to organization change, it was found that they were less likely to feel victimized and ignored by the change process if they had an opportunity to express their views and to participate in the change.[31] Chairman of P&G's board of directors and retired CEO, A. G. Lafley, says of his approach to bringing about change, "I avoided saying P&G people were bad. I enrolled them in change."[32]

A change program "prepared on high and cast as pearls before swine" will most certainly be destined to failure. Captain Queeg, in the following excerpt from *The Caine Mutiny,* very enthusiastically expounds a policy of dictated change that later contributes to the crew's mutiny:

> Now, there are four ways of doing a thing aboard ship—the right way, the wrong way, the Navy way, and my way. I want things on this ship done my way. Don't

worry about the other ways. Do things my way, and we'll get along—okay. Now are there any questions?" He looked around. There were no questions. He nodded with smiling satisfaction.[33]

If there is a union in the workplace, it needs to be involved and supportive of the change program. Some OD interventions, such as self-managed work teams (discussed in Chapter 13), may directly involve a union. When potential resisters are drawn into the planning and implementation process, their resistance to the change may be reduced or eliminated.

## Reward Systems

Reinforcing the change process and providing support for those involved in it is another way managers advocating change can deal with resistance. If the situation allows, managers can arrange promotions, monetary rewards, or public recognition for those who participate in the change program. UPS is one of many companies that has some form of employee ownership. UPS has a philosophy of employee ownership that dates back to 1927 when the founder, Jim Casey, instituted a policy that UPS should be "owned by its managers and managed by its owners." Today, all United States employees, both managers and hourly workers, can purchase stock at a discounted price, and at least half of a manager's bonus is paid in UPS shares.[34]

Flexible reward systems that take account of the differences between individual employees can win acceptance of changes. Profit sharing, bonuses, skill- and knowledge-based pay, gain sharing, and stock-ownership plans have recently become more common in large and small businesses.[35] **Profit sharing** uses the performance of the business to calculate pay. **Knowledge-based pay** or skill-based pay uses the knowledge or skills a worker has to determine pay. **Gain sharing** recognizes the value of a specific group of workers based on measurable characteristics that become the basis for calculating pay. The members of the group typically share the rewards equally. **Employee stock-ownership plans (ESOPs)** use formulas of various kinds to grant stock or stock options to a broad segment of employees. Profit sharing, knowledge-based pay, gain sharing, and ESOPs often use sophisticated and elaborate formulas to calculate the pay or amount of stock. Compensation consultants and lawyers are often brought in to help set up the plans.

Employee ownership plans are likely to be found in organizations where the nature of the work makes it difficult or costly to evaluate and measure employees' performance. Typically, these organizations are large, have or expect to have high growth rates, and have high levels of investment in intellectual capital. For example, at Google, where about half of its employees are engineers, every employee owns stock in the company. On the other hand, organizations that tend not to have employee ownership plans are more likely to be small, where employees' performance can be readily observed or the work is such that there is little investment in intellectual capital.[36] The trend in the U.S. economy is in the direction of firms that are far more intellectual-capital-intensive and abandoning the traditional production-line model of the industrial age. Likewise, the number of employees participating in employee-ownership plans is rising.[37]

The trend toward more flexible reward systems and employee ownership plans will probably continue. To date, one of the most comprehensive studies on employee ownership is from the General Social Survey (GSS). The GSS is a series of studies conducted for the Shared Capitalism Project of the National Bureau for Economic Research. Based on GSS data, estimates are that 20 percent of all U.S. employees in the private sector (approximately 25 million Americans) report owning stock in their companies. Additionally, it was found that employee ownership was more likely to be successful when it was combined with employee empowerment and good employment relations.[38]

## Negotiation, Agreement, and Politics

Another technique to lessen resistance is to negotiate with potential resisters. Some examples include union agreements, increasing an employee's pension benefits in exchange for early retirement, transferring employees to other divisions instead of laying them off, and negotiating agreements with the heads of the departments that will be affected by the change. In some organizations, the change may be so difficult for employees that they self-select and leave the organization voluntarily. Cisco's CEO John Chambers made a major change in the way Cisco was structured and managed after the burst of the Internet bubble in 2000. Chambers estimates that about 10 percent of the managers could not make the transition and left.[39]

Voices of dissent and opposition to a change program should not be interpreted as a rejection of the change. If resistance is construed by the change agent as an absolute refusal of the change, then the opportunity to listen to complaints and questions is lost. It may be possible to accommodate some of the positions of those resisting the change. It is also very possible that through negotiations and discussions, contributions of those being asked to change may improve the change program, and their participation may increase the likelihood of the changes being accepted.[40]

Political alliances can help reduce the resistance to change, but leadership based on politics will not garner the support of workers.[41] Building a coalition, just as politicians do, of people who hold divergent points of view can be a powerful force for change.[42] To win an election or get a piece of legislation passed requires that a politician reach out and get support not only from his or her core base but also from other individuals and groups. Similarly, a manager seeking to make a change on the production line or a CEO implementing a strategic change must not only go to the loyal following but should forge alliances with many other people and groups. Compromise, reciprocity, and trade-offs may be necessary parts in building political alliances.

## Power Strategies

OD practitioners have historically been reluctant to deal with the use of power in organizations. To some extent, power strategies are antithetical to OD values. But most organizations operate within a system that sanctions and uses power, and the organization's members are motivated to some extent by the perceived power of the organization. It may be necessary to use the power structure in an organization to persuade its members of an OD program's worthiness.

A power strategy, albeit fairly low key and nonthreatening, was adopted in an OD program being implemented in one of the branches of the U.S. military. For more than a year, an OD practitioner group had been seeking a unit to participate in an OD program. A volunteer unit was finally obtained. Once the program was in progress, it was decided to arrange a visit by that branch's chief of operations to communicate his personal appreciation for the unit's participation in the OD program. The visit served a dual purpose: It built a high degree of enthusiasm within the unit for the OD program, and it convinced other units that were sitting on the sidelines that the OD program was to be taken seriously. This was certainly not the only reason for the successful spread of the OD program throughout that military branch, but it gave added impetus when the future of the program was at a crucial and pivotal stage.

People are sometimes forced to go along with a change by explicit or implicit threats involving loss of jobs, loss of promotion, or raises. In some situations, employees who refuse to change may be dismissed or transferred. Such methods, though infrequent, pose risks and make it more difficult to gain support for future change programs. Organizations that introduce teamwork have found that a few employees cannot make the transition to working cooperatively with others in teams. In some organizations these workers are given the opportunity to transfer to work situations where they do not have to work interdependently with others. Samsung Group provides an illustration of a more direct way of dealing with change. In the early 1990s, Samsung was confronted with a reputation for poor-quality products. According to corporate lore, Chairman Lee Kun Hee summoned top executives and made them watch a 30-minute video documenting shoddy production of Samsung washing machines. "Change everything," Lee ordered, "except for your wife and children."[43]

In the hyperturbulent environment of the 2000s, change is the norm. The need to change for both profit and not-for-profit organizations became painfully obvious during a severe worldwide recession that began in late 2007 and the collapse of financial markets that began the following year. A radically new environment demands radically new forms of organizing and ways of managing. In this chapter, we have examined some of the forces that motivate individuals toward change, some factors that restrain the likelihood of change, and some change strategies that foster acceptance.

Subsequent chapters will cover some of the OD techniques and programs that can reduce resistance to change and increase the likelihood of acceptance. Some approaches for change are directed at the individual, others are more team and interteam oriented, and still other approaches are at an organization-wide level.

## Summary

- **Change.** The process of change is made complex by the interaction of social, technical, and psychological factors. Both people and organizations have vested interests in the status quo. The advocates of change must deal with the possible resistance to change before implementing any OD strategy or technique.
- **Life Cycle of Change.** The response to change tends to move through a life cycle. Five phases typical of change are (1) introduction of the change, (2) identification of the forces for and against the change, (3) conflict between the forces, (4) residual resistance to the change, and (5) establishment of change.
- **Factors Affecting Success.** Major factors affecting the success of change include strong advocates of change, degree of change, time frame, impact on culture, and evaluation of change.
- **Driving Forces.** These are forces that lead the organization to implement a change. The forces include the organization and its members being dissatisfied with the current situation, external pressures such as market forces, and encouragement and motivation by management.
- **Restraining Forces.** Resistance to change is usually a reaction to the methods used in implementing a change rather than an inherent human characteristic. People tend to resist changes that do not make sense to them or that are forced upon them against their will. Certain factors, such as loss of security or status, lead to resistance to change. There are ways to reduce this resistance, including good communication and participation in the change process.
- **Strategies for Change.** Acceptance of change can be improved when certain conditions are present that minimize the threat or discomfort of a proposed change. These conditions include careful planning and thorough communication of the change to the target individual, group, or system. The degree of acceptance also increases when others are allowed to participate in making a self-designed change program. The probability that a change will be accepted is increased if the manager can create a climate in which people feel free to change rather than coerced.

## Review Questions

1. Trace the life cycle of change in an organization or an event occurring in society (suggestions are smoking in public places, energy conservation, or driving smaller automobiles).

2. What are major forces in the change process?
3. What strategies might be used in gaining acceptance for an OD program?

## Key Words and Concepts

Driving Forces
Employee Stock-
   Ownership Plan (ESOP)

Gain Sharing
Knowledge-Based Pay

Open-Book Management
Profit Sharing

Restraining Forces
Vision

# OD Skills Simulation 6.1

## Downsizing in the Enigma Company

*Total time suggested: 60 minutes.*

## A. Purpose

This chapter discusses how people react to the possibility of change. In this simulation, you will be involved in a team decision on change. Thanks to your participation in this process, you will experience how different individuals tend to perceive the same situation differently. The goals include:

1. To examine how you and others attempt to exert influence in order to change another person's position.
2. To understand the relationship between motivation and the acceptance or rejection of change.
3. To consider how change situations are influenced by multiple criteria and by subjective versus objective considerations.

## B. Procedures

*Step 1.* Before coming to class, read the Company Situation for Enigma Engineering Company. Use the data in Table 6.2 to fill in the Enigma Individual Decision Form or develop your own decision form with your own criteria. Each participant should then make an individual ranking of the employees from 1 (the first to be laid off) to 8 (the last to be laid off). Record your answers in column 1 of the Rating Form.

*Step 2.* Form teams consisting of five or six members with one member serving as an observer. Additional class members can serve as observers. Each team is to reach a consensus on the ranking. Remember that a consensus decision involves reaching mutual agreement by discussion until everyone agrees on the final decision. Follow these instructions for reaching a consensus:

1. Try to reach the best possible decision.
2. Do not change your mind simply to reach an agreement and avoid conflict, but support solutions with which you are able to agree.
3. Avoid "conflict-reducing" techniques, such as majority vote, averaging, or trading in reaching your decision.
4. View differences of opinion as a help rather than a hindrance in decision making.
5. Record your team's decision in column 2 on the Rating Form. The observer can use the Observer Form at the end of the simulation.

*Time suggested for Step 2: 30 minutes.*

*Step 3.* List each team's ranking on the board and compare and discuss the differences in ranking. The observer will provide feedback using the Observer Form as a guide. Also consider the following questions, with the observers leading the discussion:

1. How did members differ in the criteria they used to lay people off?
2. Did any of the team members resist changing their positions?
3. What strategies were used to influence and change team members' positions?
4. How were the differences resolved? To what extent was the group decision really based on consensus?

*Time suggested for Step 3: 20 minutes.*

*Step 4.* Record the answers given by your instructor in column 3 on the Rating Form. (The answers are based on nonscientific survey results provided by "experts.") Score your individual and team answers. Where the actual and correct answers match, put +10 in columns 4 and 5. If the actual and correct answers do not match, put 0 in columns 4 and 5. Total the points to calculate individual and team scores. The maximum score is 80 and the minimum is 0. Column 4 gives an indication of the individual participant's "correctness," and column 5 provides an equivalent measure of each team's performance.

Compare the individual and team scores. Individuals come to teams with varying degrees of preparation, so the final score may not reflect how the team made decisions. As a class, compare the scores of the teams. As a class, discuss the following:

1. Do you agree with the answers given by the experts?
2. What are some other ways to measure team effectiveness?

*Time suggested for Step 4: 10 minutes.*

## Company Situation: Enigma Engineering Company

The Enigma Engineering Company is a medium-sized engineering and manufacturing company located in the suburbs of Chicago. Enigma specializes in designing and manufacturing circuit boards and other electronic products. The products it manufactures have low production runs and are utilized as components in products (such as computer-controlled drill presses) made by other companies. This specialization has permitted Enigma to avoid competing with larger companies such as Intel.

Enigma is not unionized. Over the past two years, it has been trying to incorporate an objective performance-review system that provides feedback to employees. The system is designed to be objective and time-oriented.

The loss of a contract bid to a competitor has forced Enigma's management to consider laying off one, two, or three of the poorest performers in the circuit board production unit. The layoff, scheduled for next week, may be only temporary, but the management wants to be sure that it is fair in presenting an objectively based decision to the employees.

The people in the unit to be cut back are:

1. Albert Banks: white, age 42, married, three children, two years of high school, and 14 years with the company.
2. Bob Brown: black, age 37, widower, two children, high school graduate, and eight years with the company.
3. Christian Newton: black, age 24, single, high school graduate, and two years with the company.
4. Dave Fram: white, age 50, single, finished junior college while working, and 15 years with the company.
5. Carla Peters: Native American, age 36, married, four children, high school graduate, and three years with the company.
6. Ray Salgado: Hispanic, age 40, married, one child, high school graduate, and four years with the company.
7. Valerie Green: white, age 39, divorced, two children, two years of college, and seven years with the company.
8. Richard Chu: Asian, age 42, married, no children, one year of college, and nine years with the company.

In previous performance reviews, the employees have been evaluated on the basis of a number of factors listed in Table 6.2. The ratings shown have been averaged over the past two years of performance evaluation.

**TABLE 6.2** Enigma Performance Review Data; Factors Evaluated by Supervisor

| Employee | Average Weekly Output[a] | (%) Rejects[b] | (%) Absences[c] | Cooperative Attitude[d] | Loyalty[d] | Potential for Promotion[d] |
|---|---|---|---|---|---|---|
| Albert Banks | 39.6 | 4.9 | 6.3 | Good | Good | Fair |
| Bob Brown | 43.4 | 5.3 | 7.9 | Poor | Fair | Fair |
| Christine Newton | 35.2 | 0.9 | 0.4 | Excellent | Good | Good |
| Dave Fram | 40.4 | 4.7 | 13.2 | Excellent | Excellent | Fair |
| Carla Peters | 40.2 | 9.6 | 9.3 | Poor | Fair | Poor |
| Ray Salgado | 39.6 | 3.4 | 6.1 | Good | Fair | Poor |
| Valarie Green | 36.2 | 4.8 | 5.0 | Good | Good | Fair |
| Richard Chu | 45.2 | 7.0 | 3.6 | Fair | Fair | Good |

[a]Higher Score = more output.
[b]Lower score = fewer rejects.
[c]Lower score = fewer absences.
[d]Possible ratings: poor, fair, good, excellent.

## ENIGMA INDIVIDUAL DECISION FORM

| | Education | Working Output | Seniority | Rejects | Absences | Attitude | Loyalty | Promotion Potential | AVERAGE |
|---|---|---|---|---|---|---|---|---|---|
| A. Banks | | | | | | | | | |
| B. Brown | | | | | | | | | |
| C. Newton | | | | | | | | | |
| D. Fram | | | | | | | | | |
| C. Peters | | | | | | | | | |
| R. Salgado | | | | | | | | | |
| V. Green | | | | | | | | | |
| R. Chu | | | | | | | | | |

**Education**
No H.S. Diploma = 2
High School Diploma = 4
1 Year College = 6
2+ Years College = 8

**Seniority**
2 Years = 1   8 Years = 5
3 Years = 2   9 Years = 6
4 Years = 3   14 Years = 7
7 Years = 4   15 Years = 8

**All other criteria**
Poor = 2
Fair = 4
Good = 6
Excellent = 8

## RATING FORM

| Employee | Individual Rating Col. 1 | Team Rating Col. 2 | Correct Rating Col. 3 | Individual Score Col. 4 | Team Score Col. 5 |
|---|---|---|---|---|---|
| 1. A. Banks | | | | | |
| 2. B. Brown | | | | | |
| 3. C. Newton | | | | | |
| 4. D. Fram | | | | | |
| 5. C. Peters | | | | | |
| 6. R. Salgado | | | | | |
| 7. V. Green | | | | | |
| 8. R. Chu | | | | | |
| Total Scores (maximum score is 80, minimum score is 0) | | | | | |

**OBSERVER FORM**

| Low | : | | : | | : | | : | | : | | : | | : | High |
|---|---|---|---|---|---|---|---|---|---|---|---|---|---|---|
| 1 | | 2 | | 3 | | 4 | | 5 | | 6 | | 7 | | |

Based on the above scale, rate the team on how it performed. Record your choice in the blank.

1. Cooperative teamwork          _____

2. Member satisfaction           _____

3. Team motivation               _____

4. Information sharing           _____

5. Consensual decision making    _____

6. Conflict directly faced and resolved   _____

7. Participative leadership      _____

8. Clearly defined goals         _____

9. Trust                         _____

10. Encouraged openness          _____

Additional observations:

_____

_____

_____

_____

_____

_____

_____

_____

_____

_____

_____

## OD Skills Simulation 6.2

### Driving and Restraining Forces

*Total time suggested: 25 to 50 minutes.*

### A. Purpose

This simulation draws on the change situation posed in Simulation 6.1. The simulation should help you further understand the diagnosis process and overcoming resistance to change.

### B. Procedures

*Step 1.* Form into the same teams as for Simulation 6.1 and identify the operating problems your team encountered in solving the task. Then make two lists on the Force Field Analysis Form: one on driving forces (behaviors and actions that helped in solving the problem) and the other on the restraining forces (behaviors and actions that hindered in solving the problem). Make additional charts depending on the number of problems identified.

*Time suggested for Step 1: 25 minutes.*

*Step 2.* Meeting as a class, report on the significant problems and the driving and restraining forces. Determine to what extent the problems are similar and different between groups.

*Time suggested for Step 2: 25 minutes.*

**FORCE-FIELD ANALYSIS FORM**

Problem: _____

| Driving Forces | Restraining Forces |
|---|---|
| _____ | _____ |
| _____ | _____ |
| _____ | _____ |
| _____ | _____ |

Problem: _____

| Driving Forces | Restraining Forces |
|---|---|
| _____ | _____ |
| _____ | _____ |
| _____ | _____ |
| _____ | _____ |

Problem: _____

| Driving Forces | Restraining Forces |
|---|---|
| _____ | _____ |
| _____ | _____ |
| _____ | _____ |
| _____ | _____ |

Problem: _____

| Driving Forces | Restraining Forces |
|---|---|
| _____ | _____ |
| _____ | _____ |
| _____ | _____ |
| _____ | _____ |

# OD Skills Simulation 6.3

## Strategies for Change

*Total time suggested: 60 minutes.*

### A. Purpose

The purpose of this simulation is to experience a change situation in which you attempt to influence another person.

### B. Procedures

*Step 1.* Form teams of three to four members and select a controversial topic (for example, outsourcing jobs out of a company or the country, free trade, gay marriage, drilling for oil in environmentally sensitive areas, political candidates). Two members take opposing points of view on the topic selected, while the third takes a neutral or undecided position. Extra class members can be observers to groups. See Figure 6.4.

*Step 2.* Within a preselected time, usually about 10 minutes, members A and C try to convince member B of their position. Member B should remain relatively silent but can ask questions for clarification.

*Step 3.* At the end of the allotted time, member B decides which person (A or C) has been most persuasive and explains why.

*Step 4.* Repeat Steps 1–3 until everyone has had a chance to be member B. It is suggested that in each of the rounds, the team select a different controversial topic.

*Time suggested for Steps 1–4: 45 minutes.*

*Step 5.* In class session, discuss what strategies were used to persuade and change member B's opinion. How would these strategies of change apply in an organizational change situation?

*Time suggested for Step 5: 15 minutes.*

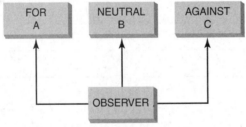

**FIGURE 6.4**

# CASE: THE HEXADECIMAL COMPANY

The Hexadecimal Company is a medium-sized manufacturing firm supplying computer components to many international computer manufacturers. Initially, the company produced traditional computer keyboards, but competition from cheaper labor markets in other countries forced it to change its products. It now licenses OLED (organic light-emitting diodes) technology from Kodak and designs and produces high-tech products such as thin film keyboards for hand-held computers and flexible electronic pages (less than 1/100 inch thick) used in e-books. With John Zoltan as president, the company has experienced rapid growth since its beginning and is now moving into nanotechnology and advanced electronics from the electromechanical assembly of the past.

John Zoltan recently attended a university executive seminar and was so impressed by it that he brought in the professor as an OD practitioner. At one of their meetings, they decided that Zoltan should start an internal OD group to help achieve the organizational excellence he desired for his company. Zoltan ran an ad in human resources and trade magazines, and he and the practitioner selected four young applicants. These four, and one young internal prospect from the human resources department, were formed into what was called the OD Group. See Figure 6.5.

## The OD Group

The OD group was housed in an old conference room and began with a high level of enthusiasm and energy. The members of the group ranged in age from 23 to 34. The members were Pete Loomis, 25, a behavioral specialist who had done training in industry; Kay Hughes, 27, who had been a sales representative prior to graduate school; Bill Heller, 26, specializing in group dynamics, with no industry experience; Indar Kripalani, 34, with OD experience in the military; and George Kessler, 23, with three years of experience in Hexadecimal's human resources department.

The group spent its first month getting to know the members of the organization. They held weekly conferences with John Zoltan, who was very interested and active in the planning stages of the OD program.

At that point, the group (the "hot-shots," as they were known in some areas of Hexadecimal) started a company-wide training program focusing on managerial style. The program involved three-day training sessions at an offsite location, a resort motel with good meals and other attractive features. This was called the "country club" by disapproving employees.

The group itself was a highly cohesive work team. Because of their open office, they spent long hours tossing ideas around and providing support and enthusiasm for one another's ideas. They were all involved in the design of the program (as was Zoltan) and worked hard to make it a success. Often the group would sit around until nine or ten o'clock or even midnight, critiquing the sessions and planning new approaches for change.

The group was characterized by diversity of dress, individuality, and openness. Pete, George, and Bill usually dressed informally in Levi's and sport shirts, while Indar and Kay dressed in more of an executive style, wearing sport jackets and the like. The difference in dress reflected a division of thought within the group. Pete, George, and Bill were more confrontational and aggressive in approach. They wanted innovative changes and an overhaul of the firm's production operations. The other two felt that they needed to be accepted first and favored more gradual changes. They felt that the group needed to start "where the system was" if it was to be effective. About this time, Zoltan left for a visit to Asia to look into new marketing opportunities.

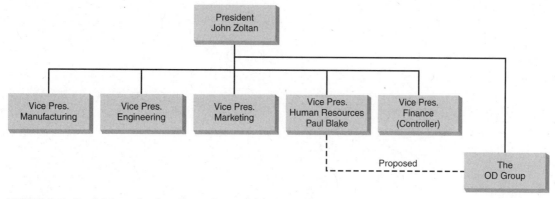

**FIGURE 6.5    Partial Organization Chart of Hexadecimal Company**

## The Activities

As the training continued through all levels of the organization, the group was also collecting organization survey data to be used in planning the next phase of the OD program. Here the controversy began to emerge. Some wanted to hold feedback sessions and confront the members with the data, then begin a job-design program leading to improving the effectiveness of work teams. The second group, including Indar and Kay, suggested a slower and more gradual approach. They thought that given their low level of acceptance in the organization, they should start with something less threatening, such as data gathering and feedback.

A second rift occurred when the group began to see less of Zoltan as the training progressed. However, Kay could call the president's office and get an appointment anytime, which she often did. Indar also held a weekly briefing session with Zoltan when he was in town.

The other members, particularly Pete, made a lot of jokes about this fact, but there was often an edge of seriousness under the humor. For example, Pete and Bill had been trying for two weeks to see Zoltan to explain their ideas, but he was unavailable. Yet his secretary called Kay Hughes to join him for coffee. When the group discussed this, Indar and Kay simply stated that they were trying to maintain and develop the group's relationship with the client. Peter replied, "I thought the whole organization was our client."

Unfortunately, the evaluation of the training program was mixed. Some managers and departments were full of praise for it, whereas others were highly negative, dismissing it as "a waste of time and money."

In a meeting with John Zoltan, the controller said that in view of the disappointing results, it would be a good idea to move the OD group to the human resources section for budgeting purposes. The group was currently charging more than $700,000 per year to overhead, and this was very unpopular among the line managers because overhead costs of the OD group were prorated to the managers' departments. Zoltan said he would give the matter some thought and discuss this possibility with the executive committee.

## The Meeting

Shortly after this (and approximately a year after the group was formed), the members of the group were invited to an executive committee meeting where the performance of the OD program was discussed and evaluated. John Zoltan and others expressed high praise for the work of the group, but the executive committee had suggestions for improving the group in the future.

Because Zoltan suggested that there was a need for more coordination and integration of training activities and for improved budgetary control, the committee recommended that the group be placed in the human resources department for budgeting purposes, reporting to Paul Blake. The committee insisted that this would not affect the way the group operated. The committee also suggested that the group designate a central contact person. It recommended Indar Kripalani for the role, claiming that he was the only member acceptable to a majority of the company's managers, but left the decision up to the group.

As the members of the group walked back to their office, several angry comments were made to the effect that Zoltan "could take this job and shove it!" Kay and Pete said they were considering resigning from the company. (Use the Case Analysis Form on the following page.)

**THE HEXADECIMAL COMPANY CASE ANALYSIS FORM**

Name: _____

I. Problems

  A. Macro

    1. _____
_____

    2. _____
_____

  B. Micro

    1. _____
_____

    2. _____
_____

II. Causes

    1. _____
_____

    2. _____
_____

    3. _____
_____

III. Systems affected

    1. _____
_____

    2. _____
_____

    3. _____
_____

IV. Alternatives

    1. _____
_____

    2. _____
_____

    3. _____
_____

V. Recommendations

_____
_____
_____
_____
_____
_____

## Chapter 6 Endnotes

1. Emily Thorton, "The New Rules," *Business Week*, January 19, 2009, p. 32.
2. Jena McGregor, "There Is No More Normal, Breakthrough Management Ideas for a World in Which the Game Will Never Be the Same," *Business Week*, March 23 & 30, 2009, p. 30.
3. For additional information, see Michael Beer and Nitin Nohria (eds.), *Breaking the Code of Change* (Boston, MA: Harvard Business School Press, 2000); Charles H. Bishop Jr., *Making Change Happen One Person at a Time: Assessing Change Capacity within Your Organization* (New York: AMACOM, 2001).
4. William Bridges, *Managing Transitions: Making the Most of Change* (Cambridge, MA: Da Capo, 2003), p. 32.
5. Goodwin Watson, "Resistance to Change," in *Concepts for Social Change: Cooperative Project for Educational Development Series*, vol.1 (Washington, D.C.: National Training Laboratories, 1967).
6. John F. Welch, "A Master Class in Radical Change," *Fortune*, December 13, 1993, pp. 82–90.
7. For additional information, see Kerry A. Bunker and Michael Wakefield, "The Balance Needed to Lead Change," *Harvard Management Update*, November 2008, pp. 3–5; John P. Kotter, "Leading Change," *Harvard Business Review*, January 2007, pp. 96–103.
8. Yukari Iwatani Kane, "Toshiba's Plan for Life after HD DVD," *Wall Street Journal*, March 3, 2008, pp. B1–B2.
9. Steven Prokesch (interviewer), "Creating a Growth Culture at GE: An Interview with Jeffrey R. Immelt," *Harvard Business Review*, January 2009, p. 104.
10. Don Clark, "Can a Hard Drive Make a Fashion Statement?" *Wall Street Journal*, January 4, 2008, pp. B1 and B6.
11. Michael Malone, "Intel Reboots for the 21st Century," *Wall Street Journal*, September 27–28, 2008, p. A17.
12. For additional information, see John Covington, "Eight Steps to Sustainable Change," *Industrial Management*, vol. 44, no. 6 (November/December 2002), pp. 8–12; Charles H. Bishop Jr., "How Does Change Management Need to Change?" *Harvard Management Update*, vol. 6, no.1 (January 2001), pp. 4–5.
13. See Larry Bossidy and Ram Charan, *Confronting Reality: Master the New Model for Success* (New York: Crown Business, 2004), and *Execution: The Discipline of Getting Things Done* (New York: Crown Business, 2002).
14. Welch, "Master Class in Radical Change," pp. 84–6.
15. For additional information on world competition and global organizations, see Thomas L. Friedman, *The World Is Flat, A Brief History of the Twenty-First Century* (New York: Farrar, Straus and Giroux, 2007); and Thomas L. Friedman, *Hot, Flat, and Crowded: Why We Need a Green Revolution, and How It Can Renew America* (New York: Farrar, Straus and Giroux, 2008).
16. For information on *Fortune*'s Global 500 list, see http://money.cnn.com/magazines. The list is usually available in the July issue of the magazine; George Mellon, Gabel Medard and Henry Brune, *Global Inc.: An Atlas of the Multinational Corporation* (New York: New Press, 2003); Richard Siklos, "The Iger Difference," *Fortune*, April 28, 2008, p. 94.
17. Scott Thurm (interviewer), "Managing Innovation," *Wall Street Journal*, September 24, 2007, p. R6.
18. Jeffrey D. Ford and Laurie W. Ford, "Decoding Resistance to Change," *Harvard Business Review*, April 2009, p. 103.
19. Ibid., pp. 99–103; Jeffrey D. Ford, Laurie W. Ford, and Angelo D'Amelio, "Resistance to Change: The Rest of the Story," *Academy of Management Review*, April 2008, pp. 362–377; D. T. Wegener, R. E. Petty, N. D. Smoak, and L. R. Fabrigar, "Multiple Routes to Resisting Attitude Change," in E. S. Knowles and J. A. Linn (eds.), *Resistance and Persuasion* (Mahwah, NJ: Lawrence Erlbaum Associates, 2004), pp. 13–38.
20. Geert Devos, Marc Buelens, and Dave Bouckenooghe, "Contribution of Content, Context, and Process to Understanding Openness to Organizational Change: Two Experimental Simulation Studies," *Journal of Social Psychology*, vol. 147, no. 6 (December 2007), pp. 607–29; R. A. Jones, N. L. Jimmieson, and A. Griffiths, "The Impact of Organizational Culture and Reshaping Capabilities on Change Implementation Success: The Mediating Role of Readiness for Change," *Journal of Management Studies*, vol. 42, no. 2 (March 2005), pp, 361–86; B. Schneider, A. P. Brief, and R. A. Guzzo, "Creating a Climate and Culture for Sustainable Organizational Change," *Organizational Dynamics*, vol. 24, no. 4 (Spring 1996), pp. 7–19.
21. Scott McCartney, "How US Airways Vaulted to First Place," *Wall Street Journal*, July 22, 2008, p. D3.
22. For additional information, see J. A. O'Shea, E. McAuliffe, and L. A. Wyness, "Successful Large System Change: At What Cost?" *Journal of Change Management*, vol. 7, no. 2 (June 2007), pp. 107–20.
23. Phred Dvorak, "How Understanding the 'Why' of Decisions Matters," *Wall Street Journal*, March 19, 2007, p. B3.
24. John P. Kotter, "Leading Change, Why Transformation Efforts Fail," *Harvard Business Review*, January 2007, pp. 96–103.
25. Rick Mauer, "Making a Strong Case for Change," *Journal for Quality and Participation*," vol. 26, no. 3 (Fall 2003), pp. 41–42; John Case, *The Open-Book Experience: Lessons from Over 100 Companies Who Successfully Transformed Themselves* (Reading, MA: Addison-Wesley Longman 1998); John Case, "Four Fears About Open-Book Management," *Management Review*, vol. 87, no. 5 (May 1998), pp. 58–61; Tim Davis, "Open-Book Management: Its Promise and Pitfalls," *Organizational Dynamics*, vol. 25, no. 3 (Winter 1997), pp. 7–21; Leon Rubis, "Playing by the Books," *HR Magazine*, vol. 40, no. 5 (May 1995), p. 38.
26. Joann Muller, "Can Delphi Tune Up in Time?" *Business Week*, March 15, 1999, pp. 68–70.

27. Malone, "Intel Reboots for the 21st Century," p. A17.

28. James M. Kouzes and Barry Z. Posner, "To Lead, Create a Shared Vision," *Harvard Business Review*, January 2009, pp. 20–21.

29. Devos, Buelens, and Bouckenooghe, "Contribution of Content, Context, and Process to Understanding Openness to Organizational Change: Two Experimental Simulation Studies"; M. H. Kavanagh and N. M. Ashkanasy, "The impact of leadership and change management strategy on organizational culture and individual acceptance of change during a merger," *British Journal of Management*, vol. 17 no. S1 (March 2, 2006), pp. S81–S103; W. H. Bommer, G. A. Rich, and R. S. Rubin, "Changing Attitudes about Change: Longitudinal Effects of Transformational Leader Behavior on Employee Cynicism about Organizational Change," *Journal of Organizational Behavior*, vol 26, no. 7 (November 2005), pp. 733–53.

30. Mike Eskew, "Stick with Your Vision," *Harvard Business Review*, July 2007, p. 57.

31. N. L. Jimmieson, D. J. Terry, and V. J. Callan, "A Longitudinal Study of Employee Adaption to Organizational Change: The Role of Change-Related Information and Change-Related Self-Efficacy," *Journal of Occupational Health Psychology*, vol. 9, no. 1 (January 2004), pp. 11–27.

32. Robert Berner, "P & G: How A. G. Lafley Is Revolutionizing a Bastion of Corporate Conservatism," *Business Week*, July 7, 2003, p. 63.

33. *The Caine Mutiny: A Novel of World War II* (Garden City, NY: Doubleday, 1951), p. 131. Copyright 1951 by Herman Wouk.

34. Eskew, "Stick with Your Vision," pp. 56–57.

35. For a more detailed discussion of reward systems, see Joseph Blasi, Douglas Kruse, and Aaron Bernstein, *In the Company of Owners: The Truth about Stock Options (and Why Every Employee Should Have Them)* (New York: Basic Books, 2003).

36. Maya K. Kroumova and James C. Sesil, "Intellectual Capital, Monitoring, and Risk: What Predicts the Adoption of Employee Stock Options?" *Industrial Relations*, October 2006, pp. 734–52.

37. See The National Center for Employee Ownership Web site, www.nceo.org for current data.

38. Statistics are from the latest year available, a 2006 random sampling of working adults. The GSS study was performed by the National Opinion Research Center of the University of Chicago. Joseph Blasi and Douglas Kruse of Rutgers University and Richard Freeman of Harvard University, all affiliated with the Shared Capitalism Project of the National Bureau of Economic Research, organized the questions and their analysis. The survey was reported at the web site of The National Center for Employee Ownership, www.nceo.org. Refer to this Web site for more current data.

39. Rik Kirkland, "Cisco's Dixplay of Strength," *Fortune*, November 12, 2007, p. 96.

40. Jeffrey D. Ford, Laurie W. Ford, and Angelo D'amelio, "Resistance to Change: The Rest of the Story," *Academy of Management Review*, April 2008, pp. 362–77.

41. Devos, Buelens, and Bouckenooghe, "Contribution of Content, Context, and Process to Understanding Openness to Organizational Change: Two Experimental Simulation Studies"; M. H. Kavanagh and N. M. Ashkanasy, "The impact of leadership and change management strategy on organizational culture and individual acceptance of change during a merger"; W. H. Bommer, "Changing Attitudes about Change: Longitudinal Effects of Transformational Leader Behavior on Employee Cynicism about organizational change."

42. Larry Hirschhorn, "Campaigning for Change," *Harvard Business Review*, vol. 80, no. 7 (July 2002), p. 98.

43. Moon Ihlwan, "Samsung Under Siege," *Business Week*, April 28, 2008, p. 46.

# PART THREE

# Improving Excellence in Individuals

Understanding the need for planned change

Building an OD background and developing an increased knowledge of OD

Personal and interpersonal OD concepts

Team and interteam OD concepts

Organization and system-wide OD concepts

Significant changes in managing have been thrust upon lower and middle managers. In organizations, the traditional ways of managing are giving way to managers acting as coaches for their teams. While these managers are making evaluations, promoting, and performing some of the other traditional roles of a manager, they are also mentoring, teaching, communicating, developing, and empowering.

As the work team becomes a greater part of the way organizations function, managers require new methods for working with teams. A better understanding of group behavior will enable managers to help the team understand how it can function more effectively. This new manager assists the team to improve in areas that include communications, problem solving, decision making, and leadership.

A major responsibility of a manager is to empower other people with whom the manager works. Central to empowerment is the delegation of power and decision making, creating or passing along a shared vision of the future, and engaging all employees so that they develop a sense of pride and ownership. Organizations increasingly realize that the individual employee or organization member is a fundamental element that will make an organization successful or a failure.

In this *Part 3: Improving Excellence in Individuals,* Chapter 7 discusses integrating behavioral, structural, and technological OD intervention strategies. The first OD interventions that we will study, covered in Chapter 8, are personal and interpersonal interventions. This includes learning skills in team and group process interventions. In chapter 9 the emphasis is upon employee empowerment, learning more about personal and interpersonal interventions, and how these interventions can help a work team better understand how it functions.

# OD Intervention Strategies

## LEARNING OBJECTIVES

**Upon completing this chapter, you will be able to:**

1. Identify and understand the range of major OD intervention techniques and how they can be applied.
2. Identify the ways various interpersonal, team, and intergroup techniques fit into an OD program.
3. Understand the change strategies.

## PREMEETING PREPARATION

1. Read Chapter 7.
2. Prepare for OD Skill Simulation 7.1. Prior to class, form teams of eight members and select roles. Complete Step 1.
3. Read and analyze Case: The Farm Bank.

## ORGANIZATIONAL CHANGE

Organizational change attempts to increase organizational efficiency. The purpose is to increase productivity through invigorated employees who are able to develop creativity, performance, and innovation beyond traditional levels. Managing organizational change is an important and complex challenge. "The world has changed so much because of, among other reasons, deregulation, lowering of trade barriers, rapid technological advances, demographic shifts, and greater urbanization, that strategies worked a decade ago are unlikely to do so anymore," according to Peter Williamson and Ming Zeng, university professors from University of Cambridge and Cheung Kong Graduate School of Business, respectively.[1] In attempting to increase organizational and individual effectiveness, managers must understand the nature of the changes needed and the possible effects of various alternative change strategies.

The starting point for setting a change program in motion is the definition of a total change strategy. After the problem areas associated with current performance are diagnosed, the opportunities for improvement are identified and a strategy to apply techniques and technologies for change is selected. The strategies are the overall plans and direction that the OD program will take. An **OD strategy** may be defined as a plan for relating and integrating the different organizational improvement activities engaged in over a period to accomplish objectives. The type of strategy selected will be greatly influenced by the diagnosis of the organization's problems.

There are several major categories of OD strategies: structural, technological, and behavioral. Structural strategies emphasize the organization's design and workflow, such as who reports to whom and how the work is structured. Technological strategies implement new developments in areas related to technological innovations. Examples of technological strategies are new manufacturing equipment and computerized information systems. Behavioral strategies improve the use of human resources, such as empowering people at lower levels of the organization to make decisions without seeking upper-level approval.

Developing a strategy includes the planning of activities intended to resolve difficulties and build on strengths in order to improve the organization's effectiveness and efficiency. From the strategies, the OD process moves to the stage of selecting intervention techniques and technologies. Intervention techniques are the specific means, activities, and programs by which change goals can be attained.

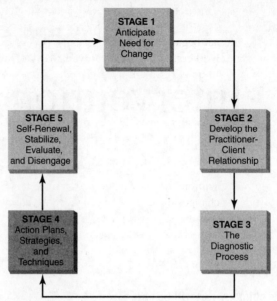

**FIGURE 7.1**   Stage 4 of Organization Development's Five Stages

This chapter, as well as the next eight chapters, discusses the fourth stage—action plans, strategies, and techniques—of an OD program. This is illustrated in Figure 7.1. Here we will describe several major OD strategies for setting up a program of change. The chapter concludes with an overview of major OD interventions.

## BASIC STRATEGIES TO CHANGE

The three basic strategies for organization change are structural, technological, and behavioral.[2] We will discuss these three strategies separately, but in practice changes made using any one strategy will very likely require some use of the other two. The sociotechnical-systems approach discussed in Chapter 2 speaks to the interconnection between structural, technical, and behavioral change approaches.

### Structural Strategies

Organization structure is important because it provides the framework that relates elements of the organization to one another. **Structural strategies** attempt to change an organization's design by modifying the lines of authority, span of control, and arrangement of work functions.

Restructuring corporations to make them more competitive has been a major goal of corporations over the past two decades. Major corporate restructuring was initially concentrated in the United States. Because of global markets, what happens in one country can have repercussions in other countries. In order to remain competitive, corporations in other countries have also undertaken major restructuring efforts. At some point, the restructuring evolved into mega-mergers, as with Daimler-Chrysler, where the restructuring was global in scope. But as is the case with some larger mergers between organizations that have different cultures, Daimler-Chrysler's merger was not successful, and Daimler sold the Chrysler operations after nine years and at a substantial loss. In another example of restructuring large organizations, The Bill and Melinda Gates Foundation invested approximately eight years and $2 billion in 40 U.S. school districts. Most of the money went to improve public education primarily by breaking up big, urban high schools and creating smaller, friendly schools to remake them scholastically sound. A *Fortune* article reported that overall it has not worked. Bill Gates said, "We had a high hope that just by changing the structure, we'd do something dramatic. But it's nowhere near enough."[3] The new program will spend $3 billion over five years focusing on what's inside the classroom: the quality of the teaching and curriculum.

Structural changes include downsizing and removing or adding layers to an organization's hierarchy. Downsizing and layoffs are frequently used during recessions, and especially serious recessions, where a cash-starved organization is desperately fighting to stay in existence.

Zappos, a quirky retailer with an upbeat culture, has core values that include "Create Fun and A Little Weirdness," "Build a Positive Team and Family Spirit," and "Deliver WOW Through Service."[4] But with the recession that began in late 2007, Zappos, two years later, was hard hit by the economy and had to lay off workers. To date, the company has had to lay off 124 employees out of 1,500. To get the news out quickly and minimize stress, Zappos used e-mail, blogs, and Twitter. The blogs and Twitter created a surprisingly positive reaction among the employees who were avid users of these communication methods.[5] Generous severance benefits were given to help the laid off employees and to provide the best possible message to the remaining employees. "The motivation was," says CEO Tony Hsieh, "let's take care of our employees who got us this far."[6]

Other structural changes include organizations adding layers that produce tall organizations, but more typically organizations are restructured to reduce the layers of the hierarchy, making them flatter. Structural changes of another type involve decentralization and centralization. In decentralization, operations are split up and departments are given more autonomy and power to make decisions. At other organizations, especially those where there have been mergers, operations have been made more centralized, with decision making increasingly taking place at the home or corporate office. For example, Ford Motor Company is attempting to integrate the operating regions around the world: the United States, Europe, Asia, South America, and Australia.[7] A similar strategy is used at Renault and Nissan Motor (Renault owns a controlling interest in Nissan) where Carlos Ghosn, CEO of both companies, is integrating the two companies with major joint ventures.[8] Other structural strategies rearrange departments, workflows, and lines of authority.

## Technological Strategies

**Technological strategies** implement new technologies, such as new computer systems and machinery. These strategies are often required to bring an organization up to the state-of-the-art in machinery, methods, automation, and job design. The need to improve on technological strategies is illustrated in Figure 7.2.

Companies such as Briggs & Stratton Corp., a manufacturer of small gasoline engines, have changed their U.S. manufacturing plants to smaller and flexible factories. The factories depend heavily upon integrated networked computers and machine tools coupled with small new facilities. The plants normally specialize in small production runs of high-margin products. Timken Co., maker of industrial bearings, shifted its product line from high-volume runs to small batches of advanced specialized bearings. Technicians—the company refers to them as shop-floor associates—can call up a 3-D digital model from the library, modify the model if necessary, and enter the instructions into the networked machine tools. The plant can change a production run in as little as 15 minutes, versus half a day with the old method.[9]

Organizations are increasingly implementing sophisticated computerized management-information systems (MIS). These systems help employees with their jobs, in addition to helping the organization's customers. In many cases, the systems use the Internet as well as an organization's internal Internet, sometimes called an Intranet. For example, technological strategies are involved when a university implements a new computerized registration system that allows students to use the Internet to view course descriptions and syllabi, view the semester course listing, register for classes, print their transcripts, participate in chat rooms with other students and the instructor, and see student evaluations of instructors. The so-called virtual

**FIGURE 7.2**  Improvements in Technology Can Help Improve Customer Service
*Source:* CROCK © NORTH AMERICA SYNDICATE

university is having a significant impact on the more traditional universities and their approach to using technology.[10]

### Behavioral Strategies

Another approach, **behavioral strategies,** emphasizes the use of human resources. In the past, managers concentrated on fully analyzing an organization's technological and mechanical capacities, but often neglected a vast untapped resource: its human assets. Employees generally have higher morale and are motivated toward organization goals when their personal resources and talents are fully used. Increasing the morale, motivation, and commitment of members can also improve an organization's performance.

Although OD traditionally has been associated with behavioral strategies, this chapter attempts to provide a balanced description of the change process by including structural and technological strategies. OD techniques are an effective means for carrying out many change strategies, including those that are technological and structural. Any major change effort, regardless of emphasis, must deal with the total organization system, which includes structure, technology, and human behavior. Each of these approaches appears in most OD strategies, but they receive varying degrees of emphasis.

Structural, technological, and behavioral change strategies are not OD change strategies per se. The determining feature of an OD strategy is the process used to arrive at and carry out the strategy. As Edgar Schein, a leading OD practitioner, said in an interview, "I believe OD is a philosophy of how you do things, not a technology of what you do."[11] In an OD program, the members of the organization develop their own problem solutions. The flow is from the diagnosis of problems and opportunities for change (where we are now) to the setting of objectives (where we want to be). The program then moves to deciding upon change strategies and finally to selecting specific intervention techniques (how we get from here to there). OD intervention techniques, such as goal setting, confrontation meetings, survey feedback, total quality management (TQM), and team building (discussed in detail in later chapters), are then implemented systematically to revitalize the organization.

## THE INTEGRATION OF CHANGE STRATEGIES

Organization development has evolved during the past several decades from a narrow viewpoint favoring one specific intervention strategy to a more integrated or systematic approach to change. Historically, OD was seen as predominantly using behavioral-oriented interventions. Today, the trend in OD is to deal with the total organization through an integration of behavioral, structural, and technological strategies. Figure 7.3 illustrates the integration of the three approaches to change.

For OD strategies to be successful, the organization must consider the interdependencies among its various subelements. A change in one subsystem will have some impact upon other elements of the system. An integration of strategies is missing in many organizations, according to Edward E. Lawler III, professor of business and director of the Center for Effective Organizations at the University of Southern California. He writes in an article for the *Wall Street Journal*, "While most companies say they value human capital, in reality, few are run that way. They may have systems in place for hiring talented people, but their organizational structures aren't designed to develop, motivate and retain the best ones."

An integration of technical, behavioral, and structural changes is the open-office concept that is used at companies such as Hewlett-Packard, Pixar (part of Disney), Intel, and Cisco. These companies are abandoning the cubicle and office-with-door model of work arrangements in favor of open-layout designs. These arrangements typically include open areas of tables, multiworker desks, and lounge-like settings where employees gather to work. Employees typically bring their project materials and laptops with wireless Internet connections to the open meeting areas. Quiet zones are available when needed. Hewlett-Packard says that this arrangement improves productivity by providing more contact and collaboration.[12]

A comprehensive approach needs to consider the system's technological and structural variables as well as its behavioral variables. One approach is to use a diagnosis based on the analogy of an iceberg. There are surface or overt organizational elements that are easily observed, such as organization structure and policy; and there are subsurface or covert elements, such as

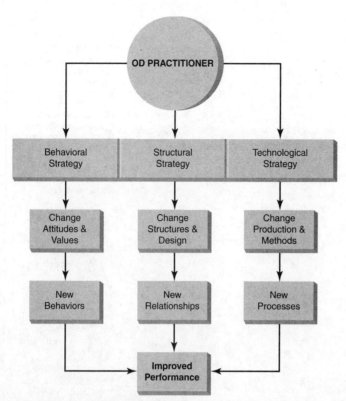

**FIGURE 7.3** An Integrated Approach to Change

patterns of communication, trust, and openness that are often obscured or hidden. For additional information, refer to Figure 7.4. Often the diagnosis examines only the more visible and overt aspects of the organization and ignores the many powerful but hidden problem areas. It is essential in any change program to consider all possible problem areas, both overt and covert, if the strategy is to be successful.

Structural, technological, and behavioral change strategies do not exist in isolation of one another. For example, a structural change in an organization eliminates a layer of the organization's hierarchy. The decisions and work of the employees who were removed are delegated to lower levels. To make quality decisions that are timely, these employees need access to additional information that should be but is currently not available. Technological changes in the form of a new management-information system are thus made. This entails a larger computer system with more remote terminals for the increased number of lower-level employees needing access to information. In addition, people at lower levels making decisions mean behavioral changes in the form of working more closely with other employees involved in the decisions and forming points where information can be exchanged with other people in the company.

Technology alone is not the answer for a company to attain quality improvement. To reach the true potential of technological changes, management must also carry out structural and behavioral changes. Similarly, a company that has set up finely tuned structural and behavioral innovations but uses outdated technology cannot operate at full potential. By an integration of fewer levels involved in making decisions (structural), team development (behavioral), and video conferencing (technological), companies can get more return on their investment than if they implemented just one strategy. The combination permits work teams to communicate and collaborate easily with one another, even across long distances and organizational boundaries, such as departments (structure). Software that goes by various names but is often called groupware is available and being used to make **virtual teams** and real-time collaboration a reality. Virtual teams and their meetings occur electronically over telecommunications lines and reduce the need for face-to-face meetings.[13]

It is increasingly evident that organizations involve complexity and contingencies. Simple cause-and-effect diagnosis and intervention strategies may overlook critical interrelationships that influence the change effort. As a result, it is often difficult to isolate changes to the relation-

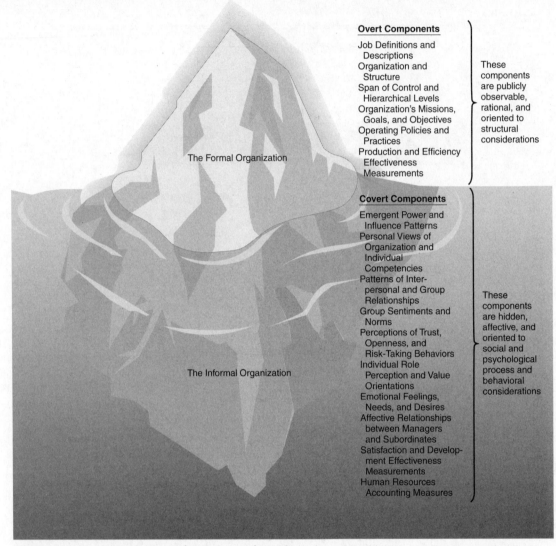

**Overt Components**

Job Definitions and Descriptions
Organization and Structure
Span of Control and Hierarchical Levels
Organization's Missions, Goals, and Objectives
Operating Policies and Practices
Production and Efficiency Effectiveness Measurements

These components are publicly observable, rational, and oriented to structural considerations

**Covert Components**

Emergent Power and Influence Patterns
Personal Views of Organization and Individual Competencies
Patterns of Interpersonal and Group Relationships
Group Sentiments and Norms
Perceptions of Trust, Openness, and Risk-Taking Behaviors
Individual Role Perception and Value Orientations
Emotional Feelings, Needs, and Desires
Affective Relationships between Managers and Subordinates
Satisfaction and Development Effectiveness Measurements
Human Resources Accounting Measures

These components are hidden, affective, and oriented to social and psychological process and behavioral considerations

The Formal Organization

The Informal Organization

**FIGURE 7.4  The "Organization Iceberg" Approach to OD**
*Source:* Adapted from Richard J. Selfridge and Stanley I. Sokolik, "A Comprehensive View of Organizational Development," *Business Topics*, Winter 1975, p. 47. Reprinted by permission of the publisher, Division of Research, Graduate School of Business Administration, Michigan State University.

ship between any two single variables. The interrelationships between organizational variables are often complex and unclear, and the OD strategies must be comprehensive enough to provide interventions that deal with such situations.

**Second-order consequences** is a significant aspect to be considered in the selection of a change strategy. This refers to the indirect or deferred consequences that result from the immediate change actions. A change in one aspect of a system to solve one problem may result in newly created problems.

The organization's problems should emerge from the diagnosis. The most effective strategy is then selected from these findings. This can be termed an integrative approach to organization change and involves combining structural, technological, and behavioral change approaches to achieve the desired goals.

In summary, the change strategy selected must collectively consider structural, technological, and behavioral issues. The use of an inappropriate or limited strategy of change will probably lead to ineffective results and the emergence of new problems. **OD Application: Changing P&G** provides insight into some of the ways that Procter & Gamble (P&G) Company is changing to remain competitive in a highly competitive consumer market.

## OD Application: Changing P&G[14]

Procter & Gamble Company (P&G), one of the largest consumer product companies in the world and a major manufacturer of home-cleaning products, has a long history of over 170 years in business and a well-established culture and way of doing things. The culture is so rigid that some employees jokingly call themselves "Proctoids." With the chairman of the board and retired CEO, A. G. Lafley, the emphasis has been to build upon the culture but also to bring some much-needed changes to keep the company relevant in a developing world.

Lafley came to P&G in 1977 right after getting his MBA from Harvard Business School. Like a lot of other people at P&G, he has never worked anywhere else. While retaining a sense of humility, through the years he earned a reputation of giving his staff ample responsibility and asking a series of insightful questions. He calls this "peeling the onion." He spends a major part of his day communicating his vision of P&G and how he wants P&G to change. Lafley often uses slogans when he talks about his vision of P&G. One slogan, "the consumer is boss," is coincidently the title of an article he coauthored for *Fortune* magazine. "It's *Sesame Street* language—I admit that," he said in a *Business Week* interview. "A lot of what we have done is make things simple because the difficulty is making sure everybody knows what the goal is and how to get there."

Part of the strategy at P&G has been to focus on building strong brands, such as Tide and Pampers, and at the same time bring new products to market. P&G has changed its tradition of developing new products from within by acquiring new technology from outside the company. The strategy has been complicated by a severe worldwide recession where shoppers began trading down by substituting cheaper private-label brands for the premium-priced P&G brands. As a consequence, P&G has increased its offerings of lower-priced products in anticipation that consumers' price sensitivity will outlast the recession. But even with the recession, P&G has increased spending on innovating new products, engineering and manufacturing technology, and understanding the consumer. It has also delivered more messages to consumers with fewer dollars because the price of media has gone down. The success of P&G can, in part, be measured by the numbers. In 2000, P&G served about 2 billion of the then 6 billion consumers in the world with one or more P&G brands. In 2009, it served 3.5 billion of the 6.7 billion consumers in the world.

Corporate headquarters, particularly the eleventh floor, where the senior executives were located, has also undergone changes. The office walls were knocked down and the division presidents moved to other locations in the building to be closer to their teams. The executives who remained share an open area. Lafley said, "They are open so we can talk to each other, and we will constantly collaborate and work on things." In addition, the changes were made without alienating employees. Lafley's style is to listen more than he talks. Lafley said, "I'm not a screamer, not a yeller. But don't get confused by my style. I am very decisive."

In an interview, Lafley was asked to explain his philosophy on change. He responded, "The first thing is that change is accelerating. It is pervasive, affecting all parts of our consumers' lives, our industry lives, our business lives. It's highly unpredictable and volatile. In that context, you only have three choices: You can hide from change and hope it goes away. That's a losing game. You can try to resist change, and I believe that's a losing game, too. So the only real choice is to lead change, especially where leading that change turns into some type of competitive advantage. I am quite a believer that leaders are change leaders. . . . And I have made a lot of very symbolic and very physical changes so people understand that we are in the business of leading change."

**Questions**

1. Of behavioral, structural, and technological change strategies, how would you describe P&G's strategies?
2. Does P&G integrate the three change strategies and, if so, how?
3. Based on current information, evaluate the success of P&G.

## STREAM ANALYSIS

**Stream analysis** is one method used in planning the implementation and analysis of behavioral, structural, and technological changes.[15] Stream analysis begins by identifying behavioral, technological, and structural interventions that the organization can implement as part of the OD program. Through the planning process, interventions are scheduled to begin and end at specific times, and the relationships between the interventions are determined. Because of the number and complexity of the variables (interventions, times, interrelationships), a chart is made to better visualize the OD strategy. The chart is the major document used in stream analysis change strategy. It shows the interventions plotted over time with arrows showing the relationship of interventions to one another.

Figure 7.5 shows a portion of a stream analysis chart for a hypothetical OD program. The key features in such a program could include installing a robotic production system (technological), implementing self-managed work teams (structural), and holding team-building sessions (behavioral). As an example, team building takes place to introduce the new technology before a robotic production line can be installed and changes made in work teams. Team building will begin at Month 1 and continue through Month 6. Robotic systems will be installed beginning Month 4 and completed by Month 7. A revised chain of command will be introduced in Month 1, and so on. Stream analysis presents a visual representation of the OD program. Stream analysis

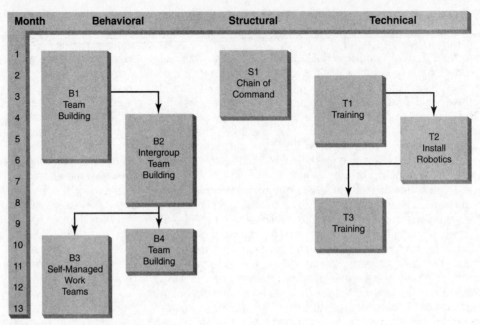

**FIGURE 7.5** Stream Analysis Chart

charts bear some resemblance to a combination of modified Program Evaluation and Review Technique (PERT) and Gantt planning charts. Complex change programs may benefit from the use of software programs that manage and keep track of the program and its many interrelated elements.

Stream analysis is useful from several perspectives. It helps the organization to diagnose and plan interventions, and keeps track of progress once the change program is underway. The client is better able to keep the organization operating as effectively as possible during the change. It may show "holes," or periods of time when there is little activity (Month 9), and periods when there is a good deal of activity (Month 5). This information may be used to redesign the change program or to schedule time appropriately. Stream analysis shows a pattern of triggers, with one activity triggering or causing another activity to follow. For complex OD projects, it is especially helpful to visually represent the change program and show "where we've been and where we have to go." If modifications are required in the OD program, the consequences of the changes on other interventions can more easily be ascertained by referring to the stream analysis chart.

In one OD program, more than two dozen practitioners were working with several operating divisions of a very large client system. By using the stream analysis approach, it was possible to plan and monitor the change program and build the necessary coordination among the practitioners and the operating divisions of the client system. The approach was also useful to top management because it could keep track of change activities occurring in the field. An entire room was devoted to charts wrapped around its walls so that top managers could drop by and see what had been accomplished and that the change program was moving on schedule. The charts gave a certain degree of legitimacy to the OD program because top management could see that something was going on out in the field. Additionally, the practitioners were better able to coordinate their activities and see areas of opportunity or potential problems that needed to be addressed.

Top management must be prepared to lead its company through a period when people are being asked to change not only structure, technology, and behaviors but also, more important, their cultural values. Changing values is often a gut-wrenching and agonizing experience. Once there is an awareness of a need for change and the organization develops a change strategy, it is necessary to decide what specific action intervention will be most appropriate. A range of activities, practices, and techniques for intervening are available to enhance the effectiveness of the organization.

## SELECTING AN OD INTERVENTION

There are many strategies, methods, and techniques for intervening during the action phase of an OD program. An OD strategy involves the planning and direction of change programs, whereas intervention techniques deal with the operational aspects of the change—the specific means by which the OD goals are attained. An **OD intervention** encompasses the range of actions designed to improve the health or functioning of the client system. The interventions are the specific means, activities, and programs by which change can be determined. The OD practitioner must be aware of the range of diverse intervention techniques available to be applied to a given target system. The major OD intervention techniques will be described in the next several chapters. All OD interventions aim at changing some specific aspect of an organization: its climate, members, structure, or procedures. An organizational practice is inefficient if it fails to further the organization's objectives; however, inefficiency may emerge slowly and become ingrained in the climate of the organization and the behaviors of its members.

When an organization is inefficient, it is necessary to alter the values, beliefs, and behaviors of the individuals who make the system work. OD intervention techniques are based upon the idea that the relationships between organization groups and organization members are one of the principal reasons for inefficiency problems and that certain activities do not contribute to organization objectives.

In **Parkinson's Law,** the satirist C. Northcote Parkinson summarizes the inherent problems of inefficient practices.[16] Parkinson proposed several principal reasons for organizational inefficiency: (1) work expands so as to fill the time available for its completion; (2) the law of multiplication of subordinates—managers want to increase the number of subordinates they direct rather than create rival organization members; and (3) the law of multiplication of work—members of an organization make work for one another. There are many, similar kinds of inefficient operations that OD techniques seek to change.

In selecting a specific OD technique, the practitioner and the client consider several factors, including the nature of the problem, the objectives of the change effort, the culture and norms of the client system, and the expected degree of resistance. Selecting a technique involves comparing and testing possible intervention techniques against some criteria. Three broad aspects are of concern to the OD practitioner in selecting the appropriate intervention:

**Potential Results of the Technique**

- Will it solve the basic problems?
- Does it have any additional positive outcomes?

**Potential Implementation of the Technique**

- Can the proposed technique actually work in a practical application?
- What are the actual dollar and human costs of this technique and the impact of the costs upon the client system?
- How do the estimated costs of the technique compare with the expected results (cost versus benefit)?

**The Potential Acceptance of the Technique**

- Is the technique acceptable to the client system?
- Is the technique adequately developed and tested?
- Has the technique been adequately explained and communicated to members of the client system?

The selection of any given technique is usually a trade-off between advantages and disadvantages because there is no precise way to answer all of these questions in advance. After comparing the advantages and disadvantages, specific techniques are selected for the action phase of the OD program. What is more, OD programs generally utilize a multifaceted approach with a combination of interventions.

## THE MAJOR OD INTERVENTION TECHNIQUES: AN OVERVIEW

This section presents an overview of the basic OD intervention techniques. Because OD is a dynamic discipline, the boundaries between "what is OD" and "what is not OD" are ambiguous and changing. The interventions included in this discussion provide examples of the diverse techniques that are available, but they are not intended to be all-inclusive.

All planned OD activities or interventions are specifically aimed at correcting inefficiencies, solving problems, developing strengths, and creating areas of opportunity. A basic assumption

**TABLE 7.1** An Overview of OD Interventions

| | Types of Interventions | | | |
|---|---|---|---|---|
| Category | Individual | Team | Intergroup | Total Organizational System |
| **Behavioral** | Employee empowerment | Team building | Intergroup development | Goal setting |
| | Process interventions | Process interventions | Third-party intervention | Grid OD (Phases 4, 5, 6) |
| | Laboratory learning | Quality control | Organization mirror | Survey research and feedback |
| | Career planning | Role negotiation | Process interventions | Action research |
| | Managerial Grid (Phase 1) | Role analysis | Grid OD (Phase 3) | Likert's System 4 |
| | Stress management | Grid OD (Phase 2) | Total quality management | Total quality management |
| | Biofeedback | Goal setting | | High performing systems |
| | Management by objectives | Third-party intervention | | Reengineering |
| | Goal setting | | | Learning organization |
| **Structural** | Employee empowerment | Job enrichment | Job enrichment | Grid OD (Phases 4, 5, 6) |
| | Job enrichment | Team building | Goal setting | Survey research and feedback |
| | Stress management | Role negotiation | Total quality management | Action research |
| | Management by objectives | Self-managed work teams | | Likert's System 4 |
| | | Role analysis | | Total quality management |
| | | Grid OD (Phase 2) | | High-performing systems |
| | | | | Reengineering |
| **Technological** | Employee empowerment | Job design | Job design | Grid OD (Phases 4, 5, 6) |
| | Job design | Quality control | Grid OD (Phase 3) | Survey research and feedback |
| | | Grid OD (Phase 3) | Total quality management | Action research |
| | | Virtual team | Virtual team | Likert's System 4 |
| | | | | Total quality management |
| | | | | High-performing systems |
| | | | | Reengineering |
| | | | | Virtual team |

underlying any intervention activity is that the client organization already has most of the basic resources for change. The primary role of the OD practitioner is to energize these forces by helping the client system to diagnose and resolve its own problems.

One way to categorize intervention techniques is in terms of the target system. Some of the major OD interventions are shown in Table 7.1. OD intervention techniques include activities focusing on several organizational levels, ranging from (1) the individual or interpersonal level, (2) the team or group level, (3) the intergroup level, and to (4) the total organizational system level. The interventions, as previously discussed, are used in behavioral, structural, and technological strategies. Certain interventions are aimed primarily at individual improvement, and others are aimed at groups, but a single intervention may fit into several or all categories. The aspect of the organization that is being changed and the problem conditions will determine the type of intervention that is selected.

Table 7.1 does not list every possible OD intervention technique, but this grouping represents a range of possible activities. Many intervention techniques do not fit distinctly into one category, and often there are overlaps. For example, TQM can be implemented as an intergroup or total system approach and can use behavioral, structural, and technological strategies. Usually, the specific intervention that is used depends upon the nature of the target system.

These different types of change techniques suggest the wide range of possible interventions available within an OD program. The discussion includes the major categories but does not cover all the possible interventions. There are also differences among OD practitioners over what is and what is not an OD technique. Depending upon the orientation of the OD practitioner, some of the OD interventions discussed may not be considered part of an OD program. In the chapters that follow, major OD interventions will be described, moving from techniques aimed at the individual, team, between teams, and system-wide.

## Summary

This chapter examined some of the major organization development interventions. OD is a long-term effort to introduce planned change on a system-wide basis. Therefore, the selection of specific strategies and techniques is an important action step.

- **OD Strategy.** The OD strategy involves the planning and direction of intervention activities. A comprehensive approach involves the way the organization is managed, the way jobs are designed, and the way people are motivated. The practitioner and the client determine the appropriate strategy to best attain the change objectives. There are also a number of possible OD techniques. Based upon the change strategy, specific action interventions that will best resolve problem conditions and increase organizational effectiveness are set in motion. A more detailed description of these techniques will be presented in the following chapters.
- **Basic Strategies.** Three basic approaches to change are structural, technological, and behavioral. Structure provides the framework that relates elements of the organization. Technological strategies implement new technologies that bring an organization up to the state-of-the-art in machinery, automation, and job design. Behavioral strategies emphasize the use of human resources to improve an organization's performance. These units are engaged in some task or technological accomplishment and are bound together in an interrelated network of social and behavioral relationships.
- **Integration of Strategies.** An organization must consider the interdependencies among its various subelements. Structural, technological, and behavioral change

strategies do not exist in isolation of one another. A change in one subsystem will have some impact upon other elements of the system. A comprehensive approach needs to consider the system's technological and structural variables as well as its behavioral variables.
- **Stream Analysis.** This is one method used in planning the implementation and analysis of behavioral, structural, and technological changes. Stream analysis identifies interventions that the organization can implement as part of the OD program. Interventions are scheduled to begin and end at specific times, and the relationships between the interventions are determined. A chart is made to better visualize the OD strategy. It shows the interventions plotted over time with arrows showing the relationship of interventions to one another.
- **Interventions.** There are many possible intervention techniques that may be used in organization development. Although these techniques differ, they aim at the same basic goals: (1) to improve the functioning of the client system, (2) to increase the organization's adaptive capability toward a more anticipative system, and (3) to enhance the development and potential of the individual members of the organization.
- **Major OD Interventions.** Intervention techniques may be classified in terms of the target system. The intervention may focus on organizational levels, ranging from the individual, team, and interteam levels to the total organizational system. The aspect of the organization that is being changed and the problem conditions will determine the type of intervention that is selected.

## Review Questions

1. Compare and contrast the basic OD strategies.
2. Identify and give examples of OD interventions for various target systems.
3. Explain how stream analysis can be used in an OD program.
4. Describe an integrated approach to change.
5. Explain three factors that should be considered in selecting a technique.

## Key Words and Concepts

| | | | |
|---|---|---|---|
| Behavioral Strategies | Parkinson's Laws | Stream Analysis | Technological Strategies |
| OD Intervention | Second-Order | Structural Strategies | Virtual Teams |
| OD Strategy | Consequences | | |

# OD Skills Simulation 7.1

## The Franklin Company

*Total time suggested: 70 to 80 minutes.*

### A. Purpose

In this simulation, you will plan and implement structural, technological, and behavioral strategies in an organization. You will also critique and receive feedback on the effectiveness of your strategies. The goals include:

1. To determine an appropriate intervention strategy.
2. To experience diagnosing and contacting a client system.
3. To provide feedback on practitioner approaches.

### B. Procedures

*Step 1.* Prior to class, form teams of eight members and assign roles. Five of these members will serve as the Franklin management team, two as the OD practitioners, and one or more as observers. Everyone reads The Franklin Company Background. The members of the Franklin management team read their role description. The practitioners become familiar with the OD practitioner guidelines (see the Role Descriptions for the guidelines) and the Practitioner Diagnostic Form. Observers can use the Team Rating Form and Observer Form to record their observations. The roles are:

1. President
2. Vice President of Human Resources
3. Vice President of Manufacturing
4. Vice President of Marketing
5. Vice President of Finance
6. OD Practitioners (two)
7. Observer(s)

*Step 2.* The Franklin management team meets with the practitioner(s) to diagnose and propose solutions to the current problems.

*Time suggested for Step 2: 30 minutes.*

*Step 3.* The OD practitioner team prepares an OD strategy and then presents it to the Franklin team, who may ask questions. The Practitioner Diagnostic Form can help the practitioner team make a presentation.

*Time suggested for Step 3: 15 minutes.*

*Step 4.* All team members critique the Franklin team meeting and the role of the consultants. The observers provide information using the Team Rating Form and Observer Form as a guideline. After feedback from the observers, the Franklin management team completes the Team Rating Form and discusses the following questions:

1. How was a decision reached? (By consensus, vote, etc.)
2. What type of process skills did the practitioners use? (Try to give examples.)
3. What did the practitioners do or say that was helpful?
4. What did the practitioners do or say that was dysfunctional?
5. Any suggestions of improvement for the Franklin team and the practitioners?

*Time suggested for Step 4: 15 minutes.*

*Step 5.* As a class, discuss and evaluate the strategies presented by each of the practitioner teams.

*Time suggested for Step 5: 10 to 20 minutes.*

### The Franklin Company Background

The Franklin Company, a medium-sized company with about 1,800 employees, manufactures radar units for use in small aircraft and police cars. The company is about 100 years old and initially manufactured wind vanes and lightning rods, but since World War II it has manufactured only radar units. Growth in sales has been stable over the past four years, and profits have decreased slightly, as contrasted to the previous 20 years of steady growth in sales and profits. Industry sales continue to show a steady growth, but new competitors have entered the field with new products and features, cutting into the firm's market share. Franklin has 12 distinct products with an average of three different models per product. New products have been brought online, but usually several years after the newer competitors. To make matters worse, several key Franklin managers, researchers, and salespeople have joined the competition.

The current abbreviated organization chart is shown in Figure 7.6. All of the company's operations are conducted from one location. Salespeople are also physically based at the plant, but they make calls throughout the United States.

The president has called in an OD practitioner team to diagnose and propose solutions to the current problems.

## Role Descriptions (Read Only Your Role)

**President.** You have been the president of Franklin for the past 14 years, and large part of its growth and success have been due to your ability to select and motivate others. You are a college graduate and have attended many executive seminars. You have tried to apply these concepts to Franklin. You still maintain close contact with day-to-day operations because you believe in hands-on management.

Over the past few years, growth has slowed, sales and earnings have declined, and turnover problems have emerged. You feel the rapid early growth may be the cause of current problems.

You are convinced that the lack of coordination between the four vice presidents and their operating groups is the major problem and that a more decentralized operation will help resolve this. You believe that a newer computerized MIS may improve coordination and communication. You would also like to know whether doing business on the Internet would improve Franklin's bottom line. You have asked the vice president of finance to look into MIS.

You believe that the organization needs better morale and improved bottom-line results. Your vice president of human resources has suggested that you try something new: an organization development program. The vice president has invited a team of consultants to meet with your executive committee. You believe in modern techniques, so perhaps these practitioners can get the various members to find an agreeable compromise to solve the problem.

**Vice President of Human Resources.** You have an MBA. and were brought in five years ago to serve in your current position. You see the key problem as poor organizational structure, a lack of coordination among departments, weak managerial competence, and poor training at all levels.

All of the other vice presidents worked their way up to their present positions, and you consider their professional managerial training somewhat remiss, with the exception of the vice president of marketing, who has attended many of your management-development training sessions. This is even more of a problem in the mid- and lower-level managerial ranks.

You feel that the answer to the problem is a decentralized operation with increased integration and coordination between departments and a participative team style. You have read about organization development and have talked to a colleague at another company who had high praise for its OD program. You have discussed implementing an OD program with the vice president of manufacturing, but there was little response. You feel a need to get conflicts out into the open where they can be resolved rather than each unit seeking its own best interest. A unified team effort is needed.

You have attempted to initiate several training and leadership development programs. Managers, including some of the vice presidents, have undercut these programs. You got word that one vice president was openly attacking the programs, even though the president has been strongly supportive. You suggested bringing in some OD practitioners in the hope of initiating some badly needed changes. Even though this might add to costs in the short run, you are sure that long-term effectiveness will be improved.

**Vice President of Manufacturing.** You have been with the company for 22 years and have worked your way up through the ranks. You have a degree in engineering and feel that you are competent and run a tight ship, and that your department is the main reason for the company's past success. You believe that most problems are due to rapid growth that has resulted in loose structure, lack of coordination, and lack of control.

You feel that the company has too many meddling staff managers (particularly in marketing and human resources) who do not contribute to profits and only cause problems for your managers. Several times the vice president of human resources has tried to discuss with you management practices such as leadership and some new kind of organization development program. You listened politely enough, but you got several good laughs out of it at your department meetings. The management-training programs offered through the human resources division have been a waste of time, and you have told your people you prefer they stay on the job instead of going to more meetings. The vice president of marketing continually wants product modifications or comes up with some goofball idea for a new product. You have made it clear that you run manufacturing, and that includes R&D. You can't run a smooth operation and keep costs down if you are constantly making special modifications. You believe you manufacture enough models to allow customers to find suitable products; if not, the customer can easily make some minor modifications. You have heard about just-in-time inventory being used in some companies but are against it at Franklin. Even though just-in-time inventory attempts to reduce raw material inventory by having as little as possible of Franklin's cash tied up in inventory, you are concerned that production lines will run out of critical items and cause downtime in manufacturing.

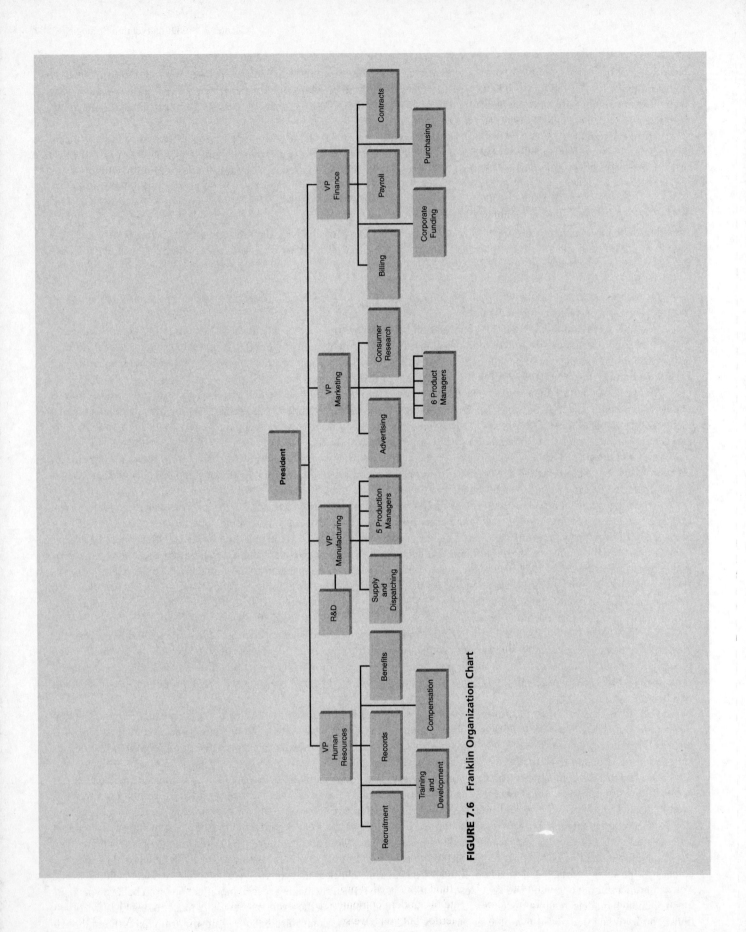

**FIGURE 7.6 Franklin Organization Chart**

You feel the solution is to move into a more highly centralized structure and appoint an executive vice president to centralize cost control (like yourself, for example) and lay off some of the deadwood.

You've heard that the president has invited some OD practitioners in, against your advice. You do not know much about OD, but it sounds like pouring money down a rat hole to you. Besides, this OD business is a bunch of "touchy-feely" nonsense anyway, which is the last thing you need.

**Vice President of Marketing.** You have been with the company for 10 years. You are a college graduate with a major in psychology, but you have gained your knowledge of marketing from experience. You feel that marketing is the major factor in the company's growth, and if your product managers were given greater authority, they could turn the profit picture around.

You see the major problem as the lack of communication among departments and the failure to utilize talented managers. You have tried to get the manufacturing division to make some special modifications in radar units, but they have been willing to comply only on very large orders, and then it generally took them so long that you almost lost several of the orders from your customers. Several of your product managers have met with representatives of manufacturing to discuss new product ideas, but nothing ever comes of the meetings until your competitors start marketing a similar product. Then it takes manufacturing a couple of years to design the unit.

Your people are bringing back word from the field that the excellent reputation once enjoyed by Franklin is beginning to fade. It has been discouraging for you and your people to fight an uphill battle with the manufacturing division for new products, and the real kicker is learning that the competition comes out with your product idea. Sales have also been hindered, you believe, by a lack of an Internet presence. You know about companies that have Internet capabilities that tie in with ordering inventory automatically from suppliers, allowing customers to track the progress of their orders with expected delivery dates, and permitting salespeople in the field to see current inventory levels with projected delivery times. All of Franklin's top competitors have well-developed Web sites.

Despite the problems with the manufacturing division, you find that if you treat your people well, they will perform well for you. You have attended most of the management-training sessions offered by the human resources department and have encouraged, though not mandated, your managers to attend. Your department meetings even have follow-up discussions of the training sessions.

Even though marketing has been accused of being run like a "country club," you feel your department performs well. The answer, you believe, is to decentralize the firm into major independent groups and utilize more of the "whiz kids" in product management by giving them more authority over product operations. You would like to see yourself as executive vice president over the product managers.

You understand that some newly established organization development practitioners are coming in, and you see this as a great opportunity to implement your ideas.

**Vice President of Finance.** You have a degree in finance from a regional college. This and prior banking experience led to your successful 17 years at Franklin. You instituted all the financial systems and made it a smooth operation.

You feel that the problems are the result of too many changes in too short a time. The company has too many bright young kids and too many wasteful practices. You suggest going back to the basics by instituting a tighter, centralized system of financial control and cutting about 10 percent of the deadwood. With yourself as an executive vice president (with other vice presidents reporting to you), this job could be done. You would set up some basic company rules, then force the department heads to enforce them.

You would like to see people be required to follow the chain of command. You have heard too many stories about people at lower levels cutting across the formal structure and meeting with employees in another division. This may sound good on the surface, but it usually screws up the operation later on. You would like to see all communications go up through their appropriate vice president and then back down the chain of command. This type of centralized control is necessary to coordinate everything. You believe there are too many committees throughout the company, and you find it amazing that anything gets accomplished. Further, with all these committees making decisions, it's hard to figure out whom to blame when something goes wrong. As far as you are concerned, a camel is a horse designed by a committee.

Recently you have been reading in the finance journals about just-in-time inventory. Last week, you talked to a colleague at another company who had nothing but praise for the just-in-time inventory model at her company. The program works closely with suppliers of raw materials to ensure that inventory is delivered in time for the production line but not so far in advance that Franklin will have money needlessly tied up in inventory. The downside is that making the system tie in closely with suppliers could require a new management information system (MIS) with Internet capabilities. Franklin has a commercial line of credit to finance the inventory, but, of course, the lower the inventory levels, the lower the interest. Interest savings can boost the bottomline and help fund other needed projects.

You realize that you are not as up-to-date on modern computerized systems as you might be. The president has asked you to look into a new MIS system and the Internet, but you have serious reservations about the technology. A new MIS system would call for a new computer, and you have heard horror stories about Internet-based systems and believe your current system to be excellent. As for the Internet, you don't believe anyone would buy radar units off the Internet.

You would like to avoid changes and keep things pretty much the way they are. You hear that some organization development practitioners are coming, and your reaction is: "Why do we need them?" They represent just the kind of wasteful practice you oppose.

**OD Practitioner Guidelines.** You hope to accomplish several things at this meeting:

1. To develop a practitioner-client relationship with all of the committee members.
2. To make a preliminary diagnosis of possible problems.
3. To gain support for a possible OD project and convince committee members of the advantages.
4. To introduce committee members to some of the goals of OD, by doing some process consultation during the meeting.

**Observer(s).** Do not take part in the committee meeting. Your role as an observer is to provide information later in Step 4. Use the Team Rating Form and the Observer Form to record your observations.

**PRACTITIONER DIAGNOSTIC FORM**

1. Who is the client?

   a.  Who has the most influence in the client system? _____
      _____
      _____
      _____

   b.  Who do you feel is the client? Why? (Example: a specific person or the team)_____
      _____
      _____
      _____

2. Identify major formal and informal problems of the organization. (Use Figure 7.4)

   a. _____
      _____
      _____

   b. _____
      _____
      _____

   c. _____
      _____
      _____

   d. _____
      _____
      _____

3. What strategy(s) might you select?

   a. Structural: _____
      _____

   b. Behavioral: _____
      _____

   c. Technical: _____
      _____

   d. Integrated: _____

4. Identify possible target systems and interventions.

   a. _____
      _____
      _____

   b. _____
      _____
      _____

   c. _____
      _____
      _____

   d. _____
      _____
      _____

**TEAM RATING FORM**

Based on the following scale, rate your team on how it performed. Record your choice in the blanks.

| Low | | | | | | High |
|---|---|---|---|---|---|---|
| 1 : | 2 : | 3 : | 4 : | 5 : | 6 : | 7 |

| Factor | Individual Rating | Team Rating |
|---|---|---|
| 1.  Cooperative teamwork | _____ | _____ |
| 2.  Member satisfaction | _____ | _____ |
| 3.  Team motivation | _____ | _____ |
| 4.  Information sharing | _____ | _____ |
| 5.  Consensual decision making | _____ | _____ |
| 6.  Conflict directly faced and resolved | _____ | _____ |
| 7.  Participative leadership | _____ | _____ |
| 8.  Clearly defined goals | _____ | _____ |
| 9.  Trust | _____ | _____ |
| 10. Encouraged openness | _____ | _____ |

**OBSERVER FORM**

Instructions: Complete this sociogram on the team you are observing. Draw direction arrows for communication flow. Identify behaviors shown.

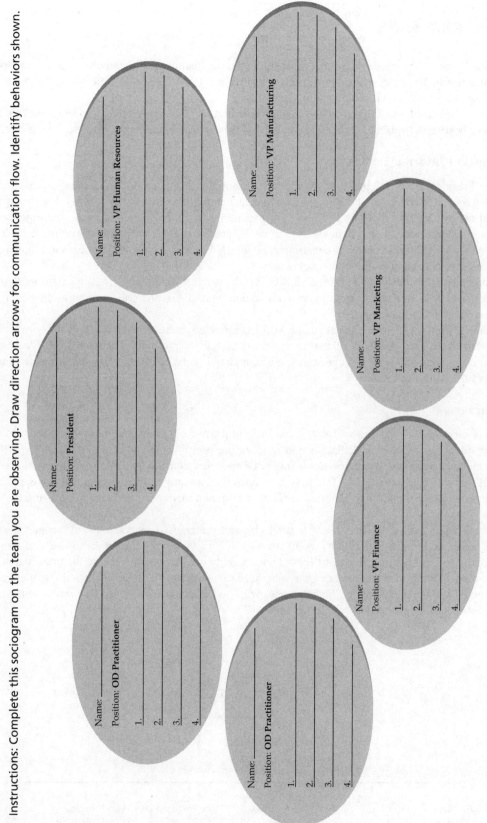

Name:
Position: VP Human Resources
1.
2.
3.
4.

Name:
Position: VP Manufacturing
1.
2.
3.
4.

Name:
Position: President
1.
2.
3.
4.

Name:
Position: VP Marketing
1.
2.
3.
4.

Name:
Position: OD Practitioner
1.
2.
3.
4.

Name:
Position: OD Practitioner
1.
2.
3.
4.

Name:
Position: VP Finance
1.
2.
3.
4.

# CASE: THE FARM BANK

The Farm Bank is one of the state's oldest and most solid banking institutions. Located in a regional marketing center, the bank has been active in all phases of banking, specializing in farm loans. The bank's president, Frank Swain, 62, has been with the bank for many years and is prominent in local circles.

The bank is organized into six departments, as shown in Figure 7.7. A senior vice president heads each department. All six of them have been with the bank for years, and in general they reflect a stable and conservative outlook.

## The Management Information System

Two years ago, President Swain felt that the bank needed to modernize its operations. With the approval of the board of directors, he decided to design and install a comprehensive management information system (MIS). The primary goal was to improve internal operations by supplying necessary information on a more expedited basis, thereby decreasing the time necessary to service customers. The system was also to be designed to provide economic operating data for top management planning and decision making. To head this department, he selected Al Hassler, 58, a solid operations manager who had some knowledge and experience in the computer department.

After the system was designed and installed, Mr. Hassler hired a young woman as his assistant. Valerie Wyatt was a young college graduate with a strong systems analysis background. She is the only woman at this level and considerably younger than any of the other managers.

In the time since the system was installed, the MIS has provided thousands of documents of operating information, including reports to all the vice presidents, all the branch managers, and the president. The reports provide weekly, monthly, and quarterly summaries and include cost of operations, projected labor costs, overhead costs, and projected earnings figures for each segment of the bank's operations.

## The MIS Survey

Mr. Swain was pleased with the system but noticed little improvement in management operations. In fact, most of the older vice presidents were making decisions and functioning pretty much as they did before the MIS was installed. Mr. Swain decided to have Ms. Wyatt conduct a survey of the users to try to evaluate the impact and benefits of the new system. Ms. Wyatt was glad to undertake the survey, because she had long felt the system was too elaborate for the bank's needs. She sent out a questionnaire to all department heads, branch managers, and so on, inquiring into their uses of the system.

As she began to assemble the survey data, a pattern began to emerge. In general, most of the managers were strongly in favor of the system but felt that it should be modified. As Ms. Wyatt analyzed the responses, several trends and important points came out: (1) 93 percent reported that they did not regularly use the reports because the information was not in a useful form, (2) 76 percent reported that the printouts were hard to interpret, (3) 72 percent stated that they received more data than they wanted, (4) 57 percent reported finding some errors and inaccuracies, and (5) 87 percent stated that they still kept manual records because they did not fully trust the MIS.

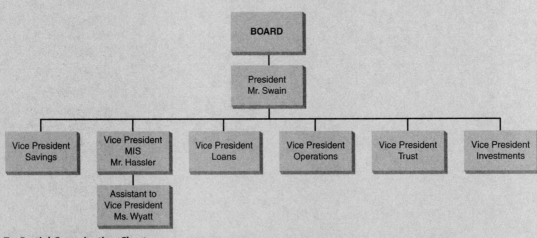

**FIGURE 7.7** Partial Organization Chart

**The Meeting**

Ms. Wyatt finished her report, excitedly rushed into Mr. Hassler's office, and handed it to him. Mr. Hassler slowly scanned the report and then said, "You've done a good job here, Val. But now that we have the system operating, I don't think we should upset the apple cart, do you? Let's just keep this to ourselves for the time being and perhaps we can correct most of these problems. I'm sure Frank wouldn't want to hear this kind of stuff. This system is his baby, so maybe we shouldn't rock the boat with this report."

Ms. Wyatt returned to her office feeling uncomfortable. She wondered what to do. (Use the Case Analysis Form on the following page.)

**THE FARM BANK CASE ANALYSIS FORM**

Name: _____

I. Problems

  A. Macro

    1. _____

      _____

    2. _____

      _____

  B. Micro

    1. _____

      _____

    2. _____

      _____

II. Causes

    1. _____

      _____

    2. _____

      _____

    3. _____

      _____

III. Systems affected

    1. _____

      _____

    2. _____

      _____

    3. _____

      _____

IV. Alternatives

    1. _____

      _____

    2. _____

      _____

    3. _____

      _____

V. Recommendations

_____

_____

_____

_____

_____

# Chapter 7 Endnotes

1. Peter J. Williamson and Ming Zeng, "Value-for-Money Strategies for Recessionary Times," *Harvard Business Review*, March 2009, p. 68.

2. Purnendu Mandal, Andrea Howell, and Amrik S. Sohal, "A Systemic Approach to Quality Improvements: The Interactions Between the Technical, Human and Quality Systems," *Total Quality Management*, vol. 9, no.1 (February 1998), pp. 79–90; F. Friedlander and L. D. Brown, "Organization Development," *Annual Review of Psychology*, vol. 25 (February, 1974), pp. 313–41; Harold Leavitt, "Applied Organization Change in Industry: Structural, Technical and Humanistic Approaches," in *Handbook of Organizations*, ed. James March (Chicago: Rand-McNally, 1965).

3. Claudia Wallis, "Bill & Melinda Gates Go Back to School," *Fortune*, December 8, 2008, p. 114.

4. See www.zappos.com/, Zappos.com culture blog, www.youtube.com/, and http://twitter.com/.

5. Jeffrey M. O'Brien, "Zappos Knows How to Kick It," *Fortune*, February 2, 2009, pp. 55–60.

6. *Ibid*, p. 60.

7. David Kiley, "Ford's Savior?" *Business Week*, March 16, 2009, pp. 31–34.

8. David Kiley, "Ghosn Hits the Accelerator," *Business Week*, May 12, 2008, pp. 48–49.

9. For additional information, see Adam Aston and Michael Arndt, "The Flexible Factory," *Business Week*, May 5, 2003, pp. 90–91; Michael Arndt, "How Briggs Is Revving the Engines," *Business Week*, May 5, 2003, p. 92.

10. Gurmak Singh, John O'Donoghue, and Claire Betts, "A UK Study into the Potential Effects of Virtual Education: Does Online Learning Spell an End for On-Campus Learning?" *Behaviour and Information Technology*, vol. 21, no. 3 (2002), pp. 223–9.

11. Fred Luthans, "Conversation with Edgar H. Schein," *Organizational Dynamics*, Spring 1989, p. 66.

12. Don Clark, "Why Silicon Valley Is Rethinking the Cubicle Office," *Wall Street Journal*, October 15, 2007, p. B9.

13. Elizabeth Agnvall, "Meetings Go Virtual," *HR Magazine*, vol. 54, no. 1 (January 2009), pp. 74–77; Bronwyn Fryer and Thomas A. Stewart, "Cisco Sees the Future," *Harvard Business Review*, November 2008, pp. 72–79; Rik Kirkland, "Cisco's Display of Strength," *Fortune*, November 12, 2007, pp. 90–100.

14. Ellen Byron, "P&G Looks Beyond Premium Goods," *Wall Street Journal*, May 29, 2009, p. B1; A. G. Lafley, "What Only the CEO Can Do," *Harvard Business Review*, May 2009, pp. 54–62; Roger O Crockett (ed.), "How P&G Plans to Clean Up," *Business Week*, April 13, 2009, pp. 44–45; Ellen Byron, "A New Odd Couple: Google, P&G Swap Workers to Spur Innovation," *Wall Street Journal*, November 19, 2008, p. A1; A. G. Lafley and Ram Charan, "The Consumer Is Boss," *Fortune*, March 17, 2008, pp. 121–6; Robert Berner, "P&G: New and Improved. How A. G. Lafley Is Revolutionizing a Bastion of Corporate Conservatism," *Business Week*, July 7, 2003, pp. 52–63; For additional information, see A. G. Lafley and Ram Charan, *The Game Changer: How You Can Drive Revenue and Profit Growth with Innovation* (New York: Crown Business, 2008).

15. Jerry I. Porras, *Stream Analysis* (Reading, MA: Addison-Wesley, 1987); D. D. Warrick (ed.), *Contemporary Organization Development: Current Thinking and Applications* (Glenview, IL: Scott, Foresman, 1985); Jerry I. Porras, Joan Harkness, and Coeleen Kiebert, "Understanding Organization Development: A Stream Approach," *Training and Development Journal*, vol. 37, no. 4 (April 1983), pp. 52–63.

16. C. Northcote Parkinson, *Parkinson's Law* (Boston, MA: Houghton Mifflin, 1957).

# Process Intervention Skills

## LEARNING OBJECTIVES

**Upon completing this chapter, you will be able to:**

1. Understand the key OD process skills and determine how they can be applied.

2. Practice using OD process skills.

3. Identify and gain insights into your own OD style.

## PREMEETING PREPARATION

1. Read Chapter 8.

2. Prepare for OD Skills Simulation 8.1. Prior to class, form teams of seven and assign roles. Complete Step 1.

3. Read and complete Steps 1 and 2 of OD Skills Simulation 8.2.

4. Read and prepare for Step 1 of OD Skills Simulation 8.3.

5. Read and analyze Case: The OD Letters.

## A NEW PARADIGM

The leadership role of managers is increasingly being transformed into a coaching relationship with their subordinates. Depending on the need of the moment, the manager will be a teacher, a counselor, a cheerleader, an adviser, or a coach.[1] This change in leadership style has come about largely because of the increasing importance of teams in today's organization. Subsequent chapters will look at the role of teams, including such concepts as empowerment, team development, interteam development, goal setting, total quality management (TQM), and self-managed work teams. Research on effective organizations shows that more and more organizations are relying on the team approach to managing.

"Casey Stengel, one of baseball's most famous managers, said the way to manage a team was to keep the guys who hate you away from the guys who haven't made up their minds. This strategy apparently worked for Stengel, who guided the New York Yankees to a record five World Championships in a row in the 1950s. But it's woefully outdated for the business world."[2] In the 2000s, effective managers will need a team that works well together and with the manager—not a situation where team members are isolated from one another.

Major changes in managing have been thrust upon both lower and middle managers. Michael Hammer, a management consultant, says, "Middle management as we currently know it will simply disappear." He believes that three-quarters of middle managers will vanish and return to the work they did before they were promoted into management. The remainder "will fill a role that will change almost beyond recognition."[3] More simply, there will be two types of new-style managers. The first will oversee, beginning to end, a reengineered process, such as order fulfillment or product development. They will need skills in performance management and work redesign. Hammer calls the second type of manager employee coaches. "Employee coaches will support and nurture employees—much as senior managers do in corporate America today."[4]

Chairman of the board and retired CEO A. G. Lafley of Procter & Gamble (P&G) provides a stark contrast to the more traditional method of managing employees. When Lafley was CEO he met with P&G's 12 other top executives every Monday at

8:00 AM to review results, plan strategy, and set the goals for the week. A writer for *Business Week*, Robert Berner, was allowed to sit in on one of these meetings. An excerpt from his account follows:

> The table used to be rectangular; now it's round. The execs used to sit where they were told; now they sit where they like. At one of those meetings, an outsider might have trouble distinguishing the CEO: He occasionally joins in the discussion, but most of the time the executives talk as much to each other as to Lafley. "I am more like a coach," Lafley says afterward. "I am always looking for different combinations that will get better results."[5]

The new role of the manager will not come easy. Organizations often put their managers in difficult and seemingly no-win situations. Managers are expected to coach their employees and let them grow and learn from their successes and failures, but at the same time they are expected to deliver evaluations, promote employees, and adjust salaries.

A better understanding of group and team behavior is needed to help managers adapt to the new role of coach. The traditional manager was probably an expert on the task of the group. Managers knew the "what and how" of the job positions reporting to them, and probably had been promoted to managerial positions because of their expertise in the job. The task is still important, but the stronger reliance on work teams means that the manager must also have the ability to help the team become more keenly aware of how it operates. For example, the emphasis in the work of a computer programmer is changing substantially from task to people skills. Traditionally a programmer sat in isolation writing computer code. But much of the writing of code has now been outsourced to countries with cheaper labor markets, such as India and Romania. The stereotype of the computer geek with few social skills needs to be updated. The programmers who remain in the United States will need to master people skills, work with and manage teams, and act as a link between customers and code writers spread around the world. Some universities have introduced special programs to teach the skills needed to manage teams.[6] One such example is Carnegie Mellon University's master computer-science program.

A work team that is more keenly aware of how it operates will be better able to analyze and solve its own problems. This chapter describes some interventions and skills that a manager and OD practitioner can use to help a team and its members develop. Because these interventions tend to focus on the processes that a work team is using, the interventions are called process interventions.

## PROCESS INTERVENTIONS

**Process interventions** are an OD skill used by OD practitioners, whether managers or OD professionals, to help work groups become more effective. The purpose of process interventions is to help the work group become more aware of the way it operates and the way its members work with one another. The work group uses this knowledge to develop its own problem-solving ability. Process interventions, then, aim at helping the work group to become more aware of its own processes, including the way it operates, and to use this knowledge to solve its own problems.

Possibly the best description of process consultation is the one by Edgar Schein in *Process Consultation: Its Role in Organization Development* and *Process Consultation: Lessons for Managers and Consultants.*[7] Schein defines process consultation as a "set of activities on the part of the consultant [practitioner] that help the client to perceive, understand, and act upon the process events that occur in the client's environment in order to improve the situation as defined by the client."[8]

The OD practitioner practicing process interventions observes individuals and teams in action and helps them learn to diagnose and solve their own problems. The practitioner refrains from telling them how to solve their problems but instead asks questions, focuses their attention on how they are working together, teaches or provides resources where necessary, and listens. With experience and training, the manager and group members will become more aware of group processes and become capable of making process interventions. One of the major advantages of process interventions is that teams learn to identify problems and then initiate their own solutions. The teams become more independent and do not have to look to the practitioner to solve problems. Self-managed work teams have team leaders and coaches who rely largely on process interventions. In one survey of OD practitioners, it was found that 80 percent of the practitioners used process-consulting skills more than any other OD skill mentioned.[9]

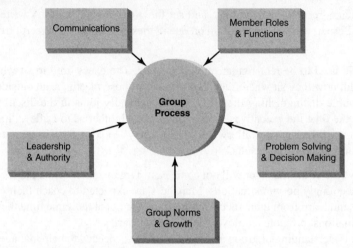

**FIGURE 8.1** Group Process Interventions

In addition to the discussion of teams in this chapter, team development is discussed in Chapter 10, and self-managed work teams are discussed in Chapter 13.

## GROUP PROCESS

The foundation of process interventions is the study of how groups and the individuals within groups behave.[10] Whereas **group content** is *what* a group does (its task), **group process** is *how* the group goes about accomplishing its task. Process interventions help the work group solve its own problems by making it aware of its process. The interventions focus on five areas crucial to effective organization performance: communication, member roles and functions in groups, group problem solving and decision making, group norms and growth, and leadership and authority (see Figure 8.1).[11]

### Communications

The OD practitioner uses several techniques to analyze the communications processes in a work group.

- *Observe.* How often and how long does each member talk during a group discussion? These observations can be easily recorded on paper and referred to later when analyzing group behavior. It is also useful to keep a record of who talks to whom or to use a sociogram (discussed in Chapter 5).
- *Identify.* Who are the most influential listeners in the group? Noticing eye contact between members can give insights on the communication processes. Sometimes one person, and perhaps not even the person who speaks most frequently, is the one focused on by others as they speak.
- *Interruptions.* Who interrupts whom? Is there a pattern to the interruptions? What are the apparent effects of the interruptions?

The practitioner will probably share this information with the group to enable the members to better understand how they communicate with one another. The actual timing of when to provide feedback to members is a judgment call by the practitioner. Feedback may be given intermittently during the meeting or at the conclusion of the meeting. And the information need not be based on a formal team meeting; it may have been gathered outside of meetings, such as during the normal workday. The purpose of feedback is to enable group members to learn about the way they communicate with one another. Research conducted on the effectiveness of feedback indicates that a positive effect on the perceptions of leadership occurs and commitment to the organization is enhanced when there is feedback and it is accompanied with action plans.[12]

### Member Roles and Functions

The practitioner must also be aware of the different **member roles** that individuals play in the group. Roles are parts, similar to those of actors in a play, except that this is real life for the members. Group members have several issues to resolve while they are working on their

**FIGURE 8.2  The Role of an Executive**
*Source:* B.C. by permission of Johnny Hart and Creators Syndicate, Inc.

task.[13] Members will be working on acting out the roles in which they feel most comfortable. Many of these roles will probably not be explicitly stated but will evolve. Typically, roles include such elements as who is the technical expert, who is aggressive, who initiates the conversation, and who is the joke teller or tension reliever. The group will also resolve control, power, and influence issues. Figure 8.2 illustrates the role of decision maker that managers traditionally held.

Members of existing groups take on roles that can be categorized as group task functions, group-building and maintenance functions, or individual functions **Group task functions** include member behaviors that directly help the group solve its task. These behaviors include initiating and suggesting what the goal of the group should be and how the group can proceed to accomplish its goal. Other behaviors include seeking opinions and information from other members and giving opinions and information. Asking questions for clarification and elaborating on information help the group to work on its goal. Summarizing occurs when a member pulls together and reviews briefly what the group has said or done thus far. A related function is testing for group consensus by asking such questions as "What I seem to be hearing the group say is . . . is this correct?" or "Are we ready to make our decision?"

**Group-building and maintenance functions** include behaviors that help the group grow and improve its members' interpersonal relationships. Harmonizing and compromising behavior helps to reduce conflict and tension between members. Encouraging behavior helps people to

**TABLE 8.1** Group Members' Behaviors

| | Group Task Functions | Group Building and Maintenance Functions | Individual Functions |
|---|---|---|---|
| | | | Satisfy individual's needs. Not germane to group's task and maintenance. |
| | Help group solve its task. | Help group grow and improve. | |
| Behaviors | Initiating and suggesting | Harmonizing | Dominating |
| | Seeking opinions | Compromising | Acting the playboy |
| | Asking questions | Encouraging | Blocking |
| | Elaborating | Gatekeeping | Seeking recognition |
| | Summarizing | Following | Pleading for special interest |
| | Testing for consensus | | |

better develop their ideas and allows the quieter members to make more contributions. Gatekeeping, another maintenance function, gives everyone a chance to be heard.

**Individual functions** are behaviors that satisfy individual needs and are dysfunctional or inconsequential to the group's task and maintenance. Dominating behavior attempts to assert superiority by displaying flattery, behaving authoritatively, and interrupting others. The playboy displays a lack of involvement through horseplay, cynicism, and other inappropriate behavior. Blocking behavior carries disagreement and stubbornness beyond reason. Seeking recognition calls attention through such acts as bragging so as to avoid being placed in an inferior position. Pleading for a special interest is behavior that disguises the person's own beliefs or biases by projecting them through others, such as "The union guy down on the floor says . . ." or "the average consumer believes . . ." Refer to Table 8.1 for an overview of group functions.

## Problem Solving and Decision Making

An effective work group must be able to identify problems, examine possible actions, and make decisions. Problem solving begins with gathering the necessary information and identifying problem areas. Alternatives are then generated, along with forecasts of possible results. An alternative is chosen, and a detailed plan of action is formulated. The decision is implemented, and finally an evaluation of the decision is made.

Groups can use several methods to reach decisions. One common method is to take a vote and let the majority rule. Although often expedient, this may leave issues unresolved and some members disenfranchised. When the decision is implemented, some participants may not be completely supportive. Another method that groups use to make decisions is consensus. A decision made by **group consensus** is one that all the members have shared in making and one they will support and buy into even though they may not be totally supportive. This is the ideal decision method, but it is the most difficult to obtain. Group consensus is *not* the manager getting advice from subordinates and then making the decision. Group consensus is especially effective if the acceptance and cooperation of the group members are required because they are the ones who will carry out the decision. A practitioner's process interventions help the group to understand how it makes decisions and the possible consequences of making decisions in that way. Process interventions do not involve the content of the decisions; they focus on how decisions are made.

## Group Norms and Growth

**Norms** are the organized and shared ideas regarding what group members should do and feel, how this behavior should be regulated, and what sanctions should be applied when behavior does not coincide with social expectations. Process interventions help the group understand its norms and whether they are helpful or dysfunctional. As the members of the group continue to meet, they move forward from the acquaintance stage to become an effectively functioning team. The group will grow as the members become more supportive, use member talents and resources, and understand how the group operates and improves upon its decision-making process.

## OD Application: Leaders Shape the Culture at Disney[14]

"The actions of one leader, multiplied by thousands of leaders, can reshape a culture. True leaders create an environment that inspires and motivates everyone with whom they come in contact . . . whether they be employees, peers, or even their own bosses." This quotation is from the head of Walt Disney Attractions (which operates the amusement parks) and represents the philosophy of managing Walt Disney World. The attitude reflected in this statement permeates the Magic Kingdom and the culture at The Walt Disney Company, one of the world's most deeply rooted corporate cultures.

Disney World has formal leaders, but they are not of the traditional "charge that hill" with the generals remaining at a safe distance. The leadership is inclusive. Many leaders choose to hold their weekly meetings in an open format rather than as executive sessions. And management spends 70 to 80 percent of its time in the operating areas, working frontline shifts during peak periods. The managers are not there to judge and evaluate others but to "walk the front" as partners. This means observing and gathering firsthand information that can be shared with the frontline "cast members," as Disney calls employees who come in direct contact with the guests (customers). By sharing information, the leaders encourage employees to feel a sense of ownership in their specific spheres of influence. The cast members then apply the information to improve the experience of the guests.

Does this work? Disney seems to think so, and it has conducted studies that bear out the validity of its leadership approach. In areas of Walt Disney World where guests' satisfaction ratings are the highest, cast members rate their leaders as outstanding in such behaviors as listening and coaching. Disney has also found that in areas where it has implemented leadership

improvement, the guest return rate has risen by more than 10 percent and cast member turnover rate has dropped.

Disney's methods of leading and managing the theme parks, which have been around since the mid 1950s, were so unique and successful that other organizations were interested in learning more about its approach. In 1986, the Disney Institute was established. The participants in the programs have an opportunity to learn the Disney approach to benchmarking best practices, visiting onstage and behind-the-scenes locations, and meeting with Disney leaders to learn firsthand how they transfer management philosophy into practice. The topics of the institute include:

- Leadership excellence
- People management
- Quality service
- Loyalty
- Organizational creativity

The programs are based upon long-standing practices used at Disney that the institute believes other organizations could use. The professional development programs permit other organizations to "experience the business behind the magic" or "Goofy management," as some participants call it.

### Questions

1. Research the programs at the Disney Institute. See its web site at www.disneyinstitute.com/ for additional information.
2. Compare Disney's practice, where leaders "walk the front," with other companies where their employees directly meet the customer (examples: other amusement parks, department stores, and restaurants).

## Leadership and Authority

Process interventions help the work group understand the impact of leadership styles and authority issues. As a team goes about its task, a member will emerge to perform a leadership function, then move back into more of a follower role. Another person will emerge and perform another leadership function, and so on. Consequently, leadership functions are widely shared among team members. As the earlier example of the top-executive meeting at P&G illustrates, an outside observer might have trouble distinguishing the CEO. A manager practicing process interventions encourages others to take leadership roles instead of dominating all the leadership functions. Although the work group is likely to have a formal leader, there will probably be informal leaders. Group members will share the leadership functions; for example, the members who perform the functions of gatekeeping, summarizing, or some other task or maintenance function are all behaving in the role of leader.

The Walt Disney Company's theme parks have a long history of being well known for the experience they provide to their guests. Refer to **OD Application: Leaders Shape the Culture at Disney** to learn how leadership has helped to accomplished this.

## TYPES OF PROCESS INTERVENTIONS

Process interventions differ in many ways, but they never involve the work-group's task. Process interventions are all about *how* the group is going about accomplishing its task. A practitioner's process interventions should be as brief and crisp as possible and focus on only one level of behavior at a time. They should provide maximum impact with minimum interruption.

The types of process interventions that may be used include clarifying, summarizing, synthesizing, generalizing, probing, questioning, listening, reflecting feelings, providing support, coaching, counseling, modeling, setting the agenda, feeding back observations, and providing structural suggestions.[15]

### Clarifying and Summarizing

Clarifying refers to resolving misunderstandings or incorrect perceptions in what members are saying. For example, "Mary, I seem to be hearing you say . . . is this correct?" Providing a summary of the major points and accomplishments of a discussion may be helpful. This sometimes helps the group to understand where it is and also provides a link to the next topic on the agenda.

### Synthesizing and Generalizing

Synthesizing occurs when several points and ideas are put together in a common theme. Generalizing refers to taking the ideas or feelings of one person and attaching them to the entire group. For example, when one person expresses reservations about dealing with a particular issue, a process observation is, "Am I correct in assuming the rest of you share Irwin's position?"

### Probing and Questioning

When the group needs additional information or needs to explore additional ideas, it may be important to seek additional information and ask questions. As an example, "Carlos, you mentioned . . . I'm not sure everyone understands your point. Could you explain it in more detail?" Probing and questioning may be especially useful at the beginning of a discussion if members are reaching hasty conclusions.

### Listening

Listening is one of the most important process interventions. In this context, listening is a very complicated activity. It is not simply passively hearing what another person is saying. One must use nonverbal communication (eye contact, nods of the head, body posture) to indicate that the speaker is being listened to. Listening refers to hearing the entire message, including any feelings. The speaker's feelings are rarely expressed in words but are often communicated nonverbally: tone of voice, facial expressions, hand and arm movements, body posture, eye movements, and so forth. As an example, an interviewer of Bill Gates, formerly CEO of Microsoft and currently cohead of the Bill and Melinda Gates Foundation, observed, "When Bill Gates gets worked up about something, his body language changes. He suspends his habit of rocking forward and back in his chair and sits a litter straighter. His voice rises in pitch."[16]

### Reflecting Feelings

Most messages have two parts: the content of the message and the speaker's feelings, often expressed nonverbally. The listener needs to practice **empathy** by trying to see the world from the speaker's point of view. Reflecting feelings refers to communicating back to the speaker the feeling part of the message that has been heard. For example, "By the looks on most of your faces, you seem confused by what Carlos has said. Is this correct?"; and after seeing a member slowly push her chair back from the table and fold her arms tightly, "Shannon, am I correct in assuming you have a problem with what Murphy has just reported?" The purpose of reflecting feelings is to check out perceptions and get members more involved in the discussion.

It is important for process interventions to test constantly for an understanding of what others are saying. Empathizing with and then reflecting back what the speaker seems to be saying from both a content and feeling point of view builds positive relations with the speaker and is at the foundation of problem solving and change.

### Providing Support, Coaching, and Counseling

Providing support includes encouraging group members to talk and express their ideas. It also includes complimenting the group for a particularly productive meeting. A practitioner who is coaching asks the team or individuals for their ideas about how to improve a work process instead of just telling them what to do. The team is encouraged to think about the problem and develop solutions. Coaching and counseling may occur in a private meeting with individuals, particularly the formal manager or supervisor of the group. It is important to remember that the objective of process interventions is to help the work group to be an active participant in identifying and solving its own problems.

## Modeling

Because practitioners have many responsibilities and thus will be working with the work group for only a limited time, it is important for group members to learn how to make process interventions. These interventions can be very helpful to the group on a regular basis, not just at sessions when the practitioner is present. One of the better methods for learning how to give process observations is through observing someone else doing so. Members should be encouraged to take over the role of providing process interventions. Ideally, and with time, the practitioner's role in process interventions will become less frequent until group members are providing their own process interventions. To some extent, the practitioner is attempting to make their role of making process interventions obsolete.

## Setting the Agenda

**Agenda-setting interventions** include setting aside time when process issues will be specifically discussed apart from content issues. Agenda-setting interventions do not include determining the task items to be discussed. The practitioner may encourage the work group to allocate time at its regular meetings to discuss the processes of the meeting or may suggest that the group hold a separate meeting just to deal with process issues. These issues may include how well members communicate with each other, how satisfied members are with the meeting, and how involved they are in the meeting.

## Feeding Back Observations

Feedback to work groups can occur at meetings or be given to individuals after meetings. The practitioner is often strongly tempted to share interesting observations regardless of the group's ability to receive and absorb feedback. There should be no feedback given to individuals or groups until they are ready to receive it. The feedback may be more useful if it is limited in scope and quantity, and given over a period of time. This will better enable the receivers to gradually integrate the feedback into their behavior.[17]

## Structural Suggestions

The practitioner also makes structural suggestions about work group membership, communication patterns, allocation of work, assignment of responsibility, and lines of authority. He or she often makes suggestions about how work should be organized, who should be on what committees, and who should be working on specific projects. It is critical for the practitioner to avoid stepping in and taking over, otherwise the group will not learn to solve its own problems and may develop a dependency relationship upon the manager.

## RESULTS OF PROCESS INTERVENTIONS

Process intervention skills can be helpful to OD practitioners, be they managers or OD professionals. Edgar Schein, who has taught middle-level executives at the Sloan School of Management at the Massachusetts Institute of Technology, says that students frequently report that as managers they often use process skills with their subordinates and superiors. Process interventions, they say, are a method useful in relating to people where organization members can learn to solve their own problems.[18]

Richard Walton, in *Managing Conflict, Interpersonal Dialogue and Third-Party Roles,* maintains that whereas process skills were once the domain of OD specialists, they are now a part of normal managerial activity.[19] Major corporations like General Electric (GE), IBM, and 3M bring process skills to the managerial level, regularly sending managers to workshops designed to help participants become more effective in working with teams and analyzing group process. These managers use process skills as a part of their daily activities. This will be more common as companies come to rely more on the team approach in managing their companies.

While OD consultants, such as Edgar Schein, report improved organization health and functioning as an outcome of process interventions, there is little empirical evidence to document such changes. The assumption is that a group that is aware of and acting upon its problems is likely to be more effective than a group that is not. Also, process interventions are usually practiced as part of an ongoing OD program, and it is often difficult to evaluate process interventions separately from the total OD program. Nonetheless, process interventions are increasing relied upon by OD practitioners. As organizations, such as Cisco and P&G, increasingly rely upon teams, process interventions are becoming a method more frequently relied upon by managers and supervisors in their daily interactions with their teams.

Subsequent chapters will discuss OD techniques that use process interventions, such as empowerment, team building, and self-managed work teams. You will also be participating in simulations where the application of process interventions will be appropriate. Use these skills to the point that they become natural and comfortable.

## Summary

- **OD Process Interventions.** This chapter has presented an overview of process interventions, one of the most used OD skills. Process interventions are often utilized to develop more effective teams. They are used to assist work groups in diagnosing and solving their own problems and to increase the functioning of work groups by helping team members work together.
- **Own Solutions.** One of the major characteristics of process interventions is that people learn to identify problems and then initiate their own solutions. Process interventions help individuals and teams to diagnose and solve their own problems.
- **Group Process.** The foundation of process interventions is the study of how groups and the individuals within groups behave. Five areas crucial to effective organization performance are communication, member roles and functions, group problem solving and decision making, group norms and growth, and leadership and authority.
- **Types.** The types of process interventions that may be used include clarifying, summarizing, synthesizing, generalizing, probing, questioning, listening, reflecting feelings, providing support, coaching, counseling, modeling, setting the agenda, feeding back observations, and providing structural suggestions. Interventions should be as brief and crisp as possible. The concern is how the group is going about accomplishing its task.
- **Interventions.** Managers must examine several factors in deciding upon an intervention. They must determine not only the depth of the desired intervention but also the relative advantages and disadvantages of various possible interventions. Process interventions can often be used to enhance team functioning and performance.

## Review Questions

1. Explain how process interventions can be used in an OD program.
2. What is the difference between group task functions and group maintenance functions?

3. Identify and explain the communication processes that a manager can use in a work group.

## Key Words and Concepts

| | | | |
|---|---|---|---|
| Group Consensus | Empathy | Group Task Functions | Member Roles |
| Individual Functions | Group Content | Group-Building and | Norms |
| Agenda-Setting Interventions | Group Process | Maintenance Functions | Process Interventions |

# Od Skills Simulation 8.1

## Apex Oil Spill

*Total time suggested: 70 minutes.*

## A. Purpose

To identify the forces acting upon individuals as they interact with others and to practice using process interventions. The goals include:

1. To examine behaviors that facilitate and inhibit group functioning.
2. To identify the functions and roles of group members.
3. To explore group processes.

## B. Procedures

*Step 1.* Prior to class, form into groups of seven members and make role assignments. Extra class members act as additional observers. The seven roles are:

1. Assistant to the Governor
2. State Economic Development Director
3. State Environment Director
4. Petroleum Industry Representative
5. Coalition of Environmental Groups' Representative
6. OD Practitioner
7. Observer(s)

Before class, read the APEX Oil Spill Background Information and your role description. Do not read the role description of other members. Record your individual position and support for your position on the APEX Oil Spill Decision Form. The observer should become familiar with Observer Forms A and B before class.

*Step 2.* The committee (including the OD practitioner and the observers) meets to decide on its recommendation. Each person should make a nametag with the name of the role he or she is playing. The OD practitioner will assist the committee in arriving at a decision, but the observer will not take part in the committee decision. Record your team position and support on the APEX Oil Spill Decision Form.

*Time suggested for Step 2: 40 minutes.*

*Step 3.* After the committee reaches its decision, meet with your group and discuss the process. The observer will also share information recorded on the Observer Forms. All members are encouraged to provide feedback. Answer the following questions:

1. How was a decision reached? (By consensus, vote, etc.)
2. What type of process interventions did the OD practitioner use? Try to be specific and give examples.
3. What types of process interventions did the other team members use?
4. Did the OD practitioner make the client feel at ease? How?
5. What did the practitioner do or say that was helpful?
6. What verbal and nonverbal communications seemed to help the meeting?

*Time suggested for Step 3: 15 minutes.*

*Step 4.* As a class, discuss the questions in Step 3.

*Time suggested for Step 4: 15 minutes.*

## APEX Oil Spill Background Information

Several months ago, one of APEX Oil Corporation's underwater oil pipelines split open and allowed 4 million barrels of heavy crude to spill into coastal waters. The pipeline carries oil from offshore platforms where the oil is pumped through another pipeline to a refinery 75 miles inland. The spill is the largest to ever hit your state, and the damage to the wildlife and coastal towns has been significant.

APEX says through its representatives that the equipment monitoring the pipeline had periodically registered false alarms of a pipeline leak for the past three months. When technicians saw that the gauges showed a problem, they assumed that it was another false alarm and did not take any action. It was not until 10 hours later, when local fishermen reported an oil slick, that the pipeline was shut down. The oil, however, continued to drain out of the pipe for another six hours.

A 100-mile stretch of state beaches and state coastal wildlife preserves was moderately to heavily fouled with the oil slick. Cleanup is proceeding by crews hired by APEX and a large number of volunteers organized by environmental groups. A great many fish were killed, and lobster and crab had been virtually wiped out. Seals, porpoises, otters, and many species of birds suffered large losses. Attempts to remove the oil from these animals have been proceeding, but most efforts have been largely unsuccessful because of the ingestion of oil by the animals.

The oil spill also affected the human population. The economies of four coastal towns in the area depend on a combination of commercial and recreational fishing and tourism. The fishing industry became nonexistent overnight when the state's environment director acted immediately to bar commercial and recreational fishing in an area that affects one-third of the state coastal fishing waters. The restriction will probably be effective for at least two years, and the time it will take for fish production to be close to normal will probably be ten years. Tourism, including out-of-state tourism, is down 90 percent. It will probably be four years before the beaches will be in good enough condition for tourists to return in normal numbers.

On the brighter side, a few businesses, such as motels and restaurants, were not hit as hard because of the influx of scientists, government officials, and cleanup crews. But this will last only as long as the cleanup. Some of the displaced commercial fishermen were hired by APEX to clean up the beaches, and half of the fish-processing plants have been turned into rescue facilities for some of the affected wildlife.

APEX has publicly taken responsibility for the oil spill, and a representative of the company has said that it will pay for the clean up of the beaches and the animal rescue centers sponsored by the company. In a news conference, APEX rejected any responsibility for incidental costs, such as reduced income to commercial fishermen, fish-processing plants, and local town businesses.

APEX has also said that it is not subject to laws relating to killing endangered or threatened species, because the intent of the law did not pertain to accidental killing. According to APEX, the cleanup operation is running expeditiously and should be completed in three months.

On the other hand, state officials, scientists, and environmentalists assert that APEX's cleanup operation is proceeding at a slow pace because of the company's bureaucracy, inexperience in handling operations of this type, and expectation that public concern will diminish with time.

The economy of the state as a whole has also been affected. The state receives 15 percent of its revenue from offshore oil production, and the platforms involved in the spill account for 30 percent of the state's offshore oil production. The state's environment director (all state directors are elected positions and can operate independently of the governor) obtained a court injunction to shut down all offshore oil production until a complete investigation could be conducted to determine the safe operating condition of all platforms and equipment operating in state waters.

The investigation by state engineers will take at least nine months, and meanwhile the state will lose its tax revenue from the production of the oil. The court action is very popular with the state's citizens, although the governor and the economic development director have expressed some reservations about the injunction.

There have been news reports for the past five years that the equipment of several companies with offshore facilities was old and preventive maintenance was lax. There was speculation that contributions to the election funds of members of the state legislature and a previous governor were partly responsible for the lack of enforcement of safety regulations. Recent opinion surveys show that the environment is the most important concern of the voters.

The governor has called this committee together to make a recommendation to her. Although court action may be necessary to enforce the suggestions, the governor has publicly stated that she wants all options to be explored. In addition to the recommendation, the governor would also like the following issues addressed (see APEX Oil Spill Decision Form):

1. Should the state try to shut down future offshore oil drilling operations?
2. Should the state try to shut down all offshore oil production pending an investigation of all platforms and pipelines by state authorities? Or shut down just platforms and pipelines involved in the oil spill?
3. Should the state try to shut down oil production in the area affected until the environment can be stabilized (about 18 months)?
4. Should the state go to court and try to force APEX to pay for all direct and indirect costs plus pay fines for pollution and killing wildlife?

## Role Descriptions (Read Only Your Role)

**Assistant to the Governor.** You have been instructed by the governor to make sure her interests are represented. The governor is concerned about the state's economy—especially as she hopes to be reelected in two years. That means trying to keep tax revenue from oil as high as possible in order to avoid a tax increase. The governor has repeatedly told the voters that there will be no new taxes while she is governor. You believe that the economic future of the state is dependent on increasing oil production. You must at least give the impression that the environment is important because of the voters' concern. You have received a secret preliminary draft from the U.S. Environmental Protection Agency recommending that federal legislation be passed banning new offshore oil drilling in environmentally sensitive waters under federal control. It is important, therefore, to get the committee to recommend continued production and drilling in state waters before the federal report is released. Though any federal legislation would have no legal authority in state waters, there would likely be increased pressure at the state level to pass similar legislation. In addition, the governor owes some favors to the petroleum industry because of its legal contributions to her campaign.

**State Economic Development Director.** Your job is to ensure that the economic development of the state progresses on track in order to meet its 10-year plan. Reduced tax revenues from oil, commercial fishing, and out-of-state tourism will reduce tax revenues as much as 20 percent for the next two years. An immediate problem is what to do about the economies of the four coastal towns after the cleanup crews and environmentalists leave. You believe that indirect costs, such as unemployed fishermen, fish-processing plants not operating, and loss of business to motels, restaurants, tourist shops, and other town businesses, should be pursued against APEX. The effect of future oil spills on the fishing and tourist industry concerns you. A recent study by a reliable economic think tank found that oil tax revenue is offset by the economic costs if a major oil spill occurs every 40 years. Despite these concerns, you realize that the loss of tax revenue from oil production and the jobs it brings in will mean a tax increase, reduced expenditures, or some combination of the two. Because of these conflicting concerns, you favor a compromise of some sort. However, if you learn of new and persuasive information during the meeting, you will be willing to support either the pro-oil or pro- environment forces.

**State Environment Director.** Your job is to protect the environment of the state. You would like to halt all offshore oil production in federal and state waters until a thorough investigation is made of each oil field. Only then will the oil field be brought on line. For the future, a very rigid state monitoring system of existing oil platforms and pipelines should be implemented. Future drilling in state waters should be permanently barred. You suspect that the cost to the fishing and tourist industries offsets any gains the state may make through oil tax revenues. Recent studies by scientists from your office show that a medium to major oil spill can be expected every 35 years in your state. In your opinion and that of groups that helped get you elected, you would like to see state legislation preventing all new offshore oil drilling in state waters. You believe that the oil industry in your state has a long history of acting irresponsibly and trying (through campaign contributions) to buy itself out of regulations being enforced against it. In addition to the imposition of heavy fines for pollution and killing wildlife, all direct and indirect costs should be pursued against APEX.

**Petroleum Industry Representative.** You represent all the oil companies doing business in the state. It is imperative that you get the committee to allow your companies to have unencumbered access to drilling and oil production in the state. In fact, the damage to the pipeline was so insignificant that APEX has already repaired and checked it out. Offshore drilling represents a minimum risk to the environment but one that is acceptable given the economic gains and the need for oil. Nonpublished and oil industry studies conducted by scientists and business experts from your organization show that a medium-sized spill can be expected every 45 years and that a major spill will occur only once every 75 years. You are aware of other studies by environmental groups contradicting these figures, but you seriously question the credentials of the scientists conducting the studies. You do not want any drilling and production restrictions for fear they will spread to other states. As a last resort, it may be necessary to let APEX be the sacrificial lamb to preserve oil development for the other companies. However, you must be discreet about abandoning APEX so as not to alienate it from your organization. You will need to stress the importance of oil production in terms of jobs and tax revenue to the state for both the short and long run. Legal contributions have been made by your organization to the governor's reelection campaign. You expect that the governor's representative will be helpful in the meeting.

**Coalition of Environmental Groups' Representative.** You were chosen by environmental organizations to represent them at the meeting. You have been directed to take a very strong position about protecting the environment for both the short and long term. You want APEX to pay for all cleanups and to pay heavy fines, for pollution and killing endangered and threatened wildlife. You also want APEX officers charged with criminal neglect. Some of the cleanup crews and animal rescue centers have been funded by environmental organizations, and you want to make sure they are reimbursed by APEX. You want to halt all offshore oil production and drilling now and in the future in state and federal waters. Studies by independent and highly reputable scientists show that offshore drilling is environmentally unsafe and that a major oil spill can be expected every 30 years in this state's waters. There have been recent rumors from your Washington sources that a letter was sent to the governor informing her that the Environmental Protection Agency will soon recommend that Congress enact legislation banning all new offshore oil drilling and that current production be phased out within 25 years in both state and federal waters. You want to make sure APEX pays for its negligence in order to set a strong example for other companies. The lack of enforcement of existing regulations by state agencies concerns you, and you feel that campaign contributions to elected officials are part of the problem. There is a saying among environmentalists that "the state's elected office-holders are the best that money can buy."

**OD Practitioner.** Review the section in this chapter titled "Types of Process Interventions." Use these process consultation skills to help the committee reach a decision. Be careful not to take over and run the committee. Do not take a position or support one group of people. Your job is to help them make their own decision.

**Observer(s).** Do not take part in the committee meeting. Your role as an observer is to provide information later in Steps 3 and 4. Use the Observer Forms to record your observations. Review the discussion of sociograms in Chapter 5.

**APEX OIL SPILL DECISION FORM**

1.   Shut down offshore drilling?

My decision:_____

_____

_____

Team decision:_____

_____

_____

_____

2.   Shut down offshore production pending investigation of all platforms?

My decision:_____

_____

_____

Team decision:_____

_____

_____

_____

3.   Or shut down only platforms involved in this spill?

My decision:_____

_____

_____

Team decision:_____

_____

_____

_____

4.   Shut down production in affected area for about 18 months?

My decision:_____

_____

_____

Team decision:_____

_____

_____

_____

5.   State goes to court to force APEX to pay?

My decision:_____

_____

_____

Team decision:_____

_____

_____

_____

**OBSERVER FORM A—BEHAVIOR OBSERVATIONS**

*Instructions:* Place the names of the individuals in your group in the spaces at the top of the chart. Read and become familiar with the behavior descriptions. Put a check in the appropriate block each time that you observe the behavior.

| Description of Behavior<br><br>Name | Assistant to the Governor | State Economic Development Director | State Environment Director | Petroleum Industry Representative | Environmental Groups' Representative | OD Practitioner |
|---|---|---|---|---|---|---|
| **Group Task Functions:** | | | | | | |
| Initiating | | | | | | |
| Suggesting | | | | | | |
| Seeking Opinions | | | | | | |
| Asking Questions | | | | | | |
| Elaborating | | | | | | |
| Summarizing | | | | | | |
| Testing for Consensus | | | | | | |
| **Group Building and Maintenance Functions:** | | | | | | |
| Harmonizing | | | | | | |
| Compromising | | | | | | |
| Encouraging | | | | | | |
| Gatekeeping | | | | | | |
| Following | | | | | | |
| **Individual Functions:** | | | | | | |
| Dominating | | | | | | |
| Acting the Playboy | | | | | | |
| Blocking | | | | | | |
| Seeking Recognition | | | | | | |
| Pleading for Special Interest | | | | | | |
| **Others:** | | | | | | |
| | | | | | | |
| | | | | | | |

## OBSERVER FORM B

Instructions: Complete this sociogram on the team you are observing. Draw direction arrows for communication flow. Identify behaviors shown by participants.

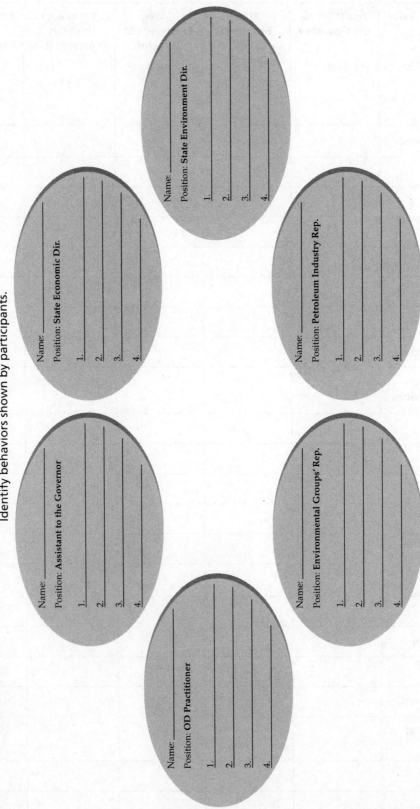

Name: _____
Position: State Environment Dir.

1. _____
2. _____
3. _____
4. _____

Name: _____
Position: State Economic Dir.

1. _____
2. _____
3. _____
4. _____

Name: _____
Position: Petroleum Industry Rep.

1. _____
2. _____
3. _____
4. _____

Name: _____
Position: Assistant to the Governor

1. _____
2. _____
3. _____
4. _____

Name: _____
Position: Environmental Groups' Rep.

1. _____
2. _____
3. _____
4. _____

Name: _____
Position: OD Practitioner

1. _____
2. _____
3. _____
4. _____

# OD Skills Simulation 8.2
## Trust Building

*Total time suggested: 25 to 35 minutes.*

### A. Purpose

The purpose of this simulation is to provide a comparison between your perceptions of trust behavior and how others perceive it.

### B. Procedures

*Note: Steps 1 and 2 may be completed out of class.*

    *Step 1.* Based on your group work in Simulation 8.1, complete and score the Self-Behavior Questionnaire for yourself. The observers in your group will also participate in this questionnaire. Transfer the responses from the Self-Behavior Questionnaire to the Individual Scoring Form. Complete the Trust Diagram by drawing horizontal and vertical lines at the numbers representing your score.

    *Time suggested for Step 1: 5 minutes.*

    *Step 2.* After completing Simulation 8.1, each member of the group rates every other group member. Record your responses on the Team Members Survey. The scoring can be anonymous if the team so elects.

    *Time suggested for Step 2: 5 minutes.*

    *Step 3.* Give each member his or her scores.

    *Step 4.* Record the scores that you received from your team members on the Scores from Team Members Form. Compute the totals and averages of the two sets of scores received from team members. On the Trust Diagram, draw dotted horizontal and vertical lines at the appropriate numbers based on your scores. You now have the results of your Self-Behavior Questionnaire and the results received from your team members. On the Trust Diagram, your perception of yourself is indicated by solid lines, and feedback from others is indicated by dotted lines.

    *Time suggested for Steps 3 and 4: 10 minutes.*

    *Step 5.* Meeting with your team, discuss the following questions:

1. How similar are the results from others and your answers about yourself?
2. Is there a close match? If not, what factors do you think contribute to the other group members' seeing your behavior differently from the way you do?
3. How could this modify your behavior?

    *Time suggested for Step 5: 15 minutes.*

### SELF-BEHAVIOR QUESTIONNAIRE

*Instructions:* The following is a series of questions about your behavior in your group. Answer each question as honestly as you can. There are no right or wrong answers. It is important for you to describe your behavior as accurately as possible. Place a number in the blank to the right representing your choice based on the following scale.

[Low   1   2   3   4   5   6   7   High]

_____ 1. I offer facts, give my opinions and ideas, and provide suggestions and relevant information to help the group discussion.

_____ 2. I express my willingness to cooperate with other group members and my expectations that they will also be cooperative.

_____ 3. I am open and candid in my dealings with the entire group.

_____ 4. I give support to group members who are on the spot and struggling to express themselves intellectually or emotionally.

_____ 5. I keep my thoughts, ideas, feelings, and reactions to myself during group discussions.

_____ 6. I evaluate the contributions of other group members in terms of whether their contributions are useful to me and whether they are right or wrong.

_____ 7. I take risks in expressing new ideas and current feelings during a group discussion.

_____ 8. I communicate to other group members that I appreciate abilities, talents, capabilities, skills, and resources.

_____ 9. I offer help and assistance to anyone in the group in order to bring up the performance of everyone.

_____ 10. I accept and support the openness of other group members, support them for taking risks, and encourage individuality in group members.

_____ 11. I share any materials, books, sources of information, and other resources I have with the other group members in order to promote the success of all members and the group as a whole.

_____ 12. I often paraphrase or summarize what other members have said before I respond or comment.

_____ 13. I level with other group members.

_____ 14. I warmly encourage all members to participate, giving them recognition for their contributions, demonstrating acceptance and openness to their ideas, and generally being friendly and responsive to them.

## INDIVIDUAL SCORING FORM

Transfer the responses from the Self-Behavior questionnaire to this form. Reverse the scoring on the questions that are starred. (Example: a score of 2 would be recorded as 6 on this form.) Calculate the totals and the averages.

| Openness and Sharing | Acceptance and Support |
|---|---|
| 1. _____ | 2. _____ |
| 3. _____ | 4. _____ |
| *5. _____ | *6. _____ |
| 7. _____ | 8. _____ |
| 9. _____ | 10. _____ |
| 11. _____ | 12. _____ |
| 13. _____ | 14. _____ |
| Total _____ | Total _____ |
| Average _____ | Average _____ |

### Trust Diagram

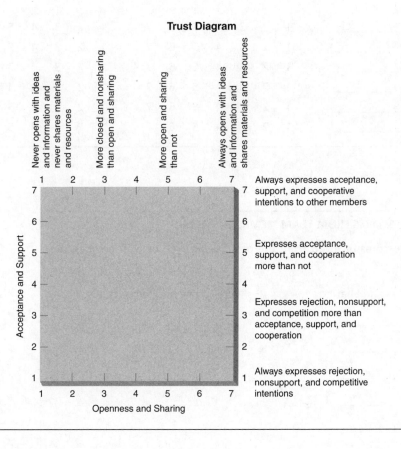

## TEAM MEMBERS' SURVEY

Write the name of your team members in the second column. Then score your team members by circling the appropriate number. To the extent possible, include the observer(s).

| Position | Team Member's Name | Openness and Sharing | Acceptance and Support |
|---|---|---|---|
| | | Low          High | Low          High |
| 1. Assistant to the Governor | _____ | 1  2  3  4  5  6  7 | 1  2  3  4  5  6  7 |
| 2. State Economic Development Director | _____ | 1  2  3  4  5  6  7 | 1  2  3  4  5  6  7 |
| 3. State Environment Director | _____ | 1  2  3  4  5  6  7 | 1  2  3  4  5  6  7 |
| 4. Petroleum Industry Director | _____ | 1  2  3  4  5  6  7 | 1  2  3  4  5  6  7 |
| 5. Environmental-Groups' Representative | _____ | 1  2  3  4  5  6  7 | 1  2  3  4  5  6  7 |
| 6. OD Practitioner | _____ | 1  2  3  4  5  6  7 | 1  2  3  4  5  6  7 |
| 7. Observer | _____ | 1  2  3  4  5  6  7 | 1  2  3  4  5  6  7 |
| 8. Observer | _____ | 1  2  3  4  5  6  7 | 1  2  3  4  5  6  7 |
| 9. Observer | _____ | 1  2  3  4  5  6  7 | 1  2  3  4  5  6  7 |
| 10. Observer | _____ | 1  2  3  4  5  6  7 | 1  2  3  4  5  6  7 |

## SCORES FROM TEAM MEMBERS' FORM

*Instructions:* Record the scores received from the other team members. Then calculate the total and average.

| Openness and Sharing | Acceptance and Support |
|---|---|
| _____ | _____ |
| _____ | _____ |
| _____ | _____ |
| _____ | _____ |
| _____ | _____ |
| _____ | _____ |
| _____ | _____ |
| _____ | _____ |
| _____ | _____ |
| _____ | _____ |
| Total _____ | Total _____ |
| Average _____ | Average _____ |

# Od Skills Simulation 8.3

## Process Interventions

*Total time suggested: 60 minutes.*

## A. Purpose

This simulation will provide you with additional practice in OD interventions in the framework of a manager working with a person in your work group who has a problem. It is your responsibility to help the person clarify the problem by formulating a diagnosis. You will also be able, as an observer, to observe the intervention process.

## B. Procedures

*Step 1.* Form into teams of three. There are three roles, and every member will play each role. Additional class members can join a group, but each group should have at least three members. The three roles are work group member, manager, and observer. Before beginning the role play, the members should read all of the following guidelines.

*Work group member:* Take a class problem or a work problem that involves you and explain this to your manager.

*Manager:* Your role is to help the work group member by practicing process interventions. See the Observer Form and the chapter discussion to familiarize yourself with appropriate and inappropriate intervention skills.

*Observer:* Your job is to observe as carefully as possible both the work group member and the manager. You will not participate in their discussion at this time. Use the Observer Form to record your observations.

At the end of each role play, the observer will share his or her observations, and the manager and the work-group member should critique one another's styles.

*Step 2.* Continue the simulation by switching roles until everyone has played each of the roles.

*Time suggested for Steps 1 and 2: 15 minutes for each role play including observer feedback. Total time for all role plays is approximately 45 minutes. The time may be longer for teams that have more than three members.*

*Step 3.* Meeting with the entire class, critique the role plays. You may want to look at the following questions.

1. As the work group member, how did you feel about the manager's responses? Were they helpful or dysfunctional? Try to be specific.
2. As the manager, how did you feel about the way the work group member behaved? Did any of his or her behaviors bother you? If so, did you share this with him or her? Try to be specific.
3. How did you feel about playing the part of the manager or the work group member? Were you able to really get into your role? Why?
4. Can you think of anything that you would like to have done differently?
5. Any other comments or thoughts?

*Time suggested for Step 3: 15 minutes.*

**OBSERVER FORM**

As an observer, score the manager on the following items. Items 1 through 6 are appropriate behaviors for process interventions, while items 7 through 10 are inappropriate behaviors.

Provide examples in the blank lines.

1.  Practiced empathy:                                    Low 1 : 2 : 3 : 4 : 5 : 6 : 7 High
    _____
    _____

2.  Made eye contact:                                     Low 1 : 2 : 3 : 4 : 5 : 6 : 7 High
    _____
    _____

3.  Practiced nonverbal communications:                   Low 1 : 2 : 3 : 4 : 5 : 6 : 7 High
    _____
    _____

4.  Reflected back content of message:                    Low 1 : 2 : 3 : 4 : 5 : 6 : 7 High
    _____
    _____

5.  Reflected back feeling of message:                    Low 1 : 2 : 3 : 4 : 5 : 6 : 7 High
    _____
    _____

6.  Demonstrated approval and acceptance:                 Low 1 : 2 : 3 : 4 : 5 : 6 : 7 High
    _____
    _____

7.  Sent solutions:                                       Low 1 : 2 : 3 : 4 : 5 : 6 : 7 High
    _____
    _____

8.  Blamed or acted in judgment:                          Low 1 : 2 : 3 : 4 : 5 : 6 : 7 High
    _____
    _____

9.  Expressed sarcasm or inappropriate behavior:          Low 1 : 2 : 3 : 4 : 5 : 6 : 7 High
    _____
    _____

10. Participated in large degree of "small talk":         Low 1 : 2 : 3 : 4 : 5 : 6 : 7 High
    _____
    _____

11. Other observed behaviors:                             Low 1 : 2 : 3 : 4 : 5 : 6 : 7 High
    _____
    _____

# CASE: THE OD LETTERS

**Larry,**

I enjoyed seeing you last month at the company picnic. I've been trying to reach you by phone, but no luck. I decided this e-mail would do until we can talk. Your secretary said you're working on another project out in the field and couldn't be reached except for emergencies. I have several projects my work teams are involved with, and managing them all gets to be pretty hectic. So I know what you must be up against. I've just been assigned a new project team to manage, the XRS Laser group, and it seems like you had some dealings with them several years back. Is that true? I could sure use someone to bounce some ideas off. I'd appreciate any insights.

*Thanks, Ryan*

**Ryan,**

Sorry to have missed your call but I was in Oklahoma City doing some work with one of my new field teams. And now that I'm back, your secretary said you were out of the area on company business. So this is what we get paid the big bucks for!

I thought I'd zap this e-mail off instead of waiting for you to get back at headquarters. Your e-mail triggered some old memories. Excuse my rambling in what I will share with you. I'll add the details when I see you. Please keep this confidential.

Yes, you were right about me working with the XRS project team. I looked in my records and it was three years ago that I worked with XRS. I have been indirectly keeping in touch with how things are going there through one of my old contacts.

Their project manager, John Everet, had been under a lot of pressure from his department head, Kate Pringle, to get the project moving at a faster pace. It seems that the team was not turning out any results, and John had been the team manager for over two years. Kate talked to me about the team. She seemed to think there was some friction among members and maybe that John was causing some problems.

Anyway, Kate contacted me to see if I would go along on the team's annual retreat and maybe help them with several issues—mainly personnel stuff—and, me being an outsider, bring in a new perspective. Because the company requires an outsider from another division to go along and help with the training on team retreats, John didn't have much choice about me being there. He sure didn't go out of his way to make me feel welcome. I decided it would be wise to go easy at first until I got the lay of the land, and retreats generally have gone pretty well. Most teams have gone away from the retreat thinking they have worked out some team issues. Well, this retreat broke the mold.

Anyway, the three-day retreat was weird. The retreat started when we were all loaded up in a bus. None of the participants were told where they were going, so it was to be a big surprise. We traveled about three hours to a dude ranch in the local mountains. I was in charge of the team meetings for the initial afternoon and through the early afternoon of the next day. We initially did a few icebreaker fun exercises, followed by some nonthreatening team exercises. This was followed by reports from the teams on what they thought were effective team skills. It was really low-key stuff and, to get them going, not specific at all about their own work team.

You know, I can remember what happened next as if it were yesterday. John remained really aloof. I had previously arranged for him, like everyone else, to be in a team. He joked around with several other men for about 30 minutes before joining his team. Meanwhile, his team went to work without him. When he finally joined them, he didn't say much. After a few minutes he got up and went over to another team and talked about getting a late-night poker game going. I did not confront him at the time, which, reflecting back on things, may have been a mistake on my part.

Well, that was the afternoon session. Not exactly a roaring success, but a number of the participants were really getting into the team exercises. The morning session of the next day went about the same. John played the part of the social butterfly. His behavior was a bit obvious to others. Reflecting back on things, I think he was intimidated. This was his first job as a project manager and I think he thought of himself as the "big cheese," the old-fashioned macho manager. I know he went through the company's team leadership courses, but he must have been sleeping.

We had a team-building exercise followed by a discussion on how team members in general could work better together—again, nothing specific. I remember that one fellow got really annoyed at John's team for joking around. He said something to the effect that this was why it took so long to get anything done. Several others agreed, but then John said that what we were doing in the teams was just a fun game and did not mean anything. That guy got the message from John and got real quiet. And so did several others. The morning session ended OK for the most part, though John and several others left early. They went for a canoe ride out on the lake. You could hear them laughing while everyone else was in their team meetings. When John and several others did not come back for the early afternoon session, everyone kind of drifted off into little groups and did what they wanted. Nothing more happened because the company structures these retreats so that the last day and a half is open for everyone to do what they want. Also, since the company provides no effective way for an outsider like me to make a report or continue to work on issues uncovered at the retreat, I had to let it go.

Well, it looks like John is no longer there and you have inherited the XRS group. There really are some good folks with a lot of potential. Sure, I'd be glad to talk to you in more detail about the situation there. Give me a call when you get back in town and you can buy me lunch.

*Larry*

(Use the Case Analysis Form on the following page.)

**THE OD LETTERS CASE ANALYSIS FORM**

Name: _____

I. Problems

  A. Macro

    1. _____

    _____

    2. _____

    _____

  B. Micro

    1. _____

    _____

    2. _____

    _____

II. Causes

    1. _____

    _____

    2. _____

    _____

    3. _____

    _____

III. Systems affected

    1. _____

    _____

    2. _____

    _____

    3. _____

    _____

IV. Alternatives

    1. _____

    _____

    2. _____

    _____

    3. _____

    _____

V. Recommendations

_____

_____

_____

_____

_____

_____

## Chapter 8 Endnotes

1. For additional information on leadership that reflects this new leadership role, see Noel M. Tichy and Warren G. Bennis, *Judgment: How Winning Leaders Make Great Calls* (New York: Portfolio, 2007); Noel M. Tichy and Nancy Cardwell, *The Cycle of Leadership: How Great Leaders Teach Their Companies to Win* (New York: Harper Business, 2004).

2. "Tips for Team Building," *Business Week Online*, October 31, 2001. See www.businessweek.com.

3. See William Bridges, "The End of the Job," *Fortune*, September 19, 1994, p. 74.

4. Ibid.

5. Robert Berner, "P&G: How A. G. Lafley Is Revolutionizing a Bastion of Corporate Conservatism," *Business Week*, July 7, 2003, p. 63.

6. Stephen Haberman, "Software: Will Outsourcing Hurt America's Supremacy?" *Business Week*, March 1, 2004, pp. 84–94.

7. For additional information, see Edgar Schein, *Process Consultation Revisited, Building the Helping Relationship* (Reading, MA: Addison-Wesley, 1999); Edgar Schein, *Process Consultation: Lessons for Managers and Consultants*, vol. 2 (Reading, MA: Addison-Wesley, 1987); Edgar Schein, *Process Consultation, Its Role in Organization Development*, vol. 1, 2nd ed. (Reading, MA: Addison-Wesley, 1988). Schein's books are considered classics in the area of process-helping skills.

8. Ibid., p. 9.

9. W. Warner Burke, Lawrence P. Clark, and Cheryl Koopman, "Improve Your OD Project's Chances for Success," *Training and Development Journal*, vol. 38, no. 9 (September 1984), p. 67.

10. In addition to the books on process consultation by Edgar Schein mentioned previously, also see Michael Donovan and Leta Letize, "Lessons from the Wizard," *Journal for Quality and Participation*, vol. 16, no. 4 (July/August 1993), pp. 44–47; John Keltner, "Catalyst for Group Problem Solving," *Management Communication Quarterly*, vol. 3, no.1 (August 1989), pp. 8–32; Benjamin J. Broome, David B. Keever, "Next Generation Group Facilitation," *Management Communication Quarterly*, vol. 3, no.1 (August 1989), pp. 107–27; Frank Luthans, "Conversation with Edgar H. Schein," *Organizational Dynamics*, Spring 1989, pp. 60–76.

11. Schein, *Process Consultation, Its Role in Organization Development*, p. 13.

12. Christina Bjorklund, Anders Grahn, Irene Jensen, and Gunnar Bergstrom, "Does Survey Feedback Enhance the Psychosocial-Work Environment and Decrease Sick Leave?" *European Journal of Work and Organizational Psychology*, vol. 16, no. 1 (March 2007), pp. 76–93; Additional information on feedback can be found in Manuel London, Henrik Holt Larsen, and Lars Nellemann Thisted, "Relationship between Feedback and Self Development," *Group and Organization Management*, vol. 24, no. 1 (March 1999), pp. 5–28.

13. For a review of one of the original articles on the roles of group members, see Kenneth D. Benne and Paul Sheats, "Functional Roles of Group Members," *Journal of Social Issues*, vol. 4, no. 2 (Spring 1948), pp. 42–47.

14. www.disneyinstitute.com/; Bruce Orwall and Emily Nelson, "Hidden Wall Shields Disney's Kingdom: 80 Years of Culture," *Wall Street Journal*, February 13, 2004, pp. A1, A8.

15. For additional information, see Schein, *Process Consultation: Its Role in Organization Development*; Paul H. Ephross and Thomas V. Vassil, *Groups That Work: Structure and Process* (New York: Columbia University Press, 1988), pp. 140–65; David Coghlan, "In Defense of Process Consultation," *Leadership and Organization Development*, vol. 2, no. 2 (1988), pp. 27–31; Carl R. Rogers and F. J. Roethlisberger, "Barriers and Gateways to Communication," *Harvard Business Review*, July–August 1952, pp. 28–34.

16. Claudia Wallis, "Bill & Melinda Gates Go Back to School," *Fortune*, December 8, 2008, p. 113.

17. Leroy Wells Jr., "Feedback, the Group Unconscious, and the Unstated Effects of Experimental Methods," *Journal of Applied Behavioral Science*, vol. 28, no.1 (March 1992), pp. 46–53; Poppy L. McLeod, Jeffrey K. Liker, and Sharon A. Lobel, "Process Feedback in Task Groups: An Application of Goal Setting," *Journal of Applied Behavioral Science*, vol. 28, no.1 (March 1992), pp. 15–41.

18. Luthans, "Conversation with Edgar H. Schein," p. 68.

19. Richard E. Walton, *Interpersonal Peacemaking: Confrontations and Third-Party Consultation* (Reading, MA: Addison-Wesley, 1969), pp. 1–5.

20. David Johnson and Frank Johnson, *Joining Together: Group Theory and Group Skills*, © 1975, p. 244. Adapted by permission of Prentice-Hall, Inc., Upper Saddle River, N.J.

# Employee Empowerment and Interpersonal Interventions

## LEARNING OBJECTIVES

**Upon completing this chapter, you will be able to:**

1. Recognize the need for employee empowerment interventions in an OD program.
2. Experience the dynamics involved in interpersonal communication.
3. Practice giving and receiving feedback on your personal communication style.
4. Describe career life planning and stress management as OD techniques.

## PREMEETING PREPARATION

1. Read Chapter 9.
2. Prepare for OD Skills Simulation 9.1. Prior to class, form teams of six or more and assign roles. Complete Step 1.
3. Complete Steps 1 and 2 of OD Skills Simulation 9.3.
4. Read and analyze Case: The Sundale Club.

## EMPOWERING THE INDIVIDUAL

A growing number of today's companies are not only concerned but are also doing something about the way they manage their employees. They recognize that empowered employees are the difference between success and failure in the long run. **Empowerment** is the process of giving employees and work group members the ability to make decisions about their work, being held accountable for the outcomes of their decisions, accepting responsibility for the outcomes of their decisions, and solving problems on their own.[1]

A range of OD intervention activities strive to enhance the development and empowerment of the individual members of the organization. These approaches are based on the underlying assumption that if the individual becomes more effective, more involved, and more skilled, the total organization will also be improved. In a general sense, organization members attempt to improve their communication abilities, interpersonal skills, and managerial performance. If managers can increase their interpersonal competence, the result should be improved organizational performance.

This chapter covers several interpersonal techniques that can help organization members become more empowered and involved. The techniques discussed include employee empowerment, laboratory learning, interpersonal style, transactional analysis, career life planning, and stress management.

## EMPLOYEE EMPOWERMENT

Employee empowerment is a technique for unleashing human potential in organizations. Central to empowerment is the delegation of power and decision making to lower levels, and the promulgation of a shared vision of the future, engaging all employees so that they develop a personal sense of pride and responsibility. Employees who are empowered are more proactive and self-sufficient in helping their organizations to achieve their goals. Management is responsible for creating a supportive climate and removing barriers.[2] In an article in *Harvard Business Journal*, the writers said of Toyota Motor Corporation, "The company [Toyota] views employees not just as pairs of hands but as knowledge workers who accumulate *chie*—the wisdom of experience—on the company's front lines. Toyota therefore invests heavily in people and organizational capabilities, and it garners ideas from everyone and everywhere: the shop floor, the office, the field."[3]

The individual is one of the most critical elements in any large-scale organizational change. Excellence is achieved by organizations that push risk taking and decision making down to the lowest possible level. The new culture of organizations is built upon the empowerment of the individual. The challenge is to empower employees to take initiative and responsibility at every level and function. Organizations are designed to use the energy and ability of individuals to do work and realize goals. Members bring to the organization their values, assumptions, and behaviors. The success of future organizations, then, depends on how effectively the needs of individual members can be integrated with the vision and goals of the organization. People and behavior-oriented changes are aimed at the functioning of the organization's psychosocial system. The **psychosocial system** includes the network of social relationships and behavioral patterns of members, such as norms, roles, and communication. Behavioral interventions may take various forms, but all are intended to improve the basic skills that enhance employee empowerment, and thus underlie managerial effectiveness.

Employee empowerment attempts to move the organization from the traditional "I just work here, I don't make the rules" type of culture to one of a shared vision and goals. The purpose is to have the individual's purpose and vision congruent with the organization's. Employees develop a feeling of psychological ownership leading to concern, interest, commitment, and responsibility. A crucial point is that empowerment must be genuine. It is not empowerment when the managers tell employees they have authority and responsibility but do not allow them to make actual decisions and carry out actions. Managers must not just "talk the talk"; more important, they must "walk the talk."

The power that can be unleashed by employee empowerment is enormous. General Electric (GE) has implemented a version of employee involvement that it calls "Work-Out." Jack Welch, retired CEO of GE, says of Work-Out:

> The only way I see to get more productivity is by getting people involved and excited about their jobs. You can't afford to have anyone walk through a gate of a factory, or into an office, who's not giving 120 percent. I don't mean running and sweating, but working smarter . . . It's a matter of seeing the importance of your role in the total process. The point of Work-Out is to give people better jobs. When people see that their ideas count, their dignity is raised. Instead of feeling numb, like robots, they feel important. They are important.[4]

Empowerment is not a natural process, and it runs contrary to traditional views held both by managers and nonmanagers about how organizations are run. From management's point of view, it looks great in theory but is contrary to the traditional command model. Similarly, some nonmanagers appreciate the opportunity to be listened to and to contribute while others resent the additional responsibilities.

Organizations that embark upon programs to empower employees need to recognize that empowerment is not a "magic bullet" that can solve every ill of the organization. Empowerment of employees is more likely to be used in an OD program in conjunction with other intervention techniques. Research has found that "empowerment is significantly influenced by the embedding organizational environment. Both organizational support and team-based HR [human resources] practices exhibited significant positive influences on empowerment beyond the influence of work design features."[5] These findings are consistent with the practice of OD as an integration of intervention techniques and that any one OD intervention does not comprise an OD program (see Chapter 7).

In many organizations—whether small or large, profit or not-for-profit, domestic or international—employee empowerment has become a basic cornerstone of change and development programs. Empowerment concepts are interwoven through team and system interventions, including total quality management (TQM), self-managed work teams, learning organizations, and high-performance systems (these topics are all covered in future chapters). To learn more about empowerment at one organization, refer to **OD Application: How W. L. Gore Empowers Individuals and Teams.**

## OD Application: How W. L. Gore Empowers Individuals and Teams[6]

Innovation and change are in the DNA of W. L. Gore & Associates. Gore is most commonly known for its Gore-Tex fabric, a fabric used to make jackets and shoes. Gore-Tex has the ability to repel water while allowing perspiration to pass through. Gore-Tex was one of the company's first inventions, but instead of becoming a textile manufacturer, Gore has gone on to produce a diverse array of products. These include guitar strings, dental floss, space suits, chemical warfare suits, fuel cells, and a medical device that can nonsurgically repair a hole in the heart. The company's products typically are raw materials that end up in products made by other companies.

Gore realizes that its products and the company itself will become obsolete in several years without continuous innovation. The climate of the company is very much free flowing and innovative. Highly innovative companies need to have a free flow of knowledge and a structure that will stimulate communications among individuals and teams.

First, a bit of history. W. L. Gore & Associates got its start in 1958 when Bill Gore, a chemist, left DuPont. Having read Douglas McGregor's management book, *The Human Side of Enterprise*, he was intrigued with Theory Y management and the lattice organization system. McGregor's book served as his model, and the lattice system is still used at Gore over 50 years later. Gore has grown to have annual sales of more than $2 billion, about 8000 associates, and approximately 45 manufacturing and sales offices around the world.

In the flat lattice system that Gore uses, there is no assigned authority, and, in keeping with this, Gore has no employees or managers. There are few job titles, no chains of command, and no predetermined channels of communication. Gore has found that the lattice organization is most effective when plants are no larger than 150 to 200 associates. The philosophy is that people who know one another work better together and any cost savings from large plants is cancelled out by the loss of efficiency and productivity when people do not know each other well. "You have to divide so that you can multiply," says the CEO, Terri Kelly. The CEO is one of the few job titles at Gore.

The system uses sponsors rather than managers, and associates rather than employees. Everyone communicates with whomever they need, and people are accountable to fellow team members. Gore lets employees figure out what they want to do. Associates make commitments to work on the projects that they believe are most worthy of their time. As a result, "People tend to be very passionate about what they're doing," says researcher Jeff Kolde. Leaders are not appointed from above; instead, they emerge as they acquire followers to work on a project. "We vote with our feet," says Rich Buckingham, a manufacturing leader in Gore's technical-fabrics group. "If you call a meeting, and people show up, you're a leader." When

projects get killed, it is the team that makes the decision. As people gravitate to a project, and if it grows, new hires may be necessary. The team does the interviewing and hiring, with the human resources group conducting in-depth reference checks.

Since the team does the hiring, its members have a vested interest in making sure that the new associate is successful. Each associate is assigned a sponsor who acts much like a mentor. Typically, 20 percent of associates are sponsors. The sponsor is normally the person who has the most at stake in making sure the new associate is successful. If you sponsor someone, you want him or her to be successful. You will offer them appropriate opportunities to sit in on meetings and seminars, and do things so that they will be successful. If you are someone who is growing people on your team, it adds to your value. In other words, the team becomes successful because it makes sure that individual members are successful.

Evaluation of performance for team members comes from other associates. Once a year, each team ranks every member to all the other members on the question, "Who has made the biggest impact on the enterprise?" The rankings are then sorted through by "contribution committees" who use the rankings as a basis for compensation. Seniority and education are not the criteria. The criterion is contribution, pure and simple. Though associates have an unbelievable amount of freedom by the standards of other companies, they know they will be reviewed by at least 20 of their associates at the end of the year.

All associates are offered a stock option plan and profit sharing. Everyone, not just salaried employees, is included. That comes back to the concept that everyone is in this endeavor together. "We all are a team."

As a footnote, W. L. Gore for 12 consecutive years has been named in *Fortune*'s list of "100 Best Companies to Work for in America."

### Questions

1. How does Gore empower teams by empowering individual associates?
2. What is the lattice system of organization?
3. Do additional research on Theory Y and Theory X.
4. Do you think other companies could use these managerial strategies and structures? Or is this something unique to Gore?
5. Using the latest edition of *Fortune*'s "100 Best Companies to Work For in America," and find out what is Gore's current ranking. See Fortune's web site at www.money.cnn.com/magazines/fortune.
6. You can find additional information on Gore's lattice system and management at the company's Web site, www.gore.com.

## LABORATORY LEARNING

**Laboratory learning** programs (sometimes called encounter groups, sensitivity training, training groups, or simply T-groups) evolved from the group dynamics work of Kurt Lewin and programs conducted by the National Training Laboratories[7] (NTL) in the United States and the Tavistock Institute in England.[8] In Japan, research at the Group Dynamics Department of Kyushu University paralleled Lewin's, and ideas were shared in what Japanese researchers called Performance Maintenance (PM) theory.[9] Although reliable data on the extent of laboratory learning are not readily available, it grew rapidly through the mid-1970s. OD programs now make less use of laboratory learning as a training technique, but they use some forms of it indirectly in other OD training techniques, such as the Managerial Grid, team building, and Outward Bound.

### The Objectives of Laboratory Learning

Managers have used laboratory learning to increase their interpersonal skills in leadership, group, and organization situations. Laboratory learning involves using a group as a laboratory for experimenting, learning, and discovering cause-and-effect relations in interpersonal communication. Laboratory learning programs usually include 10 to 12 participants who typically do not know one another and one or two experienced trainers or facilitators. The group sessions normally require a one- or two-week time span, although some last three days or less. Practitioners usually conduct the programs at a location removed from the workplace.

The focus is on what goes on in the group and on the interpersonal dynamics between group members. The learning is unstructured in the sense that there is no appointed leader and no assigned topic. The goal is for participants to develop self-insight, with greater sensitivity to their effect on others, and to become aware of their blind spots and hidden areas. The laboratory provides a safe climate away from the work organization where participants can try new behaviors and receive candid feedback from others on the effectiveness of those behaviors. Participants can then return to work with new ways of behaving and working with others.

### The Use of Laboratory Learning in OD Programs

Laboratory learning can be conducted independently of an OD program, but if so, the problem of **fade out** is more likely to occur. Fade out occurs when participants, after having learned new ways of working with others, return to their work organizations, where support is often lacking. Without a supportive environment in the workplace to reinforce the new behaviors, the laboratory learning will degrade on the job. Laboratory learning conducted as part of an OD program provides more support to the participant back in the work organization than laboratory learning conducted as an isolated program.

Robert Blake and Herb Shepard pioneered the use of laboratory learning in company-wide programs aimed at improving organizational efficiency. To date, many major corporations, including TRW, Texas Instruments, and Union Carbide, as well as the U.S. State Department, have applied these techniques in organization development programs. NTL has provided training for over 60 years to individuals and organizations around the world.

### Results of Laboratory Learning

As already noted, some major corporations have applied laboratory learning methods as a part of management development and organization development programs. There is evidence to suggest that laboratory learning provides increased self-insight and awareness of impact upon others and that observable changes in behavior do occur on the job.[10]

Several studies have found that laboratory learning is one of the most effective OD interventions in providing employees with improvements in job satisfaction and self-development. Laboratory learning improves organizational productivity just as effectively as technical and structural interventions.[11] Organizations that use some form of laboratory learning methods are more likely to combine it with other OD interventions.

## INTERPERSONAL STYLE: THE JOHARI WINDOW MODEL

Organizations are made up of individuals, each with a unique set of values, behaviors, and motivations. An organization's climate is formed by the interaction and communication between its members. If the organization uses formal communications, lines of authority, and centralized decision making, some of the communication between members may not be authentic. People will say what they think others want to hear or expect them to say. The communication is "mask to mask," from one person's facade to another person's facade. Such communication is usually distorted, inaccurate, and ineffective.

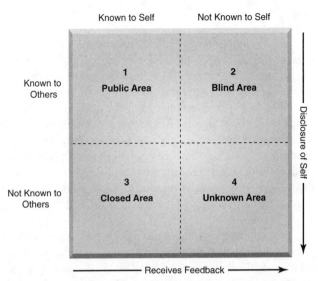

**FIGURE 9.1** The Johari Window: A Model of Interpersonal Communication Processes

Communication is a critical dimension in determining the effectiveness of organizations. The **Johari Window Model,** conceived by Joe Luft and Harry Ingram (the name Johari is formed by taking a portion of each of their first names), is a technique for identifying interpersonal communication style.[12] The model, shown in Figure 9.1, measures interpersonal style in terms of communication awareness by presenting a two-dimensional, four-celled figure based on the interaction of two sources of information: oneself and others. Each cell represents a specific area of knowledge about oneself and illustrates the quality of the interpersonal communication process.

## The Public Area

This area includes behaviors, thoughts, and feelings that are known to oneself and also known to others. This is the area of our public image and of interaction involving mutually shared perceptions (others see us as we see ourselves). One underlying assumption of the Johari Window Model is that interpersonal effectiveness is directly related to the amount of mutually shared information, or congruence. The larger this area becomes, the more effective the communication will be.

## The Blind Area

This area represents aspects of the self (behaviors, thoughts, and feelings) not known to oneself but readily apparent to others. These include mannerisms and habits that you may be unaware of but that others discover easily. The person who is red-faced and shouting "I'm not angry" and the one whose lip is twitching nervously but whose words are saying "I'm in control" are examples. Some managers act forceful and tough because they think they will look soft if they show any warmth, but others can see that in fact they do have such feelings.

## The Closed Area

This area involves behaviors, thoughts, and feelings known only to oneself and not to others. This involves a protective facade intended to protect the ego or self-image. For others to become aware of this area, you must disclose it. This area includes feelings you may perceive as possibly harmful to your self-image. For example, some people may attempt to laugh at an off-color joke even though they are repulsed by the humor.

How effective are such facades, and how effectively do people use them? When we are in a new situation or with strangers, the closed area usually represents a large part of our behavior because we and others who are present do not know much about one another and trust is low. Interestingly, people go to great lengths to conceal this part of their selves, yet it is this element that makes each of us most human. It often takes years of knowing someone before we gain insights into this area.

### The Unknown Area

Included here are behaviors and feelings that are inaccessible both to oneself and to others. According to some psychologists, unconscious, deeply repressed feelings and impulses or other hidden aspects of the personality reside here. Over time, we may become aware of some of these aspects of ourselves, but for the present purposes this area is of less importance.

As indicated in Figure 9.1, movement along the vertical and horizontal dimensions enables individuals to change their interpersonal styles by increasing the amount of communication in the public or shared area. To enlarge the public area, a person may move vertically by reducing the closed area. As a person behaves less defensively and becomes more open, trusting, and risk taking, others will tend to react with increased openness and trust. This process, termed **disclosure,** involves the open disclosure of one's feelings, thoughts, and candid feedback to others. The openness of communication leads more to open and congruent relationships.

The behavioral process used to enlarge the public area horizontally, termed **feedback,** allows us to reduce the blind area. The only way to become aware of our blind spots is for others to give information or feedback about our behavior. The blind area can be reduced only with the help and cooperation of others, and this requires a willingness to invite and accept such feedback. Almost every organization finds that poor communication is the most important problem preventing organizational effectiveness.

The Johari Window Model is a technique for examining and improving the interpersonal communication process. The ideas of the Johari Window can be used with laboratory learning to help participants understand their effect on others (disclosure) and how their behavior comes across to others (feedback).

## TRANSACTIONAL ANALYSIS

**Transactional analysis** (TA) is a practical and useful interpersonal relationship model that some OD practitioners apply in organization change programs.[13] TA, originally developed by Eric Berne, is a way for people to understand how they communicate with others and how they can improve on their communications. Although some psychologists use TA, members of organizations have adapted the ideas to improve their communication and interpersonal relationship skills. TA provides a model for analyzing and understanding human behavior using terminology familiar to many people.

### Structural Analysis

In examining interpersonal communication, we can employ structural analysis or personality analysis to understand how we get to be who we are. According to **structural analysis,** every person has three separate sources of behavior called **ego states.** The ego states are represented by circles, as illustrated in Figure 9.2. The circles may be drawn with different sizes to reflect the dominance of one ego state over another.

- *The Parent.* This ego state is a set of feelings, attitudes, and behaviors copied from a parental figure. Behavior may include prejudicial, critical, consoling, or nurturing actions.
- *The Adult.* This ego state is an independent set of feelings, attitudes, and behaviors involving the basis of objective facts. An individual who gathers facts, tests reality, and computes a rational, objective answer is in an adult ego state.
- *The Child.* This ego state is a collection of feelings, attitudes, and behaviors retained from the individual's childhood. The child ego state usually shows emotions of some kind, such as anger, excitement, sadness, and fear.

All three ego states exist within everyone, and they are not related to a person's age. A certain amount of each ego state is necessary for a well-integrated personality. When people are in an organization setting, all three ego states will be engaged and can be appropriate depending on the situation. As an example, if a sales department has just landed a major contract, it will likely be excited and celebrating its accomplishment. This child ego state is a natural and an appropriate behavior. But when two sales people are arguing over who made the biggest contribution in getting the contract, this would be an inappropriate and dysfunctional child ego state.

**FIGURE 9.2**   Ego States

The best way to examine ego states is to look at oneself and others for behavioral clues, such as words, gestures, and tone of voice. Structural analysis can enable people to better understand the source of their values, behaviors, and thoughts. This increased awareness of one's personal style can help in improving one's effectiveness in an organization.

Structural analysis can also be used by members of an organization to better understand and change their organization. The culture of an organization may emphasize or operate predominantly out of one of the three ego states. The size of the circles for the three ego states may reflect the degree that an ego state is used. An organization that relies on power strategies and manipulation to solve problems would have a larger parent ego state than adult and child ego states. In contrast, an organization that uses problem solving and consensual decision making to solve problems would have a larger adult ego state than parent and child ego states. See Figure 9.3 for an example.

## Transactional Theory

The three ego states are present in every individual and directly affect the type of transactions the person will have with others. Every interaction between people involves a **transaction** between their ego states. When one person converses with a second person, the first person is in a distinct ego state and can direct the message to any of the three ego states in the second individual. A

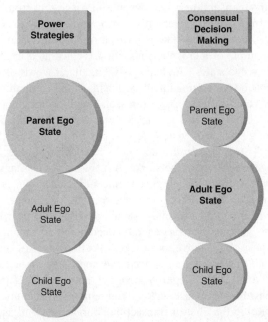

**FIGURE 9.3**   Ego States of an Organization

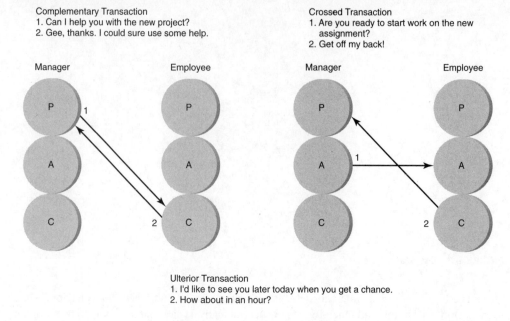

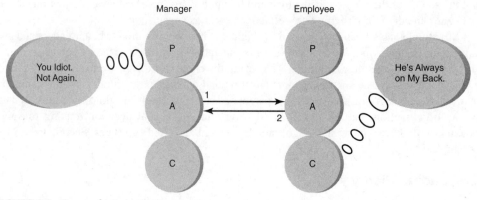

**FIGURE 9.4** Types of Interactions

transaction is the basic unit of communication. Transactions are classified as (1) complementary or open, (2) crossed or blocked, and (3) ulterior or hidden. This is illustrated in Figure 9.4.

A **complementary transaction** occurs when a message sent from one ego state receives an expected response from the other person's appropriate ego state. A **crossed transaction** occurs when a message from one ego state receives a response from an inappropriate or unexpected ego state. An example of a crossed transaction is illustrated in Figure 9.5. An **ulterior transaction** involves two ego states simultaneously: the literal words of the transaction, which may mean one thing, and the underlying intent, which may mean something entirely different. In many cases, the tone of voice, inflections, gestures, and the like determine the ego state.

**Stroking** is an important concept in transactional theory. A stroke is any form of recognition, including physical, verbal, or visual, of one person by another. Strokes are given for "doing" and for "being." Strokes given for doing are conditional strokes: They are tied to some type of performance by the receiver of the stroke. A manager ties a "thank you" to the desirable behavior by an employee. A stroke for being, or an unconditional stroke, is given to a person with no strings attached: It is given simply for being who they are. A manager who gives only conditional strokes may be regarded as artificial—saying something only when something else is wanted in return. People in organizations generally need both performance and "being" strokes.

Strokes may be positive, negative, or crooked. **Positive strokes** (in TA language, "warm fuzzies") are transactions that provide an expected response and reassure a person's worth, esteem, or competency: "You're OK!" **Negative strokes** ("cold prickles") are the reverse, resulting in an unexpected, unreassuring response with a "You're not OK" feeling. A **crooked stroke** has a double meaning similar to the ulterior transaction. It transmits a message different from the words a person uses.

**FIGURE 9.5    A Message Is Not Always What It Seems**
*Source:* B.C. by permission of Johnny Hart and Creators Syndicate, Inc

The stroking patterns of organizations tend to be closely related to the organizational culture. Effective managers are usually managers who know how to use conditional, unconditional, and positive strokes appropriately.

## Psychological Positions and Scripts

People make decisions about their own worth and the worth of others based on previous experiences. These feelings lead to **psychological positions** toward oneself and others. A psychological position is a person's general outlook on life and how he or she relates to others. The psychological positions are:

- *I'm OK, you're OK.* This position suggests an acceptance of self and others, a healthy outlook.
- *I'm OK, you're not OK.* This position suggests a tendency to mistreat, blame, and put down others.
- *I'm not OK, you're OK.* This position suggests feelings of low self-esteem or of lack of power or inadequacy compared to others.
- *I'm not OK, you're not OK.* This position suggests feelings of low self-esteem or of hopelessness and loss of interest in living, with feelings of confusion and depression.

A person's life can be compared to the script in a play, with the person being both the author and the central actor. The script is the ongoing life plan an individual has decided to follow. Organizations and units of an organization also live out scripts. The accounting department's personnel may be expected to be analytical, cold, and unfeeling in their relationships by other departments. The advertising department, on the other hand, may be perceived by others to be relaxed and dress unconventionally with always a light-hearted joke or comment to offer.

### Authentic Communication and Relationships

Transactional analysis emphasizes open, authentic communications and relationships. Muriel James and Dorothy Jongeward apply the term *winner* to "one who responds authentically by being credible, trustworthy, responsive, and genuine both as an individual and as a member of society" and the term *loser* to "one who fails to respond authentically."[14] A loser is living in the past or future, intellectualizing and rationalizing. His or her potential remains dormant. When organization members are not acting authentically, they begin to make mistakes, shift the blame, and complain about the inadequacies of other individuals or groups. TA provides a framework for carrying out change by examining how people relate, communicate, and work. Proponents of TA feel that adult-to-adult transactions make for a more effective organization and help develop employee involvement and empowerment.

A word of caution is in order. People who know very little about TA often play the "TA game": analyzing others or using the jargon on them. TA is most wisely applied to oneself before it is applied to others. If a person feels that TA can help solve a problem, it is probably better for that person to think in terms of his or her feelings and reactions, such as "I'm responding like a parent in this situation" or "I feel like a child when you treat me that way." Too often people use TA in a one-upmanship game with such statements as "Aha! That's your child showing now" or "Your parent is talking now."

Despite such problems, the TA concepts are sometimes presented in employee sessions. For some people, TA can be a useful framework for understanding and relating to others on and off the job.

## CAREER LIFE PLANNING INTERVENTIONS

OD is aimed at changing the organization's climate in order to further the integration of organizational and individual goals. The career development aspirations of the individual members are important elements. OD programs help members understand what they are good at and what their work goals are. Managerial career development is an ongoing process of change in activities, positions, and values. People often feel caught in an organizational trap because their personal goals and sense of meaning become lost. Many of these individual career problems are symptoms of larger organization problems, such as downsizing, plants closings, restructuring, a rigid bureaucratic structure, or intergroup conflict. Since workers generally expect to move from one employer to another during their career, they have become loyal to their own careers instead of the organization for which they work.

Career development in the 2000s has become an even more complicated issue. Economic conditions in industries including airlines, financial, automotive, and beer brewers have brought about mergers with the expressed purpose of combining the management ranks. As well, many companies are reducing the number of management levels and turning over more managerial responsibilities to rank-and-file employees. Simultaneously, baby boomers are crowding the ranks of management. At consumer-products giant Unilever, where a significant number of jobs have been cut, Head of Human Resources Sandy Ogg remarked, "People sitting at one level were dreaming of a job at the next level, and all of a sudden the pool has shrunk by half. The challenge is to keep them motivated when they're saying, 'Where have all the jobs gone?'"[15]

In an earlier chapter, socialization was described as the entry of the individual into a new organization. The initial entry or socialization process is an important phase leading to eventual career development and personal goals. During the course of the socialization process, individual and organization expectations are exchanged. As individuals develop within the organization, their career paths reach crisis points where they face a choice between jobs, between professions, or between organizations. At these points, the individual needs to apply some form of career life planning to decide how best to achieve his or her career goals.

**Career life planning** is the process of choosing occupational, organizational, and career paths. The purpose of career planning is to develop and promote high-potential employees in channels where their abilities will be used to the fullest. There are several different approaches to career life planning. All of them use the idea of goal setting and achievement motivation to gain greater control over one's future career development.[16]

### Steps in a Typical Career Life Planning Program

Career life planning involves (1) determining where you are now, (2) deciding where you want to be, and (3) developing a plan for getting where you want to be. The basic intervention involves a sequence of steps. Workshop participants usually work in practitioner pairs, each helping the other in the following steps:

**Step 1**   Each participant independently prepares a list of career life goals; this would usually include career, professional, personal, and relational goals (List 1).

**Step 2**   Working in a pair with the participant, the practitioner goes through the list, reality testing (are the goals realistic?), helping set priorities, and looking for conflicting goals.

**Step 3**   Each participant makes a list of important achievements or happenings, including peak experiences and satisfactions (List 2).

**Step 4**   The practitioner works through a comparison of the individual's goals (List 1) and achievements (List 2), looking for conflict or incongruence between the two lists. For example, one's goal might be to become an accountant or a research scientist, jobs that involve indoor activities, whereas the list of past satisfactions may show an emphasis upon outdoor activities. The practitioner points out the incongruence. Working with the practitioner, each participant prepares a new list of prioritized goals (List 3).

**Step 5**   The participants prepare detailed plans of action specifying how to get from where they are to where the goals show they would like to be.

Career planning can provide employees with information that will enable them to make better career decisions. Although people should continually reassess their life goals and their progress toward them, individuals usually undertake career life planning at some crisis point, as when an alternative career pattern presents itself. Career goals need to be determined often because an individual's objectives and opportunities change over time.

### The Results of Career Life Planning

There is little evidence to show the outcome of career life planning interventions. One research study found that individuals who were committed to both their organizations and their careers reported higher job satisfaction and career satisfaction. They felt more empowered than other employees did.[17] When labor markets become tighter, especially for professional employees, organizations start to do more to keep workers. And even in recessionary times, organizations try to maintain their more talented employees as the organization wants to be poised to quickly move forward when the economy begins to improve.

## STRESS MANAGEMENT AND BURNOUT

Stress seems to be everywhere: in personal lives and on the job. In a worker survey conducted by the National Institute for Occupational Safety and Health (NIOSH), more than 29 percent of American workers now describe their jobs as "extremely stressful" day in and day out.[18] These statistics were closely duplicated in a survey by the Families and Work Institute. It showed that 25 percent of all U.S. employees have "felt like screaming and shouting at times on the job," and 14 percent "felt like striking a coworker" because of work-related stress.

According to data from the Labor Department, U.S. workers average 1,942 hours on the job each year. This is an increase of 36 hours, nearly an entire workweek, since 1990. Americans are now working more hours than workers in any other industrialized nation.[19] The expressions "going postal" and "don't go postal on us" originated from violent acts on the job by postal workers. Often, workplace violence can be traced to stressed-out workers lashing out at their boss and fellow workers.

Job stress costs U.S. industry in absenteeism, diminished productivity, employee turnover, medical costs, and legal and insurance fees. Health problems associated with stress cost companies about $200 billion a year based on an estimate from NIOSH. The costs showed up in increased absenteeism, tardiness, decreased productivity, and loss of talented workers. The study estimated that between 70 and 90 percent of employee hospital visits were linked to stress, and health care costs were nearly 50 percent greater for workers reporting high levels of stress in comparison to "low risk" workers.[20] NIOSH also reported that workers with anxiety, stress, and neurotic disorders experienced "a much greater work loss than those with all nonfatal injuries or illnesses—25 days away from work compared with 6 . . ."[21] Approximately 40 percent of worker turnover is due to job stress.[22] Primary care physicians report that 75 to 90 percent of patient visits are for stress-related complaints. Stress has been linked to the leading causes of death, including heart disease, cancer, lung ailments, accidents, and suicide—and 43 percent of all adults suffer adverse health effects due to stress. In the United States, 1.5 million people have heart attacks every year, and more than 550,000 of them die. In addition, high blood pressure afflicts 58 million people.[23]

**Stress** is an interaction between an individual and the environment characterized by emotional strain affecting a person's physical and mental condition.[24] Stress refers to a reaction to a situation and not to the situation itself. Stress may also be defined as a pattern of emotional and physiological reactions in response to demands from internal or external sources. For example, having to work late one evening is not stress; stress is how a person reacts to working late. Working late, however, can be a stressor. **Stressors** are what cause stress. Stressors are events external to an individual that create a state of disequilibrium within the individual. The responses of an individual to stress may be positive, as when it causes someone to be challenged in the performance of simple tasks, or they may be negative, as when someone worries so much about doing a good job that he or she fails in the task or, worse yet, a heart attack results. In summary, stress requires two simultaneous events: an external event (stressor) and an emotional or physical reaction (normally regarded as a negative reaction) to the stressor, such as fear, anxiety, fast breathing, muscle tension, increased heart rate, and so on.[25]

## Major Sources of Stress

Stress can be traced to on-the-job activities and to events occurring away from work. But because people cannot completely separate their work and personal lives, the way people react and handle stress at work is a complex issue. Scientists long knew that stressful events could raise blood pressure temporarily, but until recently the long-term effects on heart disease were not certain. A study published in the *Journal of the American Medical Association* concludes that "job strain may be a risk factor for both hypertension and structural changes of the heart in working men."[26] The study is the first one that relates job characteristics to both hypertension and structural changes in the heart. According to the report, the jobs causing the most problems were not those with a great deal of pressure to work hard and fast, such as the high-powered executive jobs often associated with heart attacks in the popular press. Instead, the jobs causing increases in blood pressure were lower-level jobs. These were jobs where intense psychological demands were coupled with little control over the workplace and little use of skills.[27]

Today's organizational life, regardless of work that is at lower levels or at top management, can contribute in a variety of ways to the stress an individual experiences, from downsizing to worksite violence. The factors engendering stressful work activities include:

> *Technological change.*   Engineers and managers often plan advances in technology, such as introducing a new computerized system, without seeking input and involvement from the people affected by the change.

> *Downsizing.*   Layoffs, mergers, and downsizing cause incalculable levels of stress in workers who fear losing their jobs and have difficulty handling expanded job responsibilities and heavier workloads. Even employees not involved in current layoffs may fear future cuts.

> *Sudden reorganizations and unexpected changes in work schedules.*   Changes in the structure of the organization result in new work groups and changes in the way individuals work with one another. The new structures may split up workers who have formed friendships.

*Competition.*    The limited number of positions available for promotions sometimes causes people to compete excessively for the positions. As organizations restructure and remove layers of management, especially middle management, there are fewer positions available for career advancement.

*Lack of participation in decision making.*    Managers have traditionally not involved subordinates in decision making. Consequently, employees typically feel that they have little control of the work environment in their lives.

*Empowerment.*    The empowerment of employees offers advantages to the organization and its employees. Some employees appreciate the greater responsibility and decision-making authority and empowerment. But employees who have no interest in empowerment and responsibility may experience greater levels of stress. Some people find group work stressful, and their work may suffer when they work in a team setting.

*Conflicts with other people.*    Organizations, by their very nature, require people to work with one another. The current trend is for employees to be assigned to work teams where they are more dependent on one another. The interaction with more people provides more opportunities for conflicts between fellow employees. Some people like to work in teams, but there are others who find the interaction and inevitable conflicts to be stressful.

*Immediate supervisor.*    Leadership, and especially the leadership, of an employee's immediate supervisor, has a pervasive influence on organization life. A study by Hogan, Gordon, and Hogan asserted that "the reactions to inept leadership include turnover, insubordination, industrial sabotage, and malingering. Sixty to 75 percent of the employees in any organization—no matter what or where the survey was completed and no matter what occupational group was involved—report that the worst or most stressful aspect of their job is their immediate supervisor. Good leaders may put pressure on their people, but abusive and incompetent management creates billions of dollars of lost productivity each year."[28]

*Not enough time to do expected duties.*    Downsizing and layoffs can be stressful because they induce fear of losing a job. The work requirements of employees remaining at an organization are often increased: They are doing more work with fewer people.

*Violence in the workplace.*    Acts of violence committed by employees and customers may be both the cause and result of stress. According to the American Institute of Stress, homicide is the second leading cause of fatal occupational injury, and for working women it is the leading cause of death. Almost 2 million instances of homicide, aggravated assault, rape, or sexual assault are reported in the workplace. An average of 20 people are murdered on the job each week in the United States. Though much publicity is given to disgruntled former or current employees taking their anger out on coworkers or bosses, this accounts for only 4 to 6 percent of the homicides. Most violence occurs during a robbery or other crimes committed by customers or nonemployees.[29] Regardless of who commits the crime, the violence leads to a substantial amount of stress that can affect an employee.

*Nonwork-related events.*    The many different kinds of stressful events that occur away from work often include problems related to marriage, children, a serious illness, death of a family member or friend, finances, changes in social activities, impending retirement, life and career goals, and environmental pollution (noise, traffic, and air quality). These events may be out of the employer's control, but employees will nevertheless bring the stress in their lives to work.

## Job Burnout

**Job burnout** refers to the emotional exhaustion, depersonalization, and reduced accomplishment. Burnout is typically experienced by employees who work with people or do "people work" of some kind and by employees who have high levels of demands placed upon them. Job burnout is now recognized as a major work stress problem. Burnout is most common among professionals who must deal extensively with other people—clients, subordinates, and customers on the job. The professionals who seem most vulnerable to job burnout include managers, accountants, lawyers, nurses, police officers, and social workers. They tend to experience much stress because of job-related stressors, be perfectionists or self-motivating achievers, and seek unrealistic or unattainable goals.

Under the stress of burnout, the individual can no longer cope with the demands of the job and becomes less and less willing to try. The costs of job burnout, both to the organization member suffering from this syndrome and the organization, can be high. A significant consequence of burnout is that it can be an inhibitor of innovativeness of employees. The victims of burnout disengage from the organization, become disillusioned, and fail to contribute to their potential.[30] The programs for coping with stress that are examined in the last section of this chapter are also useful in reducing the causes and symptoms of job burnout.

## Stress Management Interventions and Coping with Stress

A **stress management intervention** is any activity or program that attempts to reduce the cause of work-related stresses or helps individuals to cope with the negative outcomes of exposure to stress. The OD program itself can be a stress management intervention in that OD tries to create an organization in which there are fewer harmful stressors. Research shows that OD interventions are successful in reducing stress.[31] Should an OD program include stress management interventions, it is crucial that the underlying causes of the stress be identified.[32] OD interventions like team building, goal setting, self-managed work teams, and job design will be discussed in future chapters.

The disadvantage of teaching individuals how to cope with stress is that it does not reduce the source of the stress. A program that helps employees cope with stress is not a substitute for an organization dealing with legitimate workplace issues that are creating stress. With this caution in mind, there are things that can help individuals buffer the long-term effect of living with stress. The methods used for stress management include wellness programs, relaxation programs, career life planning, stress management training, and job burnout seminars.[33]

## Wellness Programs

**Wellness programs** were initially limited to physical fitness, but recently wellness has come to include nutrition counseling and smoking cessation. A few companies have spent large sums of money to build gyms and elaborate training facilities to attract employees. Xerox, for example, has a $3.5 million fitness and recreation center in its Virginia training facility, and General Foods has health and fitness efforts for 50,000 employees in 30 locations. Other organizations, such as General Mills, Kimberly-Clark, the National Aeronautics and Space Administration (NASA), Canada Life/North American Life, AT&T, and Blue Cross and Blue Shield of Indiana, among others, have some of the better-known wellness programs. Smaller companies and nonprofit organizations provide lower-cost programs by using outside facilities, such as those offered at a local college, YMCA, YWCA, or recreational center.

The results of wellness programs are found on several levels; some are more quantifiable than others. A coauthor of a PricewaterhouseCoopers report on the cost benefits of wellness programs said, "Most programs we saw realized a positive return on their investment in three to five years."[34] Some employers are unsatisfied with the results of wellness programs offered by insurers. The PricewaterhouseCoopers survey of 350 employees shows that only half of employers are satisfied with the wellness programs. Employers said that just 15 percent of their workers participate. But the report found that 80 percent of the large employers (an average of 8,000 employees) surveyed said wellness programs are important to them compared to 20 percent for small employers (fewer than 250 employees).[35] General Mills has comprehensive wellness programs dating back over 20 years. The company's programs have resulted in medical claims that "track below national trends and other major employers" and show "dramatic" reductions in heart disease, said Dr. Timothy Crimmins, vice president of health, safety, and environment at General Mills. He said that results "are hard to attribute to a single program—it's all about the overall culture of wellness, starting with our CEO. We found out that what really matters is senior leadership modeling."[36] One of the difficulties in measuring the effectiveness of stress management interventions is that companies are continually changing the programs making it difficult to conduct longitudinal studies.

Evidence to date shows a strong positive relationship between fit employees and increased productivity, higher morale, reduced absenteeism, less turnover, fewer worksite accidents, and reduced health care costs to the employer.[37] A Harris Interactive poll conducted for the *Wall*

*Street Journal* shows that while 25 percent of those employed believed that their employers offered a wellness program of some kind, only 9 percent actually participated in programs addressing exercise (5 percent), weight loss (2 percent), diet and nutrition (2 percent), and stopping smoking (less than 0.5 percent). Although very few respondents said they actually used such programs, nearly all (99 percent) of those who participated in wellness programs found them either helpful or somewhat helpful. The poll also revealed a wide variety of wellness programs offered by employers: alcohol or drug abuse assistance programs (17 percent), psychological and family counseling (16 percent), exercise programs (14 percent), help or counseling for those with health or medical problems (14 percent), programs to help people stop smoking (13 percent), and diet and nutritional programs (11 percent).[38]

## Relaxation Techniques

Biofeedback and meditation are commonly used relaxation techniques. A **biofeedback** course will usually take from several weeks to three or four months. The course takes place in a clinic with a trained technician and will normally begin with an analysis of the person's stress points: work, family, and so on. Instruments that can measure brain waves, heart activity, temperature, and muscle activity are connected to the person to measure physical reactions to stress. The biological feedback from the monitoring machines teaches the person how to consciously control his or her autonomic nervous system by decreasing the pulse rate and blood pressure. With practice, the person no longer needs the feedback from the monitoring devices and can practice biofeedback during a stressful work or personal activity.

**Meditation** has reported outcomes similar to biofeedback.[39] People using meditation repeat in their minds a specific sound called a "mantra" during two 20-minute sessions a day—one in the morning and another in the late afternoon. Other meditators use yoga techniques. Users of meditation often report higher energy and productivity levels, ability to get along better with others, lowered metabolic rates such as heart rate, and increased creativity. The headquarters at Acacia Life Insurance Co. has an area where workers can go to be alone and meditate for a while. It is a dimly lit room, with soothing paintings, comfortable chairs, and no telephones. Other companies, including Apple Computer, Yahoo!, McKinsey Consulting, Deutsche Bank, Hughes Aircraft, and Google, have meditation benefits for their employees. Pixar Animation Studios has a masseuse and a doctor to come to its campus once a week, and animators must obtain managers' permission to work more that 50 hours a week.[40]

Corporate users are being won over to meditation according to findings from the National Institutes of Health and the Mind/Body Institute at Harvard University. The studies done by these institutions show that users have increased brainwave activity, improved intuition, better concentration, and fewer aches and pains. "These programs sound a little out there. But they have a positive impact," says Viacom International's manager of work/life, Lisa Grossman.[41]

## Career Life Planning

Some cases of stress may need to be treated with career life planning. The sessions may be in a one-to-one or group session, as explained earlier in the chapter.

## Stress Management Training

Stress management training may include instruction in time management, goal setting, delegation, counseling of subordinates, self-awareness, relaxation techniques, conflict resolution, and identification of stress situations and symptoms. Participants in six-week stress management programs report only temporary improvement in managing their stress. When the programs incorporates refresher sessions at 5 months, 11 months, and 17 months, the improvement in managing stress lasts throughout a two and one-half year period.[42]

## Seminars on Job Burnout

Seminars to help employees understand the nature and symptoms of job problems, such as workshops on role clarity and analysis (discussed in Chapter 10) have been used in many large companies, including Burlington Industries, Campbell Soup Company, IBM, Johnson & Johnson, and Xerox. The seminars typically are provided by experts and consultants from outside the company who can also integrate all components of a wellness program.

The focus in this chapter has been on interventions at an interpersonal level. The practitioner and the client must examine many factors in deciding upon an intervention. They must decide not only on the depth of the intervention desired but also on the relative advantages and disadvantages of various possible interventions. The application of a specific intervention to a client will largely depend on the problems diagnosed. The next chapter will discuss interventions based on the development of work teams.

## Summary

- **Employce Empowerment.** Interpersonal interventions are based upon improving organizational efficiency by increasing the individual's involvement, motivation, and competence. Employee empowerment is a powerful technique for unleashing human potential in organizations.
- **Laboratory Learning.** Although research on the effectiveness of laboratory learning programs shows mixed results, there is evidence suggesting that this technique can influence managerial behavior. OD practitioners often used it successfully in change programs in the past, but it is not used as frequently today.
- **Johari Window Model.** The Johari Window provides a way of thinking about ourselves in relation to other people. It also provides two major ways of getting to know and understand others and ourselves: self-disclosure and feedback. The purpose of these two strategies is to enlarge our open areas as much as possible by reducing the blind or closed areas. To the extent that we gain clearer and more accurate perceptions of others and ourselves, we can improve our ways of communicating and working together.
- **Transaction Analysis.** Transactional analysis is a technique for changing an organization's culture by getting people to think about their relationships with others and by providing a framework for improving their managerial style. One manager may assume that people are irresponsible and approach situations like a parent—critical, judgmental, and admonishing; another may act in ways that are dependent, powerless, or rebellious, like a child. Because the nature of the people in any organization is changing, the manager or OD practitioner needs to develop new skills in relating to others. These relational skills involve transactions with others, and the way you come across to others may well influence your effectiveness.
- **Career Life Planning.** Career life planning provides activities that help individuals to reassess their life and career goals and to redirect their efforts toward new goals. Now or at some time in the future you may be at a career decision point where you will want to use this technique to examine your career or life plan.
- **Stress Management and Burnout.** Stress and burnout are increasingly having an impact upon organization members. Stress management programs set up by organizations for their members include biofeedback, meditation, career life planning, training in stress management, wellness programs, and seminars on job burnout. The purpose of most of these programs is to help individuals increase their coping skills. One objective of OD programs is to improve organization situations that cause stress.
- **Choice.** The idea of choice is an important notion regarding behavioral change. We often behave in certain ways that we find effective before we become aware of their consequences. Such behaviors are essentially habitual and not by choice. A choice is opened up as you begin receiving feedback on your blind spots and on how others react to your behavior. You can choose to continue behaving the same way and accept the consequences. Or you can choose to alter your patterns of behavior in the hope of changing the consequences to modes that are more effective. Either way, more authentic and effective behavior is possible once you recognize the choices and take responsibility for your actions.

## Review Questions

1. What are the objectives of laboratory training?
2. Identify and explain the four areas of the Johari Window Model.
3. How can you use the Johari Window Model as a tool to understand interpersonal communications?
4. What is the interrelationship between the Johari Window Model and laboratory learning?
5. Explain how transactional analysis can help you better understand your communication patterns.
6. Explain the steps in a career life planning program.
7. Identify and explain stress management interventions.

## Key Words and Concepts

Biofeedback
Career Life Planning
Complementary
 Transaction
Crooked Stroke
Crossed Transaction
Disclosure
Ego States

Empowerment
Fade Out
Feedback
Job Burnout
Johari Window Model
Laboratory Learning
Meditation
Negative Strokes

Positive Strokes
Psychological Positions
Psychosocial System
Stress
Stress Management
 Intervention
Stressors
Stroking

Structural Analysis
Transaction
Transactional Analysis
Ulterior Transaction
Wellness Programs

# OD Skills Simulation 9.1

## SACOG

*Total time suggested: 60 minutes.*

## A. Purpose

In this simulation, you will learn to recognize the dimensions of group effectiveness and observe how these factors inhibit or facilitate group functioning. You will also learn to identify how OD interventions can be used to increase individual and group effectiveness. Such factors as relationships with peers, leadership, information sharing, communications, collaboration, competition, and problem solving will be studied.

## B. Procedures

*Step 1.* Form groups of six members before class and assign roles. Extra class members can be observers or become an OD practitioner team. Read the Southern Area Council of Governments (SACOG) background information and your role. The six roles are:

1. Mental Health Director
2. Marriage and Family Counseling Director
3. Employee Training and Education Director
4. Drug Abuse Director
5. Alcohol Education and Rehabilitation Director
6. OD Practitioner(s)
7. Observer(s)—optional

*Step 2.* The administrator of SACOG has called a meeting of the five area directors. Because of an emergency meeting in Washington, D.C., the administrator will not be present and has delegated the task to the directors. The OD practitioner(s) will be present to assist. The observer, if there is one, will not take part in the discussion. Through team discussion, exploration, and examination, try to reach a *consensus decision* reflecting the integrated thinking and consensus of all the members. Enter the team decision in the SACOG Team Decision Form.

Follow these instructions for reaching a consensus:

1. Try to identify the best strategy.
2. Do not change your mind simply to reach agreement and avoid conflict, but support solutions you are able to agree with.
3. Avoid conflict-reducing techniques, such as majority vote, averaging, or trading in reaching your decision.
4. View differences of opinion as helpful rather than a hindrance in decision making.

*Time suggested for Step 2: 30 minutes.*

*Step 3.* Take a moment to complete the Individual Rating column on the Team Effectiveness Profile Form. Then hold a meeting with your team using the Team Effectiveness Profile Form and the Transactional Analysis Form to critique the performance of your team. All team members, including the OD practitioner and observer, are to critique the SACOG team meeting.

*Time suggested for Step 3: 15 minutes.*

*Step 4.* Meeting with the entire class, compare the decisions made by each team. Then each team shares the results of its Team Effectiveness Profile Form and Transactional Analysis Form.

*Time suggested for Step 4: 15 minutes.*

## SACOG Background Information

SACOG, the Southern Area Council of Governments, is a regional organization of several counties and their towns in a sparsely populated region. The area covers more than 5,000 square miles. A chief administrator, who heads five social service areas that are in turn administered by directors, manages SACOG. The areas are (1) mental health, (2) marriage and family counseling, (3) employee training and education, (4) drug abuse, and (5) alcohol education and rehabilitation. These five social agencies are organized such that they are separate from one other in terms of personnel and financing. They are administered from a central office located in the largest town in the region. The five area directors work out of this office but also have their own facilities located elsewhere in the region.

Historically, the five agencies have worked closely together because they realize that people's problems are interwoven. In other words, a person abusing alcohol or drugs is likely to have difficulty holding down a job and to have family and mental problems.

SACOG receives financing from area, state, and federal governments and from private grants. The total amount for this year is $29 million. The funding has been increasing by an annual rate of 7 percent for the past five years.

Several days ago, SACOG received an invitation to apply for a special $2.4 million, five-year grant from a private foundation. The wording of the invitation indicated that only one application can be submitted and that it will have to be very specific, which means that only one of the five agencies will be able to apply for the grant. Because of the large number of disadvantaged and minority groups in the area, and because SACOG is one of the most advanced, effective, and progressive social programs, there is a good chance of SACOG receiving the grant.

Aside from the substantial increase in funding, the director of the agency selected will have increased job responsibilities and be much busier. There will likely be a sizable pay increase of approximately 8 percent during the five years of the grant.

One condition of the grant is that an advisory council be established to oversee the expenditures. The council is to include professionals (doctors, business people, educators, and so forth) and community representatives including local politicians.

The directors must arrive at a decision on these three items:

1. The agency to be named in the grant proposal.
2. A method of selecting the advisory council: either statewide or by county.
3. The length of term for council members: either two or four years.

The SACOG administrator decided to call a meeting of the five social service directors for the purpose of deciding which one of the areas will be selected to apply for the grant. The administrator did some homework and came up with six criteria believed to be relevant in the selection:

1. Past successes and failures.
2. Number of minorities served.
3. Number of people receiving services.
4. Availability of facilities in the region.
5. Anticipated results.
6. The needs of the community.

## Role Description (Read Only Your Role)

**Mental Health Director.** As director of mental health, you are responsible for administering the outpatient facilities. The mental health agency hires trained, experienced psychologists to staff the positions. The services are entirely on an outpatient basis. In fact, the area has no mental health facilities except the outpatient services provided by SACOG, so the community definitely needs the services. Records indicate that your agency has worked with 900 people in the past year.

The agency's facilities are located in the three large towns in the region. If people needing services live in outlying places, they must travel to one of the towns. Because of the large geographical region to be covered and the salaries of the staff, it has not been practical to provide mobile services though you would like to begin to offer rural services.

The department has been as successful in its work as some of the better outpatient clinics in the country. Originally, there was some reluctance to use the facilities, but time and success seem to have changed this. Future programs will probably be just as successful. Various pilot programs have been tested in conjunction with a state university, and several have received wide attention. More extensive use of these new programs is planned.

There seem to be very few minority people seeking mental health services. This can partly be attributed to a long history of misunderstanding of the services offered. Furthermore, a study, although not conclusive, shows that there are few mental problems among the minority population. You suspect that the study was flawed since minority members have a higher than average history of drug and alcohol abuse. There is a strong indication that many of the people using the services have been referred to you as a last resort.

You are strongly in favor of professionals running the council. Therefore, you support statewide selection so that the three large cities, rather than the rural areas, can dominate the selection process. Because professionals are more likely to live in the cities, the statewide selection process will more likely put professionals on the councils. You also prefer the shorter two-year term because this will lessen the impact should nonprofessionals be selected.

Although your agency is not perfect and there is much to be done, you believe that it and the community could greatly benefit from the grant.

**Marriage and Family Counseling Director.** As director of marriage and family counseling, you are responsible for administering counseling programs in such areas as child abuse, spousal relationships, and runaway children. The statistics show good past success for those cases in which your agency has been involved. Follow-up studies are favorable. In cases of spousal counseling, the divorce rate and spousal abuse are lower than average. In most of the child abuse cases, children are kept in the natural home instead of foster homes. Runaway children who have been located and brought back home usually do not run away again, and this has been attributed to counseling with the entire family.

There are centers in the three large towns, and several mobile trailers are used to serve the rural communities. The number receiving services has been increasing, up to 3,500 cases annually, although the facilities are geared to serve more people. There seems to be a feeling among staff workers that people are hesitant to confide problems that they may have with their marriage or children. National studies have shown that there are fewer reports of child and spousal abuse in rural areas because homes are widely separated from one another. Minorities use the services, although no more or no less than their numbers in the census figures would indicate.

Based on past data, there is a fairly high rate of success once a family comes in for help, but not all families that need help come in. The police reports on child abuse show a definite need for the services. The divorce rate is still high, although there are signs that it may be dropping. You would like to start working with families before their problems reach the stage of a runaway child, spousal abuse, or divorce, but you have not been successful in identifying these families and getting them to accept help. Despite this obstacle, your past success rate and the definite need for continued services by the community makes the future look promising.

You can see no particular advantage to either the statewide or the county method of selecting the advisory council or length of term, so you give your support to anyone who will back your area for the grant.

Although your agency is not perfect, you believe that it and the community could greatly benefit from the grant.

**Employee Training and Educational Director.** As director of training and education, you are responsible for assisting the so-called unemployable and those seeking new skills required for employment. Your department does not actually train people, but it arranges training and usually assists in the financing. Although the State Employment Commission has similar services, there seem to be enough people unemployed and in need of the services that all help is welcomed. Yours and the other agencies often work together and coordinate programs.

As practically everyone for whom training has been arranged has been able to obtain employment, you feel that your agency has been successful even though there is still a fairly large unemployment rate, particularly among minorities. In the case of minorities needing the services that you have been able to reach, there has been a respectable, though not overwhelming, acceptance and use of the services. But as your facilities are in the three large towns, the large minority group living in the rural areas has received almost no assistance. Furthermore, the statistics indicate that if you could arrange training for that large minority group, it might be difficult to find employment for them unless they relocated or commuted to the larger towns. And because your potential clients have limited financial resources, relocation and commuting from the rural areas will require innovative approaches and be costly.

The other day you were looking at some statistics showing that 1,400 people had used the services of your agency within the past year. Even though this was only 19 percent of the unemployed, it does seem to be a healthy indication that those needing the services are receiving them. Considering the increasing unemployment rate and your past success in training people, the future looks promising.

You feel that professionals should run the advisory council because nonprofessionals are generally less educated and more disorganized. You secretly favor statewide selection where the three large cities will control the selection. This will probably ensure the selection of professionals. Selection on a county basis will give more control to the rural areas, which will probably select nonprofessionals. You also want four-year terms so that you will have more time to develop a relationship with the council.

Although your agency is not perfect, you believe that it and the community could greatly benefit from the grant.

**Drug Abuse Director.** As director of drug abuse, you are responsible for administering programs to reduce drug abuse. At SACOG, alcohol abuse is part of the alcohol education and rehabilitation division. These programs include educational efforts in the schools, churches, recreation centers, and other parts of the community, as well as for persons who may come in contact with a drug abuser—parents, teachers, police officers, and so on. In educational efforts alone, you estimate that your agency has talked to about 10,000 children and adults in the past year. Other programs are specifically directed to the drug abuser, and these programs include one-to-one and group counseling and a 24-hour hotline service. Records indicate that you have worked with 900 people in these specific programs; there is no information available on the hotline service.

Research conducted by a private agency indicates that the harsher drugs are readily available, particularly in the larger towns. The use of marijuana is increasing in school systems. Rural areas are experiencing increased use of methamphetamines based on law enforcement reports.

The facilities are concentrated in the three larger towns in the region. A toll-free number is available 24 hours a day. Efforts are being made to serve the smaller towns and rural communities, but it is costly and there are low returns. As a result, you have decided to concentrate your efforts in the three large towns with well-equipped facilities. This strategy has caused some problems with serving minorities, as there is a large minority population living in the rural areas.

Despite some problems in gaining acceptance from the larger segments of the community, your agency is making substantial progress. Although drug abuse is increasing, studies indicate that the situation could have been much worse if your agency had not been active. Follow-up studies on people who have been counseled by your area indicate a favorable success rate. Considering the increasing availability of drugs and your agency's past success, the future looks promising for continued help to the community.

You feel that minority involvement is desperately needed on the council. You support county-based selection, which will give greater control to the rural communities where minorities are more likely to live. You also want a longer four-year term, to give the council more time to carry out their plans.

Although your agency is not perfect, you believe that it and the community could greatly benefit from the grant.

**Alcohol Education and Rehabilitation Director.** As director of alcohol rehabilitation, you are responsible for administering and coordinating many different programs. These include educational efforts directed at schoolchildren and other potential users as well as people who may interface with potential abusers, such as teachers, employers, and ministers. You estimate that your agency has talked to about 10,000 people in the past year. Another phase of the programs includes working directly with alcoholics on an individual and a group basis, and records show that about 1,100 people have used these services in the past year.

A recent independent study shows that alcoholism exists in all segments of the community and involves a variety of ages, occupations, economic levels, and ethnic backgrounds. Efforts to educate the community about the dangers of alcoholism have led to greater willingness to recognize the problem and more motivation to solve it.

The agency's programs have been highly successful. Experimental rehabilitation techniques have been tried, and several have been successful and have received wide publicity. The more traditional programs have also been used extensively. Even though you have a well-trained staff, you rely largely on volunteer workers who are often recovering alcoholics.

The services are offered throughout the area. As much as possible you rely on facilities furnished by churches, individuals, and communities. The use of volunteer workers and available facilities has provided service to the isolated rural communities where a large minority population lives. The number of minority members taking advantage of the facilities has been increasing, perhaps because minority members are now employed as part of the staff and as volunteers. Minorities are more likely to live in the rural areas, and your programs have made a strong attempt to set up programs outside the cities.

You favor a greater role for minorities, so you want the county basis for selection where minorities primarily live. Statewide selection gives more control to the three large cities, where there are fewer minorities. You also favor the shorter two-year term to get more people involved rather than the longer four-year term. You will compromise on the selection of the council in order not to alienate possible grant support for your agency.

Although your agency is not perfect, you believe that it and the community could greatly benefit from the grant.

**OD Practitioner.** You hope to accomplish several things at this meeting:

1. To develop a practitioner-client relationship with all the committee members. Try to use the concepts of the Johari Window and TA in working with the members.
2. To assist the committee by doing process interventions during the meeting.
3. To help the committee members work more effectively as a team but avoid getting involved in solving the problem for them.

**Observer Guidelines.** You are not to take part in the SACOG meeting. You are there as an observer so you can provide them information later in Steps 3 and 4. You are also to read the role description of the OD practitioner so that you may provide more useful feedback. Use the Team Effectiveness Profile Form and the Transactional Analysis Form to record your observations.

**SACOG TEAM DECISION FORM**

*Rationale or Reason*

1. Agency to be named

   Mental Health    _____

   _____

   Marriage/Family    _____

   _____

   Employee Training    _____

   _____

   Drug Abuse    _____

   _____

   Alcohol Education    _____

   _____

2. Method of selecting    _____

   _____

   Statewide    _____

   _____

   Country    _____

   _____

3. Length of term    _____

   _____

   2 years    _____

   _____

   4 years    _____

   _____

## TEAM EFFECTIVENESS PROFILE FORM

Based on the following scale, rate your team on how it performed. Record your choice in the blank.

[Never   1   :   2   :       3   :       4   :   5   :   6   :       7   Always]

| Factor | Individual Rating | Team Rating |
|--------|-------------------|-------------|
| 1. Cooperative teamwork | _____ | _____ |
| 2. Member satisfaction | _____ | _____ |
| 3. Team motivation | _____ | _____ |
| 4. Information sharing | _____ | _____ |
| 5. Consensual decision making | _____ | _____ |
| 6. Conflict directly faced and resolved | _____ | _____ |
| 7. Participative leadership | _____ | _____ |
| 8. Clearly defined goals | _____ | _____ |
| 9. Trust | _____ | _____ |
| 10. Encouraged openness | _____ | _____ |

## TRANSACTIONAL ANALYSIS FORM

Part 1

What ego state was reflected by each director and the OD practitioner? Try to give specific examples.

| | Parent | Adult | Child |
|--------|--------|-------|-------|
| Mental Health | _____ | _____ | _____ |
| Marriage and Family | _____ | _____ | _____ |
| Job Training | _____ | _____ | _____ |
| Drug Abuse | _____ | _____ | _____ |
| Alcohol Rehabilitation | _____ | _____ | _____ |
| OD Practitioner | _____ | _____ | _____ |

Part 2

What kinds of transactions were used? Complementary? Crossed? Ulterior?

| Kind of Transaction | Examples |
|---------------------|----------|
| _____ | _____ |
| _____ | _____ |
| _____ | _____ |
| _____ | _____ |
| _____ | _____ |
| _____ | _____ |
| _____ | _____ |

Part 3

Ego state diagrams can be used to explain an organization's behavior. As well, the organization can have different-sized circles to indicate the prevalence of parent, adult, and child behavior. Think of the SACOG meeting in general terms instead of specific incidents. Do one or two ego states tend to be dominating? In the space below, draw an ego state diagram of different-sized circles for the team meeting.

# OD Skills Simulation 9.2

## Johari Window

*Total time suggested: 50 minutes.*

### A. Purpose

This simulation is intended to provide you with information to compare your perceptions of your own Johari Window with the perceptions of others. The survey can be a method to initiate further thought and self-exploration about your communications and interpersonal relations.

### B. Procedures

*Step 1.* After completing SACOG (another team activity, such as a case or simulation, can be substituted for SACOG), rate your team members and yourself by following the instructions in the Johari Window Survey. Additional surveys can be conducted with other team projects. Complete the Johari Window Survey, Table 9.1, and Table 9.2.

*Time suggested for Step 1: 25 minutes.*

*Step 2.* As a team and then with the class, discuss the following:

1. Are the results for feedback and disclosure similar for the way I see myself in Table 9.1 and the way others see me in Table 9.2? If they are different, to what could this be attributed?
2. Do my scores seem reasonable?
3. Am I as public, blind, closed, and unknown in my interpersonal styles as I thought I was?
4. If I am not satisfied with my style, what can I do to change? Anything specific?

*Time suggested for Step 2: 25 minutes.*

### Johari Window Survey Rating Scale and Instructions

The six-point value scale that you are to use in rating your team members on the 10 behavioral characteristics is shown below. First familiarize yourself with the criteria for the six-point value scale and then with the 10 behavioral characteristics.

| Value Scale | Meaning |
|---|---|
| 5 | Does this consistently. |
| 4 | Does this most of the time. |
| 3 | Does this frequently. |
| 2 | Does this occasionally. |
| 1 | Does this on rare occasions only. |
| 0 | Never does this. |

### Behavioral Characteristics

1. Openly tries to influence others and control the team activities. Is not manipulative in team action.
2. Interacts with the team in an open, candid manner. Is not closed and cautious in relations with others.
3. Listens to others, respects and accepts their comments. Does not dismiss or turn a deaf ear on comments by others.
4. Says what he or she is thinking no matter how ridiculous it may be. Does not control remarks to keep them in line with ideas held by others to make them more acceptable.
5. Will press for additional information if he or she feels that others are not leveling and being honest. Does not let the matter drop, change the subject, or allow the subject to be changed.
6. Makes sure that everyone on the team agrees and is committed to the team decisions by specifically testing or questioning them. Does not assume that members agree just because they do not openly voice disagreement.
7. Takes risks in the team by exposing, when pertinent, highly personal information that may be both intellectual and emotional. Does not play it safe as if others were not trustworthy.
8. When others offer help, no matter how critical their comments may be, welcomes and appreciates their efforts to help. Does not act hurt, angered, defensive, or rejecting of their efforts.
9. Does things that allow others to participate, works to draw everyone into the team discussion, and is supportive of others. Does not just look out for self and leave participation up to each individual.
10. If angered or upset by others, will openly confront them. Does not pretend to be unaffected or overcontrolled.

**RATING SHEET**

*Instructions:* Write the names of your team members along the top of the columns on the Rating Sheet. Note that the last column is for you. Read over the behavioral characteristics and determine how much each applies to the person you are rating.

Select a value from 0 to 5 that reflects the degree to which this behavior is characteristic of the person. If an item is not applicable, leave it blank. Keep in mind that a score of "0—Never does this" is not the same thing as "not applicable." Enter the value in the column for the person and the row for the behavioral characteristic.

You may rate one person at a time on each of the 10 behavioral characteristics, or rate every person on each behavior characteristic as you go. Feel free to use any value from the value scale as often or for as many members as is appropriate.

When you have completed your evaluations, cut the sheet into separate vertical strips showing the ratings for the various team members and distribute them to the members. You, in turn, will receive a rating strip from every member of the team.

| Behavioral Characteristics | Team Members | | | | | | | | Self |
|---|---|---|---|---|---|---|---|---|---|
| 1 | | | | | | | | | |
| 2 | | | | | | | | | |
| 3 | | | | | | | | | |
| 4 | | | | | | | | | |
| 5 | | | | | | | | | |
| 6 | | | | | | | | | |
| 7 | | | | | | | | | |
| 8 | | | | | | | | | |
| 9 | | | | | | | | | |
| 10 | | | | | | | | | |

## Instructions for Table 9.1: Self-Observations

1. You have two types of feedback strips: you evaluating yourself and other people evaluating you. Divide the strips into these categories (note that the word "self" identifies your self-evaluation).
2. Record in Table 9.1 the data from the feedback strip labeled "self." Move the value score to the rectangle in Column 2 (Feedback) or Column 3 (Disclosure) depending on which rectangle is not shaded.
3. Total Columns 2 and 3.
4. Record the Column 2 Feedback part of the score on the chart by drawing a vertical line at the score. This is the degree to which you actively solicit information about yourself. Record the Column 3 Disclosure part of the score by drawing a horizontal line at the score. This is the degree to which you are open and candid about your feelings and the degree to which you share information. See the example of a completed chart in Table 9.1.

**TABLE 9.1** Self-Observations

## Instructions for Table 9.2: Feedback From Others

**1.** Add all your points from the other strips for each of the 10 behavioral characteristics. Record the totals in Column 1 (Total). See the example below.

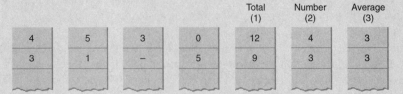

**2.** Determine the number of times you were evaluated on each behavioral characteristic and place this number in Column 2 (Number). If a behavioral characteristic was left blank, do not count the blank as one of the number of times evaluated.

**3.** Determine the average for each behavioral characteristic and record this in Column 3 (Average). See the example above for how to average a 0 and a blank.

**4.** Move the averages to the rectangle in Column 4 (Feedback) or Column 5 (Disclosure), depending on which rectangle is not shaded.

**5.** Total Columns 4 and 5.

**6.** The total in Column 4 represents your Feedback score. Record the score on the Feedback part of the chart by drawing a vertical line at the score. Record the Column 5 Disclosure part of the score by drawing a horizontal line at the score on the chart.

**7.** Compare the scores for how you think about yourself from the chart in Table 9.1 with the scores for how others perceive you from the chart in Table 9.2.

## TABLE 9.2  Feedback from Others

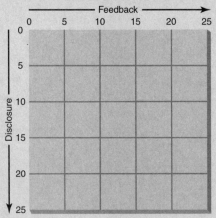

| | OTHERS' RATINGS OF ME | | | | |
|---|---|---|---|---|---|
| Behavior Characteristic | Total from "Other" Feedback Lists (1) | Number of Times Evaluated on Each Characteristic (2) | Average for Each Characteristic $\frac{\text{Col. (1)}}{\text{Col. (2)}} =$ (3) | Move Averages in Col. (3) to Col. (4) or (5) as indicated | |
| | | | | Feedback (4) | Disclosure (5) |
| 1 | | | | | |
| 2 | | | | | |
| 3 | | | | | |
| 4 | | | | | |
| 5 | | | | | |
| 6 | | | | | |
| 7 | | | | | |
| 8 | | | | | |
| 9 | | | | | |
| 10 | | | | | |
| | | | Total → | | |

## OD Skills Simulation 9.3

### Career Life Planning

*Total time suggested: 60 minutes.*

### A. Purpose

This simulation will give you experience in preparing career and life plans and in acting as a helper for someone else formulating career life plans.

### A. Procedures

*Refer to the Career Life Planning Form and complete Steps 1 and 2 before coming to class.*

 *Step 1.* Individually prepare a set of career life goals. The list can include school, career, professional, personal, and relationship goals (List 1).

 *Step 2.* Individually list important accomplishments or happenings, including peak experiences, things that have made you feel happy or satisfied, and times when you felt most alive or real (List 2).

 *Step 3.* Divide into teams of two: participant and practitioner. An extra class member may join as the third member of a team. During the simulation, you will play each role. The practitioner goes through the participant's list of career life goals testing for realistic goals, helping to set priorities, and looking for conflicting goals. Revise List 1 as necessary and mark the priority of each goal. When one person has finished, trade positions.

 *Time suggested for Step 3: 25 minutes.*

 *Step 4.* The outcome of Step 3 is a set of goals with relative priorities. Working individually, prepare a detailed plan of action specifying how to get from where you are to where the goals suggest you would like to be (List 3).

 *Time suggested for Step 4: 15 minutes.*

 *Step 5.* First in teams and then as a class, critique the usefulness of a career life planning session. Additional questions include:

 1. What things did the practitioners say or do that were helpful?
 2. What things did the practitioners think they did that were helpful?
 3. What things did the practitioners do that were not helpful?
 4. What things would the practitioners not do again?

 *Time suggested for Step 5: 20 minutes.*

**CAREER LIFE PLANNING FORM**

**Career Life Planning Form**

List 1: Career Life Goals

_____
_____
_____
_____
_____
_____
_____
_____
_____
_____

List 2: Important Accomplishments

_____
_____
_____
_____
_____
_____
_____
_____
_____

List 3: Actions Plans

_____
_____
_____
_____
_____
_____
_____
_____
_____
_____

# CASE: THE SUNDALE CLUB[43]

## Background

The Sundale Club is the largest athletic/social club in the city. It has been established for many years and has a prestigious reputation. Currently, the membership is slightly under 1,000. Sundale once had a waiting list for those wishing to join, but in the past few months the list has been exhausted and the director, Bob Watts, is considering a membership drive to fill unexpected membership vacancies.

Alice Smith was thinking about her modeling job on her way home that evening. Today had been dandy. Ted Ellis, the athletic director, had fired Pat Franklin, who had worked for Sundale for nearly nine years (see Figure 9.6).

## The Problem

The whole mess started five months ago when Ellis hired Chuck Johnson to become the men's activity manager. Shortly after Johnson arrived, rumors started that he was a homosexual. Two of the members complained to Frank Havens, the assistant athletic director, that Johnson had made verbal passes at them.

Ted Ellis and Johnson were close friends, so Havens was reluctant to approach his boss with this problem. During the next few weeks more incidents involving Johnson's behavior were reported by various staff members to Havens, in addition to complaints from club members.

Havens could sense that his staff was wondering why he had not done something about the situation, and he was aware that seven of the male members had withdrawn from the club. Finally, he requested a meeting with Ted Ellis.

## The Meeting

The meeting with Ellis did not go well. Ted Ellis was extremely defensive about Johnson and shouted, "Chuck Johnson has more savvy about this business in his little finger than the whole bunch of you put together."

That night, Frank decided to go over Ellis's head and talk to Bob Watts. Watts was due to retire next year, so he did not want to rock the boat in the final days of his tenure with Sundale. Watts tried to convince Frank that it was just a silly rumor.

Frank's working relationship with Ellis was very strained, and he continued to receive pressure from below. That week Frank quit the organization and went to work in the same capacity for the competition. The next day, Johnson, who had been working for Sundale five months now, was promoted and became the new assistant athletic director.

## The Incident

Pat Franklin was bent! The entire athletic department, with the exception of Ellis, was shocked. Pat had been very dedicated to her job and the organization. There had never been any doubt that she would get Frank Haven's job when he moved up.

**STAFF DIRECTORY**

Director—Bob Watts
Social Director—Carol Happ
Athletic Director—Ted Ellis
Asst. Athletic Director—Frank Havens
Women's Activities Manager—Pat Franklin
Mixed Activities Manager—Jim Mercer
Men's Activities Manager—Chuck Johnson
Women's Fitness Coordinator—Alice Smith

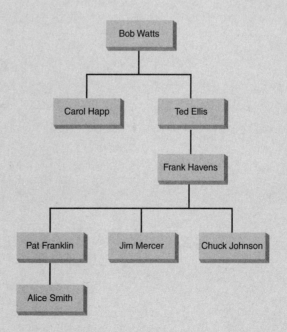

**FIGURE 9.6   Staff Directory**

Pat Franklin burst into Ellis's office and demanded to know why she had not gotten the promotion. The next few minutes were rather ugly. Pat left Ellis's office, went to her own office, and began to cry. A knock at the door stopped the flow of tears, but when she entered the office, Alice Smith could tell immediately that something was wrong. Pat explained that she had just been fired, which started the tears again. Alice was soon crying with Pat.

On her way home, although very concerned about Pat, Alice was also concerned about her own future, and her part-time job as a model. Pat had allowed her to miss up to eight hours a week from the Sundale Club to pursue her modeling duties. Although Alice did not really need the modeling money, the job itself was very important to her from a personal satisfaction standpoint; she had to keep trim and well groomed, which kept her thinking young. And besides, the glamour aspect of the modeling profession satisfied her ego.

Carol Happ, the social director, was also starting to feel the effects of the turmoil in the athletic department. Most of the Sundale Club's income was derived from its social activities. Jim Mercer, the mixer activity manager, had noticed the impact of the turmoil within his own department.

Carol, acting on her own behalf, spoke privately to all the athletic department managers with the exception of Ted Ellis and Chuck Johnson. She had hoped to arrange a meeting with Bob Watts but found little support from that department because of their fear of Ted Ellis. (Use the Case Analysis Form on the following page.)

## THE SUNDALE CLUB CASE ANALYSIS FORM

Name: _____

I. Problems

  A. Macro

    1. _____

      _____

    2. _____

      _____

  B. Micro

    1. _____

      _____

    2. _____

      _____

II. Causes

    1. _____

      _____

    2. _____

      _____

    3. _____

      _____

III. Systems affected

    1. _____

      _____

    2. _____

      _____

    3. _____

      _____

IV. Alternatives

    1. _____

      _____

    2. _____

      _____

    3. _____

      _____

V. Recommendations

_____

_____

_____

_____

_____

_____

## Chapter 9 Endnotes

1. For additional information, see John E. Mathieu and Lucy L. Gilson, "Empowerment and Team Effectiveness: An Empirical Test of an Integrated Model," *Journal of Applied Psychology*, vol. 91, no. 1 (January 2006), pp. 97–108; R. Hechanova-Alampay and T. A. Beehr, "Empowerment, Span of Control and Safety Performance in Work Teams after Workforce Reduction," *Journal of Occupational Health Psychology*, vol. 6, no. 4 (October 2001), pp. 275–82; C. Hardy and S. Leiba-O'Sullivan, "The Power Behind Empowerment: Implications for Research and Practice," *Human Relations*, vol. 51, no. 4 (April 1998), pp. 451–83; D. E. Hyatt and T. M. Ruddy, "An Examination of the Relationship between Work Group Characteristics and Performance: Once More into the Breech," *Personnel Psychology*, vol. 50, no. 3 (Autumn 1997), pp. 553–85.

2. For additional information on empowerment, see Yuen H. Chan, Robert R. Taylor, and Scott Markham, "The Role of Subordinates' Trust in a Social Exchange-driven Psychological Empowerment Process," *Journal Of Managerial Issues*, vol. 20, no. 4 (Winter 2008), pp. 444–67; Gary Hamel, *The Future of Management* (Boston, MA: Harvard Business School Press, 2007); Ananda Das Gupta and Shaji Kurian, "Empowerment at Work: The Dyadic Approach," *VISION—The Journal of Business Perspective*, vol. 10, no. 1 (January–March 2006), pp. 29–39; G. S. Sureshchandar, Chandrasekharan Rajendran, and R. N. Anantharaman, "A Conceptual Model for Total Quality Management in Service Organizations," *Total Quality Management*, vol. 12, no. 3 (May 2001), pp. 343–64.

3. Hirotaka Takeuchi, Emi Osono, and Norihiko Shimizu, "The Contradictions that Drive Toyota's Success," *Harvard Business Review*, June 2008, p. 98.

4. Jack Welch, "Jack Welch's Lessons for Success," *Fortune*, vol. 127, no. 2 (January 25, 1993), pp. 86–93.

5. John E. Mathieu and Lucy L. Gilson, "Empowerment and Team Effectiveness: An Empirical Test of an Integrated Model," p. 105.

6. www.gore.com; Robert Levering and Milton Moskowitz, "And the Winners Are . . ." *Fortune*, February 2009, pp. 67–78; Jennifer Reingold, "A Job that Lets You Pick Your Own Boss," *Fortune*, October 8, 2007; Gary Hamel, "Break Free!" *Fortune*, October 1, 2007, pp. 119–26; Ann Harrington, "Who's Afraid of a New Product?" *Fortune*, November 10, 2003, p. 189; Glenn Hasek, "The Right Chemistry," *Industry Week*, vol. 249, no. 5 (March 6, 2000), p. 36–40.

7. See http://ntl.org/ for more information on National Training Laboratories.

8. See the following for a more detailed description: L. Bradford, J. Gibb, and K. Benne, *T-Group Theory and Laboratory Method* (New York: John Wiley, 1964); Edgar Schein and Warren Bennis, *Personal and Organizational Change through Group Methods: The Laboratory Approach* (New York: John Wiley, 1965); and K. Back, *Beyond Words: The Story of Sensitivity Training and the Encounter Movement* (New York: Russell Sage Foundation, 1972).

9. Mark F. Peterson, "PM Theory in Japan and China: What's in It for the United States?" *Organizational Dynamics*, Spring 1988, pp. 22–38.

10. See the following for a more detailed description: P. Buchanan, "Laboratory Training and Organization Development," *Administrative Science Quarterly*, vol. 14, no. 3 (September 1969), pp. 466–80; J. Campbell and M. Dunnette, "Effectiveness of T-Group Experience in Managerial Training and Development," *Readings in Organizational Behavior and Human Performance*, ed. Larry L. Cummings and William E. Scott (Homewood, IL: Richard D. Irwin, 1969), p. 760.

11. George A. Neuman, Jack E. Edwards, and Nambury S. Raju, "Organizational Development Interventions: A Meta-Analysis of Their Effects on Satisfaction and Other Attitudes," *Personnel Psychology*, vol. 42, no. 3 (Autumn 1989), pp. 461–89; R.A. Guzzo, R. D. Jette, and R.A. Katzell, "The Effects of Psychologically Based Intervention Programs on Worker Productivity: A Meta-Analysis," *Personnel Psychology*, vol. 38, no. 2 (Summer 1985), pp. 275–91.

12. Joseph Luft, *Of Human Interaction* (Palo Alto, CA: National Press Books, 1961); Joseph Luft, *Group Processes, An Introduction to Group Dynamics* (Palo Alto, CA: National Press Books, 1970); J. Hall, "Communication Revisited," *California Management Review*, vol. 15. no. 3 (Spring 1973), pp. 56–67.

13. The discussion is based upon descriptions in Julie Hewson, *Transactional Analysis in Management* (Bristol, England: Further Education Staff College, 1992); Eric Berne, *The Structure and Dynamics of Organizations and Groups* (New York: Grove Press, 1963); Maurice F. Villere, *Transactional Analysis at Work: A Guide for Business and Professional People* (Upper Saddle River, NJ: Prentice Hall, 1981); Thomas Harris, *I'm OK, You're OK: A Practical Guide to Transactional Analysis* (New York: Harper & Row, 1969); Dorothy Jongeward, *Everybody Wins: Transactional Analysis Applied to Organizations* (Reading, MA: Addison-Wesley, 1973).

14. Muriel James and Dorothy Jongeward, *Born to Win* (Reading, MA: Addison-Wesley, 1974), p. 1.

15. Deborah Ball and Aaron O. Patrick, "How a Unilever Executive Is Thinning the Ranks," *Wall Street Journal*, November 26, 2007, p. B1.

16. For additional information, see Alan A. Andolsen, "Six Steps to Your Successful Career Path," *The Information Management Journal*, July/August 2008, pp. 56–60; James M. Citrin, "Be a Track Star," *Fast Company*, June 2004, p. 98.

17. Kerry D. Carson, Paula Phillips Carson, C. William Roe, Betty J. Birkenmeier, and Joyce S. Phillips, "Four Commitment Profiles and Their Relationship to Empowerment, Service Recovery, and Work Attitudes," *Public Personnel Management*, vol. 28, no. 1 (Spring 1999), pp. 1–14.

18. www.cdc.gov/niosh/.

19. Tom Nugent, "Take This Job and . . .," *Johns Hopkins Magazine*, November 2002, pp. 44–49.

20. *The Changing Organization of Work and the Safety and Health of Working People*, National Institute for Occupational Safety and Health, available at http://www.cdc.gov/niosh/.

21. *Worker Health Chartbook, 2004*, National Institute for Occupational Safety and Health, available at http://www.cdc.gov/niosh/.

22. Mara Der Hovanesian, "Zen and the Art of Corporate Productivity," *Business Week*, July 28, 2003, p. 56.

23. President's Council on Physical Fitness and Sports, *Fitness in the Workplace: A Corporate Challenge* (Washington, D.C.: U.S. Government Printing Office).

24. For additional information, see Kathryn Tyler, "Stress Management," *HR Magazine*, September 2006, pp. 79–83; Richard S. DeFrank and John M. Ivancevich, "Stress on the Job: An Executive Update," *Academy of Management Executive*, vol. 12, no. 3 (August 1998), pp. 55–67; *The Changing Organization of Work and the Safety and Health of Working People* (NIOSH Publication No. 2002–116), April 2002, National Institute for Occupational Safety and Health available at www.cdc.gov/niosh/docs/2002–116/.

25. Bruce Cryer, Rollin McCraty, and Doc Childre, "Pull the Plug on Stress," *Harvard Business Review,* vol. 81, no. 7 (July 2003), pp. 102–108.

26. Peter L. Schnall, Carl Pieper, Joseph E. Schwartz, Robert A. Karasek, Yvette Schlussel, Richard B. Devereux, Antonello Ganau, Michael Alderman, Katherine Warren, and Thomas G. Pickering, "The Relationship Between 'Job Strain,' Workplace Diastolic Blood Pressure, and Left Ventricular Mass Index," *Journal of the American Medical Association*, vol. 263, no. 14 (April 11, 1990), pp. 1929–35.

27. Warren A. Reich, Bonnie J. Wagner-Westbrook, and Kenneth Kressel, "Actual and Ideal Conflict Styles and Job Distress in a Health Care Organization," *Journal of Psychology*, vol. 141, no. 1 (January 2007), pp. 5–15.

28. R. Hogan, J. C. Gordon, and I. Hogan, "What We Know about Leadership: Effectiveness and Personality," *American Psychologist*, vol. 49, no. 6 (June 1994), p. 494. Reported in Kimberly A. Knutson and Alexis O. Miranda, "Leadership Characteristics, Social Interest, and Learning Organizations," *Journal of Individual Psychology*, vol. 56, no. 2 (Summer 2000), pp. 205–213.

29. *Violence in the Workplace: Risk Factors and Preventions Strategies*, National Institute for Occupational Safety and Health, DHHS (NIOSH) Publication No. 96–100, July 1996.

30. For additional information, see Hannele Huhtala and Marjo-Riitta Parzefall, "A Review of Employee Well-Being and Innovativeness: An Opportunity for a Mutual Benefit," *Employee Well-Being and Innovativeness*, vol. 16, no. 3 (November 3, 2007), pp. 299–306.

31. R.T. Golembiewski, R. Hilles, and R. Daly, "Some Effects of Multiple OD Interventions on Burnout and Work Site Features," *Journal of Applied Behavioral Science*, vol. 23, no. 3 (September 1987), pp. 295–313.

32. This article presents a comprehensive stress management program using an organizational development approach. Jennifer M. Kohler and David C. Munz, "Combining Individual and Organizational Stress Interventions: An Organizational Development Approach," *Consulting Psychology Journal: Practice and Research*, vol. 58, no. 1 (Winter 2006), pp. 1–12.

33. For additional information, see Katherine M. Richardson, and Hannah R. Rothstein, "Effects of Occupational Stress Management Intervention Programs: A Meta-Analysis," *Journal of Occupational Health Psychology*, vol. 13, no.1 (January 2008), pp. 69–93.

34. Louise Kertesz, "Corporate Wellness Programs Help Shape a Better Bottom Line," *Business Insurance*, vol. 41, no. 15 (April 9, 2007), pp. 15–6.

35. Rebecca Vesely, "Retooling Wellness," *Modern Healthcare*, November 17, 2008, vol. 38, no. 46 (November 17, 2008), p. 34.

36. Kertesz, "Corporate Wellness Programs Help Shape a Better Bottom Line."

37. Kizzy M. Parks and Lisa A. Steelman, "Organizational Wellness Programs: A Meta-Analysis," *Journal of Occupational Health Psychology*, vol. 13, no. 1 (January 2008), pp. 58–68.

38. "Online Poll Shows Only 9% of Employees Enroll in Corporate Wellness Programs," *Managed Care Weekly Digest*, December 1, 2003, p. 137.

39. Eduard Van Wijk, Heike Koch, Saskia Bosman, and Roeland Van Wijk, "Anatomic Characterization of Human Ultra-Weak Photon Emission in Practitioners of Transcendental Meditation (TM) and Control Subjects," *Journal of Alternative and Complementary Medicine*, vol. 12. no. 1 (January 2006), pp. 31–38.

40. Peter Burrows, "Pixar's Unsung Hero," *Business Week*, June 30, 2003, pp. 68–69.

41. Der Hovanesian, "Zen and the Art of Corporate Productivity," p. 56.

42. M. Michelle Rowe, "Skills Training in the Long-Term Management of Stress and Occupational Burnout," *Current Psychology*, vol. 19, no. 3 (Fall 2000), p. 215.

43. This case was written by Captain Pete Farmer, USAF, Fairchild AFB, and is used by permission.

# PART FOUR

# Developing High Performance in Teams

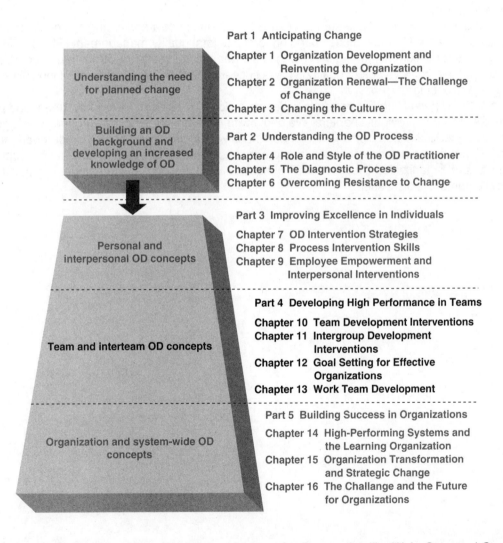

Understanding the need
for planned change

Building an OD
background and
developing an increased
knowledge of OD

Personal and
interpersonal OD concepts

Team and interteam OD concepts

Organization and system-wide OD
concepts

Teams are even more a part of organization life than in the past. Companies like W. L. Gore and General Electric (GE) have for decades made high-performance teams part of their culture. Joining them in making teams an integral part of the way they do business are newer companies like Meetup, Whole Foods Market, and Google. And a more established company like Cisco became a convert to high-performance teams in the early part of this century.

Many management theorists see the team-based organization as the wave of the future. The self-managed team could be one of the basic building blocks of the organization and may well become the productivity breakthrough of the 2000s. But high-performing work teams do not happen by an edict from upper management or the people in strategic planning shifting around departments in a restructure of the company.

Organizations have found that effective teams come with deliberate planning and training, and their implementation can take years.

Team building is a major OD technique and it is used for increasing the communication, cooperation, and cohesiveness of units to make them more productive and effective. Team building is an intervention where the members of a work group examine such things as their goals, structure, procedures, culture, norms, and interpersonal relationships to improve their ability to work together effectively and efficiently.

High-performing teams do not exist in a vacuum; they are part of a larger organization that requires teams to work effectively with one another to accomplish overall organizational objectives. One key area in the improvement of organization effectiveness involves the relation between operating groups or departments. Complex organizations tend to create situations of team interdependence, where the performance of one group is contingent upon another group.

For teams to become more effective, both within a team and between teams, requires that teams establish goals and objectives that will get them to a desired state. OD programs rely heavily upon the goal-setting process. OD, by definition, is planned change, and in order for that change to take place, goals need to be set. Early on in an OD program, managers and other employees develop ideas and goals about what the organization will be like.

Today's managers are being challenged to provide leadership in new and changing conditions. One approach that has emerged to meet these changing forces is total quality management (TQM). This is an organizational strategy of commitment to improving customer satisfaction by developing procedures and designing jobs that can improve output quality. TQM's success relies on empowerment of individuals, teamwork, and goal setting.

This *Part 4: Developing High Performance in Teams* builds upon employee empowerment and process interventions discussed in previous chapters. We begin with learning what makes for effective teams and how they can be developed in chapter 10. Chapter 11 continues with a discussion of team interdependence and ways that interdependence can be enhanced in appropriate situations. Chapter 12 covers goal setting on both individual, team, and organizational levels. Part 4 concludes with chapter 13 where improving quality through work team development is discussed.

# CHAPTER 10

# Team Development Interventions

## LEARNING OBJECTIVES

**Upon completing this chapter, you will be able to:**

1. Identify how team development techniques fit into an OD program.
2. Recognize team problems and why teams may not be operating at optimum capacity.
3. Experience the process of team development.

## PREMEETING PREPARATION

1. Read Chapter 10.
2. Prepare for OD Skills Simulation 10.1. Prior to class, form teams of six and assign roles. Complete Steps 1 and 2.
3. Complete Step 1 of OD Skills Simulation 10.2 before class but after finishing OD Skills Simulation 10.1.
4. Read and analyze Case: Steele Enterprises.

## ORGANIZING AROUND TEAMS

Teams are becoming a way of life in organizations. Some 80 percent of U.S. organizations have employees working in teams. Studies show that corporations are increasingly looking to teams as a way to organize professional work.[1] Within the last two decades, a convergence of global forces has provided the impetus for organizations worldwide to make greater use of teams. The use of teams does not occur only on the factory floor but prevails up to the highest executive levels. The prevalent use of teams in the way that work is organized and carried out has forced greater attention on issues such as when the use of a team is appropriate and what makes for an effective team.

Most of us have either participated in or watched games that involve teamwork. A **team** is a group of individuals with complementary skills who depend upon one another to accomplish a common purpose or set of performance goals for which they hold themselves mutually accountable.[2] **Teamwork** is work done when the members subordinate their personal prominence for the good of the team. Members of effective teams are open and honest with one another, there is support and trust, there is a high degree of cooperation and collaboration, decisions are reached by consensus, communication channels are open and well developed, and there is a strong commitment to the team's goals.

Many management theorists see the team-based organization as the wave of the future.[3] The self-managed team (discussed in Chapter 13) could be one of the basic building blocks of the organization and may well become the productivity breakthrough of the 2000s. Management consultant W. Edwards Deming (management guru to the Japanese and responsible for much of Japan's postwar industrial success) once said in an interview, "An example of a system well managed is an orchestra. The various players are not there as prima donnas—to play loud and attract the attention of the listener. They're there to support each other. In fact, sometimes you see a whole section doing nothing but counting and watching. Just sitting there doing nothing. They're there to support each other. That's how business should be."[4]

In this chapter, we examine some reasons for using team building and discuss several team interventions, including team development, cohesiveness, outdoor experimental laboratory training, role analysis, and role negotiation techniques. This chapter builds on employee empowerment, which was discussed in Chapter 9. Other team and interteam interventions, such as goal setting and self-managed work teams, are discussed in Chapters 12 and 13.

## THE TEAM APPROACH

Many organizations are attempting to increase productivity by implementing team-based programs. As an example, at Whole Foods Market, the basic organization unit is not the store, as is typical for a retail operation. The team is the central focus, and at Whole Foods they are small, empowered work groups that are granted a near-unprecedented degree of autonomy that is not common in retailing. There are eight teams at each store that oversee the departments. A team is responsible for key operating decisions that include hiring, promotions, staffing, in-store promotions, and pricing. The team also makes stocking decisions, with consultation of their store manager, based on products that the members feel will appeal to local customers.[5]

As well as large nationwide companies, small companies also widely use teams. One survey of small-company plants found that 68 percent of the companies used teams to varying degrees. "Small-company executives and consultants say that developing teams is necessary because technology and market demands are compelling manufacturers to make their products faster, cheaper, and better."[6]

### Interdependence

The coordination of individual effort into task accomplishment is most important when the members of a team are interdependent. **Interdependence** refers to situations where one person's performance is contingent upon how someone else performs. Sports like baseball, football, and basketball provide some useful parallels for understanding the workings of teams in other types of organizations. Among the three major professional sports—baseball, football, and basketball—basketball is more of a team sport than the other two.[7]

Baseball is a game of pooled interdependence where team member contributions are somewhat independent of one other. The players are separated geographically on a large field, they are not all involved actively in every play, and they come to bat one at a time. Football, in contrast, involves sequential interdependence. A flow of plays and first downs are required to score. The players are closer geographically than in baseball, and there is a greater degree of interdependence. Players are normally grouped together functionally (i.e., offense and defense), and the two groups do not contact one another. Unlike baseball, all the players on the field are involved in every play.

Basketball exhibits the highest degree of interdependence. The players are closely grouped together, and the team moves together on the court. Every player may contact any other player, and the player's roles or functions are less defined than in football. All the players are involved in offense, defense, and trying to score.

Organizations frequently use sport teams as a model. For example, some organizations require close teamwork similar to basketball, whereas other organizations require team involvement similar to baseball. Using sports terminology, a production manager at Procter & Gamble (P&G) expressed his vision for his work team by saying, "I have a picture of an ideal basketball team in my head that I compare to the production team. When I see people not passing to each other or when I see somebody taking all the shots, I know we have to work on teamwork. When we're not using the backboard, we need to work on skills. When only part of the team can get rebounds, we have to do cross-training."[8]

### Team Building

One major OD technique, termed **team building** or **team development** (the two terms are generally interchangeable), is used for increasing the communication, cooperation, and cohesiveness of units to make them more productive and effective. Team building is an intervention where the members of a work group examine such things as their goals, structure, procedures, culture, norms, and interpersonal relationships to improve their ability to work together effectively and efficiently.

Team building grew out of the application of laboratory learning, used principally during the 1950s and 1960s (see Chapter 9). When laboratory learning was first used in organizations, the groups were traditionally composed of strangers, often from different organizations. As laboratory learning developed and changed over the years, participants who worked with one another were brought together to deal with interpersonal issues and team functioning. This arrangement was termed "family groups." The results were often mixed and disappointing, largely because of the lack of structure in laboratory groups. However, the lack of structure gradually evolved into a defined process of training people to work effectively as teams.

There are several reasons for using team development to improve organizational effectiveness. First, the work group is the basic unit of the organization and thus provides a supportive change factor. Second, the operating problems of work groups are often sources of inefficiency.

Teams or work groups often have difficulty in operating effectively. The problems that inhibit effective operation include lack of clear objectives, interpersonal differences or conflicts, ineffective communication, difficulty in reaching group decisions, and inappropriate power and authority levels in the group. Team development techniques are used in change programs to increase work team effectiveness. The work team reviews and evaluates its own functioning and develops improved work and relational patterns. The emphasis is on the members exploring the team's functioning and processes, usually with the help of a practitioner's process interventions. If the team's manager or leader is the OD practitioner, then the manager will make process interventions. With time and team development, the members will also make process interventions.

## Virtual Teams

A new element in teams, **virtual teams,** has recently become more important and more commonplace in organizations. Virtual teams have developed out of technological advancements in the communications, computer, and electronic industries. The technology incorporates high-speed fiber optic land lines and high-end video and audio equipment. Virtual teams present some new challenges in developing teams as the members of a virtual team may never personally meet, though they may daily see and talk to one another. For large multinational companies like P&G and Hewlett-Packard (HP), the teams may have members in other countries.

Virtual teams tend to cut across all kinds of traditional boundaries, both internal and external to an organization. The internal boundaries of an organization regarding departments or divisions tend to disappear or lose their relevancy. Virtual teams also tend to be immune to a person's status or position within an organization. In some situations, virtual teams may be multiorganizational in that they may include members from more than one company or organization. This would be the situation for a company that brings in team members from a customer to solve a mutual problem or to jointly develop a product. What brings a virtual team together is that the members share a common purpose and objective. Virtual teams are geographically dispersed across time and space but otherwise share many of the same characteristics, requirements, and challenges of traditional teams. For more information on virtual teams and some examples of how organizations are using them, see **OD Application: Virtual Teams.**

### OD Application: Virtual Teams[9]

Technology and the Internet bring a double-edged sword to the workplace. While they bring together people from around the world who would probably never communicate with one another, they also inhibit genuine human interaction. People worldwide are spending an increasing amount of time at work interacting with virtual team members. For large companies like IBM, Cisco, General Electric (GE), and P&G, virtual team meetings with other people in the company, suppliers, and customers have been occurring to some extent since the beginning of the Internet. At IBM's intranet (an intranet is an organization's private and internal Internet), one of the largest in the world, they sometimes bring groups of more than 7,000 members together. But with time, the software and technology to conduct meetings has become more sophisticated. Even smaller companies with a webcam built into a laptop computer are forming their own virtual teams.

GE is using computer-based collaboration tools in a way that is changing the way it works with its 340,000 employees and with its customers and suppliers. The program is worldwide, operating across 12 divisions and thousands of suppliers and customers. The goal of the program is to improve information sharing for the company across geographic and cultural barriers. GE's program electronically brings in customers and suppliers behind the firewalls that protect its computer systems to work as part of GE's internal project teams. One example of the system is at GE Industrial Systems. There the system supports about 500 projects involving 700 users in 300 teams. Partners "will be working as if they're part of our team," says the general manager of technology at GE Industrial Systems. "We think it will change the whole paradigm of how we work with suppliers. It's going to get us a lot closer to our customers. They're going to be more involved, more frequently. We'll be much better able to meet their needs, and we think it will result in great customer loyalty."

Telepresence, an alternative to the standard videoconferencing room, is a new and still-developing technology being used by some virtual teams. The old technology often placed a rather dim but large projection screen at one end of a conference room. A signal would be beamed around the country or world. It was

*(Continued)*

common, because of time delays inherent in satellite transmission, to have participants speaking over each other. The new telepresence technology uses four to six very large high-definition monitors on one side of a room with live participants, typically seated in a semicircle, on the other side of the room facing the screens. Broadcast-quality cameras are placed above each of the screens with a camera directed at one of the participants. In some systems, cameras are placed behind the screens so that live participants are seen as staring into the eyes of the remote person. High-speed dedicated communication lines are used for the high-definition video and audio signal. This allows speakers to interrupt one another without muting the audio of the other person. More expensive fiber optic land lines are used rather than satellites to avoid the latency between speaker and listener. Equipment is used to ensure that audio and video are synchronized. A series of speakers along the walls are used to make sure that the sound from the person speaking matches the appropriate monitor.

None of this comes cheaply. Systems usually cost $250,000 to $500,000 a room, which does not include a lease on communication lines. The cost for some companies can be justified within six months. For HP's teleconference system, called Halo, the savings are even greater. In one case, HP's manufacturing managers credited their system for cutting from one year down to six months the time required to get a new inkjet cartridge plant in Singapore operational. Another user of telepresence is Pearson, PLC, a London publisher of textbooks and magazines, with major offices in New York (Pearson is the corporate owner of the publisher of this textbook). "In meetings, you can pick up real subtlety of expressions. People are much more honest," says Justine Kanter, development manager.

One of the largest users of the Internet and telepresence is P&G. It has 7,500 people located in 20 facilities in nine countries. For about a decade, it has been using its intranet as a way of bringing its researchers together on a company Web site called "communities of practice" (COP), which is a scheduled meeting devoted to a specific subject. The format of the system is Web sites, blogs, online research papers, and e-mail. People get just as much credit for giving ideas as for turning ideas into better products. The method has resulted in divisions in different parts of the company collaborating with one another to come up with new products. The homecare division came up with a new product, Mr. Clean AutoDry, thanks to help from the scientists in P&G's PUR water purification unit and Cascade scientists who know how to get dishes to dry without spotting. Other new

products that have come from COP include Glad Press'n Seal (a super-sticky food wrap) and Mr. Clean Magic Eraser (a spot remover). As an addition to P&G's company Web site, a new type of virtual meetings at P&G makes use of telepresence technology. To improve P&G's ability to conduct meetings in a virtual world, it has recently installed more than 75 of Cisco's high-end TelePresence video conferencing systems in 55 countries. The company says it will be able to hold more global consumer focus groups and to lower travel costs with the new systems.

A perfect storm of sorts has emerged that has accelerated the use of virtual teams. Consider just some of the elements that have increased their use:

- Air travel has become more expensive and less convenient. Even though air travel is fast, its speed belongs in the Stone Age when compared to the near light speed of the Internet.
- The fast pace at which organizations must operate make the time required to bring people together from different locations too time-consuming.
- The worldwide recession that developed in late 2007, and that became somewhat dire for some companies by 2008, created the necessity for reducing travel budgets.
- The hardware, software, and fiber optic lines have become more sophisticated, which enables a reasonable replication of a face-to-face meeting.
- Gen X employees grew up with the Internet, e-mail, Facebook, Blackberries, and Twitter. For them, virtual meetings are natural extensions of Internet-based technology. As Gen Xers have advanced into higher levels of organizations, virtual meetings will become common place.

With these and other unforeseen changes in society and technology, it is highly probable that we are just seeing the infancy of virtual meetings.

## Questions

1. Compare the methods used at GE, P&G, and other companies to promote virtual teams.
2. What do you see as the advantages and disadvantages of virtual meetings?
3. Visit the Web site of HP at www.hp.com and search for Halo and Cisco at www.cisco.com and search for TelePresence to research current information on telepresence technology.

## THE NEED FOR TEAM DEVELOPMENT

The team or work group is the primary unit in the organization, and there is an increasing reliance on project teams, task force groups, and committees to accomplish organizational goals.[10] Cisco has made teamwork a critical part of bonus plans, especially for top executives. CEO John Chambers has implemented a policy where 30 percent of the annual bonus would depend on how well the executive collaborates with others. "It tends to formalize the discussion around how can I help you and how can you help me," says one of the top executives.[11]

Work teams may be of two basic types. In the first type, the **natural work team,** people come together because they do related jobs or because of the structure of the organization's design. In the second type, the **temporary task team,** groups meet for limited periods to work on a specific project or problem and disband after they solve it. As task teams are designated to work on organizational and technological problems, there is an increasing need for collaboration and coordination of the resources that are brought together. Collaboration does not automatically happen, but it is possible with the use of team development techniques.

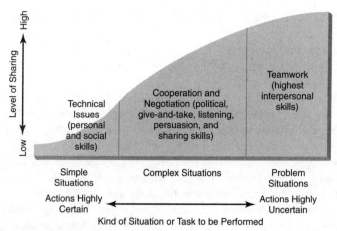

**FIGURE 10.1** Situation Determines Teamwork

Marvin R. Weisbord, who has written extensively on team development, offers a fairly straightforward description of the process of deciding whether team building is appropriate:

First, the boss calls a meeting, introduces the idea, states his or her personal goals, and asks for discussion. If, as is common, a consultant has been hired, the parties need a "get-acquainted" meeting to decide whether to go forward. Often the consultant interviews team members to discover their basic concerns. Questions might include each person's objectives, the problems each faces, and the extent and kinds of help people need from each other. The consultant, then, presents a summary of interview issues to the whole team, inviting a discussion of priorities and the pros and cons of continuing the process. If the decision is made to proceed, the group schedules one or more longer meetings specifically for team building.[12]

## Categories of Team Interaction

Some practitioners feel that team building is an overused technique. As they point out, the members of many teams say they do not want to work together, cannot work together, and have no reason to work together. Given these limitations, it is important to examine the degree of team members' interaction before beginning a team development intervention. Situations that require interaction tend to fall into three categories: (1) simple situations, (2) complex situations, and (3) problem situations. The kind of task to be performed determines whether a team is required. The type of interaction that is appropriate for a team is illustrated in Figure 10.1.

**SIMPLE SITUATIONS** A simple situation is one that can be solved by a single individual. For example, an electronic engineer may need to consult occasionally with colleagues to obtain technical information to design a routine component, but the project is one that the engineer is expected to complete alone based on technical expertise. There is no need to involve others except to pass along or obtain information. The involvement of others may slow down the organization's functions. Managers operating in a simple situation focus on their responsibilities, do not involve others in their work, and, therefore, avoid wasting valuable time. Good social skills are important, but team development is not needed for work groups involved with simple situations.

Teamwork and employee participation are not needed under the following conditions.[13]

- The work is structured so that the tasks that make it up are highly independent of other tasks.
- There is one person who is obviously more of an expert on the subject than anyone else, and those affected by the decision acknowledge and accept that expertise.
- There is an obvious correct answer.
- The task or problem is part of someone's regular job assignment, and it was not his or her idea to form the team.
- There is little or no interest in the issue.
- The involvement of others will not contribute to the issue, nor would their knowledge or expertise be increased by the team experience.

- The reward or pay is based on individual performance and not on the collective performance of the team.
- There is no time for discussion.
- Employees work more happily and productively alone.

**COMPLEX SITUATIONS** Complex situations encompass most of a group's work. There is a need to share information at a level that allows work to be accomplished, because the members cannot do the task on their own. However, input is not required from all of the group's members, and the level of the input is not deeply personal. These types of activities arise constantly in most organizations, and members handle them by cooperating with one another. For example, they assist each other in getting out the quarterly financial statements. Acting alone, no one person would have enough information or time to complete the statements, so information is shared and members help one another. Team development is not essential, but it is recommended because members need to cooperate and negotiate with one another and coordinate their activities. Good interpersonal skills are required, including the ability to compromise, to see situations from another member's point of view, to negotiate, to persuade, to listen, and to share information.

**PROBLEM SITUATIONS** Problem situations are atypical, consequential, unprecedented, and have an impact outside an individual's scope of influence. For example, a company that is planning to introduce a new product must work effectively not only in the various departments that formulate plans but also between departments to arrive at a general strategy. The uncertainty involved with these types of problems and the need to involve others in the solutions requires a team-building approach.

Different modes of working require different processes. The team approach is appropriate under the following conditions.[14]

- When the work is designed to be done by a team.
- To permit members to gain new expertise and experience and to develop and educate members.
- To allow those who know something about the subject to become involved.
- To build and enhance employee commitment, because teams offer increased levels of participation in decisions.
- To build consensus and commitment on a controversial issue.
- To work on a problem that does not belong to any one person.
- When rewards are based on team performance rather than individual performance.
- To allow more creative discussions by pulling together people of unusual and different backgrounds and interests.
- To avoid the obvious decision and explore a variety of effects.

## Operating Problems of Work Teams

When individuals are brought together to work on some problem or goal of the organization, they are likely to develop a complex pattern of behaviors, interactions, and feelings. A primary function will be to preserve the norms of the team and protect it from outside pressures perceived to be threats. Those who receive rewards from the team and support its norms represent a core of "regular" members. At the other extreme are the "isolates," who have little to do with the others and seem to have little interest in and need for observing the norms.

The team also satisfies several important individual needs. If these needs are frustrated by organizational obstacles, problems will arise both for the individual and for the work organization. The satisfaction of social needs such as affiliation, acceptance, and status is important for most people, and often these needs are partially met through the team. Work teams provide emotional support and identity for their members. The lack of support is noticeable when work teams are dissolved, as in an organization or company takeover. Work teams also serve the valuable purpose of helping individuals to attain goals and accomplish tasks.

A survey sponsored by the American Management Association found that the principal causes of conflict within organizations included value differences, goal disagreements, poor cooperation, authority and responsibility disputes, poor personal performance, frustration, competition for organizational resources, not following policies and work rules, misunderstandings, and personality clashes. The sources of team operating problems, shown in Figure 10.2, center around elements including goals, member needs, norms, homogeneous members, decision making, leadership, and size.

**FIGURE 10.2    Sources of Team Problems**

**GOALS** Individuals often have difficulty in defining and clarifying their goals, and in work teams the problem is multiplied. Objectives are often misunderstood, confused, or changed without any definite clarification. Similarly, teams tend to lose their purpose and direction, and goals require testing from time to time to figure out whether they are going full stream but in the wrong direction.

**MEMBER NEEDS** As previously noted, teams fill several needs of individuals, and frequently the satisfaction of completing the task is overemphasized at the expense of the social and personal needs of team members. Interpersonal differences, conflicts, or misunderstandings may hinder team effectiveness. Members may take sides and reject any compromise, or they may attack one another in subtle ways. Such interpersonal "garbage" or hang-ups need to be brought out and resolved.

**NORMS** The team must develop norms about its behavioral patterns. In some cases, the norms lead to behavior that is antisocial and dysfunctional for the organization. For example, groups with strongly antisocial climates appear to have significant influence on the antisocial actions of their members. If team members comprise a tightly knit group, they are more likely to match their level of antisocial behavior to that of the group.

**HOMOGENEOUS MEMBERS** Groups that are homogeneous tend to produce homogeneous ideas. Creative ideas and projects tend to come from groups that have diverse backgrounds and interests.

**DECISION MAKING** Another frequent source of difficulty in teams is the way decisions are made. Decisions may be made by authoritarian decree, by majority rule, or by unanimous rule. Each method has advantages and disadvantages. There is a good deal of evidence showing that decisions implemented by members who use consensus rules are more effective.

**LEADERSHIP** One key issue for teams is the degree of power and control that the members have over themselves and others. Groups sometimes suffer from low participation, boredom, or apathy. Some groups and individuals function better in a more structured, authoritarian situation, whereas others do not. For example, production units may operate better with more structure, whereas research groups probably do better with more independence.

**SIZE** A work team can consist of as few as two members or as many as 25 or 30, but five to seven is generally considered the most effective size. People on a small team behave differently from those on a large team. A team of two or three is generally too small to be effective, whereas 12 is probably the upper limit for the members to interact with every other member. With even larger teams, there is a greater likelihood that subteams of five to seven will form to handle specific concerns.

A leading expert in teams and a professor of organizational psychology at Harvard University, J. Richard Hackman, says, "As a team gets bigger, the number of links that need to be managed among members goes up at an accelerating, almost exponential rate. It's managing the links between members that gets teams into trouble. My rule of thumb is no double digits. In my courses, I never allow teams of more than six students. Big teams usually wind up just wasting everybody's time."[15] For example, JP Morgan Chase's CEO, Jamie Dimon, says that he prefers to work in small groups, where managers cannot hide. He says it is also easier for small groups to make changes.[16] Google prefers that those involved in product development, approximately half of its employees, work in small teams with an average of three engineers per team. A large project might have 30 engineers but the project is broken down into team sizes of three or four. As well, most team members work on more than one team and frequently "self select" by choosing the projects and teams that they work on.[17]

## COHESIVENESS AND GROUPTHINK

The term **group** (or team) **cohesiveness** refers to the unity that the members of a group have for one another. Some groups have more closeness and team spirit than others, and such groups are more cohesive than those where members are indifferent. Cohesiveness can be described in terms of task cohesiveness and interpersonal cohesiveness. Task cohesiveness is the group's shared commitment to the group task or goal and is thought to increase individual effort by the group members. Interpersonal cohesiveness is the group members' attraction to the group. Interpersonal cohesiveness permits groups to have more honest and uninhibited communication between members. Studies of group cohesiveness have shown it to have a positive relationship with performance.[18]

There is a negative component to group cohesiveness. At some undefined point, the cohesiveness can become too pronounced so that it makes the need for uniformity with the group more important than the need for high-quality decisions. This type of group behavior is called groupthink. **Groupthink** is a theoretical framework posited by Irving Janis to describe the problems of group cohesiveness. Groupthink refers to "a mode of thinking that people engage in when they are deeply involved in a cohesive in-group, when the members' striving for unanimity overrides their motivation to realistically appraise alternative courses of action."[19]

Some authorities on work group behavior, including Warren Bennis, a writer and OD practitioner, advocate appointing an official "contrarian" who is responsible for raising legitimate questions and criticisms before the team makes a key decision. "Give people license to tell the truth," Bennis said. "It's a way of stopping the folly of 'groupthink.'"[20]

Groupthink often occurs when the members of a group avoid making harsh judgments of ideas put forward by their leaders or colleagues. In their behavior and thinking, they adopt a soft line of criticism. The members are friendly to one another and seek complete concurrence on every important issue. There is no disagreement or conflict to spoil the cozy, "we feeling" atmosphere.

Irving Janis identifies eight characteristics of groupthink and the problems tending to result from it.[21]

1. *Illusion of invulnerability*. Most or all members share an illusion of invulnerability that masks obvious dangers, leads them to take extraordinary risks, and causes them to fail to respond to clear warnings of danger.
2. *Rationalization*. Members construct rationalizations that allow them to discount warnings or other negative information.
3. *Illusion of morality*. Members unquestionably believe in the inherent morality of the group's position. Other groups with opposing views are thought of as evil. This type of thinking allows the group to disregard the ethical or moral consequences of their actions.
4. *Shared stereotypes.* Views held by an opposing group, and especially by its leaders, are seen as evil or as so stupid that the opposing group could not possibly understand reasonable negotiations with one's own groups.
5. *Direct pressure.* The group applies direct pressure to any member who expresses doubts about the group's positions or questions the validity of the arguments supporting a position.
6. *Self-censorship.* Members of the group do not express views that differ from what appears to be a group consensus and minimize to themselves the importance of their doubts.
7. *Illusion of unanimity.* An illusory belief that the members of the group are all in agreement. It is partly based on the false assumption that individuals who remain silent agree with the group.
8. *Mind guards.* Self-appointed members protect the leader and other members from adverse information external to the group that might disrupt the group's cohesiveness.

The consequences of group problems are usually not clearly understood, but most managers agree that they influence motivation, morale, and productivity. Empirical investigations of groupthink do not conclusively support Janis's theory. There are, however, studies that generally support the groupthink phenomenon. One study found that in groups whose leaders promoted their own preferred solution, the group exhibited symptoms of groupthink, poor decision-making process, and poor quality decisions.[22] Other studies point to the importance of a group being composed of members with diverse personalities so that each member can contribute unique attributes to the team.[23] **OD Application: Groupthink at the White House** includes additional information about the background of groupthink and how it is a part of today's political landscape.

## THE PURPOSE OF TEAM DEVELOPMENT

Team development has the very broad objective of integrating the goals of the individual and the group with the goals of the organization. Work teams can only achieve this if they spend some time on the process of team interaction, that is, on how they work together and what they accomplish. When a baseball team executes a difficult cutoff play, a basketball team executes a precise fast break, or a football team scores on a long-pass play, it looks smooth and easy. But the ease and precision come from hours and hours of practice and attention to the details of how to run the play.

---

### OD Application: Groupthink at the White House[24]

Back in 1972, Janis Irving wrote *Victims of Groupthink: A Psychological study of Foreign Policy Decisions and Fiascoes* followed in 1983 by *Groupthink: A Psychological Study of Policy Decisions and Fiascoes*. Groupthink as a term, however, was first coined in 1952 by William Whyte in *Fortune* magazine. Irving did extensive research into the concept of groupthink during his 40 years at Yale University as professor of social psychology. Irving's books on groupthink looked at some relatively recent and major U.S. foreign policy fiascoes like the failure of being prepared for the attack on Pearl Harbor, the Bay of Pigs blunder, and the escalation of the Vietnam War. Janis also looked at some foreign policy decisions that were successful, such as the Marshall Plan and the Cuban Missile crisis, and how groupthink was avoided. In a continuation of using groupthink to help study the process of decision making in groups, in 1997 Paul't Hart edited *Beyond Groupthink: Political Group Dynamics and Foreign Policy Making*.

It has been said by reporters and those close to President Barack Obama that Obama is a student of history and tries to learn from its lessons. It is unclear if President Obama has read any of these books on groupthink but, as president-elect and then as president, it was obvious in his news conferences that he was aware of the term and the research that surrounded it regarding the making of previous foreign policy. What follows are some excerpts from three news conferences where President-elect and then President Obama used the term "groupthink."

Date: November 26, 2008

**Subject:** The economy and introduction of Paul Volcker to head the new Economic Recovery Advisory Board

Let me speak to why I think this is necessary. The reality is that sometimes policy making in Washington can become a little bit too ingrown, a little bit too insular. The walls of the echo chamber can sometimes keep out fresh voices and new ways of thinking. You start engaging in groupthink. And those who serve in Washington don't always have a ground level sense of which programs and policies are working for people and businesses

and which aren't. This board will provide that fresh perspective to me and my administration with an infusion of ideas from across the country and from all sectors of our economy, input that will be informed by members' firsthand observations of how our efforts are impacting the daily lives of our families.

Date: December 1, 2008

**Subject:** Announcing the National Security Team

One last point I will make. I assembled this team because I'm a strong believer in strong personalities and strong opinions. I think that's how the best decisions are made. One of the dangers in the White House, based on my reading of history, is that you get wrapped up in groupthink and everybody agrees with everything and there's no discussion and there are no dissenting views. So I'm going to be welcoming a vigorous debate inside the White House.

Date: February 6, 2009

**Subject:** Announcing members of the new Economic Recovery Advisory Board

I'm not interested in groupthink, which is why the board reflects a broad cross-section of experience and expertise and ideology. We've recruited Republicans and Democrats, people who come out of the government as well as the private sector.

Not everyone is going to agree with each other, and not all of them are going to agree with me. And that's precisely the point, because we want to ensure that our policies have the benefit of independent thought and vigorous debate.

#### Questions

1. Does groupthink play a part in teams and work groups of other types of organizations than governmental policy-making groups? Support your position.
2. Try to cite personal examples of groupthink.

**FIGURE 10.3** Quitting on Your Team

*Source:* B.C. by permission of Johnny Hart and Creators Syndicate, Inc.

The development of a smoothly functioning team is just as demanding and precise in an organization as in many sports activities, but few work teams ever examine their performance. A typical reason is "We're too busy." Yet it is difficult to imagine an effective basketball or football team too busy to practice or to review its performance. This is what team development is all about. It is an intensive examination of team operation focusing upon how members function as a team, and how they can overcome operating problems and improve their efficiency. The need for team development is illustrated in Figure 10.3.

The Army Rangers and Navy Seals are two organizations that are some of the best examples of world-class teamwork. But their teamwork does not happen by accident and it is not natural. They spend more time practicing as a team than on a mission. Their creeds and mottos are to the team. For example, the Rangers say, "Never shall I fail my comrades." This idea of subjugating personal prominence for the benefit of the team is expressed in the novel *North Dallas Forty*:[25]

"All right. All right. Green right pitch 29 wing T pull. On two."
My heart jumped and my mouth went dry at the call. I would have to crack back on Whitman, the outside linebacker on the right-hand side. Crawford would try to get outside of my block with the help of the strong-side tackle.

Whitman moved toward the sideline in a low crouch, stringing the play out and watching Andy and the leading tackle. At the last second, he felt me coming back down the line at him. I dove headlong as he turned. He tried to jump the block and his knees caught me in the forehead and the side of the neck. We went down in a jumble of arms and legs, my shoulder went numb, and a hot burn shot up my neck and into the back of my head. The play gained 8 yards.

Every team has its own structure, norms, and values, and members of the team tend to do things in certain ways. Team members are often more loyal to fellow team members than to the organization. Because of these characteristics, team development techniques are used to clarify goals and priorities, to examine how decisions and communication are functioning, and to recognize how the relationships among team members influence output. The goals of team development include:

- Identify objectives and set priorities.
- Examine the team's content or task performance.
- Analyze the group process, that is, how the group is functioning.
- Improve communications and relationships among group members.
- Improve the team's ability to solve problems.
- Decrease unhealthy competition and increase cooperation among team members.
- Work more effectively with other teams in the organization.
- Increase team members' respect for one another's individual differences.

It should not be inferred that conflict within a team leads to organizational ineffectiveness and, therefore, should be avoided. In some situations, conflict may be healthy and improve the performance of a work team.

Conflict is a natural social interaction, and managers should be able to recognize the types of conflicts and channel them in appropriate directions. Conflict can be healthy when it is issue-oriented rather than personality-oriented, when it sharpens people's thought processes, when it is germane to the goals of the team, and when it does not produce winners and losers with the accompanying social stigma. The OD practitioner's responsibility is to find effective methods to deal with conflicts and resolve any unhealthy conflicts.

## THE TEAM DEVELOPMENT PROCESS

As organizations are becoming increasingly complex, managing a team involves more than supervising people. In today's world, managers must bring an often-divergent group of people together to work on a common project. Since no one person can possess all the knowledge necessary to analyze and solve today's complex problems, teams or work groups are used to bring together the required expertise. The nature of work groups makes team development interventions probably the single most important and widely used OD activity.

The team development process, as described by several practitioners, recognizes two distinct types of activities.[26] *Family group diagnostic meetings*, one type of team development, are aimed at identifying group problems. *Family group team-building meetings*, another orientation of team development, are aimed at improving the team's functioning. The following description incorporates both activities. Team development is an educational process of continually reviewing and evaluating team functioning in order to identify and establish new and more effective ways of operating. Team development is an ongoing experience that occurs simultaneously with the work itself.

A team development meeting has two objectives: (1) the task or work agenda of the group, and (2) the processes by which members work on the task. The focus in a team development meeting is on the process of the team, including its working relationships and its patterns for accomplishing tasks. The team members attending a team development meeting learn how to look at their ways of behaving, diagnose any operating problems, and figure out new and more effective ways of functioning. It should be stressed that team development is not a one-time activity undertaken in the presence of a practitioner. Once a team learns how to make process interventions, it can continue to engage in team development as an ongoing part of its group activities. The main purpose is to get team members involved in solving problems and in the decision-making process.

Most team development training meetings follow a similar format, although the specific contents and activities of meetings may differ significantly. The procedure includes certain basic steps. Keep in mind when reading these steps that the practitioner may be either the team manager or an OD professional.

## Step 1: Initiating the Team Development Meeting

Within an organization, the initiating of a team development meeting may come from several different sources. A group's operating problems may have been identified and diagnosed in the earlier stages of the OD program. The team development meeting may be initiated by a manager higher in the organizational structure who is not a member of the team. The need for a meeting may also be apparent to the manager of the work group, who may initiate the team development meeting. In some situations, the team development meeting may be initiated by a practitioner if there is one working with the organization. Although the team development meeting may be initiated by any of these people, the decision to proceed is usually collaborative.

During the formation stage, the members of the team will probably discuss the degree to which they support team development. They will also discuss whether a team is necessary given the specific work situation.

## Step 2: Setting Objectives

Assuming that the team decides to proceed with team development, the next step is setting some broad objectives to be accomplished at the meeting. Such objectives might consist of evaluating the working processes of the team or improving its effectiveness. If a team development meeting is to be effective, there should be general agreement on the objectives before team development proceeds.

The practitioner may address some pertinent questions to the work group. These might well include: What is the purpose of this meeting? What do the participants and I want to do? Why this group of people at this time? How does this meeting fit into the OD program? What is the priority for this project? Are the team members really interested and committed? What does the team want to accomplish? How will team development be measured or evaluated?

## Step 3: Collecting Data

Data may be collected from the team members in various ways, but as much information as possible is gathered before the meeting. One source is the data gathered in Stage 3 of the organization change process: the diagnostic process (see chapters 1 and 5). The usefulness of this information depends on the extent to which it can be specifically identified with the team as opposed to the total organization. The members may be given additional questionnaires to fill out, or they may be interviewed by the practitioner. The practitioner may hold small group meetings with a few members at a time. The practitioner also may have a two- to four-hour preteam development meeting with all the members, designed especially to gather information.

## Step 4: Planning the Meeting

The planning session will probably be attended by the practitioner, the manager, and a few of the team members. The actual planning takes place once the data have been analyzed. It is important at this point to restate the goals and objectives as precisely as possible, incorporating information obtained during the preceding step. If the goals are specific behavioral objectives, the remaining work of planning the sequence of events of the meeting will flow more easily and logically. Going through this process will ensure a meeting that satisfies the needs of the participants.

Planning for a team development meeting includes the logistics of the meeting, such as arranging for a time and a place. The planning stage will also ensure that all necessary personnel and resources are available.

## Step 5: Conducting the Meeting

The meeting itself usually lasts two or three days. It is preferable that the physical setting be on neutral territory and away from the work area, such as at an isolated resort. A major reason for this is that it helps to put everyone—superior and subordinate—on a more equal level. It also lessens the opportunities for interruption. The nonworking setting may also help to create a climate for change and exploration of new ideas by the team members. For example, professional football and baseball teams are organizations that locate their training camps long distances from their home base of operations.

The meeting usually begins with a restatement of the previously agreed upon objectives. The data are presented to the entire team, with attention given to problem areas or issues in which the team has expressed an interest, and then the team forms an agenda ranked in order of priority. At this point, the team usually begins to work on the list of priority items. The team critiques its own performance to prevent dysfunctional actions and improve functional activities. If the members feel that this is an opportunity for them to express open and honest feelings without fear of punishment, the leader of the team may come under attack. The premeeting interviews will have shown this possibility, and the practitioner should forewarn and prepare the leader for this eventuality. The success or failure of the team development meeting may depend on how the manager reacts to the situation.

Once the team members have resolved their interpersonal issues, they can move on to the task issues that need to be discussed. The purpose is for the team to develop a specific action plan for improving the ways or processes it uses to reach its organization goals. Before the meeting ends, the team should make a list of action items to be dealt with, a list of who will be responsible for each item, and a time schedule. The team meeting is now officially over, but the list makes it possible for the team development effort to continue back in the work environment. The team agrees on a future date to meet again to evaluate progress on the action items.

## Step 6: Evaluating the Team Development Process

At this meeting, the team examines the action items, exploring those that have been or are being carried out and those that are not working.[27] It determines how well the implemented action items have aided the team's operation and what else can be done. It reconsiders any action items that are not working and discards those that seem unnecessary. Items that appear to be helpful may now be given additional attention and support. The team will also explore how to resolve ongoing problems and what can be done to enhance continuous improvement.

Topics include:

- Methods of resolving ongoing problems.
- Acquiring necessary resources.
- Continuous improvement.

## Results of Team Development Meetings

The research on team building finds that it is very effective and is a popular intervention used in many organizations. An analysis of 126 studies that used OD interventions concluded that attitudes toward others, the job, and the organization were in general positively affected. The analysis found team building to be the most effective OD intervention.[28] Other research points to the importance of team-building exercises in the development of a team, especially if managers are unable to give the team the time needed to develop on its own.[29]

## OUTDOOR EXPERIENTIAL LABORATORY TRAINING

Within the last decade, **outdoor experiential laboratory training** (sometimes called outdoor labs, wilderness labs, adventure learning, or the corporate boot camp) has become a common technique for team development and leadership training.[30] The idea is to take a group of people who normally work with one another and put them in an outdoor setting where they participate in experiential learning exercises. The outdoor setting is very different from the normal work environment; the learning exercises are so varied, and so typically foreign to the background of most participants, that no one has a distinct advantage. Thus the outdoor lab puts participants on an equal footing. This seems to encourage discussion of leadership styles, teamwork, and interpersonal relationships.

The outdoor lab experiences run the spectrum from extreme sports like technical rock climbing to spas at luxury resorts. Some of the labs require severe physical exertion in a setting of some physical danger. One type of outdoor lab has participants doing technical rock climbing where they are working in teams helping one another do climbs that none of them could do alone. Another outdoor lab has participants canoeing or rafting in white water. Rock climbing and canoeing involve physical conditioning and dangerous situations in which not all employees would be willing or able to participate.

Other outdoor labs require very modest physical exertion with almost no element of danger. These labs rely upon props such as ropes stretched between trees that participants must cross. There is an element of perceived risk but the danger has been reduced by relying on safety ropes and nets. At these labs, it is common to rely on the imagination of the participants to create the element of danger. For example, walking a twelve-foot-long, four-by-four-inch board that is one foot off the ground can be an effective learning exercise. Participants are first told to imagine that the board is spanning a moat full of alligators. Having their fellow workers cheering them on to success can build the right atmosphere for the learning exercise.

All the labs, despite the setting or the nature of the exercise, have participants involved in activities that require teamwork and allow opportunities to work on leadership and team development. After an exercise, and normally in the evening, the team spends time with a practitioner critiquing, debriefing, and discussing the exercise and the day's events, with an emphasis upon what they have learned. The learning provides participants with insights into their leadership and interpersonal styles. Participants often learn how to improve their teamwork back on the job. Interpersonal barriers that inhibit effective teamwork are often broken down, and members learn to trust and work with one another. Holding the lifeline for someone suspended off a cliff has a dramatic impact on both parties when they return to work, where they need to trust and depend on one another in a less dramatic setting.

True physical risk taking is not the goal of most outdoor labs. Perceived physical risk makes the exercises exciting so that participants are challenged to do their best. One participant explained, "It felt great. Negotiating the elements takes ingenuity and teamwork. It's about having confidence and taking risks and supporting each other. People broke down a lot of barriers on the ropes course—some of the toughest ones in the office were scared to death up there. Now we're communicating in a whole new way."[31] **OD Application: EcoSeagate and Team Development** discusses an outdoor lab program at Seagate Technology.

---

### OD Application: EcoSeagate and Team Development[32]

Seagate Technology, a manufacturer of computer hard drives, each year spends $2 million on one outdoor lab experience. It calls the lab EcoSeagate and it is where the company brings together 200 of its employees from around the world to a team development meeting in the desolate mountains and glaciers of New Zealand, close to where *Lord of the Rings* was filmed. With such a foreign and intimidating environment, everyone feels off balance and no one has an advantage over anyone else. Prework for the participants is a good deal of physical conditioning and required reading of *The Five Dysfunctions of a Team: A Leadership Fable*.

CEO Bill Watkins started EcoSeagate in 2000, soon after becoming president of Seagate. Watkins says, "They called it Slavegate. People got fired all the time. The CEO had a grenade on his desk." Watkins figured that if he showed the value of teamwork away from work, the participants would transfer the experience back into their work. He says, "I learned a lesson a long time ago in the Army. Nobody really wants to die for their god. No one wants to die for their country. Absolutely no one wants to die for money. But people put their lives on the line for the respect of their platoon mates."

The participants, who are selected from more than 2,000 applicants, consist of a cross-section of the company: top executives, managers, engineers, and factory workers. The 200 participants are split into 40 teams of 5 people. The composition of the teams is made in advance with consideration given to having a mix that includes physical ability, level within the company, sex, nationality, and personality. For five days, the teams go through a variety of competitive events that encourage each team to learn how to work together. EcoSeagate culminates in a 40-kilometer adventure race through a course consisting of biking, climbing, traversing unknown terrain with a vague map, kayaking, traversing canyons on cables, and running.

Watkins has not been able to prove or point to quantitative results of EcoSeagate. He has never won his own race and has even come in dead last. Through the years, he has received criticism from stockholders for the event, and though he can not precisely measure the results, to him there are obvious signs that it is working. "The only thing you know for sure," he says, "is that if you do nothing, then nothing will happen, and nothing will change."

**Questions**

1. What is your opinion of EcoSeagate?
2. Should the CEO attempt to quantify the results? And if so, how? Support your position.
3. Would your class teams benefit from this type of training? How?

Outward Bound, a not-for-profit organization, has been offering outdoor labs for around 70 years and has operations in 35 countries. Beginning in Great Britain in 1941, it was conceived as a program to instill greater self-reliance and spiritual tenacity in young British seamen seeing action against German U-boats. Outward Bound expanded over the years to include experience to gain self-esteem, discover innate abilities, and develop a sense of responsibility toward others.[33] The program initially focused on helping young people develop their potential and to see new possibilities. In the United States and in other countries as well, there is a professional division of OD practitioners that makes Outward Bound the largest team development training organization. It serves more than 7,500 individuals from over 400 organizations throughout the United States every year. Clients include Credit Suisse, Home Depot, JP Morgan Chase, and Pfizer. Jill Serafin, JP Morgan Chase vice president, Markets Training, says, "Outward Bound has promoted partnership, teamwork and leadership amongst our new analysts and associates. The experience has made a positive impact on new hires and demonstrates that the company is committed to developing its junior professionals in creative ways both inside and outside of the classroom. Outward Bound Day is an integral part of our analyst/associate orientation."[34]

The National Outdoor Leadership School (NOLS) is another not-for-profit organization that has a similar orientation to leadership and team development as does Outward Bound. Its consultants in the professional training division can develop a course to meet the needs of a specific organization. In some training programs, such as a week-long hiking expedition, participants will rotate serving as a designated leader for the day while others learn active followership roles to make an optimal team. Time is devoted to individual and team reflection upon the day's activities.[35]

## The Outdoor Lab Process

Outdoor labs are typically offered by specialized training companies. Some organizations that make extensive use of labs, such as Federal Express, operate them through the OD or human resource development division. An outdoor lab has to be fit into a larger program that lays the groundwork for it and follows through after it has ended. Otherwise the lab will be no more than a company retreat offering only short-term gains. Many participants in outdoor labs say that success is directly proportional to the amount of preplanning and follow-up.

Whether the company itself or an outside provider offers the lab, a preliminary assessment of the team and individual needs should be made before the lab occurs. Goals and learning objectives are drawn up. When the outdoor lab is part of an OD team development program, the assessment has already been made, and the lab becomes an integral part of the OD program, like any other OD intervention. An orientation meeting is held with the participants at their work site before the lab begins to explain what will happen at the outdoor lab and why, and to calm fears. A videotape may be shown of other team sessions.

The OD practitioner selects a series of outdoor lab experiences that fit the desired goals and the physical abilities of the team. If the lab is offered by an outside training organization specializing in outdoor labs, a training program is arranged to meet a team's specific objectives. Some providers send their trainers to a company ahead of time to research the needs of the team. In some cases, the OD practitioner may accompany the team at the outdoor lab.

The type of training will dictate the location and facilities. A backpacking trip or rafting trip may take place in the wilderness or a park, a sailboat excursion may be in the Florida Keys, but most training programs are held at private, rural facilities where ropes, platforms, and other props are in place and sleeping and eating facilities are available. A good trainer will be well versed in the organization's jargon and use process consultation techniques.

After the exercises, the trainers ask the team to reflect on the process. Constructive feedback between participants is encouraged. They discuss how they operated as a team, what behaviors were helpful and dysfunctional, what it was like to take a risk and succeed or fail, how it felt to depend on other people, what it was like to give assistance, who acted in leadership roles, and how these observations might apply to the next exercise.

Before returning to the workplace, participants summarize what they have learned and how it applies to their work. Team members draw up goals for what they hope to do back at work and make a plan for how they can accomplish the goals. Back at work, the team holds meetings to define the goals and develop more detailed plans. The trainer will often make a follow-up visit to the work site after several weeks to reinforce the learning that took place at the outdoor lab. The OD practitioner also helps the team continue to work on their goals.

## Cautions When Using Outdoor Labs

Outdoor labs are not without their risks for both the organization and the individual. Most of the problems can be minimized by taking some modest precautions.

The legal aspects of outdoor labs are beyond the scope of this discussion, but as with any work activity, the employer is liable for the health and safety of its employees.[36] Safety should be a major concern, and the safety record of the provider and the trainers should be investigated beforehand. In one case, a participant in a youth-oriented outdoor lab died of dehydration and heat exposure when the trainers and their group got lost in a remote area north of the Grand Canyon. The group consisted of troubled youths, and the trainers had designed the program to help them gain self-esteem and self-control. Although there have been no known deaths in corporate outdoor labs, safety should be a major concern. For both liability and OD philosophical reasons, participation must be voluntary and there should be no coercive pressure. Participants should feel free to decline to participate in specific exercises.

There are fundamental questions about the value of outdoor labs as management training. An AT&T spokesperson says, "These programs can be a colossal waste of money if people don't return with new thinking and an expanded ability to take risks. Unless you follow up, the afterglow tends to wear off as soon as the scabs heal."[37]

Providers of outdoor labs are not regulated, and there is no professional organization that licenses them or serves as a reference. It is easy to get caught up in the flash of the exercises and not give attention to the experiential learning that should be taking place. There should be a balance between exercises and opportunities to discuss the exercises. The trainers should be capable of more than guiding a backpacking group into a wilderness area. They should have much the same training, skills, and experiences as an OD practitioner, and should be selected with similar care.

The labs should not become too serious. Participants should have fun and do not need to be constantly drawing parallels between the lab and the work site. One trip leader on a backpacking trip in the Rocky Mountains recounted the story of a group consisting of a company's CEO and top executives. Halfway through the trip, a manager could no longer carry his pack. The lab leader pointed out that this was a team problem, just as if they were in the workplace. The CEO told the manager to pick up the pack or face being fired. The manager refused and the CEO subsequently fired him. Says the trainer, "That CEO thought everything out there related to the office. One thing it did mirror for sure is that the CEO is a _____ of a _____."[38]

## Results of Outdoor Labs

Outdoor labs have become very popular as a team development and leadership training technique. Major corporations use outdoor labs, and hundreds of smaller profit and not-for-profit organizations have sent employees to labs.

Although the outdoor labs are unquestionably popular, they are still so new that there have not been many studies documenting their effectiveness. As with many other OD interventions, the effectiveness of the techniques is diminished when they are taken out of the context of an OD program and become a fad. If labs are not introduced with planning and followed up correctly, they can become expensive topics of conversation at coffee breaks.

## ROLE ANALYSIS AND ROLE NEGOTIATION

Another team development intervention, called **role analysis** technique, is designed to clarify role expectations.[39] Because team norms influence member behavior, team members form expectations about the behavior of the other members of their team. The sets of behaviors or attitudes associated with the various positions in a team are called roles. Discrepancies sometimes arise between what is expected of a team member's role and the member's actual behavior. A consequence of organizational change is that it causes people to become uncertain about their new and changing roles. Clarifying roles as early as possible helps to reduce the stress associated with the changes. Role analysis is used to clarify such role discrepancies, leading to improved cohesiveness and functioning.

**Role expectations** are the behaviors expected or prescribed for one member of the team (the role incumbent) by the other team members. **Role conception** refers to the focal person's own ideas about appropriate role behavior. **Role ambiguity** is a role incumbent being unaware of or lacking sufficient knowledge about the expectations for the role held by the other team members. In other words, he or she does not fully know what others expect.

**Role conflict** occurs when there is a discrepancy between role expectations and the role conception. Incongruence between formal job descriptions and actual role demands is another source of role conflict. Because the team members have a stake in one another's performance, they develop attitudes and expectations about what members should or should not do in their roles. These expectations are not always in agreement, but role analysis provides a means for dealing with such problems. This intervention is based on the premise that consensual agreement about team member roles will lead to a more productive and satisfied team.

The steps in the role analysis technique are listed below.

1. *Role analysis.* The role incumbent sets forth the role as he or she perceives it, listing perceived duties, behaviors, and responsibilities: the role conception. The other team members add to or modify this list until everyone is satisfied with the role description.
2. *The role incumbent's expectations of others.* The role incumbent lists his or her expectation of other group members. This list describes expectations that affect the incumbent's role and impinge upon his or her performance. Again, the whole team adds to or modifies this list until everyone agrees upon a complete listing.
3. *Role expectations by others.* The other members list their expectations of the role incumbent. This list includes what they expect him or her to do as it affects their role performance. The work team modifies this list until everyone agrees.
4. *Role profile.* Once there is agreement on the role definition, the role incumbent is responsible for making a written summary called a role profile. He or she distributes a copy of the completed role profile to all the other members.
5. *Repeat process.* The team follows the same procedure until every member has a written role profile.
6. *Review.* The team periodically reviews role expectations and role profiles because these may change over time; the group's mission or members may also change.

As with other OD techniques, there are anecdotal reports about the effectiveness of role analysis techniques but little empirical evidence upon which to base a conclusion. According to one study, role analysis is a useful technique for reducing role ambiguity and increasing group effectiveness.[40] Another study found that where job demands were high, both high role clarity and a high degree of latitude in decision making helped individuals cope with work overload and job demands, but only in groups where there was supportive leadership.[41]

**Role negotiation** is another team development intervention similar to role analysis intervention. Role negotiation is directed at the work relationships among team members.[42] The technique involves a series of controlled negotiations between participants. During the role negotiation, team members frankly discuss what they want from one another and explain why. The steps in a role negotiation are listed below.

1. *Contract setting.* Each member prepares a list for each of the other members with three headings: (a) things to do more, (b) things to do less, and (c) things to do the same.
2. *Issue diagnosis.* Each member writes out a master list combining the lists written about him or her and posts it on the wall. Members are asked to clarify any items that need explanation.
3. *Role negotiation.* After the clarification, members decide which items they want to work on most and form into pairs to negotiate, usually with a third party to help in the process.
4. *Written role negotiation agreement.* The outcome of the role negotiation is written down and spells out the agreements and concessions that each party finds satisfactory.

This chapter has focused on developing team effectiveness. In the next chapter, the discussion of OD will move to examining the conditions for conflict and will discuss several techniques for dealing with relations between teams.

## Summary

- **Team Development.** Team development is a major OD intervention. It is a useful and successful vehicle for bringing about significant changes in a team. Team development includes outdoor experiential training, role analysis, and role negotiation Team development is used to increase the communication, cooperation, and cohesiveness of work teams, resulting in increased organizational efficiency. It is important to remember that team development is only a part of an organization-wide change program that values participation, collaboration, and the maximization of the use of human resources.

- **When to Use a Team.** Not all work situations require the use of a team. Simple situations can be solved by an individual. The use of a team in a simple situation could actually impede organizational success. However, where complex situations predominate in a group's work, team development would be highly desirable. The problem-oriented situations that a work group faces require a finely tuned team, and the work group would greatly benefit from team development.

- **Problems of Work Teams.** Problems inevitably occur when a group of people are brought together to work on a common project. Common problems center on differences in member needs, goal disagreements, norms, divergent points of view, different decision-making methods, different leadership styles and ways of administering direction, and too many or too few members.

- **Groupthink.** Work groups can benefit from cohesiveness, but too much cohesiveness can be dysfunctional. When the need for uniformity within a group is greater than the need for high-quality decisions, the situation called "groupthink" occurs. Groupthink is a type of thinking engaged in by members of a work group when they are highly involved in a cohesive in-group and their striving for unanimity overrides the motivation to realistically appraise different courses of action.

- **Team Development Process.** Team development is a process of education for the work team where the team learns new and more effective ways of operating. Team development meetings focus on the processes of how the team operates rather than the product or work of the team.

- **Outdoor Labs.** Outdoor experiential laboratory training has become a common technique used for team development. The labs permit work teams to engage in team training away from the work site and engage in activities like rock climbing and white water rafting, which are very different from work. These situations seem to hasten discussion surrounding leadership styles, teamwork, and interpersonal relationships.

- **Role Analysis and Role Negotiation.** Role analysis allows the participants to clarify their roles and relationships with one another. Role negotiation encourages participants to negotiate and arrive at an agreement on what they expect from one another.

## Review Questions

1. Identify the characteristics of an effective team. Is a golf team really a team, or just a group?
2. Identify and give examples of ways of increasing team effectiveness.
3. Identify the symptoms of groupthink. Explain how groupthink can be avoided through team development.
4. Select an example of groupthink occurring in an organization and critique the results and consequences to that organization. This could be an organization that is familiar to you or one that you have researched.
5. Identify the six steps in the team development process.

## Key Words and Concepts

| | | | |
|---|---|---|---|
| Group Cohesiveness | Outdoor Experiential | Role Conception | Team |
| Groupthink | Laboratory Training | Role Conflict | Team Building |
| Interdependence | Role Ambiguity | Role Expectations | Team Development |
| Natural Work Team | Role Analysis | Role Negotiation | Teamwork |
| | | | Temporary Task Team |

# OD Skills Simulation 10.1

## Organization Task and Process

*Total time suggested: 70 minutes.*

## A. Purpose

The two parameters of team effectiveness are (1) finding the best solution to a problem and (2) completing it in the shortest time.

The purpose of this simulation is to experience and observe parameters of interpersonal and team issues that inhibit effective organizational functioning. Specifically, it is to experience interdependence among members and to observe:

1. How team members share task information.
2. How various problem-solving strategies influence results.
3. How collaboration and competition affect team problem solving.
4. How process interventions are conducted.

## B. Procedures

*Step 1.* During the preceding class, form teams of six members. Extra class members may serve as additional observers. Each individual is to select one role from the following:

1. General Manager, United States plant
2. General Manager, Japan plant
3. General Manager, Germany plant
4. General Manager, Nigeria plant
5. General Manager, Mexico plant
6. Observer(s)

*Step 2.* Following the Energy International Briefing Sheet, you will find role descriptions and the Candidate Summary Sheet. Read the Briefing Sheet, your role description, and Energy International Candidate Summary Sheet before coming to class. Mark your individual decision on the Energy International Decision Form. Try to learn the information in your role description so that you will not have to refer to it in the team meeting.

*Step 3.* Your team is to select the correct candidate based upon the data in the Briefing Sheet, your role description, and the Candidate Summary Sheet. Try to use process interventions at the team meeting. You can refer to your role description, but do *not* read it to your team members. There is one correct solution, and decisions are to be reached independently of the other teams. Mark the team decision on the Energy International Decision Form. There are extra columns on the form that your team can use to make notes or record criteria to help make a decision.

The observers will not take an active part during this phase of the simulation. They will focus on answering the questions in Step 4 of this simulation. All teams will begin upon the signal from the instructor.

*Time suggested for Step 3: 45 minutes.*

*Step 4.* In your teams, consider the following questions, with the observers guiding the discussion:

1. What behaviors seemed to help your team successfully complete its task?
2. What factors inhibited problem solving?
3. How much time was spent on deciding how to solve the problem?
4. How was information shared among the team members?
5. How did issues of authority or power affect the team?
6. How did collaboration and competition influence the outcome?
7. Did team members make process interventions?

*Time suggested for Step 4: 10 minutes.*

*Step 5.* Discuss the questions in Step 4 with the entire class.

*Time suggested for Step 5: 15 minutes.*

## Energy International Briefing Sheet Instructions to the Team[43]

1. You are a committee made up of the general managers of Energy International (E.I.).
2. You have just flown into town.
3. This is the first meeting of the team.
4. You have just learned that E.I. intends to open a new Brazilian plant, and your first job is to select a general manager from among the seven applicants.
5. Basically, the data you bring with you are in your head.

## Assumptions That Need to Be Made Explicit

1. Assume that there is one solution.
2. Assume that all the data are correct.
3. You have 45 minutes to work the exercise.
4. Assume that today's date is April 1, 2010.
5. There must be substantial agreement when the problem has been solved.
6. You must work the problem as a team.

## Role Descriptions (Read Only your Role)

**General Manager, United States Plant.** Your team is a committee made up of the general managers of Energy International (E.I.), a young, medium-sized growing organization. The prime mission of E.I. is to locate and develop mineral claims (copper, uranium, cobalt, etc.).

The company's business has grown rapidly, especially in South America, where your organization has been made welcome by the various governments. At a recent meeting, the board of directors decided to develop a new property near Fortaleza, in northeastern Brazil. The operation will include both mining and milling production.

The date is April 1, 2010. You have come from your respective plants in different locations. This is the initial session of your annual meeting. Your first order of business today is to select a new general manager for the Brazilian plant from among the candidates on the Candidate Summary Sheet.

Fortaleza has a hot climate, one railroad, a scheduled airline, a favorable balance of trade, a feudal attitude toward women, considerable unemployment, a low educational level, a low literacy rate, and a strongly nationalistic regime.

The government has ruled that the company must employ Brazilians in all posts except that of general manager. The government has also installed an official inspector who will make a monthly report to the government. This report must be signed by the company's representative, who must be a fellow of the Institute of Mineralogy.

There are a number of schools offering degrees in mineralogy. The most recently founded is the New Mexico Institute of Earth Sciences, established under a special grant and opened in 1979.

To earn a bachelor's degree in mineralogy, the institute requires geology, seismology, and paleontology, in addition to the usual courses.

**General Manager, Japan Plant.** Your team is a committee made up of the general managers of Energy International (E.I.), a young, medium-sized, growing organization. The prime mission of E.I. is to locate and develop mineral claims (copper, uranium, cobalt, etc.).

The company's business has grown rapidly, especially in South America, where your organization has been made welcome by the various governments. At a recent meeting, the board of directors decided to develop a new property near Fortaleza, in northeastern Brazil. This operation will include both mining and milling production.

The date is April 1, 2010. You have come from your respective plants in different locations. This is the initial session of your annual meeting. Your first order of business today is to select a new general manager for the Brazilian plant from among the candidates on the Candidate Summary Sheet.

Fortaleza has a hot climate, one railroad, a scheduled airline, a favorable balance of trade, a feudal attitude toward women, considerable unemployment, a low educational level, a low literacy rate, and a strongly nationalistic regime.

The government has ruled that the company must employ Brazilians in all posts except that of general manager. It has also installed an official inspector who will make a monthly report, which must be countersigned by the general manager. By law, the general manager must have at least three years experience as a manager in charge of a mining operation.

There are a number of schools offering a degree in mineralogy, a degree essential to qualify for general membership in the Institute of Mineralogy. The smaller universities require three, the larger four, of the following special subjects as a part of their graduation requirements: geology, geophysics, oceanography, paleontology, seismology. The smallest is a women's university.

**General Manager, Germany Plant.** Your team is a committee made up of the general managers of Energy International (E.I.), a young, medium-sized, growing organization. The prime mission of E.I. is to locate and develop mineral claims (copper, uranium, cobalt, etc.).

The company's business has grown rapidly, especially in South America, where your organization has been made welcome by the various governments. At a recent meeting, the board of directors decided to develop a new property near Fortaleza, in northeastern Brazil. This operation will include both mining and milling production.

The date is April 1, 2010. You have come from your respective plants in different locations. This is the initial session of your annual meeting. Your first order of business today is to select a new general manager for the Brazilian plant from among the candidates on the Candidate Summary Sheet.

Fortaleza has a hot climate, one railroad, a scheduled airline, a favorable balance of trade, a feudal attitude toward women, considerable unemployment, a low educational level, a low literacy rate, and a strongly nationalistic regime.

The government has ruled that the company must employ Brazilians in all posts except that of general manager. It has also installed an official inspector who will make a monthly report, which must be countersigned by the company's representative. None of the government inspectors can read or write any language but their own.

There are a number of schools offering degrees in mineralogy, but a passing grade in paleontology is essential to qualify for general membership in the Institute of Mineralogy. The largest university is the New York School of Mines, which requires the following special subjects for graduation: geology, paleontology, geophysics, and seismology.

**General Manager, Nigeria Plant.** Your team is a committee made up of the general managers of Energy International (E.I.), a young, medium-sized, growing organization. The prime mission of E.I. is to locate and develop mineral claims (copper, uranium, cobalt, etc.).

The company's business has grown rapidly, especially in South America, where your organization has been made welcome by the various governments. At a recent meeting, the board of directors decided to develop a new property near Fortaleza, in northeastern Brazil. This operation will include both mining and milling production.

The date is April 1, 2010. You have come from your respective plants in different locations. This is the initial session of your annual meeting. Your first order of business today is to select a new general manager for the Brazilian plant from among the candidates on the Candidate Summary Sheet.

Fortaleza has a hot climate, one railroad, a scheduled airline, a favorable balance of trade, a feudal attitude toward women, considerable unemployment, a low educational level, a low literacy rate, and a strongly nationalistic regime.

The government has ruled that the company must employ Brazilians in all posts except that of general manager. It has also installed an official inspector who will make a monthly report, which must be countersigned by the company's representative. None of the company's employees or staff can read or write any language but Portuguese.

There are a number of schools offering degrees in mineralogy, and a passing grade in seismology is essential to qualify for a general membership in the Institute of Mineralogy. The Massachusetts Institute of Sciences requires the following special subjects for graduation: geology, seismology, oceanography, and paleontology.

**General Manager, Mexico Plant.** Your team is a committee made up of the general managers of Energy International (E.I.), a young, medium-sized, growing organization. The prime mission of E.I. is to locate and develop mineral claims (copper, uranium, cobalt, etc.).

The company's business has grown rapidly, especially in South America, where your organization has been made welcome by the various governments. At a recent meeting, the board of directors decided to develop a new property near Fortaleza, in northeastern Brazil. This operation will include both mining and milling production.

The date is April 1, 2010. You have come from your respective plants in different locations. This is the initial session of your annual meeting. Your first order of business today is to select a new general manager for the Brazilian plant from among the candidates on the Candidate Summary Sheet.

Fortaleza has a hot climate, one railroad, a scheduled airline, a favorable balance of trade, a feudal attitude toward women, considerable unemployment, a low educational level, a low literacy rate, and a strongly nationalistic regime.

The government has ruled that the company must employ Brazilians in all posts except that of general manager. It has also installed an official inspector who will make a monthly report, which must be countersigned by the company's representative, who must be an American citizen.

Fellowship in the Institute of Mineralogy can be obtained by men over 35 years of age who have otherwise qualified for general membership in the institute. St. Francis University, which is not the smallest school, requires the following special courses for graduation: paleontology, geophysics, and oceanography.

# ENERGY INTERNATIONAL CANDIDATE SUMMARY SHEET

## *Part 1*

| | |
|---|---|
| *Name:* | R. Illin |
| *Date of birth:* | March 2, 1975 |
| *Passport:* | L3452—U.S.A. |
| *Education:* | New York School of Mines, degree in mineralogy, 1995 |
| *Employment:* | Research Assistant, New York School of Mines, 1996–1998 |
| | Lecturer, Mineralogy, University of Bonn, 2004–2008 |
| | Manager, Utah Copper Mining Co. Plant, 2008 to date |
| *Language command:* | English, French, German, Portuguese |

| | |
|---|---|
| *Name:* | S. Hule |
| *Date of birth:* | May 4, 1967 |
| *Passport:* | H4567—U.S.A. |
| *Education:* | New Mexico Institute of Earth Sciences, degree in mineralogy, 1993 |
| *Employment:* | Uranium Unlimited, Management Trainee, 1993–1995 |
| | Anaconda Copper Co. (Montana area), Geology Officer, 1996–2003 |
| | Manager, Irish Mining Co. Ltd., 2003 to date |
| *Language command:* | English, French, Portuguese |

| | |
|---|---|
| *Name:* | T. Gadolin |
| Date of birth: | June 5, 1968 |
| *Passport:* | L7239—U.S.A. |
| *Education:* | New York School of Mines, degree in mineralogy, 1993 |
| *Employment:* | United Kingdom Mining Board, Management Trainee, 1993–1995 |
| | Assistant Manager, N.D.B. Cheshire Plant, 1996–2004 |
| | Manager, Idaho Cobalt Minerals, 2004 to date |
| *Language command:* | English, Portuguese |

| | |
|---|---|
| *Name:* | U. Samar |
| *Date of birth:* | April 5, 1976 |
| *Passport:* | H6259—U.S.A. |
| *Education:* | Massachusetts Institute of Sciences, degree in mineralogy, 1997 |
| *Employment:* | Junior Engineer, West Virginia Mining Research Station, 1997–2006 |
| | General Manager, Liberian State Mining Plant, 2006 to date |
| *Language command:* | English, German, Swahili, Portuguese |

| | |
|---|---|
| *Name:* | V. Lute |
| *Date of birth:* | August 6, 1973 |
| *Passport:* | K62371—U.S.A. |
| *Education:* | New York School of Mines, degree in mineralogy, 1994 |
| *Employment:* | Junior Development Mineralogist, Ontario Mining Construction Ltd., 1994–1997 |
| | Assistant Chief Mineralogy Officer, Canadian Development Board, 1998–2001 |
| | Plant Manager, Welsh Mining Co. Ltd., 2002 to date |
| *Language command:* | English, French, Welsh, Pekingese |

**ENERGY INTERNATIONAL CANDIDATE SUMMARY SHEET**

*Part 2*

| | |
|---|---|
| *Name:* | W. Noddy |
| *Date of birth:* | August 7, 1966 |
| *Passport:* | H63241—U.S.A. |
| *Education:* | St. Francis University, degree in mineralogy, 1991 |
| *Employment:* | Assistant Manager, Société Debunquant d'Algérie, 1991–1995 |
| | Manager, Kemchatka Mining Co., 1996 to date |
| *Language command:* | English, Portuguese, Russian, Arabic |
| | |
| *Name:* | X. Lanta |
| *Date of birth:* | September 8, 1973 |
| *Passport:* | Q123YB–Canada |
| *Education:* | University of Quebec, Diploma in English, 1993 |
| | Massachusetts Institute of Sciences, degree in mineralogy, 1996 |
| *Employment:* | Technical Officer, Sardinia Mining Corp., 1998–2006 |
| | Manager, Moab Valley Mining Plant, 2006 to date |
| *Language command:* | Spanish, English, Portuguese |

# ENERGY INTERNATIONAL DECISION FORM

| Candidate | Individual Decision | Notes or criteria to be developed by team (not required) | | | | | Team Decision |
|-----------|--------------------|----------------------------------------------------------|---|---|---|---|---------------|
| R.Illin | | | | | | | |
| S. Hule | | | | | | | |
| T. Gadolin | | | | | | | |
| U. Samar | | | | | | | |
| V. Lute | | | | | | | |
| W. Noddy | | | | | | | |
| X. Lanta | | | | | | | |

# OD Skills Simulation 10.2

## Team Development

*Total time suggested: 80 minutes.*

### A. Purpose

To provide an opportunity for team members to diagnose and analyze their team functioning and to work on improving team processes.

### B. Procedures

*Step 1.* Form into the same teams, including the observers, as in Simulation 10.1. Work individually. Using Simulation 10.1 as a source of information, complete the Team Development Profile and the Decision Critique Form.

*Step 2.* Working with your team, collect data on team roles from Step 1 by summarizing and categorizing the data using a blackboard or newsprint.

*Time suggested for Steps 1 and 2: 30 minutes.*

*Step 3.* Team members analyze and discuss team functioning. Members may practice process practitioner interventions (see "Suggested Process Interventions" after Step 5). The analysis may include the following questions:

1. How good was our problem-solving capability?
2. How was our decision-making done?
3. How well did we utilize team resources?
4. How did members' behavior influence effectiveness?

*Time suggested for Step 3: 20 minutes.*

*Step 4.* Working in teams, develop a list of actions that will help improve team functioning for future team projects.

*Time suggested for Step 4: 15 minutes.*

*Step 5.* Each team shares its list and action plans from Step 4, and the class discusses the team development process.

*Time suggested for Step 5: 15 minutes.*

## SUGGESTED PROCESS INTERVENTIONS

- Try to focus your questions on the problem that seems to be emerging.
- Encourage the speakers to be specific.
- Be aware of who is and who is not talking and who talks to whom.
- Questions about how people are feeling at the moment are appropriate. As an example, asking a member, "How did you feel when X said _____ to you?" might be appropriate.
- Explore feelings with the purpose of discovering how they are helping or hindering the problem's solution.

**TEAM DEVELOPMENT PROFILE**

*Instructions:* Based upon Simulation 10.1, answer the following questions:

1. Name the two team members who had the most influence on the outcome.

   _____        _____

2. Name the two team members who talked the least.

   _____        _____

3. Name the two team members who talked the most.

   _____        _____

4. Name the two team members who tried to keep the team warm, happy, and comfortable.

   _____        _____

5. Name the two team members who competed or conflicted the most.

   _____        _____

6. Name the two team members who avoided or smoothed over conflicts.

   _____        _____

7. Name the two team members you would most like to work with on another project.

   _____        _____

8. Name the two team members who were most concerned with the accomplishment of the task.

   _____        _____

9. If your team was a sports, what sporting event would best describe your team behavior (for example, golf, football, roller derby, baseball, professional tag-team wrestling, track, or basketball)? Why did you choose this sport? What would be your and your opponent's score?

   _____

   _____

   _____

   _____

10. Was it difficult for you to answer the previous questions, especially questions 1 through 8? Why?

    _____

    _____

    _____

    _____

**DECISION CRITIQUE FORM**

*Instructions:* For each item, place a number in the blank to the right representing your reaction to how your team performed based on the following scale.

[Low    1  :  2  :  3  :  4  :  5  :  6  :  7  :  8  :  9    High]

1. Cooperative teamwork                                       _____

2. Team motivation                                            _____

3. Member satisfaction                                        _____

4. Information sharing (participation)                        _____

5. Consensual decision making                                _____

6. Conflict directly faced and resolved                      _____

7. Quality of team decisions                                 _____

8. Speed with which decision is made                         _____

9. Participating leadership                                   _____

10. Clarity of goals                                         _____

# OD Skills Simulation 10.3

## Role Analysis Team Development

*Total time suggested: 80 minutes.*

## A. Purpose

To give you practice in the role analysis technique of team development.

## B. Procedures

*Step 1.* Form into the same teams as in Simulation 10.1. The observers in Simulation 10.1 will help the team using process interventions. (Observers: See "Suggested Process Interventions" in Simulation 10.2.) Select one manager at a time to serve as the role incumbent. The team works through Steps 2 through 4 until a role profile has been made for each manager. Large newsprint pads will be helpful to record the information so that all the team members can see the recorded information.

*Step 2. Role conception.* The role incumbent sets forth the role as he or she perceives it, listing the perceived duties, behaviors, and responsibilities. Other team members add to or modify this list until everyone is satisfied with the role description.

*Step 3. The role incumbent's expectations of others.* The role incumbent lists his or her expectation of other team members. This list describes those expectations of others that affect the incumbent's role and impinge upon his or her performance. Again, the team adds to or modifies this list until a complete listing is agreed upon.

*Step 4. Role expectations by others.* The other members list their expectations of the role incumbent. This list includes what they expect the incumbent to do as it affects their role performance. The list is modified until it is agreed upon by the entire team.

*Time suggested for Steps 2 through 4 for all managers: 50 minutes.*

*Step 5. Role profile.* After all the managers have participated in Steps 2 through 4, each manager working alone makes a written summary called a role profile. The managers share their profiles with the rest of the team.

*Time suggested for Step 5: 15 minutes.*

*Step 6.* As a team and then with the entire class, critique the effectiveness of the role analysis technique as a method for team development. Also consider the following questions:

1. What are its advantages and disadvantages?
2. How did the observers help? Any suggestions for improvement?
3. What would be the next step in team development if your team was a management team at Energy International?

*Time suggested for Step 6: 15 minutes.*

## CASE: STEELE ENTERPRISES

### The PR Dinner

Gene Robertson, public relations director of Steele Enterprises, knew there was trouble as soon as he saw the room. Instead of bars set up with shiny glasses and fine liqueurs, and staffed by impeccably dressed bartenders, there was chaos. Tables of hors d'oeuvres were there, but with no semblance of order. Flowers had been delivered, but were not placed. Cocktail tables and other furniture were still stacked. Thank God I'm early, he thought.

Richard Leeman (chemical, public relations chief) and Donna Olson (mechanical, public relations chief) were arguing—really going at it—while Judy Fields and Joe Maxwell stood by with looks of distress on their faces. Gene hurried over to intervene.

This was not the time for those two to get into it again. Not with more than 50 marketing representatives and buyers—ambassadors for 20 of the primary marketing outlets to which Steele Enterprises sold most of its goods—arriving in about an hour and a half. There is still time to put this thing together, he thought wearily. See Figure 10.4 for Steele's organization chart.

"OK, what's this all about?" Gene asked, as he carefully but easily slid between the two.

"God, am I glad to see you!" gasped Donna, as she tried to catch her breath. "Dick is just being unreasonable about this whole . . ."

"Unreasonable!" yelled Dick. "If Judy and I hadn't happened by, the cost of the hors d'oeuvres alone would be more than we'd planned on for the whole works! As it is, we'll exceed the budget by nearly $4,000!"

"OK, calm down," Gene soothed, as he gently but firmly eased Dick a couple of more feet away from Donna. "Now, one at a time, you first, Donna. What is going on?"

Donna, still angry, was at least breathing more normally by this time. "You told us to get the best for this party," she said accusingly." We told the catering manager to bring out his best stock and get us a classy spread of heavy hors d'oeuvres, but to stay within the $18,000 figure, with labor extra. Things were going great until Dick showed up. Then he started nosing around, asking questions, giving orders, and has things all fouled up! Just look!" She waved her arms around the room, indicating the mess.

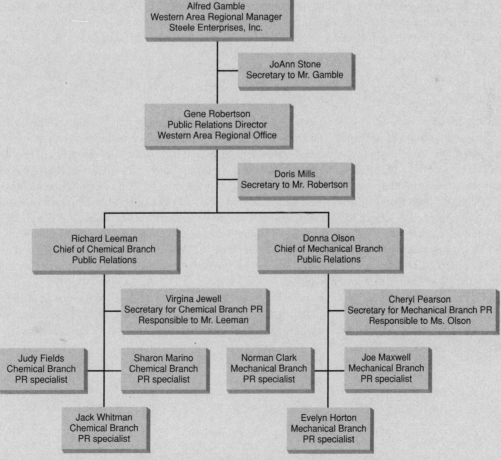

**FIGURE 10.4   Organization Chart for Steel Enterprises, Inc., Western Region, Public Relations Division**

"Not true!" gritted Dick through clenched teeth. "When Judy and I got here, neither one of these two were in sight, the catering manager was trying to find out what was going on, and his cost sheet showed $21,500 instead of $18,000. I've canceled escargot, lobster tails, and the burgundy-soaked tenderloin strips, and told them to hold the liquor prices to a maximum of $40 a bottle, except for the liqueurs. Even with the cuts, food costs are going to be nearly $4,000 above our maximum estimate, because they've already got some oysters shelled, crab legs cracked, and shrimp peeled!"

"Hold it! Time out! Stop!" said Gene, appraising the situation. "We'll sort out who did what to whom later. Right now, we still have time to pull this thing back together and keep all our necks out of the nooses! Now, here's how we're going to handle this . . ."

By the time the PR staff had been given their assignments (in clear, concise language, with no room for arguments), and by the time he had finished haggling with the catering manager (which cost him $300 under the table), getting the party cost down to within $2,000 of the estimated tab, and by the time the party was over (2:30 A.M.), Gene was really beat. It will be good to get home, he thought.

## The Aftermath

Gene came in about 11:00 A.M. the next day and, after finishing up the paperwork from the morning's mail, went to lunch. Something has to give around here, he thought. His secretary, Doris Mills, could see the consternation on his face as they sat down at the table.

"Are those two going at it again?" she asked when he finally came back to earth.

"If you mean Dick and Donna, yes," he replied. "I've just got to do something with them. I've never had two more capable people running those branches, and I don't think they've ever had a more capable staff. But this constant fighting between them just has to stop or I'm going to have to get rid of somebody, and I really wouldn't like to do that, especially with that kind of talent. Even Mr. Gamble has kind of joked around the fact that the competition must be fierce in the PR business!" Gene looked thoughtfully at Doris. "Have you heard anything from JoAnn Stone?"

"Not about the bickering between Dick and Donna," replied Doris. "And if anything was wrong at the party, it never got passed through the grapevine."

"Well, that's something," sighed Gene. "The three hundred bucks I slipped to that jerk at the hotel to fix up the bill can at least be taken care of on the expense account. I'll call it incidental expenses or something." As Doris ordered lunch, Gene thought, "How lucky I am to have an efficient, competent secretary, who keeps her eyes and ears open and her mouth shut. I think she's about due for a raise."

## The Problem

Later that afternoon, in the privacy of his office, Gene thought about the problems he was having with his staff: Dick, Ginny, Judy, Jack, and Sharon in the chemical branch, and Donna, Cheryl, Norm, Ev, and Joe in the mechanical branch. We have the business and the budget to need that many people; the boss seems pleased with what we do; good, sharp people, every one of them, and yet a hell of a lot of fighting between the two branches. So far the staff under Dick and Donna hasn't taken up the battle flags, but if I don't do something pretty soon, even that could happen, thought Gene. And the chemical/mechanical split suggested by Mr. Gamble, even though it's not working as it should, is out of my hands, isn't it? worried Gene as he reviewed the backgrounds of the respective branch leaders. Something's wrong here, but what? he wondered. Maybe it's the technical breakdown, maybe we're not definite enough about which branch should work with which companies. And that fiasco last night—why did Dick come roaring in and try to take over when I thought I had made it clear that Donna and her staff were to run that show? My orders were pretty clear, thought Gene, as he tried to assure his nagging conscience that he was doing a good job directing the PR efforts in the western region.

Good grief, I need a referee! thought Gene as he reviewed seven cases in the last six months in which he had had to intervene between Dick and Donna. Maybe I should try to trade one of them for Bob Lyons at the central region office at St. Louis, he mused, still feeling that he was, somehow, responsible for the conflicts.[44] (Use the Case Analysis Form on the following page.)

**STEELE ENTERPRISES CASE ANALYSIS FORM**

Name: _____

I. Problems

  A. Macro

    1. _____

    _____

    2. _____

    _____

  B. Micro

    1. _____

    _____

    2. _____

    _____

II. Causes

    1. _____

    _____

    2. _____

    _____

    3. _____

    _____

III. Systems affected

    1. _____

    _____

    2. _____

    _____

    3. _____

    _____

IV. Alternatives

    1. _____

    _____

    2. _____

    _____

    3. _____

    _____

V. Recommendations

_____

_____

_____

_____

_____

_____

## Chapter 10 Endnotes

1. J.A. Espinosa, J.N. Cummings, B.M. Pearce, and J.M. Wilson, "Research on Teams with Multiple Boundaries," *Proceedings of the 35th Hawaii International Conference on System Sciences*, 2002; Rob Cross, Kate Ehrlich, Ross Dawson, and John Helferich "Managing Collaboration: Improving Team Effectiveness through a Network Perspective," *California Management Review*, vol. 50, no. 4 (Summer 2008), pp. 74–98.

2. For additional information, see Steve W. J. Kozlowski and Daniel R. Ilgen, "Enhancing the Effectiveness of Work Groups and Teams," *Psychological Science in the Public Interest*, vol. 7, no. 3 (December 2006), pp. 77–124; Clayton P. Alderfer, "Group and Intergroup Relations," in J. R. Hackman and J. L. Suttle (eds.), *Improving the Quality of Work Life* (Palisades, CA: Goodyear, 1977) pp. 227–96; Jon R. Katzenbach and Douglas K. Smith, "The Discipline of Teams," *Harvard Business Review*, March/April 1993, pp. 111–20.

3. For additional information on teams and the management of teams, see Leigh L. Thompson, *Making the Team, A Guide for Managers* (Upper Saddle River, NJ: Pearson Education, 2008).

4. For additional information on teams, see Richard Hackman, *Leading Teams: Setting the Stage for Great Performances* (Boston, MA: Harvard Business School Press, 2002); Lee G. Bolman and Terrence E. Deal, "What Makes a Team Work?" *Organizational Development,* vol. 21, no. 2 (Autumn 1992), pp. 34–44; Richard Hackman, *Groups That Work (and Those That Don't): Creating Conditions for Effective Teamwork* (San Francisco: Jossey-Bass, 1990).

5. Gary Hamel, "Break Free," *Fortune*, October 1, 2007, pp. 119–26.

6. Peter Strozniak, "Teams at Work," *Industry Week*, vol. 249, no. 15 (September 9, 2000), p. 47.

7. Robert W. Keidel, "Baseball, Football, and Basketball: Models for Business," *Organizational Dynamics*, Winter 1984, pp. 5–18.

8. K. Kim Fisher, "Managing in the High-Commitment Workplace," *Organizational Dynamics*, Winter 1989, p. 38.

9. Peter Burrows, "Cisco Seizes the Moment," *Business Week*, May 25, 2009, pp. 46–8; Rik, Kirkland, "Cisco's Display of Strength," *Fortune*, November 12, 2007, pp. 90–100; William M. Bulkeley, "Better Virtual Meetings," *Wall Street Journal*, September 28, 2006, p. B1; Patricia Sellers, "P&G: Teaching an Old Dog New Tricks," *Fortune*, May 31, 2004, pp.167–74; Michael Totty, "Business Solutions," *Wall Street Journal*, May 24, 2004, p. R4; Heather Green, "The Web Smart," *Business Week*, November 24, 2003, pp. 82–106; Randy Emelo and Laura M. Francis, "Virtual Team Interaction," *T + D,* vol. 56, no. 10 (October 2002), pp. 17–19; Drew Robb, "Collaboration Gets It Together," *Computerworld*, vol. 36, no. 50 (December 9, 2002), p. 29.

10. For additional information, see Sharon Peck, "No Easy Roads to Employee Involvement," *Academy of Management Executive*, vol. 12, no. 3 (August 1998), pp. 83–85; John Syer and Christopher Connolly, *How Teamwork Works: The Dynamics of Effective Team Development* (London: McGraw-Hill, 1996); William G. Dyer, (Reading, MA: Addison-Wesley, 1987); Richard E. Walton, *Managing Conflict, Interpersonal Dialogue and Third-Party Roles* (Reading, MA: Addison-Wesley, 1987).

11. Peter Burrows, "Cisco's Comeback," *Business Week*, November 24, 2003, p. 124.

12. Marvin R. Weisbord, "Team Effectiveness Theory," *Training and Development Journal*, vol. 39, no. 1 (January 1985), p. 27.

13. For an in-depth discussion, see Rosabeth Moss Kanter, *The Change Masters: Innovation for Productivity in the American Corporation* (New York: Simon & Schuster, 1983); K. W. Thomas and W. H. Schmidt, "A Survey of Managerial Interest with Respect to Conflict," *Academy of Management Journal*, vol. 19, no. 2 (June 1976), pp. 315–18.

14. Warren Bennis, "The End of Leadership: Exemplary Leadership Is Impossible without Full Inclusion, Initiatives, and Cooperation of Followers," *Organizational Dynamics*, vol. 28, no.1 (Summer 1999), pp. 71–80; Sandra L. Robinson and Anne M. O'Leary Kelly, "Monkey See, Monkey Do: The Influence of Work Groups on the Antisocial Behavior of Employees," *Academy of Management Journal*, vol. 41, no. 6 (December 1998), pp. 658–73; Toby J. Tetenbaum, "Shifting Paradigms: From Newton to Chaos," *Organizational Dynamics*, vol. 26, no. 4 (Spring 1998), pp. 21–33; E. A. Mannix, L. L. Thompson, and M. H. Bazerman, "Negotiation in Small Groups," *Journal of Applied Psychology*, vol. 74, no. 3 (June 1989), pp. 508–17; L. L. Thompson, E. A. Mannix, and M. H. Bazerman, "Group Negotiations: Effects of Decision Rule, Agenda, and Aspiration," *Journal of Personality and Social Psychology*, vol. 54, no. 1 (January 1988), pp. 86–95; Kanter, *The Change Masters: Innovation for Productivity in the American Corporation.*

15. Diane Coutu (interviewer), "Why Teams Don't Work," *Harvard Business Review*, May 2009, p. 101.

16. Joseph Weber, "J. P. Morgan Is in for a Shock," *Business Week*, February 2, 2004, p. 67.

17. Gary Hamel, "Break Free!" *Fortune*, October 1, 2007, p. 124.

18. Kozlowski, "Enhancing the Effectiveness of Work Groups and Teams," p. 88; N. Gross, and W. E. Martin, "On Group Cohesiveness," *American Journal of Sociology*, vol. 57, no. 6 (May 1952), pp. 546–54; J. R. Hackman, "Group Influences on Individuals," in M. D. Dunnette (ed.), *Handbook of Industrial and Organizational Psychology* (Chicago: Rand McNally, 1976), pp. 1455–1525; C. R. Evans, and K. L. Dion, "Group Cohesion and Performance: A Meta-Analysis," *Small Group Research*, vol. 22, no. 2 (May 1991), pp. 175–86.

19. Irving Janis, *Groupthink*, 2nd ed. (Boston: Houghton Mifflin, 1982), p. 9. See also Karen A. Jehn, "A Multi-Method Examination of the Benefits and Detriments of Intragroup Conflict," *Administrative Science Quarterly*, vol. 40, no. 2 (June 1995), pp. 256–283.

20. Stuart Silverstein, "Corporate Communications Gap Keeps Executives, Lower Ranks in the Dark," *Los Angeles Times*, January 10, 1999, p. C5.

21. Janis, *Groupthink*.

22. Richardson Ahlfinger, and James K. Esser, "Testing the Groupthink Model: Effects of Promotional Leadership and Conformity Predisposition," *Social Behavior and Personality*, vol. 29, no. 1 (February 2001), pp. 31–42.

23. Astrid C. Homan, John R. Hollenbeck, Stephen E. Humphrey, Daan Van Knippenberg, Daniel R. Ilgen, and Gerben A. Van Kleef, "Facing Differences With an Open Mind: Openness to Experience, Salience of Intragroup Differences, and Performance of Diverse Work Groups," *Academy of Management Journal*, vol. 51, no. 6 (December 2008), pp. 1204–22; George A. Neuman, Stephen H. Wagner, and Neil D. Christiansen, "The Relationship Between Work-Team Personality, Composition, and the Job Performance of Teams," *Group and Organization Management*, vol. 24, no.1 (March 1999), p. 28–46; Glen Whyte, "Groupthink Reconsidered," *Academy of Management Review*, vol. 14, no.1 (January 1989), pp. 40–56.

24. Transcript of President-Elect Barack Obama announcing National Security Team on December 1, 2008, *Daily Compilation of Presidential Documents*, National Archives and Records Administration, available at www.gpoaccess.gov/presdocs/index.html; transcript of President-Elect Barack Obama announcing the Economic Recovery Advisory Board on November 26, 2008, *Daily Compilation of Presidential Documents*, National Archives and Records Administration, available at www.gpoaccess.gov/presdocs/index.html; transcript of President-Elect Barack Obama announcing the Economic Recovery Advisory Board on February 6, 2009, *Daily Compilation of Presidential Documents*, National Archives and Records Administration, available at www.gpoaccess.gov/presdocs/index.html.

25. Peter Gent, *North Dallas Forty* (New York: William Morrow, 1973), p. 264. Also a motion picture.

26. For additional information, see Shari Caudron, "Keeping Team Conflict Alive," *Training and Development Journal*, vol. 52, no. 9 (September 1998), pp. 48–53; Paul B. Thornton, "Teamwork: Focus, Frame, Facilitate," *Management Review*, vol. 81, no.11 (November 1992), pp. 46–47; Richard Beckhard, *Organization Development: Strategies and Models* (Reading, MA: Addison-Wesley, 1969); Jack Fordyce and Raymond Weil, *Managing with People* (Reading, MA: Addison-Wesley, 1971).

27. For additional information, see Fran Rees, "Reaching High Levels of Performance through Team Self-Evaluation," *Journal for Quality and Participation*, vol. 22, no. 4 (July/August 1999), pp. 37–39.

28. G. A. Neuman, J. E. Edwards, and N. S. Raju, "Organizational Development Interventions: A Meta-Analysis of Their Effects on Satisfaction and Other Attitudes," *Personnel Psychology*, vol. 42, no. 3 (September 1989), pp. 461–89; R. A. Guzzo, R. D. Jette, and R. A. Katzell, "The Effects of Psychologically Based Intervention Programs on Worker Productivity: A Meta-Analysis," *Personnel Psychology*, vol. 38, no. 2 (Summer 1985), pp. 275–91.

29. Brian D. Janz, Jason A. Colquitt, and Raymond A. Noe, "Knowledge Worker Team Effectiveness: The Role of Autonomy, Interdependence, Team Development, and Contextual Support Variables," *Personnel Psychology*, vol. 50, no. 4 (Winter 1997), pp. 877–905.

30. For a more complete description of outdoor labs, see Jack Szwergold, "When Work Has You Climbing Trees," *Management Review*, vol. 82, no. 9 (September 1993), p. 6; Glenn Tarullo, "Making Outdoor Experiential Training Work," *Training*, vol. 29, no. 8 (August 1992), pp. 47–52; Robert Carey, "Go Take a Flying Leap (for the Company)," *Successful Meetings*, vol. 41, no. 7 (June 1992), pp. 59–62; Jennifer Laabs, "Team Training Goes Outdoors," *Personnel Journal*, vol. 70, no. 6 (June 1991), pp. 56–63; Alex Prud'homme, "Management Training No Longer Means Seminars in Self-Discovery," *Business Month*, March 1990, pp. 61–66.

31. Prud'homme, "Management Training," p. 61.

32. Jeffrey M. O'Brien, "Team Building in Paradise," *Fortune*, May 26, 2008, pp. 113–22.

33. For additional information on Outward Bound see www.outwardbound.org.

34. Ibid; see the same Web site for case studies from corporate participants. For a description of an Outward Bound course, see Ruth Le Pla, "Outward Bound," *New Zealand Management*, vol. 49, no. 8 (September 2002), p. 54.

35. For more information on the National Outdoor Leadership School, see www.nols.edu.

36. For a more detailed discussion of the legal risks, see Susan Chesteen, Lee Caldwell, and Larry Prochazka, "Taking Legal Risks Out of Adventure Training," *Training and Development Journal*, vol. 42, no. 7 (July 1988), pp. 42–46.

37. Prud'homme, "Management Training," p. 66.

38. Ibid.

39. Wendell L. French and Cecil H. Bell Jr., *Organization Development: Behavioral Science Interventions for Organization Improvement*, 2nd ed. (Upper Saddle River, NJ: Prentice Hall, 1978).

40. I. Dayal and J. Thomas, "Operation KPE: Developing a New Organization," *Journal of European Industrial Training*, vol. 6, no. 7 (1982), pp. 25–27.

41. Paul D. Bliese and Carl Andre Castro, "Role Clarity, Work Overload and Organizational Support: Multilevel Evidence of the Importance of Support," *Work & Stress*, vol.14, no.1 (January 2000), p. 65.

42. This method of role negotiation was developed by Roger Harrison, see Roger Harrison, "When Power Conflicts Trigger Team Spirit," *European Business*, Spring 1972, pp. 27–65.

43. J. William Pfeiffer and John E. Jones (ed.), *The 1972 Annual Handbook for Group Facilitators*. Copyright © 1972 by John Wiley & Sons. Reproduced with permission of John Wiley & Sons, Inc.

44. This case was written by Major K. Funk, USAF, Fairchild AFB, and is used by permission. Modified and edited by Don Brown.

# Intergroup Development

## LEARNING OBJECTIVES

**Upon completing this chapter, you will be able to:**

1. Identify problems of intergroup conflict and suboptimization.
2. Experience the negative effects of competition on organization effectiveness.
3. Observe and develop strategies for collaborative intergroup relations.
4. Diagnose the causes of cooperative versus competitive group relations.

## PREMEETING PREPARATION

1. Read Chapter 11.
2. Prepare for OD Skills Simulation 11.1. Read and familiarize yourself with the rules and procedures of the Disarmament Game. Complete Step 1.3.
3. Read and analyze Case: The Exley Chemical Company.

## CHANGING RELATIONSHIPS

In a world of change, companies are reexamining and reinventing the way they are organized and managed. In order to improve competitiveness, increase productivity, and reduce costs, managers are concentrating their efforts on shared responsibilities among work teams. At GE Medical Systems, for example, interrelated teams are formed around core processes focusing on customer satisfaction. And at other organizations, new product development teams are globally dispersed.[1]

One key area in the improvement of organization effectiveness involves the relation between operating groups or departments. Complex organizations tend to create situations of **team interdependence,** where the performance of one group is contingent upon the assistance and performance of another group. Manufacturing depends upon engineering, production upon purchasing, marketing upon production, and so on. Consequently, managers must operate and function in an interdepartmental environment. United Technologies Corp's chairman and former CEO, George David, said of team interdependence and teamwork in a *Wall Street Journal* interview, "What goes on in a big sailboat is a combination of preparation, organization, design, strategy, tactics, rules, teamwork, individual performance and group performance. On a 50-footer, you race with a dozen people in a congested space. When you drop a new crew person in, every now and then you may get an elbow in the face. It's because you and that person don't know how you're going to move relative to one another. That's the same thing in the business; you don't want an elbow in the face."[2]

Clearly, an important dimension in organization development is the interface between operating groups. People and groups in organizations often fail to cooperate with others, and in fact may be in open conflict. Customers all too frequently go to a business, a government agency, or some other type of organization seeking help with a problem and are shunted back and forth among departments, with each employee saying, "It's not my job. You need to see someone else in another department." These situations can be very frustrating, and one may wonder whether these people ever talk to one another. As a result, the organization may lose business to a competitor. Employees of an organization seeking to resolve a problem or simply to do their job can also get the bureaucratic runaround from other employees. These are the operating problems that often lead to intergroup conflict.

All organization systems are formed of subsystems: divisions, functions, departments, and work teams. Every work team develops its own norms, goals, and behaviors, and these forces contribute to the group's cohesiveness and morale. When two teams are highly interdependent, misunderstandings or conflict may develop between them. Groups in conflict with one another spend a good deal of their effort, time, and energy on the conflict instead of on goal accomplishment.

Because of these problems, one set of OD interventions aims specifically at improving interdepartmental interfaces and intergroup operating problems. Such interventions attempt to bring underlying problems to the surface and use joint problem solving to correct misperceptions between groups and reopen channels of communication.

The emphasis in Chapter 10 was on developing an effective team. This chapter looks at developing effective working methods between teams. We examine the conditions for conflict and discuss several techniques for dealing with intergroup relations. An organization may have different functional or operating groups, each with its own specialized tasks and goals, but there must be coordinated effort if the organization is to achieve excellence.

Though Harley-Davidson Motor Co. has encountered challenges over the past 25 years, it has been able to solve its problems. But with substantial changes within the last few years in the demographics of the consumer and reductions in consumer spending on luxury goods, Harley's sales have been negatively affected. One asset that Harley has and cannot afford to lose is its reputation in the motorcycle community for building excellent quality motorcycles. So that it can maintain this reputation, one of its newest manufacturing facilities was designed and built around work teams. More about these teams and the way they work together is in **OD Application: Harley-Davidson's Plant Run by Work Teams.**

## OD Application: Harley-Davidson's Plant Run by Work Teams[3]

From humble beginnings in a Milwaukee shed where William Harley and Andrew Davidson first collaborated in 1903, the Harley-Davidson Motor Co. manufactures motorcycles that are known throughout the world. Their owners affectionately call their motorcycles Hogs, and on the New York Stock Exchange their ticker symbol is HOG.

The company has been through some rough times. It faced near bankruptcy in the mid-1980s, but then had 21 straight years of record net revenue and net income. That winning streak came to an end in 2007, and again Harley is facing significant challenges. Consumer demographics have changed, and this does not bode well for Harley. The median age of the Harley buyer has been rising and is currently around 47. He is male, has an income of $83,000, and has at least two years of college education. As the baby boomers get older, they are more likely to be moving toward recreational vehicles than riding Hogs. All of this points to a declining customer base. To reduce this effect, Harley has been trying to attract a younger and a more diverse set of riders, including women. For example, it has introduced models that are more comfortable and have less vibration. With only 20 percent of sales outside of the United States, Harley is trying to tap into new markets by increasing its sales in Europe and Asia. Further complicating Harley's declining sales and profits is a worldwide recession that has hit it on several fronts. In addition to lower demand, it is more difficult for buyers to secure loans on a motorcycle starting around $20,000. And as it turns out, Harley's in-house financing division had been fueling sales by making loans to subprime borrowers with no money down. When credit markets dried up in 2008 and 2009, so did Harley's sales.

With all of these challenges, Harley is trying to develop new strategies to build its company. Its new CEO, Keith Wandell, says that his first objective will be crafting a long-term vision for the company. "If you're only working on today and tomorrow, then things are going to stall out," he said. One example of what Harley is doing is to build on its employees' strengths. This can be seen at its relatively new Kansas City plant. Here it is empowering its employees and building a plant around work teams. This plant is unlike any of Harley's other plants and maybe unlike any other U.S. facility—no matter what company or type of business. "I'm not aware of anybody anywhere doing anything that emulates this," said the plant manager.

Before the plant opened in 1998, Harley and the two unions that represent most of the employees worked for two years on a labor agreement that defines how the plant is run. The result is "The 23 Elements of Shared Responsibility," which empower workers' teams to:

- Make their schedules and work rules.
- Train new workers and evaluate fellow workers.
- Manage the plant's operating budget.
- Approve plant strategies.

A production worker is a member of a natural work group of 8 to 15 people. Each group sends a representative to a process-operating group. The plant has four operating groups that oversee one of the plant's four operating divisions: engine production, fabrication, paint, and assembly. Each group elects a representative to serve on the Plant Leadership Group. The 14-member Plant Leadership Group also includes the plant manager, both union presidents, six managers, and an elected representative from maintenance. This committee governs the entire facility. "We're in natural work groups. We make our own decisions. We don't have bosses here," said one production worker. Each of the process groups has its own realm of authority. However, anything that affects the entire plant, such as additional employees in a group, goes to the Plant Leadership Group for approval.

*(continued)*

The physical layout of the plant is also different. There are no glass offices where management oversees the factory floor. Instead, the plant manager, the other administrators, and the two union presidents share an area in the center of the building. There are no offices and walls separating them from one another and the rest of the production floor.

The plant manager said, "We recognize there's a tremendous benefit—financially, psychologically, quality-wise, output-wise—to be gained by engaging the workforce." The increased responsibilities of the production workers are reflected by a set of financial rewards unique to this plant. Salaries can increase as much as 5 to 10 percent if short-term production goals are met, and raises of up to 3 percent are based on the previous year's performance.

The employees chosen to work at the new plant went through a rigorous hiring process. First, there was a nine-page application, then aptitude and teamwork tests, a panel interview, and a background check. From 2,000 people who were interviewed and tested, 300 were chosen. For some of the new hires, it has meant a training program lasting as long as six months. In addition to learning technical skills, employees also go through teamwork training.

**Questions**

1. Research Harley's current financial picture. Its annual reports are available at www.harley-davidson.com/.
2. Do you think the Kansas City plant is a realistic idea? Support your position.
3. What could be some problems with this type of structure?
4. Do you have any suggestions to improve the plant?

## COLLABORATION AND CONFLICT

An organization is a large system consisting of subsystems. The subsystems have internal boundaries across which members of the subsystems exchange information and materials. The points of intersection between departments are termed **interfaces.** The organization requires cooperation among its departments and divisions if it is to be effective. Teamwork implies that all the members are contributing to an overall objective even if doing so means subordinating their personal prominence. In sports, individuals play together as a team, and usually their degree of success depends on how well they cooperate and collaborate. The same is true of an organization's departments and groups. The climate of collaboration and the interface between work groups often determine an organization's effectiveness.[4] Pixar Studios, part of Walt Disney Company, is an example of an organization that has to bring together three distinct groups of people who have very different interests and skills: computer wizards, artsy animators, and Hollywood production professionals.

Richard Beckhard, an OD practitioner and one of the pioneers of OD, notes, "One of the major problems affecting organizational effectiveness is the amount of dysfunctional energy expended in inappropriate competition and fighting between groups that should be collaborating."[5] This competition and conflict originate with differences in objectives, values, efforts, and interests between groups. Some aspects of competition are consciously recognized and intentionally produced, whereas others are unconscious or unintentional. The interdependence of functions is one potential source of conflict.

Because of the possibility of group conflicts, and because work teams are often interdependent, the relationship between work teams is a crucial element in organizational efficiency. Within the organization there is a need for competition between these elements, but there is also a need for cooperation and collaboration. Success often depends upon effective sharing of resources, and many groups are interdependent; that is, they depend upon the exchange of resources with other elements to attain their objectives. **Interdependence** is the mutual dependence between groups. Often, however, interdependencies introduce conflict into the organization system.

General Electric (GE) reduces the conflict between operating divisions, departments, and teams by subscribing to interdependent teams and emphasizing the concept of being **boundaryless.** Jack Welch, former CEO and now retired, says that being boundaryless is "an open, trusting, sharing of ideas. A willingness to listen, debate, and then take the best ideas and get on with it. If this company is to achieve its goals, we've all got to become boundaryless. Boundaries are crazy."[6]

Competition among divisions for all sorts of resources (capital, labor, management, and so forth) often becomes a win-lose situation. If the company decides to build a new manufacturing plant in Texas, it cannot build a new research laboratory in California. And for some managers, their overriding mantra is, "I must not only win, everyone else must lose." There are far too many examples of competition for resources and competition just for the sake of winning.

Conflict is increasingly perceived as inevitable and common in today's organizations. Though conflict is complex and has negative forces associated with it, current research is indicating that if the conflict is managed properly, it can actually enhance working relationships and build a positive climate.[7] Thus, a manager's ability to manage or resolve conflict is important. The horizontal organization structure is becoming increasingly common, and this design intentionally builds in controlled conflict for integrating diverse activities.

Certain implications for the organization development practitioner stem from this view of interdependent subsystems. First, the OD practitioner must be able to recognize the interdependence of organizational units. He or she must be aware that these interactions result in conflicts between units. Moreover, elements often operate without feedback, or in an **open loop,** as it is termed. When this is the case, there is no mechanism for corrective action to take place.

Intergroup competition is an important aspect of the organization. Relations between groups often lead to conflicts or dysfunctional behavior affecting operating efficiency. As a result, one objective of OD is to increase cooperation among organization subsystems. These **intergroup interventions** have been described as "the deliberate interaction of two or more complex social units which are attempting to define or redefine the terms of their interdependence."[8]

## INTERGROUP OPERATING PROBLEMS

The potential for conflict depends on how incompatible the goals are, the extent to which required resources are scarce and shared, and the degree of interdependence of task activities. Figure 11.1 shows that there will be potential for more conflict between groups when their tasks are interdependent. The chance of goal conflict is somewhat low between groups that have their own resources and perform entirely different tasks directed toward completely separate goals. Computer programmers and janitors seldom conflict because their tasks are largely separate. The potential for conflict is much higher between engineers and production managers or between salespeople and credit managers. This is because such units tend to rely on common resources, their tasks are interdependent, and they frequently pursue incompatible goals (e.g., increasing sales versus reducing credit losses).

Intergroup relationships are complex, so OD practitioners need to recognize the conditions that lead to the emergence of problems or conflicts. The conditions considered in this chapter are not exhaustive or mutually exclusive, but they illustrate the important factors present in determining group relationships. The symptoms of these conflicts include complaints, gripes, verbal battles, inefficiency, and possibly sabotaging the other group in some way. An illustration of this is Figure 11.2.

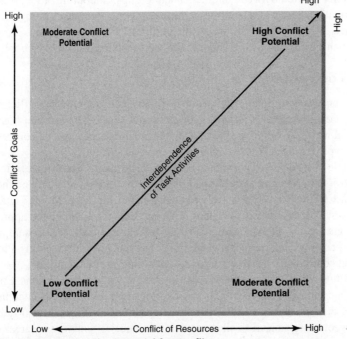

**FIGURE 11.1  Factors Involved in the Potential for Conflict**

**FIGURE 11.2**   Fighting is Senseless
*Source:* CROCK © NORTH AMERICA SYNDICATE

## Suboptimization

When the goals of operating divisions are interdependent, optimization by one group may result in decreased goal attainment for other groups and the organization. As an example, engineering may design a product very quickly and inexpensively, but the product is difficult, time consuming, and costly for the manufacturing department to produce. The financial group, by limiting hiring or overtime, may optimize its objective of cutting costs, but other departments and the organization may lose profits or customers, bringing about a net reduction in profits. This is called suboptimization. **Suboptimization** occurs when a group optimizes its own subgoals but loses sight of the larger goals of the organization as a whole.

General Motors (GM), before one of its many restructurings, had significant problems of suboptimization. Its engineering and production divisions were so autonomous that they did not interface except through the president. A car body would be designed to meet appearance and safety requirements but could not be manufactured because of physical limitations of stamping or bending metal. The design would have to be sent back to engineering to be redone. The CEO at the time described the process: "Guys in Fisher Body would draw up a body and send the blueprint over and tell the guy, 'Okay, you build it if you can.' And the guy at GMAD [production] would say, 'Well, ____, there's no damn way you can stamp metal like that, and there's no way we can weld this stuff together.'"[9] Outside experts tend to agree that GM still has problems of suboptimization. Obviously, to be effective, the old functionally oriented structures need to be altered to bring down barriers.

The objectives of OD interventions are aimed at decreasing suboptimization by increasing collaboration or integration between interdependent groups. Suboptimization, or lack of integration, is a contributing factor to decreased organizational performance. Many organizations are becoming acutely aware of how important integration is. For years, some of America's largest corporations, such as GM and Sears, failed to see the problems caused by suboptimization.

## Intergroup Competition

A second condition causing intergroup problems involves groups with conflicting purposes or objectives. The condition known as **intergroup competition** emerges when a group desires or pursues one goal while directly opposing the values of another group. The competition becomes a classic Pogo-type problem: We have met the enemy and it is us.[10]

An example of this type of conflict is between departments at pharmaceutical giant Merck & Co., Inc. "Over time Merck had developed into several fiefdoms, each doing their own thing," says an insider. CEO Richard Clark has repeatedly called for "One Merck" and has sought to unite the company operationally. Says Clark, "We needed a more integrated approach. From the moment we begin talking about a particular drug franchise, I want researchers, marketers, and manufacturing people sitting in the same room."[11] The merger with Schering-Plough has made cooperation and coordination between departments even more challenging.

Similar situations to that at Merck occur in other types of organizations. Engineering may need special hand-tooled prototypes built and developed by a limited manufacturing operation. Manufacturing, on the other hand, may see this as usurping its function and field of expertise. The subsystems of an organization all have their own special functions or areas, and they jealously guard them against intrusion as almost a territorial right.

## Perceived Power Imbalance between Groups

Differences of power between groups are another condition that may lead to intergroup conflict. The problem emerges where there is a perceived imbalance between units or when some previously established relationship is altered. This can be a serious problem in today's environment of corporate mergers and takeovers. When one group is overpowering, and its views and objectives are consistently favored, its relations with the other group are likely to deteriorate. The submissive or losing group often feels compelled to revise the power balance. It may try to manipulate the situation by means of delaying tactics or by insisting on adherence to policies and procedures.

## Role Conflict, Role Ambiguity

Role conflict (as explained in Chapter 10) also exists when an individual belongs to or identifies with two or more groups whose goals or values are in conflict. This is more typical in a matrix or project form of organization, where an individual may belong to several work groups and report to several bosses. When directives are vague or incompatible, intergroup conflict may result.

Role ambiguity occurs when an individual or the members of a group are not clear about their functions, purposes, and goals within the organization. Staff groups, such as personnel or accounting, often encounter vague or unclear situations where their functions tend to interfere or conflict with line operations. Human resources, for example, may want to control all hiring and promotion decisions, but other departments may want to have control over such matters. An individual or the members of a group may face a situation in which their job scope is being reduced for the good of the organization; this may result in noncompliance or conflict because of the intangible and multifaceted nature of what is good for the organization.

Though role conflict and ambiguity can contribute to intergroup operating problems, membership of individuals in two or more groups has the potential to reduce intergroup conflict. As organizations have become more complex, people serve on projects, committees, or the like that cut across traditional organizational lines. When partially overlapping group membership occurs, it tends to decrease the inclination of members to have biases toward the other group. Though this can enhance role conflict, it can reduce intergroup competition. People who are members of multiple categories at the same time have less need and less opportunity to make distinctions based on category membership.[12]

## Personality Conflict

Intergroup problems arise from interpersonal differences between members, usually the managers. Two individuals who are competing for promotion, rewards, or resources may elevate this to a situation of intergroup conflict. Such conflicts may result from conflicting functions, objectives, career aspirations, or personalities.

## COOPERATION VERSUS COMPETITION

Competition is normally thought of in positive terms, especially in a market-driven economic system. Some managers rationalize that the introduction of competition into their organizations helps make operations "lean and mean." Sony Corp., however, learned just the opposite: that internal competition can lead to poor performance in the marketplace. Sony has long had a highly competitive culture where divisions, especially product divisions, were encouraged to compete with one another. That competitive environment worked for many years and yielded products like the Walkman and the PlayStation. Over the years, the competition became so intense that managers working for one unit would not return phone calls from their counterparts in other units. The competition between units has led to costly mistakes for Sony. Products like the iPod, Amazon Kindle, and TiVo came from competitors. Now Sony, under the leadership of CEO and president Howard Stringer, is trying to put the pieces back together so that units are collaborating with one another. "It's about the number of silos," said Mr. Stringer at a news conference. "It's impossible to communicate with everybody when you have that many silos."[13]

The research on the results of competition and cooperation among groups is mixed.[14] The issue is not as simple as some contend. On the positive side, members of competitive groups have more self-esteem for their groups than members of noncompetitive groups. The competition produces more task orientation in groups and puts additional pressure on them to work.

Although groups competing with one another are more highly oriented toward accomplishing the task than noncompetitive groups, there is no evidence that intergroup competition results in greater productivity than cooperation. Further, the internal cohesion of groups in competition may be degraded.

One study investigated the effects of managing budgets between departments competing for limited resources.[15] In situations where resources are limited and managers are competing for their slice of the monetary pie, it is normal to expect a high degree of competition and political infighting. This study found that budget issues were resolved effectively in cases where management had developed an open-minded discussion of opposing views and cooperative goals. Conflicts and competition were not inevitable. The study pointed to the importance of managers having skills and procedures to discuss their opposing positions openly and to recognize that their goals are largely interdependent.

Group behavior research suggests that cooperation promotes productivity in some situations. This is most true when the task is complicated and requires coordination and sharing of information.[16] In somewhat simple tasks, however, competition is often superior to cooperation because it heightens interest and provides incentive. Therefore, competition can be effective between groups that do not need to share information or resources.

Just as with competitive work groups, managers must also carefully structure cooperative groups. The task of the groups should be complicated enough to justify the group effort. The formal reward system and the norms should encourage group members and the groups as a whole to help others, share information and resources, and work on the task together.

In his discussion of the effects of group competition, Edgar Schein, an OD practitioner, observes that a competing group sees the best in itself and the worst in the other group.[17] Communication decreases between groups, and hostility increases toward the other group. A competing group becomes more cohesive, structured, and organized. Concern for task accomplishment increases, and concern for the psychological needs of members decreases. Leadership styles become more autocratic and less democratic.

After the groups complete the task and there is a winner and a loser, Schein says, the winning group will be more cohesive, but its self-image of being better than the other group will make its members complacent. The winning group will become more concerned about members' psychological needs and less concerned about task accomplishment. The losing group denies the loss if the situation is ambiguous enough or rationalizes the loss by blaming it on bad luck or unclear rules. Initially, the group splinters, tries to find someone to blame, and has less concern for the psychological needs of its members. Over time, however, the losing group usually learns more about itself because its preconceived ideas about being the best group are upset. The loss can have a positive outcome in the long term if the losing group realistically accepts its loss and moves forward.

## MANAGING CONFLICT

Organizational conflict need not be reduced or eliminated, but it must be managed to enhance individual, group, and organizational effectiveness. In a research project, the authors concluded that a high degree of competitive conflict can be very damaging, whereas a cooperative approach to conflict that encourages people to argue freely about the best way to attain goals is more likely to lead to constructive effects.[18]

One element in diagnosing conflict situations involves learning the basic conflict styles used in dealing with interpersonal or intergroup conflict. A conceptual scheme for classifying conflict is illustrated in Figure 11.3 and is based on two dimensions: (1) desire to satisfy self, and (2) desire to satisfy others.[19] There are five styles representing the different levels of cooperative versus assertive behavior:

*Avoiding.*   The **avoiding style** involves a low concern for both self and others; it avoids conflict by withdrawing, buck passing, or passive agreement.

*Obliging.*   With a low concern for self and high concern for others, the **obliging style** is concerned with people satisfaction, harmony, and smoothing over conflicts.

*Dominating.*   With high concern for self and low concern for others, the **dominating style** attempts to attain personal objectives and often ignores the needs of others, forcing win-lose situations.

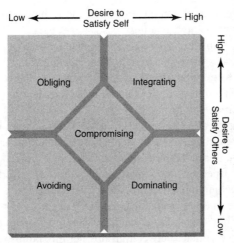

**FIGURE 11.3** Conflict Styles

*Compromising.* The **compromising style** has moderate concern for self and moderate concern for others, tending to seek out compromise between conflicting parties or elements.

*Integrating.* With high concern for self and others, the **integrating style** is concerned with problem solving; it uses openness, sharing of information, and the examination of differences to reach a consensus solution.

Although some behavioral scientists suggest that there is one best style suitable for use in all situations, most feel that any of the styles may be the most appropriate, depending on the given situation and the personal predisposition to a style.

## Intergroup Techniques

Awareness of the problem of conflict in organizations is increasing. Changes in the workforce have resulted in new situations that cannot be managed by old structures. The popularity of decentralized structures and matrix organizations, in which many organization members wind up reporting to two or more bosses, has reduced executives' reliance on authority and increased their reliance on interpersonal conflict-management skills.

Anthony Downs, a writer on the subject of bureaucracies within organizations, proposes what he calls the law of interorganizational conflict: "Every group or organization is in partial conflict with every other group it deals with."[20] Intergroup conflicts, including conflicts between line and staff, between departments, and between union and management, are very common. The merger of AOL and Time Warner was supposed to bring synergies that the two companies acting alone did not have. A key premise of the merger was that the two companies would centralize their ad-selling operations. It was expected that the units could win more ad dollars working together than they could separately. They could package an advertising deal for clients, such as Burger King and Coca-Cola, that would offer space in Time Warner units including Time Inc. magazines, airtime on Turner cable networks, spots on America Online Internet service, and licensing opportunities with Warner Bros. film studio. However, Time Warner was not able to execute the plan. An industry observer said in a *Wall Street Journal* interview, "The individual operations at AOL Time Warner have no interest in working with each other and no one in management has the power to make them work with each other. From day one, it was just wheels spinning."[21] After eight years of unsuccessful attempts to integrate and build on the strengths of the two working together, Time Warner made the decision to "finally split off AOL, fully unwinding the disastrous 2001 deal that joined a media giant and a dot-com darling," in the words of a *Wall Street Journal* article.[22]

Some companies, recognizing the existence of intergroup conflict, are encouraging team spirit by tearing down the walls that isolate departments. Now people from all the relevant disciplines, such as design, manufacturing, and marketing, get involved in new projects early on. Products are designed from the outset to be cost effective and to provide the features customers want. Similar barriers between business units are also coming down. Collaborations involving two, three, or more divisions are common. However, these things do not happen by accident; they require extensive planning and executing.

Dealing with conflicts openly provides a way to manage tensions creatively, whereas unresolved conflict usually erodes the effectiveness of an organization. It is kind of like the 800-pound gorilla in the room whose presence no one acknowledges. The OD practitioner deals with intergroup conflict by seeking interventions that increase interaction, negotiation, and more frequent communication between groups.[23]

The OD strategies for dealing with intergroup conflicts that inhibit cooperation have several goals. OD intergroup techniques seek to identify areas of commonality and **meta goals**—the superordinate organization goals. These techniques aim at avoiding win-lose situations while emphasizing the win-win aspects of the situation. They encourage interaction and negotiation and increase frequency of communication. Frequent contacts between groups reduce the degree of conflict. This is because intergroup contacts help to reduce biases, encourage external loyalties, make group membership less important, and weaken the pressures for conformity to group norms. In addition, frequent contact between groups permits points of potential conflict to be resolved as they occur, before the conflict builds.

To reduce conflict between groups, the OD practitioner examines group-to-group working relationships, applying joint problem-solving efforts that confront intergroup issues. The OD techniques for dealing with intergroup problems include third-party consultation, the organization mirror, and intergroup team building.

## Third-Party Consultation

Intervention by a third party is one method of increasing communication and initiating intergroup problem solving. The third party is usually an outside practitioner, but sometimes may be a superior, a peer, or a representative from another unit. **Third-party interventions** have the potential to solve conflicts. Confrontation of the conflict is a basic feature of this technique.[24]

**Confrontation** refers to the process in which the parties directly engage each other and focus on the conflict between them. The goals of interventions include achieving better understanding of the issues, agreeing on a diagnosis, discovering alternatives for resolving the conflict, and focusing on the common or meta goals. The third party attempts to make interventions that will open communications, equalize power, and confront the problems.

**ENSURING MUTUAL MOTIVATION** Each group needs an incentive to resolve the conflict. This may entail arranging for the organization to offer a formal reward of some kind to the participating groups. Any organizational rewards that inadvertently reward win-lose competitive behavior should be reconsidered by upper management.

**ACHIEVING A BALANCE IN SITUATIONAL POWER** If the situational power of the groups is not approximately equal, it is difficult to establish trust and maintain open lines of communication. In such a case, it may be possible to arrange for a third group, such as another work unit, to provide support to the group with less power. The third party may have to regulate discussions involving groups whose leaders are less articulate or forceful in their presentations.

**COORDINATING CONFRONTATION EFFORTS** One group's positive overtures must be coordinated with the other group's readiness to reciprocate. If one group is more highly motivated than the other, the third party may protract the discussion or encourage the more motivated group to moderate its enthusiasm. A failure to coordinate positive initiatives and readiness to respond can undermine future efforts to work out differences. A less-motivated group may perceive a higher-motivated group as weak and willing to capitulate.

**DEVELOPING OPENNESS IN COMMUNICATION** The third party can help to establish norms of openness, provide reassurance and support, and decrease the risks associated with openness.

**MAINTAINING AN APPROPRIATE LEVEL OF TENSION** If threat and tension are too low, there is little incentive for change or for finding a solution. Yet if threat and tension are too high, the parties may be unable to process information and see creative alternatives. They may become polarized and take rigid positions.

The third party provides an objective intervention for confronting or resolving issues between two disputing parties, because conflict situations are often tense and emotion laden. Diagnostic insight is provided that is not evaluative and is a source of emotional support. The third party aids in identifying conflict factors and then helps facilitate changes in the relationships.

## Organization Mirror

The **organization mirror** is a technique designed to give work units feedback on how other elements or customers of the organization view them.[25] This intervention is designed to improve relationships between teams and increase effectiveness.

A work team in personnel, engineering, production, accounting, or any other department that is experiencing interface problems with related work teams may initiate a feedback session. A practitioner or other third party obtains specific information, usually by questionnaire or interview, from other organizational groups that the work team contacts daily. The work team (also called the host group) meets to process the feedback. At this meeting, it is important that one or two spokespersons from each contacted group be present. The outside key people and the practitioner discuss the data collected in an inner circle, whereas the host group "fishbowls" and observes from the outside (therefore, the term "organization mirror"). After this the host group can ask questions that seek clarification (e.g., "Why did you say this?") but may not argue or rebut. The host unit, with the assistance of the practitioner, then discusses the data to identify problems.

Subgroups are formed of host group members and key visitors to identify specific improvements that will increase operating efficiency. Afterward, the total group hears a summary report from each subgroup, then outlines an action plan and makes specific task assignments. This completes the meeting, but a follow-up meeting to assess progress is usually scheduled.

The organization mirror provides a means for a work team to improve its operating relations with other groups. It allows the team to obtain feedback on what it is doing, identify key problems, and search for specific ways to improve its operating efficiency.

## Intergroup Team Building

The intervention technique known as **intergroup team building,** or confrontation, was originally developed by Robert Blake, Herb Shepard, and Jane Mouton.[26] The key members of conflicting groups meet to work on issues or interface. "An interface is any point at which contact between groups is essential to achieving a result."[27] The groups may be two interdependent elements of the organization, such as architects and engineers, purchasing and production, or finance and other department heads.

Role playing is frequently used to foster cross-group understanding. As in all confrontations, the practitioner must intervene to open communications, balance power, and shift from hostile to problem-solving confrontation.

Intergroup team-building meetings usually take one or two days. Members are brought together to reduce misunderstanding, open communication, and develop mechanisms for collaboration. Most OD practitioners advise intragroup team development (see Chapter 10) before intergroup team building. The purpose of this is to clear out any team issues before getting to work on interface problems. The intergroup team-building meeting usually involves the following steps:

### STEP 1: MAKE INTROSPECTIVE LISTS
When there are intergroup operating problems between two work groups, each group makes three lists before the two groups meet together:

1. How do we see ourselves?
2. How do we think the other department sees us?
3. How do we see the other department?

The groups prepare their lists written in large legible print on sheets of newsprint. Table 11.1 is a hypothetical list that a team formulated.

### STEP 2: GROUPS MEET TOGETHER
The groups meet together and tape their lists to the wall. A spokesperson for each group presents the group's lists. Neither department is permitted to defend itself, argue, or rebut while the other department is making its presentation, but it can ask clarifying questions (What do you mean by inflexible? Could you be more specific on autocratic?).

**TABLE 11.1 Intergroup Meeting Listings**

1. How do we see ourselves?

| | |
|---|---|
| a. Agreeable | e. Team oriented |
| b. Friendly | f. Participative |
| c. Trusting | g. Productive |
| d. Helpful | |

2. How do we think the other department sees us?

| | |
|---|---|
| a. Aggressive | e. Competitive |
| b. Communicative | f. Winners |
| c. Leaders | g. Independent |
| d. Rational | |

3. How do we see the other department?

| | |
|---|---|
| a. Authoritarian | d. Opinionated |
| b. Sneaky | e. Inflexible |
| c. Loud | f. Unrealistic |

### STEP 3: GROUPS MEET SEPARATELY

The groups meet separately to discuss the discrepancies in perception and react to the feedback. The feedback allows for correcting perceptions and behaviors to a more effective mode.

### STEP 4: CROSS GROUPS MEET

The groups divide into subgroups of five or six made up members of the two departments. These cross groups have the objectives of agreeing upon a diagnosis of the interface problems and developing conflict-reducing or problem-solving alternatives with action plans and follow-up activities. Together the groups develop an action plan for solving problems and assigns responsibilities for the action plan.

### STEP 5: FOLLOW-UP MEETING

The groups usually schedule a follow-up meeting to evaluate progress and make sure that the actions have achieved their purpose.

Although little hard evidence is available, there are subjective reports indicating that intergroup meetings have positive results. Blake, Shepard, and Mouton reported improved relationships in their study, and French and Bell reported working successfully with three tribal groups.[28] Bennis reported improved relationships between two groups of officials in the U.S. Department of State.[29]

The next two chapters will discuss additional ideas pertaining to team and intergroup development. Goal setting will be covered in relation to OD programs and high-involvement work teams in the next chapter.

## Summary

- **Conflict.** Conflict is inevitable in organizations. Large organizations are divisionalized, departmentalized, and segmented to increase control and effectiveness. This creates boundaries between geographic areas or functional units, such as manufacturing, engineering, and marketing. Yet cooperation and collaboration among all units is essential to attaining objectives. The complexity and size of modern organizations often leads to competition or conflict between organization units. Large-scale organizations generate increased problems of dependence between groups that often result in suboptimization and lowered general efficiency. Such problems as intergroup conflict, power imbalance, or personal conflicts inhibit coordination between groups.

- **Win-Win.** Organizations can experience situations of win-win instead of win-lose. Win-lose involves intergroup competition and conflict. Though the conditions and opportunity for a win-win collaboration are often present, many inherent factors lead organizations to define the collaboration as a win-lose situation. The consequences of win-lose situations include less communication between groups, development of negative stereotypes, and hostility and distrust toward the other group. The net result is usually dysfunctional in terms of total effectiveness. The conflict between groups may escalate, with each group attempting to win by fair means or foul.

- **Intergroup Interventions.** The OD practitioner deals with intergroup problems by seeking interventions that emphasize improved communication and relations between operating units. These interventions stress the involvement of the individual and the members of the group in the relationship between what they do and what others are doing. The practitioner uses strategies that identify areas of commonality, increase communication, and emphasize meta goals. These interventions include third-party intervention, the organization mirror, and intergroup team building and provide mechanisms for getting collaboration between competing groups. The major objectives of intergroup interventions include a better way of working together, increased recognition of interdependence, less competition, and more collaboration.

## Review Questions

1. Identify major sources of organizational conflict.
2. Many people approach conflict as a win-lose situation. Why is a win-win approach more likely to work?
3. What are the anticipated behaviors of competitive conflict that occur in work teams? Identify and compare the five major conflict styles.
4. Compare and contrast the methods used in the different approaches to resolving intergroup conflict.

## Key Words and Concepts

Avoiding Style
Boundaryless
Compromising Style
Confrontation
Dominating Style

Integrating Style
Interdependence
Interfaces
Intergroup Competition
Intergroup Interventions

Meta Goals
Obliging Style
Open Loop
Organization Mirror
Suboptimization

Intergroup Team Building
Team Interdependence
Third-Party Interventions

# OD Skills Simulation 11.1

## The Disarmament Game

*Total time suggested: 120 minutes.*

### A. Purpose

The purpose of this exercise is to simulate a situation of intergroup conflict within an organization, to observe and experience the feelings generated by such competition, and to examine strategies for developing collaboration between organization units.

### B. Procedures

*Step 1.* Form two teams with equal numbers of players. A team size of six to nine members is best, but each team should have the same number of members. Assign one or more persons to serve as observers. Other class members can assist the instructor as referee. Before class, read the Disarmament Game Rules. Cut out the "play money" at the end of the simulation or, if the situation allows, use real money and play for lesser amounts (say, 50 percent of the suggested amounts).

*Step 2.* Begin playing the Disarmament Game, keeping track of moves on the Record of Results. Play as many sets as you can within a one-hour time limit, though additional time can be allotted, if available. The observers can use Observer Forms A and B.

*Time suggested for Steps 1 and 2: 90 minutes.*

*Step 3.* Calculate all profits and losses.

*Time suggested for Step 3: 5 minutes.*

*Step 4.* The observers lead a discussion with their team on the team's performance, using the two Observer forms.

*Time suggested for Step 4: 10 minutes.*

*Step 5.* Discuss the following questions with your competing team.

1. What was the goal of your team? What kind of strategy did your team adopt to accomplish its goal? Did the strategy change at all during the simulation?
2. Did your team understand that if they collaborated with the other team, both teams could win?
3. Was your team aware of the need for and the advantages of collaborating with the other team? If so, how did you communicate the need for collaboration to the other team?
4. To make an analogy, if one of the teams was the engineering department and the other was the production department of a manufacturing enterprise, and the World Bank was the marketplace, what types of conclusions might you make about this company and the two departments?
5. What part did trust play between the two teams in this simulation?
6. How is trust built? How does it start? Where does it come from?
7. Did your team trust and collaborate with the other team so that you could try to break the World Bank? If so, what happened as a result of your trust?
8. If the simulation was run again, would you do anything differently?

*Time suggested for Step 5: 15 minutes.*

### Disarmament Game Rules[30]

The Disarmament Game is played by two teams. The World Bank, which has funds, is also part of the game. Each team can win or lose money, and in this exercise your objective, as a team, is to win as much money as you can. Both teams will have equal number of players. Each team should have at least one observer. If there is not the same number of people on both teams, one person will assist the instructor as a referee.

### The Funds

1. Each player will furnish $20 to be allocated as follows (see the end of the simulation for a description of "play money"):
   a. Initially, $15 (of your $20) will be given to your team treasury to be used in the exercise. You may need to contribute more money to the treasury, depending on the performance of your team. At the end of the game, the funds remaining in your team's treasury will be divided equally among the members of the team.

**b.** The remaining $5 will be used to supplement the funds of the World Bank, managed by the referees.

Example: Seven players on a side. Allocation of funds:
Each team—$105
World Bank—$35 from each team

**2.** The World Bank will deposit, from its own funds, an amount equal to the deposit of both teams. This money can be won by the teams.

## Special Jobs

You will have 15 minutes from the time the general instructions are completed until the first set begins. During this time, you may read and discuss the instructions and plan team strategy. You must select persons to fill the following jobs. No person may hold more than one job at any one time. The jobs can be reassigned at any time by a majority vote of the team.

**1.** Two negotiators—functions stated below.
**2.** A team representative—to communicate group decisions to the referees regarding initiation and acceptance of negotiations, moves, attacks, and so on.
  **a.** You must elect a team representative.
  **b.** Referees will listen only to the team representative.
**3.** One recorder—to record moves of the team (on the Record of Results), specifically (a) the action taken by the team in each move, and (b) the weapon status at the end of each move. The recorder should also record who initiates decisions and how the team arrives at decisions.

## The Weapons

Each team will be given 20 cards, or "weapons." Each card will be marked with an **X** on one side to designate an "armed" condition. The blank side of the card signifies that the weapon is "unarmed." To begin the game, each team will place all 20 of its weapons in an armed condition. During the course of the game, the weapons will remain in your possession and out of sight of the other team.

## The Procedure

**1.** The Set
  **a.** As many sets as possible will be played in the allocated time (from the time the first set begins). Payments will be made after each set.
  **b.** Each set consists of no more than 10 moves for each team. An attack following any move ends a set. If there is no attack, the set ends after the tenth move. Each team has two minutes to make a move. At the end of two minutes, you must have moved two, one, or none of the weapons from armed status. If you fail to move in the allotted time, the status quo counts as a move. In addition, you must decide whether or not to attack and whether or not you want to negotiate (see below). Your decision must be communicated by your representative to the referee within 15 seconds after the end of a move.
  **c.** Each team may announce an attack on the other team following any two-minute move period except the third, sixth, and ninth. You may not attack during negotiations.
  **d.** Once a set ends, begin a new set with all weapons armed. Continue with as many sets as the time allotted for the exercise permits.
**2.** The Negotiations
  **a.** Between the moves, you will have the opportunity to communicate with the other team through negotiations.
  **b.** You may call for negotiations during the 15 seconds between move periods. The other team may accept or reject your request to negotiate. Negotiations can last no longer than two minutes.
  **c.** When the negotiators return to their teams, the next two-minute move period will start.
  **d.** Negotiators may say whatever is necessary to most benefit their team.
  **e.** The team is not necessarily bound by agreements made by its negotiators.
  **f.** Your negotiators must meet with those of the other team after the third, sixth, and ninth moves. These are required negotiations.

## The Payoff

**1.** If there is an attack, the set ends. The team with the greater number of armed weapons will win 50 cents per member for each armed weapon it has over and above the number of armed weapons of the other team. This is paid directly from the treasury of the losing team to the treasury of the winning team. The World Bank is not involved in the transaction when there is an attack. If both teams have the same number of armed weapons when there is an attack, both teams pay the World Bank 50 cents per member.

2. If there is no attack, the set ends after 10 moves. If your team has more disarmed weapons than armed weapons, it will be awarded 20 cents per excess disarmed weapon per member by the World Bank. If your team has fewer disarmed weapons than armed weapons, your team will pay 20 cents per excess armed weapon per member to the World Bank.

3. The actual dollar payoff should occur at the end of each set.

## Notes to Referee(s)

1. Try to arrange separate rooms so that the teams cannot overhear each other.
2. A timer that rings at two-minute intervals will be helpful for keeping the time.
3. Be sure to permit the teams only the specified times. You will probably need to be somewhat harsh toward the teams when directing them in order to keep them on the time schedule.
4. You will manage the funds of the World Bank and check the accuracy of the teams' record keeping.
5. Do not assist either team.

## RECORD OF RESULTS

| Move | Set 1 Actual number of armed weapons | Set 1 Action taken for this move (attack, not attack, negotiate) | Set 2 Actual number of armed weapons | Set 2 Action taken for this move (attack, not attack, negotiate) | Set 3 Actual number of armed weapons | Set 3 Action taken for this move (attack, not attack, negotiate) | Set 4 Actual number of armed weapons | Set 4 Action taken for this move (attack, not attack, negotiate) | Set 5 Actual number of armed weapons | Set 5 Action taken for this move (attack, not attack, negotiate) | Set 6 Actual number of armed weapons | Set 6 Action taken for this move (attack, not attack, negotiate) | Total of all sets |
|---|---|---|---|---|---|---|---|---|---|---|---|---|---|
| 1. | | | | | | | | | | | | | |
| 2. | | | | | | | | | | | | | |
| 3. | | | | | | | | | | | | | |
| 4. | | | | | | | | | | | | | |
| 5. | | | | | | | | | | | | | |
| 6. | | | | | | | | | | | | | |
| 7. | | | | | | | | | | | | | |
| 8. | | | | | | | | | | | | | |
| 9. | | | | | | | | | | | | | |
| 10. | | | | | | | | | | | | | |
| Ending number of armed weapons of other team | | | | | | | | | | | | | |
| Line 1   $ paid to other team | | | | | | | | | | | | | |
| Line 2   $ paid to World Bank | | | | | | | | | | | | | |
| Line 3   $ received from other team | | | | | | | | | | | | | |
| Line 4   $ received from World Bank | | | | | | | | | | | | | |

Total Results
(Lines 3 + 4 − 1 − 2)

**OBSERVER FORM A—TEAM RATING**

Based on the following scale, rate your team on how it performed. Record your choice in the blank.

[Low   1   :   2   :   3   :   4   :   5   :   6   :   7   High]

| Factor | Rating |
| --- | --- |
| 1. Cooperative teamwork | _____ |
| 2. Member satisfaction | _____ |
| 3. Team motivation | _____ |
| 4. Information sharing | _____ |
| 5. Consensual decision making | _____ |
| 6. Conflict directly faced and resolved | _____ |
| 7. Participative leadership | _____ |
| 8. Clearly defined goals | _____ |
| 9. Trust | _____ |
| 10. Encouraged openness | _____ |

**OBSERVER FORM B—CONFLICT STYLES**

[Low   1   :   2   :   3   :   4   :   5   :   6   :   7   High]

| | Rating | Comments |
| --- | --- | --- |
| 1. *Avoidance*—this style involves avoiding conflict by withdrawing | | |
| 2. *Obliging*—this style is concerned with harmony, smoothing over conflict. | | |
| 3. *Dominating*—this style competes for one's own objectives in a win-lose mode. | | |
| 4. *Compromising*—this style seeks to compromise. | | |
| 5. *Integrating*—this style uses problem solving and openness to form a consensus. | | |

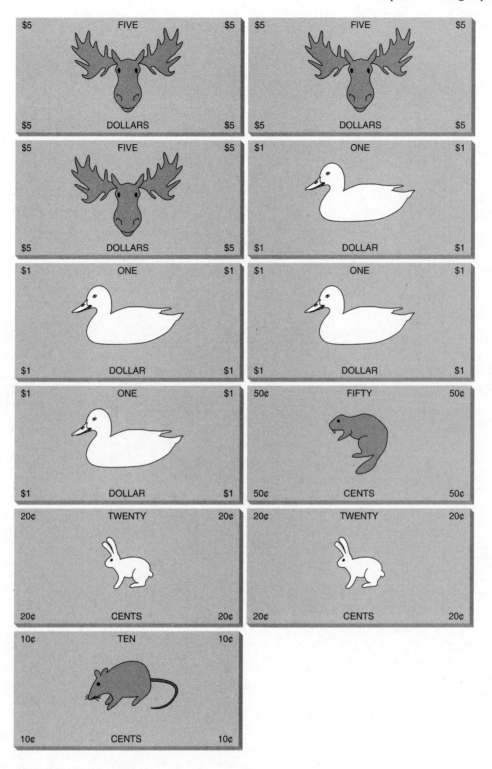

# OD Skills Simulation 11.2

## Intergroup Team Building

*Total time suggested: 75 minutes.*

### A. Purpose

To provide an opportunity for group members to clarify and analyze their interrelationships and work on improving intergroup processes.

### B. Procedures

*Step 1.* Form the same groups as in Simulation 11.1, and meet separately using a blackboard or newsprint to make these lists:

1. How do we see ourselves?
2. How do we think the other group sees us?
3. How do we see the other group?

Do not share or let the other group see the lists until Step 2.

*Step 2.* The groups meet together. A representative of each group presents the group's lists. While one group is making its presentation, the other group may not defend itself, argue, or rebut; but it does have the opportunity to ask clarifying questions (i.e., what do you mean by cutthroat? Could you give an example of two-faced?) The other group then makes its presentation.

*Time suggested for Steps 1 and 2: 30 minutes.*

*Step 3.* The groups meet separately to discuss the discrepancies in perception.

*Time suggested for Step 3: 10 minutes.*

*Step 4.* Form subgroups of four to six by combining members of the two groups. These cross groups have the objective of agreeing upon a diagnosis of interface problems and the development of conflict-reducing or problem-solving alternatives, with action plans and follow-up activities.

*Time suggested for Step 4: 20 minutes.*

*Step 5.* The subgroups report their findings, including action plans and follow-up activities to the entire group.

*Time suggested for Step 5: 15 minutes.*

# CASE: THE EXLEY CHEMICAL COMPANY

The Exley Chemical Company is a major chemical manufacturer, making industrial chemicals, plastics, and consumer products. Company sales and profits have grown, and its ratio of net profits to sales is about average for the industry, but in the last year or so, both sales and profits have been disappointing (see Table 11.2).

Because new products are constantly being introduced into the line and methods of use are constantly changing, the relative importance of different product groups is constantly shifting. For example, the major product groups experienced changes in percentage of total sales over a five-year period (see Table 11.3).

**TABLE 11.2**

| Year | Sales in Billions |
|---|---|
| 5 years ago | $81 |
| 3 years ago | 93 |
| 2 years ago | 108 |
| Last year | 111 |

**TABLE 11.3**

| | Percent of Sales | |
|---|---|---|
| | 5 Years Ago | Last Year |
| Chemicals | 61 | 55 |
| Plastics | 31 | 33 |
| Consumer | 8 | 12 |
| | 100 | 100 |

## The Organization

The general structure is shown in Figure 11.4. Production is carried on in four plants across the United States, each of which has a plant manager. The marketing vice president handles sales, advertising, and marketing services.

All research is administered and done at the corporate research laboratory, including the development section, which is responsible for the development and improvement of production processes. The engineering department handles all planning and construction and the development of new processes and pilot-plant operations.

In addition, to manage the large number of new products being developed, a product development division was established about three years ago. Before this, new products developed by the research division were passed on to the engineering division from the pilot-plant operation. The new division was established because the existing structure could not adequately coordinate complex projects. The product development division was to coordinate the development of new products, including recommending manufacturing capacity, sales programs, and so on. It was to conduct surveys to analyze market potential for new products and recommend the development or production based on these surveys. Problems began to develop in the period following the creation of the product development division.

## The Situation

Conflicts were created with several other departments. For example, the product development division started using a small force of specialty salespeople to conduct pilot marketing programs. This did not go over well with the marketing department. In addition, the product development division was given responsibility for market research, but the tasks of sales analysis and forecasting remained in the marketing division. Finally, for each separate group of products, a product manager was appointed who was responsible for the coordination of all company activities for the product. This resulted in more problems.

The product manager often needs to visit customers in order to get more realistic input on market conditions, but marketing executives resent this. They feel that all customer relations should be handled through marketing, because these visits tend to confuse the customer. "Judging from what I've seen, Product Development couldn't care less about what we are doing in terms of integrating our markets," said the marketing vice president.

Sales executives tend to question the sales estimates issued by the product managers. These estimates are usually based on the total product market rather than on Exley's share, which often tends to inflate sales estimates. "The product development group is aggressive and they want to grow, but you have to grow within guidelines. The product guys are going to have to learn to work with the other divisions," said a sales manager.

At a recent meeting of the Chemical Manufacturers Association, a product manager learned that a competitor was about to patent a new process for the production of polymers, which will presumably reduce costs by about one-third. Exley's research person in charge of polymers said that they had several interesting possibilities that might break in a few months. "I think corporate headquarters needs to integrate operations better. We can't be a bunch of entrepreneurs around here. We've got to have more teamwork on these projects," said the project manager.

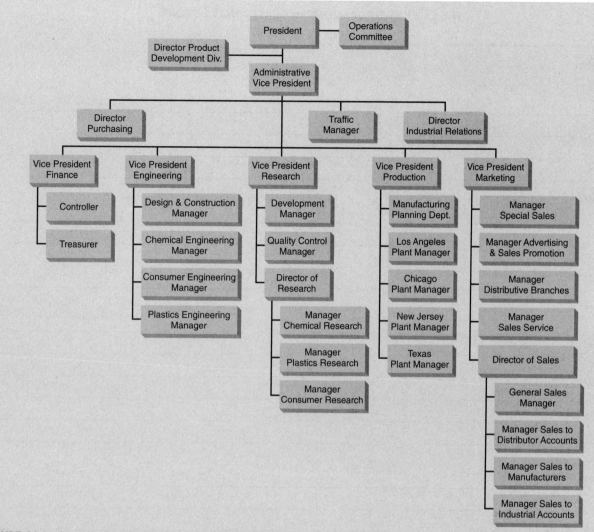

**FIGURE 11.4    Organization Chart—The Exley Chemical Company**

The manager of sales proposed to the consumer projects group that Exley's antifreeze be promoted directly to large retail outlets. He has forwarded a proposal to the project manager with a note: "Our customers feel this is a hot idea; can production supply the needed quantities at a competitive price?" The product manager has found that the two people in research and engineering who are most knowledgeable about this product are now deeply involved in a new project, so little has been done to date. "The big frustration is that you can't get help from other departments if it doesn't have a large return for them. Each division head works on the project that makes the most for them, but it doesn't necessarily help us bring new products to market," said the product manager. (Use the Case Analysis Form on the following page.)

**THE EXLEY CHEMICAL COMPANY CASE ANALYSIS FORM**

Name: _____

I. Problems

  A. Macro

    1. _____
    _____

    2. _____
    _____

  B. Micro

    1. _____
    _____

    2. _____
    _____

II. Causes

    1. _____
    _____

    2. _____
    _____

    3. _____
    _____

III. Systems affected

    1. _____
    _____

    2. _____
    _____

    3. _____
    _____

IV. Alternatives

    1. _____
    _____

    2. _____
    _____

    3. _____
    _____

V. Recommendations

_____
_____
_____
_____
_____
_____

# Chapter 11 Endnotes

1. Rob Cross, Kate Ehrlich, Ross Dawson, and John Helferich, "Managing Collaboration: Improving Team Effectiveness through a Network Perspective," *California Management Review*, vol. 50, no. 4 (Summer 2008), pp. 74–98.

2. Lynn Lunsford, "Transformer in Transition," *Wall Street Journal*, May 17, 2007, pp. B1–2.

3. www.harley-davidson.com; Ilan Brat, "Harley Picks Outsider for Chief amid Downturn," *Wall Street Journal*, April 7, 2009, p. B4; Karen Richardson, "Living High on the Hog," *Wall Street Journal*, February 5, 2007, pp. C1–C2; Geoffrey Colvin, "Wall Street's Easy Rider," *Fortune Online*, August 28, 2001; Sam Jaffe, "Harley Is Riding High on the Hog," *Business Week Online*, November 17, 2000; Stephen Roth, "New Harley Plant Spotlights Training and Empowerment," *Kansas City Business Journal*, vol. 16, no. 17 (January 9, 1998), p. 3.

4. For additional information on using collaboration, see Cross et al., "Managing Collaboration: Improving Team Effectiveness through a Network Perspective"; Alan Cannon, and Caron H. St. John, "Synergy through Collaboration: A Theory of Culture's Effects," *Academy of Management Proceedings*, August 2008, pp. 1–6; Henry Mintzberg, Jan Jorgensen, Deborah Dougherty, and Frances Westley, "Some Surprising Things About Collaboration: Knowing How People Connect Makes It Work Better," *Organizational Dynamics*, vol. 25, no. 1 (Summer 1996), pp. 60–72.

5. Richard Beckhard, *Organization Development: Strategies and Models* (Reading, MA: Addison-Wesley, 1969), p. 33.

6. "Jack Welch, "Lessons for Success," *Fortune*, January 25, 1993, pp. 86–93; See also John A. Byrne, "Jack: A Close-Up Look at How America's #1 Manager Runs GE," *Business Week*, June 8, 1998, pp. 90–111.

7. Christine A. Stanley and Nancy E. Algert, "An Exploratory Study of the Conflict Management Styles of Department Heads in a Research University Setting," *Innovative Higher Education*, vol. 32, no. 1 (June 2007), pp. 49–65; N. E. Algert and K. L. Watson, *Conflict Management: Introductions for Individuals and Organizations* (Bryan, TX: Center for Change and Conflict Resolution, 2002); and R. F. Bowman, "The Real Work of Department Chair," *The Clearing House*, January/February 2002, pp. 158–62.

8. Richard C. Walton and Robert B. McKersie, *A Behavioral Theory of Labor Negotiations: An Analysis of a Social Interaction System* (New York: McGraw-Hill, 1963).

9. Maryann Keller, *Rude Awakening: The Rise, Fall, and Struggle for Recovery of General Motors* (New York: William Morrow, 1989), p. 101.

10. Walt Kelly first used the quote "We Have Met the Enemy and He Is Us" on a poster for Earth Day in 1970. See www.igopogo.com/we_have_met.htm.

11. John Simons, "From Scandal to Stardom: How Merck Healed Itself," *Fortune*, February 18, 2008, p. 96.

12. Astrid C. Homan, John R. Hollenbeck, Stephen E. Humphrey, Dann Van Knippenberg, Daniel R. Ilgen, and Gerben A. Van Kleef, "Facing Differences with an Open Mind: Openness to Experience, Salience of Intragroup Differences, and Performance of Diverse Work Groups," *Academy of Management Journal*, vol. 51, no. 6 (December 2008), pp. 1204–22; M. B. Brewer and R. J. Brown, "Intergroup Relations," in D. T. Gilbert and S. T. Fiske (eds.), *The Handbook of Social Psychology*, vol. 2 (4th ed.) (New York: McGraw-Hill), pp. 554–94.

13. Phred Dvorak, "Out of Tune: At Sony, Rivalries Were Encouraged; Then Came iPod," *Wall Street Journal Online*, wsj.com, June 29, 2005.

14. For a comprehensive review of the research literature on competition and cooperation, see Steven M. Farmer and Jonelle Roth, "Conflict-Handling Behavior in Work Groups," *Small Group Research*, vol. 29, no. 6 (December 1998), pp. 669–714; Dean Tjosvold, "Cooperation Theory and Organizations," *Human Relations*, vol. 37, no. 9 (September 1984), pp. 743–67; A. Myers, "Team Competition and the Adjustment of Group Members," *Journal of Abnormal and Social Psychology*, vol. 65, no 5 (November 1962), pp. 325–32.

15. Dean Tjosvold and Margaret Poon, "Dealing With Scarce Resources: Open-Minded Interaction for Resolving Budget Conflicts," *Group and Organization Management*, vol. 23, no. 3 (September 1998), pp. 237–55.

16. P. R. Laughlin, "Ability and Group Problem Solving," *Journal of Research and Development in Education*, vol. 12, no. 1 (Fall 1978), pp. 114–20; M. Okun and F. Di-Vesta, "Cooperation and Competition in Coacting Groups," *Journal of Personality and Social Psychology*, vol. 31, no. 4 (April 1975), pp. 615–20.

17. Edgar H. Schein, *Process Consultation, Vol. 1: Its Role in Organization Development* (Reading, MA: Addison-Wesley, 1988), pp. 109–112. See also Barbara Meeker, "Cooperation, Competition, and Self-Esteem: Aspects of Winning and Losing," *Human Relations*, vol. 43, no. 3 (March 1990), pp. 205–19.

18. Jeffrey Barker, Dean Tjosvold, and Robert Andrews, "Conflict Approaches of Effective and Ineffective Project Managers: A Field Study in a Matrix Organization," *Journal of Management Studies*, vol. 25, no. 1 (March 1988), pp. 167–78.

19. Robert R. Blake, H. Shepard, and J. Mouton, *Managing Intergroup Conflict in Industry* (Houston: Gulf Publishing Co., 1964); K. W. Thomas, "Conflict and Conflict Management," *Handbook in Industrial Organizational Psychology*, ed. M. D. Dunnette (Chicago: Rand-McNally, 1984). See also M. A. Rahim, "A Measure of Styles of Handling Interpersonal Conflict," *Academy of Management Journal*, vol. 26, no. 2 (June 1983), pp. 368–76.

20. A. Downs, *Inside Bureaucracy* (Boston: Little, Brown, 1968).

21. Matthew Rose, Julia Angwin, and Martin Peers, "Failed Effort to Coordinate Ads Signals Deeper Woes at AOL," *Wall Street Journal*, July 28, 2002, p. A1.

22. Shira Ovide and Emily Steel, "It's Now Official: AOL, Time Warner to Split," *Wall Street Journal*, May 29, 2009, p. B1.

23. For a complementary approach, see Gini Graham Scott, "Take Emotion out of Conflict Resolution," *T+D*, February 2008, pp. 84–85.

24. Loraleigh Keashly, Ronald J. Fisher, and Peter R. Grant, "The Comparative Utility of Third-Party Consultation and Mediation Within a Complex Simulation of Intergroup Conflict," *Human Relations*, vol. 46, no. 3 (March 1993), pp. 371–93; Richard E. Walton, *Managing Conflict: Interpersonal Dialogue and Third-Party Roles* (Reading, MA: Addison-Wesley, 1987); B. H. Sheppard, "Third-Party Conflict Intervention: A Procedural Framework," in *Research in Organizational Behavior*, ed. L. L. Cummings and B. M. Staw, vol. 6 (Greenwich, CT: JAI Press, 1984); R. J. Fisher, "Third Party Consultation as a Method of Intergroup Conflict Resolution," *Journal of Conflict Resolution*, vol. 27. no. 2 (1983), pp. 301–34.

25. Sheldon Davis and his colleagues at TRW probably developed this technique.

26. Blake, Shepard, and Mouton, *Managing Intergroup Conflict*; Robert R. Blake and Jane S. Mouton, *Solving Costly Organizational Conflicts* (San Francisco: Jossey-Bass, 1984).

27. Robert R. Blake and Jane S. Mouton, "Out of the Past . . . How to Use Your Organization's History to Shape a Better Future," *Training and Development Journal*, vol. 37, no. 11 (November 1983), p. 60.

28. Blake, Shepard, and Mouton, *Managing Intergroup Conflict;* Wendell L. French and Cecil H. Bell Jr., "Organization Development," in *Behavioral Science Interventions for Organization Improvement*, 3rd ed. (Upper Saddle River, NJ: Prentice Hall, 1984), p. 11.

29. Warren Bennis, *Organization Development: Its Nature, Origins, and Prospects* (Reading, MA: Addison-Wesley, 1969).

30. I am indebted to Norman Berkowitz of Boston College and Harvey Hornstein of Columbia University for the design of this game. Used by permission of the authors. Modifications have been made to the original design including formatting, discussion questions, and forms.

# Goal Setting for Effective Organizations

## LEARNING OBJECTIVES

**Upon completing this chapter, you will be able to:**

1. Recognize how goal setting can be used as part of an OD program.
2. Apply the major findings of the research on goal setting to develop organizational and personal goals.
3. Describe how management by objectives (MBO) can be applied as a management system.
4. Practice goal-setting approaches.

## PREMEETING PREPARATION

1. Read Chapter 12.
2. Prepare for OD Skills Simulation 12.1. Prior to class, form teams of seven and assign roles. Complete Step 1.
3. Complete Step 1 of OD Skills Simulation 12.2.
4. Read and analyze Case: Valley Wide Utilities Company.

## GOAL SETTING CAN DRIVE THE BOTTOM LINE

Goals give direction and purpose. It is difficult to imagine an organization that does not have goal setting of some kind. In a large and established company, goal setting may be a formal program such as the development of an ideal model of the organization or the implementation of a management by objectives (MBO) program. On the other hand, in a newly opened business, goal setting may take the form of a mental image of what the business will be like in a year and then five years from now. Goal setting is also part of the process that a company goes through when a vision is created. As in goal setting, the vision needs to be clearly articulated and understood. Conversely, Starbucks Corp. CEO Howard Schultz has a goal for Starbucks of "re-igniting the emotional attachment with customers."[1] For employees and investors alike, it is not clear what this means and if it is happening.

OD programs rely heavily upon the goal-setting process. OD, by definition, is planned change, and in order for that change to take place, goals need to be set. Early in the implementation of the OD program, managers and other employees develop ideas, perhaps with the assistance of a practitioner, about what the organization will be like—that is, they develop goals. They then plan a series of steps that will move the organization along to accomplish the goals.

In addition to being a method for carrying out OD programs, goal setting is also a process that can be used on an individual, team, interteam, and organization-wide basis. Team building and interteam building set the foundation of trust and cooperation that are important for the establishment of goal setting.[2]

Organizations have taken several different approaches to goal setting. In this chapter, we will first discuss goal-setting concepts and then focus on one type of goal setting, MBO. For more information on how General Mills is using goal setting in a team environment, see **OD Application: Goal Setting in Teams at General Mills.**

## GOAL-SETTING THEORY

**Goal setting** is a process intended to increase efficiency and effectiveness by specifying the desired outcomes toward which individuals, teams, and the organization should work. Goal setting may be used as an intervention strategy within an OD program. An analysis of the organization may find that its divisions are not making a unified effort, that some divisions have

## OD Application: Goal Setting in Teams at General Mills[3]

General Mills has improved its teams by looking outside the company. Some of its trips look, on first blush, as if they were dreamed up by a movie scriptwriter. What do SWAT teams and NASCAR pit crews have to do with running a cereal company? That question is what the chief technical officer of General Mills, Randy Darcy, wanted to find out.

Darcy is looking at groups that take team performance to the extreme: groups that dissect their operations, analyze them, change them, and put them back together. Then the teams practice, practice, and practice some more. These extreme teams look at their processes, or how they do their work, under a microscope.

One of the target groups was a NASCAR pit crew. Darcy and his team visited the racetrack and spent time observing and studying how the crew was able to work with blinding speed. The answer: better organization. So General Mills took the lessons learned to the Betty Crocker plant at Lodi, California. The purpose was to jolt employees into thinking of new ways of doing their jobs. Here it took production line workers 4.5 hours to change from one product to another. After studying their process and applying better organization, the switch in products now takes 12 minutes. In another example, General Mills employees watched the way that Stealth bomber pilots and ground crews cooperate. At a cereal plant in Buffalo, they were able to improve their own teamwork, helping to cut costs by 25 percent.

Studying the cooperative methods between SWAT team units inspired General Mills to replace separate performance goals for engineering, purchasing, and production with a single set of goals. This eliminated the inclination of one department to cut corners to meet its own goals at the expense of the other departments. In the past, a purchasing manager had been buying thinner cartons to meet his cost-cutting goals. The downside was that the thinner cartons caused equipment in the produc-

tion department to jam, raising manufacturing costs. Now the three departments are measured against goals established for the team.

One of the people Darcy has worked with is Erik Weihenmayer, a blind mountaineer, who assembles teams to scale some of the world's highest peaks. Weihenmayer says, "The only way to cross a glacier is on a rope to which your entire team is tied. You either all plunge together or succeed together."

General Mills initially began its quest for cutting costs by looking at extreme teams in the early 2000s. It wanted to build the culture and values of extreme teams into its own organization. It doesn't take as many field trips looking for extreme teams anymore because it has its own extreme teams all over the company. The extreme teams are engaged in a fat-trimming system called "margin management." For example, several years ago, General Mills had 50 versions of Hamburger Helper. It did consumer research on what versions people liked best and eliminated half of the versions. Then it shrank the size of the box while keeping the serving size the same. The result was 10 percent lower costs to make Hamburger Helper.

Each division in General Mills has a three-year savings goal, and everyone usually meets once a week to look at costs. Margin management is prevalent on the factory floor as well as in management levels. Employees loading trucks may point to inefficient box sizes for putting in trucks. What the teams do in the different divisions of General Mills to manage margins is not as glamorous as what the Nascar pit crews do, but its teams are winning races by wringing out costs.

### Questions

1. Do you agree with Darcy's approach of going to teams that take performance to the extreme?
2. What are some other examples of extreme teams that General Mills or any organization might study?

---

little or no direction, or that individuals are dissatisfied with their performance and their careers. Besides team building, intergroup development, and other intra- and interpersonal interventions, the OD practitioner and the client may decide that goal setting will be beneficial. The goal-setting program may be carried out at the individual level to help employees improve their productivity or advance their careers. Goal setting may also be carried out on a group basis, especially if individuals are required to work with one another. Goal setting on a departmental level serves to improve productivity and gives direction to the department's efforts.

The basic premise of goal-setting theory is that the actions of individuals are regulated by their conscious intentions and values.[4] A **goal** is what an individual is trying to accomplish—the object or aim of the individual's action. Goals include deadlines, budgets, or other standards for behavior and performance. The major findings of goal-setting theory are summarized below.

## More Difficult Goals Produce Better Performance

The effect on performance of assigning easy goals is no better than the effect of not having any goals at all. A goal has to be more than the expectation that one will complete one's basic job requirements. Goals are only effective if they are difficult and challenging. In some situations, changes in external conditions may mean the goals become virtually impossible to achieve. When this occurs, it is important to recognize the new circumstances and reassess the need for new and more relevant goals. In the face of the collapse of the U.S. housing market in 2008, Home Depot sales also declined since they were directly correlated with new and used home purchases. CEO Frank Blake wanted to boost morale and set realistic goals in light of the quickly unfolding developments in the housing market. Blake extended restricted stock grants to assistant store managers and lowered sales and profit targets that hourly employees had to meet to receive bonuses. "We still challenged people to hit some pretty tough numbers," says the vice president for U.S. stores.[5]

## Specific Hard Goals Are Better than "Do Your Best" Goals

In addition to being difficult and challenging, goals should also be specific. Specific goals show exactly what constitutes acceptable performance. Motorola, General Electric (GE), Dow Chemical, and 3M have made quality a top priority and have set goals of extremely high quality for their products: Goals of this kind are specific and are expressed in quantitative terms or as specific events; that is, they include time frames, standards, quotas, monetary amounts, and the like. US Airways found that different departments did not share the same goal regarding airplane departures. Some departments thought getting the plane pushed back from the gate within 30 minutes of the scheduled departure was OK. So that everyone clearly understood the goal, US Airways came up with a rallying cry: "D-zero—every departure at or before its scheduled time."[6]

Recent research suggests that when the task is complex and there are many optimum strategies, goals should be expressed in general terms.[7] For example, the manager of a department in a constant state of change may find that setting specific goals leads to rigid behavior and neglect of new opportunities.

## People May Abandon Goals If They Become Too Hard

Although goals should be difficult, people must be able to attain or at least approach them; otherwise, they will view the goal as impossible, become discouraged, and may abandon it. An individual is more likely to accept or choose a goal when there is a high expectation of reaching it. In several studies where goals were perceived to be impossible, performance decreased. The difficulty of the goals suggests that they were not accepted in the first place.[8]

One method of reducing the negative effects of difficult goals is to adopt a strategy of adopting less difficult and shorter-term goals that provide a foundation for accomplishing the longer-term and more difficult goals. This is a method frequently used by world-class athletes. While the athlete is focusing on the long-term goal, perhaps an Olympic gold medal in four or eight years, he or she has also developed a plan where there are short-term goals. Short-term goals could include strength training, practice times, nutrition, and techniques. The achievement of short-term and interim goals can be measured by success at lower-level competitive events, all the time keeping in mind the long-term goal of winning the Olympic event.[9]

## Participation in Setting Goals Increases Commitment and Attainment of Goals

Employees are more committed to self-set goals than to goals assigned by a manager. This is not to say that the manager is a passive bystander when employees set goals but that the manager and employee are mutually involved in setting goals. In addition, job satisfaction increases when people participate in setting their goals.[10] As was discussed in Chapter 9, participation puts employees more in control of their environment and helps to reduce stress.

## Feedback and Goals Improve Performance

The combination of goal setting with feedback on individual performance has a positive effect on performance. In contrast, giving feedback on performance without having previously set goals does not lead to improved performance. Information about the outcome of the performance, such as whether a goal was met, should be included. As well, it is also important to include information about how to adjust in order to accomplish the goal. Frequent, relevant, and specific feedback is important for goal setting to be a success. The feedback should occur as soon after the work activity as possible so that the individual and the person providing the feedback remember the event and its details.[11] Figure 12.1 illustrates how not to give feedback.

Companies such as Ernst & Young LLC, IBM, and Accenture Ltd. are responding to employee demand, particularly from younger workers, for more frequent feedback. Employees at Ernst & Young can request and submit feedback at any time at an online "Feedback Zone." A survey of their employees found that 65 percent of younger workers said that providing detailed

**FIGURE 12.1  What Not to Do**
*Source:* CROCK © NORTH AMERICA SYNDICATE

guidance in their daily work was moderately or extremely important. This compared to 39 percent for older workers. Eighty five percent of younger workers wanted frequent and candid performance feedback compared to only 50 percent for older workers.[12] "There's a difference between the generations in how to provide feedback," according to one of the researchers on the project, a university professor of organizational behavior.[13] "Gen Y [those born after 1980] wanted a lot of feedback—from their immediate bosses and anyone else."

## Individual Differences Tend Not to Affect Goal Setting

Studies show that goal-setting programs are successful regardless of the education and job position of the subjects. Some goal-setting programs in organizations are limited to upper and middle management, but research findings suggest that goal setting is just as successful for positions requiring minimum education and skills. Production workers, logging crews, managers, clerical workers, students, engineers, scientists, and maintenance workers have used goal setting successfully. The success of a goal-setting program is not contingent upon how many years of service an employee has with an organization.

There are some individual differences that should be considered in goal-setting programs. People with a strong need for achievement and with high self-esteem are more likely to commit themselves to difficult goals than people with a weak need for achievement and low self-esteem. Commitment will not be forthcoming from people with a weak need for achievement simply because they have participated in setting their goals. In all probability, only external rewards or punishments will be successful in building commitment for people of this type.[14]

## Goal Setting in Teams Deserves Special Consideration

Setting difficult individual goals for an interdependent team task will likely result in poorer performance than when a team goal is set or even when there is no team goal at all. People engaged in individual goal setting tend to be more competitive and less cooperative—two conditions that were discussed in previous chapters as dysfunctional for team and interteam performance.[15] When people are engaged in interdependent work, it is important that their individual goals facilitate the attainment of the team goal. Also, team leaders and managers can improve the acceptance of team goals through active member participation. This includes fostering open feedback channels within the group pertaining to team training and performance.[16]

A manager explicitly specifying which goal is more important can achieve cooperation in goal setting. Another way to get cooperation is through participative goal setting in the context of a team-building session.

## Managerial Support Is Critical

Support for goal-setting programs by all levels of management is crucial to their success. Leaders should maintain optimism by publicizing even small steps forward. Supervisors should be present to encourage the acceptance of goals by employees, help them improve their skills, and give timely feedback on how the goals are being accomplished. At a small Illinois company, Integrated Project Management Co., managers on a regular basis provide employees with an "event summary" in which they give immediate feedback on how an employee handled a specific task and provide steps for improvement.[17] This is in addition to weekly one-on-one meetings where employees, with their manager, discuss work progress, employee's performance, and skills that need improvement.

As well as providing feedback, those who accomplish goals should be rewarded, but the rewards need to be applied consistently. If some people are acknowledged and rewarded but others are not, employees will quickly lose respect for the program.

## A MODEL FOR GOAL SETTING

Based upon the research findings previously discussed, a useful model for goal setting has been developed.[18] Goal setting will be successful only if the goals are properly developed and the individuals trying to achieve the goals are committed to them. A goal-setting program in an organization requires careful planning.

As seen in Figure 12.2, the first three factors in the goal setting process are establishing the goal, achieving goal commitment, and overcoming resistance to goal acceptance. Goals can be established in a variety of ways. Time and motion studies can provide the basis for goals involving repetitive and standardized tasks. Another approach is to base standards on past performance, but this may not result in a challenging goal, especially when past performance has been poor. Goals may also be set by joint participation between the employee and the supervisor. This method often leads to employee commitment, a crucial ingredient in effective goal setting.

Goal commitment can be achieved in a variety of ways. Trust in upper management, support by management, and an effective reward and incentive system are all helpful in obtaining commitment.[19] The work already undertaken in the OD program should have built mutual trust between employees at all levels of the organization. Past successes of accomplishing goals build excitement and a positive feeling about accomplishing future goals. Competition between employees may be useful in some cases, but managers should be careful about designing competitive situations, especially in interdependent situations. There is always the danger that employees may become so involved in competing with one another that they lose sight of the goals.

Resistance to goal acceptance can be overcome by several methods, and a combination of methods will likely result in a more successful goal-setting program. Providing special training for employees in new techniques and procedures and providing rewards and incentives can encourage goal acceptance. Participation in setting goals can lead some employees to accept goals.

The goals that work best conform to certain attributes or characteristics. They are difficult and challenging, but not impossible to accomplish. They are clear and easily understood. All the involved employees need to know what is expected of them if they are to accomplish the goals. A. G. Lafley, chairman of the board of Procter & Gamble (P&G), says of the way his firm has implemented goal setting, "A lot of what we have done is make things simple because the difficulty is making sure everybody knows what the goal is and how to get there."[20] Goals should be specific, measurable, and compatible with the goals formulated at higher levels of the organization.

**FIGURE 12.2  Goal Setting**

A period of performance follows upon the setting of specific performance goals. During this time, managers must be prepared to provide support. To achieve specific goals, employees may require training or additional resources, such as new equipment or information. Managers may need to work with employees in developing action plans. Finally, managers should provide timely and objective feedback when the goal is completed.

The results of the employees' performance can be beneficial or negative. The benefits may incur to the organization or the individual. When individuals successfully meet a goal, they feel competent and successful. Better performance and pride in the achievement of successes can be expected. Employees are more likely to have clearer roles if they more fully realize the performance expected of them. Negative consequences can be expected when the goals are not achieved. This is most problematic in situations where specific and measurable goals could not be set.

### Results of Goal Setting

Research on the effects of goal setting has shown positive results on both the personal and the organizational level.[21] One study found that in 90 percent of the cases, specific and challenging goals led to better performance than easy goals, "do your best" goals, or no goals.[22]

In a review of goal-setting studies, the median improvement in performance resulting from goal setting was 16 percent. The same study found that goal setting combined with monetary incentives improved performance by more than 40 percent. Another study found that goal setting significantly affected attitudes toward others, the job, and the organization. A review of total company strength revealed that the performance of a company is strongly related to the number of goal-setting and planning activities. Though there has been less research examining goal setting on a team level than on an individual level, the research is consistent with that of goal setting on an individual level. For example, several studies showed that more difficult team goals produced higher performance than easy goals, similar to studies of goal setting for individual performance.[23]

The remainder of this chapter will look at one specific type of goal-setting program: MBO.

## MANAGEMENT BY OBJECTIVES

**Management by objectives** (MBO) is a technique used by organizations to set goals. It is a process aimed at the integration of individual and organizational goals.[24] MBO may be defined as a system of management set up to help in planning, organizing, problem solving, motivating, and other important managerial activities. It involves the participation of subordinates and their managers in setting and clarifying the goals for subordinates. George Odiorne (a leading MBO author) defines MBO as "a process whereby the superior and subordinate managers of an organization jointly identify its common goals, define each individual's major areas of responsibility in terms of results expected, and use these measures as guides for operating the unit and assessing the contribution of each of its members."[25] The goals of this approach include improved performance, more communication and participation, higher morale and job satisfaction, and a better understanding of the organization's objectives at all levels.

MBO approaches goal setting on the assumption that people have higher-level needs for competence and achievement, and want to satisfy these higher-level needs in their work. In addition, people will work harder and perform better if they participate in setting the goals they are to achieve. In line with this, management must create a climate that encourages self-development by individuals.

### The Purposes of MBO Programs

There are two underlying reasons for implementing MBO in an organization. One is to clarify the organization's goals and plans at all levels; the other is to gain better motivation and participation from the organization's members. MBO is a way to increase the clarity of organizational planning and give subordinates more knowledge and understanding of their jobs. MBO may be used to identify organizational goals at all levels and to encourage participation in setting the standards that will be used to evaluate subordinate performance. Participation in the goal-setting process allows managers to control and monitor performance by measuring performance and results against the objectives subordinates helped to set.

Douglas McGregor suggested a modified approach to MBO under the concept of "management by integration and self-control."[26] According to McGregor, the MBO concept could be used to provide a mutual opportunity for managers and subordinates to define and agree upon areas of responsibility, specific performance goals, and the terms of the expected outcomes. He suggested that managers should establish performance goals after reaching agreement with their superiors about major job responsibilities. Then accomplishments would be appraised after a short period, usually six months. After this self-appraisal in cooperation with the superior, another set of performance goals would be established. McGregor aimed at getting organization members to commit to the goals by the "creation of conditions such that the members of an organization can achieve their own goals best by directing their efforts toward the success of the enterprise."[27] He advocated this concept for appraising performance because it shifted the emphasis from weakness and criticism to an analysis of strength and potential. In this application of MBO, the supervisor's role is one of counseling, coaching, or process consultation.

## The MBO Process

Although practitioners have different ways of implementing MBO, most of them emphasize the need for a commitment by top management. As with the overall OD program, MBO starts at the top of the organization and works its way down. One MBO program at a company begins with the top management team studying the operations. The president subsequently proposes a preliminary policy statement to the executive committee. The committee draws up a final presidential policy statement that is presented to the department managers. The department managers, working with their superiors, draw up detailed implementation plans for their departments based on the president's policy statement.

Drawing on this example, the MBO process typically begins with the management team setting up broad measures of organizational performance. Goal-setting sessions are then held at the various organizational levels, one at a time, moving from the top down. Within divisions and at each successive level, the goals are more specifically defined. MBO may be described as a process consisting of a series of five interrelated steps, illustrated in Figure 12.3.

**Step 1**   The subordinate proposes to the manager a set of goals for the upcoming time period that are congruent with the goals set at the next-higher level. The proposal sets forth specific goals and performance measures.

**Step 2**   The subordinate and the manager jointly develop specific goals and targets. These must be specific, measurable objectives for each area of responsibility. The subordinate and the manager must mutually agree upon the goals. The major responsibility, of course, lies with the subordinate. The objectives should include both performance goals and personal career goals.

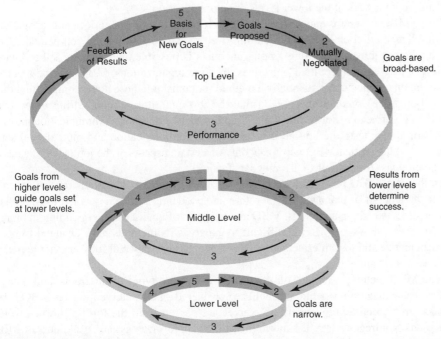

**FIGURE 12.3   Steps in the MBO Process**

**Step 3** There is a period of performance in which the individual involved attempts to accomplish the individual goals.

**Step 4** The manager feeds back results to the subordinate and gives appropriate rewards for performance. This individual performance review involves an appraisal and discussion of accomplishments and of variations in overall performance compared with targets.

**Step 5** The outcome of the performance review is the basis for setting new performance goals and recycling the goal-setting process.

MBO is a continuing self-renewal process. How long a complete cycle takes depends on the MBO program, but most programs have quarterly reviews of objectives, with a major review and new objectives set annually. Quarterly reviews facilitate quick solutions of problems and allow for considering changes in the situation. The central focus of any MBO program is the development of an agreement between supervisor and subordinate about objectives and targets.

As with other OD interventions, such as team building, MBO programs are set up in many organizations independently of an OD program. Yet MBO and goal setting are processes that OD specialists introduce into organizations. To be used as an OD intervention, MBO should include (1) a team approach to setting and reviewing targets, (2) real participation by subordinates in setting goals, with an emphasis on mutually agreed upon goals, (3) mutual trust between subordinate and manager, and (4) a real concern for personal career goals as well as for organizational goals. With such a team orientation, MBO logically follows team and interteam building in an OD program. When MBO is used in this sense, it can provide individual satisfaction and motivation, and increased organizational attainment.

Many of the guidelines used for setting objectives are the same as the ones used in other types of goal-setting programs. The subordinate and the manager should make the goals as precise and specific as possible. There must be agreement and acceptance of the objectives by both the individual and the manager. The interactions between manager and subordinate also provide a counseling and coaching opportunity and in this way provide for management development. The specific steps in the MBO process may differ among organizations and OD practitioners, but the goals are similar. They include better performance and better understanding of organization objectives at every level of the organization.

## Criticisms of MBO

Implementing MBO is expensive and time-consuming, and usually entails great effort. Because of these factors, the use of MBO has traditionally been limited to managerial and professional employees. Obtaining benefits whose value exceeds the costs is more difficult with employees performing routine work at the lower levels of an organization.

Some MBO programs encounter difficulties because management does not recognize that proper implementation of MBO requires improved managerial skills and competence. Critics question whether joint goal setting among unequals is possible, and whether subordinates at lower levels are free to select their objectives. In some organizations, MBO may be a performance evaluation tool and consequentially a method for punishing those not accomplishing the objectives. For other organizations, MBO may be too quantitative, and setting objectives as explicitly as possible may not be functional. In other MBO programs, communication may come from the top dictating to the bottom instead of open communication and mutual goal setting. There is also a danger that MBO will focus only on certain aspects of the job (such as sales) and ignore other areas (for example, customer satisfaction).[28]

In the past, MBO received a good deal of publicity, and expectations rose to unrealistic levels. If the amount of management literature and academic research devoted to MBO is any indication of its use in organizations, MBO as a program of goal setting is declining in organizations. However, the use of MBO is difficult to gauge as its methods have changed to become more participative and less intermediating, and organizations may call it by another name, such as target setting.

The MBO technique includes a multitude of different types of programs, and many OD practitioners are uncertain whether it should be considered an OD intervention. As MBO is based on the hierarchical structure (where objectives are passed from the top level down to lower levels) of an organization, there is a question as to the appropriateness and usefulness of MBO in flatter and team-based structures that are becoming more prevalent in organizations. Some OD practitioners believe that MBO is a manipulative approach and, therefore, should not be classified as an OD intervention. Others feel that OD and MBO are mutually compatible and not only fit together, but that it is impossible to have one without the other. They contend that the need to have goal setting at all levels is one of the major assumptions of organization development, and therefore that MBO is a legitimate OD intervention.

Some practitioners believe that properly designed MBO programs, based upon McGregor's ideas, can have positive results. Others believe that MBO can be improved by placing more emphasis upon individual goals and examining the underlying assumptions of motivation within these programs. There should also be an emphasis on mutual goal setting and frequent feedback and interaction between superior and subordinate. In summary, MBO programs, when implemented correctly, can systematically engage individuals in target setting and performance improvement.

## The Results of MBO

Many different types of organizations have tried MBO. One difficulty in appraising their approaches is that MBO has become an all-purpose term implying many different things in many different settings. In a study of 87 organizations using MBO, the researchers concluded that there are at least 10 different approaches to MBO, ranging from motivational to coercive.[29] There is an absence of current research on MBO, which provides some measure of its declining use in organizations.

Most research on MBO programs has reported mixed results. Some studies show that MBO has improved organizational performance, whereas others show inefficiency and weakness in application. Although the research on MBO is not conclusive, the findings are generally favorable, though much depends on how an organization defines and implements MBO. Several studies have concluded that goal setting results in improved performance and motivation. Moreover, "managers working under MBO programs were more likely to have taken specific actions to improve performance than were those who continued with the traditional performance appraisal approach."[30] Other evidence suggests that MBO is associated with positive attitudes toward the work situation, and that participation of subordinates in decision making can improve performance and job satisfaction.

This chapter has focused on what individuals, work teams, and organizations can do through OD goal-setting programs to improve performance. The next chapter deals with improving work processes for individuals and work teams through such interventions as job design, self-managed work teams, and total quality management (TQM).

---

## Summary

- **Goals.** Goals can have very beneficial results for both individuals and organizations. A goal is what an individual or organization is trying to accomplish, and goals drive behavior.
- **Goal Setting.** Goal-setting programs are more effective if the goals are difficult, specific, measurable, and achievable. The managers of an organization that introduces goal setting should provide feedback to the employees. Commitment by the individual employees is crucial; participation in designing the goal is an effective way to ensure acceptance.
- **MBO.** MBO is widely used in organizations but with mixed success. The failure of MBO programs is due in part to unrealistic expectations by management and in part to improper implementation. Despite some negative reports, MBO incorporates very sound techniques and should not be overlooked as an OD goal-setting technique.

---

## Review Questions

1. Identify and discuss the major factors in effective goal setting.
2. Discuss the role of participation in goal setting.
3. Describe Locke and Latham's goal-setting model.
4. What are the typical steps in an MBO program?
5. Compare and contrast the factors that make for successful and unsuccessful MBO programs.

---

## Key Words and Concepts

Goal

Goal Setting

Management by Objectives (MBO)

# OD Skills Simulation 12.1

## Organization Goal Setting

*Total time suggested: 60 minutes*

## A. Purpose

This simulation is intended to allow you the opportunity to set goals within an organizational setting and observe how personal and organizational goals can be in conflict. You will experience how conflicting goals can sometimes be resolved.

## B. Procedure

*Step 1.* Prior to class, form teams of seven (extra members act as additional observers), select roles, and read the Vernal Corporation Background Information and your role description. Read only your role, and mark your individual decision in Column 1 of the Vernal Corporation Decision Form. The OD practitioner and observers will not mark a decision. The roles are:

1. Project Manager
2. Accounting Systems Representative
3. Information Systems Representative
4. Technical Support Representative
5. Government Contracts Representative
6. OD Practitioner
7. Observer(s)

*Step 2.* Meet with your team members and the project manager, who conducts the meeting. The OD practitioner will also be present to help you with group process. Place the team decision in Column 2 of the Vernal Corporation Decision Form. The observers can use the Observer Forms A and B.

*Time suggested for Step 2: 30 minutes.*

*Step 3.* Critique your team meeting and the quality of the meeting. The practitioner and observer will provide feedback using Observer Forms A and B as a guide. As a team, complete the Team Rating column of Observer Form A. With the entire team providing input, consider the following:

1. Were individual goals made public, or were they concealed? Share at this point any information not previously disclosed in the team meeting.
2. Were both individual and organizational goals adequately met?
3. Was the OD practitioner helpful? Dysfunctional? What suggestions can you give for improvement?

*Time suggested for Step 3: 15 minutes.*

*Step 4.* Meet with the other teams to compare decisions.

1. Each team presents its decision and the factors most important in arriving at the decision.
2. To what extent was there members' support for the final decision? How could support have been increased?
3. How closely did the teams achieve goal agreement? If there were differences, to what could they be attributed, given that all the teams had the same base of information?
4. Did the OD practitioners make content suggestions or provide process interventions?

*Time suggested for Step 4: 15 minutes.*

## VERNAL CORPORATION BACKGROUND INFORMATION

Vernal is a medium-sized company offering consulting services for accounting information systems and a special unit specializing in local and federal government contracts. Until now, Vernal has had only one facility for all its operations, and most of the business is conducted for clients in the metropolitan area. Because of substantial contracts recently obtained in another city 200 miles away in the same state, Vernal has decided to open a field office there. The office will be headed by a project manager and will consist of representatives from Accounting Systems, Information Systems, Technical Support, and Government Contracts.

The headquarters of Vernal is a new facility located in a planned suburban community, almost a rural setting, with the most up-to-date facilities. The company has a complete health facility that is part of its wellness program, day care, company-provided van pools, bicycle and walking paths connected to the community's extensive green belts, covered and free parking lots, and a company-subsidized restaurant and cafeteria.

## Role Description (Read Only Your Role)

**Project Manager**. You have been selected as the project manager for the new facility across state. The representatives from Accounting Systems, Information Systems, Technical Support, and Government Contracts will report directly to you, and your job will be to coordinate their activities with the home office. You, as well as all the members of your team, applied for the positions. The move will mean advancement for everyone selected. The assignment is expected to last about five years, and then you will be transferred back to company headquarters. You have been led to believe that a successful operation will likely result in a promotion.

One of the first tasks facing you and your team before making the move is to select an office. Although you have reserved the right to make the final decision, you have called a meeting of those making the move to receive their input so that you can make a more informed decision. You are also interested in getting off to a good start with the other people because your success will largely be determined by how well they do their jobs; therefore, you would like to have them agree upon a decision that best meets both their goals and the company's.

You have drawn up a description of the available offices you saw on a recent fact-finding trip (see the Office Alternative List). The four offices on the list are the only choices available, and the information you have provided, although incomplete, is all that is available.

You have been informed that the maximum the company is willing to spend is $58,000 a month, but you would like to reserve $4,000 for last-minute lease changes. The offices have a monthly base lease rate and a group of options available. Most of the options have specific costs, and you will have to select options that do not exceed $58,000 less the $4,000 reserve. You have indicated to your team that the most that can be spent on the office is $54,000 a month. In addition, you would like to keep costs to a minimum to make a good impression at the home office.

You would personally like the office to be located close to the suburbs where you hope to buy a house. A private office area, such as a converted conference room, is important to you, as it will lend respect to your position with the other team members, clients, and the public. Otherwise, you are not big on amenities such as a prestigious office and furnishings. You are interested in bottomline results that look good back at the home office, not in a plush office for yourself.

**Accounting Systems Representative.** You have been selected as the representative from your division to move to the new facility across the state. You will report directly to the project manager, but you will retain close ties with your division. You applied for the position, and the move will mean advancement for everyone selected. The assignment is expected to last about four years before you are transferred back to company headquarters.

The project manager has called a meeting of those making the move to help select an office. The manager has given you a summary of the offices with pertinent information obtained on a recent fact-finding trip (see the Office Alternative List). The four alternative offices on the summary sheet are the only choices available, and the information on the sheet, although incomplete, is all there is.

The project manager has informed you that the maximum the company is willing to spend on the new office space is $54,000 a month. The offices have a monthly base lease rate and a group of options available. Most of the options have specific costs, and you will have to select options that will not exceed $54,000.

Your goal is to select an office reasonably close to your clients, many of whom are located in the downtown area. Clients will be coming to the office, so it is important to have an impressive office, at least two conference rooms, adequate parking, and proximity to restaurants. You don't like to drive, so some kind of transportation other than driving is important or else you would consider an apartment within walking distance. With your old supervisor and work team, decisions were typically made by voting after a thorough discussion. You will therefore need to build support for your choices with the other representatives and the project manager.

**Information Systems Representative.** You have been selected as the representative from your division to move to the new facility across the state. You will report directly to the project manager, but you will retain close ties with your division. You applied for the position, and the move will mean advancement for everyone selected. The assignment is expected to last about three years before you are transferred back to company headquarters.

The project manager has called a meeting of those making the move to help select an office. The manager has given you a summary of the offices with pertinent information obtained on a recent fact-finding trip (see the Office Alternative List). The four alternative offices on the summary sheet are the only choices available and the information on the sheet, although incomplete, is all there is.

The project manager has informed you that the maximum the company is willing to spend on the new office space is $54,000 a month. The offices have a monthly base lease rate and a group of options is available. Most of the options have specific costs, and you will have to select options that will not exceed $54,000.

You will often entertain your clients at the office. You believe that to entertain clients at meetings, you need a prestigious office with a good view, good furnishings, three conference rooms, and dining facilities. A downtown location close to your clients is desirable. You prefer to live in an apartment near your office. You will need to build support for your choices with the other representatives and try to convince the project manager of your position.

**Technical Support Representative.** You have been selected as the representative from your division to move to the new facility across the state. You will report directly to the project manager, but you will retain close ties with your division. You applied for the position, and the move will mean advancement for everyone selected. The assignment is expected to last about five years before you are transferred back to company headquarters.

The project manager has called a meeting of those making the move to help select an office. The project manager has indicated to you that everyone's input is important but that he or she will make the final decision. The manager has given you a summary of the offices with pertinent information obtained on a recent fact-finding trip (see the Office Alternative List). The four alternative offices on the summary sheet are the only choices available and the information on the sheet, although incomplete, is all there is.

The project manager has informed you that the maximum the company is willing to spend on the new office space is $54,000 a month. The offices have a monthly base lease rate and a group of options available. Most of the options have specific costs, and you will have to select options that will not exceed $54,000.

You believe that health and recreation are the most important factors. Therefore, your goal is to select an office with full recreational and health facilities like those at the company headquarters. It would be ideal if there were such amenities as a hair stylist and restaurants. As your work requires you to call on clients at their offices to work out technical problems, you see no reason to have a lavish office. You would like to be able to purchase a house reasonably close to the office. You will need to build support for your choices with the other representatives and try to convince the project manager of your position.

**Government Contracts Representative.** You have been selected as the representative from your division to move to the new facility across the state. You will report directly to the project manager, but you will retain close ties with your division. You applied for the position, and the move will mean advancement for everyone selected. The assignment is expected to last about four years before you are transferred back to company headquarters.

The project manager has called a meeting of those making the move to help select an office. The manager has given you a summary of the offices with pertinent information obtained on a recent fact-finding trip (see the Office Alternative List). The four alternative offices on the summary sheet are the only choices available and the information on the sheet, although incomplete, is all there is.

The project manager has informed you that the maximum the company is willing to spend on the new office space is $54,000 a month. The offices have a monthly base lease rate and a group of options available. Most of the options have specific costs, and you will have to select options that will not exceed $54,000.

You think it is important to have functionally adequate quarters, reasonably well furnished, and with a small kitchen, because you normally eat in the office. You are normally in and out of the office a lot to call on your clients, so parking close to the office is important. You also want health facilities similar to those at the home office. Because your time is important to you, you would like to get an apartment close to your work so you can ride your bike. You have heard that all members of the team will be jointly making the decision. This means that you will need to build support for your choices with the other representatives and the project manager.

**OD Practitioner.** You hope to accomplish several things at this meeting:

1. Develop a practitioner-client relationship with each of the committee members.
2. Do not get involved with the content of the problem. You will not interject your opinions as to the decision that the team should make.
3. Help the committee members carry out their task by making appropriate process interventions. See the "Suggested Process Interventions."

**Observer.** You will observe during the role-play session so that you can help the team critique their meeting in Steps 3 and 4. Observer Forms A and B may assist you in providing feedback.

## SUGGESTED PROCESS INTERVENTIONS

- Focus your questions on the problem that seems to be emerging.
- Encourage the speakers to be specific.
- Be aware of who is and who is not talking and who talks to whom.
- Ask appropriate questions about how people are feeling at the moment. For example, "How did you feel when X said _____ to you?"
- Explore feelings with the purpose of discovering how they are helping or hindering the problem's solution.

| | | OFFICE ALTERNATIVE LIST (MONTHLY EXPENSES) | | |
|---|---|---|---|---|
| **Type** | **Suburban Shopping Center Office** | **Regional Office Building** | **Downtown Office Building** | **Downtown High Rise** |
| 1 **Base lease.** | $32,000 | $40,000 | $36,000 | $50,000 |
| 2 **Size.** | Large 4 rooms | Adequate, 1 moderate size room. | Adequate, 1 moderate size room. | Large, 1 room. |
| 3 **Custodial service.** | $800 | $1,200 | $1,200 | $1,600 |
| 4 **Furnishings.** | Used carpet and furniture, fair condition, $1,200. New carpet and furniture, $2,200. | Used carpet and furniture, good condition, $1,600. New carpet and furniture, $2,200. | Used carpet and furniture, good condition, $1,200. New carpet and furniture, $2,400. | Nearly new carpet and furniture, $2,000. New carpet and furniture, $28,000 |
| 5 **Conference rooms including furnishings.** | Not available but office space has 4 rooms. | Up to 5 available, $4,000 each. | Up to 2 available, $2,800 each. | Up to 4 available, $4,400 each. |
| 6 **Prestige of building.** | Little. | Moderately high. | Some. | High. |
| 7 **Windows and view.** | Small windows with limited view. No cost. | Large windows with view, $800. Lower 5 floors, windows with poor view, no cost. | Average windows with poor view. No cost. | Large windows, with excellent view, top 5 floors, $2,000. Lower floors with moderate view, no cost. |
| 8 **Size of building.** | 2 stories. | 25 stories. | 10 stories. | 40 stories. |
| 9 **Location.** | Suburban area. Nice housing nearby. | Large regional business center in suburban area. Various types of housing in area within 1/4 hour. | Downtown business district. Few and expensive apartments in area. Driving time to affordable housing, 3/4 hour. | Downtown business district. Apartments in building and area expensive. Driving time to affordable housing, 1/2 hour. |
| 10 **Parking.** | Street and small lot in rear. No cost. | One parking lot, $200 monthly per car. Street readily available. | One car allowed in building garage, no cost. Unlimited garage space 1 block away, $120 monthly per car. No street parking. | Unlimited in building No cost for tenants and guests. No street parking. |
| 11 **Mass transportation system.** | None. Some bicycle paths. | None. Car pools. Some bicycle paths. | Bus. Building-sponsored van pools, $200 per office. Car pools. | Bus. Car pools. |
| 12 **Dining in building.** | Not available. Fast food next door. | Coffee shop in building. Okay restaurants in area. | Coffee shop and restaurant in building. Excellent restaurants in area. | Coffee shop and excellent restaurants in building. Catering available for offices. |
| 13 **Coffee machine, refrigerator, stove, kitchen.** | Small kitchen with all appliances, $400. | Small kitchen; appliances, lunch area, $800. | No kitchen. Coffee machine, small refrig, hot plate, $200. | Small kitchen, appliances and dining area, $1,200. |
| 14 **Miscellaneous services.** | Health club (gym and hot tub), 2 blocks away, $300 per member. Hair styling, 1 block away. | Hair styling. Complete health and recreation club next door, $800 per member. | Hair styling. No recreation facilities. | Hair styling. Hot tub, gym, pool, $800 per office. Guests allowed. |

**VERNAL CORPORATION DECISION FORM**

| Decision Factors | Column 1 Individual | Column 2 Team |
|---|---|---|
| 1. Lease | $_____ | $_____ |
| 2. Size | _____ | _____ |
| 3. Custodial | _____ | _____ |
| 4. Furnishing | _____ | _____ |
| 5. Conference rooms | _____ | _____ |
| 6. Prestige | _____ | _____ |
| 7. View | _____ | _____ |
| 8. Building size | _____ | _____ |
| 9. Location | _____ | _____ |
| 10. Parking | _____ | _____ |
| 11. Mass transit | _____ | _____ |
| 12. Dining | _____ | _____ |
| 13. Kitchen | _____ | _____ |
| 14. Miscellaneous | _____ | _____ |
| **Total** | $_____ | $_____ |
| **Alternatives** | | |
| 1. Suburban | _____ | _____ |
| 2. Regional | _____ | _____ |
| 3. Downtown | _____ | _____ |
| 4. High-rise | _____ | _____ |

**OBSERVER FORM A—TEAM RATING**

*Instructions:* For each item, place a number in the blank to the right representing your reaction to how your group performed based on the following scale.

[Low   1   :   2   :   3   :   4   :   5   :   6   :   7   :   8   :   9   :   10   High]

|  | Observer Rating | Team Rating |
|---|---|---|
| 1. Degree of cooperative teamwork | _____ | _____ |
| 2. Degree of team motivation | _____ | _____ |
| 3. Degree of member satisfaction | _____ | _____ |
| 4. Degree of information sharing (participation) | _____ | _____ |
| 5. Degree of consensual decision making | _____ | _____ |
| 6. Degree of team conflict or competition (i.e., conflict directly faced and resolved) | _____ | _____ |
| 7. Degree of quality of group decisions | _____ | _____ |
| 8. Degree of speed with which decision is made | _____ | _____ |
| 9. Degree of participating leadership | _____ | _____ |
| 10. Degree of clarity of goals | _____ | _____ |
| Overall rating | _____ | _____ |

Additional Observations: _____

_____

_____

_____

_____

_____

_____

_____

_____

**OBSERVER FORM B**

Instructions: Complete this sociogram on the team you are observing. Draw direction arrows for communication flow. Identify behaviors shown.

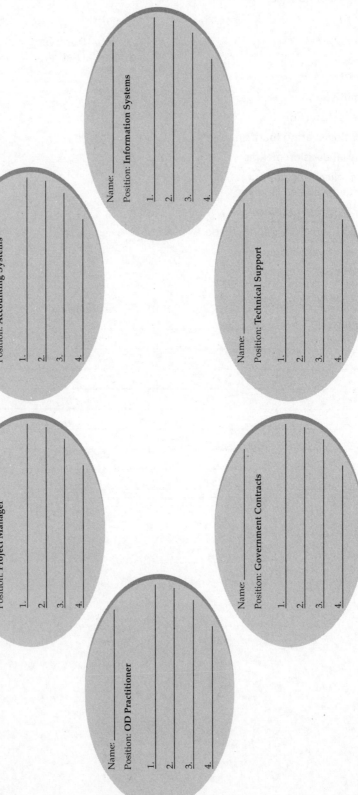

Name: _____
Position: Information Systems
1. _____
2. _____
3. _____
4. _____

Name: _____
Position: Accounting Systems
1. _____
2. _____
3. _____
4. _____

Name: _____
Position: Technical Support
1. _____
2. _____
3. _____
4. _____

Name: _____
Position: Project Manager
1. _____
2. _____
3. _____
4. _____

Name: _____
Position: OD Practitioner
1. _____
2. _____
3. _____
4. _____

Name: _____
Position: Government Contracts
1. _____
2. _____
3. _____
4. _____

# OD Skills Simulation 12.2
## Managing by Objectives

*Total time suggested: 60 minutes.*

## A. Purpose

In this simulation, you will have an opportunity to practice goal setting and apply it to your own objectives. You will be able to practice MBO-type coaching and counseling relationships, and to receive feedback in your own practitioner style.

## B. Procedures

*Step 1.* Before class, review your list of personal objectives for the course from OD Skills Simulation 2.1, Chapter 2, and determine the progress toward the goals. In Simulation 2.1, refer to the Class Performance Form and Objectives Form.

*Step 2.* Form groups of three. Additional class members can join a group, but each group should have at least three members. In a group meeting, each member in turn will have an opportunity to (1) review his or her objectives (client), (2) act as an OD practitioner, and (3) observe.

The practitioner will help the client determine specific mutual objectives, provide feedback, and review progress toward goals. Review the "Suggested Process Interventions" in Simulation 12.1.

The observer is to carefully note the interaction of the practitioner and client (see the Observer Form), looking for actions that facilitate or inhibit the MBO process.

*Step 3.* Rotate roles until all of the members have reviewed their objectives.

*Time suggested for Steps 1–3: 45 minutes.*

*Step 4.* The group should then collectively discuss the process of helping and coaching another individual in the goal-setting situation.

*Time suggested for Step 4: 15 minutes.*

**OBSERVER FORM-MANAGEMENT BY OBJECTIVES**

*Instructions:* As an observer, score the practitioner on the following ten questions. Select a number from 1 for low to 7 for high that indicates your observation. On the lines below each question, provide examples or additional information.

1.  Establish a relationship                                            Low 1 : 2 : 3 : 4 : 5 : 6 : 7 High

   _____

2.  Make eye contact                                                    Low 1 : 2 : 3 : 4 : 5 : 6 : 7 High

   _____

3.  Focus on feelings                                                   Low 1 : 2 : 3 : 4 : 5 : 6 : 7 High

   _____

4.  Encourage the client to be specific                                Low 1 : 2 : 3 : 4 : 5 : 6 : 7 High

   _____

5.  Allow the client to talk                                           Low 1 : 2 : 3 : 4 : 5 : 6 : 7 High

   _____

6.  Provide solutions                                                   Low 1 : 2 : 3 : 4 : 5 : 6 : 7 High

   _____

7.  Lead and direct the conversation                                   Low 1 : 2 : 3 : 4 : 5 : 6 : 7 High

   _____

8.  Participate in "small talk"                                        Low 1 : 2 : 3 : 4 : 5 : 6 : 7 High

   _____

9.  Show indications of judging others                                 Low 1 : 2 : 3 : 4 : 5 : 6 : 7 High

   _____

10. Use sarcasm or inappropriate humor                                 Low 1 : 2 : 3 : 4 : 5 : 6 : 7 High

   _____

# CASE: VALLEY WIDE UTILITIES COMPANY

Valley Wide Utilities Company, a privately owned utility company, is faced with financial inefficiencies resulting from an expansion of its facilities. President Robert Delgado has requested a review of the firm's operating standards. He has asked John Givens and Hilda Hirsh to provide a broad outline of MBO performance standards that would identify key standards with which to control performance. Three years ago, Valley Wide Utilities, under the direction of a management consulting firm, implemented a system of MBO for the purpose of evaluating department managers, sales engineers, and consumer service employees.

The advantage of such a system of controls is that top management can very rapidly scan a printout and detect any trouble spots in the department. Givens and Hirsh attempted to set the standards as if the personnel were working at a normal pace. After review, Givens and Hirsh raised the performance level on several items, reasoning that a standard is probably too low if it can be achieved without a challenge. Delgado had specifically asked for goals that were not easily attainable. There was a certain amount of negative reaction, but in the end, the departments agreed.

## The Situation

During the past year, however, a significant amount of dissatisfaction has emerged. In the first year, participation was encouraged and rewards were obtained. The employees set their goals high and productivity increased.

Now, however, problems are being reported in the evaluation of performance, and many managers are claiming that the standards set by Hirsh were too tight or unfair. The president said, "Yes, we have had a few operating problems, but no system is perfect." Hirsh noted that the consumer department had exceeded its monthly labor cost standards, so she called Bill Walton and "red-lined" his performance report. Walton hit the roof. He called Givens and said, "The system is grossly unfair and inaccurate as a measure of performance. The real objective is to control total costs. My department has done this, even though we were over in labor costs. There was a heavy snowstorm last month with lots of frozen lines, and we had to get people out there on overtime. The real need is to maximize customer service and keep costs to a minimum, which we have done."

Two other department managers complained that the system was unfair, and several engineers are threatening to resign. In their complaints to Givens, they pointed out that Hirsh was apparently only looking for failures to report, under the cover of the MBO system. Robert Delgado thought: "We may need to take another look at our system; maybe MBO doesn't work in a utility." (Use the Case Analysis Form on the following page.)

**VALLEY WIDE UTILITIES COMPANY CASE ANALYSIS FROM**

Name: _____

I. Problems

  A. Macro

    1. _____

    _____

    2. _____

    _____

  B. Micro

    1. _____

    _____

    2. _____

    _____

II. Causes

    1. _____

    _____

    2. _____

    _____

    3. _____

    _____

III. Systems affected

    1. _____

    _____

    2. _____

    _____

    3. _____

    _____

IV. Alternatives

    1. _____

    _____

    2. _____

    _____

    3. _____

    _____

V. Recommendations

_____

_____

_____

_____

_____

_____

## Chapter 12 Endnotes

1. Janet Adamy, "Schultz Takes Over to Try to Perk Up Starbucks," *Wall Street Journal*, January 8, 2008, p. B1.

2. For additional information, see Michael P. O'Driscoll and James L. Eubanks, "Behavioral Competencies, Goal Setting, and OD Practitioner Effectiveness," *Group and Organization Management*, vol. 18, no. 3 (September 1993), pp. 308–27.

3. Mina Kimes, "Cereal Cost Cutters," *Fortune*, November 10, 2008, p. 24; Norman T. Sheehan and Ganesh Vaidyanathan, "The Path to Growth," *Wall Street Journal*, March 3, 2007, p. R8; Pallavi Gogoi, "Thinking Outside the Cereal Box," *Business Week*, July 28, 2003, pp. 74–75.

4. For summaries of goal setting, see Edwin A. Locke, and Gary P. Latham, *A Theory of Goal Setting and Task Performance* (Englewood Cliffs, NJ: Prentice-Hall, 1990); Gary P. Latham and Edwin A. Locke, "Self-Regulation through Goal Setting," *Organizational Behavior and Human Decision Processes*, vol. 50, no. 2 (December 1991), pp. 212–47; E. A. Locke, G. P. Latham, and M. Erez, "The Determinants of Goal Commitment," *Academy of Management Review*, vol. 13, no. 1 (January 1988), pp. 23–29; E. A. Locke, L. M. Saari, K. N. Shaw, and G. P. Latham, "Goal Setting and Task Performance: 1969–80," *Psychological Bulletin*, vol. 90, no. 1 (July 1981), pp. 125–52.

5. Jena McGregor, "Keeping Talent in the Fold," *Business Week*, November 3, 2008, p. 51.

6. Scott McCartney, "How US Airways Vaulted to First Place," *Wall Street Journal*, July 22, 2008, p. D3.

7. E. A. Locke, D. C. Chah, S. Harrison, and N. Lustgarten, "Separating the Effects of Goal Specificity from Goal Level," *Organizational Behavior and Human Decision Processes*, vol. 43, no, 2 (April 1989), pp. 270–87; P. C. Earley, T. Connolly, and G. Ekegren, "Goals, Strategy Development, and Task Performance: Some Limits on the Efficacy of Goal Setting," *Journal of Applied Psychology*, vol. 74, no. 1 (February 1989), pp. 24–33.

8. M. Erez and I. Zidon, "Effect of Goal Acceptance on the Relationship of Goal Difficulty to Performance," *Journal of Applied Psychology*, vol. 69, no. 1 (February 1984), pp. 69–78; G. P. Latham and G. A. Yukl, "A Review of Research on the Application of Goal Setting in Organizations," *Academy of Management Journal*, vol. 18, no. 4 (December 1975), p. 833.

9. Graham Jones, "How the Best of the Best Get Better and Better," *Harvard Business Review*, June 2008, pp. 123–6. For research tending to validate this method, see Cornelius J. König and Martin Kleinmann, "Time Management Problems and Discounted Utility," *Journal of Psychology*, vol. 141, no. 3 (May 2007), pp. 321–34.

10. M. Erez, P. C. Earley, and C. L. Hulin, "The Impact of Participation on Goal Acceptance and Performance: A Two-Step Model," *Academy of Management Journal*, vol. 28, no. 1 (March 1985), pp. 50–66; J. R. Hollenbeck, C. R. Williams, and J. Klein, "An Empirical Examination of the Antecedents of Commitment to Difficult Goals," *Journal of Applied Psychology*, vol. 74, no. 1 (February 1989), pp. 18–23.

11. Michelle Tuckey, Neil Brewer, and Paul Williamson, "The Influence of Motives and Goal Orientation on Feedback Seeking," *Journal of Occupational & Organizational Psychology*, vol. 75, no. 2 (June 2002), p. 195; Francis J. Yammarino and Leanne E. Atwater, "Do Managers See Themselves as Others See Them? Implications of Self-Other Rating Agreement for Human Resources Management," *Organizational Dynamics*, vol. 25, no. 4 (March 1, 1997), pp. 35–45; P. C. Earley, G. B. Northcraft, C. Lee, and T. R. Lituchy, "Impact of Process and Outcome Feedback on the Relation of Goal Setting to Task Performance," *Academy of Management Journal*, vol. 33, no. 1 (March 1990), pp. 87–105; R. Vance and A. Colella, "Effects of Two Types of Feedback on Goal Acceptance and Personal Goals," *Journal of Applied Psychology*, vol. 75, no. 1 (February 1990), pp. 68–76; J. R. Larson, "The Dynamic Interplay Between Employees' Feedback Seeking Strategies and Supervisors' Delivery of Performance Feedback," *Academy of Management Review*, vol. 14, no. 3 (July 1989), p. 408.

12. Brittany Hite, "Employers Rethink How They Give Feedback," *Wall Street Journal*, October 13, 2008, p. B5.

13. Ibid.

14. Hollenbeck, Williams, and Klein, "Empirical Examination"; J. R. Hollenbeck and A. P. Brief, "The Effects of Individual Differences and Goal Origin on Goal Setting and Performance," *Organizational Behavior and Human Decision Processes*, vol. 40, no. 3 (December 1987), pp. 392–414.

15. Peter G. Dominick, Richard R. Reilly, and Jack W. McGourty, "The Effects of Peer Feedback on Team Member Behavior," *Group and Organization Management*, vol. 22, no. 4 (December 1997), pp. 508–23; Jon R. Katzenbach and Douglas K. Smith, "The Discipline of Teams," *Harvard Business Review*, March/April 1993, pp. 111–20; T. R. Mitchell and W. S. Silver, "Individual and Group Goals When Workers Are Interdependent: Effects on Task Strategies and Performance," *Journal of Applied Psychology*, vol. 75, no. 2 (April 1990), pp. 185–93; E. E. Gist, E. A. Locke, and M. S. Taylor, "Organizational Behavior: Group Structure, Process, and Effectiveness," *Journal of Management*, vol. 13, no. 2 (Summer 1987), pp. 237–57.

16. Stephen B. Knouse, "Task Cohesion: A Mechanism for Bringing Together Diverse Teams," *International Journal of Management*, vol. 23, no. 3, part 2 (September 2006), pp. 588–96; E. V. Hobman, P. Bordia, and C. Gallois, "Perceived Dissimilarity and Work Group Involvement: The Moderating Effects of Group Openness to Diversity," *Group and Organization Management*, vol. 29, no. 5 (October 2004), pp. 560–87.

17. Kelly K. Spors, "Top Small Workplaces 2008," *Wall Street Journal*, October 13, 2008, R1–5.

18. G. P. Latham and E. A. Locke, *Goal Setting: A Motivational Technique That Works* (Upper Saddle River, NJ: Prentice Hall, 1964); G. P. Latham and E. A. Locke, "Goal Setting: A Motivational Technique That Works," *Organizational Dynamics*, Autumn 1979, pp. 68–80.

19. J. A. Riedel, D. M. Nebeker, and B. L. Cooper, "The Influence of Monetary Incentives on Goal Choice, Goal Commitment, and Task Performance," *Organizational Behavior and Human Decision Processes*, vol. 42, no 2 (October 1988), pp. 155–80.

20. Robert Berner, "P&G: How A. G. Lafley Is Revolutionizing a Bastion of Corporate Conservatism," *Business Week*, July 7, 2003, p. 62.

21. Locke, Saari, Shaw, and Latham, "Goal Setting and Task Performance," p. 125; E. A. Locke, D. B. Feren, V. M. McCaleb, K. N. Shaw, and A. T. Denny, "The Relative Effectiveness of Four Methods of Motivating Employee Performance," *Changes in Working Life*, ed. K. Duncan, M. Gruneberg, and D. Wallis (New York: John Wiley, 1980).

22. Locke, Saari, Shaw, and Latham, "Goal Setting and Task Performance," p. 125.

23. Steve W. J. Kozlowski and Daniel R. Ilgen, "Enhancing the Effectiveness of Work Groups and Teams," *Psychological Science in the Public Interest*, vol. 7, no. 3 (December 2006), pp. 77–124; C. C. Durham, D. Knight, and E. A. Locke, "Effects of Leader Role, Team-Set Goal Difficulty, Efficacy, and Tactics on Team Effectiveness," *Organizational Behavior and Human Decision Processes*, vol. 72, no. 2 (November 1997), pp. 203–31; L. R. Weingart, "Impact of Group Goals, Task Component Complexity, Effort, and Planning on Group-Performance," *Journal of Applied Psychology*, vol. 77, no. 5 (October 1992), pp. 682–93.

24. For additional information, see George S. Odiorne, "MBO Means Having a Goal and a Plan, Not Just a Goal," *Manage*, vol. 44, no. 1 (September 1992), pp. 8–11; George S. Odiorne, "Chaos in Management," *Manage*, vol. 43, no. 1 (August 1991), p. 4; Paul Mali, *MBO Updated* (New York: John Wiley, 1986); S. Carroll and W. Tosi Jr., *Management by Objectives, Applications and Research* (New York: Macmillan,1973); George Odiorne, *MBO II* (Belmont, CA: Fearon-Pitman, 1979); Anthony Raia, *Managing by Objectives* (Glenview, IL: Scott Foresman, 1974).

25. Odiorne, *MBO II*, p. 53.

26. Douglas M. McGregor, *The Human Side of Enterprise* (New York: McGraw-Hill, 1960), p. 61. See also Douglas M. McGregor, "An Uneasy Look at Performance Appraisal," *Harvard Business Review*, May/June 1957, pp. 89–94.

27. McGregor, *Human Side of Enterprise*, p. 62.

28. For a critique of MBO, see Joseph F. Castellano and Harper A. Roehm, "The Problems with Managing by Objectives and Results," *Quality Progress*, vol. 34, no. 3 (March 2001), p. 39; Philip E. Quigley, "Can Management by Objectives Be Compatible with Quality?" *Industrial Engineering*, vol. 25, no. 7 (July 1993), p. 14.

29. Carroll and Tosi, *Management by Objectives*.

30. Raia, *Managing by Objectives*; H. Meyer, E. Kay, and J. French, "Split Roles and Performance Appraisal," *Harvard Business Review*, January/February 1965, p. 123.

# Work Team Development

## LEARNING OBJECTIVES

**Upon completing this chapter, you will be able to:**

1. Describe the major OD quality and productivity interventions.
2. Diagnose job design problems as part of an OD program.
3. Identify the similarities and differences in job design, total quality management, and self-managed work teams.
4. Experience how an OD practitioner can help an organization to make productivity changes.

## PREMEETING PREPARATION

1. Read Chapter 13.
2. Prepare for OD Skills Simulation 13.1. Prior to class, form teams of six to eight members and assign supervisor and observer roles. Complete Step 1.
3. Prepare for OD Skills Simulation 13.2. Form teams of six and assign roles. Complete Step 1.
4. Read and analyze Case: Wengart Aircraft.

## CONTINUOUS IMPROVEMENT PROCESSES

The organization of the twenty-first century strongly emphasizes quality and productivity. Executives striving to increase quality, enhance productivity, and reduce costs are reexamining the way companies are managed. Many organizations are changing the way they operate in such areas as organizational culture, technology, structure, and how they relate to customers and employees. Google is perhaps one of the most notable examples of applying these ideas. It has continued to develop new technologies combined with a unique culture, an egalitarian orientation towards employees, and an extremely decentralized organization that relies on small self-managing teams—all this in a company that has seen exploding growth to more than 20,000 employees worldwide in a relative short life that dates to only 1998. The message is clear: change for the better or face elimination. A key issue facing organizations is the way they respond to a changing environment of "world-class competition." OD interventions leading to improved productivity, efficiency, and quality have evolved to help organizations meet these challenges.

Total quality management (TQM) is a widely used quality and productivity intervention. Under TQM, organization members commit to continuous improvement in meeting or exceeding customer expectations. In a time of downsizing and restructuring, many North American companies are finding that they must learn to manage more effectively, and TQM involves all levels of the organization in developing practices that are customer-oriented, flexible, and responsive to changing needs. For many companies, the change involves a top-to-bottom overhauling of their corporate culture. Companies are becoming leaders by driving relentlessly for market share, focusing on high quality, cutting costs, investing in research and development, and pouring heavy resources into training and empowering their employees.

Business enterprises and nonprofit organizations are increasingly confronted with problems of stagnant or declining productivity, worker dissatisfaction and alienation, and domestic and foreign competition. Many federal regulations that once protected inefficient operations are being rescinded, and as a result companies now confront increased competition. Businesses in many countries no longer receive the trade protection once extended by their national governments. As an example, for every $5 of goods or services a country produces, it sells about $1 abroad. The marketplace is truly a global market, and with this comes ever greater competition. Witness the rapid changes in the services and products offered through the Internet, the rapid contraction and mergers of airline carriers, the radical transformation of the financial services industry, and the change in the way healthcare is offered. Worldwide market conditions are forcing these and other industries to rapidly and radically alter the manner in which they do business.

This chapter deals with improving work processes for individuals and work teams. The trend in many profit and nonprofit organizations is toward decentralization, horizontal organization, fewer levels of management, a decrease in staff positions, and broader spans of control. More of the decision-making authority is being pushed down to the lowest levels of the organization where the employees are most aware of the problems. The work team, not the individual, is becoming the mechanism for organizing work.[1] Through high-involvement management, line workers are planning, organizing, controlling, and leading. In a real sense, they are all managers. TQM postulates that *good isn't good enough!* These programs focus on continuous process improvement.

OD practitioners use structural changes like work design concepts to help organizations make productivity changes while simultaneously improving the work life of employees. First we look at how work or jobs can be redesigned, and then we continue with a discussion of two quality and high-involvement interventions: TQM and self-managed work teams.

## JOB DESIGN

**Job design** has been a concern of managers for many years, but it was Frederick Taylor in 1911 who first proposed scientifically designing jobs. Scientific management ideas emanating from industrial engineers tended to break jobs down into their smallest, simplest tasks to reduce human error and the need for training and skill. Time-and-motion studies were expected to increase productivity. There was little regard for the human element other than to make sure that it was adequately controlled and supervised. More recently, organizations have begun to discover that they often have to pay a high price in absenteeism, turnover, apathy, poor work quality, or even sabotage when they fail to consider the human element.

Job design certainly applies to production line work but does not stop there. It looks at work in general from an operational viewpoint. The objective is to find and implement innovative ways of doing work. Business-oriented newspapers and magazines frequently report on innovations at Cisco, Toyota, Intel, Apple, and Procter & Gamble (P&G).

The current trend is to redesign jobs to improve worker satisfaction and productivity. Redesigning jobs is by no means easy, because there are so many variables, such as the worker,[2] the nature of the work, the organizational climate, and the manager's style. Some of the successes in job design provide guidelines. The following is a discussion of two closely related theories of job design: job characteristics theory and job enrichment theory.

### Job Characteristics Theory

An approach to job design is the **job characteristics model**.[3] The model attempts to develop objective measures of job characteristics that can directly affect employee attitudes and work behaviors. According to the model, work motivation and satisfaction are affected by five core job dimensions: skill variety, task identity, task significance, autonomy, and job feedback.

> **Skill variety** is the degree to which a job requires a mix of activities and involves the use of different skills and talents. Employees usually see tasks that require several different skills, especially challenging skills, as being meaningful.
>
> **Task identity** refers to the degree to which the job requires completion of a whole and identifiable piece of work. It is doing a job from beginning to end with a visible outcome. An employee probably will find a task more meaningful if it entails producing the entire product rather than a small component.
>
> **Task significance** is the degree to which the job has a substantial impact on the lives of other people, whether in the same organization or in the external environment. Work will likely be more meaningful when an employee perceives the results to have a substantial effect on other people.
>
> **Autonomy** is the degree to which the job gives the worker freedom, independence, and discretion in scheduling the work and determining the procedures to be used in carrying it

out. Autonomy allows employees to take a larger part in planning and controlling their work. Employees will generally have greater commitment to and ownership of their jobs when they have autonomy over their work.

**Job feedback** refers to the degree to which carrying out the work activities required by the job results in workers obtaining direct and clear information about the effectiveness of their performance. Customers or other people internal to the organization who use the product or service can provide feedback if communication channels to the employee are provided. The feedback is directly based on how well the task was done and not on the evaluations of a peer or supervisor.

The five core job dimensions can be mathematically combined to derive a score that reflects a job's motivational potential. As skill variety, task identity, and task significance jointly determine a job's meaningfulness, these three dimensions are treated as one dimension in the **Motivating Potential Score** (MPS) formula:

*Motivating Potential Score (MPS) = Job Meaningfulness $\times$ Autonomy $\times$ Job Feedback*

The first variable in the formula, job meaningfulness, is a function of skill variety, task identity, and task significance. Thus, the formula can further be expanded:

*Motivating Potential Score (MPS) =*

$$\left[ \frac{Skill\ Variety + Task\ Identity + Task\ Significance}{3} \right] \times Autonomy \times Job\ Feedback$$

Based on the formula, a score of near zero on either the autonomy or job feedback dimension will produce an MPS of near zero, whereas a number near zero on skill variety, task identity, or task significance will reduce the total MPS, but will not completely undermine the motivational potential of a job.

When the core job dimensions are present in a job, the job characteristics model predicts certain positive effects in an employee's psychological state. High scores in skill variety, task identity, and task significance result in the employee's experiencing meaningfulness in the job, such as believing the work to be important, valuable, and worthwhile. A high score in the autonomy dimension leads to the employee's feeling personally responsible and accountable for the results of the work. A high score in the job feedback dimension is an indication that the employee has an understanding of how he or she is performing the job.

The authors of the model and other authorities suggest that research from the behavioral sciences can be used to enrich jobs and produce a positive impact on the five core job dimensions. One approach to improving jobs is to take fractionalized tasks and put them back together to form a new and larger module of work. This increases the skill variety and task identity dimensions of the work. This method has been used for several decades at General Motors (GM) and Toyota's NUMMI (New United Motor Manufacturing Inc.) plant in Fremont, California. NUMMI is a joint venture between the two companies and has been in operations since 1984. GM uses it as a way to learn lean manufacturing techniques from Toyota and to implement the techniques in other GM plants. Teams of workers are responsible for auto subassemblies, such as doors and transmissions. NUMMI has been helpful in introducing a teamwork-based working environment to the United States. NUMMI has won numerous awards for the plant and for the vehicles produced there.[4]

A second approach is to form natural work units by giving employees tasks that constitute an identifiable and meaningful whole. Doing this enables the employee to have greater ownership in the work, and to more closely identify with it and understand its significance.

A third approach is to permit the employee to have direct contact with the people who use the product or service. This means directing complaints or questions from customers directly to the involved employee or employees. The term "customer" should be broadly defined to mean anyone, inside or outside the organization, that an employee serves. For example, the finance department's customers are other divisions within the company to whom they provide financial and operational information. Other customers include investors, the Securities and Exchange Commission, and the media that reports on financial matters.

A fourth approach is to load jobs vertically by giving employees such functions as deciding on work methods, break times, and how to train new employees, and formulating budgets. Skill training in such areas as budgets, training techniques, and time management may be needed to enable employees to successfully take on these new responsibilities, which improve autonomy.

## OD Application: When Teams are 14 Time Zones Apart[5]

The sales of a small Silicon Valley software company slowed in 2001 to the point that it began laying off software engineers. In looking for ways to cut costs, the company decided that it could save millions by moving much of its programming to Bangalore, India, that country's equivalent to Silicon Valley. The company could put more people on the job at a lower cost and turn out the software faster. The motivation for this company was pure survival. But the process was difficult, and the anticipated savings was offset by other costs. The company preferred to use small teams of highly qualified and enthusiastic people working closely together.

Working with teams located in California and India, separated by 14 time zones, and with no local manager in India, turned out to be a challenge. The Silicon Valley company was looking for experienced programmers with 8 to 10 years of experience. But such programmers are hard to find in India, where many programmers are recent college grads. What's more, the company's engineers were used to working with people on the other side of a cubicle—not on the other side of the world. Engineers were accustomed to writing vague specifications for a program because everyone was familiar with the products and customers. All the programmers knew the features that customers expected and automatically included them in the software. If anyone had a question, the answer could be found down the hall.

The combination of no local manager, inexperienced Indian programmers, and vague instructions was a formula for failure. Indian programmers were frustrated by the lack of direction, followed by rejected software. Over half of the Indian programmers quit within a year. Executives in the United States went from one crisis to another. Software deliveries were delayed and revenues went down. Its reputation with customers was declining. Responses to customer requests and questions went from two days to a week.

Sitting even closer to the edge of bankruptcy than before the company began using engineers in India, the company's managers decided to streamline operations and change the way they divided work between California and India. They gave the Indian programmers entire projects instead of small parts of a bigger project, so that continual interaction with U.S. programmers was not required. U.S. team leaders started writing more detailed program specifications and communicating twice a week by telephone. Concerted efforts were made to make the Indian programmers a part of the team from the home office. Times of telephone and conferencing calls were rotated to alternate the inconvenience caused by the time difference. Employees in India were included in company-wide e-mails. Multiple sessions of company meetings were held at times convenient for the Indians. A new software engineer was brought in to the Silicon Valley office whose job was to coordinate the U.S. and Indian teams.

Other companies are using culture-awareness training to prepare employees in India and the United States to work together. American employees who will be part of an Indian/U.S. team participate in courses that educate them in cultural and communication differences. Subjects include religious and language diversity and business attire and protocol. Much of the knowledge gained from the courses may seem basic, but it can help to avoid misunderstandings.

Communication problems should not be underestimated. One suggestion is to get feedback from an Indian coworker in a different form than what was transmitted. For example, if there was a phone conversation, get feedback about what was communicated via e-mail. Though Indians know English well, it may not be their native language, and they may not be processing the information in the same way as their U.S. coworkers. This kind of training is occurring on both sides of the Pacific.

### Questions

1. What were the challenges faced in outsourcing work to India?
2. Can you think of any other things that will help Indian and U.S. teams work better together?
3. What do you think of the culture-awareness training that some companies are using?

A fifth approach is to open or create feedback channels so that employees can learn how well they are performing their work. Self-managed work teams, which will be discussed later in this chapter, combine these five approaches into a unified method of improving work. An example of lessons learned about unifying teams when they are separated by time zones and have a different culture is in **OD Application: When Teams are 14 Time Zones Apart.**

### Job Enrichment Theory

Employees at every level of an organization are interested in two facets of their work—the quality of the work itself and the benefits or rewards the job offers, based on the research of Frederick Herzberg.[6] Of the two, the quality of the work leads to job satisfaction. Job satisfaction occurs when employees experience work situations that entail increases in achievement, recognition, challenging work, responsibility, and advancement. **Job enrichment theory** holds that jobs should be redesigned to improve the motivators related to a job by permitting employees to attain more responsibility and achievement. Employees can be given appropriate recognition and advancement in their careers for a job well done, and the work itself should be challenging, interesting, and meaningful. There are many techniques for improving these motivational factors, and they must be tailored to fit specific situations. Several suggestions include:

- Give employees or work groups a natural and complete unit of work. This is in contrast to the practice of specialization of labor that dominated the structure of most organizations in the twentieth century.

- Add more difficult assignments to jobs and provide appropriate training.
- Give employees more authority. For example, let them make important or difficult decisions.
- Have peers in work groups or teams become experts in specialized areas. Work groups could have several specialists that other employees could go to for information and help.
- Make information, including company reports, directly available to employees instead of editing or censoring the information. This is particularly important where the information is related to the employees' work. An example of making more information available to employees is open-book management, discussed in chapters 3 and 6.
- Remove controls over employees but continue to hold them accountable.

Job enrichment theory holds that extrinsic rewards such as money are important accompaniments to changes in the way jobs are done. It emphasizes, however, that a system that only provides monetary incentives will not improve worker performance. Improvements in both the quality of the work and rewards are required to make a change in job design successful.[7]

## Results of Job Design Programs

The results of job design programs suggest that they can be successful if they are managed correctly and have employee involvement. In a review of the literature on work-restructuring methods, researchers have found that 90 percent of the reports on work-restructuring interventions cited improvements in productivity, costs, absenteeism, attitudes, or quality, and that an increasing number of organizations are setting up such methods.[8]

The results of job design efforts and job enrichment theory are promising in terms of positively linking improvements in the five core job characteristics and job enrichment with higher levels of team effectiveness.[9] Another study related to job enrichment theory looked at employee satisfaction and productivity. It was found that encouraging know-how among employees and providing information at the lowest levels of an organization gives employees the expertise to manage their work, recognize problems, and generate solutions.[10] Several other studies have confirmed the validity of the job characteristics theory.[11] Additional research into this theory is warranted, but until it is available the basic ideas of the theory will serve as a foundation for many changes in job design within organizations.

## TOTAL QUALITY MANAGEMENT

Today's managers are being challenged to provide leadership in new and changing conditions. Customers, competitors, employees, and stockholders are all putting pressure on management to quickly innovate and change. One approach that has emerged to meet these changing forces is **total quality management.** It is also known by other names, including continuous quality improvement (CQI) and leadership through quality (LTQ).

TQM is an organizational strategy of commitment to improving customer satisfaction by developing procedures that carefully manage output quality. TQM involves moving toward organizational excellence by integrating the desires of individuals for growth and development with organizational goals. TQM is a philosophy and a set of guiding principles for continuous improvement that is based on customer satisfaction, teamwork, and continuous improvement. It particularly relies on teamwork and empowerment of individuals, two concepts discussed in previous chapters. TQM is not so much a special OD technique as an aspect of a reinvented corporate culture—a culture with a strong commitment to improving quality in all organizational processes.

TQM applies human resources and analytical tools to focus on meeting or exceeding customers' current and future needs. It integrates resources and tools into managerial efforts by providing planned, systematic approaches to improving organizational performance. For an example of what not to expect in TQM, see Figure 13.1. This involves everyone in programs aimed at improving the total organization, so that it is more customer-oriented, quality conscious, flexible, and responsive. The purpose of a TQM program is to make the organization more effective and develop the potential of its individual members. Finally, there are a series of planned improvements that will ultimately influence the quality and productivity of the organization. TQM programs currently exist worldwide in various forms, and there are a number of professional organizations that encourage their implementation.[12]

**FIGURE 13.1   This Is Not TQM**
*Source:* CROCK © NORTH AMERICA SYNDICATE

## The Characteristics of TQM

Although there is some disagreement about what makes up TQM, several key characteristics are widely recognized. TQM is regarded as an organization-wide system that focuses on the customer and increases efficiency and reliability of work.[13] TQM is planned and broad-based. Organizations that practice TQM usually have several principles or components in common:[14]

*TQM is organization-wide.* The production line is a natural and obvious place to improve quality, but TQM also takes place in the accounting, marketing, retail sales, human resources management, information systems, engineering, and housekeeping departments, and in other service and staff areas of an organization.

*The CEO and other top managers visibly support it.* Everyone, from top managers to hourly employees, operates under TQM. There is a reward system in place that ensures continual support.

*TQM is an ingrained value in the corporate culture.* Continuous improvement penetrates the culture and values of the organization. Quality is seen as "how we do things around here."

*Partnership with customers and suppliers.* The organization encourages partnerships with suppliers and customers. The product or service must meet or exceed the customer's expectations. Results—not slogans—represent quality.

*Everyone in an organization has a customer.* The customer may be internal or external. The next person on the production line, another department, and someone outside the organization who purchases the product or service are all seen as customers.

*Reduced cycle time.* Cycle times for products and services, as well as support functions, focus on doing the job faster.

*Techniques of TQM range in scope.* The techniques used in TQM include statistical quality control, job design, empowerment, and self-managed work teams.

*Do it right the first time.* Quality is not obtained by rejecting a product when it gets to the end of a production line. It has to be built in at every stage of the production process. Nothing leaves a department unless it is right, even if the poor quality may have originated in another department. Inspections are not enough; the people making the product are responsible for product quality.

*Corporate citizenship.* The organization values and respects everyone, both those in the organization and those it serves. This includes customers, suppliers, employees, owners, the community, and the environment. These parties are often called stakeholders.

*No single formula works for everyone.* Every organization is unique, and off-the-shelf programs tend not to work. Managers often subscribe to the "follow the crowd" or "lemming" approach, but what was successful at one company may not work in another.

## Quality

Harvard professor David Garvin has identified eight dimensions that define the perspective of the quality concept. Customers, managers, engineers, line operators, and employees at every level of an organization must be involved in improving and managing quality if TQM is to succeed. The dimensions of quality that he identified are listed below.[15]

- *Performance.* A product or service's primary operating characteristic (e.g., the speed of a personal computer).
- *Features.* Add-ons or supplements (e.g., a cell phone that has built-in games, a camera, and e-mail capability).
- *Reliability.* A probability of not malfunctioning or breaking down for a specified period of time (e.g., a six-year, 60,000-mile warranty for an automobile).
- *Conformance.* The degree to which a product's design and operating characteristics meet established standards (e.g., a product test shows that the product is within 0.001 inches of the standard).
- *Durability.* A measure of a product's life (e.g., 10 years).
- *Serviceability.* The speed and ease of repair (e.g., a component for a product can be replaced by an untrained user).
- *Aesthetic.* A product's look, feel, taste, and smell (e.g., a distinctive and appealing design).
- *Perceived quality.* Quality as viewed by a customer or client (e.g., a parent who buys only one brand of baby shampoo or powder because of the company's history of providing quality products).

## Malcolm Baldrige National Quality Award

TQM has become a key concern of management. In the 1980s, much of this attention was initially focused on the U.S. auto industry, which was experiencing a decline in sales and a growing number of product defects. Companies in many other industries also became concerned about poor quality products and services. The Malcolm Baldrige National Quality Award's purpose is to increase attention to quality.[16] The award program was established in 1987 by the U.S. Congress largely in response to the qualitative challenge posed by foreign products and processes in competition with U.S. companies. The act set up a national program to recognize U.S. companies and other organizations that practice effective quality management. The program is managed by National Institute of Standards and Technology, an agency of the Commerce Department.

The **Baldrige Award** is given annually to U.S. organizations that have exemplary achievements in quality. The number of recipients has varied annually from two to five. The categories for the award include manufacturers, service companies, small business, nonprofit organizations (charity and government agencies), and education and health care organizations. Companies that receive the Baldrige Award are obligated to disseminate information about their successful strategies. The award's recipients include Cargill Corn Milling, Mercy Health System, Ritz Carlton, Chugach (Alaska) School District, U.S. Army Armament Research, Development and Engineering Center (ARDEC), and Boeing Aerospace Support (Boeing AS).

The Baldrige Criteria for Performance Excellence provide a framework for guiding and assessing organizational performance. The Baldrige Criteria are based on seven core values and concepts:[17]

*Leadership* examines how senior executives guide the organization and how the organization addresses its responsibilities to the public and practices good citizenship.

*Strategic planning* examines how the organization sets strategic directions and determines key action plans.

## OD Application: Chugach School District and the Baldrige Award[18]

The smallest organization ever to win a Baldrige Award is the 214-student Chugach School District (CSD). The CSD is not a typical school district. It encompasses 22,000 square miles in south-central Alaska. Most of its 214 students live in remote areas, accessible only by aircraft. CSD began a comprehensive restructuring effort when it introduced its own "onward to excellence" process. Indicators of student performance were well below state and national averages, with staff turnover exceeding 50 percent. Scores on the California Achievement Test were the lowest in the state, and the average student was reading three grades below grade level. Business leaders complained that CSD graduates were deficient in basic skills, and in 26 years only one student had gone on to college.

CSD pioneered a standards-based system of "whole child education" that emphasizes real-life learning situations. From the outset, the district's overhaul was undertaken collaboratively with CSD staff, current and past students, parents, school board members, and business and community leaders. Meetings yielded a core vision, shared values and beliefs, and common performance goals. Stakeholders emphasized that accountability should be built into the educational system and embedded in CSD's performance goals.

After securing a waiver from the Alaska Department of Education, the district replaced credit hours and grade levels—hallmarks of traditional schooling—with an individualized, student-centered approach. CSD created a continuum of standards for 10 content areas and established specific minimum graduation levels of mastery. Students are evaluated in the traditional areas of reading, writing, mathematics, social science, and science as well as in the nontraditional areas of service learning, career development, technology, cultural awareness and expression, and personal/social/health development. These assessments are designed to determine whether they can apply skills and knowledge in real situations. Students work at their own appropriate pace.

Highlights of the results after 10 years of the program include:

- Student's performance exceeded state and national norms. Results on the California Achievement Test rose dramatically in reading, math, and language arts.
- In the four subject areas tested in Alaska's High School Graduation Qualifying Examination, CSD topped the state average.
- A substantially larger percentage of graduates are attending post-secondary institutions.
- Faculty turnover rate, which had previously averaged 55 percent, has fallen to 12 percent.

### Questions

1. Research the Baldrige Awards at www.quility.nist.gov/ to find out what organizations are the current award winners.
2. At this Web site, research the application requirements.

*Customer and market focus* examines how the organization ascertains customer requirements and expectations, builds relationships with customers, and acquires, satisfies, and retains customers.

*Measurement, analysis, and knowledge management* examines the management, effective use, analysis, and improvement of data and information to support key organization processes and the organization's performance management system.

*Human resource focus* examines how the organization enables its workforce to develop its full potential and how the workforce is aligned with the organization's objectives.

*Process management* examines how key production/delivery and support processes are designed, managed, and improved.

*Business results* examine the organization's performance and improvement in its key business areas: customer satisfaction, financial and marketplace performance, human resources, supplier and partner performance, operational performance, and governance and social responsibility. The category also examines how the organization performs relative to competitors.

To learn about a previous recipient of the Baldrige, see **OD Application: Chugach School District and the Baldrige Award.**

### Compatibility of TQM and OD

Total quality management and organization development share certain values. Both are systemwide, depend on planned change, believe in empowerment and involvement, are self-renewing and continuous, base decision making on data-based activities, and view people as having an inherent desire to contribute in meaningful ways.

There are differences, however, between OD and TQM. Some OD practitioners argue that their core values differ, and they caution against OD practitioners assuming the role of "quality management expert."[19] The OD practitioner has to enter the organization as a neutral party and resist advocating any particular method of change. OD practitioners view organization problems as having a variety of causes with no predefined solutions. TQM consultants, on the other hand, view organization problems as having TQM solutions.

Within an OD program, TQM can be applied as one change methodology along with an accompanying array of other interventions. Some recent studies of organizations have found that TQM is more likely to be successful when combined with employee involvement.[20] The two are complementary, and the impact of either is diminished by the absence of the other.

According to some theorists, OD is becoming a "checklist" or "technology-driven approach." TQM approaches often lead even more in this direction. The OD practitioner must take care not to bring prepackaged solutions to a client. Not all change approaches are equally effective with all client systems at all points in time.

OD practitioners are often involved in setting up TQM programs. In this situation, the practitioner is being asked to act in the role of an expert. Clients are usually more comfortable with experts who can provide quick answers, but the OD approach is to build the client's self-renewal capability.

TQM is in danger of becoming another "technique" that managers believe they must use because it is used at other companies.[21] Bain & Co., a major worldwide consulting firm, has completed 12 surveys over the past 16 years of senior executives around the world to see what management tools they use. The most recent survey available is based on the findings from 1,430 companies in 70 countries. TQM was used by 34 percent of the respondents, down from 57 percent from five years prior. The satisfaction rating was 3.8 out of a possible 5, no change from five years ago.[22] Other studies of TQM programs point to poor implementation as a significant reason for failure. Frequently, for instance, TQM is formally developed at the top management level but it fails to be adequately implemented at the operational level.[23] Another study indicates that companies that implemented TQM but later discontinued its use did so because of factors related to core philosophy, commitment of senior management, ability of TQM advocates, and continuity of leadership.[24] Despite the problems with TQM, when implemented properly it has the potential to bring desirable benefits, such as improved quality, higher productivity, and enhanced employee development.[25]

## SELF-MANAGED WORK TEAMS

A **self-managed work team** is an autonomous group whose members decide how to handle their task.[26] The task of the team is an identifiable task, service, or product. The group may be a permanent work team or a temporary team brought together to solve a problem or develop a new product. Often teams are composed of people from different parts of the organization, with different skills and backgrounds. Authority has been vested in the teams by upper management to manage their group processes, including production and personnel matters, in order to accomplish their objectives. The diversified background of members and the necessary authority gives the teams the ability to move around the bureaucratic organization and get the job done.

Increased responsibility is placed on team members. Work teams are assigned a wide range of tasks, including setting work schedules, budgeting, making job assignments, developing performance goals, hiring and selecting team members, assessing job performance of fellow members, purchasing equipment, and controlling quality.

Self-managed work teams also go by other names, including self-regulating work groups, cross-functional teams, sociotechnical systems, autonomous work groups, high-performance work teams, and high-commitment work teams. Such companies as Cisco, Xerox, Boeing, DuPont, Google, Cummins Engine Company, Harley-Davidson, Dana Corporation, and W.L. Gore use them either throughout their companies or in specific facilities.

DuPont's plant in Towanda, Pennsylvania, is a good example of self-managed work teams. The plant lets employees find their own solutions to problems, set their own production schedules, and have a say in hiring. Managers call themselves "facilitators." Their main job is to coach workers and help them understand the external market forces that demand quality, teamwork, and speed.

Most companies that use self-managed teams do not do so organization-wide. They typically choose specific sites. Some companies, like Harley-Davidson Motor Company's Kansas City plant, build new plants and design the layout and production processes to fit the requirements for self-managed teams. Teams are more common in production facilities than the service sector, but they have been successfully applied in service-oriented organizations, such as life insurance companies, colleges, and government agencies.

## The Characteristics of Self-Managed Work Teams

Self-managed work teams may be used organization-wide, at a work site composed of a number of work teams, or within just a few work teams. But to whatever degree they are used, there are several characteristics that are common to all self-managed work team sites.

*The structure of the organization or work site is based on team concepts.* There are few managerial levels in the plant or work site structure and few job descriptions. The organization structure is more horizontal than vertical.

*There is an egalitarian culture and a noticeable lack of status symbols.* There are no management dining rooms, no assigned parking places, and no special furniture or decor for manager's offices. Managers may not have offices; if they do, they often become team-meeting rooms. There is no special dress code; if uniforms are required, as at Honda's U.S. plant, everyone, including the plant superintendent, wears the uniform. At other sites, no one wears ties, special badges, or other signs of power.

*A work team has a physical site.* There are functional boundaries that members can identify.

*The number of people in a team is kept as small as possible.* Typical sizes range from five to 15 members.

*Work teams order material and equipment.* They set goals, profit targets, and decide their production schedule.

*Team members have a sense of vision for their team and their organization.* A vision provides direction and energizes team behavior to accomplish goals. Most companies have a simple, understandable creed that is well communicated to all employees.

*There is strong partnership between team members and management.* If there is a labor union, the union is also a member of the partnership. Team members also help set rewards for the team members. They have a voice in who is hired and fired in the work team and the hiring of managers.

*There is a diversity in the members of a team.* Team members are different enough in their backgrounds, cultural experiences, and training so that a variety of viewpoints will be represented, and their skills will be varied enough so that members can learn from one another.

*Information of all types is openly shared.* The information system, including real-time performance data, needs to be well developed and available to all members. Members are knowledgeable in accounting and statistical concepts so they can use financial and production information to make decisions.

*Team members should be skilled and knowledgeable in their areas.* Team members should have good interpersonal skills and a desire and ability to work with others.

*Training, and especially cross-training, is a major requirement of self-managed work teams.* The success of a team depends on its members being skilled and knowledgeable in a variety of areas, including technical skills, finance, accounting, competition in the marketplace, and team process interventions.

*Team members are knowledgeable of customers, competitors, and suppliers.* The primary emphasis is to focus on customers. From the team's standpoint, a customer is someone within the organization or external to the organization who uses the team's product and service. Some organizations enter into joint-training ventures with their suppliers. They recognize that the finished product is no better than the components supplied by other companies.

*Results are tied to compensation and recognition.* Compensation, including incentive and bonus pay, for members in the team reflects the contributions and results of the team and not just individual work. In addition to monetary rewards, there is an infinite variety of noncash methods of recognition.

## The Design of Jobs

Self-managed work teams are associated with work that is high in the five core job dimensions discussed previously in job characteristics theory: skill variety, task identity, task significance, autonomy, and job feedback. Comparing a job against these five dimensions can help in evaluating the degree to which a work team is genuinely a self-managed work team.

*Skill variety* will be present in a self-managed work team when the team and its members use many different skills and talents. Many organizations that have self-managed work teams have few job classifications reflecting the ability of people to do a variety of work.

*Task identity* occurs when the team is responsible for a complete and identifiable piece of work. Examples of task identity occur when work teams do market research, engineering, design of the product, production, budgeting, and handling customer questions and complaints. Engineers' desks are on the production floor, and team members take calls from customers on the floor. At a Tektronix's plant, customers' questions and complaints are taken over a phone located on the manufacturing floor.

*Task significance* occurs in a self-managed work team when the members see that their performance has an impact on other team members, other people within the organization, and customers. Work teams are kept small so that members can identify more closely with their contributions. Members have ready access to accounting and production figures so that their individual contributions can be seen.

Self-managed work teams have *autonomy* when they have freedom to set goals, make work schedules, discipline and reward team members, and decide on work methods. At the GM's plant in Lodi, California, the night shift does not have a manager present because the work teams are self-sufficient.

In self-managed work teams, *job feedback* occurs when the members see the effect of their work through accounting and production figures, information coming to the team from outside managers and customers, and by doing the work itself. Group work that includes the five job dimensions is more likely to have fully functional self-managed work teams.

## New Organizational Structures

The structure that results from self-managed work teams is a flat one with few levels of managers and little support staff. Considerable changes are also required in organizational policies and managerial practices. Self-managed teams are not something that happens just to the employees on the lowest level; they involve the entire hierarchy. Self-managed work teams are not superimposed upon the existing structure. In most cases, they represent a substantial change in the way an organization is structured and managed.

One of the best ways to ensure that decisions are made within the work team is to have few levels of managers so that the remaining managers do not have time to make all the decisions. The work team carries out functions that would normally be performed by management. Few levels of management are needed because the work team is doing most of the work.

There are fewer support staff, such as engineering, planning departments, and purchasing, because the work team performs these jobs. Functional structures along such lines as accounting, personnel, engineering, production, and the like are counterproductive because they encourage a system where workers do not identify with the final product. These functional departments do not exist in some organizations that have implemented self-managed work teams. This does not mean that engineers and accountants are not needed, but that these functions and the people who do their work are integrated into the work team.

## Management and Leadership Behavior

There are usually three distinct levels of management at a work site that have implemented self-managed work teams: upper management, coordinator, and internal team leader. The work team has an **internal team leader** who is usually elected by the members, but sometimes is appointed by higher management. The work team also has an external leader, sometimes called a **coordinator.** This position is similar to that of a first-level supervisor in a traditional organization, despite considerable differences. The coordinator may have a few to several dozen teams to coordinate.

Upper management, sometimes called the **support team,** is similar to a site manager or plant manager in traditional organizations. This level is responsible for general planning, setting broad goals, and dealing with outside parties (such as the rest of the organization for multiple-site organizations and outside clients).

Some organizations have a council made up of representatives from throughout the company to deal with substantial organization-wide concerns. The council may be elected by all the members of the organization or appointed by management.

When an organization uses self-managed work teams, a question often arises about the role of external leaders and managers. Organizing, planning, and directing, which would normally be managerial functions, are mostly carried out by the work team. The external coordinator's role is ambiguous, and so is the internal leader's role.

The coordinator's role is innovative, and there are no parallels to draw upon in a traditional organization.[27] The coordinator functions largely as an energizer, teacher, and facilitator, encouraging the team's self-managing behaviors, learning, goal setting, creativity, self-evaluation, feedback to one another, new ways of problem solving, and group problem solving. In these ways, the coordinator is similar to a practitioner using process interventions. The objective is to promote the team's independence and problem-solving skills. For example, the coordinator does not run meetings and instead coaches the team on how to run meetings. The coordinator encourages the team to take responsibility for accomplishing its work and enhances the members' self-management skills. The coordinator also helps the team obtain equipment and training, conveys communication to and from management, and provides channels of communications between teams.

Some organizations uses the term "chimney buster" or "barrier buster" to describe how the coordinator runs interference for the team by breaking up rigid and narrow (therefore the term "chimney") bureaucratic obstacles. The coordinator helps build trust and openness within the team, helps to fashion its culture, helps the team develop a sense of direction, and makes the team aware of the total organization's vision.

The internal team leader makes sure that equipment and supplies are available, helps the team organize itself, and serves as an additional team member doing work similar to other members. Like the external coordinator, the internal team leader also serves as an encourager and facilitator.

## The Reward System

The reward system for self-managed work teams is usually different from what is found in traditional organizations. Research has shown that rewards should accrue to both individual and team performance.[28] For example, ICU Medical Inc., a maker of medical devices consisting of approximately 2,000 employees, uses employee-initiated teams to drive the company's progress and growth. ICU rewards successful teams a percentage of the cumulative salaries of their members. The payment system has been altered over the years to set the size of the reward to the importance of the project. The team work is in addition to an employee's regular work, but team participation is voluntary.[29] Studies show that in self-managed teams rewards should be associated with team performance rather than individual performance. These reward systems are typically called **gain sharing.** A general guideline is that at least 80 percent of the available rewards should be distributed equally among team members.[30] The teams should be small enough for an individual's performance to be obviously reflected not only in his or her own paycheck but also in the paycheck of everyone else on the team. At ICU, for example, team size is typically five to seven members. Some companies permit the team leader to distribute small rewards to individual members who have done things that supported the team. Rewards may also be given to the team as a whole, and then the team decides how they should be distributed among the members. In some cases, there are no hourly workers, and all employees are salaried.[31]

An example of how wages are distributed among team members comes from Thor Industries, the world's largest manufacturer of recreational vehicles (RVs). On the factory floor at many of Thor's plants, workers are paid by how many RVs they get out the door. Each group along the line—say plumbing and cabinetmaking—makes a percentage of the pool. It's up to the workers and the group's leader in the division to figure out faster and better ways of doing things and weed out slow or sloppy workers. If a group figures out a faster way of doing a process, it gets a bigger cut of the pool.[32]

Knowledge-based pay is another common approach, but it is usually not as successful. It rewards people based on their skills or knowledge. This involves paying members more for additional skills or tasks they can do.[33] The profit-sharing approach is a reward system based on the entire organization's performance, intended to make people understand the importance of everyone working together. Normally, this type of reward loses relevancy to the individual and the work team because of the size of the organization. Rewards tend to be more successful when the individual and the work team can easily identify the work and contributions of an individual on their own paycheck. That is, when an individual's performance excels or is poor, not only does that individual see the consequences in his or her paycheck, but the other team members see the impact in their own paychecks.

## Role of Labor Unions

If a union is present, it will need to be highly involved from the very beginning, including the planning stages. Facilities that have self-managed work teams do not have the typical adversarial relationship between management and workers. The success of creating a collegial relationship will depend on the union's support and acceptance of self-managed work teams.

Unions often keep management honest about participative management and make sure that all sides to an issue are heard. Union support for self-managed work teams helps in the acceptance of the teams. Most union contracts covering plants that have self-managed work teams are brief and open-ended. Harley-Davidson's approach to setting up self-managed work teams at its plants is to begin working with the unions in the plant's planning stages. Policies are set by a joint union-management structure similar to the council discussed previously.

## Warning Signs

There are several problems associated with self-managed work teams. Most of these can be solved or circumvented. Some of the problems and cautions that should be considered are:

*Self-managed work teams may not be appropriate to the task, people, and context.* Where people and jobs are not interdependent, work teams may not be necessary. Some employees do not like self-managed teams. In many cases, teams are time-consuming and require frequent meetings. Teams normally work best with people who like to work in groups. Many companies are finding that with the greater complexity of technology and rapid development of products and services brought on by more intense competition, self-managed work teams are becoming more appropriate.

*The organization does not perceive a need to change.* This does not mean that installing self-managed work teams should be abandoned, but the driving forces for change within the organization will need to be set in motion.

*Managers and leaders are vague and confused about their roles.* Training for managers, leaders, and team members can resolve the confusion.

*Organizations that do not reward performance are likely to run into problems.* A "thank you" and a wall plaque are not enough. Teamwork is time-consuming, and companies that add team responsibilities to a person's existing responsibilities will probably meet with resistance. Organizations that share the wealth are more likely to have successful teams.

*A lack of training can cause self-managed work teams to fail.* Some practitioners believe that lack of training is a major reason for failure, especially for team members in group processes and team building.

*Because there are fewer layers in an organization, there are fewer opportunities for advancement into managerial positions.* Companies that have not altered their career-planning programs to address shorter career ladders will face long-term resistance from their workers. Some companies can get the team to focus on building an effective team, the challenge of the product, and beating the competition.

*Building self-managed work teams is not a one-shot activity.* Once the teams are installed, people cannot go back to work at their old jobs. The team is their job.

## Results of Self-Managed Teams

Self-managed teams are a relatively new practice, and the techniques are still being developed. Many organizations, for competitive reasons, are unwilling to allow academicians in to study their plants. Some companies know that self-managed work teams are having a positive effect on earnings and are not inclined to pass along their techniques to competitors.

The available research indicates that self-managed teams are effective for the organization and have appeal for employees. These teams are generally more effective than traditionally managed work teams.[34] Other research has built upon these studies and found that self-managed teams are more competent in completing tasks that are related to improving quality and work performance than are traditional work groups.[35]

To be successful, the teams need to be carefully implemented. Not all employees find them appealing, but research indicates that employees experience greater satisfaction from their work and may perform better when supervisors encourage self-direction. According to most practitioners who specialize in helping organizations implement self-managed work teams, the quality of the work is high and productivity is increasing. Plant managers, employees, and union officials enthusiastically describe their effectiveness.

In this chapter, we have examined several quality and productivity interventions that are often part of an OD program. Some interventions have been used over many years with varying degrees of success, whereas other methods are somewhat new. In the last few years, productivity and quality interventions have received much more attention and seem to be having a positive impact in improving organizations. Though there are several methods that will help managers and practitioners to improve productivity, there is a definite need for additional research into work-design programs.

The next chapter will focus on system-wide interventions where change is implemented within the total system. System-wide interventions examine an organization's structure, its work processes, and the interaction of individuals and teams within the structure.

## Summary

- **Job Design.** Job design applies to work in general from an operational viewpoint. The current trend is to design jobs to improve worker satisfaction and productivity. Some of the variables to consider are the worker, the nature of the work, the organizational climate, and the manager's style. Job enrichment and job characteristics are two different views of job design.
- **Job Enrichment.** Job enrichment involves increasing the motivators by permitting employees to attain more responsibility and achievement. Employees are given recognition and advancement in their careers, and the work itself should be challenging, interesting, and meaningful.
- **Job Characteristics.** This method of designing jobs attempts to develop objective measures of job characteristics that can directly affect employee attitudes and work behaviors. Work motivation and satisfaction are affected by five core job dimensions: skill variety, task identity, task significance, autonomy, and job feedback.
- **Total Quality Management.** Quality issues are an important managerial concern. This has led to the development of TQM. TQM programs are comprehensive, integrated, and led by top management. TQM is an organization-wide intervention that focuses on the customer and increases the efficiency and reliability of work.
- **Malcolm Baldrige National Quality Award.** The Baldrige Award is given annually to U.S. organizations that have exemplary achievements in quality. The number of recipients has varied annually from two to five. Companies that receive the Baldrige Award are obligated to disseminate information about their successful strategies.
- **Self-Managed Work Teams.** Self-managed work teams represent a new method of organizing and managing an organization. Most businesses that use this approach apply it to specific plants or work sites instead of the entire organization. Self-managed work teams require a major commitment from the organization, both managers and workers. The long-term effectiveness of the teams has not been clearly established, but many organizations and their members are enthusiastic about the approach. Self-managed work teams are one of the most popular interventions and one that major corporations are hoping will make them competitive as the twenty-first century progresses.

## Review Questions

1. Explain total quality management and how it can be used to improve quality and productivity.
2. What are some problems that organizations might have in implementing total quality management?
3. What are the characteristics of self-managed work teams?
4. Would you like to work in a self-managed work team? Explain your answer. Are classroom team project similar to self-managed teams? Why or why not?

## Key Words and Concepts

| | | | |
|---|---|---|---|
| Autonomy | Internal Team Leader | Job Feedback | Support Team |
| Baldrige Award | Job Characteristics Model | Motivating Potential Score | Task Identity |
| Coordinator | Job Design | Self-Managed Work Team | Task Significance |
| Gain Sharing | Job Enrichment Theory | Skill Variety | Total Quality Management |

# OD Skills Simulation 13.1

## Paper House Production

*Total time suggested: 150 minutes.*

### A. Purpose

This simulation is designed to give you an opportunity to participate in a complex situation involving a great deal of interaction among competing teams, each striving to accomplish a specific objective. You will work in a traditional production environment and then in a self-managed work team. This will provide you with a basis for comparing the two different methods of managing. In the process of interaction, you will have an opportunity to experience:

1. Leadership patterns.
2. Evaluation of jobs using the job characteristics model.
3. Implementation of a self-managed work team and the redesign of jobs.
4. Group process skills in a stress situation.
5. Patterns of interaction among competing teams.

In addition, you will have the opportunity to analyze your team behavior as a member of a system engaged in a complex task.

### B. Procedure

*Step 1*. Before class, form into teams of equal size with six to eight members. The number of people producing the houses should be the same on each team. Extra class members can serve as observers. Select one person from each team to be a supervisor/team leader and another to be an observer. The supervisor reads the Note to Supervisor and Note to Team Leader. The observer reads the Note to Observer and refers to the Observer Form. Everyone reads the Paper House Production Description and becomes familiar with the remaining steps in the simulation before coming to class.

*Step 2*. In a team meeting, plan for Production Period 1. The meeting should be formal and structured, with the supervisor conducting the meeting. The production of the houses should show a high division and specialization of labor among the tasks involved in house production. The observer is not to make any suggestions during the planning and production stages and is not to help in any manner. The equipment and supply purchases will be made and recorded on Lines 3 through 7 of the Cash Position Statement—Production Period 1.

*Time suggested for Step 2: 25 minutes.*

*Step 3*. Teams will construct houses for 20 minutes. Closely adhere to the plans made during Step 2. At the end of the production period, the Federal Housing Administration (FHA) will purchase houses meeting the specifications. Complete the Cash Position Statement—Production Period 1, and determine which team is the winner. Return all equipment, supplies, and houses.

*Time suggested for Step 3: 30 minutes.*

*Step 4*. With the work team (excluding the supervisor's job), look at the jobs as a whole and evaluate them using the job characteristics model. Calculate the MPS for each of the five core job dimensions by using a ranking from 0 (low) to 10 (high). The MPS can range from a low of 0 to a high of 1000.

Skill Variety score (SV): _____
Task Identity score (TI): _____
Task Significance score (TS): _____
Autonomy score (A): _____
Job Feedback score (JF): _____

$$MPV = \left[\frac{SV + TI + TS}{3}\right] \times A \times JF$$

*Time suggested for Step 4: 10 minutes.*

*Step 5*. Plan for Production Period 2. Using the same teams as for Production Period 1, form a self-managed work team with the meeting, closely following the suggestions for self-managed teams discussed in the text. The supervisor from Production Period 1 will be the team leader and operate as close as possible to the text description of a team leader. The team leader should read the Note to Team Leader at the end of this simulation. Redesign the jobs using suggestions from the theory of job enrichment and the job characteristics model. The observer will not assist in the meeting. The equipment and supply purchases will be made and recorded on lines 3 through 7 of the Cash Position Statement—Production Period 2. No cash, supplies, or equipment will be carried forward from Production Period 1.

*Time suggested for Step 5: 25 minutes.*

*Step 6.* Teams will again construct houses for 20 minutes. At the end of the production period, the FHA will purchase houses meeting the specifications. Complete the Cash Position Statement—Production Period 2, and determine which team is the winner.

*Time suggested for Step 6: 30 minutes.*

*Step 7.* As you did in Step 4, look at the jobs as a whole (excluding the team leader's job) and evaluate them using the job characteristics model. Calculate the MPS.

Skill Variety score (SV):          _____
Task Identity score (TI):          _____
Task Significance score (TS):      _____
Autonomy score (A):                _____
Job Feedback score (JF):           _____

*Time suggested for Step 7: 10 minutes.*

*Step 8.* With the observer leading the discussion in your team and then with the other teams, focus on feedback from the Observer Form and the following questions:

1. Was there any difference in the MPS for the two production periods?
2. Was there any difference in the Cash Position Statements of the two production periods? How do you explain this?
3. If there was an improvement in the Cash Position Statement in Period 2 over Period 1, to what extent could the improvement be the result of the experience of having built these houses during the first production period? And to what extent could the improvement be the result of any changes made in the job design during the team meeting?
4. What kinds of problems did you encounter in improving the job design?
5. Were there any compromises made between improving the quality of the jobs and improving productivity?
6. Try to project working in this company for several years. What would be the advantages and disadvantages of the two different production procedures?

*Time suggested for Step 8: 20 minutes.*

## Paper House Production Description

The members of this team have just formed a corporation. The supervisor/team leader will direct the meeting. You must decide on a name for your corporation. At this point, you do not have any organizational structure or production plans. Take the next 25 minutes to become better acquainted with this business. Organize your corporation and plan your strategies for the 20-minute production period that will immediately follow this planning period.

Your corporation is, needless to say, in the paper house construction business. You produce quality paper houses, but in large quantities. Your goal is, very simply, to make the most money you can. Your corporation has $500,000 in cash available to purchase certain supplies and equipment. It may not spend more than this amount. The only source of supplies and equipment is your instructor (you may not use your own pen, ruler, etc.); the supplies and equipment are available during this planning period and during the 20-minute production period (but at a higher price).

Following is a price list of supplies and equipment available.

| | Price When Purchased During | |
|---|---|---|
| Equipment | Planning Period | Production Period |
| Scissors | $7,000 | $8,000 |
| Cellophane tape | 4,000 | 5,000 |
| Ruler | 5,000 | 6,000 |
| Marking pen | 2,000 | 3,000 |

**Price When Purchased During**

| Supplies | No. of 5 × 8 Cards per | Planning Period | Production Period |
|---|---|---|---|
| Micro package | 1 | $ 2,000 | $ 3,000 |
| Mini package | 5 | 8,000 | 10,000 |
| Small package | 10 | 15,000 | 18,000 |
| Medi package | 20 | 25,000 | 30,000 |
| Large package | 40 | 45,000 | 53,000 |
| Mogo package | 80 | 80,000 | 90,000 |

Any number or combination of packages may be purchased. Equipment and supplies unused at the end of the production period will be considered unrecoverable salvage and will be collected. Completed houses built according to specifications will sell for $20,000 each, and you will be able to sell all you can build. Houses deviating from the specs as judged by the FHA (the FHA could be your instructor or an extra class member) are not marketable. The house plans provided are your specifications. Your house should appear as described except that it should not have any dimensions written on it. Your company's name should be neatly printed on the roof.

A Cash Position Statement for the first and second production periods is provided for you to keep a record of your financial status.

You have 20 minutes for the first production period. At the end of this time, qualifying houses will be bought and the cash position determined.

*Note to Supervisor—First Planning Meeting (Other class members should not read.).* Conduct the meeting in Step 2 in a highly formal and structured manner. You should have the production procedures carefully planned before coming to the meeting. During the meeting, you will simply tell others of your plans and make sure your subordinates know what is expected of them. You may choose to let others make suggestions, but the decision to implement them is yours. You may perform your job as a supervisor in an autocratic manner. During the production stage of Step 3, you are not to do the work of producing the houses (production is the job of your workers). You are to make sure your subordinates are doing their jobs correctly.

*Note to Team Leader—Second Planning Meeting (Other class members should not read.).* Conduct the meeting in Step 5 using the discussion in the text on the role of the coordinator and internal team leader in a self-managed work team as your guide. During the production stage of Step 6, you are to make sure equipment and supplies are available, help the team organize itself, and serve as an additional team member who does the same work as the other members. You will also serve as an encourager and facilitator.

*Note to Observer.* As an observer, you are only *to observe* during both production periods. Note the differences in the behaviors of members during the two production periods. Read the Notes to the Supervisor and Team Leader so that you will understand the roles of the supervisor and leader. Record your observations on the Observer Form. Read the questions in Step 8, and be prepared to help the team discuss them.

## House Specifications

1. The sides of the house each measure 4 inches high by 7 inches long. The front and back of each measure 5 inches wide and 4 inches high (or 7⅛ inches high at the top of the gable).
2. The total height of the house is 7⅛ inches from the base to the highest point of the roof.
3. The roof is V-shaped and is 7 inches long. It measures 4 inches along the ends.
4. Your corporation's name appears in letters ½ inch high on both sides of the roof. Neatly print name with the marking pen.
5. The two sides each have one window measuring 2 inches long and 1½ inches high, centered. Draw the windows.
6. There is a door at the front (a gable end) measuring 3 inches high and 1½ inches wide centered along the base of the wall. Draw the door.
7. There is no floor.

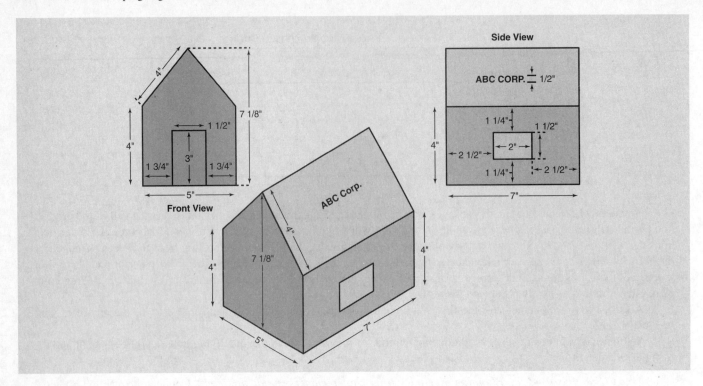

**CASH POSITION STATEMENT—PRODUCTION PERIOD 1**
_____CORPORATION

1. Beginning cash      $500,000

2. Cost of purchases during planning period:

3. Scissors      _____

4. Cellophane tape      _____

5. Ruler      _____

6. Marking pen and pencil      _____

7. Supplies (cards)      _____

8. Total cost of purchases during planning period:
   (add Lines 3 through 7)      _____

9. Cost of purchases during production period:

10. Scissors      _____

11. Cellophane tape      _____

12. Ruler      _____

13. Marking pen and pencil      _____

14. Supplies (cards)      _____

15. Total cost of purchases during production period: (add Lines 10 through 14)      _____

16. Total cost of purchases: (add Lines 8 and 15)      _____

17. Adjusted cash balance after purchases: (subtract Line 16 from 1)      _____

18. Cash inflow from sale of houses:

19. Number of houses sold    times    selling price    equals    sales receipts
         _____      ×      $20,000      =      _____

20. Ending cash balance: (add Lines 17 and 19)      _____

**CASH POSITION STATEMENT—PRODUCTION PERIOD 2**
_____CORPORATION

| | |
|---|---|
| 1. Beginning cash | $500,000 |
| 2. Cost of purchases during planning period: | |
| 3. Scissors | _____ |
| 4. Cellophane tape | _____ |
| 5. Ruler | _____ |
| 6. Marking pen and pencil | _____ |
| 7. Supplies (cards) | _____ |
| 8. Total cost of purchases during planning period: (add Lines 3 through 7) | _____ |
| 9. Cost of purchases during production period: | |
| 10. Scissors | _____ |
| 11. Cellophane tape | _____ |
| 12. Ruler | _____ |
| 13. Marking pen and pencil | _____ |
| 14. Supplies (cards) | _____ |
| 15. Total cost of purchases during production period: (add Lines 10 through 14) | _____ |
| 16. Total cost of purchases: (add Lines 8 and 15) | _____ |
| 17. Adjusted cash balance after purchases: (subtract Line 16 from 1) | _____ |
| 18. Cash inflow from sale of houses: | |
| 19. Number of houses sold   times   selling price   equals   sales receipts | |
| _____      ×      $20,000      = | _____ |
| 20. Ending cash balance: (add Lines 17 and 19) | _____ |

**OBSERVER FORM**

Based on the following scale, rate your team on how it performed. Record your choice in the blanks.

[Low   1   2   3   4   5   6   7   High]

| Factor | Production Period 1 | Production Period 2 |
|---|---|---|
| 1. Cooperative teamwork | _____ | _____ |
| 2. Member satisfaction | _____ | _____ |
| 3. Team motivation | _____ | _____ |
| 4. Information sharing | _____ | _____ |
| 5. Consensual decision making | _____ | _____ |
| 6. Conflict directly faced and resolved | _____ | _____ |
| 7. Participative leadership | _____ | _____ |
| 8. Clearly defined goals | _____ | _____ |
| 9. Trust | _____ | _____ |
| 10. Encouraged openness | _____ | _____ |

# OD Skills Simulation 13.2

## TQM in the University Setting

*Total time suggested: 60 minutes.*

### A. Purpose

If there is one constant in today's world, it is change. The purpose of this simulation is to apply the TQM process to your university or organization. The goals are:

1. To compare decisions made by individuals with those made by the group.
2. To practice effective consensus-seeking techniques.
3. To gain insights into the concept of TQM values.

### B. Procedures

*Step 1.* Prior to class, form into teams of six members, each group constituting an executive committee. Assign each member of your group as one of the committee members and an observer. (Extra class members act as observers.) Use the TQM Decision Form. Observers may use the Team Profile/Observer Form to gather data on group process.

1. Dean
2. Professor
3. Student
4. Student
5. Student
6. Observer

Participants are to enter their individual decisions in Column 1 on the TQM Decision Form.

*Step 2. Executive Committee Meeting.* Through group discussion, exploration, and examination, try to reach a consensus decision reflecting the integrated thinking and consensus of all members. Remember, a consensus decision involves reaching mutual agreement by discussion until everyone agrees on the final decision.

Follow these instructions for reaching a consensus:

1. Try to reach the best-possible decision, but at the same time defend the importance of your position.
2. Do not change your mind simply to reach agreement and to avoid conflict, but support solutions with which you are able to agree.
3. Avoid conflict-reducing techniques, such as majority vote, averaging, or trading, in reaching your decision.
4. View differences of opinion as a help rather than a hindrance in decision making.

At this point, meet together as the executive committee and enter your results in Column 2 on the TQM Decision Form. The observers use the Team Profile/Observer Form.

*Time suggested for Step 2: 35 minutes.*

*Step 3.* Each team lists its results on the board, and the instructor or a class member leads a comparison of TQM approaches.

*Time suggested for Step 3: 15 minutes.*

*Step 4.* With the observer leading the discussion and providing input, meet as a team and discuss your team processes using the Team Profile/Observer Form.

*Time suggested for Step 4: 10 minutes.*

**TQM DECISION FORM**

Individual (Column 1)   Team (Column 2)

1. **Process Improvement**

   How can we make administrative processes faster, easier, and better?

   1. _____   _____
   2. _____   _____
   3. _____   _____
   4. _____   _____
   5. _____   _____

2. **Quality Improvement**

   How can we improve the quality of our education?

   1. _____   _____
   2. _____   _____
   3. _____   _____
   4. _____   _____
   5. _____   _____

3. **Customer Student Satisfaction**

   How can we measure and improve student satisfaction levels and attract new students?

   1. _____   _____
   2. _____   _____
   3. _____   _____
   4. _____   _____
   5. _____   _____

## TEAM PROFILE OBSERVER FORM

Team Profile: Rate the team on these dimensions.

| | (Low) | | | | (Moderate) | | | | (High) |
|---|---|---|---|---|---|---|---|---|---|---|
| A. Involvement | 1 | 2 | 3 | 4 | 5 | 6 | 7 | 8 | 9 | 10 |
| B. Leadership | 1 | 2 | 3 | 4 | 5 | 6 | 7 | 8 | 9 | 10 |
| C. Competence | 1 | 2 | 3 | 4 | 5 | 6 | 7 | 8 | 9 | 10 |
| D. Communication | 1 | 2 | 3 | 4 | 5 | 6 | 7 | 8 | 9 | 10 |
| E. Goals | 1 | 2 | 3 | 4 | 5 | 6 | 7 | 8 | 9 | 10 |
| F. Decision making | 1 | 2 | 3 | 4 | 5 | 6 | 7 | 8 | 9 | 10 |
| G. Collaboration | 1 | 2 | 3 | 4 | 5 | 6 | 7 | 8 | 9 | 10 |
| H. Openness | 1 | 2 | 3 | 4 | 5 | 6 | 7 | 8 | 9 | 10 |
| I. Listening | 1 | 2 | 3 | 4 | 5 | 6 | 7 | 8 | 9 | 10 |
| J. Motivation | 1 | 2 | 3 | 4 | 5 | 6 | 7 | 8 | 9 | 10 |

# CASE: WENGART AIRCRAFT

President Ralph Larsen of Wengart Aircraft has become increasingly concerned about profits. Though he is not fearful of a company takeover, he does feel an obligation to maximize shareholders' return on their investment. He and about a dozen top executives receive sizable stock bonuses, so it is to their advantage to obtain a high share price.

Wengart manufactures private and military aircraft. It is number two in its industry, which consists of seven companies. Its profits, however, are ranked sixth. It is disturbing to Larsen and his top management team that they are not able to maximize profits. Refer to Figure 13.2 for Wengart Aircraft's organization chart.

## Quality Problems

The top management team has identified quality as one of the major problems at Wengart. Aircraft have to be reworked even after they are sent to the customer. The federal government, one of Wengart's largest customers, shares the concern about quality. The Secretary of Defense has sent Larsen several letters warning that unless quality is improved by 20 percent within six months, the government will exercise its contract provision to withhold partial payment as a penalty. This will place even more pressure on profits. Nongovernmental customers have also expressed serious concerns about quality. There have been major stories in the *Wall Street Journal* and *Business Week* about Wengart's quality problems and deteriorating financial condition.

The Department of Defense, in its latest letter to Larsen, said it would look favorably upon Wengart's implementing a "TQM program similar to programs at other aircraft, automobile, and electronic firms. By Presidential Executive Order 12552 applying TQM to all federal executive agencies, the Department of Defense is encouraging all defense contractors to adopt TQM."

## Total Quality Management and the OD Practitioner

Larsen, in an effort to learn more about TQM, hired an OD practitioner to explain it. The practitioner made several points at a two-hour meeting with Larsen:

- Customer, engineering, production, and product support functions are integrated into a team.
- The customer is the next person in line. Therefore, for someone within the company, the customer can be the next person on the production line, and for the company the customer is the purchaser of Wengart's planes. Everyone in the company is both a customer and a producer.

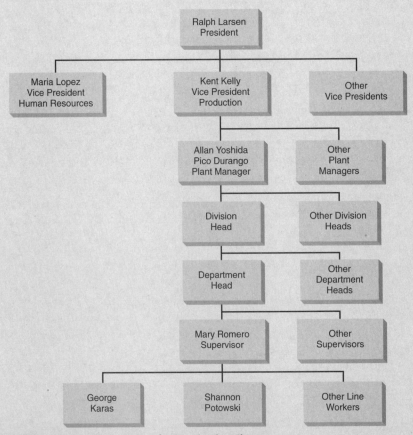

**FIGURE 13.2  Wengart Aircraft Organization Chart**

- Quality is giving customers what they have a right to expect.
- Substantial increases in education and training are required.
- Teamwork is a basic building block of TQM.
- As the CEO, Larsen and his top management team must be committed to TQM and communicate its importance by word and deed at every opportunity.
- TQM will have to become part of Wengart's culture. The CEO must believe in work principles that include improved leadership, working conditions, and job security.

Larsen thanked the practitioner and said he would take it from here. To Larsen, TQM was a matter of common sense. It was what they were doing or should be doing.

Larsen decided that the company had no other choice but to implement TQM. He called a meeting of his vice presidents and explained TQM. Larsen put Kent Kelly, vice president of production, in charge of the program. Maria Lopez, vice president of human resources, tried to convince him that TQM should be a joint project between human resources and production, with the president's office coordinating the program. Larsen explained, however, that he didn't have time to get involved with TQM personally because he wanted to spend his time and energy improving profits.

Mary Romero, a supervisor of the wire harness assembly team for the drone aircraft, is responsible for 11 people on the swing shift. Her people put together the thousands of color-coded electrical wires that make up a "harness." Another production team sets the harness in place in the aircraft by running the harness from the aircraft's central computer to the other sections of the aircraft. The drone is a new and highly advanced unmanned aircraft for the U.S. Air Force using the latest in electronic and computer controls in combination with a stealth design. Romero's team, like every team working on the drone, is critical to the plane's ability to meet specifications.

Two months ago, all the managers and line supervisors at the Pico Durango plant, including Romero, attended a meeting called by the plant superintendent, Allan Yoshida, who explained TQM to them. Managers and supervisors came away from the meeting with various interpretations of TQM, and thus the line workers tended to get different ideas about TQM. Within a day after the meeting, all the workers in the plant received a brief memo from Yoshida in which he outlined TQM, said that the managers and supervisors had the details, and that everyone was to support the program.

Romero was very enthusiastic about TQM. She was taking a management course at a local university, and her class had recently spent several class meetings learning about TQM. She was, however, confused at the brevity of the TQM information she and the other supervisors got from Yoshida.

Two of Romero's veteran workers, George Karas and Shannon Potowski, said it sounded just like the other management programs where the union workers did all the work and management, especially top management, got the credit—and the bucks. Both of the workers made some rough calculations and figured that under the old system, at least 20 percent of their time was spent reworking a defective harness after it had been installed in a plane, waiting on products coming from the preceding production team, or waiting on delayed inventory items. The waiting time, which was about the same for other teams, was a good opportunity to go to the company store, take a longer coffee break, or visit with friends on other production teams. After comparing notes with other workers around the plant, plant workers generally concluded that Allan Yoshida was trying to speed up production so that the midnight shift could be cut.

This morning, Romero and several other supervisors went around their department and division heads to see Yoshida. They explained the rumors they had heard about a worker plan to get the job done right the first time but make sure it took so long that no one would be laid off. Yoshida, unsure about what to do, referred to the seven-page memo Kent Kelly had sent him on how to implement TQM. Yoshida's knowledge of TQM was limited to the memo he had received from Kelly. The situation the supervisors were explaining was valid, said Yoshida. Unfortunately, Kelly's memo did not address the problem.

After looking at the way Kelly had set up the plant goals, Yoshida decided that quality was what mattered most. Yoshida quickly reasoned that his next promotion was dependent on meeting his quality goals, not on improving productivity. Getting the workers mad at you was a sure-fire way to lose both quality and production. He told the supervisors at the meeting to pass the word that layoffs were not the purpose of TQM and just make sure quality was top-notch.

After the meeting, Yoshida wondered if he should call Kelly and see if there was any more to TQM he should know about. But he decided after several minutes that if the program was very important, he surely would have heard something more. He reasoned that it was best not to make waves. (Use the Case Analysis Form on the following page.)

**WENGART AIRCRAFT CASE ANALYSIS FORM**

Name: _____

I. Problems

  A. Macro

    1. _____

    _____

    2. _____

    _____

  B. Micro

    1. _____

    _____

    2. _____

    _____

II. Causes

    1. _____

    _____

    2. _____

    _____

    3. _____

    _____

III. Systems affected

    1. _____

    _____

    2. _____

    _____

    3. _____

    _____

IV. Alternatives

    1. _____

    _____

    2. _____

    _____

    3. _____

    _____

V. Recommendations

  _____

  _____

  _____

  _____

  _____

  _____

## Chapter 13 Endnotes

1. Steve W.J. Kozlowski and Daniel R. Ilgen, "Enhancing the Effectiveness of Work Groups and Teams," *Psychological Science in the Public Interest*, vol. 7, no. 3 (December 2006), pp. 77–124.

2. Nitin Nohria, Boris Groysberg, and Linda-Eling Lee, "Employee Motivation, A Powerful New Model," *Harvard Business Review*, July-August 2008, pp. 78–84.

3. The model was conceived by J. R. Hackman, G. R. Oldham, R. Janson, and K. Purdy, "A New Strategy for Job Enrichment," *California Management Review*, Summer 1975, pp. 57–71. The model was based upon the work of A. N. Turner and P. R. Lawrence, *Industrial Jobs and the Worker* (Boston, MA: Harvard Graduate School of Business Administration, 1965).

4. See the NUMMI Web site for more information at www. nummi.com

5. Jena McGregor and Steve Hamm, "Managing the Global Workforce," *Business Week*, January 28, 2008, pp. 34–51. Scott Thurm, "Lesson in India: Not Every Job Translates Overseas," *Wall Street Journal*, March 3, 2004, pp. A1, A10.

6. For additional information, see Frederick Herzberg, Bernard Mausner, and B. Synderman, *The Motivation to Work* (New York: John Wiley, 1959); Frederick Herzberg, *Work and the Nature of Man* (Cleveland: World, 1966); Frederick Herzberg, "One More Time: How Do You Motivate Employees?" *Harvard Business Review*, January/February 1968, pp. 53–62; M. Scott Meyers, "Conditions for Manager Motivation," *Harvard Business Review*, January/February 1966, pp. 58–71; M. Campion, "Interdisciplinary Approaches to Job Design: A Constructive Replication with Extensions," *Journal of Applied Psychology*, vol. 73, no. 3 (1988), pp. 467–81.

7. Katherine A. Karl and Cynthia L. Sutton, "Job Values in Today's Workforce: A Comparison of Public and Private Sector Employees," *Public Personnel Management*, vol. 27, no. 4 (Winter 1998), pp. 515–28; Hackman, "A New Strategy for Job Enrichment." See also J. Richard Hackman and J. Lloyd Suttle, *Improving Life at Work* (Santa Monica, CA: Goodyear Publishing Co., 1977), pp. 130–1.

8. See William A. Pasmore, "Designing Work Systems for Knowledge Workers," *Journal for Quality and Participation*, vol. 16, no. 4 (July/August 1993), pp. 78–84; William A. Pasmore, "Overcoming the Roadblocks in Work-Restructuring Efforts," *Organizational Dynamics*, Spring 1982, p. 55.

9. Kozlowski, "Enhancing the Effectiveness of Work Groups and Teams," p. 100; M. A. Campion, E. M. Papper, and G. J. Medsker, "Relations between Work Team Characteristics and Effectiveness: A Replication and Extension," *Personnel Psychology*, vol. 49, no. 2 (Summer 1996), pp. 429–52.

10. For a related study of job satisfaction, see M. West, and M. Patterson, "People Power: The Link between Job Satisfaction and Productivity," *Centre Piece*, vol. 3, no. 3 (Autumn 1998), pp. 2–5. Also see Paul Gollan, Erik Poutsma, and Ulke Veersma, "New Roads in Organizational Participation?" *Industrial Relations*, vol. 45, no. 4 (October 2006), pp. 499–512.

11. For additional studies on the validity of the job characteristics theory, see Brian D. Janz, Jason A. Colquitt, and Raymond A. Noe, "Knowledge Worker Team Effectiveness: The Role of Autonomy, Interdependence, Team Development, and Contextual Support Variables," *Personnel Psychology*, vol. 50, no. 4 (Winter 1997), pp. 877–905; J. E. Champoux, "A Multivariate Test of the Job Characteristics Theory of Work Motivation," *Journal of Organizational Behavior*, vol. 12, no. 5 (September1991), pp. 431–46; Gary Johns, Jia Lin Xie, and Yongqing Fang, "Mediating and Moderating Effects in Job Design," *Journal of Management*, vol. 18, no. 4 (December 1992), pp. 657–76; Turner and Lawrence, *Industrial Jobs and the Worker*; J. R. Hackman and E. E. Lawler III, "Employee Reactions to Job Characteristics," *Journal of Applied Psycholog*, vol. 55, no. 3 (June 1971), pp. 259–86; Y. Fried and G. Ferris, "The Validity of the Job Characteristics Model: A Review and Meta-Analysis," *Personnel Psychology*, vol. 40, no. 2 (June 1987), pp. 287–322; P. Bottger and I. Chew, "The Job Characteristics Model and Growth Satisfaction: Main Effects of Assimilation of Work Experience and Context Satisfaction," *Human Relations*, vol. 39, no. 6 (1986), pp. 575–94; E. Hogan and D. Martell, "A Confirmatory Structural Equations Analysis of the Job Characteristics Model," *Organizational Behavior and Human Decision Processes*, vol. 39, no. 2 (April 1987), pp. 242–63.

12. Navin Shamji Dedhia, "Global Perspectives on Quality," *Total Quality Management*, vol. 12, no. 6 (September 2001), pp. 657–68; Irina Selivanova and Jan Eklof, "Total Quality Management in the West, East and Russia: Are We Different?" *Total Quality Management*, vol. 12, nos. 7 (December 2001), pp. 1003–09.

13. For detailed information, see Paul Lillrank, A. B. (Rami) Shani, and Per Lindberg, "Continuous Improvement: Exploring Alternative Organizational Designs," *Total Quality Management*, vol. 12, no. 1 (January 2001), pp. 41–56; Appa Rao Korukonda, John G. Watson, and T. M. Rajkumar, "Beyond Teams and Empowerment: A Counterpoint to Two Common Precepts in TQM," *S.A.M. Advanced Management Journal*, vol. 64, no. 1 (Winter 1999), pp. 29–37; Kenneth R. Thompson, "Confronting the Paradoxes in a Total Quality Environment," *Organizational Dynamics*, vol. 26, no. 3 (Winter 1998), pp. 62–75; W. Edwards Deming, *Out of Crisis* (Cambridge, MA: MIT Press, 1986); Joseph M. Juran, *Journal on Leadership for Quality: An Executive Handbook* (New York: Free Press, 1989); *Academy of Management Review*, special issue on total quality, vol. 19, no. 3 (July 1994).

14. Additional information can be found in Chris Moon and Chris Swaffin-Smith, "Total Quality Management and New Patterns of Work: Is There Life Beyond Empowerment?" *Total Quality Management*, vol. 9, nos. 2/3 (May

1998), pp. 301–11; Richard M. Hodgetts, Fred Luthans, and Sang M. Lee, "New Paradigm Organizations: From Total Quality to Learning to World-Class," *Organizational Dynamics*, Winter 1994, pp. 5–18; Robert M. Grant, Rami Shani, and R. Krishnan, "TQM's Challenge to Management Theory and Practice," *Sloan Management Review*, vol. 35, no. 2 (Winter 1994), pp. 25–35.

15. See J. Bank, *The Essence of Total Quality Management* (Upper Saddle River, NJ: Prentice Hall, 1992).

16. For additional information, see www.quality.nist.gov/; Statement of Harry S. Hertz, Director, National Quality Program, National Institute of Standards and Technology, Technology Administration, U.S. Department of Commerce, before the Subcommittee on Social Security and the Subcommittee on Human Resources, Committee on Ways and Means, U.S. House of Representatives, February 10, 2000 (www.nist.gov/testimony/2000/hhssaf10.htm; Public Law 100–107), Malcolm Baldrige National Quality Improvement Act of 1987; Robert Bell and Bernard Keys, "A Conversation with Curt W. Reimann on the Background and Future of the Baldrige Award," *Organizational Dynamics*, vol. 26, no. 4 (Spring 1998), pp. 51–61.

17. www.quality.nist.gov.

18. Ibid.

19. Nicolay A. M. Worren, Keith Ruddle, and Karl Moore, "From Organizational Development to Change Management," *Journal of Applied Behavioral Science*, vol. 35, no. 3 (September 1999), pp. 273–87; Ira M. Levin and Jonathan Z. Gottlieb, "Quality Management: Practice Risks and Value-Added Roles for Organization Development Practitioners," *Journal of Applied Behavioral Science*, vol. 29, no. 3 (September 1993), pp. 296–310.

20. K. F. Pun, K. S. Chin, and R. Gill, "Determinants of Employee Involvement Practices in Manufacturing Enterprises," *Total Quality Management*, vol. 12, no. 1 (January 2001), p. 95; E. E. Lawler III, "Total Quality Management and Employee Involvement: Are They Compatible?" *Academy of Management Executive*, vol. 8, no. 1 (February 1994), pp. 68–76; E. E. Lawler III, S. A. Mohrman, and G. E. Ledford Jr., *Creative High Performance Organization: Practices and Results of Employee Involvement and Total Quality Management in Fortune 1000 Companies* (San Francisco: Jossey-Bass, 1995); S. A. Mohrman, E. E. Lawler III, and G. E. Ledford Jr., "Do Employee Involvement and TQM Programs Work?" *Journal for Quality and Participation*, vol. 19, no. 1 (January 1996), pp. 6–10.

21. For additional information, see Rhonda K. Reger, L. T. Gustafson, S. M. Demarie, and J. V. Mullane, "Reframing the Organization: Why Implementing Total Quality Is Easier Said than Done," *Academy of Management Review*, vol. 19, no. 3 (July 1994), pp. 565–84; O. Harari, "Ten Reasons Why TQM Doesn't Work," *Management Review*, vol. 82, no. 1 (May 1993), pp. 33–38.

22. www.bain.com. The most recent annual survey is available at this Web site.

23. For additional information, see Gerald Zeitz, Russell Johannesson, and J. Edgar Ritchie, Jr., "An Employee Survey Measuring Total Quality Management Practices and Culture," *Group and Organization Management*, vol. 22, no. 4 (December 1997), pp. 414–45.

24. P. Venkateswarlu and V. Nilakant, "Adoption and Persistence of TQM Programmes—Case Studies of Five New Zealand Organizations," *Total Quality Management & Business Excellence*, vol. 16, no. 7 (September 2005), pp. 807–25.

25. Denis Leonard and Rodney McAdam, "Developing Strategic Quality Management: A Research Agenda," *Total Quality Management*, vol. 13, no. 4 (2002), pp. 507–22; Joseph Taiwo, "Systems Approaches to Total Quality Management," *Total Quality Management*, vol. 12, no. 7 (December 2001), p. 967; Mark J. Zbaracki, "The Rhetoric and Reality of Total Quality Management," *Administrative Science Quarterly*, vol. 43, no. 4 (September 1998), pp. 602–37; Edward Lawler, III, Susan Albers Mohrman, Gerald E. Ledford, Jr. *Creating High-Performance Organizations* (San Francisco: Jossey-Bass, 1995).

26. For additional information on self-managed work teams, see Mark E. Haskins, Jeanne Liedtka, and John Roseblum, "Beyond Teams: Toward an Ethic of Collaboration," *Organizational Dynamics*, vol. 26, no. 4 (Spring 1998), pp. 34–51; Susan G. Cohen, "A Hierarchical Construct of Self-Management Leadership and Its Relationship to Quality of Work Life and Perceived Work Group Effectiveness," *Personnel Psychology*, vol. 50, no. 2 (Summer 1997), pp. 275–309; Susan G. Cohen and Diane E. Bailey, "What Makes Teams Work: Group Effectiveness Research from the Executive Suite," *Journal of Management*, vol. 23, no. 3 (June 1997), pp. 239–90; Edward E. Lawler III, *High-Involvement Management* (San Francisco: Jossey Bass, 1986), pp. 170–233; K. Kim Fisher, "Managing in the High-Commitment Workplace," *Organizational Dynamics*, Winter 1989, pp. 31–50; Charles C. Manz and Henry P. Sims, "Leading Workers to Lead Themselves: The External Leadership of Self-Managing Work Teams," *Administrative Science Quarterly*, vol. 32, no. 1 (March 1987), pp. 106–28; Richard Hackman and Greg R. Oldham, *Work Redesign* (Reading, MA: Addison-Wesley, 1980), pp. 161–90.

27. For additional information, see Michael E. McGill and John W. Slocum Jr., "A Little Leadership, Please?" *Organizational Dynamics*, vol. 26, no. 3 (Winter 1988), pp. 39–49; Robert E. Quinn and Gretchen M. Spreitzer, "The Road to Empowerment: Seven Questions Every Leader Should Consider," *Organizational Dynamics*, vol. 26, no. 2 (Autumn 1997), pp. 37–50; Robert M. Fulmer, "The Evolving Paradigm of Leadership Development," *Organizational Dynamics*, vol. 25, no. 59 (Spring 1997), pp. 59–73; Susan G. Cohen, "A Hierarchical Construct of Self-Management Leadership and Its Relationship to Quality of Work Life and Perceived Work Group Effectiveness," *Personnel Psychology*, vol. 50, no. 2 (Summer 1997), pp. 275–309.

28. Kozlowski, "Enhancing the Effectiveness of Work Groups and Teams," p. 99.

29. Erin White, "How a Company Made Everyone a Team Player," *Wall Street Journal*, August 13, 2007, pp. B1.

30. Ruth Wageman, "Critical Success Factors for Creating Superb Self-Managing Teams," *Organizational Dynamics*, vol. 26, no. 1 (Summer 1997), pp. 49–63. In this study, teams were considered to have team rewards if at least 80 percent of the rewards were distributed equally among team members.

31. For additional information of types of team pay, see Leigh L. Thompson, *Making the Team, A Guide for Managers* (Upper Saddle River, NJ: 2008), pp. 46–56.

32. Jonathan Fahey, "Lord of the Rigs," *Forbes*, March 29, 2004, pp. 67–72.

33. For more information, see Dale E. Yeatts and Cloyd. Hyten, *High-Performing Self-Managed Work Teams: A Comparison of Theory to Practice* (Thousand Oaks, CA: Sage Publications, 1997); Bradley R. Hill, "A Two-Component Approach to Compensation," *Personnel Journal*, vol. 72, no. 5 (May 1993), pp. 154–61; Henry Tosi and Lisa Tosi, "What Managers Need to Know About Knowledge-Based Pay," *Organization Dynamics*, Winter 1986, pp. 52–64.

34. E. Sundstrom, M. McIntyre, T. Halfhill, and H. Richards, "Work groups: From the Hawthorne Studies to Work Teams of the 1990s and Beyond," *Group Dynamics: Theory, Research, and Practice*, vol. 4 , no. 1 (March 2000), pp. 44–67; Yeatts and Hyten, *High-Performing Self-Managed Work Teams*; Susan G. Cohen and Diane E. Bailey, "What Makes Teams Work: Group Effectiveness Research from the Executive Suite," *Journal of Management*, vol. 23, no. 3 (June 1997), pp. 239–90; Susan G. Cohen, "A Hierarchical Construct of Self-Management Leadership and Its Relationship to Quality of Work Life and Perceived Work Group Effectiveness," *Personnel Psychology*, vol. 50, no. 2 (Summer 1997), pp. 275–309.

35. Simone Kauffeld, "Self-directed Work Groups and Team Competence," *Journal of Occupational and Organizational Psychology*, vol. 79, no. 1 (March 2006), pp. 1–21.

# PART FIVE

# Building Success in Organizations

Understanding the need
for planned change

Building an OD
background and
developing an increased
knowledge of OD

Personal and
interpersonal OD concepts

Team and interteam OD concepts

Organization and system-wide OD
concepts

With the worldwide and severe recession that began in late 2007, it is more important than ever that organizations reduce costs, develop innovative new products and services, shorten process cycles and response times, and increase customer satisfaction. The recession certainly proved to be a time when organizations must be great just in order to survive.

Though all OD interventions are aimed at improving organization effectiveness, some interventions are intended for the implementation of change within the total system. System-level interventions examine the way an organization is designed, its work processes, and the interaction of individuals and teams within the system. Some of the most widely used total organization change techniques are survey research and feedback, the learning organizations, the system 4 approach, and high-performing systems.

There is a body of change methods that are general in nature and broad-based in scope. One such approach to change, organization transformation, is a drastic, abrupt change to total structures, managerial processes, and corporate cultures. As corporate culture defines an organization's very essence, it may be necessary for the culture to be changed deliberately and consciously. For example, the culture of Google has been instrumental in its success just as the culture at American Internationl Group (AIG) was instrumental in its downfall. Changing the corporate culture takes on increased importance in the light of evidence that suggests that firms with effective corporate cultures have increased productivity, increased employees' sense of ownership, increased profits, and enhanced customer satisfaction.

The final stage of the OD process occurs when the program's basic change objectives have been accomplished and either the practitioner or the client or both feel that the system can continue the change effort without outside assistance. One of the fundamental objectives of an OD program is for the organization to create within itself a self-renewal capability. Change will then be viewed as a natural and desirable process.

As change in our world has accelerated to what appears at times to be unmanageable, a criticism of OD is that it has become less effective in helping organizations. For example, the changes required of General Motors (GM) when confronted with bankruptcy in 2009 was that it change rapidly and in some very fundamental ways. These are total system changes required of GM's stakeholders: employees, debt and stockholders, suppliers, dealers, and customers. As is discussed in the last chapter of this book, there is a lack of evidence that OD can be effective for an organization where its survival is of immediate concern. The field of OD is currently, and will likely always be, in transition if it is to remain relevant.

This *Part 5: Building Success in Organizations* continues the discussion of OD by covering system-wide interventions, stabilizing an OD program, and the future for OD. Chapter 14 is a discussion of system-wide interventions that includes survey research, the learning organization, reengineering, and high-performing systems. In chapter 15, we will continue to cover system-wide interventions including organization transformation, corporate culture, and the importance of strategic change management to an OD program. In chapter 16, the final chapter, monitoring and stabilizing the OD program will be discussed. The chapter will conclude with a look at some of the emerging issues, values, and future trends in OD.

# High-Performing Systems and the Learning Organization

## LEARNING OBJECTIVES

**Upon completing this chapter, you will be able to:**

1. Describe what a system-level intervention is.
2. Identify the survey research and feedback process.
3. Recognize characteristics of learning organizations.
4. Recognize the steps of reengineering.
5. Describe the four systems of system 4 management and explain why the fourth system is likely to be more successful in today's environment.
6. Explain the characteristics of a high-performing system.
7. Recognize the six phases of the Grid OD program.
8. Experience and practice system approaches.

## PREMEETING PREPARATION

1. Read Chapter 14.
2. Prepare for OD Skills Simulation 14.1. Form into teams of seven to eight members and select roles. Complete Step 1.
3. Read and analyze Case: Tucker Knox Corporation.

## SYSTEM-WIDE INTERVENTIONS

In today's Internet-speed economy, successful organizations are doing what was once considered impossible. They are increasing customer satisfaction, shortening process cycles and response times, reducing costs, and developing innovative new products and services—all at the same time. In the past, managers aimed for success in a relatively stable and predictable world. Today, however, managers confront accelerating change that has been accentuated with a recession and financial crisis that began in late 2007. Managers as change agents are facing constant innovation in computer and information technology and a chaotic world of changing markets and consumer lifestyles. Today's organization must be able to transform and renew itself to meet these changing forces. Mark Herd, CEO of Hewlett-Packard (HP), is aware of the legacy of Bill Hewlett and Dave Packard but simultaneously recognizes his responsibility to keep HP ever forward looking. "We can't live in the past," he says. "At Hewlett-Packard, we want to be on the news channel, not the History Channel."[1]

All OD interventions are aimed at improving organization effectiveness, but certain interventions aim at the successful implementation of change within the total system. As noted in previous chapters, OD is essentially a system approach to better understand the complex set of interpersonal team and interteam relationships that are found in organizations. The **system-level intervention** may be described as a structural design framework for viewing an organization that examines (1) the way the organization is designed, (2) the organization's work process, and (3) the interaction of individuals and teams within the flows and structures of the system. The major system-level interventions include survey research and feedback, the learning organizations, reengineering, the system 4 approach, high-performing systems, and Grid organization development.

Organizations inevitably change because they are open systems in constant interaction with their environment. Although the impetus for change may arise from internal or external forces, the underlying factor is the degree of openness of the organization to the changing demands, technologies, and values that influence the system.

This chapter presents an overview of the most widely used total organization change techniques. Note that the system can either be an organization or a reasonably well-isolated unit, such as a large segment or subsystem, within the total organization. For example, the organization to be changed could be the Federal Bureau of Investigation (FBI), which is part of the Justice Department, which is part of the Executive Branch of the federal government.

## SURVEY RESEARCH AND FEEDBACK

As employee attitude surveys are gaining popularity worldwide, the key to a successful survey is for management to clearly define the survey's purpose and explain what will be done with the results. Once the data are collected, the results must then be translated into action plans.

Employee attitude surveys have two important functions. First, they are an improvement tool. Surveys identify opportunities for improvement and evaluate the effectiveness of change programs. Second, surveys are a communication tool. They provide a communication channel and facilitate dialogue between managers and employees.

Employee surveys may be used to:

- Assess the state of the organization, department, or work team.
- Evaluate policies, procedures, and work processes.
- Assess job satisfaction and morale.
- Identify problems that hinder employees from doing their jobs and satisfying customers.

The questions on the survey should cover such areas as whether employees know what direction the organization is going, what are its objectives, and how their department fits into these goals. It is the manager's responsibility to provide employees with feedback once the survey is conducted. After the results are collected, the organization should not fall into the common trap of comparing scores with other companies. Instead, the data should be analyzed to see how the results relate to its own overall needs.

**Survey research and feedback** is a widely used process in which the OD practitioner and members of the organization collaboratively collect data and use them as a basis for changing organizational relationships.[2] The survey feedback method, as developed by the Survey Research Center at the Institute for Social Research, University of Michigan,[3] consists of collecting data by questionnaire on a number of organizational dimensions and then feeding the data back to work groups at successively lower levels. The work groups use the data to diagnose problems and to generate action plans altering organizational structure and work relationships. The questionnaire probes into such dimensions as leadership, communication, decision making, superior-subordinate relations, and job satisfaction. The data generated by the questionnaire are then used as a basis for further change efforts.

This method provides techniques for changing work relationships and a means for measuring the effects of such changes within organizations. The client system is usually involved in the data-collection activities, and managers and other organization members are usually asked to submit questions for the survey and to plan the data collection. The data are usually fed back to the organization through work teams, that is, the superior and those immediately reporting to him or her in a work-related group. These feedback conferences then provide the system with data about problems, leading to specific action plans and programs to improve effectiveness.

### The Steps in Survey Feedback

The survey feedback approach as developed by the Survey Research Center usually includes the following steps.

**Step 1**   The involvement of top management in preliminary planning of the survey questionnaire. Other organization members may be involved, if appropriate.

**Step 2**   The survey questionnaire is administered to all organization members by the outside staff.

**Step 3** The data are summarized by the outside staff and then fed back to work teams throughout the hierarchy of the organization, usually beginning with the top management team and flowing down to successive levels of the organization, a so-called waterfall effect. Some guidelines for providing survey results include:
- Managers should receive the results for their own work teams.
- Results should be shared with the whole work team.
- Everyone should see the results for the organization as a whole.

**Step 4** Each manager and work team meet to diagnose problems from the data presentation and to develop an action plan and program for improvement. An outside practitioner involved in the survey usually attends each work team meeting, using process interventions or acting as a resource person. This process may be described as a series of interlocking conferences or meetings structured in terms of organizational family units—the superior and immediate subordinates—considering the survey data together. The data presented to each group are those pertaining to the group as a whole or to the subunits for which members of the organizational unit are responsible. The survey feedback is intended to (1) develop an understanding of the problems, (2) improve working relationships, and (3) identify factors and opportunities for change or to determine areas where more research is required.

In one such company-wide study of employee and management attitudes and opinions over a period of two years, three different sets of data were fed back: (1) information on the attitudes and perceptions of 8,000 nonsupervisory employees toward their work, promotion opportunities, supervision, and fellow employees; (2) first- and second-line supervisors' feelings about various aspects of their job and supervisory beliefs; and (3) information from intermediate and top levels of management about their supervisory philosophies, roles and policy information, and problems of organizational integration.[4]

### The Results of Survey Research and Feedback

Survey feedback techniques, widely used in organization change, often provide the foundation for change programs. Most of the evidence pertaining to the results of survey research and feedback, obtained by the Survey Research Center, indicated positive changes in employee attitudes and perceptions.[5] The observations of the Survey Research Center showed that these methods are a powerful process for creating and reporting changes within an organization. They also demonstrated that the greater the involvement of the members of the organization, the greater the change. Other research showed that when the results of an OD intervention are fed back properly and action plans are made, factors associated with leadership and commitment to the organization are enhanced.[6] This research found that action plans with concrete objectives are essential for there to be improvement in the organization and leadership. When survey feedback interventions are the only type of intervention used, the success is usually short-range; but when feedback is combined with other interventions, the effects are usually more substantial and long-range.

## THE LEARNING ORGANIZATION

Competition is changing the way organizations do business. Internet technology means that new competition can come from anywhere and at any time. Globalization has dramatically increased the need for more responsive organizations. Successful organizations will be the ones that can develop new technologies and products rapidly, and get them to market immediately. This requires a flexible and responsive workforce able to adapt rapidly to constantly changing competition—in short, a learning organization.

The learning organization builds on a number of ideas, some of which have already been discussed in this and previous chapters. It has its roots in OD and uses the ideas and philosophies of action research, systems approach, organizational culture, continuous problem solving, self-managed work teams, collaboration, participative leadership, and interpersonal relations. The **learning organization** (or knowledge management as it is called in some organizations) is a system-wide change program that emphasizes the reduction of organizational layers and the involvement of all employees—management, nonmanagement, professional, line functions, staff, and so forth. The learning organization is a continuous state of self-directed learning that will lead toward positive change and growth in the individual, team, and organization.

### Learning Organizations Are Pragmatic

The ideas and theories of the learning organization have been around for some time. The learning organization, as the concept has come to be used and applied to organizations, has as its basis three schools of thought represented by Edgar Schein,[7] Chris Argyris,[8] and Peter Senge.[9] The three schools bring to learning organization theory the experiences of management, research, articles, books, and OD practitioners dating back to the 1960s.[10] Each of the schools of thought has made valuable contributions to the theories and use of learning organizations. Organizations like MetLife, General Electric (GE), Federal Express, Lafarge, and Cisco have implemented the ideas in ways that fit their specific situations. For an example of learning organizations refer to **OD Application: The Learning Organization at Lafarge.**

An approach frequently used in learning organization theory is to bring together key members of the organization in a collaborative process to discover the problems and then to develop a model of the system. According to Senge, "Leaders in learning organizations are responsible for building organizations where individuals continually expand their capabilities to shape their future—that is, leaders are responsible for fostering learning and are themselves learners."[11] Learning in organizations means the continuous testing of experience and the transformation of that experience into knowledge accessible to the whole organization and relevant to its core purpose.

Changing the way members interact means redesigning not just the formal structures of the organization, but also the hard-to-see patterns of interaction between people and processes. The disciplines of shared vision, systems thinking, and team learning are specifically aimed at

---

## OD Application: The Learning Organization at Lafarge[12]

Yves Cantat is a 20-year electrical maintenance worker at Lafarge's plant in France. Gone are the days when mixing cement was like making a huge cake. Now it is all computerized. The equipment and production processes have changed over his 20 years, but not many of the employees. He says, "In 20 years I have seen only two people leave."

Lafarge is the world's biggest cement producer and is on *Fortune*'s "Global 500" list, with over $15 billion in revenues from 133 cement plants in 46 countries. It traces its origins to 1833 when it was founded by the Lafarge family. The founders were committed to a form of humanism that still prevails in the company today even though the family no longer controls it. Since the end of World War II, Lafarge has had only five CEOs, and two of them have written books about the company's culture. Now retired CEO and current board member Bertrand Collomb says, "Lafarge will not work in situations where we are required to deny our values and participate in practices that we abhor." Collomb is an advocate of the "Lafarge way," a philosophy of participative management.

The Lafarge way says in part:

- A key responsibility for managers is to develop their people. They expose employees to challenging assignments, help them to learn from their achievements and mistakes, and support them to outperform themselves.
- We expect our people to share their experiences and to seek those of others. Best practices derive from our ability to recognize and share our local successes, regardless of their scale.
- Dealing with conflict is an integral and productive part of teamwork. Teamwork is not about reaching consensus on every issue. It is about each individual contributing, accepting, and seeking differences of opinion as a source of progress.
- Effective teamwork creates an environment of trust and confidence. This is built daily through professionalism,

personal commitment, shared goals, and respect for common rules.

There are three trade unions at the French plant, and despite recent strikes, things seem amicable between management and labor. As one employee said about the strike, "After all, this is France." Many of the workers are shareholders in Lafarge. Several years ago, more than half the employees bought Lafarge stock when they were given an opportunity to buy it at a price subsidized 60 percent by the company.

Lafarge's organization development program incorporates the principles of learning organizations. For them it means that they promote the sharing of best practices and experiences through networking, cross-functional, and international ways of working. Self renewal is part of the process where they increase the ability of all employees to adapt to new conditions, solve problems, and learn from experiences.

An important element at Lafarge is training. Managers are required to monitor the development of employees. "Our aim is to become a learning organization," says the training manager of the cement division. Given the global nature of the company, managers are expected to speak English, with Lafarge offering language classes.

The company practices intensive communication to make sure that its worldwide businesses understand its operations. Lafarge operates a Web site for employees and publishes a monthly magazine in French and English.

### Questions

1. Can you explain how a culture can persist in an organization for over 170 years across different owners?
2. Visit the Lafarge Web site at www.lafarge.com to read and critique the "Lafarge way" and other company practices and philosophies. Based on your research, is Lafarge a learning organization? Support your position.

changing interactions. Once members become conscious of how they think and interact, and begin developing capacities to think and interact differently, the organization will change for the better. The changes will ripple through the organization and reinforce a growing sense of capability and confidence.

Learning organizations realistically and pragmatically emphasize creating "knowledge for action" and not "knowledge for its own sake." They focus on acquiring knowledge, sharing it across the organization, and using it to achieve organizational goals. Participants must liberate themselves from such mental traps as blaming the competition, the economy, or other factors beyond their control. Learning organizations realize that they are part of a larger system over which they have little or no control. Instead of complaining, they seek out opportunities and "ride the wave."

## Core Values and Behaviors

A strong set of core values and behaviors is normally present in learning organizations. These include:

- Value different kinds of knowledge and learning styles.
- Encourage communication between people who have different perspectives and ideas.
- Develop creative thinking.
- Remain nonjudgmental of others and their ideas.
- Break down traditional barriers within the organization.
- Develop leadership throughout the organization. Everyone is a leader.
- Reduce distinctions between organization members (management versus nonmanagement, line versus staff, doers versus thinkers, professional staff versus nonprofessional, and so on.)
- Believe that every member of the organization has untapped human potential.[13]

Becoming a learning organization increases the size of an organization's "brain." Employees throughout the organization participate in all thinking activities. The boundaries between the parts of the organization are broken down. GE calls this "boundarylessness" and has made it part of the corporate culture. When everyone communicates and works together, there is enormous intelligence and flexibility present to deal with rapidly changing conditions.

## Characteristics of Learning Organizations

There are some common characteristics that define a learning organization though there is no set formula for how they are implemented. Constant readiness, best knowledge available, collaboration, continuous planning, improvised implementation, and action learning are typical characteristics of learning organizations.[14]

*Constant readiness.* The organization exists in constant readiness for change. By staying in tune with its environment and being willing to question its ways of doing business, the organization is ready to take advantage of new opportunities. There are new products and ideas in the pipeline. Research, development, and innovation do not occur just when times are good and there is money available in the budget. Some of the best and boldest strategic moves came from companies during recessions because they were ready to execute. IBM, for example, in a recession in 1981, introduced the personal computer.

*Best knowledge available.* The best knowledge, including real-time data, is available to implement changes. The knowledge is widely gathered and widely disseminated. Knowledge is power, and in the learning organization no one owns or monopolizes knowledge. The knowledge is gathered from inside and outside the organization which means going to experts, research journals, conferences, and other organizations. Many of the best experts may already be in the organization, but at lower levels, where they are not often heard. A person on the production line may have a bit of knowledge that would help a researcher solve a problem who is working on a new product. A challenge is how to share the knowledge between people who may not know each other and are not likely to come into contact with one another.

Learning organizations do not depend on "accidental sharing" of knowledge but instead they develop sophisticated mechanisms to assure that people and their ideas are brought together. An account of how Cisco does this comes from *Fast Company* magazine:

"Pull back the tent flaps and Cisco citizens are blogging, vlogging, and virtualizing, using social-networking tools that they've made themselves and that, in many cases, far exceed the capabilities of the commercially available wikis, YouTubes, and Facebooks created by the kids up the road in Palo Alto."[15] Cisco calls it a "human network effect" that extends both on and off the Cisco campus to operations throughout the world. Other than sharing information internally, other situations may call for learning from other companies, maybe even a competitor. For example, Toyota occasionally opens up its training classrooms to non-Toyota people such as home builders and U.S. soldiers. Here they learn about Toyota's unique business philosophy and "lean-thinking" approach. GE also offers programs for non-GE employees at their Crotonville, New York, management development center.[16] And even a relatively new company, Zappos, offers Zappos Insights where, for $39.95 a month, entrepreneurs have Internet access at Zappos.com to the company's management. "We're happy to share pretty much anything," says CEO Tony Hsieh.[17]

*Collaboration across the organization.* Dissemination of knowledge through technology, as in the example of Cisco, is common. In addition, successful learning organizations, including Cisco, foster opportunities for face-to-face collaboration. This occurs in meetings that cut across boundaries. All kinds of boundaries exist within organizations including one of the most obvious, geographical; but other types of boundaries exist because of departments, professional affiliations, and levels within the organization. In solving problems in the learning organization, collaboration occurs between people throughout the organization: vertically, horizontally, and diagonally. Knowledge knows no boundaries and coordination and collaboration of everyone involved is required.

*Continuous planning.* Instead of a few top executives formulating fixed plans, the learning organization creates flexible plans that are fully known and accepted by the entire organization. The plans are constantly reexamined and rewritten by those involved with their implementation—not just top management. The old adage that "the top thinks and the bottom acts" has given way to the need for "integrated thinking and acting at all levels."

*Improvised implementation.* The learning organization improvises. Instead of rigidly implementing plans, it encourages experimentation. To "stay the course" when confronted with changing conditions might have merit if the organization consisted of nonthinking and nonreasoning robots, much like the assembly lines of Henry Ford where tasks were broken down into small and repetitive motions. But the organizations of today, where conditions can change rapidly and without warning, require people actively thinking and contributing.

*Action learning.* Successes are identified and institutionalized within the organization. Change is reevaluated continually, not just at annual planning sessions. The learning organization collects data to understand better what went wrong, what went right, and what could have gone better. It constantly takes action, reflects, and makes adjustments. Things learned are widely shared, and there are no reprisals from admitting mistakes. It is similar to the football team that meets the day after the game and watches videos so that its members can learn what they did right and wrong. Even the winning team will have a lot to critique. In short, learning organizations constantly undergo a reexamination that questions and tests assumptions. They do not wait for problems to arise.

The idea and theory behind learning organizations is promising; however, the problem has been in the execution—that is to say, how learning is shared. To date, organizations have tried a variety of ways; many of them are technology and computer-oriented, such as databases, e-mail, blogs, and Web sites. It has proved challenging for large organizations to institutionalize the sharing of information that historically occurred informally around the water cooler and at coffee breaks. Surveys by consulting firm Bain & Company show 41 percent of managers worldwide report the use of learning organizations but also reveal a satisfaction rate of 3.66 out of a possible 5 (the average satisfaction for all types of tools used by organizations is 3.82). The figures for recent years have been fairly consistent, which seems to indicate that despite the lower satisfaction rate, managers are still trying to implement the objectives of a learning organization. "We don't necessarily understand enough yet about optimizing the conditions for knowledge work, even though we've been doing it for 25 years," says the research director for Delphi Group, a consulting firm. "Most organizations are still managing as if we were in the industrial era."[18]

## REENGINEERING: A RADICAL REDESIGN

**Reengineering,** or "business process reengineering" as it is sometimes called, is a system-wide change approach focusing on the basic processes of an organization.[19] Reengineering may be defined as the fundamental rethinking and radical redesigning of business processes to achieve drastic improvements in performance. Organizations that use reengineering do not look at existing processes and search for ways to improve; they begin with a blank sheet of paper. This gives them an opportunity to look at their operations in totally new ways without the baggage of "this is how we do it now."

Reengineering, as the name implies, focuses on the design of work activities or processes: how the task is accomplished. It is like designing a circuit, examining the flows or sequences of activities from input to output in an attempt to eliminate inefficiencies and improve productivity. Reengineering seeks to make all processes more efficient by combining, eliminating, or restructuring tasks without regard to traditional methods. Reengineering emphasizes products, customer satisfaction, improvement in processes, and creation of value. It is radical change with the objective of gaining a large or quantum leap in performance.

The focus is the customer. Companies like Verizon Communications, the largest phone company in the United States, have reengineered the process used to implement telephone service to new customers. The results have been faster, better, and easier for both customers and employees. The CEO of Verizon, Ivan G. Seidenberg, says, "When you're the market leader, part of your responsibility is to reinvent the market."[20] Seidenberg is determined to transform what was once just another sleepy phone company into the leader of the industry. Reengineering does not refer to minor modifications of current practices. Instead, it means rethinking existing processes to deliver more value to the customer, identifying the way things can be done best, and right now. This includes radical changes in work processes and work relationships. The main emphasis in reengineering is upon serving the customer.

The first step is to identify the key business processes of a department or work team. The next step is to identify performance measures in terms of customer satisfaction and to examine current processes to meet these measures. The customer does not care about internal rewards or "turf wars"; the customer just wants the product or service done right, and on time. The third step is to reengineer the process, organizing work around the process, not around functions or departments. Work is simplified by combining related tasks and eliminating any elements that do not directly add customer value. Finally, the redesigned process is implemented, and all activities are subjected to an ongoing reevaluation. Work processes are continually reexamined as technology, competitors, and customers change.

Reengineering examines each process and evaluates it in terms of how it affects the customer. In this sense, reengineering is similar to job design. It is different in that job design usually focuses on incremental changes, whereas reengineering seeks a radical reexamination aimed at large-scale increases in productivity. Some OD practitioners criticize reengineering as a top-down, or numbers, approach, but it lends itself to OD by involving all employees in the reengineering process. In its use of employee involvement, empowerment, and teams, reengineering is similar to the sociotechnical approach to change that was discussed in Chapter 2.

## SYSTEM 4 MANAGEMENT

**System 4 management** is a system-wide intervention developed by Rensis Likert.[21] Likert found through extensive research that organizations can be described on a continuum, with traditional bureaucratic organizations (ineffective) at one end and participative (effective) organizations at the other. Likert then identified four systems, as follows:

- *System 1*—exploitative-authoritative (autocratic, top-down approach).
- *System 2*—benevolent-authoritative (top-down/less coercive-autocratic).
- *System 3*—consultative.
- *System 4*—participative (based upon participative methods of decision making and supervision, emphasizes employee involvement and participation).

Likert devised a measurement device to determine the degree to which an organization approximates the system 4 parameters. Employees indicate their perception of the organization on

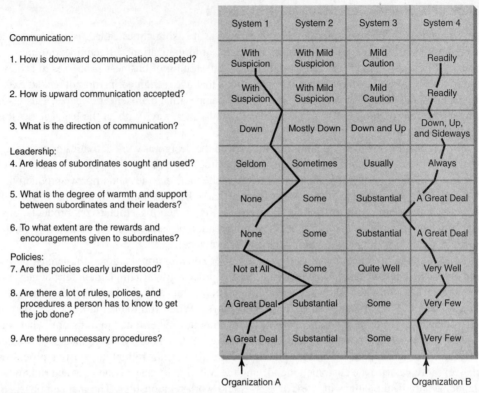

Communication:

1. How is downward communication accepted?

2. How is upward communication accepted?

3. What is the direction of communication?

Leadership:
4. Are ideas of subordinates sought and used?

5. What is the degree of warmth and support between subordinates and their leaders?

6. To what extent are the rewards and encouragements given to subordinates?

Policies:
7. Are the policies clearly understood?

8. Are there a lot of rules, polices, and procedures a person has to know to get the job done?

9. Are there unnecessary procedures?

| | System 1 | System 2 | System 3 | System 4 |
|---|---|---|---|---|
| 1 | With Suspicion | With Mild Suspicion | Mild Caution | Readily |
| 2 | With Suspicion | With Mild Suspicion | Mild Caution | Readily |
| 3 | Down | Mostly Down | Down and Up | Down, Up, and Sideways |
| 4 | Seldom | Sometimes | Usually | Always |
| 5 | None | Some | Substantial | A Great Deal |
| 6 | None | Some | Substantial | A Great Deal |
| 7 | Not at All | Some | Quite Well | Very Well |
| 8 | A Great Deal | Substantial | Some | Very Few |
| 9 | A Great Deal | Substantial | Some | Very Few |

Organization A                           Organization B

**FIGURE 14.1   Profile of Organization Characteristics**
*Source:* Adapted from Rensis Likert and Jane Gibson Likert, *New Ways of Managing Conflict* (New York: McGraw-Hill, 1976).

this questionnaire. The results are plotted on a profile, as shown in Figure 14.1. The profile illustrates the differences that can occur in organizational functioning. According to Likert's model, the profile indicated by Organization A tends toward system 1 design; Organization B tends toward system 4 functioning.

Two contrasting examples will illustrate a company working largely from system 1 and another company working from system 4. Based on a *Business Week* report, Bob Nardelli appears to develop system 1 types of organizations.[22] As CEO of Home Depot for about seven years and then at Chrysler for about two years, he tended "to ram through his ideas" according to the *Business Week* article. At Home Depot, he bought a wholesale business despite objections from executives that this would deflect focus on the retail stores. At Chrysler, he cut capital spending on engineering and product development that resulted in few new products in the pipeline. When in 2009, the feds showed up to ascertain Chrysler's viability prior to a federal loan, they found only four new models were planned for the next five years. Procter & Gamble (P&G), in contrast, tends to exemplify system 4. Another *Business Week* article reports of an executive meeting: "At one of those meetings, an outsider might have trouble distinguishing the CEO [currently chairman of the board] Alan Lafley: He occasionally joins in the discussion, but most of the time the executives talked as much to each other as to Lafley. 'I am more like a coach,' Lafley says afterward."[23] It should be pointed out that the examples of Bob Nardelli at Home Depot and Chrysler and Alan Lafley at P&G are strictly anecdotal and not based on survey instruments.

Likert has found that system 1 organizations tend to be the least effective, whereas system 4 organizations tend to be very effective. Consequently, to improve an organization, the OD practitioner tries to move its pattern of functioning closer to the right, toward the system 4 operation.

In today's changing environment, organizations that encourage individual ability and hold employees accountable for achieving goals are more likely to succeed. These empowered organizations attract high performance from the outside. Under this empowerment approach to system 4 management, subordinates are allowed to make decisions, and employees are given personal responsibility instead of strict rules to follow. Such organizations promote individual ability and encourage their members to grow personally and professionally.

Several elements should be looked for in analyzing empowered organizations:

- Action rather than further analysis.
- Decisions involving subordinates rather than by superiors.
- Individual accountability rather than rigid policies.
- Specific recognition of team and individual accomplishments rather than blanket expressions of thanks.

Managers in empowered system 4 organizations are demonstrating the importance of these values to themselves as individuals and as managers. Empowerment is not the simplest or easiest managerial option. In fact, an extensive commitment is required if its benefits are to be fully realized.

OD programs utilizing system 4 approaches, then, measure the present state of the system and design training interventions that foster empowerment, participative goal setting, and shared decision making. In this way, one attempts to shift the key organizational factors toward the system 4 framework. Likert presents evidence that system 4 is the most effective management system for all organizations, and explains how a system 4 organization, in contrast to systems 1 and 2, leads to greater effectiveness. He maintains that the causal variables that comprise system 4 managerial practices can be altered or changed by members of the organization to affect the end-result variables related to performance and quality. Several organizations have reported using system 4 theory as an approach to change, including one OD program that uses system 4 approaches.

## HIGH-PERFORMING SYSTEMS

The concept of a **high-performing system (HPS),** a term originated by Peter Vaill, is another development in large-scale change.[24] The idea is that today's organizations need continuing excellence and renewal as a way to bring innovation into our systems.

HPS calls for the removal of excessive layers of structure within the organization and the creation of a climate that encourages participation and communication across functional barriers. The most important element in creating a successful HPS is the leaders' abilities to display energy and zest for the task being worked on, the products and processes being developed, and fellow team members. These ideas are similar to those of international management professor and author, Gary Hamel, who writes in a *Harvard Business Review* article, "In Management 2.0, leaders will no longer be seen as grand visionaries, all-wise decision makers, and ironfisted disciplinarians. Instead, they will need to become social architects, constitution writers, and entrepreneurs of meaning. In this new model, the leader's job is to create an environment where every employee has the chance to collaborate, innovate, and excel."[25]

Leading by example is a popular way for managers to create excitement and electricity within the workplace. Displays of enthusiasm tend to improve the morale and productivity of the workforce. An HPS has been defined as an excellent human system—one that performs at an unusually high level of excellence. However, as Peter Vaill points out, how we define excellence and performance depends upon our values. Figure 14.2 provides a good lesson in how not to lead in order to build an HPS.

### HPS Criteria

Vaill has identified a set of eight criteria that may be used to examine systems:

1. They are performing excellently against a known external standard.
2. They are performing excellently against what is assumed to be their potential level of performance.
3. They are performing excellently in relation to where they were at some earlier point in time.
4. They are judged by informed observers to be doing substantially better qualitatively than other comparable systems.
5. They are doing whatever they do with significantly fewer resources than are assumed to be needed for what they do.
6. They are perceived as exemplars of the way to do whatever they do, and thus they become a source of ideas and inspiration for others.
7. They are perceived to fulfill at a high level the ideals of the culture within which they exist.
8. They are the only organizations that have been at all able to do what they do.[26]

**FIGURE 14.2** **Leaders Need Enthusiasm to Develop High-Performing Systems**
*Source:* CROCK © NORTH AMERICA SYNDICATE

The OD practitioner can use these criteria to examine client systems and identify how well they measure up.

## HPS Characteristics

Based on his experience, Vaill has also identified eight characteristics that typify high-performing systems. Note that an HPS can be either an organization as a whole or a subsystem within a larger organization. For example, an HPS can be an entire organization, such as GE, or, alternatively, a unit, division, or smaller work group within GE.

1. An HPS is clear on its broad purposes and on nearer-term objectives for fulfilling these purposes. It knows why it exists.
2. Commitment to these purposes is never perfunctory. Motivation, as usually conceived, is always high.
3. Teamwork in an HPS is focused on the task.
4. Leadership in an HPS is strong and clear.
5. An HPS is a fertile source of inventions and new methods within the scope of the task it has defined.
6. An HPS is separated from its environment by a clear boundary. There is a strong consciousness that "we are different."
7. Other subsystems in the environment often see the HPS as a problem, even elements in the environment that may have power over the HPS. This is because the HPS avoids external control and produces its own standards.
8. Above all, an HPS is a systems that has "jelled"; it is a cohesive unit.

As Vaill suggests, the phenomenon of the HPS poses a complex conceptual challenge—how to analyze human interdependency in more descriptively accurate terms. Vaill has also formulated what he terms a "Time-Feelings-Focus" theory of HPS. It reflects his observation that HPS leaders tend to put in extraordinary amounts of time, have very strong feelings and dedication to attaining the system's goals, and focus on key issues and variables. Executives at Harley-Davidson and International Specialty Products (manufacturer of chemicals and pharmaceuticals) credit HPS with helping them to revitalize inefficient factories.[27] To learn more about Cisco Systems Inc., another example of an HPS, see **OD Application: Cisco and High-Performing Teams.**

## THE GRID OD PROGRAM

Grid organization development, a change model designed by Robert R. Blake and Jane S. Mouton and marketed by Grid International Inc., is a widely used approach to system-wide planned change.[28] This program, which has been around for over 40 years, is a systematic approach

## OD Application: Cisco and High-Performing Teams[29]

The tech wreck of the first few years of the 2000s caught many companies—especially tech companies—off guard. More than a few companies were in a state of denial, including Cisco Systems Inc. and its CEO, John Chambers. Cisco went from being the most highly valued company in the world to a poster child of the excess of bubbles in the tech sector. Finally, in 2001 Chambers decided it was time, and hopefully not too late, for a massive overhaul. This was not a time for evolutionary change; revolutionary change was the company's only chance. "Explaining to people why we needed to change things was the hard part," says Chambers years later reflecting on the radical and massive change at Cisco that was at times tumultuous.

The low point came in 2001 with a net profit loss of $1 billion, but by 2003 Cisco was back in fighting trim—stronger than ever, with record profits of $3.6 billion, while some of its competitors were just beginning to see black ink. Cisco could be a case study of how a discredited industry leader can use a slump to clean house and build a better foundation. Chambers took the opportunity of a downturn to rethink every part of the company, including operations, priorities, and culture. Chambers says, "We went through a life-threatening experience in 2001. At first, there is disbelief, then understanding . . . then how do you position yourself for the future?" Cisco seems to have learned its lessons, if the recession that began in late 2007 offers an indication. For the latest year available, in 2008 Cisco had record net profits of $8.1 billion on record sales of $39.5 billion. This occurred at a time when there was a world-wide and severe recession. With cash reserves of $26.2 billion, Cisco has been expanding by adding new product lines, purchasing other companies, and helping their customers to finance Cisco products and services.

Cisco's culture before the changes could best be described as a wild-west cowboy culture. Executives were encouraged to compete with one another. "All decisions came to the top 10 people in the company, and we drove things back down from there," says Chambers. Executives were too busy taking orders to bother with efficiency or teamwork. Any idea was pursued with little discipline or accountability. But today is a different situation. The market changed dramatically in terms of what customers expected. As the market changed, engineering, manufacturing, professional services, and sales had to work together in a way that was not required before.

The changes that Chambers implemented permeated the entire company and not just the top managers. Previously, where Cisco had a top-down structure, it now has a network of councils and boards empowered to launch new businesses and products. A council is a team of executives who have decision-making authority on $10 billion or greater opportunities. Boards are teams of managers who make decisions on $1 billion opportunities. Working groups, similar to ad hoc committees, deal with a specific issue for a limited time. The teams that work on major initiatives of specific product lines cut across functional lines and are interdepartmental. In many cases, the teams are aimed at achieving international where Cisco uses its TelePresence technology in the meetings. Chambers is rarely involved with any of the decision-making groups. This structure allows Cisco to operate on a variety of major projects simultaneously and quickly respond to new opportunities. In a fast-paced global marketplace, being able to move quickly is required from the initial conceptual stage of a product or service to bringing it on line. Chambers says, "Fifteen minutes and one week to get a [business] plan that used to take six months!"

As the new structure required trust and openness and the old system required cut-throat competitiveness in order to gain Chambers' attention, changing the culture was paramount. To reinforce the new culture, Cisco put into place a new financial incentive system that encouraged executives and rank-and-file employees to work well together. Executives are compensated on how well the collective of businesses perform and not how well their unit performs. To do this, Chambers says, "I now compensate our leadership team based on how well they do on collaboration and the longer-term picture. If we take the focus off of how they did today, this week, this quarter, it will work."

Cisco also learned that it needed a way to bring people and their ideas together. This is not an easy task with 66,000 employees plus customers and partners. This is where its vice president of IT Communications and Collaboration comes in. For this to happen, Cisco is using the technology that it sells, like routers, switches, servers, digital billboards, telephony, Flip video recorder, data centers, TelePresence, and mobile devices. One tool that Cisco developed is WebEx Connect, a virtual workplace that supports online meetings, audio and video conferencing, file sharing, presence notification, instant messaging, and online chat. What's more, tools like WebEx Connect are not only used by Cisco's employees to help them collaborate internally on projects, but are also used to encourage collaboration between its partners and customers. WebEx Connect is an example where Cisco has become a laboratory for developing and using technology that it later went on to sell. Mike Mitchell, who is charged with encouraging the company's rank and file to adopt new technology, says, "We want a culture where it is unacceptable not to share what you know."

### Questions

1. Identify the changes at Cisco that tend to be more structural, behavioral, and technological in nature. How are the three categories of change interconnected at Cisco?
2. Cisco's Web site at  www.cisco.com/ has information on its products, services, and applications. Its corporate annual reports have both financial and product information. Research this site to learn of its latest products for online collaboration. Its site for webcasts, which is continuously updated, may have some helpful topics.
3. What is its current financial data for profits, sales, and cash reserves?

---

aimed at achieving corporate excellence. Blake and Mouton feel that managers and organizations can only be made more effective if the basic culture of the system is changed. Grid organization development starts with a focus on individual behavior, specifically on the managerial styles of executives, using what Blake and Mouton call the Managerial Grid. The program then moves through a series of sequential phases involving the work team, the relationships between groups or subunits, and finally the overall culture of the organization. The Managerial Grid and **Grid**

**OD** comprise an approach to organization improvement used by major corporations throughout the world. Grid International reports that over 700 organizations and 250 multinational companies have participated in its programs.[30]

Blake and Mouton assembled data on corporate excellence from some 200 organizations. They found that Managerial Grid seminars could be used as a starting point for a planned change program called Grid OD. Grid OD has as its objectives the maximizing of managers' concerns about both their subordinates and the organization. In order to make individual managers more effective in dealing with subordinates, changes must take place in the organizational culture. Grid OD is a systems approach that addresses the whole organization from the CEO down. The Grid OD program consists of the following six **grid phases.**

## Phase 1: Grid Seminars

Organizations get involved in a Grid OD program in various ways, but involvement usually begins with someone in a responsible managerial position reading an article or book about the Management Grid. This person may decide to become more familiar with the Grid by attending a public seminar to gain first-hand knowledge. The seminars are a week long, held both day and evening, and are conducted at various locations around the country and the world. There are about 30 or 40 hours of paperwork in addition to the work at the seminar. The learning objectives for the week include:

- Learning the Grid as a way to analyze thinking.
- Increasing one's personal objectivity in appraising oneself.
- Achieving clear and candid communication.
- Learning and working effectively in a team.
- Learning to manage intergroup conflict.
- Analyzing one's corporate work culture by applying the Grid framework.
- Gaining an understanding of the phases of Grid OD.

The seminar is highly structured, with most of the activities devoted to short lectures and team projects. It is highly intensive and emotionally demanding, because it encourages competition between teams and confrontation between team members. Participants who leave the seminar committed to the precepts of the Grid will probably encourage other key members of their organization to attend a similar seminar.

Participants in the seminar analyze their own managerial approaches and learn alternative ways of managing. In addition, they study methods of team action. They measure and evaluate team effectiveness in solving problems with others. A high point of the seminar learning is reached when the participants critique one another's styles of managerial performance. Another is when managers critique the dominant style of their own organization's culture, its traditions, precedents, and past practices. A third is when participants consider steps for increasing the effectiveness of the whole organization.

## Phase 2: Teamwork Development

An organization is composed of many subgroups or teams whose members range from top management to assembly-line workers. Phase 2 is concerned with improving teamwork and includes a boss and his or her immediate subordinates meeting together for a one-week session. Teamwork development begins with the organization's top manager and the employees who report directly to him or her. These people later attend another team meeting with their own subordinates. This continues down through the entire organization.

Teamwork development is a planned activity that begins with each team member completing various Grid instruments. The teams deal with subjects directly relevant to their daily operations and behaviors. The team members also receive feedback from participants on their Grid styles in real situations. Before the conclusion of the week, the team sets group and individual goals.

## Phase 3: Intergroup Development

The teamwork development meetings that occur in Phase 2 cut vertically through the organization by encompassing natural work teams, but people also relate to others along a horizontal dimension: people interact with others in different teams, departments, divisions, and sections. Unintended competition between departments may develop into a win-lose contest resulting in a loss of organization effectiveness. Coordination, cooperation, and collaboration between elements are necessary for an effective organization, and to accomplish this, intergroup development meetings are held and attended by the key members of two segments or divisions where barriers exist. Intergroup development involves group-to-group relationships where members of interfacing teams meet for three or four days to identify those things that would be present in an ideal relationship between their two segments. The objective is for the two segments to agree on the elements for an ideal relationship and then develop specific actions to attain the ideal. As in Phase 2, participants leave the meetings with actual goals and objectives plus an increased understanding of communication with one another.

## Phase 4: Development of an Ideal Strategic Model

The development of an **ideal strategic model** provides an organization with the knowledge and skills to move from a reactionary approach to one of systematic development. This phase is concerned with the overall norms, policies, and structure of the organization. The responsibility for these matters is with the top manager and those reporting to him or her. During a week of study, the key people in the organization define what the organization would be like if it were truly excellent. Moderate-sized organizations normally spend six months to a year perfecting the ideal strategic model. During this time, other people at various levels have the opportunity to contribute to the model. This helps build the commitment needed for implementation of the model.

## Phase 5: Implementing the Ideal Strategic Model

The manner in which the ideal strategic model is implemented determines the success of Grid OD in the organization. An edict coming from above will probably fall on deaf ears and be doomed to failure from the beginning. The Grid OD program has an implementation model that can be adapted to any organization. Organizations can be divided into identifiable segments, such as products, profit centers, or geographical areas. Once the segments are identified, the top management team assigns one planning team to each segment, one team to the corporate headquarters, and a coordinator of Phase 5. The coordinator recommends implementation tactics to the topline executive. The task of each planning team is to analyze all aspects of its section's operations and determine how it would act ideally. The design is based on the ideal strategic model determined in Phase 4 but is interpreted and implemented for each section by the planning team. The task is aided by the skills attained during Phases 1, 2, and 3. The studies to convert the ideal model into reality for each section may take three months to a year, and the actual conversion may take six months to five years or even longer.

## Phase 6: Systematic Critique

The final phase in Grid OD is a systematic examination of progress toward change goals. The systematic critique determines the degree of organizational excellence after Phase 5 compared with measurements taken before Phase 1. The basic instrument is a 100-question survey investigating managerial behavior, teamwork, intergroup relations, and corporate strategy. With instruments administered at each phase, it is possible to observe the degree of change and gain insight into the total process of change. Because change never ceases, discovery sets the stage for a new beginning.

This chapter has presented some system-wide approaches to OD. The approaches to change of several of these models are contradictory, which perhaps should be taken as a reminder that there is no one best way for all organizations to manage change. Because there is insufficient research evidence supporting any one approach or model, it is difficult to make meaningful comparisons, and therefore our knowledge of system-wide approaches to change and high-performing systems is incomplete. The purpose here is to make you aware of these new approaches and models. Given a certain situation or set of conditions, you may decide that one approach will be more effective than others for a particular application. In the next chapter, we will explore and describe several major OD strategic interventions including organization transformation, the strategy-culture matrix, and strategic change management.

## Summary

- **System wide.** This chapter has examined six different system-wide approaches to organization development: (1) survey research and feedback, (2) learning organization, (3) reengineering, (4) system 4 management, (5) high-performing systems, and (6) Grid OD.
- **Survey research and feedback.** This method uses attitudinal surveys of employees as a means of identifying and communicating organizational problems. The survey data are provided to work teams as a way of improving performance.
- **Learning organization.** This embodies a vision of more humane workplaces and organizations built around learning. It emphasizes the reduction of organizational layers and the involvement of all employees in continuous self-directed learning.
- **Reengineering.** This system-wide approach implements a fundamental and radical redesign of all business processes to achieve a higher level of performance.

- **System 4 management.** Organizations can be described on a continuum with traditional bureaucratic organizations (ineffective) at one end and participative (effective) organizations at the other.
- **High-performing systems.** Developing a new corporate culture is a process of continuous improvement. A more participative, empowered, HPS can lead to a successful organization.
- **Grid OD.** This approach to change focuses on improving managerial skills and developing a new strategic model. It uses methodologies similar to those of the action research model. It often involves the collection of data, the feeding back of data to appropriate individuals, and the generation of action plans by system members.

## Review Questions

1. Identify and give examples from your experience of the major system-wide OD intervention techniques.
2. Compare and contrast the reasons for successful and unsuccessful change programs.
3. How can managers develop an organizational culture that encourages an HPS or a learning organization?

## Key Words and Concepts

Grid OD
Grid Phases
High-Performing System (HPS)

Ideal Strategic Model
Learning Organization
Reengineering

Survey Research and Feedback
System 4 Management
System-level intervention

# OD Skills Simulation 14.1

## Brentwood Division

*Total time suggested: 85 to 100 minutes.*

## A. Purpose

The purpose of this simulation is to provide a situation where you will need to influence others and to observe how information affects team decision making. During and after the simulation, you are encouraged to become aware of the processes you use in your attempts to influence and relate with others. You will also be given an opportunity to design an OD program. You will experience:

- How task information is shared.
- How problem-solving strategies influence results.
- How collaboration and competition affect team problem solving.

## B. Procedures

*Step 1.* All participants should read the Brentwood Division Background Information. Prior to class, form teams of seven to eight members and select roles. Additional class members will serve as OD practitioners, but ideally there should be at least two and no more than three practitioners per team. Each player should read only his or her role and the Brentwood Division Background Information.

1. Brentwood General Manager
2. Director of Marketing
3. Director of Production
4. Director of Human Resources Development
5. Director of Engineering
6. OD Practitioner Team (two or three)

*Step 2.* Executive committee meeting. Your team is to use the information to arrive at a decision. Practitioner teams and the executive committee meet in an executive meeting. The meeting is scheduled to last 30 minutes. The practitioners use the Team Profile Form to help them analyze the organization.

The decisions facing the committee are:

1. What should be the basic goal—efficiency or effectiveness, short-term profit or long-term market share?
2. What should the decision be on pricing policy—to stay with the policy or to become more flexible?
3. How should people be retained by increasing salaries, by bonuses, or in other ways?

*Time suggested for Step 2: 30 minutes.*

*Step 3.* After the executive meeting, the OD practitioner team completes the diagnosis and formulates an OD program to present to the executive committee for its consideration. While the practitioners are designing the OD program, the executive committee of Brentwood should discuss questions to ask the practitioners and determine the criterion for rating the proposal.

*Time suggested for Step 3: 10 minutes.*

*Step 4.* The practitioners present the diagnosis and OD program to their respective companies. Then each company with its practitioners jointly develops an OD program.

*Time suggested for Step 4: 15 minutes.*

*Step 5.* At the conclusion of the role play, the team discusses and critiques the team process and the practitioner style. Did the practitioner team:

1. Establish a relationship?
2. Take over the problem and the meeting?
3. Focus on feelings?
4. Encourage the client to be specific?
5. Allow the client to talk?
6. Lead and direct conversation?
7. Show indications of judging the client?
8. Take sides?

*Time suggested for Step 5: 15 minutes.*

*Step 6.* As a class, each practitioner team should present its company's OD program for class discussion and critique. Discuss the eight questions in Step 5.

*Time suggested for Step 6: 15 to 30 minutes, depending on the number of teams.*

## Brentwood Division Background Information

The Continental Manufacturing Company is a leading manufacturer of industrial and military equipment. The company is divided into several major functional groups, each headed by a vice president. One of these groups is the Products Group, which is divided into a number of product divisions, each headed by a division general manager. See Figure 14.3 for its organization chart.

The Brentwood Division's general manager oversees the directors for engineering, marketing, production, and human resources development. Brentwood's performance has been excellent, especially over the past 10 years, but with the exception of the most recent two years. In fact, Brentwood has a record of being one of the most profitable divisions of Continental in terms of amount of profit and return on investment. However, two years ago profits dropped by 4 percent, and last year they dropped by 11 percent, reflecting a decline in sales of 6 percent and 13 percent, respectively. Continental uses cost centers, and its divisions are relatively autonomous in their operations; but each division is expected to be self-supporting.

Brentwood employs about 1,200 people and operates from one plant location. The number of employees has increased rapidly within the past 10 years but leveled off this year because of the sales decline. So far there have not been any layoffs, but if the current sales trend continues, layoffs may have to be considered as a possibility to reduce costs. The employees are unionized, as is common in this industry, but both Brentwood and Continental have exceptionally positive relationships with the unions. This is largely due to the diligent work by the human resources development department at corporate headquarters, where contracts are formulated. At the local level, leadership training has been helpful, but quality improvement circles had some problems after a half year and were discontinued.

The major problem with sales has been attributed to the new major competitors that have entered the field. To date, the product line has faced little competition, probably because of the expensive and technologically advanced processes used in the fabrication. Because of the technological orientation of the products, it is important that Brentwood be able to respond quickly to the changing customer demands. In addition, to be competitive, it is increasingly necessary for Brentwood to anticipate the needs of its customers and bring in technologically superior products before its competitors. Most recently, Brentwood's ability to respond effectively to competitors has been diminished because several dynamic middle managers in engineering and production as well as other key employees were lost to competitors.

A key engineer recently left Brentwood and formed a competing company—Infiniti Engineering. He has been recruiting many key people from Brentwood—primarily engineers, marketing, and production specialists. Infiniti offers a bonus and stock options, but mainly recruits employees based on its free-form corporate culture and upon personal growth for the individual. However, Infiniti employees often work much longer hours than employees at Brentwood.

Brentwood products are used at workstations in the production of industrial and military products. The military contracts have been declining at a slightly greater rate than the civilian sales. The products themselves are very high-tech and

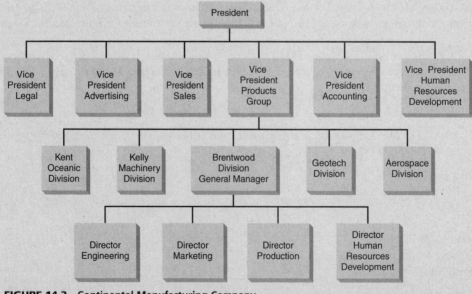

**FIGURE 14.3 Continental Manufacturing Company**

require strong engineering and software support. Many of the materials used in the manufacturing process are exotic metals, plastics, and titanium matrix composites that are very difficult to fabricate. In many cases, the products must be extremely lightweight and have high strength. In some cases, the products and the processes used in manufacturing are the result of inventions developed at Brentwood to which it owns the patent rights.

Brentwood recently submitted a proposal to one of its major customers (a large aerospace corporation) for a very large order involving 10,000 machines. This could involve much more over the long term. This company has always used the Brentwood product because of its fine support systems—especially its training and customer service. However, the purchasing agent of the aerospace firm has informed Brentwood that it has proposals from two competing firms—one of which is Infiniti—that are lower than Brentwood's standard $110,000 price by as much as 20 or 25 percent. The bottom line is: If Brentwood cannot meet the competition, the contract will probably go to a competitor.

Corporate headquarters recently formed a new OD division within the human resources development department. The vice president of the Products Group has suggested that Brentwood Division consider using the services of the OD group. Because Continental believes it is important to allow its divisions to be fairly autonomous, Brentwood has the authority to choose to participate, and if Brentwood does participate, it will help design an OD program that best fits its own culture and needs. The OD practitioners will be present at the executive committee meeting.

## Role Descriptions (Read Only Your Role)

**Brentwood General Manager.** You have been with the company for eight years, five in your current job. Although you started fast, things have slowed down in the past two years. Your goal is to be promoted to group vice president, and to do this, you need to turn things around right now and show a good profit profile. To accomplish this, you want to cut labor costs by 10 percent, cut expenses to the bone, and get rid of any fat or deadwood that exists. You operate best in a directive, structured, and centralized situation and feel that the current problems stem from a lack of control and coordination among the four departments that report to you. Your goal now is to increase short-run profits at any cost.

You basically would like to retain the pricing policy because the real question is value and support, which your company has always provided. However, in this instance you'd rather cut price than lose the order because Infiniti is involved. You feel that the way to keep people from leaving is to appeal to their loyalty to Brentwood.

During the meeting, you want to persuade the directors to voluntarily cut costs by 10 percent, which will directly and quickly affect the bottom line. You also hope to sell them on a more centralized and controlled operation: a "taut ship." You feel that the current problems are basically caused by the operating relations between departments and the lack of proper controls on spending.

You see the OD practitioners as a possible ally in achieving your goal of promotion. A good word back at corporate headquarters would undoubtedly increase your chances. Consequently, you want to appear to be highly competent and dynamic.

**Director of Marketing.** You are an MBA and have been with the company for 14 years. You feel that a decentralized organization is most effective and believe that dividing Brentwood into major product groups instead of the current functional arrangement would be best suited for the company. Organizing along product groups will enable Brentwood to be more focused on the customer. You are very concerned with good relationships as well as goal accomplishment and are known as a "super salesperson." You feel strongly that what the organization needs to solve its problems is a greater marketing and promotional effort. You recognize that the established market is important, but also that a firm must be innovative and adapt to changing markets with new products and promotions. A decentralized, product-oriented organization will best allow Brentwood to respond quickly to changing markets.

You feel that competitors are forcing you to change your pricing policies; therefore, you must change or lose the business. This does not mean that Brentwood will compete on price alone, but rather that you must change to meet the new competition. You feel that growth and being the best is the way to hold people—you can't keep good people with money alone, they need a challenge.

At the meeting, you wish to push strongly for an aggressive marketing campaign aimed at increasing market share as a way to solve current problems. This requires increasing the sales force by 10 percent, and a 15 to 20 percent increase in advertising. The only way to halt a sales decline is to increase the marketing effort. You feel strongly that a decentralized, product-oriented organization is the way to go, with a product manager responsible for each major product line. The past problems were largely due to high manufacturing costs, poor product quality, and an inability to quickly respond to customer demands. You hope to persuade the OD practitioners to support the major products group structure.

**Director of Production.** You have been with the company for over 20 years. You worked your way up through the ranks and have found that a structured, decisive-leadership style works best. You see increased efficiency as the major goal, because excessive spending in marketing and engineering is needlessly raising costs. You are convinced that costs can be reduced drastically by limiting engineering changes and the number of products, and by slowing down the introduction of new products (which marketing always wants). This will allow a more stable and efficient production-line operation, rather than the hectic, constantly changing situation you have now.

You feel that Infiniti and others will go out of business because of their own low prices; therefore, Brentwood should stick with its pricing policy. This policy has been critical to its success over the years. Training the customers in how to use

Brentwood's technical products and providing onsite, next-day repair has played a significant part in Brentwood's success. You feel that employees should be loyal to Brentwood, the company should keep its key people by providing bonuses or stock options, and anyone who threatens to leave should be fired for disloyalty.

At the meeting, you are going to push for some "no-nonsense" cost controls on overhead, particularly in marketing and engineering. You strongly oppose any layoffs in production, because skilled workers are hard to get and you are forced to pay overtime now. You also need a more automated assembly line, which in the long run will cut production costs and reduce the need for overtime. You would like to cut out the employee development programs initiated by the Brentwood's director of human resources. Although the leadership programs were helpful, the self-managed team idea nearly caused a small rebellion when you did not approve of some production changes, and the quality control circles were a total disaster. You suggest a more centralized operation with tighter financial controls. For example, you feel that salespeople pad their expense reports beyond reason. You hope to get support from the practitioners for a more efficient and centralized form of operation.

**Director of Human Resources Development.** You have a master's degree in human resources management and have been with the company for five years. You favor a more decentralized organization and a type of leadership that is concerned with human needs, and you have been working toward this goal. You feel strongly that people are the organization's most important resource. Morale and the satisfaction of individuals are the primary goals, as you see it. You have already initiated several OD-type programs (communication, self-managed teams, and leadership training) and would like to see more innovative OD programs to improve the organization's long-term effectiveness. You feel that all of the programs have been successful except for the quality circles, which turned out to be a hyped-up suggestion system. In the use of self-managed teams, some production-line employees got upset when their suggestions were not implemented by the director of production. They came to see you about initiating the manufacturing changes they had proposed, but you explained that it was the production director's decision to make.

You see a real problem in the changing competitive marketplace and feel that pricing policies may need to be changed. You wish to retain key people and feel Infiniti is a real threat because it has informal networks to find out who the key people are and then go after them. You feel that Brentwood has to offer a better culture and more personal growth for its employees, as well as financial incentives, if it is to attract and retain good people.

At the meeting, you strongly oppose layoffs of any kind. The negative effects on morale would be almost irreversible. What is needed, you feel, is a raise in pay and improved coordination between departments instead of the constant bickering and fighting that prevails. You want to urge implementation of more self-managed work teams (SMWT) throughout Brentwood, which will solve these problems. This would improve the communication and coordination between groups. Naturally, you would be designing the SMWT program. If it is successful, this could lead to the application of the teams in the whole company. You see the OD practitioners as allies in gaining support for the SMWT program, and you hope to make a favorable impression as a dynamic manager who could head up a company-wide SMWT program.

**Director of Engineering.** You have an M.S.E.E. and have been with the company for three years. You feel that a highly decentralized structure with a participative leadership is most effective. You see long-term effectiveness as the most important goal. Both profit and market share depend on the ability to remain innovative in R&D. In your view, the company must become more innovative and improve marketability to survive. Successful companies can't stand still and rest on past successes in your fast-moving industry.

You feel that the key to sustained performance is the relationship between Brentwood and its customers—the ability to meet customer needs with innovative new products and to produce them at competitive values. You feel that we must get this order in an attempt to stop Infiniti before it can get its foot in the door. You see the key to increasing markets and retaining key people as the challenge of being on the leading edge of designing and producing the best, where new approaches and risk taking are encouraged.

At the meeting, you wish to propose increased expenditures on R&D for the next two years. You also need two new engineers (in stress analysis and thermal dynamics) for these advanced projects. You feel that a reduction in manufacturing costs, less overtime, and reducing advertising budgets will allow for this. You feel that the current problems are due to stagnant, low-risk strategies, front-office interference, and a lack of R&D in emerging fields. The production department is old and obsolete in both methods and equipment. You have suggested new methods, but your advice has been rejected. You hope to gain the practitioner's support for creating a more innovative, R&D-oriented organizational climate. You recently lost several of your key researchers to other companies. You think Brentwood's lack of incentive system tends to stifle innovation. You would like to see the company use some of the techniques you used when you were at your previous employer, such as team building and reengineering.

**Practitioner Team Guidelines.** You are the practitioner team from the company's newly formed OD practitioner group. You hope to accomplish several things at this meeting:

1. Develop a practitioner-client relationship with all the committee members.
2. Assist the committee by doing process interventions during the meeting.
3. Avoid making decisions for the committee—after all, they and not you must live with the decisions.
4. Make a preliminary diagnosis of possible problems.

Use the Team Profile Form to analyze group processes and assist you in making a diagnosis.

**TEAM PROFILE FORM**

*Team Profile:* Rate the team on these dimensions.

| | (Low) | | | | (Moderate) | | | | | (High) |
|---|---|---|---|---|---|---|---|---|---|---|
| A. Involvement | 1 | 2 | 3 | 4 | 5 | 6 | 7 | 8 | 9 | 10 |
| B. Shared leadership | 1 | 2 | 3 | 4 | 5 | 6 | 7 | 8 | 9 | 10 |
| C. Know their facts | 1 | 2 | 3 | 4 | 5 | 6 | 7 | 8 | 9 | 10 |
| D. Communication | 1 | 2 | 3 | 4 | 5 | 6 | 7 | 8 | 9 | 10 |
| E. Goal oriented | 1 | 2 | 3 | 4 | 5 | 6 | 7 | 8 | 9 | 10 |
| F. Shared decision making | 1 | 2 | 3 | 4 | 5 | 6 | 7 | 8 | 9 | 10 |
| G. Collaboration | 1 | 2 | 3 | 4 | 5 | 6 | 7 | 8 | 9 | 10 |
| H. Openness | 1 | 2 | 3 | 4 | 5 | 6 | 7 | 8 | 9 | 10 |
| I. Listening | 1 | 2 | 3 | 4 | 5 | 6 | 7 | 8 | 9 | 10 |
| J. Motivation | 1 | 2 | 3 | 4 | 5 | 6 | 7 | 8 | 9 | 10 |

## CASE: TUCKER KNOX CORPORATION

Ed Leonard sat slumped behind his desk at Tucker Knox Corporation (TKC). It was 6:00 p.m., and everyone else had left for the day. Ed recalled the progress he had made in just over three years. He had joined TKC to help the company develop a new automation design department. In the first two years, he had designed and developed the new department and had helped to automate the production process to the point where new products were very competitive and profitable. The final year had been filled with political turmoil due to changes in top management.

A new challenge and a new set of goals were what Ed needed. He sat there at his desk staring at a phone-call message from another company. Ed had been pursuing his personal goals at Tucker Knox, but felt that the phone message was the moment he had been waiting for. Ed had been planning a move away from Tucker Knox and this was his chance. Where did it all go wrong? he wondered.

### Company Background

Tucker Knox Corporation is a world leader in automotive breaking-systems design and manufacturing, supplying breaking systems to car manufacturers. Since 1994, TKC held the number-one position in market share (sales volume) of automotive breaking systems. The number-one position was not easy to come by for a company that had been founded by a retired corporate executive in a rented garage in 1982.

Larry Henderson, a strong-willed entrepreneur, had pledged his personal assets, mortgaged his home, and called on five of his closest friends and business associates to build and grow the company into a world market leader with sales over $110 million. See Figure 14.4 for the company's original organization chart. Larry, president and CEO, had always clearly been the father figure for TKC and for everyone whom he had personally selected to join him at the senior management level. Like sons answering to their father, each of the senior vice presidents would always look to Larry for his "nod of the head" of approval or disapproval.

### Tucker Knox Goals

At an executive board meeting, the major topic of discussion was once again focused on the continual challenge to retain market share in an aggressively price-competitive market. Larry started the meeting as he always had, by setting the issues directly on the table. "Our current challenge is (1) to compete in the world market with private and captive manufacturers, (2) have efficient manufacturing facilities in locations in the United States and overseas as required to meet price/cost demands, and (3) retain our corporate headquarters in the United States while the other manufacturers are moving their entire operations overseas. These challenges mean that besides the usual corporate functions of marketing, sales, finance, and engineering, we will also have to provide those functions required to support our unique product design."

In the automotive breaking business, the major area of product uniqueness is the design of the "piece parts" comprising the physical and mechanical portion of the breaking systems. The unique features in each manufacturer's part design lead to very high labor costs for assembly. Because the designs are unique, there are no readily available automated assembly machines on the market that will aid in reducing the high cost of assembly labor. "I've waited patiently for you boys to come up with a solution to this world competition issue, and I trust that the solution will be presented today," continued Larry.

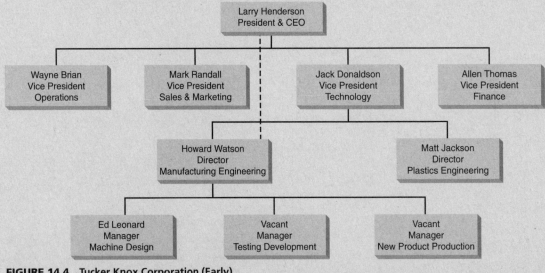

**FIGURE 14.4**   Tucker Knox Corporation (Early)

Much to Larry's pleasure, the skilled fatherly coaching paid off once again as Howard Watson announced, "Beginning next year, I will develop a corporate automation engineering department. The new department will be responsible for the concept, design, manufacture, installation, and maintenance of all custom automation for TKC's five manufacturing facilities: three in the United States, one in Ireland, and one in Taiwan." Larry was pleased, not only with the decision, but because Howard had been the one to announce it. With this new advanced technology department, Larry Henderson envisioned keeping his company ranked number-one in world sales.

## Development of the Department

Howard Watson, director of manufacturing engineering, worked closely with Larry in developing the automation engineering department. Howard not only knew of Larry's fondness for equipment but was eager to move up in TKC. Howard was a very aggressive manager with a positive attitude toward his job, traits that Larry liked in his managerial staff. Although his responsibilities were many, and growing, Howard had not yet selected a manager to develop and run the new department.

In fact, Howard had not filled either of the two vacant managers' positions in his division. Howard was not a distrustful manager, but a great deal of convincing was always required before he would delegate control. Howard knew that for the automation engineering department to be successful, he would need a manager with a strong technical background as well as a good understanding of the business.

The manager he hired would be very visible to the corporate staff, including Larry. The manager would eventually have to develop and "sell" his own cost-saving automation programs to the vice presidents. There were several people in the manufacturing engineering department who had the qualifications to manage the new department, but none with the technical background and none with the desire to have such a visible position.

Through a friend of his at Tucker Knox, Ed Leonard learned of the decision to develop an automation engineering department. In June, Ed began discussing with Howard the need to build the new department and the potential of joining the TKC team. Ed, a mechanical engineer with an MBA and both management and manufacturing experience, was seeking a new career challenge. Ed's engineering degree and experience easily satisfied the technical requirements of the position. However, his managerial skills were mainly in the project management area with some personnel management. Ed's managerial style was not as aggressive as Howard's, but his highly motivated, hard-work ethic, and commitment to the project appeared to be the balance that Howard was looking for. In November, Ed joined the Tucker Knox team, not as the automation engineering department's manager, but as a machine design engineer.

Howard wanted Ed to first prove his technical ability in the seven-person machine design department that Howard had created as a beginning for the automation department. Ed would then progress through the step of department supervisor before moving to manager and further developing the department. This progression was important to Howard for two reasons. "The performance and success of this department is very important to the future of TKC. The employees in the department must function as a close-knit team. It is essential that each team member accept and be accepted by every other member. "Therefore," Howard continued, "each person functions in their new position for a period of time to demonstrate their ability and to become accepted by the team."

The second reason for this slow progression (which Howard did not discuss) was Howard's nature of being very slow to delegate and relinquish authority. This plan, being agreed upon by both Ed and Howard, was the beginning of a very strong management team that was about to develop at Tucker Knox. Within a year, Ed had proven his abilities and was promoted to manager of machine design.

Soon after Ed Leonard's arrival at Tucker Knox, the machine design team was divided in two by Howard's boss, Jack Donaldson. Jack was a relatively new member of the Tucker Knox team whom Larry Henderson had brought in as the vice president of technology. Larry Henderson was planning on retiring in a few years and had tried to groom several candidates to take over his position. Jack Donaldson was the latest of these candidates. In attempting to imprint his "signature" on the Tucker Knox organization, Jack decided to reduce some of Howard's power within TKC by splitting the machine design team.

The multiple-copy manufacturing group was split off from the manufacturing engineering group and assigned to Matt Jackson, plastics engineering director. Matt was not only one of Howard's peers, but also his strongest rival.

Howard was not the type to take such a change lightly. He disagreed with the decision not just because some of his organization was given to his strongest rival, but also because the decision, in his opinion, was not founded on sound financial information. Howard and Ed worked closely to develop the cost-saving justification that Ed used to convince Larry Henderson and Jack Donaldson to recombine the multiple-copy manufacturing group with the manufacturing engineering group. By allowing Ed Leonard to present the data and plan to Jack, Howard once again demonstrated his ability to achieve his own goals through skillful managing of people at all levels within the organization. He also put Ed Leonard in the middle of an internal political conflict.

## Growth of the Department

Ed continued to build the machine design department into a 23-person automation engineering department through corporate organization streamlining. The test equipment department, responsible for designing and building custom test equipment, was merged with the automation engineering department in January of Ed's second year at TKC. The plastics engineering department, part of Matt's division, was merged into the automation department six months later. The plastics automation department, also part of Matt's division, was merged into the automation engineering department in December of the same year. Ed had now been at TKC for just over two years, and his career looked promising. The rapid growth of the automation engineering department was due to the efforts of both Ed and Howard. Ed provided the technical expertise for the department's growth. He also presented the justifications for cost reduction, increased output, and increased response to the ever-changing customer demand in the marketplace for new breaking-systems designs.

The new breaking-systems designs resulted in demands from the vice presidents that the production facilities have the automation in place at the same time that the new breaking-systems design arrived in production. The automation was viewed as essential to provide the low production costs necessary to stay ahead of the competition. Howard's contribution to the team was not only his position as director, but more so his natural ability to understand people almost better than they understood themselves and his ability to use internal politics to achieve his goals.

Howard had an ability to deal with peers and superiors in a way that bordered on manipulation. His intent was to influence decisions by communicating with each person in a unique way, so that each person was comfortable with the decisions. Howard used his position and communication skills to present the development steps to Larry Henderson and Jack Donaldson for their approval. He often presented the idea to Larry Henderson first, and then to Jack Donaldson as a "fait accompli!"

## Change in Senior Management

In June of Ed's third year, a change took place in the vice president assignments. Jack Donaldson was promoted to a newly created position of senior vice president. But as the corporate staff members were expecting Howard and Ed also to be promoted, trouble arose in the Ireland plant.

The managing director of the Ireland plant was unexpectedly forced to retire for health reasons with no time to groom a replacement. The Ireland plant played a major role in the European market. Howard possessed the most in-depth knowledge of the manufacturing part of the plant because he was responsible for having set it up. Jack Donaldson, as a relatively new member of the Tucker Knox top management team (and possibly being displeased with Howard because of his political maneuvering in the machine design department), decided to assign Howard to the Ireland plant.

Howard moved to Ireland in August. Jack Donaldson filled his own vacated position of vice president of technology with Sam Martin. Jack handpicked Sam from outside TKC so that he could begin building his own loyal management team. Sam came from a high-tech firm in California with the experience of high-volume manufacturing of custom products made from "standard piece parts." Sam also brought several years of experience in worldwide competition, including the creation of two foreign production facilities.

During his first couple of months at TKC, Sam Martin made no changes, no promotions, and no attempt of any kind to fill personnel vacancies. After acquainting himself with his new departments, Sam Martin recommended promoting Ed Leonard to the position left vacant by Howard, but was overruled by Jack Donaldson. There was much discussion between Jack and Sam over Ed Leonard's record of continued cost reductions and excellent performance of timely installation of new equipment in the critical manufacturing facilities. However, without explaining his decision, Jack Donaldson overruled Sam. Sam Martin was ordered to fill the vacancy from outside the company. See Figure 14.5 for the organization chart after the changes.

## Conclusion

In the next few weeks, it became apparent that Jack was trying to fill the vacant positions in the senior management staff with people who would be loyal to him. Another newcomer, Art Hodges, was brought in to fill Howard Watson's position as director of manufacturing engineering. Although Jack hand-selected the team, he made sure that Sam Martin actually did the hiring so that it would appear that the "team" was selecting its own members. Art had been the manager of a packaging design department for a scientific instruments company in Portland, Oregon, where he had worked since graduating from college 10 years previously. He did not have the years of managerial experience that Sam had and could, therefore, be easily manipulated by Jack.

Three weeks after arriving at TKC, Art Hodges (at the direction of Jack Donaldson) reassigned Ed Leonard to the company's largest manufacturing facility to set up a maintenance department. Ed was told by Jack and Art that after successfully completing the assignment he would be able to return to his own department. With virtually no experience at TKC, Art followed Jack's directions without question and four weeks later assigned Ed's automation engineering department to Matt Jackson. Ed was now completing his third year, and his career was taking a very precarious turn. Within about a half a year, Jack

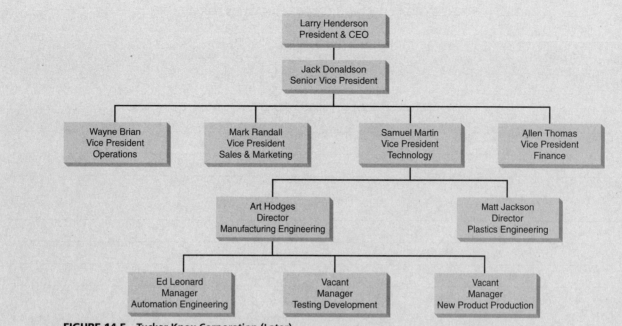

**FIGURE 14.5**   **Tucker Knox Corporation (Later)**

Donaldson had managed to rearrange the manufacturing engineering department and surround himself with managers he had hand-selected and who he felt would be loyal to him. Six months after being given the assignment to set up the maintenance department, Ed was brought back to the corporate facility and given six weeks to find another job in the company or be laid off.

Ed Leonard sat slumped behind his desk. It was late in the day, and everyone had gone home. Ed recalled the progress he had made over the last few years as well as the lessons in management that he had so painfully been taught. Routine was not what Ed wanted, and routine was certainly not what he got.[31] (Use the Case Analysis Form on the following page.)

# TUCKER KNOX CORPORATION CASE ANALYSIS FORM

Name: _____

I. Problems

  A. Macro

    1. _____

      _____

    2. _____

      _____

  B. Micro

    1. _____

      _____

    2. _____

      _____

II. Causes

    1. _____

      _____

    2. _____

      _____

    3. _____

      _____

III. Systems affected

    1. _____

      _____

    2. _____

      _____

    3. _____

      _____

IV. Alternatives

    1. _____

      _____

    2. _____

      _____

    3. _____

      _____

V. Recommendations

  _____

  _____

  _____

  _____

  _____

  _____

# Chapter 14 Endnotes

1. Michael S. Malone, "The Un-Carly," *Wall Street Journal*, April 14–15, 2007, p. A9.
2. For one of the first books on the use of survey research and feedback as it applies to organization development, see David Nadler, *Feedback and Organization Development: Using Data-Based Methods* (Reading, MA: Addison-Wesley, 1977).
3. www.isr.umich.edu/home/
4. See Tony Condeni, "The Survey Solution," *Management World*, vol. 12, no. 4a (May 1993), pp. 30–31, which describes the use of an OES survey.
5. www.isr.umich.edu/home/
6. Christina Björklund, Anders Grahn, Irene Jensen, and Gunnar Bergström, "Does Survey Feedback Enhance the Psychosocial Work Environment and Decrease Sick Leave?" *European Journal of Work and Organizational Psychology*, vol. 6, no. 1 (Mar. 2007), pp. 76–93.
7. Edgar Schein, *Organizational Culture And Leadership: A Dynamic View* (Oxford: Jossey-Bass, 1991); Edgar Schein, "On Dialogue, Culture, and Organizational Learning," *Organizational Dynamics*, vol. 22, no. 2 (1993), pp. 40–52.
8. Chris Argyris and Donald. Schön, *Organizational Learning II: Theory, Method, and Practice* (Reading, MA: Addison-Wesley, 1996); Chris Argyris, "Good Communication That Blocks Learning," *Harvard Business Review*, vol. 72, no. 4 (July/August 1994), pp. 77–86; Chris Argyris and Donald. Schön, *Organizational Learning: A Theory of Action-Perspective* (Reading, MA: Addison-Wesley, 1978).
9. Peter Senge, *The Fifth Discipline, The Art and Practice of the Learning Organization* (London: Random House, 1990); Peter Senge, *The Dance of Change: The Challenges of Sustaining Momentum in Learning Organizations* (New York: Currency, Doubleday, 1999); Peter Senge, *The Fifth Discipline Fieldbook: Strategies and Tools for Building a Learning Organization* (New York: Currency, Doubleday, 1994); Peter Senge, *Elegant Solutions: The Power of Systems Thinking* (Pleasanton, CA: New Leaders Press, 1999).
10. Robert Holmberg, "Organizational Learning and Participation: Some Critical Reflections from a Relational Perspective," *European Journal of Work and Organizational Psychology*, vol. 9, no. 2 (June 2000), pp. 177–88.
11. Senge, *Fifth Discipline*, p. 3.
12. www.lafarge.com/; Milton Moskowitz, "100 Best Companies to Work For," *Fortune*, January 20, 2003.
13. Laura Roper and Jethro Pettit, "Organization: An Introduction," *Development in Practice*, vol. 12, nos. 3 and 4 (August 2002), pp. 258–72.
14. For additional information, see Amy C. Edmondson, "The Competitive Imperative of Learning," *Harvard Business Review*, July–August 2008, pp. 60–7; Robert W. Rowden, "The Learning Organization and Strategic Change," *Advanced Management Journal*, vol. 66, no. 3 (Summer 2001), p. 11; David A. Garvin, Amy C. Edmondson, and Francesca Gino, "Is Yours a Learning Organization?", *Harvard Business Review*, March 2008, pp. 109–116.
15. Ellen McGirt, "Revolution in San Jose," *Fast Company*, December/January 2009, pp. 93.
16. Steven Prokesch, "How GE Teaches Teams to Lead Change," *Harvard Business Review*, January 2009, pp. 99–106.
17. Jena McGregor, "Zappos' Secret: It's an Open Book," *Business Week*, March 23 and 30, 2009, p. 62.
18. Scott Thurm, "Companies Struggle to Pass on Knowledge that Workers Acquire," *Wall Street Journal*, January 23, 2006, p. B1.
19. Michael Hammer and James Champy, *Reengineering the Corporation: A Manifesto for Business Revolution* (New York: Harper Business, 1994); Michael Hammer, *Beyond Reengineering* (New York: Harper Business, 1997).
20. Steve Rosenbush, "Verizon's Gutsy Bet," *Business Week*, August 4, 2003, p. 53.
21. Rensis Likert and Jane Gibson Likert, *New Ways of Managing Conflict* (New York: McGraw-Hill, 1976); Rensis Likert, *New Patterns of Management* (New York: Garland, 1987).
22. David Welch, "Bob Nardelli's Wrong Turns," *Business Week*, May 4, 2009, p. 26.
23. Robert Berner, "P&G: How A. G. Lafley Is Revolutionizing a Bastion of Corporate Conservatism," *Business Week*, July 7, 2003, p. 63.
24. See Peter Vaill, *Learning as a Way of Being: Strategies for Survival in a World of Permanent White Water* (San Francisco: Jossey-Bass, 1996); Peter Vaill, *Managing as a Performing Art: New Ideas for a World of Chaotic Change* (San Francisco: Jossey-Bass, 1989); Peter Vaill, "The Purposing of High-Performing Systems," *Organizational Dynamics*, Autumn 1982, p. 23–39; Peter Vaill, "Toward a Behavioral Description of High-Performing Systems," in M. W. McCall, Jr. and M. M. Lombardo (eds.), *Leadership* (Durham, NC: Duke University Press, 1982); Also see Robert T. Golembiewski, "Linking Interaction and Techno-Structural Emphasis: A Synthesis for High-Performing Organizations," *Public Administration Quarterly*, vol. 10, no. 2 (Summer 1986), pp. 138–70.
25. Gary Hamel, "Moon Shots for Management," *Harvard Business Review*, February 2009, p. 93.
26. Vaill, "The Purposing of High-Performing Systems," p. 25.
27. Stanley Holmes, "Boeing: Putting Out the Labor Fires," *Business Week*, December 29, 2003, p. 43.
28. Robert R. Blake, *The Supervisory Grid* (Austin: Grid International, 1998); Robert R. Blake and Jane Srygley Mouton, *The Managerial Grid* (Houston: Gulf Publishing Co., 1985 and 1994); Robert R. Blake and Jane Srygley Mouton, *Leadership Dilemmas: Grid Solutions* (Houston: Gulf Publishing Co., 1991).
29. www.cisco.com/; Ellen McGirt, "Revolution in San Jose," *Fast Company*, January 2009, pp. 89–136.
30. See www.gridinternational.com/index.html for the most current information.
31. This case was written by Don Harvey and Mel Hartwig, Eastern Washington University, 1991. Edited and modified by Don Brown.

# Organization Transformation and Strategic Change

## LEARNING OBJECTIVES

**Upon completing this chapter, you will be able to:**

**1.** Identify and define organization transformation in relation to the change process.

**2.** Understand the basic strategy-culture matrix and other approaches to changing the culture to fit the strategy.

**3.** Recognize the importance of corporate culture and its relation to strategy.

**4.** Experience these concepts in a management simulation.

## PREMEETING PREPARATION

**1.** Read Chapter 15.

**2.** Prepare for OD Skills Simulation 15.1. Prior to class, form teams of six and select roles. Complete Step 1.

**3.** Read and analyze Case: The Space Electronics Corporation.

## STRATEGY AND TRANSFORMATION

In a world of unpredictability and rapid change, what makes one organization a winner and another unable to adjust to the same opportunities? How do some smaller companies move forward and seize new product and market opportunities, while large companies sometimes fail to take advantage of their size and situation? How did Sam Walton and others lead Wal-Mart from an obscure Bentonville, Arkansas, retailer to the world's largest retailer while at the same time Kmart and more established retailers went bankrupt? The answers are multifaceted but partially lie in the ability and inability of these firms to change their strategies to meet changing conditions.

The corporate landscape is rapidly changing in this new millennium. The overwhelming success of many great companies starts to work against them when "pride of position" begins to erode their base. Customers become fuzzy entities, then nonentities, as corporations stop earning their loyalty. Then corporate visions become blurred as well; the ideas for new products and services become overdrawn; and bloated corporate bureaucracies hinder employees from doing "productive work." An article in *Forbes* argues, "Powerful companies get complacent and staff-bloated, like General Motors in the 1960s or Xerox in the 1970s. They have too much invested in old ways of doing business to see the threat from new ways, like mainframe-dependent IBM in the 1980s or film-addicted Eastman Kodak in the 1990s. They become prey to antitrust attack, losing lawsuits (Standard Oil, AT&T) or just agreeing to be less feisty (Microsoft)."[1] Kodak is desperately trying to reinvent itself for the digital age but realized it needed to bring in outside managers. CEO Antonio Perez says, "We needed leaders who had 'been there, done that' because this is not a turnaround. It's a transformation."[2]

Organization transformation refers to these drastic changes in how an organization functions and relates to its environment.[3] Good management does not mean trying harder by using old, out-of-date methods. It involves developing strategies for coming up with new products, making sure they are what the customer wants, and getting them to market in time to gain a competitive advantage. Accelerating changes in technology, shorter product life cycles, and unexpected new competition make succeeding in business harder than ever. The evidence indicates that managers play a major role in whether or not an organization performs. Managers make strategy, and strategy determines business success or failure.

The new excellent companies must be able to transform the way they operate and reorganize the importance of corporate culture in devising and executing new strategies. In fact, the biggest obstacle in the path of strategic change is usually an old and inflexible corporate culture. CEO Fred Hassan of Schering-Plough Corp., a drug maker with problems on a number of fronts, said soon after he became CEO, "This company was lulled into a false sense of comfort for too long. We need to change the culture."[4] A culture that prevents a company from meeting competitive threats, or from adapting to changing economic or social environments, can lead to the company's stagnation and ultimate failure unless it makes a conscious effort to change. Cultural change efforts include activities designed to improve the skills, ability, structure, or motivation of organization members. The goals are improved technical skills (planning and so forth), more effective work processes, improved interpersonal competence, and faster communications. Implementation efforts may also be directed toward improved leadership, decision making, or problem solving among organization members. The assumption underlying such efforts is that developing an improved culture will result in a more effective organization.

The strategy-culture matrix provides one model that can be used to access the readiness of a corporate culture for strategic changes. A growing body of research indicates that culture affects strategy formulation and implementation, as well as the organization's ability to achieve a high level of corporate excellence. Strategic change management, another type of intervention, involves integrating the organization's strategy with its structure, technology, and people and aligning these factors to the competitive environment.

This chapter will describe several major OD strategic interventions, including:

- Organization transformation
- The corporate culture
- Strategic change management

## ORGANIZATION TRANSFORMATION

In a general sense, OD strategies represent more gradual approaches to strategic change, focusing on developmental and participative change processes. **Organization transformation** (OT), on the other hand, may be defined as drastic, abrupt change to total structures, managerial processes, and corporate cultures.[5] It requires a redesign of everything in the organization, including the norms and the culture, the very soul of the organization. Nothing is sacred, and there are few, if any, guidelines.

An example of organization transformation is Cummins Inc., maker of diesel engines. It hit a recession in 2000 through 2003 where demand in its core markets dropped by about 70 percent. The company was highly leveraged and sales had substantially declined. Top management, with virtually no other options, implemented a radical plan where they closed the original manufacturing plant in the company's hometown of Columbus, Indiana, restructured the truck engine business, and laid off a substantial number of the employees. But the CEO, Tim Solso, and his management team did not stop with radical surgery. The next step was to transform Cummins with a new mission and strategy. The remaining employees undertook learning new skills that would lead to Cummins' ability to develop new products and services that were less cyclical and less subject to future economic downturns. The strategy included focusing on service, distribution, and green technology that took advantage of Cummins' long-standing expertise in pollution-control devices. By 2007, Cummins' sales had more than doubled, net earning had increased more than five times, and the workforce was committed to the new strategy.[6] What's more, the engine plant in Columbus has now reopened. An example of transformation that was not so successful is The Home Depot, Inc. Within a period of ten years, the company has had three CEOs, and transformation seems to still have eluded Home Depot. To learn more about the transformation efforts at Home Depot, see **OD Application: Transformation at Home Depot.**

Organization transformation is more revolution than evolution. Since transformations strive for organizational survival in a competitive environment, the changes may or may not subscribe to the values of organization development and, in many instances, are not accomplished by participative processes. Organization transformations include such changes as takeovers, mergers, and plant closures, which often involve large-scale downsizing, employee layoffs, and massive restructuring. The changes undertaken by General Motors (GM) and Chrysler in 2008 and 2009 prior to their declaring bankruptcy are examples of organizational transformation, though not examples of successful transformations.

## OD Application: Transformation at Home Depot[7]

Home Depot is the number-one home-improvement retail chain in the United States and second-largest retailer in the U.S., after Wal-Mart. For more than 22 years, it was known for having an unstructured and entrepreneurial culture. Stores were set up, encouraged to be independent, decentralized, and managed with independent-minded managers. The company's cofounders told store managers to ignore messages from headquarters and do what they thought would be best. Each store was a separate operation, and headquarters was called the store support center. Without a central buying system, Home Depot could not take advantage of its buying power with suppliers. The company did not even have the technology for headquarters to send e-mail to store managers. And this was as recent as 2000, when e-mail was hardly a novelty.

Things began to deteriorate, and by the late 1990s it became obvious to the board of directors that they had a problem. Sales growth was declining, and same-store sales were on a downward spiral. Older stores looked shabby, and customers did not like the narrow aisles and hard-to-find sales staff. Competitor Lowe's began taking market share. Lowe's stores were new and the service was better. To help correct the problems, Bob Nardelli was brought in as CEO of Home Depot. Nardelli, who had worked at General Electric (GE) for 30 years, was steeped in GE's culture of highly structured management and data-driven decision making.

Nardelli's experience at GE had taught him that leaders are the glue that holds a company together—no matter how large the company. The leader has the power to turn around a dysfunctional corporate culture. If it worked at GE with CEO Jack Welch, it would work at Home Depot with CEO Bob Nardelli. With the blessings from the board, Nardelli began his disciplined approach. However, what happened at Home Depot shows how transformation from the top down comes at a price if there is no support from the lower levels. In an entrepreneurial type of culture, the stores were not prepared for top-down edicts for change.

On taking over at Home Depot, Nardelli quickly began installing managerial practices that he had seen work at GE. He started with straightforward changes—at least they were straightforward to him. He instituted centralized purchasing to take advantage of Home Depot's large purchasing power with suppliers. Stores were cleaned and spruced up. Store displays and personnel practices like hiring and evaluation were standardized. Store managers were required to submit store performance data to headquarters. Store managers were measured on metrics such as average hourly labor rate. Once seeing the performance data, Nardelli embarked on a strategy to cut costs. The stores were required to lower their employee costs by replacing more expensive employees like veteran hardware experts and retired tradesmen with less experienced and cheaper employees. The strategy worked for the short term, but things at Home Depot began to deteriorate even more than before the changes.

As the saying goes: beware of unintended consequences. Nardelli, being data-driven, used to say, "Facts are friendly," but he had a tendency of not looking beyond the facts. What did not show up on the data was customer service. When store managers were told to increase the speed with which products flowed through the stores, some responded by cutting back on inventory levels. This sparked customer complaints, not to mention lost sales. Customers, accustomed to having helpful experts around in an orange apron, were fortunate to find anyone, and technical questions from do-it-yourselfers remained unanswered by unknowledgeable and indifferent employees. Stores became dirty and check-out lines were long. With store managers no longer able to make orders based on the needs of their local communities, stores had inventory ill-suited to customer demands. Stores in Phoenix had rows of riding lawn mowers where home owners typically have little or no grass. And Kansas City stores had beach chairs for sale during a snow storm. Some employees, used to running their own operations, quit rather than submit to the demands from headquarters. The sense of ownership among employees declined. A longtime human resource manager says, "It was revolution, not evolution." On the University of Michigan's American Customer Satisfaction Index, over seven years that ended in 2007 while Nardelli was CEO, Home Depot's index fell from 75 to 67. Rival Lowe's score remained steady at 75.

Though Home Depot's profits and sales figures looked good under the cost cutting, by 2005 Home Depot was beginning to struggle. Nardelli's pay reached $30 million. With Home Depot's performance continuing to slide, in early 2007, the board asked to renegotiate his pay. Instead of negotiating, Nardelli quit and collected a severance payout of $210 million.

Several postscripts: Nordelli was hired in 2007 by the privately held Cerberus Capital Management, the company that bought Chrysler from Daimler AG, to fix Chrysler as its CEO. Nardelli resigned after Chrysler filed for Chapter 11 bankruptcy protection in 2009. Home Depot hired Marvin Ellison as CEO. Soon after he took over, the U.S. housing market collapsed. As home sales drive a lot of the sales at Home Depot, the collapse accentuated Home Depot's problems. Ellison seems to be making a methodical and long-range approach to change.

### Questions

1. Evaluate the positive and negative changes that Nardelli made at Home Depot.
2. To get a sense of the current customer and employee dissatisfaction of Home Depot, enter "I hate Home Depot" or similar words into Google. Observe the dates of the postings to see if the postings have changed in frequency and degree of criticism.
3. Research Home Depot's current performance and what the company is doing to bring change. Financial and other company information is available at www.homedepot.com/

## Strategies of Change

OT approaches tend to use directive rather than participative approaches. Typically, a senior manager initiates the transformational change, deciding when to initiate change, what the changes shall be, how the change is to be implemented, and who is responsible for the change program. This is usually a top-down, top-management–driven process. Figure 15.1 illustrates transformational change.

**FIGURE 15.1   Transformational Change: Immediate and Direct**
*Source:* B.C. by permission of Johnny Hart and Creators Syndicate, Inc.

There are several possible approaches to large-scale change programs depending upon existing conditions. One approach, which may be termed the **incremental approach,** refers to long-term planned change that relies upon collaboration and participation by organization members. The second approach, **transformational change,** refers to immediate drastic change accomplished by directive methods.

Dunphy and Stace have identified a model of large-scale strategies based upon three key dimensions: the time frame of the change, long or short; the level of support of the organizational culture; and the degree of discontinuity with the environment.[8] From these three dimensions, four process change strategies have been identified, as shown in Figure 15.2.

1. *Participative Evolution.* This incremental strategy is used to keep an organization in sync with its environment in anticipation of changes, when minor adjustments are needed, and when sufficient time is available. Such change is achieved by collaborative means with the support and participation of organization members.
2. *Charismatic Transformation.* This transformation strategy is used to accomplish radical change in a short time frame, with support from the organization's culture. Fred Smith of Federal Express and Steve Jobs, founder of Apple Computer, are two examples of leaders who used such strategies to accomplish change.

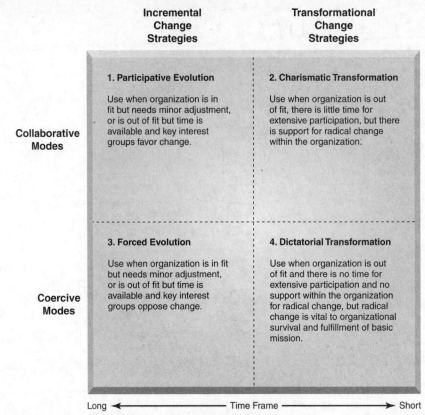

**FIGURE 15.2** **Strategies for Planned Organizational Change**
*Source:* Adapted from Dexter C. Dunphy and Doug A. Stace, "Transformational and Coercive Strategies for Planned Organizational Change Beyond the OD Model," *Organizational Studies*, vol. 9, no. 3 (1988), pp. 317–34.

3. *Forced Evolution.* This strategy is used to make minor adjustments over longer periods but without the support of the organization's culture.

4. *Dictatorial Transformation.* This transformation change strategy is used in times of crisis, when a major restructuring is needed that may run counter to the entrenched interest of the internal culture. In these conditions, authoritative direction may be the only option to ensure organizational survival.

A company that transformed itself is General Electric Corporation (GE) under the leadership of Jack Welch. When Welch first took over as CEO in 1981 and looked at the books, he was appalled. Two-thirds of sales were made by aging business. Sales were dropping for the first time in 22 years. GE was increasing productivity by a mere 1.5 percent a year, compared with the 8 percent of its Japanese competitors. Pay and bonuses depended on seniority, not merit. GE was in trouble. Welch gave the managers of every GE business an ultimatum: make your business number-one or number-two in its industry or get out.[9]

## Results of Organization Transformation

Research evidence suggests that the political dynamics of transformational change tend to be shaped more by directive or coercive methods (the use of power) rather than more collaborative, participative approaches. This may be the best way, or the only way, to rapidly bring an organization under immediate threat back into fit with its environment. The evidence also indicates that outsiders (externally recruited executives) are more likely to initiate transformational change than the existing management team. For example, GM and Chrysler had new CEOs upon exiting their reorganization under Chapter 11 bankruptcy proceedings.

Though terms such as "transformational change" commonly appear in the mass media, research has shown this method of change is risky and its performance outcomes are uncertain.[10] The conclusion of one research study found that "the lack of financial performance benefits stemming from organizational transformation suggests that . . . executives should be cautious in their expectations about the results of transformation."[11] The study also found organizational transformation is not a panacea, and the desired benefits are neither certain nor necessarily forthcoming. AOL is an example of attempts at organizational transformation that never seemed to be successful. "AOL has reinvented itself so many times. It is hard to keep track," says a senior partner in a media-planning firm.[12] Time-Warner, after about eight years, finally abandoned its attempts of integrating AOL into the mega-media conglomerate and spun off AOL as an independent company.

The key point of OD practitioners is that the selection of an appropriate change strategy depends on a strategic analysis of the change situation. OD practitioners should select the most effective change process and strategy rather than rely on a strategy simply because it is compatible with their personal values. Just as important, however, is the fact that large-scale change in times of crisis can be more effectively implemented if it is combined with the behavioral skills of the OD approaches.

## THE CORPORATE CULTURE

The concept of corporate culture has become a very important factor in large-scale interventions. Every organization has its own distinct culture. As noted in Chapter 3, an organization's culture includes the shared values, beliefs, and behaviors formed by the members of an organization over time. The leadership style of top management and the norms, values, and beliefs of the organization's members combine to form the corporate culture. Organizational effectiveness can be increased by creating a culture that achieves organizational goals and at the same time satisfies members' needs.

The CEO's words alone do not produce culture—the actions of managers do; a corporation's culture can be its major strength when consistent with its strategies. Some of the most successful companies clearly demonstrate this fact, including Genentech Inc., which has a work-hard/play-hard culture. Scientists wearing cut-off jeans and torn shirts often work 100-hour weeks. Then they blow off steam by playing pranks on one another at the company's wild Friday afternoon parties.[13] With the purchase of Genentech in 2009 by F. Hoffmann-La Roche, it is unclear if Genentech's unique culture will survive as part of a much larger pharmaceutical company with over 110 years of experience and based in Switzerland. Culture can also lead to major problems for an organization or even an industry. In *The End of Detroit*, author Micheline Maynard suggests that the Big Three's well-intentioned managers are paralyzed by a dysfunctional culture. They are a product of an era when their companies dominated the auto world. She says, "The great tragedy of Detroit's decade-long demise is that it's self-inflicted."[14]

The corporate culture reflects the organization's past and is often deeply rooted in its history and mythology. The corporate culture influences how managers approach problems, react to competition, and implement new strategies. Many cultures were started by the firm's founders, such as Fred Smith of Federal Express and Larry Page and Sergey Brin of Google, and the cultures have been reinforced by successful operations and strategies. In another example, Steve Jobs, a cofounder of Apple Computer, has built Apple into a driving force of change in computer and consumer electronics. With his turtleneck shirt, jeans, and sneakers at Apple PR events, Jobs has infused a culture of innovation within Apple that has resulted in a near cult-like following by some of Apple's customers.

### The Strategy-Culture Fit

Corporate culture is important because of its relationship to organizational effectiveness. There is increasing evidence that firms with effective corporate cultures have increased productivity, boosted employee camaraderie, increased employees' sense of ownership, increased profits, and enhanced customer satisfaction.[15]

**Strategy** refers to a course of action used to achieve major objectives. This includes all the activities leading to the identification of the objectives and plans of the organization and is concerned with relating the resources of the organization to opportunities in the larger environment. Organizations are finding it increasingly necessary to change their business strategy to meet emerging discontinuities in the environment.

Culture provides a set of values for setting priorities on what is important and "the way things are done around here." Because of this, culture is a critical factor in the implementation of a new strategy. An organization's culture can be a major strength when there is a fit with the strategy and can be a driving force in implementing a successful change. The challenge of the new millennium is the need to replace bureaucratic obstacles with speed, simplicity, constant change, and improvement.

Every organization evolves a unique culture. However, this culture must also change to meet new conditions. "When you deal with a company that has a great legacy, you deal with decisions and conflicts that arise from the clash of heritage vs. innovation vs. relevance," says the CEO of Walt Disney Company, Bob Iger. "I'm a big believer in respect for heritage, but I'm also a big believer in the need to innovate and the need to balance that respect for heritage with a need to be relevant."[16]

A number of studies indicate that corporate strategy alone cannot produce winning results. Management consultants say that only 1 company in 10 can successfully carry out a complex change in strategy. However, the need to devise and execute strategic changes is rapidly increasing. A study of firms whose cultures support employee participation in decisions found that they performed significantly better than firms where this was not the case.[17] The best way to execute strategic change is by empowering employees. Even single acts by individual employees can be critical to the achievement of total quality, customer satisfaction, and continuous improvement.

## Core Characteristics

There is widespread agreement that organizational culture refers to a system of shared values held by members that distinguishes one organization from another. An organization's **culture** may be described by a set of core characteristics that include:

- *Individual autonomy.* The degree of responsibility, independence, and opportunities for exercising initiative for members of the organization.
- *Sensitivity to the needs of customers and employees.* The degree of responsiveness to changing needs.
- *Support.* The degree of assistance and warmth provided by managers.
- *Interest in having employees initiate new ideas.* The degree to which employees are encouraged and empowered to come up with better quality and productivity suggestions.
- *Openness of available communication channel.* The degree of freedom of communication between members and teams and levels.
- *Risk behavior.* The degree to which members are encouraged to be aggressive, innovative, and risk seeking.[18]

By combining these characteristics, then, a composite picture of the organization's culture is formed. The culture becomes the basis for the shared understanding that members have about the organization, how things are done, and the way they are supposed to behave.

An organization's success rests on its ability to change its strategy in order to meet rapidly changing market conditions. Under these conditions, the culture must be adjusted so the firm can confront and deal with factors that may contribute to its failure, stagnation, or success. The culture influences each member's adjustment to these changes. Productive corporate changes increase the company's capacity to meet new challenges. To be effective, managers must be able to motivate their employees and help them adapt to changing conditions. Success depends on management's skills and strategy, and on the acceptance of change by the organization members.

Organizations operating in different environments with different competitive situations may need to develop distinct cultures focused upon the goals of their strategy and competitive arena. Similarly, organizations existing in several markets may need to have differing subcultures to meet the unique strategies of each specific business environment. A corporate culture reinforcing innovation, entrepreneurship, and participation, for example, may be necessary for a high-tech firm competing in a highly dynamic and complex industry. On the other hand, a more traditional firm in a mature, smokestack industry may develop a culture focusing on stability, quality, and extra productivity.

## Sharing the Vision

The development of a vision is an important element in organizational and cultural change. Many management theorists feel that vision is the very essence of leadership. Any attempt at changing a culture should begin with a clear vision of the new strategy and what it will take to make it work. Organizations are driven by a vision, not by directives from the chain of command.

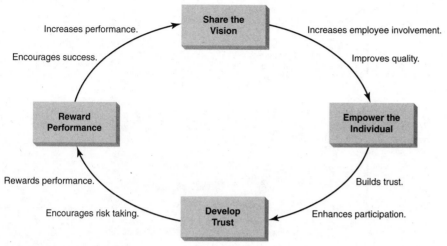

**FIGURE 15.3** Sharing the Vision

According to a widely used definition, **vision** is "a mental image of a possible and desirable future state of the organization . . . that articulates a view of a realistic, credible, attractive future for the organization, a condition that is better in some important ways than what now exists."[19] An effective vision should be challenging, inspiring, and aimed at empowering people at all levels.

In one study, it was found that sharing the vision—that is, making certain that every level of the organization is involved and communicated with—is critical.[20] The fact of the matter is that the McDonald's employee flipping burgers and waiting on the customer is the one who will ultimately carry out the vision, not the store's owner and management team at McDonald's corporate headquarters.

Developing a shared vision involves several stages, as shown in Figure 15.3.[21]

- *Share the Vision.* People will buy into a clear challenging vision that has meaning for them and will improve society. Communicate the vision clearly and unambiguously including an image of the future.
- *Empower the Individual.* People need to feel they have a stake in the outcome and have participated in defining the vision. This involves listening to others and bringing them in to the conversation of creating and adopting the vision. The idea is to have individual purposes congruent with the organization's vision.
- *Develop Trust.* An effective vision must set goals for challenging performance, but must also allow people to "buy in" to the vision and provide feedback on performance.
- *Reward Performance.* High performers need to be recognized. This element also includes support for taking risk, providing the freedom to fail, and pushing decision-making information downward to the lower levels.

A shared vision provides a starting point for cultural and organizational transition. A shared vision should be simple, easily understood, clear, and energizing. "Without a sensible vision, a transformation effort can easily dissolve into a list of confusing and incompatible projects that can take the organization in the wrong direction or nowhere at all," according to Professor John Kotter, retired from the Harvard Business School.[22]

## Strong versus Weak Cultures

Every organization has a culture, but some cultures are stronger than others. IBM, for instance, has a more tightly held culture than a conglomerate of newly acquired companies or a very young firm such as Google. Harvard University has a more cohesive culture than many newer universities offering online Internet-based classes. In a strong culture, the behavior of members is constrained by mutual accord rather than by command or rule.

It is becoming popular to classify cultures as "strong" or "weak." The evidence suggests that strong cultures have more impact on employee behavior and are more directly related to lower turnover. Research evidence also suggests that a strong culture helps workers march to the same drummer, creates high levels of employee loyalty and motivation, and provides the company with structure and controls without the need for an innovation-stifling bureaucracy.[23]

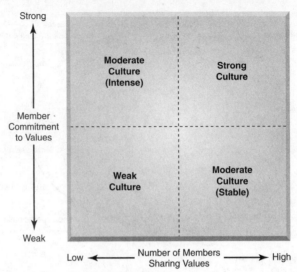

**FIGURE 15.4** Relative Strength of Corporate Cultures

A strong culture is characterized by the organization's basic values being intensely held and widely shared, as shown in Figure 15.4. Each dimension can be envisioned as existing along a continuum from low to high. The more members share the basic values and the greater their commitment to them, the stronger the culture. Once an organization develops a "strong" culture, it should be noted, there is considerable resistance to changes that affect the culture. The organization can survive high turnover in the lower ranks because new members can be strongly socialized into the organization.

Cultural strength does not necessarily guarantee corporate effectiveness. Although many current writers argue that strength is desirable, the fact remains that the relationship between culture and effectiveness is not simple. The definition of the culture and the degree to which its solutions fit the problems posed by the environment seem to be the critical variables here, not strength alone. A strong culture may also encourage the organization's members to adhere to the demonstrated methods of the past and to blind members to new opportunities.

Managers often have a difficult time recognizing the relationship between culture and the critical performance factors on which excellence depends. There are several components of the organization—structure, systems, people, style—that influence the way managerial tasks are performed. Culture is the product of these components. Strategic change is largely concerned with adjustments in these components to accommodate the perceived needs of a new strategy. Therefore, managing the strategy-culture relationship requires sensitivity to the interaction between the changes necessary to implement strategy and the compatibility of the fit between the changes and the organization's culture.

## The Strategy-Culture Matrix

Implementing strategic changes can be done more effectively when the culture of the organization is taken into consideration. In an effort to minimize the risks inherent in a proposed change, the extent of the need for change and the degree to which the change is compatible with the culture should be viewed together as each impacts upon the other. The **strategy-culture matrix** is one way of understanding the relationship between an organization's strategy and its culture. There are four basic alternatives in determining strategy changes:

1. Manage the change (manageable risk).
2. Reinforce the culture (negligible risk).
3. Manage around the culture (manageable risk).
4. Change the strategy to fit the culture (unacceptable risk).[24]

The need for strategic change and the compatibility of the change, viewed together as a strategy-culture matrix, will largely influence the method used to manage the strategic change. Refer to Figure 15.5 for additional information.

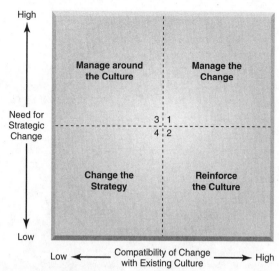

**FIGURE 15.5    The Strategy-Culture Matrix**

**MANAGE THE CHANGE (MANAGEABLE RISK)**  An organization in quadrant 1 of Figure 15.5 is implementing a strategy change that is important to the firm, where the changes are compatible with the existing corporate culture. Therefore, the company can pursue a strategy requiring major changes and should manage the change by using the power of cultural acceptance and reinforcement. The change strategies should emphasize these basic elements:

- Share the vision. The changes must be related to the overall goals and mission of the organization. This builds on existing strengths and makes any changes legitimate to members.
- Reshuffle power or raise key people to positions important in implementing the new strategy. Key people make visible the shared values and norms that lead to cultural compatibility.
- Reinforce the new value system. If the new strategic direction requires changes in marketing, production, and so forth, the changes should be reinforced by the organization's reward structure.

**REINFORCE THE CULTURE (NEGLIGIBLE RISK)**  An organization in quadrant 2 needs relatively little strategic change, and the changes are very compatible with the existing culture. Here the practitioner should emphasize several factors:

- Forge a vision of the new strategy that emphasizes the shared values to make it work.
- Reinforce and solidify the existing culture.

**MANAGE AROUND THE CULTURE (MANAGEABLE RISK)**  Organizations in quadrant 3 need to make some strategic changes, but the changes are potentially incompatible with the corporate culture. Here the critical point is whether the changes can be implemented with a reasonable probability of success. The key element is to manage around the culture, without confronting direct cultural resistance. The approaches include:

- Reinforce the value system.
- Reshuffle power to raise key people.
- Use any available levers of change, such as the budgeting process and reorganization.

**CHANGE THE STRATEGY (UNACCEPTABLE RISK)**  An organization in quadrant 4 faces a different type of challenge. The proposed changes are incompatible with the entrenched corporate culture and there is little need for strategic change. The initial reaction is to do nothing because there is little need for change and if change was implemented, it would likely be incompatible with the existing culture.

When an organization is in this situation, facing a large-scale change with a high probability of cultural resistance, the OD practitioner and management must determine whether strategic change is really needed and whether it is a viable alternative. The challenge of changing the

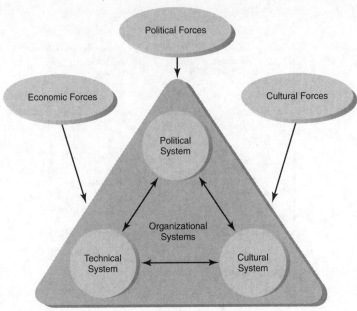

**FIGURE 15.6** **Environmental Forces and Organizational Systems**
*Source:* Reproduced by permission from N. Tichy, "Strategic Change Management" (Working paper, GSBA, University of Michigan, April 1982, p. 7).

culture is an explosive long-term undertaking that is very difficult to achieve. The key questions are: Can the strategic change be made with any possibility of success? Is there really a need to make a large-scale strategic change? If the answers are no, the organization should modify its strategy to fit more closely with the existing culture.

## STRATEGIC CHANGE MANAGEMENT

Noel Tichy proposed the **strategic change management** model as an important integration of the strategic interventions discussed earlier.[25] The model seeks an alignment among an organization's strategy, structure, and human resource systems, and a fit between them and the organization's environment. Strategic change is a function of how well an organization manages these alignments.

According to Tichy, organizations are composed of **technical, political, and cultural systems.** Three basic managerial tools—organizational strategy, organizational structure, and human resource management—may be used to align the three systems with one another and with the larger environment (see Figure 15.6).

Organizations are experiencing ongoing environmental change and uncertainty. This turbulence often causes existing structures and strategies to become obsolete, requiring major strategic changes. For example, the banking industry, long regarded as a stable and unchanging industry, faced monumental changes during the 1980s through 2007 because of deregulation, international banking, and globalization. Moreover, with the collapse of the banking industry in 2008 and 2009, the banking industry once again, and this time over a period of days instead of decades, experienced even more intense change.

Tichy describes the three organizational systems as follows:

- *The technical system* is designed to solve the organization's production problems. It includes the mission, strategy, and organizational structure necessary to become effective.
- *The political system* resolves the allocation problem: how to distribute resources and power, including reward system, career succession, budgets, and power structure.
- *The cultural system* is designed to solve the value/belief problem: what values members share, what objectives should be pursued, and so forth.

The technical, political, and cultural systems are interrelated and form an organizational system, as discussed in Chapter 2. Strategic change management involves the alignment of these systems to meet environmental pressures.

This approach to change suggests that initially an image is developed of the desired organization with the technical, political, and cultural systems aligned. Change must start with a strategic vision of a desired organizational state. This vision should include a futuristic view of each of the three systems (technical, political, and cultural), as well as what the organization will look like when the systems are aligned. Secondly, the three systems are separated and intervention occurs in each one. Because the systems tend to be mutually reinforcing, it is necessary to unlock them from one another before strategic change can occur. And third, a plan for reconnecting the three systems is developed. After strategy interventions have been made in the three systems separately, it is necessary to determine how they will be reconnected. This reconnecting plan determines how the three systems will achieve the desired state or strategic vision that was initially developed.

## CHANGING THE CORPORATE CULTURE

It is generally agreed that an effective corporate culture can result in superior performance. There is also considerable agreement that organizations facing discontinuity—out of fit with the environment—may need large-scale cultural change. However, changing the corporate culture is often very difficult because the culture is based upon past success. As a result, organization members may hold deeply entrenched beliefs and strong personal investments in the existing culture. Research by Jay B. Barney suggests that a firm's culture can be a source of sustainable competitive advantage if it is difficult to imitate, thus making it difficult for less successful organizations to imitate a more successful culture.[26]

The organization culture may inhibit the implementation of the strategy and prevent a firm from meeting competitive threats or from adapting to changing economic conditions. This can lead to the firm's decline, stagnation, or even ultimate demise unless the culture is changed.

Terrence Deal and Allan Kennedy suggest that there are only five reasons to justify large-scale cultural changes.

1. When the company has strong values that do not fit the changing environment.
2. When the industry is very competitive and changes with lightning speed.
3. When the company is mediocre or worse.
4. When the firm is about to join the ranks of the very largest.
5. When the firm is small but growing rapidly.[27]

An organization facing any of these situations may need to change its culture in order to adapt to a changing environment or to perform at higher levels of effectiveness. However, implementing cultural change can be extremely difficult and time-consuming. Given the problems associated with culture change, most OD practitioners suggest that major changes to the culture should be attempted only after less difficult and costly solutions have been ruled out.

Meshing different cultures or subcultures within the same organization can also be problematic. This cultural clash becomes even more evident in the case of mergers or takeovers when two differing cultures must be integrated.[28] There are some recent examples of unsuccessful and very costly mergers that were partly the result of widely disparate cultures: Chrysler with Mercedes Benz, Citibank with Travelers, and AOL with Time-Warner. Conversely, when Google acquired YouTube, a very conscious decision was made at Google to let the two retain their existing cultures. "YouTube has remained largely separate from Google. They're in San Bruno [north of the main Google campus in Mountain View, California] and have their own culture which is different and cool," says Larry Page, cofounder of Google.

In summary, leadership in today's fast-changing world involves developing an innovative corporate culture: a culture that recognizes employees' needs, the firm's history, the marketplace, and the company's products and services. Top managers invariably try to develop a framework for transmitting the corporate culture and for adapting to change. Unfortunately, a strong culture may often prove to be a liability if it fails to respond to changing market forces. When the corporate culture is resistant to change, OD strategies can be used to move the culture in a more innovative direction.

The next and final chapter will discuss the last stage in an OD program: self-renewal, stabilize, evaluate, and disengage. In addition, we will look at emerging issues and future trends in the field of organization development.

## Summary

- **Organization Transformation.** This chapter has presented several interventions for helping organizations transform to meet new strategic directions. Large-scale change programs typically occur in response to, or in anticipation of, fundamental environmental or technological changes. Environmental discontinuities often require a dramatic shift in organizational strategy, which, in turn, necessitates changes to organization structure, corporate culture, and managerial processes. These strategy interventions are aimed at relating the organization to its broader environment and achieving a higher level of corporate excellence.

- **Corporate Culture.** Corporate culture includes the shared values and beliefs of organization members and determines how they perform. Corporate culture is a key determinant of how an organization implements strategic change and what strategies and techniques the OD practitioner may bring to such interventions. Changing the corporate culture starts with developing a shared vision, the empowerment of members, and the development of a trust relationship at all levels.

- **Vision.** The development of a vision is important in organizational and cultural change. An effective vision should be challenging, inspiring, and aimed at empowering people at all levels.

- **Strategy.** The strategy-culture matrix provides one tool that the OD practitioner can use in implementing strategic changes. Changing the corporate culture can be an extremely challenging task. It requires a clear strategic vision, reinforcement of new values, and reshuffling the power-reward system to fit the new strategy.

- **Strategic Change Management.** Strategic change management presents a view of the organization as technical, political, and cultural systems, and involves aligning these systems with the environment.

- **Changing the Culture.** Organizational excellence in a rapidly changing world requires an innovative and adaptive corporate culture. Strategic change has become increasingly important in recent years and often influences the very survival of an organization in a volatile environment. The corporate culture can be a force in reinforcing or resisting strategic changes. When the culture is resistant to innovations, OD techniques and strategies may be used to enhance successful strategic changes.

## Review Questions

1. Compare and contrast organization development and organization transformation. How are they similar or dissimilar?
2. Suppose you receive a new job offer. What cultural factors would you consider in making a decision?
3. How does the culture affect an organization's ability to change?
4. Can you identify the characteristics that describe your organization's culture? Or the culture of this class?
5. Select an organization and critique how the president or its CEO has articulated a vision to its members?
6. Find an article from *Business Week, Fortune*, the *Wall Street Journal*, or another publication that discusses an organization's culture and identify the strength of the corporate culture using Figure 15.4 as a frame of reference.

## Key Words and Concepts

Culture
Incremental Approach
Organization
   Transformation (OT)

Strategic Change
   Management
Strategy
Strategy-Culture Matrix

Technical, Political, and
   Cultural Systems
Transformational Change
Vision

# OD Skills Simulation 15.1

## The GenTech Company

*Total time suggested: 90 minutes.*

## A. Purpose

The purpose of this simulation is to experience and observe how information affects strategic decision making. In this simulation, you will be able to develop strategy and culture in an organization. You will receive feedback on your risk-taking level. The goals include:

- Comparing strategic decisions made by individuals with those of the team.
- Learning how task information is shared among group members.
- Identifying how individual risk-taking levels influence results.
- Learning how collaboration and competition affect team problem solving.

## B. Procedures

*Step 1.* Prior to class, form teams of six. Additional members may serve as practitioners. Each member selects one role and reads the company and strategy information. The roles are:

1. Executive Vice President, Corporate Strategy
2. Vice President, Human Resources
3. Vice President, Manufacturing
4. Vide President, Marketing
5. Vice President, Engineering
6. OD Practitioner(s)

Individually, read the GenTech Company background, terminology, and strategy descriptions that follow. There are four basic strategies, and within each strategy there are two implementation alternatives. For the four strategies, allocate a percentage of investment to each strategy that reflects the degree of emphasis you want to place on it. Record your choices on Form 1: My Individual Strategic Decisions, Column 1 (Individual Strategy). The four strategies should vertically add to 100 percent.

Next, for each of the four basic strategies, allocate a percentage of resources between Implementation Alternatives A & B. Record your percentages in Column 2. The sum of the percentages for Alternatives A & B within each of the four strategies will total 100 percent. (As an example, you may give "Market Penetrations" 30 percentage points, and within this strategy you may give Alternative A 80 percentage points and Alternative B 20 percentage points. You would then go through the other three strategies and allocate percentage points in a similar manner.)

*Step 2.* The executive committee meets to select a strategy. Through team discussion, exploration, and examination, try to reach a consensus decision reflecting the integrated thinking and consensus of all the members. During the meeting, try to use the OD skills that you have learned during the course. The OD practitioner may make interventions to assist the team. Follow these instructions for reaching a consensus:

1. Try to identify the best long-term strategy.
2. Do not change your mind simply to reach an agreement and to avoid conflict, but support solutions with which you are able to agree.
3. Avoid conflict-reducing techniques such as majority vote, averaging, or trading in reaching your decision.
4. View differences of opinion as a help rather than a hindrance in decision making.

There are at least three possible strategies that your team can follow:

- High risk, high growth.
- Low risk, low growth, cost control.
- Some trade-off between the first two strategies.

At this point, meet together as the executive committee and enter your committee's decision on Form 2: Executive Committee Strategic Decisions.

*Time suggested for Step 2: 30 minutes.*

*Step 3.* Each team lists its results on the board and compares and discusses the team decision rankings.

*Time suggested for Step 3: 10 minutes.*

*Step 4.* Based upon your own decision style, individually rate your risk-taking level on Form 3: Individual Risk Assessment. If you feel you are a low risk taker (risk-averse), select a rating at the low end of the scale; if you feel you are a high risk taker (risk-taking), then you will rate yourself on the high end of the scale. On Form 4: Risk Taking—Individual and Team write in the names of the team members including the OD practitioners, rate the members' risk levels and record it in Column 1 (My Assessment of Others).

*Time suggested for Step 4: 10 minutes.*

*Step 5.* Meeting with your team and the practitioner leading the discussion, reach a team consensus on each team member's risk level and record it in Form 4, Column 2 (Team Consensus). Share feedback and collect ratings from each member on your style. Record this risk-level assessment made by others on Form 5: My Risk-Taking Summary.

*Time suggested for Step 5: 15 minutes.*

*Step 6.* You now have three risk-level ratings: (1) ratings by other individuals, (2) the team consensus rating; and (3) your own. Calculate the average of the ratings, and compare the assessments of your risk-taking levels on Form 5.

Individual and team risk can be compared based on these scores. However, individuals have different degrees of risk taking, and the final score may not reflect how decisions were made during the team discussion.

*Time suggested for Step 6: 10 minutes.*

*Step 7.* As a class, consider the following questions, with the practitioners leading the discussion.

1. What behaviors seemed to help your group successfully complete its task?
2. How was information shared among the group?
3. How did issues of risk taking affect the decision?
4. How did collaboration/competition influence the outcome?

*Time suggested for Step 7: 15 minutes.*

## The GenTech Company Background

The GenTech Company is a medium-sized high-tech firm developing and selling industry-specific software and information systems. Software, for example, is developed for specific industries, such as home-improvement stores, hotels, restaurants, and amusement parks. GenTech has had a strong, steady growth record, and its software products have traditionally been highly rated by customers. GenTech has a sound financial position, but during the last five years it has been losing market share because new competitors are entering the field with more advanced features in their software products and at lower prices.

In the past, GenTech was noted for its fast growth. Employees always knew where they stood at GenTech. However, recently several of the newer and more promising managers and engineers have quit to join competitors. As a relative newcomer to the computer industry (it was founded 11 years ago), GenTech is still a medium-sized company in its industry, but it has been moderately successful in competing with larger firms like Ovation. GenTech is a fast-moving company, and employee behavior is somewhat unorthodox in that it is highly flexible. GenTech has always operated on the concept of "Let's get it done now and we'll worry about company rules and regs tomorrow."

The executive vice president of corporate strategy has called a meeting of key managers to form a new corporate strategy based upon the goals of the company. One key factor is how to allocate the investment funds into a total company strategy.

## Terminology

1. A market penetration strategy involves an attempt to increase market share in an existing market niche, one in which the firm already offers software.
2. Market development introduces existing software into new market areas, often by expansion into new market segments or geographic areas.
3. Diversification involves the development of new software and entry into new markets. The degree of change often makes this a high-risk strategy.
4. Software development is a technology-based strategy that involves developing new or advanced software features for existing markets.

The CEO has suggested four basic strategies, with two implementation alternatives within each basic strategy (see Figure 15.7—Strategy Alternatives):

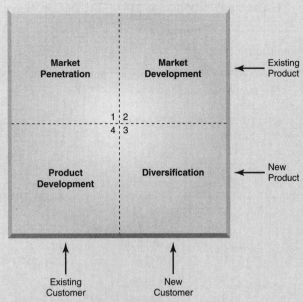

**FIGURE 15.7   Strategy Alternatives**

### Strategy 1. Market penetration.

**a.** Increase advertising expenditures, number of sales reps, and promotional activities, and possibly cut prices. This strategy will focus on the software with the greatest profit margin. There is an estimated 80 percent probability that this strategy will increase demand for currently profitable software.

**b.** Increase advertising and introduce new sophisticated software into existing lines. This may improve the company's image and lead to customer acceptance of these higher margin products in existing markets and increased market share and profits with an estimated 75 percent probability of success.

### Strategy 2. Market development.

**a.** Identify and develop new markets for existing software by promoting software in markets not currently served—new demographic or geographic markets. Market research estimates a 75 percent probability that increasing demand in new markets would add to sales growth, profits about the same (possibly slightly lower), but with increased volume of sales.

**b.** Identify and develop new markets by differentiating our existing software to tailor them to new geographic markets, or new market niches. The profit margins are likely to be high with this strategy, even with relatively low volume of sales with an estimated 70 percent probability of success, since uncertainty in the industry could result in low sales.

### Strategy 3. Diversification.

**a.** There is an opportunity to acquire a firm that has developed antivirus software for servers running Linux and Windows operating systems. The software would complement and widen our line of products. This would allow a more complete line of software and would increase volume, but involves a segment of the software industry in which we have little expertise. The estimate of success is rated at about 65 percent, but could increase total sales volume and profitability.

**b.** The company has a chance to develop a new line of software, such as environmental control software for large buildings, by acquiring a small company in the field. This would move the company into entirely new markets and increase its potential return and profitability. It builds on existing expertise, although much of the technology comes from the acquired company, and thus the estimated probability of success is only 60 percent, but it has become a very attractive, high-growth industry (representing a potentially fast growing segment of the market) and offers high rewards if successful. Our risk is that of operating in a totally new market.

### Strategy 4. Product development.

**a.** The software development group has proposed a new, low-cost, low-price software to meet competition. In the past, the firm has developed only high-quality software. Low-cost software with fewer features could result in increased sales to the low-end market, estimated at a 70 percent probability of success.

**b.** The software development group will develop a new line of software that is highly sophisticated and uses advanced algorithms engineered by GenTech. This would provide an increase in market share at the high-end market and help protect against competition. This requires up-front design investment, but has a 65 percent probability of considerably higher profit margins and increased market.

**FORM 1: MY INDIVIDUAL STRATEGIC DECISION**

| Strategy | Individual Strategy (Column 1) | Implementation Alternatives A & B (Column 2) |
|---|---|---|
| 1. Market Penetration | _____% | A_____% |
| | | B_____% |
| | | 100% |
| 2. Market Development | _____% | A_____% |
| | | B_____% |
| | | 100% |
| 3. Diversification | _____% | A_____% |
| | | B_____% |
| | | 100% |
| 4. Product Development | _____% | A_____% |
| | 100% | B_____% |
| | | 100% |

**FORM 2: EXECUTIVE COMMITTEE STRATEGIC DECISIONS**

| Strategy | Team Strategy (Column 1) | Implementation Alternatives A & B (Column 2) |
|---|---|---|
| 1. Market Penetration | _____% | A_____% |
| | | B_____% |
| | | 100% |
| 2. Market Development | _____% | A_____% |
| | | B_____% |
| | | 100% |
| 3. Diversification | _____% | A_____% |
| | | B_____% |
| | | 100% |
| 4. Product Development | _____% | A_____% |
| | 100% | B_____% |
| | | 100% |

---

### FORM 3: INDIVIDUAL RISK ASSESSMENT

Risk Taking. The ability to take risks to accomplish what one feels is necessary, to dare to be different, to follow one's conscience, to be creatively different.

In the space below, indicate whether you are a risk taker or risk averter. If you avoid risk in most or all situations, pick a number closer to 0. If you are a high risk taker, choose a number close to 100. Circle the number that best describes your approach to risk situations.

**Risk Level**

| Risk Averse | 0 | 10 | 20 | 30 | 40 | 50 | 60 | 70 | 80 | 90 | 100% | Risk Taking |
|---|---|---|---|---|---|---|---|---|---|---|---|---|

This is your "individual risk estimate."

---

### FORM 4: RISK TAKING—INDIVIDUAL AND TEAM

Risk Taking. The ability to take risks to accomplish what one feels is necessary, to dare to be different, to follow one's conscience, to be creatively different.

| Risk Averse | 0 | 10 | 20 | 30 | 40 | 50 | 60 | 70 | 80 | 90 | 100% | Risk Taking |
|---|---|---|---|---|---|---|---|---|---|---|---|---|

| Team Members' Names | Column 1<br>Individual<br>Risk Level<br>(My Assessment<br>of Others) | Column 2<br>Risk Level<br>of Members<br>(Team<br>Consensus) |
|---|---|---|
| 1. _____ | _____ | _____ |
| 2. _____ | _____ | _____ |
| 3. _____ | _____ | _____ |
| 4. _____ | _____ | _____ |
| 5. _____ | _____ | _____ |
| 6. _____ | _____ | _____ |
| 7. _____ | _____ | _____ |
| 8. _____ | _____ | _____ |

**FORM 5: MY RISK-TAKING SUMMARY**

Record the risk level assessment made by other individuals and the team from Form 4. Record your self-assessment from Form 3.

| **From Team Member** | **Risk Level Rating** |
|---|---|
| 1. _____ | _____ |
| 2. _____ | _____ |
| 3. _____ | _____ |
| 4. _____ | _____ |
| 5. _____ | _____ |
| 6. _____ | _____ |
| 7. _____ | _____ |
| 8. Individual Average | _____ |
| 9. Team Assessment (Form 4, Column 2) | _____ |
| 10. My Assessment (Form 3) | _____ |
| 11. Overall Average (average of lines 8, 9, and 10) | _____ |

# CASE: THE SPACE ELECTRONICS CORPORATION

The Space Electronics Corporation is a subsidiary of a major firm with sales in excess of $300 million. Space Electronics holds substantial positions in commercial and military electronic systems markets, but profitability and market position have been declining. About a year ago, it became apparent that two R&D projects were coming up: a new electronic guidance system for the stealth bomber, and electronic control systems for a remote-controlled military airplane. These appeared to be the only two major projects coming up in the next few years. The executive committee had to decide whether or not to pursue these two projects. This would involve taking a radically new course of action, going after the prime contract for the electronic systems, whereas in the past, the company had operated as a subcontractor to other primes.

## The Executive Committee Meeting

In mid-September, Reade Exton, the president, opened the meeting. "As you all know, our profitability and market position have been declining. We have landed only one new proposal during this period, and there is great pressure from headquarters to go after these major projects. We have all had an opportunity to review a copy of the proposals, and I'll let Glenn start the discussion."

Glen Overton, vice president, engineering. "About a year ago, it became obvious that our engineering activity was going to decline. The decision was made that a joint effort with marketing would be undertaken, and after a series of meetings, it was decided that our best course of action was to aggressively pursue these two large contracts."

Oliver Whittier, vice president, finance. "Frankly, Glenn, I have reservations about such a major departure from our past policies and by the magnitude of these projects. I'm worried about the increased overhead and the drain on our current profits. And I have a gut feeling that our probability of getting those contracts is less than you seem to think."

Ted Byron, vice president, marketing. "Although you may estimate that the probability of gaining these projects is low, the payoff is enough to turn our whole picture around. These contracts will put us on the map. My best 'guesstimate' is that our chances are closer to 75 percent than 60 percent. Don't forget, I have a lot of personal contacts back in Washington, and while that is no guarantee, it sure doesn't hurt."

Paul Brown, vice president, industrial relations. "I agree with Oliver. I have my doubts as to our chances of getting such a large-scale project, and I am worried about our people. If we should fail to get these contracts, people could get hurt. We may have to have layoffs and that is a bad business. I think we have a certain responsibility to the people here."

Mort Jenson, vice president, manufacturing. "Let's face it, if we pull these two proposals out of the hat, they will love us at headquarters. We'll be superstars! But on the other hand, we could take a real beating if these projects fizzle out. I think we have to consider the risk factor and what might happen to the company if we fail. And, like Paul says, a number of our line employees could take a beating if things don't work out."

Glen Overton. "Listen, fellows, there are no lead-pipe cinches in this business. But don't you think Ted and I have a better feel for our probabilities than people in personnel? If a downturn were to occur, our company will be hard-pressed anyway. Frankly, I'm not quite as optimistic as Ted here, but I still think our chances are in the 60 percent range. Even at that, it seems like a good risk because even if we only get one of the projects, our company will benefit greatly. Plus our R&D will stand to gain a heck of a lot by being involved in the state of the art. We'll be able to attract new talent."

Mort Jenson. "One of our past problems was the isolation of R&D from the rest of the organization. I feel that we should seek to achieve more interdepartmental cooperation. So I think it is important to get all the differing viewpoints out on the table."

Reade Exton. "I think we have had a good discussion, but now what is our decision? As you know, there is a lot of pressure from headquarters to go after these projects, but it has to be a team decision. Frankly, we are between a rock and a hard place. There will have to be a significant expenditure just to pursue these major contracts, and our R&D activity will be almost exclusively devoted to the proposals for about three months, and that will include 10-hour days and seven-day work weeks. There definitely is a degree of risk involved, although the exact odds are hard to predict. One thing is sure: if we don't go after the projects, we won't get them." (Use the Case Analysis Form on the following page.)

**THE SPACE ELECTRONICS CORPORATION CASE ANALYSIS FORM**

Name: _____

I. Problems

  A. Macro

    1. _____

    _____

    2. _____

    _____

  B. Micro

    1. _____

    _____

    2. _____

    _____

II. Causes

    1. _____

    _____

    2. _____

    _____

    3. _____

    _____

III. Systems affected

    1. _____

    _____

    2. _____

    _____

    3. _____

    _____

IV. Alternatives

    1. _____

    _____

    2. _____

    _____

    3. _____

    _____

V. Recommendations

_____

_____

_____

_____

_____

_____

## Chapter 15 Endnotes

1. Stephane Fitch, "Soft Pillows and Sharp Elbows," *Forbes*, March 10, 2004, p. 78.

2. Faith Arner, "No Excuse Not to Succeed," *Business Week*, May 10, 2004, p. 98.

3. Patricia McLagan, "Success with Change," *T + D,* vol. 56, no. 12 (December 2002), pp. 44–54; Richard Leifer, "Understanding Organizational Transformation Using a Dissipative Mode," *Human Relations*, vol. 42, no. 10 (October 1989), pp. 899–916.

4. Amy Barrrett, "Schering's Dr. Feelbetter?" *Business Week,* June 23, 2003, p. 56.

5. McLagan, "Success with Change," p. 44; Leifer, "Understanding Organizational Transformation," p. 899.

6. Russell A. Eisenstat, Michael Beer, Nathaniel Foote, Tobias Fredberg, and Flemming Norrgren, "The Uncompromising Leader," *Harvard Business Review*, July–August 2008, pp. 51–7.

7. David Welch, "Bob Nardelli's Wrong Turns," *Business Week*, May 4, 2009, p. 26; Jennifer Reingold, "Home Depot's Total Rehab," *Fortune*, September 29, 2008; Carol Hymowitz, "Home Depot's CEO Led a Revolution, But Left Some Behind," *Wall Street Journal*, March 16, 2004, p. B1.

8. Dexter C. Dunphy and Doug A. Stace, "Transformational and Coercive Strategies for Planned Organizational Change: Beyond the O.D. Model," *Organization Studies*, vol. 9, no. 3 (July 1998), pp. 317–334.

9. Noel Tichy and Stratford Sherman, "Control Your Destiny or Someone Else Will," *Economist*, February 1993, p. 94.

10. K. L. Newman, "Organizational Transformation during Institutional Upheaval," *Academy of Management Review*, vol. 25, no. 3 (July 2000), pp. 602–19.

11. J. Daniel Wischnevsky and Fariborz Damanpour, "Organizational Transformation and Performance: An Examination of Three Perspectives," *Journal of Managerial Issues*, vol. 18, no. 1 (Spring 2006), p. 122.

12. Emily Steel, "AOL Ad Project, 'Platform A,' Plots Plan B," *Wall Street Journal*, March 26, 2008, p. B6.

13. Arlene Weintraub, "Genentech's Medicine Man," *Business Week*, October 6, 2003, pp. 72–80.

14. Micheline Maynard, *The End of Detroit: How the Big Three Lost Their Grip on the American Car Market* (New York: Currency/Doubleday, 2003); review by Adam Aston, "Running Out of Road," *Business Week*, December 15, 2003, p. 24.

15. Michael A. Gillespie, Daniel R. Denison, Stephanie Haaland, Ryan Smerek, and William S. Neale, "Linking Organizational Culture and Customer Satisfaction: Results from Two Companies in Different Industries," *Organizational Psychology*, vol. 17, no. 1 (March 2008), pp. 112–32; Daniel. R. Denison, *Corporate Culture and Organizational Effectiveness*, (New York: Wiley, 1990); John Kotter and James Heskett, *Corporate Culture and Performance*, (New York: Free Press, 1992); Barbara Block, "Creating a Culture All Employees Can Accept," *Management Review*, July 1989, p. 41.

16. Richard Siklos (interviewer), "The Iger Difference," *Fortune*, April 28, 2008, p. 92.

17. Daniel R. Denison, "Bringing Corporate Culture to the Bottom Line," *Organizational Dynamics*, vol. 13, no. 2 (Autumn 1984), pp. 4–22; Daniel R. Denison, "The Climate, Culture, and Effectiveness of Work Organizations," Ph.D. dissertation, University of Michigan: Ann Arbor, 1982.

18. See J. Martin, *Culture in Organizations* (New York: Oxford Press, 1992).

19. John R. Latham, "Visioning: The Concept, Trilogy and Process," *Quality Process*, vol. 28, no. 4 (April 1995), p. 65.

20. Howard E. Butler, "Strategic Planning: The Missing Link in TQM," *Quality Process*, vol. 28, no. 5 (May 1995), p. 105.

21. James M. Kouzes and Barry Z. Posner, "To Lead, Create a Shared Vision," *Harvard Business Review*, vol. 87, no. 1 (January 2009), pp. 20–21; John W. Alexander, "Sharing the Vision," *Business Horizons*, May/June 1989, pp. 56–59.

22. John Kotter, "Leading Change," *Harvard Business Review*, vol. 85, no. 1 (January 2007), p. 99.

23. John Kotter and James Heskett, *Corporate Culture and Performance*.

24. Howard Schwartz and Stanley M. Davis, "Matching Corporate Culture and Business Strategy," *Organizational Dynamics*, Summer 1981, p. 43.

25. Noel M. Tichy and Nancy Cardwell, *The Cycle of Leadership: How Great Leaders Teach Their Companies to Win* (New York: HarperBusiness, 2002); Noel M. Tichy and Andrew R. McGill (eds.), *The Ethical Challenge: How to Lead with Unyielding Integrity* (San Francisco: Jossey-Bass, 2003); Noel M. Tichy, *Managing Strategic Change: Technical, Political, and Cultural Dynamics* (New York: John Wiley, 1983); Noel M. Tichy, "Revolutionize Your Company or Someone Else Will," *Fortune*, December 13, 1993, p. 114.

26. Jay B. Barney, "Organizational Culture: Can It Be a Source of Competitive Advantage?" *Academy of Management Review*, vol. 11, no. 3 (July 1986), pp. 656–65.

27. Terence E. Real and Alan A. Kennedy, *Corporate Cultures* (Reading, MA: Addison-Wesley, 1982).

28. For additional information, see Micahel Gibbs, Kathryn Ierulli, and Valerie Smeets, "Mergers of Equals and Unequals," working paper, The University of Chicago Booth School of Business, 2008, available at www.faculty.chicagobooth.edu/michael.gibbs/research/.

# The Challenge and the Future for Organizations

## LEARNING OBJECTIVES

**Upon completing this chapter, you will be able to:**

**1.** Understand the basic issues in using organization development as an approach to planned change.

**2.** Recognize ways of maintaining, internalizing, and stabilizing a change program.

**3.** Identify some of the future trends and problems facing the OD practitioner.

**4.** Understand the process of terminating the practitioner-client relationship.

## PREMEETING PREPARATION

**1.** Read Chapter 16.

**2.** Complete the Profile Survey and Profile Form in Simulation 16.1, Part A, Step 1.

**3.** Complete Step 1 of OD Skills Simulation 16.2.

## THE ORGANIZATION OF THE FUTURE

The organization of the future will be different from today's organization. In a world of global competitiveness and technological innovation, organizations are reengineering, restructuring, and flattening the hierarchy to meet market pressures. Leading companies now envision an endlessly changing organization. The new term is **reconfigurable**—an organization that is flexible and able to change on an annual, monthly, weekly, daily, or even hourly time frame. Unchanging systems will become dinosaurs. Singer and poet Bob Dylan prophetically said in his 1963 album and song of the same name, "The times they are a changin'."[1]

There is a continuing need for long-range strategies to improve organizational decision making and work relationships to meet these changing conditions. Organization development, the newest discipline in planned change techniques, has emerged from these needs. OD is viewed by organizations of all types—industrial, governmental, and health care—as a field of expertise that can provide a viable option for planned change.

Change is a continuing process. Every organization exists in a continuous state of adapting to change. Nissan Motors is a company that learned its lesson the hard way. By the mid-1990s, Nissan was facing a quick demise unless it acted quickly. It did not have the deep pockets of well-healed backers to rescue it; it had to change if it was going to stay in business. "We were a collapsing company," recalls CEO Carlos Ghosn. He quickly shut down five plants, reduced the workforce by 23,000, and shifted production of more models to the United States.[2] Ghosn has become a corporate hero in Japan and is even the admired subject of comic books.[3]

External competitive forces usually cause downsizing changes, whereas other changes to work processes come about because of shifting forces within the organization. Many management theorists feel that authoritarian or bureaucratic systems are too rigid to adapt to the increasing rate of change and, therefore, become reactive organizations, reacting drastically after problems emerge. More and more organizations are finding that employees are no longer satisfied to simply fill a slot in the organization chart.

Just as organizations are in a continuous state of change, so too OD is a continuing process. As one set of change objectives is achieved, new standards of excellence and new challenges arise. As a result, the OD practitioner has two primary criteria of effectiveness. One criterion is the stability of the OD effort after the practitioner stops working with the client system; the other is the ability of the client system to maintain innovation within the system or the development of a self-renewal capability.

Because an OD program is an approach to improving effectiveness, its results have to be evaluated. The organization members involved in the change need feedback on the outcome of their efforts in order to determine whether to modify, continue, or discontinue these activities. At this point, there is also usually a disengagement between the OD practitioner and the client—a termination of the change program relationship.

Organization development is an ongoing process because an organization cannot remain static and be effective. In today's changing environment, organizations must develop adaptive mechanisms and anticipative management systems. To cope with these changing conditions, an OD practitioner needs to be able to monitor and assess progress toward change goals so as to have the ability to recognize when these efforts may be phased out. The participants and teams involved in an OD program need feedback to measure their progress toward goals and to stabilize change efforts. This continuing assessment also acts to prevent deterioration or degradation of earlier behaviors, attitudes, or values. An organization might implement total quality management (TQM) and initially feel that the program is successful. A year later, however, most managers may have discarded TQM and returned to their former management methods unless there is some stabilization and continued reinforcement of the TQM program.

Because OD is a continuous improvement process, the completion of one change cycle leads to another cycle in the process of development. In this chapter, we examine monitoring and stabilizing the OD program, discuss several emerging issues, and examine the future of the OD field.

## MONITOR AND STABILIZE THE OD PROGRAM

After an OD program has been implemented, the emphasis must be placed upon internalizing and **stabilizing** the changes so that the new behavior becomes part of the organization's cultural norms. This chapter discusses the fifth stage of an OD program and is illustrated in Figure 16.1. In the five-stage model of the organization development process, Stage 5 involves four factors: (1) generate and communicate information through feedback to participating members so that they can measure their progress; (2) stabilize and monitor the change or desired behavior so that it will be continued; (3) evaluate the OD program's results; and (4) disengagement of the practitioner's help and a transition to internal resources.

### Feedback of Information

The members of an organization involved in an OD program need feedback on the results of the change in order to determine whether to modify, continue, or discontinue their activities. Without feedback on the consequences of a change program, the client system may perceive the program

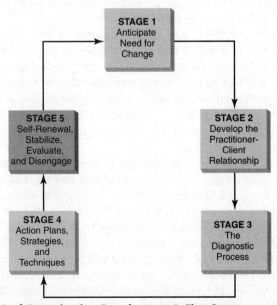

**FIGURE 16.1   Stage 5 of Organization Development's Five Stages**

as a failure and discontinue it. Therefore, part of the OD practitioner's job is to see that necessary information is made available to participating members and groups. Research on TQM programs shows that the more successful programs have early payoffs that the participants can see and be encouraged by.[4]

The feedback of information can also create commitment among organization members. Commitment to change emerges from open communications and management's ability to reinforce new behaviors so that members can see how their contributions affect outcome.

One criterion for determining the effectiveness of a change program is whether system problems are corrected. In certain instances, data will be readily available, particularly around operational indices of performance or productivity. In other instances, the practitioner may gather after-the-fact interview or questionnaire data to verify the degree of change in less tangible factors, such as morale, leadership style, or job satisfaction. At one consulting firm, for example, client firms are first evaluated by developing hypothesis problem statements about the client firm's current operations. These hypotheses are then researched and proven or disproven with information, not opinions. The research process includes all of the possible alternative actions that could logically be incorporated into the firm's culture. From this review and elimination process, recommendations are then forwarded and suggested for adoption by the client.

Some companies hold team meetings to share information on productivity, backlog, and person-hours per unit. Each month financial statements, including a chart tracking operating profits (a key measure for profit sharing) are posted for all members. Setpoint Systems, a small but growing custom-manufacturing company, has a system where spreadsheets showing financial and production data are posted on a large board for all employees to see and use. The company has built a culture that has everyone involved in the process of controlling cash. Not only does the company have a standard once-a-week meeting to go over the figures, but employees, and not just management, are involved. Says a project engineer, "We monitor the spreadsheets throughout the week, and we make decisions based on them. Should we buy component x or y, considering the price difference? Should we put an extra 15 hours into this project to do such-and-such? It's a constant, daily process."[5]

## Stabilize and Monitor Change

When a performance problem has been corrected and the change objectives have been achieved, some means must be devised to ensure that the new performance level is stabilized. If this is not done, there will be a tendency for the individual or the system to deteriorate and revert to previous ineffective behaviors. As an example, an individual may desire to discontinue some habit, such as smoking, and actually change for a short period of time. However, the change objective is not accomplished if the person begins smoking again six months later. One criticism of some of the OD interventions is "fade-out." Fade-out, or deterioration of change, may occur in an OD program when the change is not stabilized into the system and behavior gradually slips back into previous ineffective modes. Obviously, one measure of success is whether the change is permanently assimilated into and accepted by the client system.

The change program itself may have a stabilizing effect because of its advantages and support. There is also an effect surrounding many change methods, such as with self-managed work teams or TQM techniques, which makes participating employees feel they are an elite group and sell the benefits of the OD program to other members, thus stabilizing the acceptance of change. Sometimes an OD program is initiated in one division or subsystem of an organization, and the performance results are used to demonstrate the effectiveness of the new techniques to another division. Where results about such matters as decreased turnover or costs are obtainable, this recognition may act as a stabilizing force.

Once a change effort is fully accepted, the change may become institutionalized or internalized by group members. The acceptance and adoption of a change effort depend upon practice and familiarity, so that the innovation becomes a routine part of the organization's activity. Managers continue to level with one another over on-the-job performance, and they are constantly critiquing one another over quality goals. In other words, the change has been integrated into the organization structure, norms, and culture. Innovation and change is in the DNA of W. L. Gore & Associates. Gore realizes that its products and the company itself will become obsolete in several years if it does not continually innovate. Finally, some form of continuing assessment of the change effort in later periods should be included to guard against degradation over time. The greater the investment in the OD program, the more detailed the reappraisal mechanisms should be.

## Evaluate the OD Program

The need to develop better research designs and methods is a major problem in OD. If the practice and theory of OD are to merge into a broader field of planning change, research will play a crucial role.

Many OD practitioners feel that the evaluation method should be designed into the change process itself. OD evaluations will be important in the future for three groups:

1. *Decision makers* of an organization will want to see evidence that the expenditures are providing the desired results.
2. *Participants* in an OD program will need feedback about their change efforts.
3. *OD practitioners* need the evaluation so that they can develop their expertise.

The success of an evaluation will depend upon the degree of support provided by the decision makers, participants, and practitioners. Decision makers will need to provide the financial resources to pay for a rigorous evaluation. Participants will need to cooperate by providing the data necessary for the evaluation. And the practitioner will need to have the professional capacity and self-confidence to accept criticism and use it to improve his or her skills.

Evaluating OD program outcomes involves making an assessment about whether the OD intervention has been satisfactorily implemented and, if so, whether it is bringing about the desired outcomes. When client systems invest resources in major OD efforts, there is an increasing need for data on the results. OD practitioners are frequently asked to justify OD programs in terms of basic productivity, cost savings, or other bottomline measures. Consequently, organizations are constantly seeking more rigorous evaluations of OD interventions.

## Terminate Practitioner and Client Relationship

The final stage of the OD process occurs when the program's basic change objectives have been accomplished and either the practitioner or the client or both feel that the system can continue the change effort without outside assistance. That place may be reached when there is a diminishing rate of return for efforts expended. The practitioner may feel that little more can be accomplished, the evaluation indicates that desired change levels have been achieved, and the client system feels able to continue renewal processes on its own.

It is likely that the disengagement of the practitioner will be a gradual one and the organization will transition to using internal resources. An important objective is to ensure that the changes are not short term or temporary and are not followed by a regression to former operating patterns. Another objective is to prepare for continuous improvement with periodic follow-ups and a gradual phasing in of new change objectives. If the organization has internal OD practitioners, then they can continue to monitor and to provide support to the organization.

It should be emphasized that continued involvement is usually advisable. The practitioner is available for emergency help or special consultation. Continued formal or informal contacts are always possible, and the practitioner may become involved again in some new change effort.

## Self-Renewal

The OD practitioner considers disengagement when the benchmarks used to evaluate change have been achieved and the client system seems capable of continuing self-renewal and innovation; that is, the client system has the resources and competence necessary to continue change efforts. One of the basic objectives of the OD practitioner from the beginning of the OD program has been to help the client system develop the ability to innovate constantly. The client system needs a self-sustaining capability to devise and implement change programs without outside support. If the organization and its members have accepted and value innovations and perpetual growth, change will be viewed as a natural and desirable process. The culture of the organization will become one of self-renewal. **Self-renewal** means building innovation and commitment to change into the organization's values. Change is the only constant in today's world, and leaders need to find continuing ways to renew and revitalize their teams, departments, and organizations. Change is not a one-time event that gets checked off of a "to-do" list.

The mechanism for this self-renewal capacity is usually an internal OD practitioner or OD group. Internal practitioners can continue collecting, diagnosing, and evaluating new data to determine the need for further change strategies and programs. The OD practitioner needs to continue

**FIGURE 16.2 Self-Renewal Is Difficult**

*Source:* B.C. by permission of Johnny Hart and Creators Syndicate, Inc.

to provide members' awareness of emerging competitive problems and use this as a means of developing a willingness to move rapidly to introduce needed changes. The self-renewing organization is constantly able to initiate new strategies leading to continued innovation and adaptation. In a changing, chaotic world, there is a need for constant innovation and continuous change.

As the client system develops a self-renewal capability, its need for an external practitioner should decrease. If the client system has successfully developed a self-renewal capacity, the gradual termination of the practitioner-client relationship should be a smooth transition; however, if the client system has become overly dependent upon the OD practitioner, termination of the relationship may be difficult. The challenge of developing a self-renewal capability is illustrated in Figure 16.2.

## EMERGING ISSUES AND VALUES

OD is a growing, developing, and changing field of study. Consequently, there are a number of evolving theories and concepts that have contributed to the field, and a number of approaches that have emerged from it. The field of OD is currently and will likely always be in transition if it is to remain relevant. This state of flux makes it difficult to define exact boundaries of what is or is not an OD intervention. As a result, two key issues will be examined in the following sections: (1) OD: fad or discipline? and (2) the role of values.

## OD: Fad or Discipline?

A number of writers disagree about whether OD will become a long-term contribution to management and organization theory or will soon fade away into the dusty archives together with scientific management and other short-lived trends. This is a little like asking the question: "Is air travel a fad?" After all, it has only been around for 60 years or so. Similarly, OD now has some 50 years of background history and, at this point, has not yet reached its apex in either quantity or quality of effort.

OD has already developed and experimented with a variety of new approaches to organization innovation and renewal, and the state of the art is still evolving. While OD builds on its roots, it also discards old ideas and methods that are no longer relevant. Concurrently, OD incorporates new and evolving methodologies and philosophies. OD is an exciting new field. As with any discipline, there are unsolved issues, problems, and controversy.

Rather than being a fad, OD appears to be a primary method for helping organizations adjust to accelerated change. As a result, OD is not a fad but it is an emerging discipline. OD practitioner and author Warren Bennis points out that OD rests on three basic propositions. The first is the hypothesis that every age adopts the organizational form most appropriate to it and that changes taking place in that age make it necessary to "revitalize and rebuild our organizations." The second basic proposition is that the only real way to change organizations lies in changing the "climate" of the organization—the "way of life," the system of beliefs and values, the accepted modes of interaction and relating. It is more important to change the climate of the organization than the individual if organizations are to develop. The third basic proposition is that "a new social awareness is required by people in organizations," since social awareness is essential in our current world. In short, the basic thrust behind OD is that the world is rapidly changing and that our organization must follow suit.

Some executives like to latch on to almost any new concept that promises a quick fix for their problems.

- Having trouble developing new products? Try employee empowerment, the process for giving employees the power to make decisions about their work.
- Having a tough time competing against foreign competition? Try TQM, a way to involve workers in finding ways to increase productivity and ensure quality.
- Having trouble building teamwork, increasing communication skills, or boosting self-esteem? Try outdoor experiential training, a way to build trust and instill teamwork through off-the-job exercises.
- Having trouble linking a firm's daily operations to its vision? Try open-book management, a process that opens the financial books to employees so they can understand the problems and help solve them.

There is nothing inherently wrong with any of these methods, but too often managers treat them as gimmicks or quick fixes rather than face the basic problems. What's more, little or no objective research may have been conducted to find out what are the problems. Unless problems are identified and solutions are systematically thought out and supported by the commitment of management, the "fixes" may become another fad in a long series of fads.

OD is contributing a technology that will be required even more as the rate of change increases. OD emerged as a response to the needs of organizations and individuals seeking innovative ways to employ change. OD presents the technology for creating and seeking organizational excellence, which is the underlying goal of the modern manager and organization. Successful organizations are seeking to practice "anticipative" management styles rather than using "reactive" styles, that is, waiting until after the fact to react to change.

As the rate of change increases, so has the range of interventions used in OD. Organization development has moved far beyond its historical antecedents and is continually adding new approaches and techniques as new problem areas emerge. As noted earlier, new system-wide approaches are needed to tie together the basic OD approaches. Every OD intervention is aimed at solving technical or human problems, but what is needed are comprehensive, long-term approaches that integrate the systems into long-term solutions.

## The Role of Values

OD practitioners also differ about how OD techniques should be applied to improve organizational functioning. In the application of OD, practitioners face several complex dilemmas.

**THE PROFESSIONALISM OF OD**  Many theorists question OD because it is ill-defined and presents a "moving target." They point to the lack of a common body of knowledge, research, and techniques. It is generally recognized that because of its rapid emergence, there is not enough empirical evidence to provide scientific validation of all, or perhaps any, of the major OD intervention techniques. OD's basic thrust arises from its face validity; it seems to work in making the organization more competitive.

**THE CERTIFICATION OF OD PRACTITIONERS**  There are currently a number of professional organizations with OD orientations or OD divisions, but no single organization that accredits or certifies OD practitioners. Some theorists feel that the rapid growth of the OD field will lead to the possibility that unqualified persons (or charlatans) may represent themselves as professionals but that a certifying agency could prevent this. Others feel that many certifying bodies are less than effective and suggest reliance on the free enterprise system.

**OVEREMPHASIS ON HUMAN AND SOCIAL INTERVENTION**  OD approaches seem to overemphasize changing the behavioral patterns of members, with a consequent lack of recognition of other significant factors, such as structural and technological elements. Many practitioners call for a broadening of OD practices to a more systematic, comprehensive, or integrated approach to change.

What is important is that we proceed with our study of OD with a questioning, inquiring, and irreverent attitude. Many practitioners suggest that new vitality, potency, and creativity are needed if OD is to grow and evolve.

**CONTROVERSY OVER WHAT ARE OD TECHNIQUES**  The field of OD has grown rapidly. Many innovative techniques have been developed, and many more are still being developed. Because of this rate of growth, there are also many problems and disagreements among practitioners over what is and what is not an OD technique and what interventions or strategies should be used. Although OD strategies, especially in the 1960s and 1970s, emphasized the behavioral aspects of change, OD practitioners are increasingly using an integrated, eclectic, or systems, approach that includes structural and technical strategies in addition to behavioral strategies.[6] One thing is clear. The field of OD is itself developing and changing.

**DEALING WITH POWER**  OD relies upon the use of collaboration models, which frequently increase cohesion within units but fail to deal with organizational power issues or with relations to external systems. OD efforts seem to be successful under conditions of trust and collaboration, but are less able to deal with conditions of distrust, power, and conflict.

**LIMITATIONS OF TIME AND TERMINALITY**  As George Allen, former coach of the Washington Redskins, states: "The future is now!" OD interventions are generally regarded as a long-term, two- to five-year process. What about a system that requires immediate change? OD at this point offers few short-term improvement techniques that allow rapid change to occur. Could OD have helped Chrysler, General Motors (GM), Circuit City, Lehman Brothers, and American International Group (AIG) when they confronted bankruptcy?

OD is usually undertaken in relatively healthy organizations that desire to become more effective. What does OD offer for the self-destructing system? What does it offer organizations in crisis that may be fighting for survival? Is there a need for short-term, crisis OD interventions that can help introduce change under conditions where urgency and survival may be the immediate concern?

## Conclusion for the Future

Organization development represents a major change from traditional methods of management development and training. OD is a means for changing organization systems and revitalizing them in line with the needs of the individuals within the system and environmental constraints.

Because of the changing environment, it is important that managers be aware of and understand the advantages and disadvantages of the techniques and strategies available for managing in this changing context. OD is not a panacea, but it provides a dynamic and powerful methodology for helping people and organizations to work together collaboratively and become a winning team.

## FUTURE TRENDS IN ORGANIZATION DEVELOPMENT

The application of OD technology is growing rapidly. New models, techniques, and approaches are constantly being developed and old techniques are being discarded. OD itself is facing future shock.[7]

An awareness of the complex environment in which organizations exist is evidenced by the popularity of new trend books in management, such as *How the Mighty Fall, The Five Dysfunctions of a Team, Outliers, The Snowball, StrengthsFinder 2.0, The Compassionate Samurai, Strengths-Based Leadership, The Black Swan, Tribes, The 21 Irrefutable Laws of Leadership,* and *Hot, Flat, and Crowded.* As shapers of change, OD practitioners will play a critical role in helping organizations adjust to the changing forces and trends that affect them. These future trends include organization transformation, empowerment, learning organizations, and organization architecture.

*Organization Transformation (OT).* This recent advance in change strategies is used in situations of drastic, abrupt change when the organization's survival is at stake. These situations include mergers, takeovers, product changes, and plant closures, which often involve large-scale layoffs and restructuring.

*Shared Vision.* This approach to organizational change involves getting all levels of management to identify the strategic vision of the future and what it takes to make it work.

*Innovation.* Organizations are focusing more effort on innovating—creating new products, goods, and services—and on new ways of organizing and relating among organization members. W. L. Gore and Cisco, for example, have corporate cultures that encourage and support innovation. Harvard Business School professor Clayton Christensen, in *The Innovator's Solution: Creating and Sustaining Successful Growth,* says that "no company has been able to build an engine of disruptive growth and keep it running and running."[8] However, he also makes a strong case that a company does not have much choice but to try.

*Trust.* The critical factor in changing organizations is the development of trust within and between individuals, teams, and organizational units and levels. Without trust, there can be no sustainable excellence with an organization.

*Empowerment.* In order to develop high-performing systems, organization members must be empowered—given the autonomy to do things their own way, to achieve recognition, involvement, and a sense of worth in their jobs. This allows for member ownership of ideas and strategies, and for "buy-in" management. The payoff to employee empowerment and involvement is that it allows individuals to discover and use their own potential.

*Learning Organization.* A conceptual framework for the organization of the future, the learning organization is the notion that learning is central to success. Management needs to see the big picture, escape linear thinking, and understand subtle interrelationships.

*Reengineering.* This fundamental rethinking and radical redesigning of business systems urges an overhaul of job designs, organizational structures, and management systems. Work should be organized around outcomes, not tasks or functions.

*Core Competencies.* The idea is for companies to identify and organize around what they do best. Corporate strategy should be based not on products or markets, but on competencies that give a company access to several markets and are difficult for competitors to imitate.

*Organizational Architecture.* A metaphor that forces managers to think more broadly about their organization in terms of how work, people, and formal and informal structures fit together. This often leads to autonomous work teams and strategic alliances.

Because of the rapid changes, predicting the future trends in OD is difficult, if not impossible. However, a number of "cutting-edge" trends appear to be affecting the future directions of OD.

## Macrosystem Trends

Organizations are becoming ever more complex and are affected by competitors and conditions globally. A small machine shop in Topeka, Kansas, is affected by another machine shop in Mumbai, India. Macrosystem trends focus on the organizational system.

*The impact of culture change.*    It will become increasingly important to understand the impact of culture on morale, productivity, competence, organizational health, and especially the relationship of culture to strategy.

*Total resource utilization.*    Another trend is the need for a system approach to ensure efficient use of the organization's resources.

*Centralization versus decentralization.*    In organizations of the future, it will be necessary to both centralize and decentralize functions, structure, and governance. Organizations decentralize so that they can respond quickly to changes. Yet, the organization must be centralized to ensure that units are coordinated and working together.

*Conflict resolution.*    Conflict management has become an important element in today's complex organizations, and value and goal differences are continuing problems. Future OD activities should include helping managers to diagnose conflicts and resolve disputes.

*Interorganization collaboration.*    As limited resources and increased complexity confront the manager of the future, increased sharing, collaboration, and cooperation among organizations will be necessary. Networking offers alternative routes for organizational action.

## Interpersonal Trends

Interpersonal trends focus on team and group dynamics. Teams are a way of life for most of the members of an organization, and teamwork is required where members subordinate their personal prominence for the good of the team. Not only must individuals work together as a team, but increasingly, teams are required to work together. Team interdependence occurs when the successful performance of one team is dependent upon other teams. As teams become even more critical to the success of organizations, there are multiple emerging issues facing how teams are formed, managed, and used within organizations.

*Merging line and staff functions.*    There is a trend toward reducing layers of management, increasing participation, and developing temporary systems for problem solving. OD practitioners may facilitate teamwork, assist in downsizing, and manage the transition to "do more with less" systems.

*Linking resources among teams.*    As problems become more complex, it becomes important to develop ad hoc problem-solving groups.

*Integrating quality and productivity.*    The growing emphasis on productivity and quality suggests future trends for OD practitioners to develop links between the goals of management and improving productivity systems. Some organizations have become painfully aware that productivity without quality has severe consequences.

*Diversity.*    There are increasing trends toward greater diversity of the workforce, including multinational corporations and a need for the integration of diverse cultures, values, and skills.

*Networking.*    In order to benefit from knowledge and innovation, organizations will need efficient systems for identifying and accessing information. The learning organization is an example of a change program that addresses the problem of communicating and working effectively across the organization.

*Rewarding.*    "You get what you reward" is a truism reminding managers to reward smart work, simplification, loyalty, teamwork, and risk taking. Rewards may include stocks, trips, bonuses, and fun.

## Individual Trends

Individual trends center on empowering individuals by giving them the power to make decisions about their work. To do this requires improving communication abilities, interpersonal skills, technical competence, and managerial performance of individuals. Organizations are trying on a number of fronts to improve the capabilities of their individual members.

*Intrinsic worth.*   Evidence suggests that increasing intrinsic, not extrinsic, motivation is a factor in reducing stress and its symptoms. The OD practitioner can assist in shared understanding and training to deal with these problems.

*Change in individuals.*   With an increased emphasis on corporate training and development efforts, the OD practitioner will need to make this process easier and more effective.

*The effects of thinking.*   The concept of the thinking individual raises the question of corporate values and cultures as belief systems, and offers the OD practitioner a vehicle for creating a positive, research-based value system in the organization.

*Health and fitness.*   Currently, fitness models focus on organizational and individual health; such models will provide an increase in self-selected excellence and fitness approaches for the OD practitioner in the future.

*Interdependence.*   Finally, the increasing complexity emphasizes the interdependent relationship between the individual and the organization. The OD practitioner attempts to develop synergy among organizational elements.

## THE FUTURE OF OD

Organization development has been described as a process designed to increase organization effectiveness by integrating the needs of the individual members for growth and development with the organization's goals. In a changing environment, OD provides strategies to alter beliefs, attitudes, values, and structures of organizations, making them more anticipative and adaptive to deal with problems of future shock.

The course of change anticipated for OD will predominantly surround the issues of a changing workforce, global competence, and transformation within the organization. The changing workforce will encompass a positive change toward productivity and involvement with enhanced training and technological awareness. Global competence will mean shared values and similar organizational structures to compete in a highly competitive arena. Advances in media and communication technologies will influence all of these organizational transformations.

Organization development is an expanding and vital technology. A great deal was accomplished during its past growth, and certainly much more will be done in the future. OD is being applied in a multinational framework and in a variety of organizational settings, including industrial, governmental, and health care institutions. Most theorists agree that there is a need for more empirical studies on the relationship of intervention processes to other organizational variables. It is widely acknowledged that techniques to deal effectively with external systems and power-coercive problems have yet to emerge. Yet the different views about the myths and rituals of OD are in themselves an indication of a healthy discipline. When OD practitioners become complacent, when the controversies over approaches and techniques subside, and when the discipline becomes stagnant, then perhaps there will be an even deeper need to worry about the future of OD.

Managers need to understand that OD interventions have the potential to make the biggest difference in human development and bottomline performance. These interventions are based on the same truths that have led us to see democracy as a superior form of governance for our society.

**OD Application: No Job Is Safe and Never Will Be** discusses some suggestions for how to remain professionally viable and competitive in today's workplace.

---

### OD Application: No Job Is Safe and Never Will Be[9]

As we have seen throughout this book, organizations must constantly change and innovate if they are to remain viable and competitive. This also applies on the individual level. Will Rogers once said, "Even if you're on the right track, you'll get run over if you just sit there." The nature of work and what you will be doing in the future will constantly be changing. To anticipate changes in your career rather than react to them, you will need to be running your own personal organization development program. The mantra is planned change.

The career that you are preparing for today will not likely be the career you pursue for much of your life. The shift in jobs to cheaper overseas labor markets that first began in manufacturing, textiles, autos, and steel is now moving up the labor food chain, making college-educated professional workers increasingly nervous. It seems that no job or career is safe from outsourcing to another country with cheaper labor. The list of professions moving offshore includes software engineers, lawyers and legal professionals, accountants and CPAs, financial

*(Continued)*

analysts, customer support, and medical specialists. Service jobs were once considered safe, but, for example, income tax returns are being prepared in India by $500-a-month CPAs, then reviewed and signed by a CPA in the United States. Microsoft employs programmers in countries from India to Ireland. Dell Computer's customer help centers are in India. Even physicians are not safe from outsourcing. Patients from around the world, including North America and Europe, are checking in to hospitals in Thailand and India for planned surgeries that include everything from heart surgery to hip replacement.

No matter how much we hear from talk-show hosts and politicians about the downside of outsourcing jobs, legislation is not likely to be a solution, nor is it likely to be forthcoming. Pleas to companies to keep jobs in-country based on patriotism are also not likely to get large-scale results. Even U.S. state and local governments are going out of the country to manage things like food-stamp programs. The U.S. Postal Service contracts for work that is performed in India. Governments, like profit-making organizations, are trying to minimize their costs. A vice president at Hewlett-Packard (HP) said what most companies have said about outsourcing: "We have to outsource in order to stay competitive."

Fortunately, individuals can do some things to help themselves better meet the challenge of a changing workplace. But just like companies trying to remain competitive, being innovative and on the cutting-edge is a never-ending and always vigilant activity. Here are some suggestions.

*Avoid jobs that can be broken down into repeatable steps.* Research from the Massachusetts Institute of Technology and Harvard University concludes that jobs that can be "routinized," or broken down into repeatable steps that vary little from day to day, are good candidates to either be replaced by computer software or sent to a lower-paid worker in a cheaper labor market. "If you can describe a job precisely, or write rules for doing it, it's unlikely to survive. Either we'll program a computer to do it, or we'll teach a foreigner to do it," says Frank Levy of the Massachusetts Institute of Technology.

*Attractive jobs include those requiring teachers, college professors, factory floor management, health care professionals, and law enforcement.* All of these jobs require flexibility, problem solving, creativity, and a lifetime of learning. Actually, a substantial majority of the jobs remaining in the economy are in this category. Improvements in productivity have already removed many of the routine jobs in manufacturing and clerical work.

*The factory workers who are more likely to keep their jobs will probably be those who excel in computer-controlled equipment or can quickly respond to one-of-a-kind customer orders.* Other jobs likely to remain include work that cannot be performed off the

work site, such as repairing a complicated machine. Until copying machines become obsolete, the person who services the paper jams will be needed. Pay will, of course, vary depending on the complexity of the work.

*Work that relies on complex communication skills will probably not be outsourced.* Jobs that require frequent interactions with other people, often face-to-face, will remain and flourish. These include managers of people and those who sell expensive equipment, such as Internet infrastructure equipment and automated manufacturing equipment. Occupations that are good bets include manager, management consultant, teacher, artist, designer, sales, and generally jobs that require good people skills. The good programming jobs that remain will go to those who have the ability to be the managers of teams of programmers scattered around the world. The information technology industry is hungry for workers with good people skills who can act as liaison between customers and programmers. Gone are the days when a programmer could sit working alone in an office all day.

*Multicultural teams have a big advantage over homogeneous teams.* This is particularly the case when the teams will need to deal with customers and suppliers throughout the world. Multicultural teams are already built into Canadian, United Kingdom, and U.S. teams, because their societies are already a global mix. A team of engineers in New Delhi, China, Norway, or Japan will probably be less multicultural.

*Get a college education.* Prior to the recession that began in late 2007, statistics showed that the unemployment rate for people with a bachelor's degree or better was 2.2 percent, versus 4.4 percent for people who had graduated from high school but not college. By mid 2009 when the economy was in the recession more deeply, the unemployment rate for people with a bachelor's degree or better was 4.4 percent, versus 9.3 percent for people who had graduated from high school but not college.

A final piece of advice from Warren Bennis, OD practitioner, author, and University of Southern California professor: "No job is safe. Never will be. The half-life of any particular skill is, at most, five years. And that's on the long side. What will keep you alive? Be curious, be willing to learn, have a moral compass, and know what gives your life meaning."

## Questions

1. What are you doing to become or remain competitive in the job market?
2. Can you think of some other careers that are safe from being outsourced?

## Summary

- **Monitor and Stabilize.** After an OD program has been implemented, the emphasis turns to stabilizing the changes so that the new behavior becomes part of the organization's culture and norms. This encompasses feeding data back to organization members so that they

can measure their progress and evaluate the program's results.

- **Self-Renewal.** The members of the organization need a self-sustaining capability to implement change programs without outside support. The self-renewing organization is constantly able to initiate new strategies leading to continued innovation.

• **Emerging Issues.** OD has come a long way in the past five decades since its inception by Douglas McGregor, Richard Beckhard, Robert Blake, and Herbert Shepard in their early work with organizational systems. Since that time, an array of new intervention techniques, methodologies, and applications have evolved. Nonetheless, many practitioners feel that OD has become too ritualized, that the field lacks rigorous empirical foundations and fails to deal with critical issues. As you have probably noted, there is a wide divergence of opinion over what are or should be called OD interventions and whether or not certain interventions lead to successful outcomes.

• **Future of OD.** OD's growth will not result from more practitioners moving into the OD field or because more techniques become available, but because the problems of adapting to a more rapidly changing world create the need for expanded use of OD. The increasing need for organization transformation, high-performing systems, innovation, self-managed work teams, and empowerment suggests that speed in making transitions is the critical issue facing organizations. OD practitioners must be able to develop new and innovative ways of adapting organizations to high-speed change. As more organizations seek to achieve organizational excellence, there will be a parallel growth in the future for new OD models, new OD strategies, new OD interventions, and new OD practitioner roles.

## Review Questions

1. Identify some of the conditions for the success of an OD program.

2. Is OD an emerging discipline or only a passing fad?

3. Do you agree or disagree with the criticisms of OD?

## Key Words and Concepts

| | | | |
|---|---|---|---|
| Fade-out | Individual trends | Macrosystem trends | Self-renewal |
| Feedback | Interpersonal trends | Reconfigurable | Stabilizing the changes |

# OD Skills Simulation 16.1

## OD Practitioner Behavior Profile II

*Total time suggested: 45 to 60 minutes*

## A. Purpose

In most organizations, there is a lot of untapped human potential. In an excellent, renewing organization, this potential can be released, resulting in personal growth for the individual. Personal development and organization renewal involve changes in attitudes and behavior that are related to your self-concept, role, goals, and values.

The purpose of this profile is to help you gauge for yourself some aspects of your behavior. During this course, you have had many opportunities to obtain information about yourself and how you behave in organizational situations. This feedback may provide the impetus for you to change, but the ultimate responsibility for the change is with you.

In this simulation, you will experience:

- Developing skills in goal setting and changing behaviors.
- Developing skills in listening and using feedback. Exploring the OD practitioner role in an ongoing situation.
- Increasing your self-renewal capability.

## B. Procedures

### Part A. Profile Survey and Assessment with Practitioner

*Step 1.* Before class, complete the Profile Survey and the Profile Form (Table 2.1 in Chapter 2).

Your responses to the Profile Survey reflect how you view yourself, which in turn reveals something about your behavioral style. Based on the profile scale of 1 through 10, select the number that indicates the degree to which you feel each description is characteristic of you. Record your choice in the blank to the right.

In Chapter 2, OD Skills Simulation 2.1, is Table 2.1, the Profile Form. Record your responses on this Profile Form and in the "Score" column for Chapter 16. Shade in the bar graph for Chapter 16 in the appropriate line based upon your score. Note that the 30 descriptions have been reordered to fit into five categories. Calculate and record on the Profile Form the averages for the five categories and an overall profile average.

Review the Profile Form to determine if there are any changes in your responses in Chapter 16 and when you initially took the Profile Survey in Chapter 2. Look to see if there are patterns within the five categories.

The profile may indicate items on which your score is less desirable than you would like. You may also find categories in which you have generally low ratings. These may suggest areas for improvement in the future and for assessing the kinds of changes you may wish to make in order to become a more effective practitioner or manager.

*Step 2.* Form into trios (preferably the same groups as in Simulation 2.1), with one person acting as the client, a second as the practitioner, and the third as observer. Extra class members may join an existing group. Working with the practitioner, complete the Class Performance Form. Then compare this Class Performance Form with the one you completed in Chapter 2 to gauge how well you have accomplished your goals. Share the information from the Chapter 2 Profile Form and obtain feedback and perceptions from your practitioner. Compare the changes in your answers from Simulation 2.1 and, with your practitioner, discuss whether the changes reflected on the Profile Form seem accurate. The observer will observe the practitioner relationship using the Observer Form. After each of the practitioner sessions is completed, each observer shares the information on the Observer Form. Rotate roles so that each person is in each of the three roles.

*Time suggested for Step 2: 15 to 20 minutes per session. Total time is 45 to 60 minutes.*

### Part B. Goal Setting—Personal Objectives for Career

*Step 1.* After completing Part A of the simulation, outside of class, list on the Objectives Form some of the specific objectives and expectations you have for your career. These objectives should describe what you will be able to do and the time required. This Objectives Form is for your own use, and you do not need to share it with other class members unless you care to.

*Step 2.* After you have completed the Objectives Form, you can refer to the Objectives Form from Chapter 2 to compare your current objectives to those you selected at the beginning of the course.

**PROFILE SURVEY**

        1    2    3    4    5    6    7    8    9    10

     Not at All      Somewhat      Very
   Characteristic   Characteristic   Characteristic

1. Having the ability to communicate in a clear, concise, and persuasive manner   \_\_\_\_\_

2. Being spontaneous—saying and doing things that seem natural on the spur of the moment   \_\_\_\_\_

3. Doing things "by the book"—noticing appropriate rules and procedures and following them   \_\_\_\_\_

4. Being creative—having a lot of unusual, original ideas; thinking of new approaches to problems others do not often come up with   \_\_\_\_\_

5. Being competitive—wanting to win and be the best   \_\_\_\_\_

6. Being able to listen to and understand others   \_\_\_\_\_

7. Being aware of other people's moods and feelings   \_\_\_\_\_

8. Being careful in your work—taking pains to make sure everything is "just right"   \_\_\_\_\_

9. Being resourceful in coming up with possible ways of dealing with problems   \_\_\_\_\_

10. Being a leader—having other people look to you for direction; taking over when things are confused   \_\_\_\_\_

11. Having the ability to accept feedback without reacting defensively, becoming hostile, or withdrawing   \_\_\_\_\_

12. Having the ability to deal with conflict and anger   \_\_\_\_\_

13. Having written work neat and organized; making plans before starting on a difficult task; organizing details of work   \_\_\_\_\_

14. Thinking clearly and logically; attempting to deal with ambiguity, complexity, and confusion in a situation by thoughtful, logical analysis   \_\_\_\_\_

15. Having self-confidence when faced with a challenging situation   \_\_\_\_\_

16. Having the ability to level with others, to give feedback to others   \_\_\_\_\_

17. Doing new and different things; meeting new people; experimenting and trying out new ideas or activities   \_\_\_\_\_

18. Having a high level of aspiration, setting difficult goals   \_\_\_\_\_

19. Analyzing a situation carefully before acting; working out a course of action in detail before embarking on it   \_\_\_\_\_

20. Being effective at initiating projects and innovative ideas   \_\_\_\_\_

21. Seeking ideas from others; drawing others into discussion   \_\_\_\_\_

22. Having a tendency to seek close personal relationships, participating in social activities with friends; giving affection and receiving it from others   \_\_\_\_\_

23. Being dependable—staying on the job; doing what is expected   \_\_\_\_\_

24. Having the ability to work as a catalyst, to stimulate and encourage others to develop their own resources for solving their own problems   \_\_\_\_\_

25. Taking responsibility; relying on your own abilities and judgment rather than those of others   \_\_\_\_\_

26. Selling your own ideas effectively   \_\_\_\_\_

27. Being the dominant person; having a strong need for control or recognition   \_\_\_\_\_

28. Getting deeply involved in your work; being extremely committed to ideas or work you are doing   \_\_\_\_\_

29. Having the ability to evaluate possible solutions critically   \_\_\_\_\_

30. Having the ability to work in unstructured situations, with little or no support, and to continue to work effectively even if faced with lack of cooperation, resistance, or hostility   \_\_\_\_\_

**CLASS PERFORMANCE FORM**

### 1. ATTENDANCE

What percentage of the class meetings did you attend?

| 100%–95% | 94%–90% | 89%–80% | 79%–70% | 69%–60% | 59%–50% | 49%–0% |
|---|---|---|---|---|---|---|
|  |  |  |  |  |  |  |

### 2. PREPARATION

What percentage of the time did you come prepared?

| | 100%–95% | 94%–90% | 89%–80% | 79%–70% | 69%–60% | 59%–50% | 49%–0% |
|---|---|---|---|---|---|---|---|
| Chapters read |  |  |  |  |  |  |  |
| OD Skills Prepared |  |  |  |  |  |  |  |
| OD Cases Prepared |  |  |  |  |  |  |  |

### 3. PROBLEM SOLVING

What percentage of the time did you:

| | 100%–95% | 94%–90% | 89%–80% | 79%–70% | 69%–60% | 59%–50% | 49%–0% |
|---|---|---|---|---|---|---|---|
| Understand key terms |  |  |  |  |  |  |  |
| Prepare text assignments |  |  |  |  |  |  |  |
| Develop correct answers |  |  |  |  |  |  |  |

### 4. INVOLVEMENT

What percentage of the time did you contribute to team performance by:

| | 100%–95% | 94%–90% | 89%–80% | 79%–70% | 69%–60% | 59%–50% | 49%–0% |
|---|---|---|---|---|---|---|---|
| Showing interest in meeting |  |  |  |  |  |  |  |
| Initiating discussion |  |  |  |  |  |  |  |
| Getting along with other team members |  |  |  |  |  |  |  |

## OBSERVER FORM

Your role during this part of the simulation is important because your goal is to give individuals feedback on their strategies of change. Following are listed 10 criteria of helping relationships. Rate the practitioner by circling the appropriate number.

1. Level of involvement:
   Cautious                            Low 1: 2: 3: 4: 5: 6: 7: 8: 9: 10 High    Interested

2. Level of communication:
   Doesn't listen                      Low 1: 2: 3: 4: 5: 6: 7: 8: 9: 10 High    Listens

3. Level of openness, trust:
   Shy, uncertain                      Low 1: 2: 3: 4: 5: 6: 7: 8: 9: 10 High    Warm, friendly

4. Level of collaboration:
   Authoritative                       Low 1: 2: 3: 4: 5: 6: 7: 8: 9: 10 High    Seeks agreement

5. Level of influence:
   Gives in                            Low 1: 2: 3: 4: 5: 6: 7: 8: 9: 10 High    Convincing

6. Level of supportiveness:
   Disagrees                           Low 1: 2: 3: 4: 5: 6: 7: 8: 9: 10 High    Supports

7. Level of direction:
   Easygoing, agreeable                Low 1: 2: 3: 4: 5: 6: 7: 8: 9: 10 High    Gives directions

8. Level of competence:
   Unsure                              Low 1: 2: 3: 4: 5: 6: 7: 8: 9: 10 High    Competent

9. Reflects feelings and summarizes:
   Never                               Low 1: 2: 3: 4: 5: 6: 7: 8: 9: 10 High    Often

10. Overall style:
    Ineffective                        Low 1: 2: 3: 4: 5: 6: 7: 8: 9: 10 High    Effective

NOTES:
Words,
behaviors      _____

               _____

               _____

               _____

               _____

**OBJECTIVES FORM**

Communicating Skills:

1. _____
   _____
2. _____
   _____
3. _____
   _____

Interpersonal Skills:

1. _____
   _____
2. _____
   _____
3. _____
   _____

Aspiration-Achievement Levels:

1. _____
   _____
2. _____
   _____
3. _____
   _____

Problem-Solving Skills:

1. _____
   _____
2. _____
   _____
3. _____
   _____

Leadership Skills:

1. _____
   _____
2. _____
   _____
3. _____
   _____

Other:

1. _____
   _____
2. _____
   _____
3. _____
   _____

## OD Skills Simulation 16.2

### The OD Practitioner

*Total time suggested: 90 minutes.*

### A. Purpose

To provide an opportunity to apply the skills you have learned in this course.

### B. Procedures

*Step 1.* Read The Bob Knowlton Case and answer the seven questions at the end. Record your answers in the "Individual" columns on the Bob Knowlton Record Form. Complete the "Individual Section" on the Diagnostic Strategy Form.

*Step 2.* Form into teams of three to four members each and answer the questions. Record your answers in the "Team" column on the Bob Knowlton Record Form. Also complete the "Team Section" of the Diagnostic Strategy Form. Your instructor may have you provide an analysis of the case.

*Time suggested for Step 2: 30 minutes.*

*Step 3.* With the instructor playing the role of Dr. Jerrod, each team presents its analysis using the Diagnostic Strategy Form as a basis for the analysis.

*Time suggested for Step 3: 30 minutes.*

*Step 4.* As a class, compare and discuss the team answers. How many different problems were identified? What different interventions might have been used? Try to reach a class consensus on an OD intervention strategy?

*Time suggested for Step 4: 30 minutes.*

# THE BOB KNOWLTON CASE[10]

Bob Knowlton was sitting alone in the conference room of the laboratory. The rest of the group had gone for the day. One of the secretaries, who had stopped by and talked for a while about her husband's coming induction into the army, had finally left. Bob, alone in the laboratory, slid a little further down in his chair, looking with satisfaction at the results of the first test run of the new photon unit.

He liked to stay after the others had gone. His appointment as project head was still new enough to give him a deep sense of pleasure. His eyes were on the graphs before him, but in his mind he could hear Dr. Jerrold, the project head, saying again, "There's one thing about this place that you can bank on. The sky is the limit for a man who can produce!" Knowlton felt again the tingle of happiness and embarrassment. "Well, damm it," he said to himself, he had produced. He wasn't kidding anybody. He had come to the Simmons Laboratories two years ago. During a routine testing of some rejected Clanson components, he had stumbled on the idea of the photon correlator, and the rest had just happened. Jerrold had been enthusiastic; a separate project had been set up for further research and development of the device, and he had gotten the job of running it. The whole sequence of events still seemed a little miraculous to Knowlton.

He shrugged himself out of the reverie and bent determinedly over the sheets when he heard someone come into the room behind him. He looked up expectantly; Jerrold often stayed late himself, and now and then dropped in for a chat. This always made the day's end especially pleasant for Bob. It wasn't Jerrold. The man who had come in was a stranger. He was tall, thin, and rather dark. He wore steel-rimmed glasses and had on a very wide leather belt with a large brass buckle.

The stranger smiled and introduced himself, "I'm Simon Fester. Are you Bob Knowlton?" Bob said yes, and they shook hands. "Doctor Jerrold said I might find you in. We were talking about your work, and I'm very much interested in what you are doing." Bob waved to a chair.

Fester didn't seem to belong in any of the standard categories of visitors: customer, visiting fireman, or stockholder. Bob pointed to the sheets on the table. "There are the preliminary results of a test we're running. We've got a new gadget by the tail and we're trying to understand it. It's not finished, but I can show you the section that we're testing."

He stood up, but Fester was deep in the graphs. After a moment, he looked up with an odd grin. "These look like plots of a Jennings surface. I've been playing around with some autocorrelation functions of surfaces—you know that stuff." Bob, who had no idea what he was referring to, grinned back and nodded, and immediately felt uncomfortable. "Let me show you the monster," he said, and led the way to the work room.

After Fester left, Knowlton slowly put the graphs away, feeling vaguely annoyed. Then, as if he had made a decision, he quickly locked up and took the long way out so that he would pass Jerrold's office. But the office was locked. Knowlton wondered whether Jerrold and Fester had left together.

The next morning, Knowlton dropped into Jerrold's office, mentioned that he had talked with Fester, and asked who he was. "Sit down for a minute," Jerrold said, "I want to talk to you about him. What do you think of him?" Knowlton replied truthfully that he thought Fester was very bright and probably very competent. Jerrold looked pleased. "We're taking him on," he said. "He's had a very good background in a number of laboratories, and he seems to have ideas about the problems we're tackling here." Knowlton nodded in agreement, instantly hoping that Fester would not be placed with him. "I don't know yet where he will finally land," Jerrold continued, "but he seems interested in what you are doing. I thought he might spend a little time with you by way of getting started." Knowlton nodded thoughtfully. "If his interest in your work continues, you can add him to your group. "Well, he seemed to have some good ideas even without knowing exactly what we are doing," Knowlton answered. "I hope he stays; we'd be glad to have him."

Knowlton walked back to the lab with mixed feelings. He told himself that Fester would be good for the group. He was no dunce, he'd produce. Knowlton thought again of Jerrold's promise when he had promoted him: "The man who produces gets ahead in this outfit." The words seemed to carry the overtones of a threat now.

That day Fester didn't appear until midafternoon. He explained that he'd had a long lunch with Jerrold, discussing his place in the lab. "Yes," said Knowlton, "I talked with Jerry this morning about it, and we both thought you might work with us for a while." Fester smiled in the same knowing way that he had smiled when he mentioned the Jennings surfaces. "I'd like to," he said. Knowlton introduced Fester to the other members of the lab. Fester and Link, the mathematician of the group, hit it off well together, and spent the rest of the afternoon discussing a method of analysis of patterns that Link had been worrying over for the last month.

It was 6:30 P.M. when Knowlton finally left the lab that night. He had waited almost eagerly for the end of the day to come, when they would all be gone and he could sit in the quiet rooms, relax, and think it over. "Think what over?" he asked himself. He didn't know. Shortly after 5:00 P.M., they had all gone except Fester, and what followed was almost a duel. Knowlton was annoyed that he was being cheated out of his quiet period, and finally resentfully determined that Fester should leave first.

Fester was sitting at the conference table reading, and Knowlton was sitting at the desk in the little glass-enclosed cubby that he used during the day when he needed to be undisturbed. Fester had gotten the last year's progress reports out and was studying them carefully. The time dragged. Knowlton doodled on a pad, the tension growing inside him. What the hell did Fester think he was going to find in the reports?

Knowlton finally gave up and they left the lab together. Fester took several of the reports with him to study in the evening. Knowlton asked him if he thought the reports gave a clear picture of the lab's activities. "They're excellent," Fester answered with obvious sincerity. "They're not only good reports; what they report is damn good, too!" Knowlton was surprised at the relief he felt, and grew almost jovial as he said good night.

Driving home, Knowlton felt more optimistic about Fester's presence in the lab. He had never fully understood the analysis that Link was attempting. If there was anything wrong with Link's approach, Fester would probably spot it, "And if I'm any judge," he murmured, "he won't be especially diplomatic about it."

He described Fester to his wife, who was amused by the broad leather belt and the brass buckle. "It's the kind of belt the Pilgrims must have worn," she laughed. "I'm not worried about how he holds his pants up," he laughed with her. "I'm afraid that he's the kind that just has to make like a genius twice each day. And that can be pretty rough on the group."

Knowlton had been asleep for several hours when he was jerked awake by the telephone. He realized it had rung several times. He swung off the bed muttering about damn fools and telephones. It was Fester. Without any excuses, apparently oblivious of the time, he plunged into an excited recital of how Link's patterning problem could be solved. Knowlton covered the mouthpiece to answer his wife's stage-whispered "Who is it?" "It's the genius," replied Knowlton.

Fester, completely ignoring the fact that it was 2:00 in the morning, proceeded in a very excited way to start in the middle of an explanation of a completely new approach to certain of the photon lab problems that he had stumbled on while analyzing past experiments. Knowlton managed to put some enthusiasm in his own voice and stood there, half-dazed and very uncomfortable, listening to Fester talk endlessly about what he had discovered. It was probably not only a new approach, but also an analysis that showed the inherent weakness of the previous experiment and how experimentation along that line would certainly have been inconclusive. The following day, Knowlton spent the entire morning with Fester and Link, the mathematician, the customary morning meeting of Bob's group having been called off so that Fester's work of the previous night could be gone over intensively. Fester was very anxious that this be done, and Knowlton was not too unhappy to call the meeting off for reasons of his own.

For the next several days, Fester sat in the back office that had been turned over to him and did nothing but read the progress reports of the work that had been done in the last six months. Knowlton caught himself feeling apprehensive about the reaction that Fester might have to some of his work. He was a little surprised at his own feelings. He had always been proud—although he had put on a convincingly modest face—of the way in which new ground in the study of photon measuring devices had been broken in his group. Now he wasn't sure, and it seemed to him that Fester might easily show that the line of research they had been following was unsound or even unimaginative.

The next morning, as was the custom, the members of the lab, including the secretaries, sat around a conference table. Bob had always prided himself on the fact that the work of the lab was guided and evaluated by the group as a whole, and he was fond of repeating that it was not a waste of time to include secretaries in such meetings. Often, what started out as a boring recital of fundamental assumptions to a naive listener, uncovered new ways of regarding these assumptions that would not have occurred to the researcher who had long ago accepted them as a necessary basis for his work.

These group meetings also served Bob in another sense. He admitted to himself that he would have felt far less secure if he had had to direct the work out of his own mind, so to speak. With the group meeting as the principle of leadership, it was always possible to justify the exploration of blind alleys because of the general educative effect on the team. Fester was there; Lucy and Martha were there; Link was sitting next to Fester, their conversation concerning Link's mathematical study apparently continuing from yesterday. The other members, Bob Davenport, George Thurlow, and Arthur Oliver, were waiting quietly.

Knowlton, for reasons that he didn't quite understand, proposed for discussion this morning a problem that all of them had spent a great deal of time on previously, with the conclusion that a solution was impossible, that there was no feasible way of treating it in an experimental fashion. When Knowlton proposed the problem, Davenport remarked that there was hardly any use in going over it again; he was satisfied that there was no way of approaching the problem with the equipment and the physical capacities of the lab.

This statement had the effect of a shot of adrenaline on Fester. He said he would like to know what the problem was in detail and, walking to the blackboard, began setting down the "factors," as various members of the group began discussing the problem and simultaneously listing the reasons why it had been abandoned.

Very early in the description of the problem, it was evident that Fester was going to disagree about the impossibility of attacking it. The group realized this, and finally the descriptive materials and their recounting of the reasoning that had led to its abandonment dwindled away. Fester began his statement, which, as it proceeded, might well have been prepared the previous night, although Knowlton knew this was impossible. He couldn't help being impressed with the organized analogical way that Fester was presenting ideas that must have occurred to him only a few minutes before.

Fester had some things to say, however, which left Knowlton with a mixture of annoyance, irritation and, at the same time, a rather smug feeling of superiority over Fester in at least one area. Fester was of the opinion that the way that the problem had been analyzed was typical of group thinking and, with an air of sophistication that made it difficult for a listener to dissent, he proceeded to comment on the American emphasis on team ideas, satirically describing the ways in which they led to a "high level of mediocrity."

During this time, Knowlton observed that Link stared studiously at the floor, and he was very conscious of George Thurlow's and Bob Davenport's glances toward him at several points of Fester's little speech. Inwardly, Knowlton couldn't help feeling that this was one point at least in which Fester was off on the wrong foot. The whole lab, following Jerry's lead, talked, if not practiced, the theory of small research teams as the basic organization for effective research. Fester insisted that the problem could be approached and that he would like to study it for a while himself.

Knowlton ended the morning's session by remarking that the meetings would continue and that the very fact that a supposedly insoluble experimental problem was now going to get another chance was another indication of the value of such meetings. Fester immediately remarked that he was not at all averse to meetings for the purpose of informing the group of the progress of its members; the point he wanted to make was that creative advances were seldom accomplished at such meetings, that they were made by the individual "living with" the problem closely and continuously, a sort of personal relationship to it.

Knowlton went on to say that he was very glad Fester had raised these points and was sure the group would profit by reexamining the basis on which they had been operating. Knowlton agreed that individual effort was probably the basis for making the major advances, but said he considered the group meetings useful because of the effect they had on keeping the group together and on helping the weaker members of the group keep up with the ones who were able to advance more easily and quickly in the analysis of problems.

It was clear as days went by and meetings continued that Fester was coming to enjoy them because of the pattern that they had assumed. It became typical for Fester to hold forth, and it was unquestionably clear that he was more brilliant, better prepared on the various subjects germane to the problems being studied, and more capable of going ahead than anyone there. Knowlton grew increasingly disturbed as he realized that his leadership of the group had been, in fact, taken over.

Whenever the subject of Fester was mentioned in occasional meetings with Dr. Jerrold, Knowlton would comment only on the ability and obvious capacity for work that Fester had. Somehow he never felt that he could mention his own discomforts, not only because they revealed a weakness on his own part, but also because it was quite clear that Jerrold himself was considerably impressed with Fester's work and with the contacts he had with him outside the photon laboratory.

Knowlton now began to feel that perhaps the intellectual advantages that Fester had brought to the group did not quite compensate for what he felt were evidences of a breakdown in the cooperative spirit he had seen in the group before Fester's coming. More and more of the morning meetings were skipped. Fester's opinion concerning the abilities of others of the group, with the exception of Link, was obviously low. At times, during morning meetings or in smaller discussions, he had been on the point of rudeness, refusing to pursue an argument when he claimed it was based on the other person's ignorance of the facts involved. His impatience of others led him to also make similar remarks to Dr. Jerrold. Knowlton inferred this from a conversation with Jerrold in which Jerrold asked whether Davenport and Oliver were going to be continued on; and his failure to mention Link, the mathematician, led Knowlton to feel that this was the result of private conversation between Fester and Jerrold.

It was not difficult for Knowlton to make a quite convincing case on whether Fester's brilliance was sufficient recompense for the beginning of this breaking up of the group. He took the opportunity to speak privately with Davenport and with Oliver, and it was quite clear that both of them were uncomfortable because of Fester. Knowlton didn't press the discussion beyond the point of hearing them in one way or another say that they did feel awkward and that it was sometimes difficult for them to understand the arguments he advanced, and that they were often embarrassed to ask him to fill in the background on which his arguments were based. Knowlton did not interview Link in this manner.

About six months after Fester's coming into the photon lab, a meeting was scheduled in which the sponsors of the research were coming in to get some idea of the work and its progress. It was customary at these meetings for project heads to present the research being conducted in their groups. The members of each group were invited to other meetings that were held later in the day and open to all, but the special meetings were usually made up only of project heads, the head of the laboratory, and the sponsors.

As the time for the special meeting approached, it seemed to Knowlton that he must avoid the presentation at all cost. His reasons for this were that he could not trust himself to present the ideas and work that Fester had advanced, because of his apprehension as to whether he could present them in sufficient detail and answer such questions about them as might be asked. On the other hand, he did not feel he could ignore these newer lines of work and present only the material that he had done or that had been started before Fester's arrival. Knowlton also felt that it would not be beyond Fester at all, in his blunt and undiplomatic way—if he were present at the meeting, that is—to make comments on Knowlton's presentation and reveal Knowlton's inadequacy. It also seemed quite clear that it would not be easy to keep Fester from attending the meeting, even though he was not on the administrative level of those invited.

Knowlton found an opportunity to speak to Jerrold and raised the questions. He remarked to Jerrold that, with the meetings coming up and with the interest in the work and with the contributions that Fester had been making, he would probably like to come to these meetings, but there was a question of the feelings of the others in the group if Fester alone were invited.

Jerrold passed this over very lightly by saying that he didn't think the group would fail to understand Fester's rather different position, and that he thought that Fester by all means should be invited. Knowlton then immediately said he had thought so, too; Fester should present the work because much of it was work he had done; and, as Knowlton put it, this would be a nice way to recognize Fester's contributions and to reward him, as he was eager to be recognized as a productive member of the lab. Jerrold agreed, and so the matter was decided.

Fester's presentation was very successful and in some ways dominated the meeting. He attracted the interest and attention of many of those who had come, and a long discussion followed his presentation. Later in the evening, during the cocktail period before dinner—with the entire laboratory staff present—a little circle of people formed about Fester. One of them was Jerrold himself, and a lively discussion took place about the application of Fester's theory. All of this disturbed Knowlton, and his reaction and behavior were characteristic. He joined the circle, praised Fester to Jerrold and to others, and remarked on the brilliance of the work.

Knowlton, without consulting anyone, began at this time to take some interest in the possibility of a job elsewhere. After a few weeks, he found that a new laboratory of considerable size was being organized in a nearby city, and that the kind of training he had would enable him to get a project head job equivalent to the one he had at the lab, with slightly more money.

He immediately accepted it and notified Jerrold by a letter, which he mailed on a Friday night to Jerrold's home. The letter was quite brief, and Jerrold was stunned. The letter merely said that he had found a better position; that there were personal reasons why he didn't want to appear at the lab any more; that he would be glad to come back at a later time from where he would be, some forty miles away, to assist if there was any mix-up at all in the past work; that he felt sure that Fester could, however, supply any leadership that was required for the group; and that his decision to leave so suddenly was based on some personal problems—he hinted at problems of health in his family, his mother and father. All of this was fictitious, of course. Jerrold took it at face value but still felt that this was very strange behavior and quite unaccountable, for he had always felt his relationship with Knowlton had been warm and that Knowlton was satisfied and, as a matter of fact, quite happy and productive.

Jerrold was considerably disturbed because he had already decided to put Fester in charge of another project that was going to be set up very soon. He had been wondering how to explain this to Knowlton, in view of the obvious help Knowlton was getting from Fester and the high regard in which he held him. Jerrold had, as a matter of fact, considered the possibility that Knowlton could add to his staff another person with the kind of background and training that had been unique in Fester and had proved so valuable.

Jerrold did not make any attempt to meet Knowlton. In a way, he felt aggrieved about the whole thing. Fester, too, was surprised at the suddenness of Knowlton's departure, and when Jerrold, in talking to him, asked him whether he had reasons to prefer to stay with the photon group instead of the project for the Air Force which was being organized, he chose the Air Force project and went on to that job the following week. The photon lab was hard hit. The leadership of the lab was given to Link with the understanding that this would be temporary until someone could come in to take over.

## Questions

1. The self-managed work team violates which of the following principles?
   a. Importance of decentralization.
   b. Unit of command.
   c. Keeping the chain of command limited.
   d. Mixing types of departmentation.
2. Fester's role in the organization was determined by:
   a. A set of expectations.
   b. The formal organizational structure.
   c. The authority of the position.
   d. Largely his personality.
3. Jerrold's approach to leadership included:
   a. Providing direction and performing management functions.
   b. Influencing others and setting goals.
   c. Providing direction and influence.
   d. Influencing and pressuring to produce.
4. Jerrold's decision to promote Fester was based upon:
   a. Leadership traits.
   b. Leadership behavior.
   c. Situational factors.
   d. Contingency factors.
5. In Bob's group, which of the following is most correct?
   a. Conflict was successfully managed.
   b. Conflict indicates that problems exist in the organization.
   c. Conflict is something to be avoided.
   d. Conflict is only damaging when it is unresolved.
6. In this organization, one problem was:
   a. Getting too many people with conflicting opinions involved in the decisions.
   b. Collecting yes men who did not encourage diversity of opinion.
   c. Considering how others would react to decisions.
   d. Delegating too many decisions for others.
7. The main cause of the problem is:
   a. Jerrold.
   b. Knowlton.
   c. Fester.
   d. The organization.

## BOB KNOWLTON RECORD FORM

| Question | Individual | | Team | |
|---|---|---|---|---|
| | Answer | Support | Answer | Support |
| 1 | | | | |
| | | | | |
| | | | | |
| | | | | |
| | | | | |
| 2 | | | | |
| | | | | |
| | | | | |
| | | | | |
| | | | | |
| 3 | | | | |
| | | | | |
| | | | | |
| | | | | |
| | | | | |
| 4 | | | | |
| | | | | |
| | | | | |
| | | | | |
| | | | | |
| 5 | | | | |
| | | | | |
| | | | | |
| | | | | |
| | | | | |
| 6 | | | | |
| | | | | |
| | | | | |
| | | | | |
| | | | | |
| 7 | | | | |
| | | | | |
| | | | | |
| | | | | |
| | | | | |

# DIAGNOSTIC STRATEGY FORM

## Individual Section

| | Problem | Target System | Intervention |
|---|---|---|---|
| 1 | | | |
| 2 | | | |
| 3 | | | |
| 4 | | | |
| 5 | | | |

## Team Section

| | Problem | Target System | Intervention |
|---|---|---|---|
| 1 | | | |
| 2 | | | |
| 3 | | | |
| 4 | | | |
| 5 | | | |

## Chapter 16 Endnotes

1. Copyright © 1963 Columbia Records; renewed 1991 Special Rider Music.

2. Brian Bremner and Gail Edmondson, "Japan: A Tale of Two Mergers," *Business Week*, May 10, 2004, p. 42.

3. Robyn Meredith, "Encore," *Forbes*, April 26, 2004, pp. 72–74.

4. See Howard E. Butz Jr., "Strategic Planning: The Missing Link in TQM," *Quality Progress*, vol. 28, no. 5 (May 1995), p. 166.

5. Bo Burlingham, "Business, What's Your Culture Worth?" *Inc. Magazine*, September 2001, (www.inc.com).

6. Chris Piotrowski and Stephen J. Vodanovich, "Theoretical Orientations of Organizational Development Practitioners," *Social Behavior & Personality: An International Journal*, vol. 29, no. 3 (March 2001), pp. 307–12.

7. For a critique of the relevancy of organization development, see David L. Bradford and W. Warner Burke (eds.), *Reinventing Organization Development: New Approaches to Change in Organizations* (San Francisco: Pfeiffer, 2005).

8. Clayton M. Christensen and Michael E. Raynor, *The Innovator's Solution: Creating and Sustaining Successful Growth* (Boston, MA: Harvard Business School Press, 2003).

9. Jenny Mero, "The Evolution of Work," *Fortune*, September 29, 2008, pp. 223–25; Jena McGregor and Steve Hamm, "Managing the Workforce," *Business Week*, January 28, 2008, pp. 34–51; David Wessel, "The Future of Jobs: New Ones Arise, Wage Gap Widens," *Wall Street Journal*, April 2, 2004, pp. A1, A5; Peter Coy, "The Future of Work," *Business Week*, March 22, 2004, pp. 50–52; Rebecca Buckman, "HP Outsourcing: Beyond China," *Wall Street Journal*, February 23, 2004, p. A14; "No Job Is Safe. Never Will Be," *Business Week*, April 28, 2003, p. 58; Labor statistics from U.S. Bureau of Labor Statistics are for April 2009 and April 2006. See www.dol.gov/ or www.bls.gov/data/

10. I am indebted to Professor Alex Bavelas of Stanford University for the use of this case, and it is used with his permission.

# INDEX